Right: Maynard Dixon's May 1930
cover illustration suggests the joys of
Western commercial flying.

Frontispiece: May 1906 "Emergency Edition"
cover following the great San Francisco
earthquake, also by Maynard Dixon.

Cover Illustrations

Top row:
May 1898 (illus.: M.P.)
February 1911 (illus.: John Jay Baumgartner)
April 1914 (illus.: Jules Guerin)

Middle row:
February 1921 (illus.: Paul Farnham)
February 1929 (illus.: Maurice Logan)
September 1932 (illus.: Heath Anderson)

Bottom row:
October 1957 (photo: Ernest Braun)
July 1979 (photo: Glenn Christiansen)
June 1996 (photo: William Neil)

SUNSET

THE WESTERN MAGAZINE OF GOOD IDEAS

NOW
10¢

MAY
1930

In
This Issue

Practical
Suggestions *for*
Western
Gardeners

Two
Vacation
Cottages

Many Pages
of Travel
and
Outdoor Features

and

Lane Publishing Company ~ San Francisco

Building ▾ Decorating ▾ Recipes

Sunset Magazine

Sunset Magazine

A Century of Western Living, 1898-1998

*Historical Portraits and
A Chronological Bibliography
of Selected Topics*

*Stanford University Libraries
Stanford, California
1998*

Table of Contents

FEBRUARY 1960 * 25 CENTS

Sunset

THE MAGAZINE OF WESTERN LIVING

WINTER in the WEST

Newest Snow Highway
Squaw Valley Ski Cabins
The Winter Olympics

Foreword

Stanford University Libraries are publishing this bibliography for students of Western American life and culture as a means of tracking the growth of the modern West of the United States through the pages of the region's long-lived, distinctive, and successful chronicle, *Sunset*. This selective subject and chronological bibliography lists 9,400 significant articles printed in *Sunset* magazine from May 1898 through January 1998, documenting how the magazine reflected and communicated a range of topics of regional interest. *Sunset* is also a leading publisher of popular "how-to" books on various aspects of Western living; we provide in this volume a chronological list of *Sunset* books. The reader will also find a set of essays and images that delineate the history of the publication and place *Sunset* in the context of its times.

The first question to address is: Why the bibliography? In part, it is a celebration of *Sunset*'s remarkable publishing achievement, an uninterrupted century of regional publication. In part, this bibliography marks the start of Stanford's new multidisciplinary program, the study of the American West. In part, the bibliography with its marvelous introductory texts reveals numerous insights into the Western landscape (both natural and built) as it has evolved in the twentieth century. To assure widespread access to these fascinating articles, Stanford will distribute free copies of this bibliography to libraries with known significant holdings of *Sunset* throughout the West and to important centers of research in American Studies throughout the world.

The second question is: Why has Stanford produced this work? The simple answer is that there is a singular appropriateness in our doing so. The connection between Stanford and *Sunset* goes back to the founding of both, each a scion of the nineteenth-century railroad boom that reshaped the West. The early connection is fully described in Kevin Starr's introduction as well as Tomas Jaehn's essay on the founding of the magazine: neighbors for nearly half a century, each institution a pillar and focus of Peninsular and California culture (understood broadly); affiliates through the education of some of its early editors and writers; and very importantly through the generous loyalty to Stanford on the part of alumni Bill and Mel Lane, *Sunset*'s longtime owner/publishers. The relationship between *Sunset* and Stanford is deep, multivalent, and lasting. Our decision to prepare and publish this volume is the result of those enduring and profound connections.

The third question is: How to use it? The question is well matched to the long-term practical bent of *Sunset* itself. While this is not the only bibliographic resource for getting at the contents of *Sunset* (it has, after all, produced a detailed *Annual Index* since 1952) or at the history of the

February 1960 cover
(photo: Martin Litton)

publication, the topical-chronological listing of notable articles provides a new way of reviewing trends and directions in the West and in the magazine. The index (keyed numerically to the listing of articles) provides a more detailed and less structured way of finding articles on particular topics.

Bill and Mel Lane's contributions present firsthand insights into the workings of the publication, explaining how it achieved its definitive success. The introduction, "*Sunset* Magazine and the Phenomenon of the Far West," by Kevin Starr, the State Librarian of California, places the magazine in the context of the emerging West. Dr. Starr is, of course, uniquely qualified to write such an essay as he is the pre-eminent historian of California, with five scholarly monographs about California published by Oxford University Press, an aerial-photography essay, *Over California*, in addition to numerous articles in learned society journals and other historical introductions. Tomas Jaehn, American and British History Curator of the Stanford University Libraries, provides a four-part essay on the eras of ownership which reveals much insight into how *Sunset* survived, changed, and prospered. The list of *Sunset* Books, closely linked to the magazine by content and emphasis, provides another bibliographic resource, while shedding light both on popular publishing and on the markets *Sunset* addresses.

To the serious student of the West, to the self-avowed lover of *Sunset*, to the thinking, reading Western public, I encourage you to read each of the texts, scan the graphics, and peruse the topical listings and index. What will emerge from these forays together will likely be a different and surely richer perception of the magazine itself and of Western living in the twentieth century. When your imagination is so piqued that you need to consult the cited articles, you can find *Sunset* in almost 1,500 libraries in the 13 states of the Far West; alternatively you might use interlibrary loan procedures to obtain articles or even send a request to a document delivery company (the West's principle such service is Information Express, whose contact numbers and procedures are cited at the end of this Foreword).

There may also be questions about how the bibliography was compiled. In its 100 years of existence, *Sunset* magazine has published more than 18,000 feature articles, secondary articles, regular monthly columns, news notes, poetry, and fiction. We have listed about 9,400 of these, according to the following guidelines.

Multiple ownership, evolving formats, and policy changes provided some challenges in the compilation of this bibliography. The editors had to limit this bibliography in several ways. Of the four current regional editions of *Sunset*, it seemed most appropriate to use the Northern California edition (and its predecessor, the Central West edition), for this bibliography, as the magazine's home has always been in Northern California. The overwhelming number of potential entries required further exclusion: monthly columns, freestanding recipes, brief notices, primarily pictorial layouts, floor plans, fiction (short stories, serial stories, and poetry), and artwork have been excluded in favor of "feature" articles, of which over 9,400 are represented. Poetry and fiction have been excluded as well.

Finally, in order to allow this volume to be issued during the centennial month of May, the selection of articles herein ends with the January 1998 issue. Note, however, that an on-line version of the bibliography will also include future articles selected per the criteria described below through the May 1998 issue. This Web site, http://www.sunsetmagazine.stanford.edu, has an anticipated launch date in May 1998 and will provide text-searching capabilities, free to the world.

Over the years, the extent of typical feature articles, which at some, but not all, stages in the magazine's history were identified as such in the magazine, has varied from fewer than two to five or more pages. We have excluded some articles that were significantly shorter than the norm for the time. From 1962 on, the tables of contents specifically identified "feature" articles, and the bibliography accepts such designation by *Sunset* editors as definitive. Elsewhere in this volume, the term "notable" refers to these selection criteria.

It is important to note that these selection criteria undoubtedly resulted in the omission of materials of historic interest; truly noteworthy, indeed "notable," topics are to be found throughout the columns, brief listings, sidebars, one-page articles, and other editorial content not listed in this volume (and the advertising, moreover, is raw material for any number of scholarly or popular inquiries). We can only suggest that serendipity is an invaluable tool and encourage the reader to use the bibliography as a starting point for hands-on investigation of the magazine.

Frequently, titles in the table of contents differed from those used on the actual articles. At various times, article titles were merged imperceptibly into introductory segments of text or were discarded in favor of enlivening phrases used as page composition elements, making it problematic to identify an authoritative title. In practice, we relied heavily on the tables of contents, but often adapted the caption title in the interest of clarity. In line with general editorial and business plans, authors were frequently credited with bylines up to about 1930, and again from 1990, but rarely in the intervening (i.e., Lane) years, and the bibliography reflects this pattern.

The bibliography is divided topically into 10 major categories (most of which are further divided into subcategories), within which articles are listed chronologically. Each item indicates the author (if applicable), title, month and year, volume, issue number, and pagination. Each major category of the bibliography begins with an introductory statement giving some perspective on the category as a whole, with notes indicating the relation of the subjects covered relative to other categories. It is recommended that readers interested in the development or history of a particular topic review these introductory statements to ascertain other areas that might pertain to their inquiry. Assignment of articles to these categories had to be somewhat arbitrary, as many of the contributions might easily have been included in two or more categories. All but the most cursory users of this bibliography would be well advised to read the introductory statements for all categories, and refer to the index, which brings together references for subjects, place names, and authors. The reference numbers listed in the index refer to the sequential numbering of articles throughout the bibliography.

Note that the index does not replicate the category in which each article appears. For example, an article listed in the category of general gardening will not be indexed under "gardening." However, an article in the topical listing for domestic architecture which also bears on gardens would be indexed under "gardening" (but not under "home design" or the like). When an article is indexed under a specific term (say, "plums"), it is probably not indexed under a more general term encompassing the specific term used (in this instance, "fruit"), unless the article also addresses the general subject. We have tried to provide as many index points as necessary to reflect the subject matter of the article, but not to burden the index with excessive numbers of common terms. For example, we could have had a thousand or more reference numbers listed under the index term "recipes." Not only would this abundance be daunting to a reader, it would have been largely redundant with the chronological listings for food-related articles.

It is worth noting that *Sunset* has, since the early 1950s, published an *Annual Index* of the magazine's contents. These indexes are very specific–down to the level of each variety of sandwich described in an article on cold buffets–and are clearly intended to accompany working sets of the magazine. They point directly to the issue and page, rather than to an article title or bibliographical citation. The present volume, with its longer chronological scope and more historical orientation, does not attempt to replicate either the detail or the purpose of the *Sunset Annual Indexes*, which continue to be of considerable utility.

The bibliography may seem to appear at times overly selective, because it reflects the vicissitudes and varieties of editorial policies. For example, readers will find a variety of articles from the 1890s to the 1990s in the subcategory "Environmental Issues and Concerns," although the meaning of "Environment" was decidedly different in the era of Teddy Roosevelt from its meaning today. There are voids apparent in certain chronologies, due to changes in editorial direction. The fact that works of fiction and artwork are excluded from the bibliography makes the Field years appear quantitatively less significant than they actually were. Authors like Jack London, Upton Sinclair, Mary Austin, and John Steinbeck wrote stories for *Sunset*, but appear here mainly to the extent that they may also have provided nonfiction articles; even prominent artists such as Maynard Dixon will not often be found in the bibliography listing (but try the table of illustrations). While the bulk of this bibliography (roughly two-thirds) represents the Lane Publishing Company years that turned *Sunset* into a profitable and well-recognized Western magazine, the topical listings clearly indicate how distinctly the Lanes' editorial direction differed from that of the previous management.

Sunset gave rise to a variety of monographs early in its history, but the book program became far more organized and successful under the Lanes' Book Division, as described in the piece by Mel Lane, longtime head of the Book Division. The Lane Publishing Company created a *Sunset* Book Division circa 1950, which produced not only a large body of books published for *Sunset* readers and for sale to the general public but also numerous books and booklets on behalf of other businesses–such as appliance manufacturers–to be used for promotional or instructional purposes. On the other hand, *Sunset* Books collaborated editorially with some firms (spice importers and barbecue manufacturers come to mind) to produce works for sale to the public. *Sunset* has also published some dozens of video programs, language instruction cassettes, and a few multimedia works on CD-ROM.

A chronological list of over 900 *Sunset* books follows the article bibliography. This list, based primarily on information supplied by *Sunset* Books, includes only books made available to *Sunset* readers or to the general public. As such, we have not included non-print publications, calendars, or various other ephemera also published by *Sunset*. During the mid-1970s, the *Sunset* Book Division produced a series of publications in magazine format for seasonal newsstand sales, such as *Christmas Ideas & Answers '75* ; these short-lived materials are not reflected in the listing. Several *Sunset* titles dealing with home repair and remodeling have more recently been translated into Spanish and published by a Mexican publisher (which is no longer active); as these were not *Sunset* imprints, we felt they were outside the scope of the present volume. Among the many *Sunset* titles scheduled for release in 1998, we listed only those already produced and available for inspection in early January.

Many *Sunset* books have gone through numerous editions and re-issues, often with ambiguous or incomplete edition statements and often with variations in title or binding, making something of a challenge for the bibliographer. Some apparent reprints were, in effect, new editions, while some "new" editions were, in essence, reprints. In general, we have taken a middle ground in distinguishing releases, looser than national standards for bibliographic description, but more restrictive than the publisher's lists. We chose not to include a number of titles which appear in lists provided by *Sunset* Books, but which are neither represented in the major national bibliographical utilities nor to be found in *Sunset* Publishing Company's archives. In some cases, new titles have been applied to books previously released under different titles, a common enough practice. Conversely, there appear to be cases where an entirely new work appeared under an older title. More often than not, *Sunset* books provide a choice of several variant titles; in the vast majority of cases, the word (or logo) *Sunset* appears in or above the title on the title page or the cover. We have credited and indexed prominently named authors, editors, and other contributors; for technical reasons, the listing treats all named individuals (and some firms) equivalently, whether they are the primary author or not. It would be fair to say that most, but by no means all, *Sunset* books have been collaborative efforts. All listed books are indexed along with articles in the single master index, and are identifiable by numbers beginning with "B."

Naturally, many *Sunset* book titles and editions are now out of print. Readers interested in purchasing out-of-print books are encouraged to seek out booksellers which are members of the Antiquarian Booksellers' Association of America, a self-regulating trade group. These booksellers are reliable concerns, adhering to a strong code of ethics. We recommend any of them. For assistance in locating member booksellers, please contact:

Antiquarian Booksellers' Association of America
20 West 44th Street, Fourth Floor
New York, NY 10035
(telephone) 212-944-8291
(fax) 212-944-8293
http://www.abaa-booknet.com/booknet.html

Sunset is, of course, well known for its intense use of graphics, and we felt it important to document this aspect of the magazine. A series of over 20 visual themes, running parallel to the essay texts in the outer margins, provides a complementary, but separate, narrative about Western life and *Sunset* through its illustrative matter. The graphics used throughout this book (with the exception of one or two group portraits of the Lane family) were scanned directly from either the pages of *Sunset* or book covers. We felt it important to use the illustrative material from the actual source, though there were some technical challenges to overcome in so doing. Credits to the photographers are indicated as published in the original issues. We thank here the photographers for permission to reproduce their pictures in this bibliography.

Finally, there is the question of obtaining copies of articles. Few individuals will have direct access to (to say nothing of possessing) a continuous set of *Sunset* since 1898, but virtually anybody can obtain photocopies of articles from the pages of *Sunset*, by any of various means.

Depending on where the reader lives, the simplest course of action might be to go to the local public library. Many public libraries throughout the Western states (and elsewhere) have extensive sets of *Sunset* back issues. As most copies of this bibliography will be placed in such institutions, access to some or most *Sunset* articles may be immediately at hand: Ask a reference librarian for assistance. Similarly, many Western college, university, and state libraries have holdings (whether or not complete) of *Sunset*. For example, this bibliography was prepared using the complete sets at the Stanford University Libraries and at the California History Room in the California State Library, Sacramento.

Should the local library not have the specific issue desired, it may be possible to obtain it or a copy of the specific article through Interlibrary Loan; procedures, policies, delivery time, and costs may vary from place to place.

Alternately, the reader can obtain a copy of an article through one of several enterprises specializing in document retrieval services. Depending on the reader's requirements, copies can be delivered via mail, express mail, telefacsimile (fax), or Internet. Costs for this service, of course, may vary and may also include payment of copyright fees. One such service is prepared to handle requests for *Sunset* articles conveniently by citing the reference numbers listed in this bibliography:

Information Express
Customer Service: 650-494-8787
3221 Porter Drive
Palo Alto, CA 94304
Electronic mail address: service@express.com

Services offered, including Web-based searching and ordering procedures, are cited at the Internet address: http://www.express.com. Information Express offers its many services at competitive rates.

Sunset now has a presence on the World Wide Web, at http://www.Sunsetmagazine.com/. This site provides information about *Sunset* magazine, books, garden tours, special events, as well as a means of subscribing to the magazine. Alternately, readers of the bibliography desiring to subscribe to *Sunset* may call 800-777-0117.

Clearly, this volume is the result of much effort on the part of many individuals. First of all, this volume would not have been possible without the interest, commitment, and support of L.W. "Bill" Lane, Jr., Stanford alumnus of the Class of 1942 and a former publisher of *Sunset*. Many hands were involved over the course of a year of development. The contributors of the essays–Kevin Starr, Tomas Jaehn, and Stanford alumnus of the Class of 1944 Melvin B. Lane–provided needed context for the article and book listings and set forth a hitherto untold narrative history. The article database, on which the bibliography was based, was compiled primarily by Shana Bernstein, Jennifer Chin, Shawn Gerth, Camilla Lindsay, and Chad Martin–all graduate students in the Department of History at Stanford–under the direction of Tomas Jaehn, Curator of American and British History, supported by John McDonald, both members of the superb staff of the Stanford University Libraries. Much additional review and refinement of the database was performed by Karen Abbott and Kathy Hudson, with clerical support from Nathan Pudewell. Lois Shumaker made heroic efforts in shaping and augmenting the index. The book list owes much to the research and cooperation of Bob Doyle, Lisa Anderson, and Britta Schwartz at *Sunset* Books. *Sunset* Publishing Corp. management was helpful and supportive, most notably CEO Steve Seabolt and CFO James E. Mitchell, assisted by Lorraine Reno and Carole DeLong, respectively. Chuck Moses, also at *Sunset*, has been very helpful in locating materials. Ideas and materials were generously shared by Elena Danielson and Cecile Dore Hill, of the Hoover Institution of Stanford University, during their concurrent work on a centennial exhibit about *Sunset* at the Hoover. The design of the book is Chuck Byrne's work, with assistance on scanning the *Sunset* images and graphics from Jeong Kim. The copy editor was Madeline Johnson. The publication's managing editor and the one responsible for keeping all of the many threads necessary for weaving such a complex fabric is Andrew C. Herkovic. Support for the development and publication of this book came from a source which prefers to remain anonymous. It is with gratitude that I acknowledge this insightful philanthropy.

Richard Strauss's delightful tone poem, *Till Eulenspiegels lustige Streiche* (opus 28), refers in its title to a German peasant figure whose family name, Eulenspiegel, is a compound word meaning "true mirror." *Sunset* has been for its readers, for its advertisers, for the culture and values of the Far West, a true mirror. Strauss's tone poem is witty, colorful, vigorous, exactly as is and has been *Sunset*. We hope that this centennial bibliography will be a useful tool for an audience as broad as that *Sunset* itself has acquired over these past 100 years and will be of interest to many aficionados and students of Western Americana. The bibliography gives an overview of the achievements, the wide range of topics, and the often trendsetting stories that make *Sunset* uniquely The Magazine of Western Living.

Michael A. Keller
University Librarian & Director of Academic Information Resources
Stanford University
May 1998

FEBRUARY 1929

SUNSET

10 CENTS

Preface

by L. W. "Bill" Lane, Jr.
Former Publisher of Sunset Magazine, Class of '42

With most successful endeavors, for humans as well as organizations, there is a recognizable life span of achievement and distinction, in addition to whatever other ways success is measured. *Sunset* magazine is a story of success, by any definition, in achieving a 100-year history of continuous publication without missing an issue. Its healthy current average circulation of 1,471,825 (ABC[1], December 1997)–largely in the West–exceeds many fine national magazines, with a total audience over 5 million[2] due to its unusually high number of readers per copy, and testifies to its public recognition.

This feat is further significant, given its focus on only one geographical region of the nation: Western America. It is important to keep this regional emphasis in mind: National and worldwide conditions often had far different immediate and long-term repercussions in the West than the rest of the U.S. and were accentuated for *Sunset*'s readership beginning with the first issue in May 1898. For example, Yosemite and other Western attractions were much more difficult to visit from east of the Sierra and Rocky Mountains, and *Sunset*'s early goal was to make "coming West" much more comfortable and cheaper–which just might encourage a decision by some passengers to settle down out West! The early popularization of the automobile and airplane, the opening of the Panama Canal, concerns about the Empire of Japan, World Wars I and II, the great Depression, the wonders of radio earlier and later television, and the economic boom and population shifting taking place over the last 50 years are issues bearing witness that the West was not marching in sync step with the national agenda. They and many more examples are reflected in this bibliography of over 9,000 major *Sunset* magazine articles and some 900 *Sunset* book titles, editions, and reprints, the latter often with new, updated material. Many of these East-West differences are put in a historical context by Dr. Kevin Starr in his perceptive introduction and by Dr. Tomas Jaehn in his well-researched essay, "Four Eras: Changes of Ownership." My brother, Melvin Bell Lane, gives his experienced overview of *Sunset* Books. The magazine and books continue to reinforce each other.

Thus, the primary function of this bibliography is to recognize a century of "notable" editorial content in *Sunset* magazine under its four owners. But, make no mistake, senior editorial staff and team efforts are a critical part of the magazine's performance. Several early editors are mentioned elsewhere. It is worth noting, however, from the launch of the first Lane issue, there have been remarkably few changes in

[1] Audit Bureau of Circulation.
[2] Mediamark Research Institute, Inc. (1997).

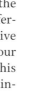

The first Lane cover, February 1929.
From original oil painting by Maurice
Logan, collection of Bill and Jean Lane.

senior magazine editorship in the ensuing seven decades. Co-editors Genevieve A. Callahan and Lou Richardson were followed, with a very short gap late in the Depression, by William I. Nichols, Walter T. Doty, Proctor Mellquist, and William R. Marken. The Lane family greatly appreciates their contributions. Rosalie Muller Wright now serves as editor-in-chief. These senior editors, with their dedicated and creative staffs—as well as many fine book editors—deserve tremendous credit for what this bibliography represents.

A successful magazine personifies "team effort." Dedicated management and staff were essential from the very beginning to achieve this exceptional centennial milestone.

Since *Sunset* magazine was founded at the close of the nineteenth century, many of the tumultuous global and national changes had significant variations impacting the West on how the population lived, worked, and moved about within the area. In recent history, as California has been the magnet to draw the largest share of domestic and foreign population growth, some old and new Californians have moved to other states with smaller populations for a number of reasons. But the large majority move to nearby Western states. Very few relocations go off the Western "reservation"! And, at times, a few of these regional differences created a special challenge of survival for *Sunset*, unique in the history of successful magazines—granted that all have had their own rocky road and certainly with the relatively few magazines still being published that exceed *Sunset*'s longevity of uninterrupted publication. According to the MPA,[3] only 39 magazines started publication before 1898 (*Outdoor Life* joined *Sunset* in 1898), and many are no longer published or had interruptions in their normal publication frequency. *Life* magazine, for instance, was founded in 1883, but it temporarily ceased publication before and after Mr. Henry Luce purchased the title for Time Inc.[4] However, it is important to note that there are more magazines in the U.S. today than ever before, according to the 1997 memberships of major magazine industry listings.[5] I'm not surprised. The high-tech/computer/Web industry alone has spawned a great many new magazines. My brother, Mel, and I often heard our father say, "A new magazine is the easiest to start up by an editor with a bright idea meeting over a couple of martinis with a printer who will advance paper and printing!" The two-martini lunch is not as fashionable and the "easy" part is not so, of course, with a touch of our Dad's humility, and is only relative to the costs of starting up a new radio station, TV station, or daily newspaper. That comment, also, was usually followed by "And to keep a magazine successful is harder than getting it started" and then a warning, "Don't kill the goose that's laying the golden eggs."

To succeed with a new magazine is always a risky business: editorial appeal, gaining circulation vitality with rising direct mail costs for subscriptions and newsstand display competition, and advertising acceptance. But, as the socio-economic trends with a growing population become more diversified, and new technologies become more available, there are growing opportunities for the selectivity advantage of magazines. Dad wrote to a friend shortly after buying a failing magazine in 1928, only a year before the Depression, "The *Sunset* deal, of course, is a gamble." Indeed it was, but it won big.

Topographical map often used to distinguish the West geographically from the rest of the United States.

---

[3] Magazine Publishers of America.

[4] The American Magazine, MPA & American Society of Magazine Editors (1991).

[5] including Standard Rate and Data Service (SRDS) Consumer and Farm Magazines, Audit Bureau of Circulation (ABC) General and Farm Magazines, and Publisher's Information Bureau (PIB) Measured Magazines.

Because editorial content is so critical in the founding and survival of magazines, this scholarly and beautifully produced bibliography is a dream come true for me. Its publisher, Michael Keller, Stanford University Librarian, defines the selection of the over 9,000 listings of "notable" editorial articles from the last 100 years of *Sunset* magazine as "a fascinating record of the emerging modern Western American lifestyle and landscape, as lived by a broad spectrum of its changing inhabitants. That numerous aspects of the Western life influenced and foreshadowed life and styles elsewhere in the United States makes *Sunset*'s editorial history as reflected in this bibliography even more valuable."

This 100-year bibliography was inspired by and benefited from a long history of *Sunset*'s publishing an *Annual Index*, beginning in 1952, listing all articles from each year, in three regional editions. In 1964, a new Desert edition was added for the more arid Southwest. The first priority of regional editions was editorial. Advertising was not initially accepted in regional editions. Today, there are more regional breakouts for editorial changes and for local advertising. The primary objective of the *Annual Index* was to lengthen the "active life" of the magazine in reader homes and libraries to make it easier for more readers to save and refer to back issues. Also, our research made us aware of the benefits of increasing response to advertisers, especially those with coupon or bound-in reply requests, which were often acted upon weeks, months, or even years after the issue was first published. This was a "plus benefit" for magazines generally and a few especially–*Sunset*, *National Geographic*, *Better Homes and Gardens*, *Reader's Digest*, and others that were saved by readers. We did not want nor sell "pass along" readership figures to advertisers, including *Sunset* Books. We wanted *Sunset* to remain in the households of primary readers. Even so, some copies eventually ended up in doctors' offices, beauty and barber shops! As a marketing tool, the *Annual Index* benefited readers but, in turn, strengthened circulation and further gave *Sunset* a competitive edge with advertisers. We were able to present hard evidence of the confirmed "long life" of *Sunset* magazine, vis-à-vis broadcast media and newspapers, of course, and most other magazines. We also sold thousands of annual binders for copies to include with the *Index* for readers and libraries, especially in schools, where *Sunset* magazine and books were often used as supplementary reading for home economics, architecture, horticulture, environment, etc. Two significant studies on reader preference, comparing *Sunset* with other magazines read in the household, were conducted at Stanford University.[6] Older issues, back to the first issue, have always been valuable resources, especially for editors in researching anniversary issues and articles up through this centennial year.

So, as the years passed since the first *Annual Index*, we were missing a much-needed index from the first issue. This bibliography by Stanford University reflects the full century of publication, with continuity of editorial coverage in the major categories listed. Such continuity of editorial policy is significant, recognizing that *Sunset* magazine's destiny has been held by four different owners. And its fundamental editorial mission continues to adapt with the times from the new ownership of Time Warner with management through Sunset Publishing Corporation.

This last change of ownership is unique in maintaining the basic editorial and marketing objectives. The merger in June of 1990 was based

Critical information on regional characteristics and Sunset *readers, for advertisers and market analysts. 1989.*

[6] David Ernest Faville, *How Sunset Magazine Subscribers Evaluate The Magazines They Read* (Stanford, Calif.: Stanford Graduate School of Business, 1940), and Chilton Bush, *Studies of Magazine Preference in Palo Alto, California* (Stanford, Calif.: Stanford Institute of Journalism Studies, 1954).

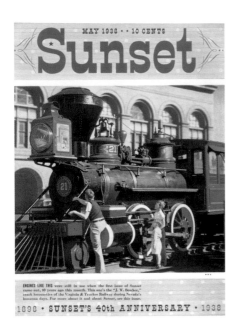

May 1938 40th Anniversary cover

May 1948 50th Anniversary cover

upon a commitment to the editorial mission of the past 60 years, but recognizing the reality of continuing changes that had been the modus operandi for all the years of Lane ownership. Also, the Lane Publishing Company had no debt, owned its headquarters real estate plus a cattle ranch and suburban properties, and had a sizable cash surplus. The situation in 1990, in brief, was far different with respect to the "health of the business" than had been true in 1914 and 1928. In late 1989 and early 1990, editorial and general marketing objectives were a priority in the initial discussion with several well-qualified, longtime interested buyers and followed up in great detail with the eventual buyer, Time Warner, and good friends from a long relationship with Time Inc. Indeed, the long-established formula–a Western family service magazine with a record of remarkable achievements–was the chief asset, as well as the potential for continued growth. That assurance of confidence and respect by the buyer far exceeded in importance any discussion of financial values by the sellers. As Reginald Brack, Jr., Chairman, President, and CEO of Time Inc., which shortly before had become a part of Time Warner, explained at a meeting with *Sunset* employees on April 18, 1990: "One of the first things we discussed with Bill and Mel when we sat down in New York was the respective position of our companies as leaders in their fields. Clearly, you are the leader in the West ... It was the sheer size and growth of your market in the West and of California, in particular." An earlier news release from Time Inc. Magazines, dated March 27, 1990, regarding the upcoming sale, quoted Brack: "Lane Publishing is the preeminent publishing franchise in the country's fastest growing market, the 13 Western states."

Independently of ownership issues, however, *Sunset*'s fate has also been determined over the century of publication by a backdrop of significant regional differences that have influenced all four owners, going back to its founding, that are distinctly Western: topography and weather; early geographic isolation of the West; the nation's last continental frontier facing the new emerging world of the Pacific and Asia; pioneer exploration and settlement with many lasting cultural differences; the dramatic and sudden impact of the discovery of gold 150 years ago; the May 1906 San Francisco earthquake and fire (*Sunset*'s eighth anniversary!); and the massive, unequaled, voluntary migration from East to West beginning with the Gold Rush. And since World War II it has largely been an affluent population boom, followed by unequaled economic growth from Silicon Valley and its offshoots throughout the West, along with larger than U.S. average rate of growth of the inland Western states. Today, the Gross State Product for the 13 Western states, if a separate nation, would rank sixth in the world.[7] Not to be overlooked has been the important political fallout from the surging population growth that has triggered far larger and more influential representation in Congress. (It will jump again with the census in 2000.)

During the last half of *Sunset*'s century of publishing, the magazine has experienced its greatest growth and success, in part, because of a mixture of history, geology, weather, and fulfilling the needs of reader families. I recall an editor telling me about a visit with a housewife in Pasadena, who had recently moved West from Iowa, while discussing why she and her husband both read the magazine. Her quick response was "*Sunset* is all about the West that we came out here for!" For a lot of queries from Eastern advertisers, that statement said it all. Neil Morgan supported this sometimes hard-to-explain phenomenon in his popular book *Westward Tilt: The American West Today*, with his early-on recognition in the early 1960s of the suburban revolution taking place in the West: "*Sunset* has been both a symbol and symptom of the West... it is now the bible of the Westerner. It has sensed and capitalized on Western regionalism." I would have preferred "responded to" instead of his second verb! However, encouraging migration was not a part of the mission, à la the Southern Pacific creed published in the first issue–subscriptions were long refused from non-*Sunset* states and later at higher, one-year-only rates and no newsstand sales out of the West. An irate lady from Boston wrote to my father, "How snooty can you get?" after her subscription order was returned. Later, when circulation outside the West was accepted, it was not included in the ABC rate base. But the out-of-the-West readers, often recipients of Christmas gifts from Western family members or friends wanting to share their "good life," became very responsive readers for many advertisers–and, I am sure, helped make the West a more desirable place to live for some family visitors who later moved out West! And *Sunset* was one of the few magazines that did not rent or exchange subscription lists.

Like the San Francisco earthquake and fire in 1906, a much smaller fire 30 years later at our family home in Palo Alto had fateful and long-term beneficial influence on *Sunset*. While Mel and I finished high school, our parents rented an apartment and bought Quail Hollow Ranch in the Santa Cruz Mountains. Its history went back to the Ohlone Indians and the Spanish Zayante Rancho. During the late Depression and World War II, up to the company's move from San Francisco to Menlo Park in 1951, many editorial projects and key business meetings were conducted at the beautiful and peaceful ranch where Dad kept a "country office." Many business meetings took place there with staff, advertisers, and others. Early discussions were held there that led to the founding of the Advertising Council, which is still flourishing today. Mom was an avid gardener and a home economist, so her gardens and kitchen were a beehive (and we had them, too!) for many experiments. Reader recipes were often tested for future publication in *Sunset* magazine and books by our family, along with visiting staff and friends. Brother Mel was often the barbecue chef, and our first staff family picnic was held there. Fortunately, Quail Hollow Ranch is now preserved as a Santa Cruz County Park.

The uniquely Western regional and socio-economic conditions have given impetus to the evolution of prominent demographics that have further set the West apart from the rest of the U.S.: higher per capita levels of education, income, home and car ownership, passports, etc. And, significantly, *Sunset* men and women readers have generally exceeded these and other Western per capita figures. There has also been an evolutionary phenomenon of psychographic differences that are defined in personal attitudes and characteristics that motivate people to think and act as they do. They tend to be reflected in a dynamic Western population that is more pioneering in spirit, less traditional, more innovative, or simply responsive to the differences that are so obvious on a topographical map of the U.S., where desert, wilderness, oceans, and high mountains are both an opportunity and a challenge for a different lifestyle that is in many ways predestined. Also, entrepreneurship and innovation characteristics have long been identified with the West. Interestingly, some 34 percent of the members of the National Academy of Sciences[8] currently live in the 13

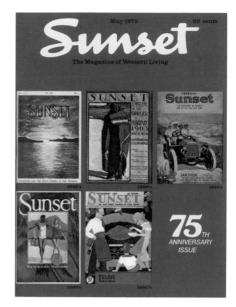

May 1973 75th Anniversary cover

May 1978 80th Anniversary cover.
(photo: Don Normark)

---

[7] As of 1994, per Tables 696 and 1347, *Statistical Abstract of the United States* (Washington, D.C.: Government Printing Office, 1997).

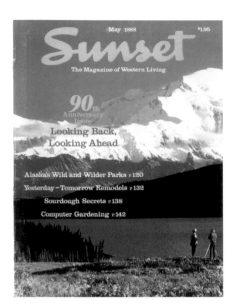

May 1988 90th Anniversary cover
(photo: Mark Kelly, Alaska Photo)

Western states with 21 percent of the U.S. population.

For sure, not all Western differences are better for human happiness: smog (which is getting better), unpredictable earthquakes and mud slides, water shortages and floods, increasing traffic congestion, and ocean damage along our coast, to name a few. *Sunset* has tackled many of these "problems," giving *Sunset* editors an opportunity to help readers find better answers. *Sunset*'s editorials have helped families with ideas for minimizing damage from earthquakes and unstable building sites, brush fire prevention, conservation of water, solar energy, nonpolluting garden products, and many ways to help achieve better environmental goals. Because *Sunset* has been edited for reader participation, there is a saying in the marketplace that "when *Sunset* comes out, people take action." And *Sunset* ideas have been used by planning commissions and building inspectors, park and environmental planners, and other governing agencies to benefit a far broader population than just the many millions of *Sunset* readers over the years. Thousands of reprints of many articles have been distributed by local governments, garden clubs, and often other media that, again, have benefited a far wider group of people than only *Sunset* readers.

The Holy Grail of truly successful magazines–beyond the understandable pride and bias of the founder–starts with an editorial mission. Editors fulfill that editorial mission, starting a chain reaction to attract and hold readers. Reaching that goal must, in turn, develop a solid and marketable volume of circulation that is impressive enough for prospective advertisers to join with editors to provide the total service for readers. The most brilliant editorial content does not go it alone in commercial magazines. To fulfill the business mission of conventional magazines- for-profit requires that both circulation and advertising play critical complementary and synergistic roles in varying degrees of importance for the bottom line profit. Magazine publishers generally have a finger on the pulse of their reader audience for research and adjusting the formula to continue publication. Henry Luce is reported to have taken 10 years to reach a profit with Time Inc.'s now fantastically successful *Sports Illustrated*. Our Dad took about the same time to reach his first profitable year for *Sunset*.

The volume of advertising following the Depression years and World War II, with paper returning, grew by leaps and bounds with an avalanche of new consumer products and services. And the new television medium was taking an increasing lion's share of the dollars. *Look, Collier's, Life,* and *The Saturday Evening Post* folded. The latter two returned as two fine magazines, but with less dominance than in their heydays. However, *Sunset* continued to achieve solid gains through this very tough competition of television and later regional editions of national magazines. *Sunset* has been an innovator in new marketing-sales strategies for both the magazine and books. The magazine grew in circulation, exceeding Western population gains in rate of growth and established many magazine-industry records in pure volume of advertising and several key categories: automotive, travel, garden products, etc. In the midst of the battle for the prime consumers, *Sunset* published several issues over 300 pages–340 pages in April 1960, which was the maximum capacity of the presses at the time–and many in the 200-plus range. These postwar years gave *Sunset* editors the opportunity to write hundreds of long, in-depth articles, and many more that were shorter

[8] National Academy of Sciences Membership List (July, 1997).

than a page, but carried a real wallop for readership. (These shorter articles are not included in this bibliography, as explained by the publisher in his Foreword.) The editorial-advertising ratio remained close to constant at 45 percent to 55 percent through the post–World War II Lane years. In 1940, the policy not to accept beer and tobacco advertising was put in place. Liquor was never accepted. Wine advertising was accepted and continues to be, while tobacco advertising is still not accepted. Some 30 categories of advertising were not accepted and several on a one-time decision, like the American Rifle Association and many others that we did not deem appropriate for a family magazine.

In the earlier tough and lean years, tightly written articles with black-and-white photographs and illustrations simply gave more helpful how-to-do-it information to readers and supported the growing number of advertisers to present their "what-to-do-it-with" advertising. The first editorial color under Lane appeared in December 1954 illustrating Christmas ideas in baking and decorating. I recall very clearly that in January 1961, my second year as Publisher, we ran a full-color page on Sonora, Mexico, followed by a four-color spread in April on varieties of citrus. It was reprinted as a poster by demand from nurseries. From then on, four-color photographs were in every issue, made possible by the great growth of advertising and improvements in printing and binding. *Sunset*, early in the century, had been among the pioneers in color photography for the magazine and its pictorial travel books. Under Lane, during the Depression and the war years, paper and space were precious, and color was not used, because more information could be conveyed in less space using how-to-do-it text and smaller line drawings and black-and-white photographs. And readers approved with a steady growth in circulation with very high renewals–which we monitored carefully. In fact, black-and-white editorial was developed into a strong marketing tool for selling four-color advertising, which stood out more facing the high readership of black-and-white editorial, and gained exceptionally high advertising readership figures.

As Dr. Tomas Jaehn points out in his essay, "Four Eras: Changes of Ownership," changes to the editorial mission and marketing objectives did not take place to the same extent in the 1990 change of ownership as had prevailed in 1914 and 1928, because Time Warner, as it announced, was eager to continue many of the profitable values already in place. However, and make no mistake, every single successful magazine must constantly adapt to change to stay healthy and keep and gain new readers as well as appeal to the advertisers. Actual readers inevitably change, conditions change, priorities change, technology changes, the status quo does not survive–and every one of *Sunset*'s owners has changed procedures during their tenures. During the Lane years, we used to say *Sunset* magazine "changed by evolution, not revolution." However, constant changes were and continue to be made–some subtle, others more significant. But the "mission" stays firm.

For 100 years, *Sunset* has been a magazine reporting on and helping to make history in the West. It was founded with great enthusiasm as a new century was emerging, one bringing challenges anticipated and often unknown. It is my deepest hope that, with this extensive centennial bibliography and historical analyses, the experiences of failure and success from the past will help *Sunset* magazine and its readers meet the challenges of the future and continue to benefit Western America by representing the very best family values as a dynamic part of our great nation.

The evolution of Sunset *cover logos over the decades.*
June 1996, p. 8.

A *Sunset* BOOK

Western Ranch Houses
by *Cliff May*

A Commentary on Sunset Books

by Melvin B. Lane
Former Publisher, Sunset Magazine and Books, Class of '44

During the Southern Pacific ownership of *Sunset* magazine (1898–1914), it was a literary magazine of articles by prominent Western writers. There was little book publishing. The most notable was a series of paperback booklets on each of the counties in California. This was part of *Sunset*'s self-appointed Chamber of Commerce role promoting real estate and commerce in California. The primary market for the magazine was in the Midwest and East. The magazine also published a few picture books of the beauty of the West to promote tourism and Western migration but did very little to convert magazine editorial content into books.

There is no record of any peripheral publishing activity during the Woodhead-Field ownership (1914–1929), even though many of the magazine's articles were written by some great early Western literary talents (e.g., Jack London, Peter B. Kyne, Sinclair Lewis).

When *Sunset* was purchased by L.W. Lane, Sr., and his Iowa friends in 1928, it was changed to a magazine for Westerners, with some staff-written and freelance "how-to" articles on gardening, cooking and entertaining, architecture and landscaping, and travel.

After a few years, the accumulated inventory of *Sunset* magazine articles lent itself to packaging some of these articles into booklets. These booklets were offered as premiums for new subscribers or renewals by existing subscribers. They were saddle-stitched and 6" by 9" in size. The editorial content was created by magazine editors and some freelance writers under the direction of *Sunset* editors.

The use of booklets to aid subscription sales was phased out in the late 1930s, and a few of them were converted to hardbound books (often with significant revisions and enlargements), which were sold by filler ads in *Sunset* magazine and a few Western bookstores and specialty retail outlets in the West.

Lane Publishing Company began to take more interest in book publishing in 1938, and about a dozen titles were published before this effort was curtailed by World War II. The market continued to be Westerners who were *Sunset* magazine readers (home owners looking for how-to-do-it, etc.), with nearly all the content coming from magazine articles or created for the books by magazine editors and freelance special-interest writers. These were initially used to promote circulation. Some of the booklets in time were enlarged into books and became mainstays of the book-publishing wing of the company in later years, e.g., *Barbecue Cook Book, Kitchen Cabinet Cook Book, The Sunset Visual Garden Manual.*

In 1946 a separate Book Division was created with directions to expand the program. New offerings included three or four new titles a year and some major revisions of earlier titles. The market and distribu-

Western Ranch Houses. *The definitive 1958 edition.*

Sunset *travel articles and books have always featured Asian and Pacific travel opportunities, a trend accelerated in the early 1950s and continuing to the present.*

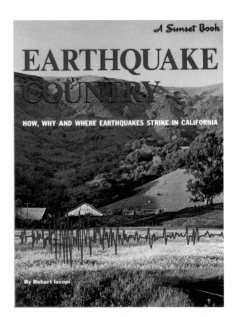

Earthquakes, a regionally important subject that gave rise to three book editions between 1964 and 1971.

tion were the same, i.e., Westerners involved in the *Sunset* way of living. Bookstore sales were expanded. After World War II nearly all new titles were the same trim size as *Sunset* magazine, and this format began to create more of a series. In 1950 the Book Division program was enlarged to a dozen or more new titles and major revisions per year.

There was some early testing of sales in nontraditional outlets (wholesalers and retail chains, stores that traditionally did not sell books, e.g., hardware stores, large discount stores, supermarkets, garden and nursery stores, craft shops, etc.). *Sunset* provided racks. A major effort was made on all the existing and new titles to fit into a series (same trim size, cover design, paperback) in the four magazine editorial fields (building and crafts, cooking and entertaining, gardening and landscaping, and travel).

In 1949 a professional book publisher from the East, George Pfeiffer, was hired as the manager of the Book Division. He greatly increased the number of new titles within the magazine's four editorial fields. He started using direct mail to sell the books and expand sales in bookstore and newsstand outlets in the West. The expansion of distribution into nontraditional outlets was continued.

This set the stage for *Sunset* Books sales and profits to skyrocket in the late 1960s and '70s. Sales went from $3 million to $4 million a year in the mid-1950s to over $50 million in the late 1960s, with nearly half the sales outside the West.

The formula revolutionized this type of book marketing. Most of these sales were through jobbers and wholesalers who would place the racks in stores and service (refill) the racks on a schedule, usually one or more times a week. Many of these were stores that carried the products needed to implement projects in the books. *Sunset* added sales staff in all parts of the United States to sell the line to different kinds of wholesalers and then monitor and help them. In many cases *Sunset* hired part-time people to help the jobbers and wholesalers inventory the racks and refill them. Sales were slowly expanded into Canada, Australia, and New Zealand through special distributors.

In the late 1950s, *Sunset* Books launched a very successful mail order business of coffee table books on Western subjects in the $9.95 to $14.95 price range. This preceded the boom of coffee table books in the publishing industry. Sales were primarily by mailings to *Sunset* magazine subscribers and bookstore sales. Examples would be *National Parks of the West, Earthquake Country, California Missions, Ghost Towns of the West, Back Roads of California, Beautiful California, The Sea of Cortez,* and many others. Sales by mail order ranged from 100,000 to 250,000 copies.

There were also some specialty books that were done to benefit *Sunset* magazine or for publisher fun or satisfaction in filling a societal need, even though little profit would result. A line of *Sunset* Junior Books was created as a test in the early 1960s in the hope of being adopted by the California State Department of Education as grade school supplemental books. This line met with only a modest success in the political jungle and was dropped after a few years. A large-format book called *Peter McIntyre's West* was created by the famous New Zealand artist and was published in 1970.

After World War II, *Sunset* magazine staked out travel to Pacific countries as a major expansion of editorial coverage and potential advertising sales. The Book Division assisted by publishing a *Pacific Area Travel Guide* which covered all the major tourist or business destinations. This was followed by a series of guidebooks to each major destination country, which filled a badly needed niche in bookstores in the United States.

The one title that has prevailed from the 1930s to today is *The Western Garden Book*. It is the unchallenged how-to book for gardeners in the West. Sales have exceeded 5.5 million copies. It started from booklets in the 1930s (*The All Western Garden Guide* of 1933 and other booklets). The real beginning was in 1939, with *The Complete Garden Book*, followed by *The Western Garden Book* of 1954, which was organized around different climate zones in the West.

In summary, *Sunset* was a leader in book publishing in several respects: regional how-to publishing specifically for Westerners; large volume coffee-table book publishing sold by mail order; distribution of a series of books in racks by jobbers and wholesalers into retail outlets

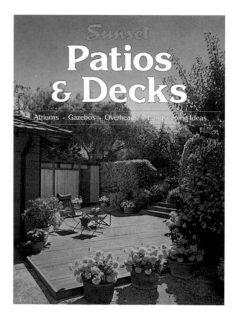

One of many how-to-do-it titles for home owners (1986).

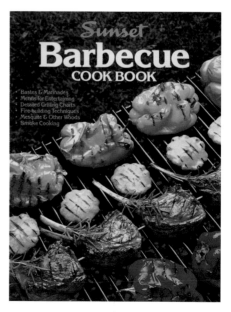

The 1986 version of a perennial favorite.

which normally do not sell books; and travel guidebooks to Asian and Pacific countries. Most notably, however, *Sunset* led the field by launching a highly successful book publishing business based on the innovative idea of using editorial content and expertise of a well-known magazine, and benefiting from a valuable mailing list and the *Sunset* name recognition.

SEPTEMBER 1934   10 CENTS

SUNSET

Sunset *Magazine and the Phenomenon of the Far West*

by Dr. Kevin Starr
State Librarian of California

Through the influence of the thousands of articles documented in this bibliography, *Sunset* has shaped the way people live in the Far West and exercise their stewardship of the environment. Without *Sunset*, in fact, it would be much more difficult to document the evolution of Far Western lifestyle and values. With *Sunset*, it is possible to understand not only what these values and ways of life are but how they evolved over the course of a century. Very often, the subjects covered in the magazine influence national magazines and lifestyles across the nation. Founded a century ago, *Sunset* began its existence serving a Far West on the verge of large-scale settlement. In 100 years it has never missed an issue, even when earthquake and fire destroyed its printing press in April 1906. It has enjoyed, moreover, during this century a significant and generally increasing circulation. Today, it continues to serve an expanded Far West, which has become a region of global importance, with powerful connections to Latin America and the Asia Pacific Basin. As *Sunset* reported to its advertisers in 1989[1], were the Far West a nation, it would be the sixth largest economic power on earth.

Like the *Atlantic Monthly, Harper's Magazine,* and the *Overland Monthly*,[2] *Sunset* has helped its readers–in this case, the educated people of the Far West–discover and define, in the course of the thousands of articles presented in this bibliography, the values and lifestyles; the intellectual, emotional, and imaginative context; indeed, the very psychological center of the region in which they were pursuing their lives. Like these and other great periodicals–the *North American Review, Scribner's Monthly, The New Yorker*–*Sunset* has helped its readers define their intellectual preferences and tastes. Like *The Saturday Evening Post, Colliers, Look,* and *Life, Sunset* verified for them the unfolding pageant of life. Like the *Ladies' Home Journal,* the *Woman's Home Companion,* and *McCall's* magazine, *Sunset* has helped them articulate and direct their emergent tastes, guiding them through a thousand domestic decisions. Like such partisan reviews as *The Nation, The New Republic,* and *The National Review, Sunset* also stands for something–a cluster of values and ideals, a program of action–although *Sunset* rarely preaches overtly (except in matters of conservation), preferring, rather, in the Lane era to allow ideas and values to emerge ever so subtly by implication from staff-written articles tightly controlled by the editorial process.

[1] *Sunset Western Market Almanac* (1989), p. 7. As reported in the *Statistical Abstract of the United States,* the 13 Far Western states in 1994 were the sixth largest international economy; see Tables 696 and 1347 (Washington, D.C. : Government Printing Office, 1997).

[2] Some of the magazines cited in this paragraph have ceased publication (e.g., the *Overland Monthly* and *Scribner's*), while others have changed editorial direction (e.g., *The New Yorker* and *The Saturday Evening Post*).

September 1934 Maynard Dixon cover hearkens to a traditional Western landscape.

Railroad Heritage

It is no surprise that railroad themes appear in the pages of Sunset, *given its initial raison d'être, or that properties owned by the Southern Pacific, such as hotels, are similarly visible. Even in more recent times, railroads appear as part of the Western heritage and as vacation opportunities, whether as attractions or modes of travel.*

Early issues of Sunset *never failed to present the amenities of SP's prime hostelry, the Hotel Del Monte.*
March 1899, p. 116.

The Southern Pacific used the magazine as a showplace not only of Western attractions but of its accommodations as well, as in this picture of "The tourist car by day."
November 1898, p. 8.

In its journey to identity and success, *Sunset* had to find its own distinctive path and format. Energized by, and serving, the drama of the unfolding Far West–a region without precedent and with few certainties, struggling for idea and metaphor–*Sunset* was embarked upon a pioneering journey, an odyssey of travel and exploration, as vivid as any of those described by its articles. By the time that journey was nearing completion, in the flush and expectant years following the Second World War, *Sunset: The Magazine of Western Living* had become more than a magazine. It had become a key prism through which the people of the Far West were glimpsing the possibilities and futures of themselves and their region. *Sunset* entered the twentieth century primarily as a tourist magazine. *Sunset* ends the twentieth century as a Far Western institution, its Menlo Park headquarters a place of near-pilgrimage. Through 100 years of *Sunset*, the Far West, now expanded to include the Mountain states, Hawaii, and Alaska, had voiced, and continues to voice, its deepest hopes and dreams: its collective pursuit of happiness through an equally intense pursuit of the good life.

The railroad hauled people and goods, linking marketplaces throughout the U.S. with the Far West. The Southern Pacific Railroad founded *Sunset* with the premier issue of May 1898, naming the magazine in honor of its crack overland Sunset Limited, operating between New Orleans and Los Angeles. The Southern Pacific, in establishing *Sunset*, promoted travel and migration to the states it served. Quite naturally, the Southern Pacific had an interest in promoting travel to the states it served: California, Oregon, Nevada, Texas, Louisiana, and the territories of Arizona and New Mexico, together with hotel resorts en route, culminating in the Hotel Del Monte in Monterey, one of the great resort hotels of turn-of-the-century California. It was a time when all California, especially the Southland, with its favorable climate, was attracting visitors and developing its economy via such impressive resort hotels as the Coronado off San Diego, the Horton House in San Diego, the Hotel Virginia in Long Beach, the Hotel Green in Pasadena, the Hotel Wentworth in Santa Barbara, and, later, the Beverly Hills Hotel in the lima bean fields west of Los Angeles. Catering to elite visitors from the Eastern and Midwestern United States, these great resort hotels–so many of them destined to stimulate cities in their immediate environs–were intimately dependent upon the Southern Pacific, which offered package tours, with an emphasis upon long winter sojourns. The Southern Pacific, in fact, owned outright the Hotel Del Monte, and beginning with the first issue, *Sunset* helped to promote that property. Dedicated to providing, in the words of its founding motto, "Publicity for the attractions and advantages of the Western Empire," Volume One Number One of *Sunset*, rather expectedly, devoted its lead article to the Yosemite, one of several primary tourist attractions of the Far West. The Yosemite was the Niagara Falls of California, the one place which had emerged in the nineteenth century as the primary icon of all that the Far West offered in the way of scenic grandeur and subliminal release. Ironically, the reference to Yosemite was balanced by the use for the first several issues of the cover image of the Golden Gate, later the setting for two national parks.

There were also chatty descriptions of hotel life throughout the state. At the Hotel Del Monte, for example, Mr. B.F. Jones and a party of Pennsylvanians had arrived in their private railroad car, the Cleopatra, and spent the month of March enjoying the delights of the season. On hand as well were other Pennsylvanians, including Governor Daniel H.

Hastings and Mr. J.T. Brooks, second vice president of the Pennsylvania Railroad. From Southern California there was news of the recently remodeled and enlarged Hotel Metropole at Avalon on the island of Santa Catalina. Mrs. Robert Louis Stevenson, widow of the author, had made a visit to the Glenwood Tavern in Riverside, en route to Scotland, where she was traveling to settle the estate of her late husband. The Hotel Del Coronado, meanwhile, seemed packed with New Yorkers arriving on the Sunset Limited. California, in short, provided a delightful destination for Easterners and Midwesterners anxious to escape the wintry rigors of the East and Midwest via a luxurious transcontinental journey on the Sunset Limited to hotels on the shores of the Pacific,

C. P. Huntington and H. E. Huntington, father and son and successive presidents of the Southern Pacific Railroad. August 1900.

Left: Namesake and raison d'être, the Sunset *Limited. "The most perfect example of the luxury of modern railway travel. Equipment consists of Composite Buffet Library Car, Ladies' Compartment and Parlor Car, elegant Double Drawing-room Sleeping Cars and Dining Car. It is broad vestibuled throughout, gas lighted and steam heated, and runs solid from ocean to ocean." February 1899, p. 82.*

Top: Southern Pacific motive power. February 1899, p. 78.

Bottom: "The latest railway motor car." August 1906, p. 193.

where one awoke each morning, as one visitor to the Hotel Del Monte put it, to "see one hundred acres of lawn and flowers from my window while the air is fragrant with the perfume of roses, violets, heliotropes, and other flowers."[3]

Even amidst such gentility in the pages of *Sunset,* aimed so precisely at the patrician and upper-middle classes, another aspect of the Far West managed to assert itself alongside the discussions of hotels, re-

[3] *Sunset* (May 1898), inside cover advertisement for Hotel Del Monte.

33

"Dedication of Claus Spreckels music
stand, Golden Gate Park, September 9,
1900." Civic, cultural, civilized architecture
in a favorite public park.
September 1900, p. 251.

New City Hall, San Francisco, exemplifying
a worthy destination for Eastern travelers,
whether as visitors or settlers.
July 1899, p. 90.

Mission Dolores, San Francisco, a
modest reminder of the Spanish history
of California.
November 1900, p. 26.

sorts, and rose gardens. Gold had been discovered in Alaska and the Klondike, and the Southern Pacific was anxious to point out that it might arrange a direct connection from San Francisco to the Far North via the Pacific Coast Steamship Company for adventurers en route to the Klondike via the Chilcoot Pass. (Did young Jack London of UC Berkeley read this notice? He would, in any event, be shortly embarking upon this very journey and later writing about it for *Sunset*, to the benefit of American literature.) *Sunset* published arrivals and departures from San Francisco of steamers of the Pacific Mail Steamship Company and the Occidental and Oriental Steamship Company for Honolulu, Yokohama, Kobe, Nagasaki, Shanghai, and Hong Kong. Thus even in its first issue, *Sunset* magazine, founded primarily to promote the genteel pleasures of scenic travel and resort life, was noting as well the surviving frontier of the Pacific Northwest, the Yukon and Alaska, the enchanted islands of Hawaii, and the mysterious lands of the Far East. Here from the very start, then, was *Sunset* country, if only by inference: the Far West as it swept to the Pacific, leapt north to Alaska, and rolled majestically westward toward the Hawaiian Islands, which were the northern edge of Polynesia, and beyond the islands encountered the vast and mysterious lands of the Far East. It would take not even a half-century for *Sunset* fully to possess on the level of engaged journalism this vast area, this Far West as pivot of continental and Asia-Pacific Empire; but it was there from the first, glimpsed through a glass darkly: the gorgeous and heroic spectacle of an empire that began in the Spanish Southwest and, later, embraced the Rocky Mountain states, the Pacific Northwest, including the Alaskan territory, and the lands and islands of the Pacific.

For nearly 16 years the Southern Pacific continued to operate *Sunset* on this basis, headquartered in a Mission Revival–style building near the Southern Pacific offices in San Francisco. From one perspective, the magazine, because it was limited to promotional and travel writing, was narrowly focused; yet because the region it covered was so vast and full of future promise, even this promotional magazine possessed imaginative implications. *Sunset* was about an empire and a way of life in the making. *Sunset* was about the next great stage of American development.

Reinvention as a Literary and General Review

As of the January 1912 issue, *Sunset* absorbed its northern counterpart, the *Pacific Monthly*, founded in 1898 in Portland, Oregon, to promote travel to and settlement of the Pacific Northwest. For the century to come, no matter what subtitle *Sunset* happened to be using at the time on its cover–The Pacific Monthly, The Magazine of the Border, The Magazine of the Pacific and All the Far West, The West's Great National Magazine, and finally and most successfully The Magazine of Western Living–the rubric Pacific Monthly remained fixed on the table of contents page, suggesting this first merger, which brought *Sunset* into the Pacific Northwest and foreshadowed its eventual editorial regionalization. When *Sunset* grew, it absorbed a magazine. Later, when the Far West had grown, *Sunset* partially subdivided itself better to cope with regional diversity. *Sunset*'s most heroic moment in these years was its issue of May 1906, less than a month after the great earthquake and fire of April 18 had destroyed much of San Francisco, including the *Sunset* offices. Fortunately, despite the loss of its drawings, photographs, and engravings, its building and printing press, the mailing list and contract records were rescued. Within a few short weeks the more than 65,000 *Sunset* families in all parts of the world were holding in their hands the New San Francisco Emergency Edition of May 1906, with a cover by Maynard Dixon depicting the enduring spirit of San Francisco rising from the conflagration. No matter, wrote Southern Pacific president E.H. Harriman in the issue's lead article (an issue hastily printed on presses used ordinarily for tickets and schedules in the SP-owned Ferry Building), San Francisco would be rebuilt on a new and better basis. Editor Charles Sedgwick Aiken agreed. Not only would San Francisco be rebuilt, *Sunset* would reappear more excellent than ever. Aiken made good on his word, and within two years a thoroughly re-established *Sunset* was publishing an eight-page photographic panorama by H.C. Tibbitts, astonishing in its printing and binding virtuosity, depicting the rebuilt City by the Bay.

By 1914 the Southern Pacific was deciding to get out of the magazine business. *Sunset*, after all, had been established in great measure to promote the settlement of the Far West, which now stood at 6 million inhabitants and climbing. The economy of the Far West, moreover, was generally booming. The Far West, the Southern Pacific decided, no longer required the promotional efforts of an expensive magazine. Besides, the staff was interested in buying the property, led by editor Charles K. Field, who had succeeded Aiken after Aiken's death in 1911. And so in 1914 *Sunset* passed from the Southern Pacific to the ownership of its new publisher, Woodhead, Field and Company.

Some of the willingness, indeed eagerness, of the Southern Pacific to divest itself of its magazine property came, no doubt, from the fact that

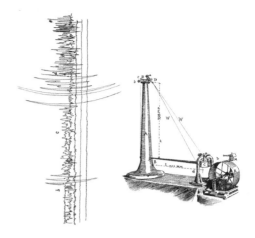

Left: "The record of the San Francisco earthquake as recorded on Professor Omori's Seismograph at Tokyo, Japan." Portrait of a killer.
June-July 1906, p. 43.

Right: "The Bosch-Omori horizontal pendulum seismograph," a technology of some importance in San Francisco.
June-July 1906, p. 42.

the editorial staff and contributors had long since grown restive with the subordination of *Sunset* to the corporate policies of the railroad. Editor Charles Sedgwick Aiken, after all, who had guided the magazine from 1902 to 1911, stated that it was his goal to make *Sunset* "a combination of the *Atlantic Monthly, Outing,* and *McClure's* magazines," which is to say, a magazine that would combine literary and intellectual distinction with an outdoor emphasis and an orientation toward usefulness in daily living.[4] Even while carrying out the general editorial policies of the Southern Pacific ownership, Aiken began to intensify the literary identi-

"Panorama photograph of San Francisco, taken from Nob Hill on the morning of April 18th, 1906, a short time after the fire started, showing the comparatively insignificant damage done by the earthquake."
June-July 1906, pp. 16-17.(photos: Stewart and Rogers)

---

[4] Paul C. Johnson, "Introduction," *The Early Sunset Magazine 1898-1928* (1973), p.11.

"Wagon loads of bread awaiting distribution." Large-scale relief efforts were necessary in San Francisco while the City rebuilt itself.
June-July 1906, p. 33.(photo: Frankish and Smart)

"Bread line on Guerrero street, showing open air kitchens along the curb. All the city's cooking was done in these kitchens for a month after the fire."
June-July 1906, p. 32. (photo: Frankish and Smart)

"Passing the grotesque curb-stone kitchens we heard low murmurings of lovers." Street scenes in the aftermath of the San Francisco quake and fire.
October 1906, p. 322.(drawing: Maynard Dixon)

ty of *Sunset* by publishing, among other writers, the naturalist Charles Norris (brother of the late great novelist Frank Norris, author of *The Octopus* (1901), a powerfully anti-railroad novel); humorist Gelett Burgess, one of the demi-urges of the fin de siècle magazine *The Lark* and the author of the ever-surviving poem "Purple Cow"; a young writer by the name of Jack London, back from the Klondike; London's friend, San Francisco poet George Sterling; prose stylist Mary Austin, whose *Land of Little Rain* (1903) pioneered the aesthetic appreciation of the high desert plateau and arid back country; and–here from the very founding of California literature itself a half-century earlier–a poem by Bret Harte and several poems by Harte's colleague Ina Coolbrith, the poet laureate of California. Aiken also published such established California figures as John Muir, herald of the Sierra Nevada; the renowned historian Theodore Hittell; the poets Joaquin Miller and Charles Warren Stoddard, survivors alongside Bret Harte and Ina Coolbrith of the post–Civil War San Francisco literary frontier; the renowned horticulturist Luther Burbank of Santa Rosa; the San Francisco-born novelist Gertrude Atherton, then living in Europe; poets Vachel Lindsay, William Rose Benet, Witter Bynner, and Yone Noguchi, each at various stages of an emergent reputation; the young novelist Kathleen Norris, Charles's wife, destined to develop by the 1930s into the highest-earning novelist in the United States; and other aspiring writers–Sinclair Lewis, James Hooper, Stewart Edward White, Peter B. Kyne, Earl Stanley Gardner, Damon Runyon, Frederick Lewis Allen–each destined to win national reputation.

All this proved especially exhilarating to Aiken's protégé and successor, Charles K. Field, who headed the group buying the magazine and continued as editor-owner in the new regime. Now, if anything, the roster of notable writers expanded even further as Field sought to make *Sunset* the *Atlantic Monthly* of the Pacific Coast. Writing on nature and Native American life were such renowned figures as Charles Francis Saunders and George Wharton James. Professor E.J. Wickson of Berkeley wrote most gracefully on agriculture. From Stanford came articles by David Starr Jordan, the founding president. Other social commentators included Chester Rowell, later editor of the *San Francisco Chronicle* and a driving force in California Progressivism; Berkeley socialist Herman Whitaker, whom Jack London so admired; and reporters Rufus Steele, Will Irwin, and Lewis Stellmann, among the best journalists San Francisco has ever produced. Michael Williams, the future founding editor of *Commonweal*, covered the missions and religious life from San Francisco and Carmel. The renowned Charles Fletcher Lummis, himself the editor of his own regional publication, *Land of Sunshine*, later *Out West*, wrote from Los Angeles. Literary and cultural life was covered by Henry Meade Bland, a poet-professor from San Jose, Nellie Van de Graft Sanchez, a respected historian of California, and Rose Wilder Lane. Other writers included Charles Shinn, historian of the mining era, naturalist Galen Clark, artist Maynard Dixon, who contributed poetry as well as cover and other art, cowboy writer Will James, and Western novelist Zane Grey. Writer Walter Woehlke, secretary to the board of owner-publishers, wrote what seemed like hundreds of articles through the 1920s on every conceivable topic.

What did these writers, and hence, *Sunset*, have in common? The answer to this query is significant because these writers, who today might seem a mere roll call of half-forgotten names, were bound together by shared values and assumptions which would never be lost to the *Sunset* ethos, despite what may be seen as drastic changes in editorial policy once the magazine was acquired by Laurence W. Lane in late 1928.

First of all, with the exception of such older Literary Frontier figures as Miller, Stoddard, Hittell, and such an arch-conservative figure as Gertrude Atherton, most of the *Sunset* writers from the Aiken-Field era were Progressives. Whether or not they were overtly political, that is, each of these writers adhered to and exemplified a cluster of values regarding public and private life which in the political world, more formally designated as Progressivism[5], was then in the process of reforming California. Progressives were white, Protestant, tending toward the upper-middle class. Instinctively they gravitated toward a reforming middle ground in politics, avoiding corporate monopolies (such as the railroad!) on the one hand, and immigrant-dominated big labor and big city political machines on the other. Progressives valued taste and efficiency in the arts and private life. In the two decades before the First World War, and to a lesser extent after, their sensibility accounted for the simplification and harmonizing of architecture and interior design. They came to a new respect for Native Americans and wrote of Native American culture. They preserved the missions and appropriated, indeed semi-Protestantized, the Hispanic heritage of California as their own. To the Progressive point of view, the entire Far West–California especially–offered a tabula rasa upon which might be projected and achieved a society based upon values of education, taste, beauty, and restraint. Today, at the end of the century they began, a significant percentage of the enduring books defining the California and Southwestern heritage–books by John Muir, Charles Fletcher Lummis, E.J. Wickson, Charles Francis Saunders, Charles Holder, George Wharton James, Joseph Le Conte (whose photographs of the Yosemite appeared in the first issue), and other *Sunset* writers–bear their names on the title page.

Above all else, they were conservationists. In 1892 they had organized the Sierra Club as the key expression of their conservationism, with *Sunset* author John Muir, the single greatest figure among them, serving as founding president. Gifted writers in the main, they were skilled at describing the scenic beauties of California and the Far West. Committed activists, they joined forces with their colleagues in the East to help found the National Park Service in 1916 and fought a score of local skirmishes on behalf of conservation throughout the Far West. The loss of one such battle, the fight to prevent the Valley of the Hetch Hetchy from being dammed, is said to have cost John Muir his life.

They were, in the main, university men, although not all of them, for in that era self-educated men and women were more than capable of rising to intellectual careers and good prose. This was the era between 1880 and 1920, when the American university, blending the Germanic ideal of research and the English ideal of collegial instruction, invented

Two views of San Francisco "taken from almost the same elevated point" 17 years apart: April 1906 and 1923. June 1923, p. 8.(photos: Gabriel Moulin)

"Burning of the Call Building April 18th. This tower like structure, which is 315 feet from sidewalk to tip of dome, suffered small damage from the earthquake. Its frame was unhurt by fire and the interior is being speedily restored." And Sunset *was there. June-July 1906, p. 25.(photo: Haley)*

General Frederick Funston, whose troops attempted to save San Francisco with strategic use of explosives. June-July 1906, p. 26.(photo: J.D. Givens)

[5] It was as if social awareness had reached a critical mass around 1900 that set reform activity going as a major, self-sustaining phenomenon of early twentieth-century America. Interpretations of the Progressive Era (1900-1914) differ sharply ranging from conservative, Richard Hofstadter's *The Age of Reform: From Bryan to F.D.R.* (New York : Alfred A. Knopf, 1959), to liberal, Robert H. Wiebe's *The Search For Order, 1877-1920* (New York: Hill and Wang, 1967), to left-wing, Gabriel Kolko's *The Triumph of Conservatism: A Re-interpretation of American History, 1900-1916* ([New York]: Free Press of Glencoe, [1963]). Other works that interpret particular Western aspects of the period are William Deverell and Tom Sitton, eds., *California Progressivism Revisited* (Berkeley : University of California Press, 1994); Robert Paehlke, *Environmentalism and the Future of Progressive Politics* (New Haven: Yale University Press, 1989); Tom Sitton, *John Randolph Haynes: California Progressive* (Stanford, CA: Stanford University Press, 1992); Robert E. Hennings, *James D. Phelan and the Wilson Progressives of California* (New York: Garland, 1985); and Hiram Warren Johnson, *The Diary Letters of Hiram Johnson, 1917-1945*, edited by Robert E. Burke (New York: Garland, 1983).

Stanford University

There was never any doubt that Stanford was Sunset's favorite temple of learning; the links between them were numerous and profound, as discussed in the essays. This became less visible over time, but persists to the present.

itself. Without the presence of such university-educated men and women, in fact, Progressivism would not have gained the momentum it did, nor, indeed, existed at all; for it was the educated classes, the professionals, doctors, lawyers, university professors and administrators–the clerisy as Samuel Taylor Coleridge described them–who provided the intellectual structure and moral force of the Progressive movement. In a very real sense, they were new men and women. Just prior to their generation, it must be remembered, a college or university degree was in general not required, even for many of the learned professions; but from the turn of the century onward, as the American university and its graduate and professional schools emerged on the horizon of American life, university men and women would increasingly take hold of professional and managerial positions. Theirs was a sense of caste, true, as testified to by the founding of University Clubs throughout the

Panorama of the early Stanford campus. May 1899, p. 23.

major cities of the nation in this era; but it was not a sense of caste based on lineage–but on service. "Princeton in the Nation's Service" was the way that Woodrow Wilson, president of that university, described this Progressive ideal.

The Stanford Connection

Hence an all-important and enduring *Sunset* trait from the very beginning: the Stanford University connection. True, *Sunset* writers had other university affiliations, and over the years *Sunset* would publish articles on the University of California at Berkeley, its second favorite campus, together with articles on such emergent institutions as the California Polytechnic Institute at San Luis Obispo, the University of Nevada, the University of Arizona, and other state universities in the Far West; but it was Stanford–as place, as alma mater, as another legacy of the Southern Pacific Railroad–which most nurtured and structured the emerging *Sunset* ethos. Charles K. Field, after all, had been a member of Stanford's first (and brilliant), Pioneer graduating class of 1895, whose first citizen and lifelong leader was Herbert Hoover, the Chief, as he came to be known in later years. Throughout his life–as a mining engineer in Australia and China, as director of the Commission for Relief of Belgium, as food administrator in the war and postwar period, as secretary of commerce, as president of the United States, as senior statesman and library-builder–Herbert Hoover would surround himself with Stanford classmates, Stanford graduates of other years, and Stanford faculty, whose names (Vernon Kellogg, Will Irwin, Charles K. Field, Rose Wilder Lane, and, above all, David Starr Jordan, founding president and continuing avatar of the Stanford spirit) continued through the 1920s to appear so conspicuously in *Sunset*. Many, quite naturally, being outdoors

Campus scene, Stanford. May 1899, p. 23.

men, were early members and supporters of the Sierra Club. Many of the men, such as Herbert Hoover, were lifelong members of the Bohemian Club of San Francisco and spent part of each July in the Bohemian Grove on the Russian River in Sonoma County. Charles K. Field wrote much of the book and lyrics for the annual Cremation of Care ceremony in the Grove, where an amphitheater was later named in his honor.

Stanford University, founded by Leland Stanford, first president of the Southern Pacific, offers a key expression of Progressivism in the Far West. Here was a university which admitted men and women on the same basis and where a significant percentage of students were on scholarship. Here was a university which from the start excelled in such Far Western subjects as mining engineering, geology, economics, and the emergent science of business management. Here was a university whose founding president, David Starr Jordan, a physician by training and an ichthyologist by practice, preached his own version of the strenuous life, based on values of physical fitness, outdoor activity, conservation, a gracious but restrained lifestyle, internationalism, and public service: a prefigurement, it might be said, of the emergent *Sunset* ethos. All great university campuses–the Palladian grandeur of Jefferson's Virginia, the Gothic spires of Yale, Princeton, and Chicago, the Georgian, Federalist, and Romanesque solidity of Harvard Yard–are in their own way utopian statements of regional life and value. For Jordan and for the first generations of students he produced into the 1920s, so many of them *Sunset* writers, the Romanesque quadrangles of Stanford University, admixed with Mission Revival (designs first sketched out by the great H.H. Richardson shortly before his death), embodied a shimmering ideal of Far Western life refined and intensified to a new plateau of style, efficiency, and proper social value.

Not surprisingly, then, Stanford found its way into *Sunset*, for Stanford had shaped so profoundly the founding generation at the magazine. As this bibliography indicates, Stanford received more than its fair share of articles through the early period, including numerous articles by David Starr Jordan and Herbert Hoover, dual embodiments of the Stanford spirit and the Stanford man in the founding generation. This Stanford orientation would continue down to the present, through the two generations of Lane management. Mr. and Mrs. Laurence W. Lane settled in Palo Alto. Each of the Lane sons graduated from Stanford. *Sunset* would eventually locate its mission-style headquarters in Menlo Park near the Stanford campus, in buildings designed by Cliff May very much in keeping with the Stanford style.

From this perspective, the *Sunset* spirit and the Stanford spirit, while not fully synonymous, were powerfully and continuously linked not only by the Stanford connections of the Lane family but by deeper connections that came from the founding era of each institution. The same entrepreneurial drive, the same pioneering and adventuresome spirit, and the same family values that nurtured Stanford spilled over into *Sunset* and remained. The early Stanford style, as preached by Jordan and practiced by the first generations of graduates, was partially transmuted into the *Sunset* style as well. Like Stanford, *Sunset* cherished values of education, conservation, social responsibility, and a slightly understated yet enthusiastic lifestyle. Aesthetically, more specifically in terms of architecture and design, *Sunset*, like the Stanford campus before it, favored a certain dryness of style in dialogue with the water-scarce, semi-arid realities of the Far West. Like Stanford University, destined to nurture twentieth-century engineering sciences and to generate the computer

"*Looking from an archway into the quad, showing artistic adaptation of mission architecture.*" Part cloister, part varsity quad, part SP station: It could only be Stanford University. *December 1902, p. 94.(photo: Donaggho)*

Memorial Church, Stanford University, "*a marvel of architectural beauty.*" Survivor (barely) of two major quakes since this photo, it is an enduring and peaceful highlight of the campus and region. *December 1902, p. 95.*

"*Two great universities*"–Stanford and Berkeley, twin beacons of enlightenment in the Bay Area, shown in a montage-type layout typical of the time. *May 1899, p. 10.*

In its early years, weighty matters of the world and the region were treated in Sunset's *pages, resulting in a fascinating trove of photographs and even political cartoons. With the region's frontier heritage, its facing the vast (and potentially hostile) Pacific, and the drama of World War I, military affairs were well represented, in text and photos.*

"Which troops are safer, those in the dugouts or those on top? The question and the drill will soon have more than an academic significance for the huskies who are getting ready to fight for democracy."
September 1917, p. 9. (photo: International Film Service)

Far right, top: "The armored coast line battleship 'Wisconsin,' in the San Francisco bay after her world record breaking trial trip. Built by Union Iron Works, San Francisco." A strong naval presence was vital to a Pacific-facing coast in an era of increasing international engagement.
October 1900, p. 274.

Right: "The Wings of war. For a little over two years the Signal Corps Aviation School of the United Sates Army has been in operation at North island, in San Diego bay..." Military aviation coexisting with luxury resort, both beneficiaries of the Southern California climate.
March 1916, p. 9.

Far right, bottom: "One of the machine-gun trucks manned by discharged soldiers." Civic unrest on Western American streets in the aftermath of WWI.
April 1919, p. 15.(photo: Webster & Stevens)

revolution, *Sunset* had a continuing belief in practical technology, whose fundamental assumption was: The simpler way of doing things was frequently the better way.

Concerns and Interests in the Early Years

But that was for the years to come. In the meanwhile, *Sunset* continued as a general interest magazine until February 1929, when Larry Lane's first issue was published with completely revised editorial direction. A perusal of this bibliography will reveal how certain subjects treated in these pre-Lane years did not make the transition into the new era. Aiken, for example, published articles on Spanish art in Texas and an essay by Bruce Porter (Henry James's nephew-in-law) on Arthur Putnam's animal sculpture. During the Panama Pacific International Exposition, Michael Williams wrote a key article on Western artists, and sculptor A. Stirling Calder covered sculpture. Other art-oriented articles covered art, bookplates, fabrics, mosaics, and tiles. All this was very much in the Arts and Crafts mood of the early 1900s. *Sunset* also reviewed the many instances of outdoor drama, and both Charles K. Field and Rose Wilder Lane submitted film criticism. There were also book reviews and literary chitchat aplenty, as befitting a journal which had the *Atlantic Monthly* as its model. This rapidly disappeared with Lane's new editorial direction.

Social questions–by which is meant politics, economics, industrial relations, and various sociological topics–which occupied a reputable percentage of *Sunset* pages in the pre-Lane era, did not survive into the 1930s. Between 1914 and 1928, *Sunset* published 119 notable articles on politics, and only 6 in the ensuing decade. Most of these, however, with the exception of Walter Woehlke's four-part series on the Tom Mooney case in 1919 and an article or two on the IWW, were not gritty, engaged

pieces, but more philosophical essays such as David Starr Jordan's "What of the Nation?" series running through 1916 and early 1917 and Jordan's essays on the peace process following World War I. Other writers on politics included Governor, later Senator Hiram Johnson and *San Francisco Call* editor Fremont Older. After the war, Senator Johnson took over the "What of the Nation?" column. Jordan, Johnson, Older: solid Progressives all, and very much indicative of the politics of *Sunset* in these early years.

Between 1898 and 1931 *Sunset* ran 177 notable articles on business and industry, many of them by Walter Woehlke. Interest in these early years was very much on mining, a survival from the frontier Far West, but also upon such new industries as electricity and telephone service,

irrigation, oil drilling, ship building, dam building, timber, and cattle ranching in Hawaii (a 1927 article most charmingly entitled "Ukulele Cowboys"). *Sunset*'s coverage of ranching and agriculture, especially the articles by Walter Woehlke, were among the glories of the magazine in its first two decades. Here, after all, was the long-desired Garden of the West being brought to fruition. At the same time that Jack London was ranching in the Valley of the Moon in Sonoma County, and setting some of his fiction there, *Sunset* was also on the scene covering the very same agriculture which London had now declared to be his life's work along with writing. Sheep and cattle raising throughout the Far West; the raising of chickens and ducks; the introduction of rice into the marshy regions of the Delta; the growing of prunes in the Santa Clara Valley; the planting of onions and celery; the growing of olives, almonds, walnuts in the Central Valley (increasingly under irrigation); the spreading orange and lemon groves of the Southland; the hardscrabble life of ranching in the Imperial Valley, so recently seized from the desert; the patient, Virgilian work of bee-keeping–in article after article, the writers of *Sunset* were there, on the spot, creating a prose Georgic of California and Far Western agriculture for the ages to come.

Nor was this an exclusively California-centered perspective. *Sunset*, after all, had absorbed the Portland-based *Pacific Monthly* in 1912 and thus moved easily into coverage of Oregon, Washington, Idaho, and even Alaskan agriculture. One is constantly impressed, moreover, by the continuing high-mindedness of the coverage: of seeing agriculture as moral science and art as well as an economic activity. Who else but *Sunset* could publish such articles as "Among Oregon Apples" by "A Harvard Man" or Walter Woehlke's "The Soul's Awakening and the Price of Prunes"?

Biography and military studies were other editorial categories that did not survive into the 1930s. Historical articles did not represent a large category, only 92 notable entries in this selective bibliography, of which a third appear after 1928; yet such reputable Western writers as the novelist Eugene Manlove Rhodes, *Los Angeles Times* columnist Harry Carr, and budding journalist John Considine, who would eventually gain

Far left: "Starting something." While this cartoon does not quite convey the 800-year history of Anglo-Irish relations, it does remind us that Sunset's *outlook was then cosmopolitan, as much as regional. March 1919, p. 10.(credit: McCall, Portland Telegram)*

Left: "Love at first sight." Realpolitik and women's suffrage. November 1920, p. 20.(credit: Wahl, The Sacramento Bee)

The impact of new technology on warfare, the rise of aviation, the global-strategic importance of the Panama Canal (and Pacific lines of communication): all major themes of the West and of Sunset *at this time, depicted dramatically on this April 1914 cover. (Artist: Jules Guerin)*

"'The Makin's'": Fresh recruits for European battlefields, ready to make the world safe for democracy? March 1918, p. 22.(photo: Mark Larkin)

41

Commerce

The early Sunset *was bullish on Western commerce, agriculture, transportation, and industry. Whether to promote a land of limitless opportunity or to investigate issues of the day,* Sunset *tells us much about the economic West of the early century.*

Pampas plumes, a minor crop in California. November 1899, p. 23.

Right, top: All that is mined is not gold; the salt industry.
July 1900, p. 137.

Right, bottom: "A feature of the wine industry" long before Prohibition.
February 1900, p. 152.

Far right: "Fresh catch is hoisted ashore Eureka, center of California's crab-fishing industry." Regional favorites.
March 1978, p. 264.(photo: Richard A. Duning)

a national reputation, submitted articles in this genre. Since 1929, historical context, including military ones, became a significant sub-theme in travel and other articles; such inclusion made *Sunset* attractive for educational use, especially in the Lane years. Biographical articles, by contrast, received much more attention in the pre-Lane years, 343 notable biographies in all. Some of these–UC Professor Edward Wickson on Luther Burbank, David Starr Jordan on Jane Stanford, Michael Williams on Junipero Serra, Hamlin Garland on Joaquin Miller, Walter Woehlke on Abbott Kenny, Flora Hines Longhead and Madera Holt on Ina Coolbrith, Charles Fletcher Lummis on Theodore Roosevelt, Rose Wilder Lane on Jack London, Lewis R. Freeman on Calamity Jane, Will Irwin on Hiram Johnson, Charles K. Field and Rose Wilder Lane on Herbert Hoover, and Aimee Semple McPherson on herself–remain classics of their kind, possessed as they are of what Edmund Wilson called the shock of recognition: the moment, that is, when writer and subject collaborate in mutual recognition and statement. In Theodore Roosevelt, after all, Charles Fletcher Lummis saw in his Harvard classmate, so quintessentially Eastern in his origins, very much the man of the Far West. In Junipero Serra, Michael Williams, a recent convert to Catholi-

cism, en route to becoming one of the foremost Catholic journalists of his generation, perceived the Roman Catholic dimensions of European culture in California. The articles on Herbert Hoover by Charles K. Field and Rose Wilder Lane are especially interesting; for by this time, Herbert Hoover was on the verge of taking the Stanford style (dare one say the *Sunset* style?) eastward to the White House itself.

In one pre-Lane genre, military affairs–so seemingly remote from the normal concerns of *Sunset*–the magazine made a startling contribution. But then again, from the perspective of *Sunset*'s dynamic relation to the Far West, this is not so surprising; for both the Army and the Navy had played major roles in the exploration of the Far West and the conquest of California during the Mexican War. Between 1846 and 1850, in fact, California remained a military territory, with the highest- ranking officer on the coast serving as the de facto civil governor, since Congress, divided on the slavery issue, had proven unable to grant California territorial status. Following the granting of statehood in September 1850, the United States Navy established a yard on Mare Island in San Francisco Bay, which represented the nation's strategic naval presence on the Pacific. Such distinguished Civil War generals as Ulysses Grant, William Sherman, William Halleck, and Albert Sidney Johnston all spent time in California before the war. The military, in short, was the midwife of California and the Far West's American identity in the mid-nineteenth century, and for the half-century to come the Army, and to a lesser extent the Navy, continued to play important roles in the governance and economy of this region, especially in the territories. Generals Lew Wallace, author of *Ben Hur*, and John Charles Fremont served as territorial governors of Arizona. The Army administered the Yosemite until the creation of the national park system. The Army Corps of Engineers exercised enormous influence and jurisdiction over the rivers, lakes, and inland waterways of the entire region.

The military emphasis of *Sunset*, then (between 1902 and 1928 the magazine published 116 notable articles on military topics), must be seen in this context. The states and territories of the Far West, especially California, Arizona, and Hawaii, had been and continued to be intimately dependent upon the military presence for the development of its society and economy. Hence, when *Sunset* covered, as it did, the Spanish American War, the Philippine Rebellion, the last phases of Apache resistance in the Far West, the growing naval presence on the Pacific Coast, the acquisition of Pearl Harbor and the creation of the Pacific Fleet, and the expedition against Pancho Villa, it was not only advancing a strategic argument, it was covering one of the important components of Far Western society and identity.

In naval and aviation matters, moreover, *Sunset* published articles of strategic importance. More than any other state, California, with its more favorable climate, welcomed the new art and science of aviation, beginning with the Los Angeles County Air Show at Dominquez Field in January 1910. Within a few short years both the Army and the Navy had centered their major aviation efforts on the Pacific coast. Hence the importance, among other articles, of "Can the Panama Canal Be Destroyed From the Air?" by Riley E. Scott, published in April 1914. Eight years before Brigadier General Billy Mitchell was court-martialed for advancing the same notion, Scott suggested that great battleships and shore installations were highly vulnerable to air assault. Likewise, in the matter of the projection of Japanese naval presence into the Pacific, *Sunset* was glimpsing, along with others, the probability of a trans-Pacific clash between the United States and Japan.

The more diversified *Sunset* became, however, the more it lost its focus. Already, *Sunset* had defied the odds by remaining in business as a Pacific Coast–based general interest magazine in competition with national magazines for the Far Western dollar. With the exception of the

"Wouldn't she make a fine figure as a major of a Battalion of Death!" Far from the battlefield, WWI ushered changes in Western culture, economics, and attitude. February 1918, p. 7.

"Old and young, grave and gay work side by side." Then as now, agriculture was highly labor-intensive, especially at harvest time. January 1904, p. 242.

"They are young Americans though married eleven years, city dwellers until a year ago and never out of debt. For a year they have followed the fruit in their own automobile, earning ten dollars for every day in the year and spending two and a half. They are out of debt and planning to buy a ranch of their own." December 1920, p. 28.

"*Laurence W. Lane (1890-1967). As a publisher for 31 years, Larry Lane always
made his guidelines for the magazine unmis-
takably clear ... 'To render a regional service
not duplicated by other media,* Sunset *must
adhere to a policy of not being all things
to people.'*"
May 1973, p. 328.

Overland Monthly, no Far Western–based general interest magazine had
lasted longer; and yet by the late 1920s, *Sunset* was in financial trouble.
The difficulties facing *Sunset* were more than a matter of focus, although
it could honestly be said that *Sunset* was trying to be too many things to
too many people. On a deeper level, the exhilaration of the early Progressive years had not survived the shock of World War I. Increasingly,
middle-class Americans–traumatized by the casualties the United States
had experienced in two short years of the AEF–were withdrawing from
their previous stance of optimistic internationalism and becoming more
cautious, isolationist, and conservative. And besides, the high-mindedness of the Progressive era seemed increasingly out of touch with the
cynical syncopations of the Jazz Age. America had become frenzied and
materialistic in contrast to the more philosophical and aesthetic stance
of the pre–World War I Progressives. It was not so much that their time
had passed. Far from it: Had Herbert Hoover been elected president
in 1920, or even 1924, he might have emerged as the Progressive
Triumphant. Although, even in this speculation one must take into consideration the figure of another shaken and defeated Progressive,
Woodrow Wilson, stung by his nation's rejection of the League of
Nations, felled by stroke, serving the final months of his presidency as
a stricken recluse in an upstairs White House bedroom. Progressivism
would never disappear, but it was losing momentum as a full-fledged
social and political program. Magazines serve as arsenals, true; but

by the late 1920s it was uncertain at *Sunset* which audience ought to be
targeted, and circulation figures and the bottom line began to show the
effects of the confusion.

A New Owner, A New Vision

Enter Laurence W. Lane, advertising director of the Des
Moines–based Meredith Publications, owner of the widely read *Better
Homes and Gardens, Successful Farming,* and two other magazines. With
the help of six other Des Moines investors, Lane purchased *Sunset* from
the Field group in September 1928 for $60,000. (Soon thereafter,

Charles K. Field went into the radio business, winning fame and fortune as the commentator Cheerio.) Immediately, Lane laid down a new editorial policy. "'The magazine,' he said, 'will be maintained as a strictly western one, designed to serve western and national advertisers in reaching the substantial homes of the western states. Editorially, a large portion of the magazine will be devoted to the home and outdoor life of the west.'" [6] *Sunset* would no longer resemble *Harper's* and the *Atlantic* as a writer-driven literary review. And he leaned on President-Elect Hoover's family values plank, excerpted in the first Lane issue, to create

Larry and Ruth Lane, 1966.
(Oil painting by Arthur W. Palmer, collection of Bill Lane)

Left: The Lanes on the lawn at Sunset, *circa 1956. From left: Bill, Jean, Larry, Ruth, Mel, and Joan.*

Mel and Bill Lane, circa 1989.

Sunset magazine's editorial policy of service to the whole family with attention to men readers. That same issue included a piece entitled "The House a Man Calls Home," suggesting the importance of the man in the home. It would eventually become a staff-written magazine, with no by-lines, focusing on the Far West lifestyle–meaning homes, gardens, cuisine, travel, and leisure.

Conventional opinion claims that Laurence W. Lane saved *Sunset* by changing it. Yes and no. True, Lane drastically altered the nature of the magazine. Paradoxically, however, Lane saved the magazine by channeling values and energies of an earlier era into a precise pattern of highly useful topics. Indeed, it can be claimed that Laurence W. Lane saved *Sunset* by tightening its focus and keying it to the next Far West, suburban and middle-class, in the making.

A successful magazine publisher (which Laurence W. Lane certainly became) uses his or her magazine to explore a set of personal preoccupations as well as to meet the needs of a market. Lane formulated new editorial policies and recruited as senior editors two talented women from *Better Homes and Gardens* to help him implement those policies. The two, Miss Genevieve A. Callahan and Miss Lou Richardson, had top editorial responsibility and, together with the counsel of Lane's wife, Ruth Bell Lane, proceeded to fulfill those editorial objectives. These were pioneering roles for women in the magazine industry. At their high point, successful magazines are energized by the dialogue between editor and readership. In assigning stories, the publisher defines the prod-

Bill and Mel Lane outside the new Sunset *building with their father, Laurence W. Lane.*

[6] *Des Moines Register*, Sept. 15, 1928, p. 11.

"Visitors walking past the demonstration gardens get this view back toward main building. Barbecue, left. Reception room, center."
August 1952, p. 54.

Right: "Aerial view of the Sunset Grounds in Menlo Park, looking south. Along San Francisquito Creek, which forms the irregular boundaries of the property to the west (right) and the south is Sunset's demonstration garden. Here you can see, in a quarter mile garden walk, typical plants of Pacific Coast from Canada to Mexico growing side by side. Main entrance is at lower left." GHQ for a Western lifestyle. Significant remodeling has taken place since this photograph was first published.
August 1952, p. 47.

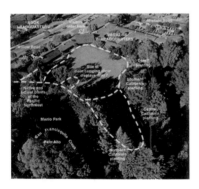

"Helicopter's view shows Willow and Middlefield roads, the two buildings, and the 27-year-old garden at the Magazine Headquarters–with its native and typical plant areas labeled." A new view of the familiar grounds for the 80th Anniversary issue.
May 1978, p. 128. (photo: Glenn Christiansen)

uct according to his own vision and what he understands the audience wants. When the vision and the audience's needs coincide, and the other aspects of publishing are in place–good writing, good design, good business practices–the stage is set for success. Good business practices include adequate and responsive circulation, a successful advertising program, and efficient and ever-modernizing production practices. Such figures as William Shawn at *The New Yorker*, Condé Nast at *Vogue* and *Vanity Fair*, and Clay Felker at *New York* magazine exemplify this process. From this perspective, there could have been no more suitable purchaser of *Sunset* in 1928 than the 37-year-old Midwesterner, Laurence W. Lane. He had acquired *Sunset*, after all, as the key instrument and source of energy for his own journey to Far Western identity.

Born in Horton, Kansas, in 1890, Larry Lane grew up in an ethos of self-reliance and Midwestern values. His father died when Larry was a boy, and he and his mother moved to northern Illinois, where they lived with relatives. At the age of 16 the young man had gone to work as part-time salesman at a hardware supply company to support himself through school. After moving to Iowa with his mother, he attended Drake University and worked summers with the Meredith Publishing Company. He also found time to court Ruth Bell, daughter of the univer-

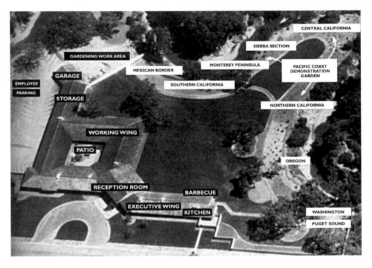

sity president, whom he married upon graduation at the somewhat advanced age of 27. Shortly thereafter, Lane entered the Army, achieved the rank of first lieutenant, and served throughout the First World War.

Even with these sketchy details, a portrait emerges as if from a novel by Booth Tarkington: an ambitious Midwestern lad, forced into self-reliance by the early death of his father, eager for education and upward mobility, earns a college degree, marries his college sweetheart, earns an officer's commission in the Army. Of equal importance, he discovers his lifetime work, magazines, initially on a part-time basis, and then after the war as a full-time employee of Meredith Publishing Company, where he quickly rises up the ladder–personnel, research, and sales–to become advertising director for all Meredith publications. *Successful Farming* was a practically oriented, can-do magazine, equally aimed at the Midwestern farming husband and wife. After the war, Meredith purchased a defunct Seattle magazine, *Better Homes, Fruits, & Gardens*, which it re-designed, and, under Larry Lane's direction, brought back into circulation and renamed as *Better Homes and Gardens*.

Practical by temperament, formed in the school of hard knocks, yet not hardened by the process, managing to move himself solidly into the corporate upper-middle class by dint of his own efforts, socially connected to his local milieu through a happy and advantageous marriage, Laurence W. Lane had absorbed unto himself the best of the Midwest experience. He might have remained, in fact, in Iowa for a long, happy, and fulfilled lifetime, except for the fact that he fell completely, totally, in love with the Far West. With almost paradigmatic clarity, it happened during a visit to Yosemite National Park.

As advertising director, Lane traveled extensively throughout the country setting up sales offices, dealing with major clients, exploring new possibilities for advertising and circulation growth. Already, as advertising director for the hugely successful national publication *Better Homes and Gardens*, Lane had become sensitive to just how important regional matters were to his readership. What grew in Massachusetts, and when, was an entirely different matter to what grew in Illinois, and when, or Salt Lake City, Tacoma, Palo Alto, or Pasadena. Likewise was the question of home design and improvement dependent upon regional variation. Of all the regions he was visiting, Lane decided, the Far West–its terrain and climate, its flora and fauna, the special challenges and opportunities of its settings–was the most distinctive; and nowhere was this more true than in California, where Ruth's retired parents had settled, in Los Angeles. At one point in the early 1920s, Lane's boss Ed Meredith invited him to come along on a ride through the great San Joaquin Valley in the private car of the president of the Southern Pacific Railroad. Meredith–secretary of agriculture in the Wilson administration–was especially interested in the agricultural vitality of the Great Valley. Near Fresno the luxurious private car was transferred to a spur track leading to the El Portal terminal outside the Yosemite Valley. The party then transferred to a motorized open bus for the final stage of the journey to that place which had been symbolizing in the American imagination the special possibilities of the Far West ever since the 1860s. Thus within a few hours Lane had experienced the maritime setting and urban sophistication of San Francisco, the vast expanse of the irrigated San Joaquin Valley, the Sierra Nevada foothills, then the mountains themselves, and finally the great Yosemite Valley. "The dramatic transition from sea coast to broad valley to high mountains in only a few hours' travel," his son Laurence William Lane, Jr., later remembered, "made a lasting impression on Dad and convinced him that travel and recreation would increasingly play a significant role in the lives of Western families as one of the viable differences from the rest of the country." [7]

Because Larry Lane tended to see life in terms of magazines, he was soon seeing his growing interest in the Far West from this perspective as well. Already, he had been keeping his eye on the embattled *Sunset*, then up for sale. With the help of six other Des Moines investors, he acquired the company in September 1928. Within a month, he had moved to San Francisco to take over his new venture.

Definitive Rededication to a Fourfold Path

When Larry Lane stepped off the ferryboat at the foot of Market Street, a brass band was playing and a parade was passing by. It was, however, the annual Columbus Day celebration by the city's Italian community and not a welcoming demonstration for an Iowa publisher

[7] Laurence W. Lane, Jr., *The Sunset Story* (1973), p. 18.

"From the garden you look into the reception hall and along the roofed corridor that leads to the barbecue. Note that the corridor ramps up gradually with the rise in ground level." Interior of the Sunset *headquarters. August 1952, p. 48.*

"You enter through these four-inch-thick carved pine doors. Inside is the reception desk where hostesses are on duty to take visitors through the building, patio, and garden." The tours are now self-guided, but the ambiance is unchanged. August 1952, p. 48.

Sunset*'s test kitchen: "Looking through kitchen and freezer into pantry. Trick was to give space to many cooks without destroying efficiency when used by only one. Sink, work surfaces stainless steel. Cupboards blue, ceiling off-white. Natural redwood above cabinets." August 1952, p. 52.*

In its first three decades, Sunset *boasted a gallery of prominent contributors, some of whom were also the subject of biographical pieces. Here are a few faces from that period.*

Above left: "Herbert Hoover, the Far Western engineer who served in Europe as the economic director for the Supreme War Council and who has come home convinced about the Treaty and the League." Not yet president, Stanford alumnus Hoover was both author and topic in the pages of Sunset. *November 1919, p. 15.*

Above right: Stanford University president David Starr Jordan, contributor to the early Sunset. *December 1902, p.103. (photo: Vaughan & Keith)*

Above left: "Two famous nature-lovers and authors in a California garden–John Muir (by the fern) and John Burroughs. Muir, 'Psalmist of the Sierra,' was a pioneer in Yosemite Valley where he once tended flocks of sheep, discovered scores of living glaciers and helped create the Park. Muir Glacier in Alaska is also one of his famous 'finds.'" August 1914, p. 356.(photo: King)

Above right: Joaquin Miller, Western Romantic, at Fremont Park. February 1902, p. 164.

determined to become a citizen of the Far West. But the band might have been celebrating Lane's arrival as well, for a process was being set in motion that would eventually present the Far West with its most successful magazine and book publisher, from whom millions would learn how best to live in this still-new region, where the Lanes would now be rearing their two young sons, Laurence W. (Bill) Lane, Jr., and Melvin Bell Lane.

In buying *Sunset*, Larry Lane inherited the Progressive traditions of the magazine, its good will and reputation, and its flair for graphics and typography. *Sunset* had long since excelled, for example, in color. The April 1914 issue, for example (in which Riley E. Scott's pioneering article on air power also appeared), presented colored photographs of the Panama Pacific International Exposition under construction; an orange-sailed felucca sailing off Mt. Tamalpais on San Francisco Bay; Shoshone Falls on the Snake River; a buckboard rider in an idyllic Idaho countryside; a girl in a blossoming orchard in Washington; a steamer entering the Port of Columbia; motorists enjoying scenic Lake Tahoe; and Mrs. Phoebe Apperson Hearst's Hacienda del Pozo de Verona near Pleasanton, its white walls and red-tiled roof gleaming in the sun, its entrance pathway ablaze in blooming flowers. The covers of *Sunset* were likewise polychromatic and engaging. Many of them–produced by such noted artists as Maynard Dixon, Ed Borein, Maurice Logan, and Will James–were works of art. Covers by Maynard Dixon before and after the Lane acquisition, many of them depicting Native Americans in the Southwest, are especially notable. Taken cumulatively, *Sunset* covers from the first four decades of the century yield some of the finest iconography and image-making dealing with Western life. Across scores of covers was achieved an almost utopian presentation of the landscape, people, and pleasures of the Far West.

Larry Lane retained, indeed enhanced, this graphic tradition. Appropriately for a magazine celebrating beauty, *Sunset* would always itself be a beautiful instance of print, graphics, and photography. When it came to the editorial policy, however, Lane rejected the existing identity of general review and declared that henceforth *Sunset* would concern itself with four major fields: home, gardening, travel, and cooking. Each article, moreover, had to be useful to the reader. It had to teach a reader how to do something–prepare a certain dish, plant a certain tree, repair a window pane, make Halloween costumes for children. In contrast to *Better Homes and Gardens* and other home service magazines, the new *Sunset* suggested where a reader might travel and what sights could be visited there. Larry Lane was bringing to *Sunset*, in some measure, the practical orientation that had made *Successful Farming* and *Better Homes and Gardens* so successful.

Was Larry Lane transforming *Sunset* into a women's magazine? Not really. In his "Mission Statement" published in the January 1929 issue, Lane specifically noted that he would be publishing a magazine for both men and women. Many of the articles–how, for example, to build a brick backyard barbecue, how to weatherproof an attic–would more than likely interest and instruct male readers. On the other hand, given the emphasis upon food and upon food preparation in the home as being largely women's work in that era, Lane was making the magazine more relevant to women. A more subtle analysis, however, might see that, as in so many other aspects of the Progressive tradition so evident in the pre-Lane publication, the new orientation of *Sunset* was being coaxed from its previous identity. Women, first of all, held an equal place among *Sunset* readers and subscribers. Women, that is to say, formed at least half the audience for *Sunset*'s general interest articles. And then there was the question of articles expressly about women. Between 1902 and 1937, *Sunset* published over 100 notable articles about women and many more articles for women. These articles dealt with a variety of topics, some of them–such as Gladys Johnson's 1926 article on "Divorce and the American Home"–rather daring for their era, in contrast to those after 1928, such as Genevieve A. Callahan's "It Takes Two to Make a Home" in 1935.

In any event, *Sunset* ran articles on how to run a house without servants, how to get by on a secretary's salary, how to combine motherhood and a career, how to learn to fly fish, or run a ranch on one's own, or travel solo across the continent, or, in one instance, run a small regional railroad. In 1912, *Sunset* ran an article by the noted feminist Louise Bryant, companion of John Reed. Another contributor was the second Mrs. Woodrow Wilson, whom many consider to have been the de facto president of the United States during the last 18 months of her husband's second term.

Larry Lane, in short, was bringing to the fore a previously implicit aspect of the *Sunset* identity. Since women were primarily responsible for the home in that era, and since *Sunset* was concerned with the home as one of its four major editorial policy directions, *Sunset* was becoming in part a magazine appealing to women. It was not, however, becoming a women's magazine; for so many of the other articles–travel articles, for example–were gender neutral, while other articles were male-oriented. In time, *Sunset* would run an increasing number of articles oriented toward children and child care. By that time *Sunset* had very much become a family magazine.

But first Larry Lane had to get *Sunset* through the Depression. One of his techniques was a pioneering use of department store charge ac-

Jack London, both a contributor of stories and essays and himself the subject of articles. May 1907, p. 7.(photo: Arnold Genthe)

"With more than 1,000 completed designs, perhaps the most influential popularizer of the Western ranch house is designer Cliff May. His first book on the subject, coauthored with Sunset editors in 1945, sold more than 50,000 copies." August 1988, p. 144. (photo: Chad Slattery)

counts to pay for subscriptions. That way, *Sunset* enjoyed a convenience akin to the credit card long before the invention of that credit device and a pre-existent screening process. Customers, moreover, enjoyed the convenience of being able to order *Sunset* through their department store. Launched in 1932, regional editions–one for the Pacific Northwest, one for Northern and Central California, one for Southern California, and, later, one for the Desert Southwest–also helped *Sunset* weather the economic crisis; for these regional editions not only opened *Sunset* to more focused articles, they would also later bring in local businesses as advertisers. In time, *Sunset* would carry more regional advertisements than any other magazine.

Left: "Monitoring the progress of our birthday report, from left to right, are Bill Lane, Ken Cooperrider, and Proctor Mellquist." Senior staff show hands-on managerial style preparing 80th Anniversary issue. May 1978, p. 4.

Yosemite and the National Parks
*A state park from 1864, Yosemite became
one of the first National Parks in 1890.
From the first issue of* Sunset, *Yosemite has
taken pride of place among natural won-
ders, appearing repeatedly on its pages.*
Sunset *has not only covered National
Parks, it has helped create several of them.*

*Right: "The Bridal Veil falls in the spring, is
one of the most exhilarating of sights." See
your Southern Pacific ticket agent for details.
June 1904, p. 109.(photo: Tibbitts)*

*Far right: "El Capitan, 3,500 feet above the
floor of the valley." Yosemite was a constant
presence in the early* Sunset .
June 1904, p. 107.

*As in 1898, so in May of 1990, Yosemite is
the lynchpin of the* Sunset *West.
(photo: Renee Lynn)*

Sunset helped its readers cope with the Depression through its selection of how-to-do-it articles and by keeping the prices of the magazine
and growing book list low. As a business, *Sunset* was struggling along
with everyone else, negotiating a deferred payment plan for paper with
Crown Zellerbach. (Not until 1938 did *Sunset* experience an operating
profit,10 years after Lane bought the magazine.) But within the pages of
the magazine there unfolded a panoramic pageant of gardening, architecture, regional cuisine, patio dining, golf, tennis, horseback riding,
and other leisure pursuits, which represented, in its own way, a cunning
strategy for economic success. *Sunset* fought the Depression by holding
before the middle classes opportunities to enjoy life even in dire times.
At the very depth of the Depression, 1933, *Sunset* had more than 200,000
subscribers, home owners in the main, who were paying a mere dollar a
year for their subscription.

Larry Lane also fought the Depression through the bold device
of launching *Sunset* Books, although this enterprise remained on a rela-

tively small scale until after World War II. In time, however, under
the direction of his son Mel as publisher, *Sunset* Books became an impressive publishing force. Since 1933, more than 900 titles and revisions
have been issued.

Between 1934 and 1951 *Sunset* operated out of a slender, tower-like,
seven-story building at 576 Sacramento Street in San Francisco. Gradually, the magazine was evolving. After 1936, photographs tended to re-
place original art on the cover. Yet artistic standards were not relaxed.
Photographers of the stature of Ansel Adams and Imogen Cunningham
were commissioned for *Sunset* covers. By the late 1930s, *Sunset* was reflecting the editorial character that persists to this day. *Sunset* made its
first operating profit in the decade in 1938, thanks, in part, to Ruth,
who remained close to the editorial process and personally tested
many *Sunset* recipes and gardening ideas. Keeping with a family tradition, the Lane sons sold *Sunset* and several other magazines door
to door. That year, everyone on the staff received an unexpected but
welcome $500 bonus.

Period of Rapid Growth

During the Second World War, Larry Lane's sons, Bill and Mel,
Stanford graduates, served as Navy officers. A major problem in these

years was paper. Yet the War Ration Board allowed *Sunset* extra paper for its *Sunset Vegetable Garden Book* (1943), which promoted Victory Gardens. In the face of wartime staffing shortages, Ruth Bell Lane became managing editor in 1944 as an additional contribution to the magazine. Returning from the service in 1946, the Lane brothers began an intense apprenticeship in every aspect of the publishing business. Their youth and energy would be very much needed. In the decades ahead the Far West, California and Arizona especially, would add millions of new residents, brought there by a booming economy and the desire for a better life free of Eastern winters and offering new job opportunities. Now more than ever, the classic work of a magazine–to provide information and guidance, to serve as a useful form of reference, to suggest and instruct–became the renewed *Sunset* mission and challenge. And as the West grew in population, competition for readers and advertisers became fierce, but *Sunset* thrived.

Literally millions of new homes would be built; whole cities and suburbs created, almost overnight. Millions of Americans who were born and raised elsewhere would now be seeking to transform themselves into Far Westerners. What kinds of homes should they build? What foods should they prepare? What trees, shrubs, and flowers should they plant in their new environment? Where should they go on family vacations? *Sunset* began to answer these questions in its own way, and by 1947, circulation, which had remained in the 200,000s during the war, increased by 100,000, and reached 400,000 in 1948 as more and more neophyte Far Westerners, together with longtime residents, were finding *Sunset* truly, as it described itself, The Magazine of Western Living. For many years, the rate of *Sunset* circulation grew even faster than that of the population.

In 1946, *Sunset* published its first large-format, hardcover *Sunset* book, *Western Ranch Houses*, written by *Sunset* editors with Cliff May and illustrated with May-designed houses. Ten years before, *Sunset* editors had discovered this San Diego home designer and began publishing his homes in the magazine. No single *Sunset* book before or since has had such a profound effect on the architectural environment of the Far West as it was being so rapidly actualized.

In 1951, Cliff May designed new headquarters for *Sunset* on the former Timothy Hopkins property in Menlo Park on the edge of San Francisquito Creek, originally part of a land grant made to Don Jose Arguello, governor of Spanish California, in 1815. The renowned landscape architect Thomas Church laid out the gardens. Working with the magazine's garden editors, Church created a garden with distinct areas representing the major climate zones of the West: Northern California, Central California, the Southwest Desert and Southern California, and the Northwest. He also helped establish a Test Garden for use by the editors. All this was centered around a 1.2-acre lawn, planted in colonial bent grass of the Astoria strain. At one end of the lawn stood the Old Man, a magnificent coast live oak hundreds of years in age. All in all, more than 300 kinds of shrubs, trees, vines, ground covers, annuals, and perennials were growing–and blooming!–in the garden at any given time. Eventually, after 1977, this entire garden would be irrigated from a well dug on the property.

Cliff May and Thomas Church: Each designer was a master in expressing an enchanted, almost dreamlike ambiance for gracious living in the West. (Thomas Church, after all, had invented the deck, first recognized in *Sunset*, perhaps the Far West's most notable contribution to do-

Glacier Point, Yosemite.
April 1899, p. 124.

"Bridal Veil Fall, Yosemite Valley."
April 1899, p. 121.(photo: Argenti)

El Capitan.
April 1899, p. 120.

mestic architecture after the Spanish-inspired patio.) In its headquarters, then, *Sunset* was making in architecture and landscaping an idealized presentation of the values for which it stood. Here at last was room and facilities not only for the editorial process but for what the magazine was soon calling a Laboratory of Western Living, including extensive kitchens and barbecue area where recipes could be tested. Not surprisingly, the *Sunset* headquarters itself became an object of tourist interest and soon averaged some 75,000 visitors a year.

In June 1952, the Territory of Hawaii became part of the editorial and circulation domain of *Sunset*, which took over the circulation of *Hawaii Farm and Home*, a magazine published by the *Honolulu Star-Bulletin*. The magazine now had editorial offices in Menlo Park, Seattle, Los Angeles, and Honolulu. In March 1952, the names of Bill and Mel Lane appeared on the *Sunset* masthead for the first time, Bill as advertising

"There are only three National Parks of the United States where the automobilist is permitted. This wonderful trip [to Mt. Ranier] may be made easily from either Seattle or Tacoma, Washington." The National Parks have grown and changed, with the help and support of Sunset *.*
January 1912, p. 41.

"The road to Mt. Rainier runs through magnificent forests of Douglas spruce; some of the trees are fifteen feet in diameter. As the altitude increases, the beautiful Alpine hemlocks appear."
January 1912, p. 42.

Right: One of the last Lane issues, this November 1989 cover features the larger cursive-style logo as well as the Golden Gate Bridge.
(photo: Glenn Christiansen)

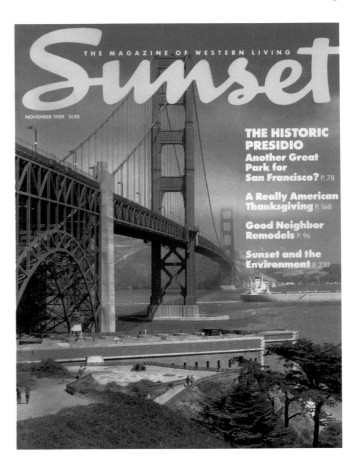

manager, Mel as business manager, with both involving far broader operating responsibilities than these titles imply. In fact, they were running the company, though under the watchful eye of their father. Adding Hawaii to the *Sunset* coverage was their first major policy decision. Now ensued a decade-plus of astonishing growth. As advertising manager, Bill Lane brought out back-to-back record-size 336-page issues in April and May 1956. Circulation topped 700,000 by 1957, more than 800,000 by 1965, in spite of the rapid growth of television and regional editions of national magazines. In 1957, the magazine began a series on the major cities of the Far West which began with San Francisco in November 1957 and ended with Salt Lake City in April 1965. In 1959, while Larry Lane remained chairman of the board, Bill Lane became publisher of *Sunset* magazine, and Mel Lane assumed the direction of *Sunset* Books. It was a new and continuously expanding era. In 1967 alone *Sunset* Books sold an astonishing 1.5 million copies.

On February 20,1967, just short of his 77th birthday, Larry Lane passed away. Modified and updated, but steadily adhered to, the editorial direction and business policies he had established nearly 40 years earlier had guided the enterprise into an era of unprecedented success. Lane's fourfold editorial policy of 1928–building, gardening, travel, and cooking–had brought discipline to a magazine that had lost its way. It did not, however, cut off variety within each category. Surveying the articles in this bibliography, in fact, one can see at once how Larry Lane's makeover of the magazine has been kept consistent across 70 years, but also how certain aspects of the previous *Sunset* identity, travel and recreation, for example, found congenial re-expression in the Lane editorial policy.

Heralding a New West

Sunset had begun as a vehicle to promote the West as place, for both settlement and travel. That orientation continued more vigorously than ever, following Larry Lane's editorial credo that it should be a magazine for the West, not about the West. This bibliography reveals an almost heroic inventory of the geography, flora, and fauna of the Far West. Even poison oak received its own article in 1960! And as early as 1930, the threat to the California live oak received attention. In each instance, following the *Sunset* editorial program, articles not only described the Far West but brought readers to it, as visitors or as settlers in a most engaged and practical, how-to-do-it way. *Sunset* was interested in scenery for its own sake, true; but the magazine was also concerned with the human equation: in bringing scenery, flora, and fauna together with people in an atmosphere of respectful enjoyment. Whether coming as tourists from one region of the West to another, or staying close to home (where the regional editions emphasized localized information), *Sunset* readers were encouraged to learn to live with nature, side by side, and absorb nature's gifts in a respectful, caring manner. This orientation toward the human equation no doubt accounts for the large number of notable articles, 408, devoted to landscaping and landscape architecture, which is to say, the human art form of working with nature to bring forth even further beauty.

When it came to landscapes, moreover, *Sunset* was no snob. Respecting wilderness, *Sunset* did not insist that only wilderness represents nature in its truest form. *Sunset* was interested in the irrigated landscapes of the California Central Valley and Arizona, as well as in the dry deserts of the Southwest, the wilds of the Snake River, or the glacial regions of Alaska. In each instance, whether wilderness preserve or urban park, *Sunset* was concerned with proper stewardship, use, and enjoyment: a direct continuity of its progressive heritage. Hence, *Sunset*'s continuing interest in national parks, places of natural beauty set specifically aside for human enjoyment. Two important national parks, in fact, Redwood National Park in Del Norte County on the Northern California coast and the North Cascades National Park in Western Washington at the Canadian border, partially owe their creation in 1968 to the advocacy of *Sunset* editors and readers. Hence also *Sunset*'s interest in urban parks. Golden Gate Park in San Francisco received frequent coverage, as did parks in other Western cities. *Sunset* played a major role in the establishment of the American River Parkway running through Sacramento. In

"A meadow of flowers" at Yosemite. *May 1900, p. 23. (photo: Tibbitts)*

"Thundering herd. To see this big a herd of bison in Yellowstone you leave the main highway and go by horseback over park trails. You can see a smaller herd of them from your car at Antelope Creek south of Tower Falls." *July 1938, p. 10.(photo: Haynes, Inc.)*

"Who can describe the ascent of Mount Shasta; its fields of eternal snow; its glaciers, its immensity," and who makes the ascent these days wearing skirts? *November 1902, p. 37.*

Environment

Wildlife has been the bellweather for Sunset's visual coverage of environmental issues, and editors use is a variety of approaches to make readers more aware of the imperiled West, such as how progress or degradation is measured.

"'Piping' in a hydraulic placer mine in southern Oregon," long after this destructive practice had been banned in California. While gold rushes come and go, mining for precious metals has always been part of the West. August 1906, p. 139.

"Rare trumpeter swans, so white they glisten, but with shiny black bills, glide silently across a pond. These were transplanted from wild bird refuge in Montana as experimental project." Awareness of nature fostered through pictures. March 1958, p. 45.

"Sharp-shinned hawk, above, kinglet and bushtit, below, are banded for migration and lifespan studies." Readers learn about the study and conservation of Western wildlife, a persistent thread over the years. April 1978, p. 61.(photo: David Stubbs)

its May 1973 75th Anniversary edition, *Sunset* ran a long article encouraging its readers to enjoy Griffith Park in Los Angeles. In November 1989 *Sunset* published a pioneering article outlining not only how visitors could enjoy the Presidio of San Francisco, but also its possible future as a public park, together with a rare signed editorial by Bill Lane entitled "*Sunset* and the Environment: Working With You to Help Conserve and Improve the West."

Hence also *Sunset*'s continuing interest in cities and especially their suburbs, where much of *Sunset*'s readership had homes. Over the years *Sunset* has given regular coverage to the older cities of the Far West, especially San Francisco and Los Angeles in their home state. As Northwest cities achieved greater prominence–Portland, Seattle, Tacoma, Boise, Salt Lake City–*Sunset* was on hand, providing early coverage; indeed, a significant number of articles deal with Portland and Seattle, two cities in which the Garden City ideal seemed especially promising of realization. *Sunset* introduced its readers to the overnight phenomenon of Phoenix, and later, when the Mountain states were added to *Sunset*'s territory, such cities as Denver and Albuquerque appeared in the pages of the magazine. Nor was *Sunset* neglectful of smaller cities, for here as well were significant variations of the Far Western dream. When San Jose made its dramatic comeback in the mid-1970s, *Sunset* announced, "San Jose–Nowheresville in Renaissance."

In covering cities, *Sunset* also managed to introduce its readership to various ethnic groups in the Far West, new and old: the Chinese of Chinatown, and the Italians of North Beach, San Francisco; the Japanese of Los Angeles; the East Asian Indians and Basques of Central California and Nevada; the Mexican Americans of the Southwest. *Sunset* approached ethnicity not as part of the problem, but as part of the solution. Each ethnic group was frequently presented in terms of its food, traditions, and celebratory customs, in an effort to capture the poetry of heritage and identity.

In the matter of Native Americans, moreover, *Sunset* from the start and continuing through its 100-year career has presented these nations and peoples with great sympathy. As this bibliography indicates, *Sunset* paid attention to the diversity of Native American cultures from Alaska to New Mexico. It was the Native Americans of the Southwest, however–the Apache, the Hopi, the Navajo, the vanished Anasazi, their arts and architecture, their customs and rituals–which claimed the bulk of *Sunset*'s attention, in both articles and stunning covers by Maynard Dixon. *Sunset* exhibited one of the finest collections of vegetable-died Navajo rugs at its Menlo Park headquarters.

An Expanding, Pacific-Oriented World to Explore

Over the years, moreover, *Sunset* expanded its territory, which is to say, its definition of the Far West. Alaska was on the mind of *Sunset* from the very first issue, with its reference to the Klondike Gold Rush. Then came editorial coverage of the Southwest and Mexico itself, 171 notable articles from 1898 to 1994. In fact, Southern Pacific had run a line into Mexico. When *Sunset* first began publication, New Mexico and Arizona were still territories. Writing about Mexico and the Spanish Southwest, including Native American culture, attracted many noted authors to *Sunset* in the early years. In California, *Sunset* returned again and again to the missions as tourist destinations. (Its popular pictorial, *California Missions*, is still available.) By the late 1960s, *Sunset* was carrying articles on Mexico in nearly every issue. Among *Sunset* Books' best-sellers were the *Travel Guide to Mexico* (under various titles and editions dating from 1955) and *The Sea of Cortez* (1966).

While the focus of these articles remained, in the usual *Sunset* fashion, fixed on travel and tourism, a cultural statement was nevertheless being made. Mexico and the United States, *Sunset* was suggesting, were neighbor republics in North America. Through California and the Spanish Southwest, they shared a common heritage and, increasingly, as the Hispanic population in these regions grew, a common people. Thus without preaching, *Sunset* advanced a notion of United States–Mexican dialogue, not through diplomacy but through tourism and a mutual appreciation of heritage, especially as expressed through crafts, cuisine, and south-of-the-border plants.

The first issue of *Sunset* announced steamship departures for the Pacific and informed the reader that tickets to Yokohama, Kobe, and Shanghai could be purchased at Southern Pacific's offices. The Asia Pacific Basin had always been linked to the Far West. In fact, the earliest support in the East (and by Congress) for a transcontinental railroad was mainly to encourage trade between the Eastern industrial areas and the Pacific Far East. The acquisition of California and the Spanish Southwest and of the Oregon Territory in the mid-nineteenth century made the United States a Pacific nation. San Francisco and Honolulu were linked from the late nineteenth century onward through travel, trade, and investment. Following the Second World War, Hawaii, the territory and then the state, became *Sunset* country. Beginning in the 1950s and continuing thereafter, *Sunset* paid special attention to Japanese gardening, Japanese bathing practices, Japanese interior design, and Japanese cuisine. Staying within its own editorial policy, in other words, *Sunset* was making its connection with that Japanese-California link which, on the level of architecture, cuisine, and aesthetics (as well as financial investment), was subtly transforming the Californian way of life. It was a process, moreover, under way since the early decades of the century, when Japanese architecture and building practices, absorbed by the Craftsman movement, had had such a dramatic effect on domestic design in the Golden State.

By the late 1960s *Sunset* publisher Bill Lane was publicly stating: "The magazine never publishes an issue without reporting on one or more Pacific Ocean countries, and the Book Division keeps a dozen

books on the area constantly updated."[8] Books such as the *Sunset Travel Guide to Australia* and the *Sunset Travel Guide to New Zealand*, both first published in 1964, together with articles on this region in *Sunset* itself, coaxed forth and further articulated in terms of travel the long-standing

[8] Ibid., p. 27.

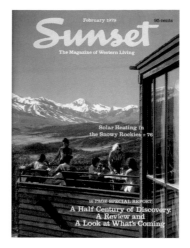

A solar-heated Colorado home graces the cover of the February 1979 issue, which focused on this alternate form of energy. (photo: Glenn Christiansen)

Sunset *staff were very involved in the design and development of the urban park in Portland, Oregon, shown on this July 1976 cover. (photo: Glenn Christiansen)*

Left: The scientific study of Lake Tahoe water quality is one aspect of a complex and contentious issue with conflicting conservancy, property, public access, and recreational issues, each addressed in Sunset's *coverage. June 1978, p. 92. (photos: Charles R. Goldman/Robert C. Richards)*

Homes

The history of twentieth-century domestic Western architecture is thoroughly represented in Sunset *(albeit with more emphasis on single-family houses than on multiple dwelling units). From the simple weekend cabin, to Craftsman-style bungalow, through the trademark Western ranch house, to highly self-conscious modernism,* Sunset *shows us how Western homes look and function.*

Right: "Tall native trees frame the low rambling cottage" and serve as sentinels to the new priorities of home and garden, Portland, Oregon.
February 1929, p. 15.

"Five rooms, bath, hall and screened porch for $2300 at present prices." An architectural archetype of its time and place: the Craftsman-style bungalow.
May 1918, p. 51.

"Floor space similar to second bungalow. Concrete basement with furnace. Cost, $2600." A stony variant on a theme that still dominates some older neighborhoods in Western cities.
May 1918, p. 51.

connection between the Far West and the South Pacific. The parallels between Australia and New Zealand and the Far West were many, Australia especially. Like the Far West of the United States, Australia was generally an arid to semi-arid region dependent upon irrigation, though it had an even greater scarcity of surface water, lacking winter snows, and far fewer people. Each region had begun its economy in the nineteenth century with cattle raising, followed by agriculture. Each region found itself by the late twentieth century highly urbanized and highly suburbanized, with its populations pursuing a decidedly similar version of the good life. In 1985, President Ronald Reagan named *Sunset* publisher Bill Lane United States Ambassador to Australia and Nauru.

In 1952 *Sunset* became a founding member of the Pacific Area Travel Association (PATA, now the Pacific Asia Travel Association), promoting travel and tourism in this region. Indeed, *Sunset* must be considered a pioneer in alerting Americans to the possibilities of Pacific Basin travel. In 1899, *Sunset* published "A Trans-Pacific to the 'Land of Aloha' and Beyond" by J. Sloat Fassett. After all, *Sunset* was founded at a time when Teddy Roosevelt and others were trumpeting the new Century of the Pacific. In 1924 the magazine published pioneering articles on travel to Australia and New Zealand. In 1927 it introduced its readership to the even more exotic locale of Fiji, and after World War II, *Sunset* helped a boom in tourism in Hawaii. Both the magazine and *Sunset* Books pioneered in introducing Americans to travel in the Pacific, including exotic locales off the beaten path of most tourists. Several *Sunset* Book titles further drew attention to Pacific island destinations.

Such interest in Hawaii and the South Pacific was part of *Sunset*'s ongoing commitment since the very beginning to travel as one of the most engaging forms of leisure activity. *Sunset*, after all, had been founded in May of 1898 as a vehicle to promote travel to the West–and the Del Monte Hotel in Monterey!–via the Southern Pacific Railroad. Such travel by the upper classes was not a new phenomenon. As time went on, however, *Sunset* opened and supported the possibility that the middle classes might also make travel an important part of their leisure program. Once again, *Sunset* was echoing a Progressive ideal, in this case, the belief that the good life, including travel, should be available to as many people as possible.

Indeed, travel (even without counting closely related articles listed under national parks and outdoor recreation) constitutes the second largest category in the magazine across 100 years, some 1,388 notable articles, ranging from day trips to expeditions to Bora Bora and the Greek islands. Cumulatively, these travel articles reflect the rising prosperity of the nation and the expanding opportunities middle-class Americans were experiencing in the twentieth century. This was especially true in the West, where incomes were higher, and there was a greater propensity for year-round travel. Across the years, *Sunset* has advised its readers on how to travel by train, mule, horse, touring car, skis, snowshoes, houseboat, Ford Tri-motor, jet liner, cruise ships, and recreational vehicle to places worth seeing throughout the Far West, Mexico, Central America, Latin America, Europe, the South Pacific, the Far East– even Disneyland. In article after article, *Sunset* advised its readers on how best to enjoy the Rose Bowl Parade in Pasadena, ski across the Truckee River in Nevada, see the aspens turn to gold along the Corona-do Trail in Arizona, retrace the mining trails and bask in the midnight sun of Alaska, explore the jungles of the Yucatan, walk the beaches of Waikiki, or range through the Hawaiian back country by bicycle, picnic in Sonoma, view the Pacific from a promontory in Big Sur, search out new restaurants in Tokyo, shop for handicrafts in Mexico City, or just spend a day sampling the delights of Phoenix, Tucson, Reno, Denver, Boise, San Diego, Pasadena, Los Angeles, Fresno, San Jose, San Francisco, Oakland, Portland, Seattle, or Vancouver. In 1952 *Sunset* introduced its readers to the San Juan Islands. Who else but *Sunset* would advise its readers, as the magazine did in 1988, to explore Sawtooth, Idaho? But then again, in 1960, at the height of the Cold War, *Sunset* had even suggested a trip behind the Iron Curtain! Whether in the West or abroad, *Sunset* coined the term "Discovery Trip" to highlight hitherto-undiscovered travel destinations. *Sunset* championed what is now known as eco-tourism long before the term became fashionable, with features on out-of-the-way wildlife and wilderness areas, emphasizing stewardship of the natural environment.

The rise of tourism as a lead element in the Western economy can be documented and placed in context through numerous *Sunset* articles across a century. *Sunset* pioneered travel to Alaska as well as to Hawaii and in so doing helped these territories along the road to statehood. It recommended travel to the affiliated Commonwealth of Puerto Rico as well, suggesting the summer off-season, and in so doing was perhaps encouraging the evolution of yet another American state. *Sunset* was among the first to discover Santa Fe as a stylish tourist destination, with early recognition of its now-famous outdoor opera and music seasons, and a source of new imagery for the Western lifestyle. In time, Santa Fe became a resort of international repute, as did Colorado, another *Sunset* favorite. (As an adolescent Larry Lane had first spent time on a relative's Colorado ranch during a tuberculosis scare, which fortunately turned out to be a false alarm.) *Sunset* also pioneered interest in Baja, California, showing a continuing fascination with that then-unsettled region, especially the Sea of Cortez, as demonstrated by its book on the region. Mexico remained a longtime *Sunset* favorite, and the magazine pioneered in promoting travel to Central America, a tradition honored today, as in the October 1997 "Colors of Oaxaca." Although *Sunset* ran a number of articles on travel to China in the 1920s, this option naturally diminished with the protracted wars in that nation through 1949, fol-

"An old live oak, carefully preserved, adds beauty to this new California home." The idea of building around trees (if not always so closely) recurs both in the pages of Sunset and later in the siting of its headquarters. *April 1938, p. 50.*

"Bedroom corner adjoins stake-covered porch for orchid growing." Ever promoting a discourse between interior and exterior. *November 1946, p. 26.*

"Corner garden in an alcove formed by kitchen, dining room, and maid's room. Low porches, board and batten, typical ranch-house details." The maid's room may be a rarity today, but the other features are very much part of an enduring style. *November 1946, p. 27.*

This "home in Los Angeles demonstrates many of the virtues of the Western ranch house. It also testifies to the often-overlooked fact that space, color, flowers, fences–the things that any of us can give to a house–are the controlling factors in changing a house to a home." Integration of house, site, and landscaping is always stressed.
November 1946, p. 1.

Touches of Mondrian and traditional Japanese shoji in a stark and dramatic modern interior.
August 1938, p. 14.(photo: Dapprich)

Right: A bit of color enlivens this futuristic home.
May 1948, p. 25.

October 1937 cover

lowed by the establishment of an initially tourist-hostile government. In its early years, *Sunset* promoted travel to Japan, then recently opened to the West, and it resumed its Japanese interest after the Second World War. Other destinations appearing occasionally in *Sunset* included Spain, the Canary Islands, Argentina, France, and Great Britain. In such articles, *Sunset* reflected the ability of middle-class Americans, especially from the advent of jet travel in the 1960s, to visit locales once reserved for the affluent.

On the other hand, *Sunset* never lost touch in its travel articles with an emphasis upon nature and a family-oriented enjoyment of the outdoors as opposed to typical travel-guide emphasis on archeology or historical monuments. Beginning in the 1950s, in fact, there emerged an emphasis upon accessible, family-oriented vacations in the many travel articles published in the magazine and in such books as *Sunset Western Travel Adventures* (1979) and *Sunset Western Campsites* (first published in 1955). (Many destinations were mentioned in articles of less than one page, and while their impact was often immediate and strong, these shorter pieces could not be listed in this bibliography.)

The travel emphasis of *Sunset* also implied a continuing interest in transportation. All in all, *Sunset* published more than 174 notable articles on transportation in the Far West: on horseback and burro, by coach or

skiff, or deep-water yacht (such as Jack London's *Snark*, described by Allan Dunn for *Sunset* in 1907 as it embarked for the South Seas), or biplane and Ford Tri-motor, foreshadowing the rise of airline travel in the Far West, to the touring automobile and the Sunset Limited train. Obviously, a railroad-founded magazine promoted the railroad as the primary means of tourist travel, including photographs of the beautiful Southern Pacific and Santa Fe Railroad stations throughout the Far West. Yet very soon, *Sunset* found itself introducing its readers to the wonders and delights of the touring automobile. A long article in the February 1907 issue, "Motoring in the West," is in and of itself an important document in the history of motor travel in America, then as now a more popular form of travel in the West because of the variety of destinations, proximity to scenic or rugged terrain (hence the regional preference for four-wheel-drive vehicles), and climate favorable to the open touring vehicle and its successor, the convertible. The cumulative pages of *Sunset* contained a near-complete inventory of automobiles through the twentieth century, including that cherished leisure-oriented suburban vehicle, the station wagon. When small foreign cars became all the rage in the late 1950s, *Sunset* was on hand with an article in 1959 on how best to camp with such a vehicle. Almost from the start, *Sunset* promoted the building and maintenance of high quality roads and highways. As the age of the automobile began to show some of its limitations, especially in the area of commuter travel, *Sunset* turned its attention to the problem of over-crowded freeways with an article in May 1988 on van-pooling. It also ran an article advising its readers to try travel on the newly built BART system.

A New Frontier: Leisure and the Western Middle Class

Through these many travel articles one can glimpse what is perhaps the single greatest benefit (other than home ownership) coming to the middle classes of the Far West in the twentieth century, especially the second half–leisure. In nineteenth-century America, significant leisure was in the main the prerogative of the more affluent classes. Increasingly, however, in the twentieth century more and more middle-class Americans had more and more time–weekends, national holidays, paid vacations–in which to travel or otherwise to enjoy recreational activities. Here was time for family life, for sport and other forms of recreation, for the cultivation of the inner landscape through enjoyable hobbies, for time to enjoy the sheer goodness of life. And no region had opportunities for using that time comparable to the West. Here again was a Progressive ideal: a belief in balance between work and leisure, money-making and soul-making activities. Hence arises another major category in this *Sunset* bibliography, recreation and leisure, 568 notable entries in all, covering every conceivable kind of activity. Taken together with travel, this allied category brings to over 2,000 the notable leisure-oriented articles published by the magazine.

Fly-fishing on Lake Tahoe, yachting on San Francisco Bay, duck hunting in the Delta country, tennis in Santa Cruz, golfing at Del Monte, and like activities in other areas served by the Southern Pacific: Initially, *Sunset* tended to emphasize upper-end, upper-class sorts of pursuits. As the century progressed, however, these activities–especially after the Lane family took over the magazine–became much more middle-class in their orientation; indeed, in the more than 500 notable articles dealing with recreation and leisure is evident a process through which the good life was being democratized. (For example, the once-elite subject of playing polo becomes in 1986, in an article entitled "Fast Polo and Relaxed Picnicking," an entirely accessible spectator sport for a family outing.) In general, one follows a path of development in *Sunset* in which leisure activities become more and more available to a broader and broader audience, though one which stays within *Sunset*'s primary public of Western home-owning families.

Winter sports, for example, especially skiing, can be traced as they are being enjoyed by more and more Far Westerners. While fly-fishing remains a pursuit of the few, the swimming pool, once a prerogative of the more privileged, became a rather common backyard amenity. The *Sunset* book on swimming pools became a best-seller. Hence, the spate of articles from the 1950s onward suggesting ways of enjoying one's backyard, one's swimming pool, one's poolside barbecue, perhaps enjoyed with a spa and followed by a sauna, both early championed by the magazine. Golf, another prerogative of the affluent in the early years, becomes a municipal event with the rise of city-owned golf courses in the Far West. Outdoor life–camping, back-packing, hiking, pack trips

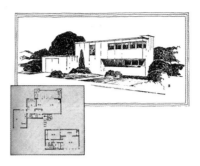

"Note pleasant spacing of windows, and (plan) the generous deck and terrace. Estimated cost, $6,000." Though not the classic Western ranch, this boxy structure does provide opportunities for outdoor living.
February 1938, p. 23.

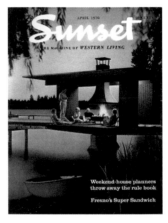

An appealing vision of an extraordinary recreational home on the April 1970 cover. (photo: Glenn Christiansen)

"Children have direct access to garden, don't have to troop through house." Many Sunset *home improvement ideas focus on maximal use of limited space, as in this town house.*
November 1968, p. 110.

City living in a studio apartment, "just above the broom factory. A large, sheet-metal hood makes the fireplace into an exceptionally efficient heater."
May 1938, p. 29.

Right: "Lake Arrowhead, the green of pine trees, the changing moods of sky, are all part of the living room in this mountain home." The quintessential Sunset home, reveling in an easy intimacy with the Western landscape, complete with "large sliding door."
January 1958, p. 42.

Far right: "Open living room through glass wall and up to sky through skylight, this house shows that ranch house can be airily and freely spacious and yet keep its character." Variants on the archetypical ranch house.
February 1958, p. 58.

"The low, close-to-the-earth, rambling quality of the... home, and its livability, are typical of the early Western ranch house" and equally typical of the Sunset style.
November 1946, p. 26.(photo: Maynard L. Parker)

with horses, river rafting–which once seemed the prerogative of the elite Sierra Club in the early years of the century (professional people, capable of mounting expensive expeditions into the Sierra Nevada) increasingly became an affordable family-oriented affair in state and federal lands that were far more abundant and available to more people. Every now and then (a 1975 article on hot air ballooning, for example) *Sunset* reverted to the once privileged and the exotic, and also as a travel opportunity for all reader families to enjoy as spectators. In the main, however, its activities–family sailing, bird watching, gathering driftwood on the beach, observing sea otters, arranging a chuck wagon party for teenagers, making and flying kites, hunting for exotic rocks, bicycling, skiing, snowshoeing, kayaking, rafting on the Klamath River–were within the financial reach of mid-America, but again, with greater interest and participation in the West, and particularly on the part of *Sunset* readers. In 1970, *Sunset* introduced its readers to the pleasures of playing boccie ball on the lawn. In 1975, serving the physical fitness craze, it introduced its readers to the PAR course. In fact, *Sunset* had installed its own PAR course at its headquarters; magazine employees served as models for an article in their own backyard, the Laboratory of Western Living.

Increasing Environmental Awareness and Activism

Travel and many of the leisure activities promoted by *Sunset*, moreover, were linked to conservationism. "Through travel in the West," Bill Lane pointed out in May 1969, "we also believe that people gain interest and courage to fight ugliness by appreciating beauty in both their homes and travels."[9] Both Bill and Mel had been reared in an instinctively conservationist environment, shaped by both the love of their parents for the outdoors and the pervasive conservationism of the *Sunset* ethos. Long before the term ecology surfaced in American discourse, *Sunset* had been advancing in both the pre-Lane and Lane eras a conservation ethos that was at the very center of the pre–World War I Progressive ideal. With the enthusiastic support of Bill and Mel Lane and their editors, *Sunset* magazine, books, and films advanced a steady, if occasionally subtle, program of conservation advocacy. The "Lane boys," as they were sometimes referred to, became active in conservation activities when they felt their efforts coincided with their own interests and those of the Lane publications. The magazine, for example, was among the first to see the possibilities of transforming the Presidio of San Francisco into one of the most distinctive national parks in the nation, a desig-

[9] Ibid., p. 27.

nation that has been achieved and is now being implemented. Two such activities that set a national precedent were the San Francisco Bay Conservation and Development Commission and the California Coastal Commission, on both of which Mel Lane served as the first chairman.

In all these efforts, Yosemite National Park has remained for three generations of Lanes and *Sunset* staff both the reality and the symbol of all that great national parks have to offer. On a trip to Yosemite in the early 1920s, Larry Lane made the decision to leave Iowa and become a citizen of the Far West; and in later years the Yosemite, which Bill and Mel Lane first saw as boys on their first summer vacation trip with their parents, remained for each of them–and later their families–a beloved place throughout a lifetime.

As Wallace Stegner and others have pointed out, the big question west of the 100th meridian is water, water, water. Both directly and indirectly, *Sunset* has been constantly addressing the water problem; indeed, like the Stanford campus nearby, the Cliff May–designed *Sunset* headquarters in Menlo Park, to which the company moved in 1951, favors the dry look. Beginning in the 1930s, use of water became more home-oriented. Water conservation has more recently been a frequent theme in *Sunset* gardening articles. On a more macroscale, *Sunset* has addressed itself since its earliest years (e.g., "Phoenix, Born of Water," by J.O. Dunbar, August 1904) to the continuing question of water in the West, which is to say, the future of the West itself; for water constitutes the fundamental resource and environmental premise of *Sunset* country.

It is not, however, the only question. Among other causes, *Sunset* has realistically aligned itself behind the cause of solar heating, especially in the home. It first addresses solar power as early as April 1903, with "Sunshine as Power" to pump water for irrigation, by Arthur Inkersley. The February 1979 issue (celebrating the 50th anniversary of the first Lane *Sunset*), featuring a cover-story article on a Colorado home of country singer John Denver, focused on solar heating. It also included an analysis of how the Native American pueblo cultures of the Spanish Southwest practiced this art. The articles in this issue–giving illustrated examples of solar-heated homes in New Mexico and Colorado and, in the usual *Sunset* fashion, providing extensive guidance for readers wishing to avail themselves of this nonpolluting, non-resource-consuming energy source–built upon the more ambitious treatment of the *Sunset Homeowner's Guide to Solar Heating*, published in 1978. In 1980, Pacific Gas & Electric cooperated with *Sunset* editors to build a demonstration of solar technology at *Sunset*'s headquarters for public viewing. Solar heating had an international dimension as well, for Swedish architect and solar heating expert Varis Bokalders and Swedish journalist Barbro Larsson were brought aboard as consultants. (While importing such expertise from Sweden was unusual, the practice of engaging outside experts has long been a routine editorial practice.)

A Distinct Identity for the Western Home

The focus of these solar heating articles, in both book and magazine, was upon the home. So many of the categories in this bibliography–gardening, landscaping, architecture and home design, home improvement, workshop projects and crafts, and food preparation–directly serve the *Sunset* ideal of the home as balanced, rational, aesthetic, promotive of family life and personal development. It was the desire for a home and land of one's own, it must be remembered, which so powerfully motivated Far Western migration in the nineteenth century. Then, the

"Ranch-house interiors should have no style but your way of living." Never force a decorating scheme or theme on a way of life; decorating ideas are for do-it-yourself mix-and-match.
November 1946, p. 26.

"Cabinlike bunk is suspended a foot above floor; it has a drawer bed with foam mattress, other drawers for clothing." Space saving and creative storage are characteristic of Sunset *home improvement ideas.*
October 1968, p. 104.

October 1957 marks the first annual Sunset-AIA *Western Homes Awards with a cover story.*
(photo: Ernest Braun)

Do-It-Yourself

For 70 years, Sunset has emphasized "how-to-do-it" in its approach to all subjects, from travel to remodeling to holiday decorations, and its approach to graphics has reflected this orientation. A strange and wonderful collection of crafts, hobbies, and workshop projects have appeared throughout the years, including the following.

"When the 10 pairs of wheels are piled in a pyramid, the levels rotate in opposite directions. Stretched out as at right, the toy slithers upstairs." Many workshop projects focus on things for children.
March 1978, p. 122.(photo: Peter O. Whiteley)

Right:"An array of food gifts and containers" convey thoughts of holiday gift-giving, pride in the results of one's own efforts: practical, thoughtful, attractive, and tasty.
December 1968, p. 70.(photo: Ernest Braun)

Far right: "This 'tool box' keeps everything together, handy and ready, for wrapping presents."
November 1968, p. 158.(photo: Darrow M. Watt)

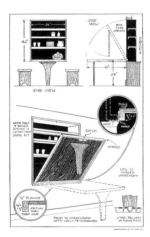

A practical, affordable, do-able, space-saving home improvement project suited the times.
July 1938, p. 40.(credit: Hi Sibley)

goal was largely rural and agricultural, a 160-acre land grant and the chance to build a farmhouse and barn. Later, while remaining agricultural, that ideal transmogrified itself into urban and suburban circumstances: a family-owned house with a backyard in a decent neighborhood. In the highly suburbanized Far West, such ambitions took on the intensity of a crusade. A home of one's own and a flourishing family life became the popular image of what the Far West, beginning with California, most dramatically offered and thus was and is the natural focus of *Sunset*'s editorial coverage and advertising–even though by no means all readers own their own home but find the spectrum of ideas stimulating and useful: They may be planning a home (or getaway home) or hoping to buy one, already using food and travel ideas, or enjoying container gardening. The ideal of a well-kept and aesthetic home for the Western family went hand in hand with a concern for the broader community and social responsibility. As Bill Lane would put it in 1969: "The family that maintains and improves its home, shares it with friends, goes traveling together, and pursues constructive hobbies, is relating in a very positive way to the social and natural environment of its community and country. Any responsible minister, psychiatrist, or probation officer can document that statement with very strong statistics."[10] Among the

Progressives and even more so in *Sunset*, the focus was suburban over urban (though *Sunset* did run occasional articles on downtown or midtown multiple dwellings, which receive recognition via *Sunset*'s Western Home Awards program, cosponsored with the American Institute of Architects). *Sunset* early began coverage of cluster dwelling development within the suburban milieu, thereby preserving open space in the planning process. For the suburban ideal, so redolent with Jeffersonian implications, expressed an America that was neither a landed patriciate nor an urban proletariat but was, rather, a flourishing middle ground, especially in the West, where suburban growth has been particularly pronounced.

In its architectural articles, as in the case of its travel and leisure articles, *Sunset* had a tendency in its early years to focus on the upper end of the economic spectrum, such as Porter Garnett's "Stately Homes of California" series in 1913–1914, describing the great estates of the San Francisco Peninsula, or Mira Maclay's description of James Duval Phelan's Villa Montalvo farther south, near Saratoga. Here were homes in

[10] Ibid., p. 28.

the grand style, true, but available only to an affluent elite.

Fortunately, such an emphasis did not remain long in force. Almost simultaneously Charles Francis Saunders was describing "bungalow life" in 1913. When the Spanish Revival came in the 1920s, *Sunset* was there to cover it; indeed, it would not be difficult to piece together examples from nearly every phase of domestic architectural development in California and the Far West from *Sunset* articles and illustrations. (Even the condominium would receive some consideration in 1952.) In 1956, *Sunset* inaugurated, in conjunction with the Western chapters of the American Institute of Architects, its Western Home Awards program with a panel of noted professionals serving as jury. Interestingly, the suggestion that *Sunset* partner with AIA in this program came from Time Inc., which had earlier cosponsored similar award programs. Many of the homes recognized by *Sunset* went on to win national awards, and a number of architects recognized in the program achieved regional or national reputations. This program also brought landscape architects and interior designers as judges and was the first to include remodeling and recreational homes as separate categories. This biennial awards program continues to thrive under *Sunset* Publishing Corporation.

If the truth be told, *Sunset* was not much concerned with historicity in Spanish or other Revival styles. Its persistent preference, rather, if one is to judge from homes and architects recognized, was for homes in a simple, straightforward manner, devoid of historical fussiness, a style that can be generically described as California Ranch. Cliff May, for instance, worked in this idiom, although his homes did possess a strong Spanish or Mexican ambiance, as did other popular designers and architects featured in *Sunset*. This ambiance came, however, not from historical detail but from the emphasis on roof line, wall, mass, and volume in dialogue with, but not slavishly repeating, the best elements in the Southwestern and Southern Californian adobe. The concept of a home ranged across the entire space between property lines, encompassing both interior and exterior in a single living space. Thus, fences and landscaping for privacy became important concerns and prompted several *Sunset* books. Ditto patios and decks, as witnessed, among numerous examples, by 1993's "Best Owner-built Deck."

Sunset also paid attention to the second home, a growing phenomenon in the Far West. *Sunset* began to cover second homes in 1920, then often called "vacation cabins," and Lane published a book on the topic in 1932. Through its coverage of second, or recreational, homes, *Sunset* is credited with launching the A-frame design and the hillside or waterfront deck, which again extended living space into the outdoors.

Home Improvement and Remodeling: A Continuous Stream of Practical Solutions

Homes, whether primary or secondary, not only have to be designed and built (and *Sunset* ran a number of articles on building materials and techniques), they also have to be adapted and improved over the years, often by adding additions or remodeling. For *Sunset*, fixing up one's home constituted a near-ritual. Here, after all, is a celebration of both the home as the locus of family togetherness and as one's individual responsibility for maintaining the house, while often inspiring community pride and engagement through a virtual contagion of visible improvement. And besides: Home improvement is both fun and practical,

How-to-do-it, step by step: setting up the station wagon "tail-gate kitchen," travel and food interests conjoined in the affordable family outing.
January 1958, p. 26.
(photo: Clyde Childress)

Sunset has long striven to provide practical information in clear and concise ways, in part a legacy born of the lean Depression years, matured with wartime paper scarcity. Its characteristic graphic treatments– including how-to cartoon-strip instructions and superimposition of text on photographs and drawings–realize this mandate.

This paper cut-out illustration, the July 1935 cover, brings together recreational activity, a rather rustic vacation home, and a Western landscape.

Right: Proper pruning technique is a continuing theme, frequently illustrated with diagrams.
December 1948, p. 80.

Far right: Floral border landscaping design explained through clear diagramming juxtaposed with text.
November 1948, p. 121.

particularly in adding value to the owner. All in all, this bibliography lists 780 notable entries in the home improvement category. In the early Lane years of the Depression, the emphasis was upon such basic but still new items as electrical wiring, refrigerators, and water heaters. (It is not coincidental that these were years when advertisement was less abundant. Later, as advertising volume grew, expansion of editorial content followed.)

From the start, *Sunset* is interested in roofing design and materials and in the development of unused space. When new construction products such as plywood come on line, *Sunset* responds with suggestions. *Sunset* sees glass as a positive construction material that both delineates space and enables visual possession of the outdoors. In the 1950s *Sunset* began to introduce its readers to the advantages of sliding glass doors and the skylight: another case of allowing the light of the Far West to stream into the home.

Sunset, however, remains more than slightly suspicious of air conditioning, which closes off the home and consumes vast amounts of electricity. *Sunset* tries to emphasize as much as possible, rather, designs and materials facilitating natural ventilation, along with landscaping for shade. On the other hand, *Sunset* embraced early the microwave oven, prototype models of which were tested in *Sunset* kitchens. These became especially popular in the West with its higher incomes and more active lifestyle, and in turn, furthered the use of frozen foods, which were consumed proportionately more than in other regions. The computer, too, which made its appearance in the May 1988 90th Anniversary issue, was enthusiastically welcomed, as were many technological ad-

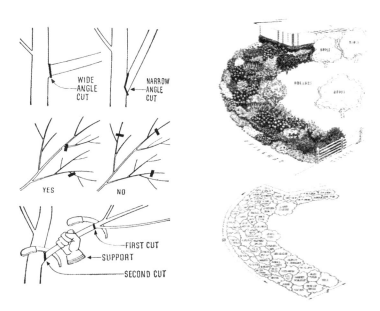

vances which improved the safety, utility, and comfort of the home. Just a few blocks away from *Sunset* headquarters, Silicon Valley was in the process of taking the Far West and the world into cyberspace and bringing cyberspace into the Far Western home. *Sunset* practiced what it preached, too; its own production was one of the earliest magazines to be automated with the Atex computer system for editing and composition. To the *Sunset* way of thinking, high technology and conservationism (in such forms as efficient programmable heating/cooling and sprinkler systems) went hand in hand. *Sunset* publications had a high penetration among high-tech research and technical professionals, who, with their families, were often home owners in traditional *Sunset* areas.

Sunset also made many valuable suggestions on how to integrate the storage, display, and use of books into the home, as both a source of knowledge and adornment. Some *Sunset* housing suggestions, the decorative use of stained glass, for example, were very much part of an era, in this case the revival of the 1970s; but in general, home improvement articles tended not to be overly faddish. There are a number of realistic suggestions as well–burglar alarms and security systems, for example–reflecting the more noir aspects of contemporary life.

Sunset served as a leader in the development of the American kitchen after the Second World War from a hidden workplace, peopled by either servants or an isolated woman, to an active positive space where the family, not just the cooking mother, came together. Its kitchen books were among its best-sellers. *Sunset* was an early popularizer of how-to-do -it solutions, such as open kitchens with adjoining family room, island counter spaces, built-in appliances, glassed-in herb or kitchen gardens. *Sunset* also paid close attention to the bathroom, which like the kitchen was being rapidly developed in the second half of the twentieth century, another trend initiated in the West and first reported by *Sunset*. Among other innovations, *Sunset* introduced its readers to the Finnish sauna and the Japanese hot tub, in the forefront of national trends. In the case of its articles dealing with the renovation of older homes, with respect for their architectural integrity, *Sunset* showed a strong preservationist commitment.

Coming outdoors, *Sunset* returned again and again to the enclosed patio as a distinctively Far Western form of indoor/outdoor space. Closely allied to the patio, and also an indoor/outdoor construction, was another *Sunset* favorite, the deck. Then there was the poolside, which was also in the mind of *Sunset* a form of outdoor living space connected to the house itself, far more popular in the West because of extended swimming seasons.

The Suburban Freeholder's Domain: Intensifying One's Plot of Land as Living Space

In a tradition that went as far back as Thomas Jefferson, who built a serpentine wall at Monticello, *Sunset* made many valuable suggestions as to how brick, stone, and Mexican-inspired adobe walls might protect and enhance the garden. Here again is another major category in this bibliography, gardening, 1,170 notable entries in all. As metaphor and ideal, the garden offered one of the most powerful images associated with the Far West in the nineteenth century. As the theory of Manifest Destiny suggested, it was the destiny of the American people to settle the Far West and make the desert bloom: as agriculture, of course (as ardently promulgated by the Southern Pacific), but also as horticulture and landscape architecture and parks, such as those set aside by San Francisco in 1855 (Golden Gate Park) and San Diego in 1870 (Balboa Park). The search for the Garden of the West was central to the epic of Western settlement and migration: made all the more challenging by the fact that a significant percentage of the Far Western environment was arid or semi-arid. To seek the Garden of the West, then–whether as agriculture or horticulture–was to seek to redeem the land, to make the desert bloom, with all that such biblical imagery implied. Planting the West was nothing less than a search for redemption itself. With the ad-

Add-on wings, protected spaces, characteristic features of the ranch house.
November 1946, p. 27.

"Thanks to our climate, the West has become the horticultural crossroads of the world."
Thinking globally and locally.
May 1958, p. 4.

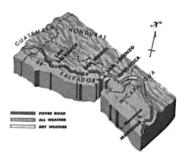

"An isolated segment of the Pan American Highway from Guatemala through Nicaragua," nicely depicted in an early example of a now-familiar style of map.
November 1948, p. 6.

"Family checks out recreational vehicles for rent on a lot in Southern California. These are average-sized models. Rates vary, but figure at least $100 a week plus a mileage charge."
May 1973, p. 69.(photo: Gerald R. Fredrick)

Right: Informational graphics' use of dramatic photography and typographic overlays convert garden entomology into art.
June 1958, p. 77. (photo: Clyde Childress)

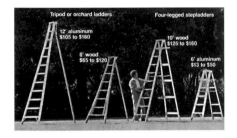

A fine crop of garden ladders, demonstrating characteristic Sunset *interplay of image and text.*
January 1981, p. 54.(photo: Norman A. Plate)

Garden pests are as constant a presence in the magazine as they are in Western gardens; this time, the Japanese beetle is the villain.
May 1978, p. 268.(photo: Bill Ross)

dition of Alaska and Hawaii to the Far West, moreover, two very dramatic and contrasting environments were added to this garden quest.

In time, especially after 1928, *Sunset* increasingly concerned itself with the domestic garden as well. As with cooking, Ruth Lane, a keen gardener before and after she came West, played a key role as a participating consultant to the garden editors. As far as garden theory is con-

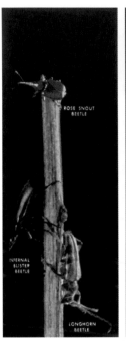

cerned, *Sunset* would seem to have preferred over the years the informal, slightly romantic garden, although it did publish a number of articles dealing with large formal gardens as well. With so much of the Far West being semi-arid, even desert, *Sunset* paid extensive attention–beginning in 1930 with such articles as "Gardening in the Land of Little Rain"–to water conservation-oriented techniques, encouraging its readers not to waste water, but to garden with nature rather than against it.

Sunset also advocated a 12-month cycle of planting, as only possible in the Far West, as evident in another 1930 article, "A Year-Round Garden Calendar," by the great landscapist John McLaren, superintendent of Golden Gate Park. Numerous articles suggested how *Sunset* readers, both men and women, might take their autumn plants into winter, their winter plants into spring, their spring plants into summer, and their summer plants back into autumn, and thus to achieve a rich and varied garden year. With gardening especially, *Sunset*'s regional editions reflected local soil, weather, and other regional differences. In numerous articles, *Sunset* helped its readers carry on a civilized warfare against garden pests, including the omnipresent deer and the medfly, which made its debut in 1981. *Sunset* also encouraged the development of gardening as a family ritual, publishing articles which encouraged parents to introduce children to gardening as early as possible and thus make of it a lifetime avocation. Paying attention to the placement, care, and cultivation of the more standard trees–maple, birch, ash–*Sunset*, beginning in 1965, also assisted the more exotic palm in making a triumphant comeback. Within 25 years, in fact, transplanted palm trees would be commanding fantastic prices. Often symbolic of stately landscaping as seen today with Palm Drive at Stanford University, planned by Frederick Law Olmsted for the original campus, the Southern Pacific promoted commercial development of date palm growing in the California desert, following the development of irrigation. *Sunset* also gave advice on the growing of fruit trees–apple, fig, pear, cherry, even the banana tree ("Bananas in Your Garden?" August 1996)–as part of the garden environment. In 1959 *Sunset* introduced its readers to the Japanese bonsai.

The edibility of garden fruit underscored another dimension of *Sunset*'s garden advice, the vegetable garden–carrots, broccoli, Brussels sprouts, tomatoes, sweet potatoes–which had provided such a main staple of the Home Front through the Victory Garden movement in the Second World War. In 1982, in far more peaceful and profitable times, *Sunset* encouraged its readers to grow their own endive (and thereby save themselves $6 a pound for this gourmet product at their local market) as well as fresh herbs, again more widely used in the West.

In its attention to flowers, *Sunset* encouraged its readers to merge native blooms (the poppy, the sunflower, lupine) with the unpretentious imported (the honeysuckle, the pansy, the geranium), the delicate imported (the hibiscus, the daffodil, the peony, the crocus, the petunia, jasmine, dahlia, and orchid), together with such luxuriant standbys as the begonia, the camellia, the lily, the magnolia, and the fuchsia. And then there was always the rhododendron and the chrysanthemum, flourishing so magnificently in the admixed sunshine and fog of the coastal regions, blooming across the year in a riot of Impressionist hue; and rich red poinsettias for Christmas, and every now and then an exotic, such as a 1930 article on the night-blooming Cereus which opens its flower between twilight and sunset, then vanishes into blossomless secrecy for another cycle. Above all, there was the rose, a variety of which, the *Sunset* Celebration, was introduced and named in honor of *Sunset* during this Centennial Year (just as the *Sunset* Jubilee was introduced during the magazine's 75th anniversary).

From the 1970s onward, *Sunset* was especially eager to integrate indoors and outdoors through flowering plants. Take shrubs, ferns, and

A gallery of beans

These heirloom beans are favorites of Elizabeth Berry and Santa Fe chefs. Characteristics of each differ somewhat among growers.

Black Valentine. Small jet-black bean with mealy texture and neutral flavor.

Cannellini. White with creamy texture; delicate sweet, nutty flavor. Larger variety may be called Italian Butterbean Cannellini, the smaller one, Eastern Cannellini.

Flageolet (also called Green Flageolet). Very slender, white to pale green bean. Mild taste; buttery, melting texture.

Flor de Mayo (also called Flor de Junio). Small red bean with medium-firm but creamy texture and subtly sweet flavor.

New Mexico Appaloosa. Mottled black and white or red and white. Smooth, creamy texture; mild, earthy flavor.

Scarlet Runner. Inch-long purple bean with black markings. Meaty, starchy texture and sweet chestnut flavor.

White Aztec (also called Pueblo). Thumb-size, plump white bean with a flavor and texture reminiscent of potatoes.

Jewel-like portrayal of bean varieties, carefully described: a classic Sunset *presentation.*
March 1997, p. 122.
(photo: Deborah Denker)

Left: "Bright and spacious, new kitchen blends into family sitting room and dining area. It opens through French doors at right to terrace, pool." There can be no doubt about what the editors want the reader to notice here.
March 1982, p. 122.(photo: Don Normark)

In the vast repertory of Sunset *garden-related images, there is a balance among three approaches: beauty for inspiration; guidance in selection of varieties and species; and technical instruction, ranging from the basics of pruning (a perennial topic in all senses of the word) to the laying out and construction of an entire backyard world.*

Getting to know one of the less desirable Western natives: poison oak. September 1968, p. 163.

"For early spring delight, plant a few pots of crocus or set corms in cracks between paving. These species crocus prefer cold winters. Dutch crocus good in warm areas." Ideas suitable for both city apartment and mountain retreat.
October 1968, p. 235. (photo: Glenn Christiansen)

flowers back into the home from the garden, *Sunset* urged its readers. Line the deck with bold earthen pots big enough to support plants that would link the indoor and outdoor environments. Create hanging gardens in the kitchen or suspend window gardens off the kitchen or the bedroom. Adorn living rooms with ficus. Live, in short, as completely as possible in the garden of the Far West, an essential component of an even larger ideal, the home. *Sunset*'s headquarters exemplified this integration of outdoors and indoors for its hundreds of thousands of visitors.

Cultivation of the Home Life: Crafts, Holidays, Food

Likewise did household crafts and food preparation serve this domestic ideal. Articles on crafts began appearing in *Sunset* increasingly from the 1930s and reached 265 notable entries by 1997. Like gardening and recipes, the vast majority of these projects–pack and ship a gift of Western fruit, build a tree house for kids with a safe exit rope, build a bird house, construct a Japanese folding bed, build your own outdoor picnic table–were home improvement and other family-oriented projects fitting into the overall *Sunset* philosophy of the home as domestic ideal and showing care for the quality and rhythms of daily life. Here again, these projects often appealed as much to readers who did not own their own homes as to home owners. The sheer variety of these projects is astonishing. Some of them involve simple skills; others, more advanced knowledge of carpentry or other skills. As in the case of gardening and food preparation, crafts suggestions were keyed to the cycle of seasons. For Halloween, for example, make costumes for children out of paper bags.

The Christmas holidays represent an especially intense season for crafts (make Christmas Magi for the windows, make homemade Christmas cards and tree ornaments); indeed, all things considered, Christmas is the favorite *Sunset* season, at least in terms of the predominance of Christmas-oriented crafts and menu suggestions. In its Christmas recipe proposals, *Sunset* adhered to tradition (bake Christmas breads) but at the same time offered over the years an intriguing number of variations on the traditional Christmas dinner. Not, however, that *Sunset* ever forgot the turkey! But *Sunset* often added a Western twist, for example, by barbecuing the holiday bird. It would seem, in fact, if one were to judge from the turkey-related items in this bibliography, that *Sunset* was making a special cause of this low-fat, low-calorie, high-protein bird: just another example of the nutritional and health awareness which pervades the 1,391 notable food, holiday, and entertaining suggestions in this bibliography.

In the case of its treatment of food themes, moreover, in both the magazine and in its many cookbooks, *Sunset* adhered to its usual philosophy of balance and practicality, the cycle of seasons, and family values. Many *Sunset* recipes originated as suggestions from readers. All recipes are thoroughly tested in the *Sunset* kitchens at the Menlo Park headquarters by a trained staff of food editors with employee and outside panels of chefs, restaurateurs, food writers, and selected members of the public, with the likes of Julia Child and Duncan Hines among the guest experts.

What is the *Sunset* philosophy of food? Like so many other aspects of *Sunset*, it is keyed to the range and variety of the Far West, the cycle of seasons, family life, and that persistent elegant simplicity that was ever part of the *Sunset* aesthetic. The formula was set by editor

Genevieve Callahan, with the help of Ruth Lane, upon the publication of the first "*Sunset* Kitchen Cabinet" feature in the first Lane issue. Most explicitly with the later addition of the "Chefs of the West" monthly feature, *Sunset* energetically brought men into the kitchen or barbecue area. Long before the rise of Martha Stewart, *Sunset* was sustaining a continuing dialogue, at once intimate and practical, with its readers as to how food preparation might help them celebrate their lives, enjoy their region, reinforce their family life, along with sharing with friends, and experience the pleasures of good taste.

"Some of the striking Ville de Nantes' petals may be red, others almost entirely white." Helping gardeners select suitable plants and varieties.
December 1948, p 76.

Left: "Wild Primrose. From original drawing by Margaret W. Buck." Printed by stone lithograph and inserted as decorative element.
July 1900, p. 110.

Each season has its special foods and recipes–summer, winter, fall, spring, the Fourth of July, Thanksgiving, Hanukkah, Christmas, Passover, Easter–and in recommending such seasonal recipes, *Sunset* was once again, as it did in encouraging its readers to plant a 12-month garden, helping its readers make life a little better, a little more caring, a little more enhanced. What kind of dishes might be served on long summer evenings, spent outdoors on the lawn? What kind of food could be served on long wintry evenings spent by the fire? What kind of foods would be fun to be served in the autumn, with football in the air, or in the spring, when the infinite variety of Far Western agriculture made itself most noticeable at the local grocery store or supermarket? Wine,

Agave, emblematic of a dry landscape.
November 1968, p. 247.
(photo: Richard Fish)

for *Sunset*'s food editors, was both a cooking ingredient and a beverage to serve for all seasons. *Sunset* built on the vineyard heritage of the Spanish missions, promoted wine regions throughout the Far West, and backed its editorial emphasis with an advertising policy that declined ads for all alcoholic beverages except wine. (Beer ads, like tobacco ads, were discontinued early in the Second World War years.)

For *Sunset*, cooking could so often be a unifying family ritual; hence, *Sunset* recommended that families cook together whenever possible, that teenagers be taught how to cook, and, by implication but powerful nevertheless, that a family "team effort" was part of a rewarding family life. Hence, *Sunset* paid attention to family vacation time as well as the rest of the year, with recipes for campfire cooking on outdoor treks or simple summer dishes to be enjoyed in mountain cabins or cottages by

A new variety of carnation, "Velvet 'N Lace." January 1997, p. 43. (photo: Norman A. Plate)

Right: The Sunset Jubilee rose was released in honor of the magazine's 75th year of publication and graced the January 1973 cover. (photo: Glenn Christiansen)

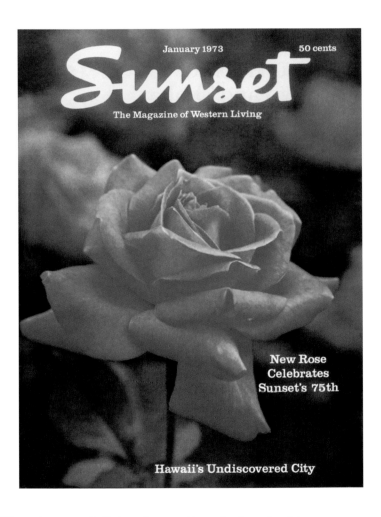

January 1973   *50 cents*

Sunset
The Magazine of Western Living

New Rose
Celebrates
Sunset's 75th

Hawaii's Undiscovered City

"Daffodil bulbs planted in early November produced this glowing display in just five months. In return for a little care they'll repeat the miracle springtime after springtime." November 1968, p. 94. (photo: Glenn Christiansen)

the sea. There is a near-infinity of suggestions for how best to prepare a picnic: family picnics in the main, but also picnics for couples, together with suggestions for an elaborate picnic buffet while tailgating before a football game.

In discussing the philosophy of the *Sunset* recipe and cookbook program, editors emphasized the variety of fruits, vegetables, and dairy products in *Sunset* country. Certainly, *Sunset* played no small role in helping to revolutionize American cuisine–such a meat-and-potatoes affair in the nineteenth century–by repeated recipes emphasizing garden vegetables and seasoning. *Sunset* also helped make such new, even exotic vegetables as the asparagus, the artichoke, the eggplant, and the avocado (actually a fruit) assimiliable to the Western, and eventually American, palate. In the case of the asparagus, a luxury vegetable was made middle-class. In the case of the avocado and the eggplant, even disrespected foods (in earlier times the avocado was used as animal feed) were upgraded in their status. If one were to judge by the number of recipes, one might say that *Sunset* practically re-invented the salad—or at the least brought the salad to the fore as a meal in itself as well as a side dish—with novel combinations of vegetables, fruits, seafood, cheeses, and wine dressings. Once again, the emphasis was upon the intrinsic healthfulness of salads as a main-course dish and the seemingly infinite variations of which salads were capable. *Sunset*'s early cookbooks were unique and promoted to the book trade for covering foods "from artichoke to zucchini," neither easily available nationally outside the West at the time.

What was true of vegetables was equally true of fruits, another bountiful product of the Garden of the West. Obviously, *Sunset* paid attention to such known fruits as the apple, the orange, the pear, the plum, and the cherry; and when such new fruits as the mango, papaya, kiwi, and, most recently, pluot were introduced, *Sunset* came forward with suggestions— for instance, not only serving papaya fresh, but also baked. It also brought its readers to a better understanding of two other genres, berries and melons, made possible by the eclectic vitality and year-round growing season of Far Western agriculture. While the strawberry was reasonably known in the *Sunset* market, the raspberry began its career as a more exotic introduction, and the blueberry seemed very much a Yankee import. As far as melons were concerned, Americans knew the watermelon, and Far Westerners knew the cantaloupe; but *Sunset* helped them appreciate even more exotic varieties of this genre—the Crenshaw, the Persian, the casaba, the honeydew—imported from the Middle East and now flourishing in the Far West amidst comparable warmer climate and soil conditions. (Thirsty crops such as melons generally benefited from Western large-scale irrigation systems, as reported by *Sunset* throughout the century.)

Not that *Sunset* lost connection with such old-fashioned standards as the sandwich, the mashed potato, and homemade bread. Over the years, in fact, *Sunset* showed great respect for the American sandwich, documenting and presenting its variations throughout the Far West; and perhaps only *Sunset* would have the courage to promote so many variations on the theme of mashed potatoes. In a number of recipes, the classic American hamburger is garnished with elements of haute cuisine. There are dozens of articles on pie-baking and jam-making; and even the prosaic cabbage takes on a certain éclat when submitted to the *Sunset* recipe treatment. Then there is the case of that ritual of Far Western identity, the barbecue. As might be expected, *Sunset* has innumerable articles on barbecuing, to include such mildly exotic variations as barbecuing a whole salmon or a whole pig, barbecuing in the Mongolian style, barbecuing on mesquite. *Sunset* often tested different types of built-in barbecue designs—both indoor and outdoor—as well as portable barbecues. Many articles, along with several books, detailed instructions for building barbecues and other outdoor cooking facilities, such as one of *Sunset*'s most popular how-to-do-it projects: a Mexican adobe baking oven.

Another luxury food brought by *Sunset* to the broad Western middle-class palate was seafood, following earlier traditions of other coastal

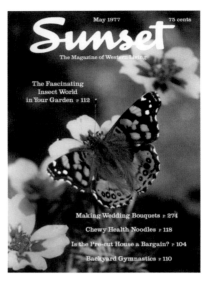

"*A young West Coast Lady—that's a kind of butterfly—on a marigold in Berkeley.*" May 1977 cover. (photo: James Carney)

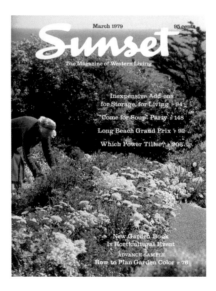

Native flowers grace the March 1979 cover. (photo: Norman A. Plate)

"One day's collection picked along State 165 to Mount Rainier National Park: Elderberry (upper left); blueberry (upper right); salal (center); blackberry (lower left); red huckleberry (lower right)." Food and travel combine in a National Park setting.
July 1968, p. 52. (photo: Don Normark)

Garden bounty and family focus: almost Eden, somewhere in Oregon.
May 1973, p. 290. (photo: Don Normark)

areas, such as New England and the Eastern Seaboard and the Gulf states. While San Francisco and Seattle had long since developed as seafood towns, Far Westerners in general did not frequently include seafood in their daily diet, with the exception perhaps of mountain trout fried in a skillet in the summertime or the tuna fish sandwich sent to school in a lunch bag. In the course of many recipe suggestions, *Sunset* patiently tutored Americans in the Far West in how to prepare and appreciate a food which, if not treated properly, dramatically loses its excellence. Thanks in part to *Sunset*, salmon, sea bass, sand dabs, abalone, crab, seafood soups, even crayfish and lobster bisque, became part of the Far Western dining vocabulary, and the many regional varieties, such as Dungeness and Alaska crab, Coho salmon, and the Olympic oyster, were recognized and made popular.

While demanding in their own way, *Sunset* recipes were never needlessly fussy or self-absorbed. Sometimes, as in the case of suggesting something as simple as a few selected spices to be added to ice tea, a *Sunset* recipe could be breathtakingly brief. One exception would be the years that "Chefs of the West" featured recipes for men only, and when recipes were often lengthy and time consuming. Rather than payment for recipes, published contributors received a chef's hat and apron. In other instances–making apple cider, cooking venison–one felt the re-emergence of an older American frontier. *Sunset* never threw itself excessively into the nouvelle cuisine movement. It did not have to, and yet some of today's "California Cuisine" has its roots in early *Sunset* magazines and books such as the 1936 *Sunset All-Western Cook Book*, largely made up of *Sunset* magazine recipes submitted by California readers. Its food philosophy already emphasized nutritiousness and simplicity. Yet it did advise its readers on how to roast their own coffee or serve pasta for breakfast, or even prepare special gourmet dishes in the microwave. In the matter of wine, *Sunset* avoided excessive connoisseurship and snobbery, preferring instead to emphasize the availability of good wines at moderate prices and how they might be served unpretentiously with food. *Sunset*'s popular wine books encouraged readers not only to use wines but to visit wineries throughout the West, as *Sunset* magazine articles continue to do today. Thus, by refusing to intimidate them, *Sunset* brought its readers forward in their taste for, and knowledge of, wine: another ambition as venerable as the wine program of Thomas Jefferson himself, who believed that Americans would never be truly civilized until they learned to enjoy wine as a daily beverage with simplicity and moderation.

Two foods–sourdough bread and Jack cheese–exercised a special fascination on the *Sunset* staff as emblems of the Far West. Each commemorative issue, in fact–May 1973 (75th), May 1978 (80th), and May 1988 (90th)–ran articles on sourdough French bread as the bread of the West. The May 1973 issue ran a very scholarly article on the history of sourdough, including a chemical analysis of sourdough starter by Professor George York of UC Davis. Needless to say, sourdough French also received due treatment in the *Sunset Cook Book of Breads* (in five editions from 1963 to 1994) and continues to be featured in the magazine, as recently as March 1998 ("Our Daily Bread: Easier Than You Think").

The same was true of Jack cheese, another product of the California frontier, in this case, the Monterey County dairy of Scotsman David Jacks, who arrived in California in 1850 and went into the dairy and cheese-making business. As in the case of sourdough French bread, Jack cheese–fresh or dry, or California teleme, a first cousin of Jack, all of it manufactured in five cheese factories, three in the San Francisco Bay Area, two in the Central Valley, which *Sunset* encouraged its readers to visit–offered late twentieth-century Americans a continuing taste of the California frontier.

By the late twentieth century that frontier had produced an extraordinarily diverse population, whose cuisines found their way into the magazine. Over the years *Sunset* has shown a total and encompassing respect for the cuisine traditions of the Far West, whether the product of Native America, the Spanish, Mexican, or American frontier, or recent immigration. Mexican food, for example, offered *Sunset* readers an opportunity to enjoy the dishes of the very civilization which had first explored and organized California and the Spanish Southwest. Enchiladas, tortillas, tamales and tamale pie, tacos, huevos rancheros, the burrito, the chilis and peppers of the Southwest, Mexican salads and vegetables, the blue corn of New Mexico, Mexican food on Christmas Eve, even Mexican fondue and Mexican Lite for weight watchers: The recipes of *Sunset* do more than justice to the food of Mexico and the Spanish Southwest. Also well represented are the dishes brought to the Far West by Basque sheepherders. As Hawaii loomed on the consciousness of Far Westerners, Polynesian recipes made their appearance. Japanese food proved an especial favorite, and *Sunset* must be given major credit for in-

Indoor gardening provides opportunities for apartment or condo dwellers, here shown at Aspen in close conjunction with home design concepts.
January 1978, p. 42. (photo: Glenn Christiansen)

Left: Dried flower arranging brings together garden and home crafts interests.
July 1957, p. 132.

troducing the middle classes to sushi. By the 1970s, *Sunset*, like the Far West itself, then in the beginnings of a global immigration, was reaching out to India, to Indonesia, to Thailand, and to Morocco for food influences. By the mid-1980s, Vietnamese cuisine was showing a strong presence. With time, these influences have recombined with other sources, for example, to produce such exotic crosses as "Bouillabaisse, Hawaii-Style" (May 1997).

Resurgence of Stewardship as Pressures Mount on Western Environment

All this suggested that the Far West had become an international place in both its peoples and its cuisine. One hundred years earlier, *Sunset* had been founded to serve a smaller and more restricted audience and a sparsely settled region. Now that audience, once almost exclusively Anglo-American, contained the cultures and ethnicities of the planet. Still, the same ambition remained at *Sunset*: to provide this audience with the information and references it needed to pursue its identity, maintain its quality of life, and exercise proper stewardship over its region. *Sunset* began as a travel magazine, then exfoliated into a general review in the pre-Lane era. The Lanes had brought focus, and from this focus had come new strength. By the May 1973 75th Anniversary issue,

"Mania for dracaenas is easy to understand. These plants are colorful, undemanding, and lush." Container gardening with a vengeance. Note use of type color over the various background colors.
February 1978, p. 78.(photo: Norman A. Plate)

"Narrow sideyard in Tokyo–planted 5 years ago with timber bamboo… Monotony of long path is broken by using old stones in various sizes and shapes, by water channel suggesting river across path."
March 1958, p. 83.

"Leisurely walking on this path–and being led by it–is esthetic pleasure, although the Japanese are always mindful that path's function is practical as well as ornamental."
February 1958, p. 88.

"Fences play an important part in this Belvedere, California, entry garden." An uncharacteristically stark and formalistic piece of landscaping.
May 1958, p. 76.(photo: Ernest Braun)

however, *Sunset* was expanding on its growing concerns with environmental considerations outside the fourfold editorial policy–building, gardening, travel, and cooking–which had served it so well.

"Can the West Grow Wisely and Well?" *Sunset* asked in its 75th Anniversary issue. Several environmentalists, including Starker Leopold, sought to answer the question. Recognizing the importance of government, *Sunset* included comments on the future by eight Western governors. Merely to ask this question implied a certain concern for the problems facing Far Western life. *Sunset* country could no longer be taken for granted. The great big Far West had its own great big problems to face, and *Sunset*, while not abandoning its nearly half-century identity, could not help but be open to the challenges of the present. Six years later, in the February 1979 issue celebrating 50 years of Lane ownership, *Sunset* took pride in its role in advocating environmental living, progressive technology, the new agriculture and aquaculture, good nutrition, preservationism, and public parks. By the May 1988 90th Anniversary issue, *Sunset* had become even more explicit regarding the social and environmental challenges facing the Far West. Hence, the articles on traffic, open space, waste management, urban design, water conservation, and other social and environmental matters in this anniversary issue. *Sunset* still stood for a better life–for travel and recreation, for building and remodeling, for food and entertainment, for gardening and landscaping, for outdoor living, for workshop and crafts–but it had also aligned itself solidly behind the effort to deal with the awesome challenges facing the region. The November 1994 issue, for example, described "Painting to Save the Land," revealing that "armed with brushes and canvases, Santa Barbara's Oak Group fights to save open spaces." Mel Lane, in a 1988 editorial celebrating the 90th anniversary of *Sunset*, wrote: "As we look toward our centennial and the beginning of the 21st century, we see more challenges ahead… *Sunset* editors are already researching solutions to these and other challenges. And as the West continues to change, so will we."

In one sense, however, while this response to challenge was receiving a more explicit acknowledgment, it was nothing new. Reminiscent of the Progressive philosophy earlier in the century, conservation, preservation, and stewardship had long been part of the *Sunset* program, whether expressly stated in the early era of the general review or reflected in the Lane era through the presentation of better ways of living and later with articles expressing strong concerns for various environmental issues. Over the years, *Sunset* had its critics, as any strong publishing institution will, such as the Stanford professor, talking to journalist Neil Morgan at a conference at Carmel in 1958, who believed that *Sunset* "… could spearhead an emerging sense of Western responsibility" and should return to its earlier identity as an intellectual review. The professor told Morgan, "*Sunset* could be a terrific force for good in the West today."[11] The unnamed Stanford professor was of course wrong on both counts, unaware or forgetting, on the one hand, that *Sunset* had gone broke as an intellectual review 30 years earlier and, on the other hand, that the formula as enunciated in the first Lane issue was very much a force for good in supporting strong family values. It also would develop a distinguished record of advocacy for the Western environment, addressing regional problems with workable solutions. In fact, *Sunset: The Magazine of Western Living* had been flourishing for three decades by

[11] Neil Morgan, *Westward Tilt, The American West Today* (1963), p. 20.

1958, not only addressing problems but helping to solve them, and its circulation was in better shape than ever. As background, it is worth noting that the Far West had never in its history supported a general review for any significant length of time. And *Sunset*'s influence for social and environmental improvements has increased greatly over the years.

Why? Because *Sunset* does not proselytize. *Sunset*, rather, for most of a century has advanced its message through adherence to context and practical, useful facts. Readers do not feel intimidated by *Sunset*. On the contrary, they feel supported and encouraged in their desire to make their lives as dignified, as purposeful, and as enjoyable as possible. And besides: At the core of *Sunset* is message enough. Here is a magazine based upon the fundamental goodness of life and the nurturing and ennobling Far West where the good life can be pursued, but with an added social responsibility to others. As Wallace Stegner stated in a 1978 video interview produced by *Sunset* Films, "*Sunset* is both traditional–in that it takes its stance from Western places, architecture, gardens, and food–and progressive in that it knows that in an all-but-experimental society like that of the West, change is going to be a constant. *Sunset*, on its record, is as competent to deal with change as to reflect the unchanging."[12]

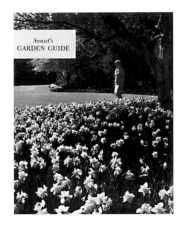

"*Daffodils illuminate* Sunset's *garden in late March and on into April.*"
October 1968, p. 230.

Far left: "*Long wood walkway leads visitors from the house to a flagstone patio in the center of the 20- by 30-foot garden. Birches underplanted with perennials surround the patio.*" *Making the most of a restricted space.*
March 1997, p. 80. (photo: Norman A. Plate)

Left: "*A low stucco wall defines one edge of a small dipping pool and forms the front side of a raised planter. An arbor and shrubs help screen the garage from view.*" *We can imagine this treatment in most Western cities.*
March 1997, p. 66. (photo: Jay Graham)

As long ago as ancient Greece, and certainly among the Founding Fathers of the American Republic, this notion–the pursuit of happiness–possessed the force of a fundamental and transforming idea. From this perspective, *Sunset* is about life, liberty, and the pursuit of happiness: life in the Far West, liberty to make that life as good as possible, happiness to pursue in a thousand simple ways, alone or with one's family, in the midst of landscapes which in the nineteenth century had beckoned Americans to cross a trackless continent. *Sunset* now, as the twentieth century turns into the next millennium, beckons the world as well to see in this Far Western region one of the most privileged and promising portions of Planet Earth.

"*Ideas for planting, screens, walls, paving, begin even as you enter these gardens at Los Angeles State and County Arboretum.*" *Note* Sunset's *participation in both experimental horticulture and public education.*
June 1958, p. 71. (photo: William Aplin)

[12] *Looking In on Sunset: With Wallace Stegner* (Sunset Video, 1978).

Vol. 5　　　MAY 1900　　　No. 1

SUNSET

W.H.BULL

10 Cents a Copy　　　　　$1.00 per Year

Four Eras: Changes of Ownership

by Tomas Jaehn
Curator for American and British History, Stanford University Libraries

The Southern Pacific Launches a New Vehicle to Develop Its Market

Any discussion of late nineteenth-century development of the West, rural or urban, social, political, or economic, inevitably involves the Southern Pacific Railroad (formerly Central Pacific). This rich and powerful strictly Western enterprise conceived in Sacramento and managed from San Francisco received from the United States government over 11.5 million acres of land in California and nearly 11 million in Nevada, Utah, and Oregon. It also received funds and land from Western states, cities, and counties and thus drew on local capital and local leadership as well. Merely the profits of building the tracks of Central Pacific have been estimated at well over $200 million.[1]

To secure the continuation of revenues and profits after completion, Southern Pacific owners and their supporters turned into enthusiastic boosters and land developers.[2] While some profits were sought in ferry and passenger train services, the Southern Pacific's larger objective was to develop suburban areas and to a lesser extent urban and rural regions throughout the West.

Advertising was one way to increase visibility. Up to the 1890s, railroads typically limited advertising to running timetables in local newspapers. Railroads not only began to advertise heavily in magazines and other high-toned media, the Southern Pacific decided to publish its own magazine.[3] In 1898 the Passenger Department of the Southern Pacific Railroad created *Sunset* magazine, essentially as publicity for railroad lands and tourism. No outside advertising was accepted in the first few issues, as the Southern Pacific expected to underwrite the entire expense as part of its advertising program.[4] In its first issue, at 5 cents a copy, editors promised their readers conveniently "information concerning the [Western states and territories]–a rich and inexhaustible field over which the dawn of future commercial and industrial importance is just breaking."

Sunset directed its information primarily toward tourists who were in the late nineteenth century, above all else, potential investors and mi-

---

[1] Earl Pomeroy, *The Pacific Slope: A History of California, Oregon, Washington, Idaho, Utah, and Nevada* (New York: Alfred A. Knopf, 1964), 96-7; Donald Worster, *Rivers of Empire: Water, Aridity and the Growth of the American West* (New York: Pantheon Books, 1985), 101.

[2] Worster, *Rivers of Empire*, 101-2.

[3] Stephen Fox, *The Mirror Makers: A History of American Advertising and Its Creators* (1984; reprint, Urbana: University of Illinois Press, 1997), 38.

[4] Charles William Mulhall, Jr., "Sunset: The History of a Successful Regional Magazine" (M.A. thesis, Stanford University, 1955), 1-2.

May 1900 cover

Native Americans

The original Westerners have been evident in the illustration of the magazine from the earliest years. At times, the portraiture has been poignant, sometimes tragic-heroic (most notably at the hands of Maynard Dixon), at other times festive, but always sympathetic.

A very late, but archetypal, Maynard Dixon illustration: the enduring Native American in an eternal Western landscape.
May 1938, p. 18.

Right: "The early period of American rule was extremely unsettled; Indian massacres and the dangerous elements which composed the population–prospectors, cow-punchers, adventurers, gamblers, bandits, horse-thieves–leading to one of the worst, though one of the most picturesque, periods of our frontier history. But today, when Arizona claims the most law-abiding population in the United States, the picturesque quality lingers in the sunny villages of the aborigines."
October 1913, p. 671.(photo: Karl Moon)

Far right:"Half-a-dozen miles outside Tucson stands the white Mission of San Xavier del Bac, still of extraordinary beauty, sole survivor of that chain of outposts of the church which the friars of the Spanish orders stretched across Arizona in their campaign of proselytism three centuries ago." The Spanish and Indian heritages of the Southwest were always part of Sunset's coverage.
October 1913, p. 666.

grants[5], and secondly to Westerners seeking economic improvement or recreational diversion.[6] The magazine sold the West's best commodity, its environmental attractions and economic potentials, to thousands of men, women, and children. It was not at all surprising that in its first issue, the magazine featured Yosemite and reassured its readers "that only by actual experience can the splendor of Yosemite be realized."

In an attempt to bring people and resources west on the Southern Pacific, *Sunset* sweepingly promoted gold mining, harvesting, and other economic ventures in California and the West. *Sunset* published countless promotional articles on "Thrifty Cities of the Pacific Coast" (January 1900) and on towns and valleys on the brink of development appealing to the communal senses of potential and actual Westerners. For instance, the magazine recruited the Fresno Chamber of Commerce to write an article interspersed with picturesque images about its resources and possibilities in *Sunset*'s pages (November 1899).

Occasionally Southern Pacific used its magazine as a corporate platform to defend freighting practices or to hint at political matters. In journalistic prose, articles describe the smoothness of how freight is transported from the East to the West, how easily it is to obtain a car for

shipment (March 1900), quite contrary to images so vividly described in Frank Norris's California epic *The Octopus*.[7]

It was because of Eastern and European clientele that *Sunset* eventually began to accept advertisement in July 1899. Its editors realized that "if our Eastern readers are to gain the knowledge they must have concerning a colony, resort, or any business, they must be placed in contact with whom they can 'talk business'" (July 1899).

Now mingling with *Sunset* editorials were pages of testimonials to the wonders and splendors of the great Western landscape and its wealth of natural resources. Baker City, Oregon, advertised itself as the

5 Earl Pomeroy, *In Search of the Golden West: The Tourist in Western America* (New York: Alfred A. Knopf, 1957), 131.

6 Southern Pacific, like other railroad companies, employed agents in Europe. Ray Allen Billington, *Land of Savagery, Land of Promise: The European Image of the American Frontier* (New York: W. W. Norton and Company, 1981), 64.

7 Frank Norris, *The Octopus* (1900; reprint, New York: New American Library, 1964).

"metropolis of the Inland Empire," and the San Jose Chamber of Commerce imposed proper pronunciation by adding "San Hosay" to its advertising.[8] Petaluma prided itself the largest poultry center on earth, and the Calistoga Chamber of Commerce praised that its "Orchadists clear from $100.00 to 350.00 per acre [and that] good fruit lands can be had from $100.00 to $200.00 per acre."

But Southern Pacific's and Chambers of Commerce's promotional and economic motives notwithstanding, by the end of the century, *Sunset* reflected the large political and communal responsibilities its owners and supporters had assumed.[9] Southern Pacific's political influence, though, was not unique. One might think of *Sunset*'s parent company as robber barons or as the evil Octopus, or one might view the owners of the Southern Pacific as benevolent empire builders, but its pages now stand as a documentary of the West's development. Regardless of view, it was in large part because of railroads like the Southern Pacific and because of their policies that the Far West emerged to a mature and more balanced economy.

The magazine promoted the abundant recreational opportunities of the West with articles and photos on fiestas in Sonora, Mexico (January 1900), fishing and hunting adventures in Oregon (August 1899), and days of frolicking and folly along Santa Cruz's beautiful shoreline (March 1903). These articles suggest the strong influence the Southern Pacific exercised in shifting American recreational habits. With or without the automobile, recreational trips were likely to involve a train trip. If anglers, campers, and sightseers could not reach their desired destinations on main lines, they were likely to use one of the local lines or stagecoach connections to reach resorts, the ocean, or the mountains. In fact, by the 1890s the Southern Pacific was advertising special campers' fares and free rental of tents, stoves, and other camping equipment.[10]

The magazine made use of the climate factor in advertising and in editorials which gave zest and optimism to health seekers. A California booster once responded to a remark that California had nothing to offer but climate: "That's right, and we sell it, too–$10 an acre, for the land, $490 an acre for the climate."[11] It was often from the ranks of these health seekers and tourists that many permanent settlers came bringing along Eastern capital and income to the West.

California's and the West's development was supported by the increasing popularity of the automobile. At first it was a rich tourist's, Eastern tourist at that, amusement rather than a major means of transportation. But the Southern Pacific and *Sunset* recognized the potential of the automobile early (just as it would identify the possibilities of air travel) and thus promoted motorcar tourism. *Sunset* anticipated the nation's automobile fever and promoted the opportunities available for "motoring" across urban and scenic landscapes. With the automobile and road development still in their infancy, *Sunset* recommended in 1903 a four-day trip from San Francisco to Los Angeles.

Opportunities for exploration grew steadily: By 1915 the Pacific

"During the last three winters many of the aged Blackfeet men and women have died of hunger diseases even while Nebraska farmers were burning corn for fuel. For instances of actual starvation we need not go to Armenia; we can find them right here in America among the 'wards of the nation.'" November 1922, p. 19. (photo: Leland J. Burrud)

Ishi, the California Native American who experienced a startling transformation, from solitary hunter-gatherer to celebrity, from the sole survivor of his culture to a museum exhibit and virtual encyclopedia of a vanished way of life. January 1912, p. 109.

---

[8] Charles Fletcher Lummis, editor of *Land of Sunshine*, a competitor of sorts to *Sunset*, fought hard (and often losing) battles to prevent the loss or disfigurement of California place names. He found the U.S. Postal Service and the railroads to be the most flagrant offenders and his campaign focused upon them. Edwin R. Bingham, *Charles F. Lummis: Editor of the Southwest* (San Marino, CA: The Huntington Library, 1955), 83-4.

[9] Gerald D. Nash, *The American West in the Twentieth Century: A Short Study of an Urban Oasis* (Englewood Cliffs, NJ: Prentice-Hall, Inc., 1973), 45.

[10] Pomeroy, *In Search of the Golden West*, 125.

[11] Cit. in Oscar Osburn Winther, "The Use of Climate as a Means of Promoting Migration to Southern California," *Mississippi Valley Historical Review* 33 (December 1946), 412.

Food

There is an almost endless variety of drawings and photographs related to food, entertaining, and kitchens in the back issues of Sunset, *balanced between the ends (the finished item, spread, or room) and the means (steps in the making) and ranging from the homely to the magnificent.*

"Gently, carefully, daughter rolls the dessert. Mother has a plate ready to slip under it. The cheese filling tends to push ahead when rolled, so it is spread more thickly at the starting end. Smooth the filling well out to the sides before rolling it into a log."
April 1958, p. 182.(photo: Esther Litton)

There is an almost abstract feeling to this May 1939 cover's table setting. "Give a garden breakfast party! It's easy, it's informal, it's Western."
(photo: Henry Seuter)

Highway connected Seattle with San Diego; the Sunset Highway crossed the Cascades into Seattle, and the old Santa Fe Trail and its extension, the California Trail, were no longer paths for ox carts and burros but routes for automobiles and motor coaches which traversed the Southwest's deserts and mountains.[12] *Sunset* recommended to its readers to take leisurely drives along the beautiful coastline, to see the majestic mountains, and to explore the blossomed roadways of the Central Valley in California.

Appropriately, in February 1907 *Sunset* featured "Motoring in the West: Fast Flying Automobile in Pastime and Trade, Helping Upbuild the Far Country of Gold and Sunshine"[13] and pointed the way to the complex connection between the automobile and the West in years to come. In an attempt to gear the magazine to a feminine clientele of leisure, the magazine cover prominently featured four women in their auto motoring across landscapes exemplifying the liberating "Westering experience."[14]

Sunset addressed women in many ways in its pages. It targeted female readers by highlighting the modernity and familiarity the West had to offer. Articles covered social news that suggested community values and respectability. Editorials such as "Famous California Women" implied possibly exaggerated opportunities for women in California and the West at a time when economic as well as political opportunities for women were still limited.[15]

Sunset also provided women with information on social groups and organizations to ensure women's access to familiar institutions and amenities such as women's clubs, which were interested in a wide variety of issues, from monitoring child labor to preserving the forests.

To counter images of the West as a cultural and educational wasteland, the Southern Pacific promoted and *Sunset* frequently highlighted events such as world expositions, museum exhibits, and theater events. The magazine endorsed cultural achievements and opportunities and featured many stories about the University of California and, not surprisingly, Leland Stanford, Jr. University. The magazine was not shy about flaunting educational excellence at both universities.

By 1902 *Sunset*'s pages featured regular columns such as "Books and Writers" and "Plays and Players," covering Western literary and dramatic developments. To spread the word about the quality of life out West, *Sunset* recruited famous writers such as Jack London (often in exchange for railroad transportation[16]), whose tales of Western drama and intrigue were world-renowned and told of the West as a land for adventures and fortune seekers.

Sunset used famous and soon-to-be famous artists such as Edward Borein, who frequently contributed pictures to the magazine from its inception. Borein's rough sketches of cowboy life confirmed Southern Pacific's vested interest in evoking images of a picturesque West.

A close friend of Borein, Maynard Dixon, one of the most distinctive Western illustrators published in *Overland Monthly* and *Harper's Weekly*,

[12] "The West: Looking Ahead... From 60 years' Experience," *Sunset*, 120 (May 1958), 3-6.

[13] *Sunset*, 18 (February 1907), 275-95.

[14] On women's relations to the automobile, see Virginia Scharff, *Taking the Wheel: Women and the Coming of the Motor Age* (New York: The Free Press, 1991).

[15] Sandra L. Myers, *Westering Women and the Frontier Experience, 1800-1915* (Albuquerque: University of New Mexico Press, 1982), 269. See also Joan M. Jensen and Gloria Ricci Lothrop, eds., *California Women: A History* (San Francisco: Boyd & Fraser Publishing Company, 1987).

[16] Earle Labor et al., *The Letters of Jack London*, 3 vols. (Stanford: Stanford University Press, 1988), 1: 502.

designed covers for Jack London's *Son of the Wolf* and other works, but did his most dramatic work before 1910 for *Sunset*. He drew traditional Western images such as cowboys, Native Americans, landscapes, and explorers, but he simplified their forms. Dixon contributed many *Sunset* covers, notably the May 1906 emergency issue (see frontispiece) and the October 1905 issue picturing a Native American in a blanket standing on a mesa, his back to a vast, desolate landscape.[17]

The pages of *Sunset* shed light upon American attitudes concerning the environment. The magazine consistently promoted the West's natural habitat. *Sunset* was a major proponent of the preservation of the West's great beauty and natural environment. Even its parent company, the Southern Pacific, played a significant role in making Yosemite

Children helping out in the kitchen; a recurring theme, one that makes explicit the relationship of food and family.
December 1968, p. 132.(photo: Darrow M. Watt)

Left: "Familiar soft 'Hachiya,' cut, and in front in basket; rarer soft 'Tamopan' at left in basket; and two firm persimmon varieties. Honey and lime are complementary flavors." Spotlight on a less-common fruit easily grown in California.
November 1968, p. 175.(photo: Glenn Christiansen)

"Western-grown examples of the four major groups of potatoes—one variety of each of the thin-skinned types and two of the russets." A particularly attractive and informative portrait of the Western spud.
April 1978, p. 126. (photo: Glenn Christiansen)

Valley a national park, as John Muir begrudgingly admitted. "Even the soulless Southern Pacific R.R. Co.," he conceded, "never counted on for anything good, helped nobly in pushing the bill for this park through Congress."[18] When in 1903 Theodore Roosevelt visited the Golden State, it gave *Sunset* the opportunity to feature a president's words that symbolized the magazine's concerns to make conservation and environmental protection a Western priority: "In California I am impressed by how great the state is, but I am even more impressed by the immensely greater greatness that lies in the future, and I ask that your marvelous natural resources be handed on unimpaired to your children and your children's children."[19]

[17] William H. Goetzman, *The West of the Imagination* (New York: W. W. Norton, 1986), 318-19.

[18] Quoted in Alfred Runte, "Promoting the Golden West: Advertising and the Railroad," *California History* no.1, vol.70 (Spring 1991), 63.

[19] *Sunset*, no.3, vol.11 (July 1903), 210.

Stir flour, then cheese, butter and seasonings into hot milk.

Remove from heat, add unbeaten eggs, beat mixture smooth ~ ~

Let stand 8 to 12 hours, then cut into 2-inch squares ~ ~

Dip in corn meal; brown in butter; serve with Tomato Sauce!

The step-by-step cartoon-strip style of instruction was successfully used over many years. Here we see that gnocchi made its way to Sunset's *West long before restaurants like Spago were conceived. October 1938, p. 21. (illus.: Ruth Taylor White)*

Under the ownership of the Southern Pacific, *Sunset* magazine pursued a dual policy of promoting its parent company's service area as well as Southern Pacific itself.[20] It was through *Sunset* that readers became aware of the many opportunities of the American West. Particularly California had everything prospective tourists and actual Westerners could want: mountains, ocean beaches, seaside resorts, deserts, urban amenities, and economic opportunities. Southern Pacific recognized the importance of the West when it purchased the Portland-based *Pacific Monthly* (also founded in 1898) in 1912 and expanded its readership area. By 1914, *Sunset: The Pacific Monthly* (as it now called itself) had become a publication of national attention and circulation, and Southern Pacific felt that it had reached its limit as a promotional magazine. The Southern Pacific sold *Sunset* to a small group of employees whose interest was to continue the promotion of the West under a less corporate influence.

The Woodhead-Field Years: Addressing a Rapidly Changing West

When the Southern Pacific Railroad sold its creation, *Sunset*, in 1914, an important era came to a close for California and the West. By the end of the Progressive Era, on the threshold of World War I, *Sunset* had accompanied a surge of new immigrants to the West, religiously providing promotional news for the newcomers. Unlike the nineteenth-century migration of individuals seeking mother lodes and farmland in underdeveloped territory, these new immigrants were largely families, often with adequate means to establish a comfortable new life in the West Coast's mild climate. In addition, they more often settled in cities and attempted to establish a familiar lifestyle and culture. This situation was an opportunity for Western-oriented magazines of national significance. *Sunset*, as a corporate promotional magazine for Western migration, tourism and development, had done its service.

Against this backdrop of progressive changes and the uncertainty of the times, a group of employees decided to take over the magazine after the Southern Pacific decided to sell it. William Woodhead, Charles K. Field, and numerous other former employees of *Sunset*, such as Walter V. Woehlke, secretary and later managing editor, formed Woodhead, Field and Company and purchased the magazine from the railroad. The new owners felt editorial and format changes were needed to make the magazine a vehicle of Western thought and to steer the magazine into a national market. Immediately, without offending the Southern Pacific Railroad, the new owners and editors distanced themselves from the railroad to minimize "the handicap of railroad ownership, in the face of all the prejudice that unavoidably attaches to a magazine so owned."[21] In 1915 *Sunset* then announced its "joining of the company of modern magazines" by changing its format from book size to the distinctive and larger magazine shape.[22]

The necessity of editorial change for magazines like *Sunset* had loomed earlier in the century. Ironically, Charles Erskine Scott Wood, onetime contributor to *Sunset* and major collaborator with *Pacific Month-*

[20] Donovan L. Hofsommer, *The Southern Pacific, 1901-1985* (College Station: Texas A&M University Press, 1986), 67.

[21] "Announcement to the Readers of Sunset," *Sunset*, October 1914, David Starr Jordan Archive, SC 58, Special Collections, Stanford University (hereafter DSJ Collection).

[22] "Sunset Gets Into Line," *Sunset*, December 1915.

[23] Jane Apostol, "Lute Pease of the *Pacific Monthly*," *Pacific Northwest Quarterly* 74 (July 1983): 104.

ly before it was absorbed into *Sunset* in 1912, predicted that "it will be necessary for the *P. M.* [*Pacific Monthly*] to be rather more radical and up-to-date. At present we are really no different from *Sunset*."[23] What had been true for the *Pacific Monthly* at the turn of the century was true for *Sunset* itself in 1914.

National magazines published on the East Coast touched only lightly–and with an Eastern, sometimes condescending, viewpoint –on Western events, creating an opportunity for a strong Western magazine. Given the competition of West Coast publications such as *Land of Sunshine* and *Overland Monthly*, Woodhead, Field and Company was convinced that *Sunset* could develop into the premier Western magazine. To that end, the editors went far beyond the original ideas of the Southern Pacific Railroad to simply advertise the beauties and opportunities of the West. As a first step, *Sunset* quietly moved away from naming its home region "Frontier West" and "Wild West" and adjusted its editorials to the more sophisticated region of the "Pacific Coast." While retaining the informational and promotional legacy of the Southern Pacific Railroad, the new owners broadened the magazine's scope and attracted national attention by adding literary, political, and cultural features:

> The Magazine will begin, each month, with a strong editorial department entitled "The Pulse of the Pacific Coast," commenting on the affairs of the West Coast and the world it faces, reflecting its politics, its sociology, its economics, its art, its recreation–all its problems, aspirations, griefs [sic] and triumphs.[24]

This change toward a national audience was driven to some extent by Westerners' resentment at being perceived as intellectually inferior to the East.

The greatest impact of the new leadership, the basis for a reputation recognized to this day, was in the caliber of writers and literature published during this era. Promising to publish the "best fiction money will buy," the "literary *Sunset*" published many great writers of its day. Or published work about them, as was the case of Jack London, *Sunset*'s most famous writer during the Southern Pacific era. Shortly after the sensational news of Jack London's death in November 1916, Charles K. Field of *Sunset*, in order to compete with other magazines for stories about London, commissioned Rose Wilder Lane to write a biography of Jack London. The working relationship among Lane, *Sunset* editors, and London's wife, Charmian, was strenuous, and the subsequent serialized article about Jack London was a "fictionalized biography."[25] Nevertheless, *Sunset*'s publication of Lane's sketches viewed Jack London as a regional writer and indicated his significance in the growing movement toward a Pacific Coast culture.

Whereas *Sunset* of the railroad days reflected an attraction to the West, Woodhead, Field and Company's magazine mirrored the seedlings of a regional culture in the West that "was to provide deep-seated roots for all American culture."[26] Succeeding Jack London, who painted early on exciting, if simplistic, pictures of the American West on *Sunset*'s pages, were authors recognized beyond the Pacific Coast, like Eugene Manlove Rhodes, Will James (as author and illustrator), and Erle Stanley Gardner. Dashiell Hammett wrote in "Ber-Bulu" (March 1925) of frontier conditions and romance on a Pacific island, and Zane

"You can have pork with orange-cranberry sauce, couscous, and broccoli on your table in less than 30 minutes." One can imagine that the first plate to bear couscous and cranberries at the same time may well have been in Sunset's West.
February 1997, p. 124.
(photo: Norman A. Plate)

"New-wave chef's salad: toss in cactus strips, tomatillos, hominy, and smoky citrus dressing." The salad may be new, the chef may be new wave, but the inspiration for the trans-border mixture is classic Sunset.
February 1997, p. 90.
(photo: Geoffrey Nilsen)

"In electric frying pan beef and bean sprouts can cook on the dining table. Meal's first course is avocado halves and mandarin oranges. Tray holds bowls of flank steak strips, fresh bean sprouts, green onions, sliced mushrooms, consomme-soy sauce, cornstarch mix." Asian cuisine fused with American technology and California produce: a nascent California cuisine?
June 1958, p. 120.

[24] "Announcement to the Readers of Sunset," October 1914.
[25] William Holtz, "Jack London's First Biographer," *Western American Literature* 27 (Spring 1992): 22.
[26] Gerald D. Nash, *The American West in the Twentieth Century* (Englewood Cliffs, N.J.: Prentice-Hall, Inc., 1973), 121.

Kitchens

Kitchens have evolved greatly in the twenti-eth-century West, and Sunset *documents that evolution in equipment, layout, decor, and importance to family life.*

"Hungry youngsters like to linger around the huge brick chimney into which is recessed a modern range. Here the gifted Caroline daily performs her mysterious culinary rites" in obeisance to the new emphasis on the home and kitchen.
February 1929, p. 17.

"The oven regulator will watch your baked foods and the electric refrigerator will take care of desserts and salads."
February 1929, p. 37.

Preparing for a weekend of entertaining: "How the refrigerator looked Friday afternoon. General Electric refrigerator from Hickey's Home Appliance Shop, Oakland."
March 1938, p. 32. (photo Moulin)

Grey shared with *Sunset*'s readers in "The Log of the Gladiator" (April 1926) his adventures in deep sea fishing and his struggles against nature off the coast of Southern California.

Some well-known writers contributed nonfiction material to *Sunset* as well. Mary Austin, best known for *Land of Little Rain*, began publishing in *Sunset* in the early 1900s, while she was still the young protégée of *Sunset* rival Charles Lummis, editor of *Land of Sunshine*.[27] In "Woman and Her War Loot" (February 1919), her single contribution to *Sunset* under the Woodhead, Field and Company leadership, she stepped away from the material about Western frontier life that had established her as an important regional writer and, instead, discussed the gains women made from World War I.[28] A Western issue only in the sense of gender frontier, she contributed a thoughtful essay on "elimination of feminini-ty from women's working clothes."

Gertrude Atherton, a native of San Francisco, was especially skilled in capturing the sentiments of many Westerners who were over-whelmed by the grandness of nature in the West. In a political piece, "West for Smith" (April 1928), concerning the upcoming presidential election between Republican Herbert Hoover and Democrat Alfred Emanuel Smith, she eloquently argued why Californians would not vote for Hoover, "the fetish of farm distress." In addition to Atherton's attack on Hoover's qualifications for the presidency and stabs toward his agri-cultural policies during the war, readers had to acknowledge inevitably that even in heavily urban California, many Westerners still relied on agriculture as a means of earning a living.

Political commentaries and articles were part of the magazine's new editorial quest for national recognition. To fulfill its promise to com-ment on the Pacific Coast's political affairs, *Sunset* began featuring a monthly column concerning—as the magazine's editors so poignantly called it—"the Pacific Coast and its hinterland, the United States" (Feb-ruary 1922). The editorials offered colorful commentaries on domestic topics such as agriculture and industry as well as on international con-cerns such as the war in Europe and racial issues. In addition to its own editorials, *Sunset* enlisted many significant writers and politicians to ex-press their views on Western issues. Naturalist Aldo Leopold counted the mixed blessings of paved roads and pleaded for the preservation of some sample wilderness ("Conserving the Covered Wagon," March 1925), and the advocate of Native Americans John Collier warned of the "Plundering of the Pueblo Indians" (January 1923). *Sunset*'s managing editor, Walter V. Woehlke, commented on a wide variety of Western is-sues. He condemned the labor unions, the "Bolshevikis of the West" (January 1918), for hindering the war efforts, and he raised his eyebrows over "Traffic Jams" (March 1926) in Western cities, showcasing Los An-geles's success in regulating foot and car traffic. California senator Hi-ram W. Johnson brought a Western perspective to *Sunset*'s readers in a year-long column "What of the Nation?" between 1919 and 1920.

In international affairs, Herbert Hoover commented on his work in Europe during the war. Although "Unto the Least of These" (February 1920), the story about his efforts to help the starving populations of France and Belgium, was not a particularly Western topic in itself, Hoover addressed values with which *Sunset* editors liked to identify

[27] Edwin R. Bingham, *Charles F. Lummis: Editor of the Southwest* (San Marino, CA: The Huntington Library, 1955), 156.

[28] Karen S. Langlois, "A Fresh Voice From the West: Mary Austin, California, and American Literary Magazines, 1892–1910," *California History* (Spring 1990): 22.

Westerners: charity, generosity, organizational talent, and ingenuity. Hoover's political foe, Senator William E. Borah of Idaho, also touted his isolationist views in *Sunset*'s pages. In "Why the [Washington] Conference Must Act" (January 1922) and "The Results of Secrecy" (February 1922), he criticized President Woodrow Wilson's ill-conceived efforts to mediate at the Versailles conferences and to create the League of Nations. Apparently, the magazine's editors were not comfortable with some of Senator Borah's remarks, and placed an annotated disclaimer in each article.

Sunset solicited many important men and women of the time to comment on the West and to place issues of national and international significance into a Western context. But its most loyal writer and possibly most influential commentator was David Starr Jordan. Jordan arrived in California from the East in 1891 to become Stanford University's first president. He began contributing to *Sunset* in 1899 with an article on Mexico. Although his specialty was ichthyology, he was well educated in national and international affairs and a strong proponent of internationalism.

A well-appointed kitchen for its time. May 1938, p. 35.

Far left: Photographic treatment verging on the abstract: interior details. March 1997, p. 112.(photo: John Sutton)

Left: "Warm wood tones complement the concrete counter." Sunset kitchens evolve continuously. February 1997.(photo: Gary Parker)

Charles K. Field, since his days as editor under the Southern Pacific ownership, counted on Jordan to enlighten readers on Asian-American relations along the Pacific Coast, a sensitive issue for the magazine because of its geographic proximity to large Asian communities in San Francisco. In 1923 managing editor Walter V. Woehlke once reminded Jordan: "We cannot spare you and you realize how important it is at this crucial time to guide public opinion into the right channel to the end that the fundamental causes of war and peace may be fully understood."[29]

Jordan frequently surveyed international politics in articles such as "The Right to Conquest" (July 1919) and "The Dark Stream of World Politics" (June 1923), in which Stanford University's president reminded readers how important fair treatment of Japanese immigrants was to the Pacific Coast's well-being. In the context of the postwar efforts to create international relations, he pointed out the complexity of annexation issues, discussed pitfalls of "the splash dash method" of the Referendum, and warned of false interpretations of patriotism. To work toward this harmonic end, he summed up, the West and the United States should not follow the political traditions of the old continent but should be-

"Island with two elements is completely efficient as cut, mix, even cook-and-serve center." Sunset was long bullish on kitchen islands. September 1968, p. 71. (photo: Richard Fish)

[29] Walter V. Woehlke to David Starr Jordan, 27 December 1923, DSJ Collection.

Outdoor Cooking and Entertaining
Sunset's vision of Western entertaining and outdoor living is reflected in extensive illustration of barbecues, patio dining, and outdoor fireplaces.

The April 1946 cover shows an outdoor fireplace and picnic area overlooking the Pacific, a windy version of the Sunset *idyll. (photo: Sam Oppee)*

"Inviting focal point of garden, teahouse is a natural place to entertain ... Pool with spill pan gives pleasant sense of separation from rest of garden. Striking thing is that everything you see in this picture was built out of formerly unused downslope at rear of property." February 1958, p. 64. (photo: Clyde Childress)

come part of newness and internationalism. Incidentally, *Sunset* editors closed his article with a sketch of Auguste Rodin's *The Thinker*, which today decorates the Stanford University Campus.

Jordan's exposés were well received among *Sunset* readers as evidenced by "fan mail" and Woehlke's comments that "it is astonishing to see how few disagree with you. I always was of the opinion that the minority, which created all the noise against you, was extremely small numerically..."[30] It is then surprising to see that *Sunset* accepted in 1921 a full-page political advertisement in which U.S. senator James D. Phelan promised to "save our State from Oriental Aggression" and sought re-election on his promise to "keep California white." Here, financial concerns may have overridden editorial policy.

Many others, along with Jordan, commented on domestic issues ranging from transportation to ethnicity to education. In an attempt to demonstrate the West's advances in education to its national readership and to promote an aura of culture and refinement, *Sunset* published several articles on the state of education and often functioned as a promoter of California's education. Articles wondered about the flappers on California campuses and asked why young women should attend college. Herbert Hoover's life during his Stanford years and Stanford University's active involvement in the war efforts were showcased prominently in *Sunset's* pages. Although *Sunset* generally promoted California's and other Western states' university campuses, it gave Stanford University preferred billing in the growing importance of Western education.

Sunset did not shy away from controversy. When Dr. W. N. Hailmann asked "Is Montessori the Educational Columbus?" (June 1915) and took the Montessori method to task, readers including David Starr Jordan were not happy with his conclusion. Jordan apparently defended the Montessori method strongly enough to warrant a defense of the Hailmann article by Walter Woehlke. Woehlke's letter to David Starr Jordan, however, is as much an excursion into the application of the Montessori method as an early insight into the *Sunset* editor's perception of the American character:

But I am also prepared to defend the position of *Sunset* Magazine in its attitude toward Dr. Montessori and her method... It also seems to me that the Montessori method, while it probably is splendidly adapted to the needs of the shrinking, quiet and overly-repressed Italian child, entirely misses its object and aim when applied to the overly-aggressive, self-assertive and excessively individual American child. I have maintained right along that a great deal of the lawlessness and a large part of the disregard for the rights of others in American life can be traced directly to the lack of self-control and discipline of the child in the American home.[31]

Since its inception, *Sunset* reflected this Western identity of boisterousness, assertiveness, and individualism–characteristic of the earliest immigration of the Gold Rush pioneers–in shaping opinion about the American West.

Growing regional identity was visible not only in *Sunset's* editorial and pictorial pages about literature, politics, and education. Advertisements, too, became a major factor in *Sunset's* portrayal of the West. Always a leader in cover illustrations that provided visual reinforcement

[30] Walter V. Woehlke to David Starr Jordan, 6 August 1919, DSJ Collection.
[31] Walter V. Woehlke to David Starr Jordan, 13 October 1915, DSJ Collection.
[32] Amy Janello and Brennon Jones, *The American Magazine* (New York: Harry N. Abrams, Inc. Publishers, 1991), 184.

of Western themes and contributed significantly to *Sunset*'s overall personality, the magazine also used advertisements to support the understanding of a distinct Western culture.[32] *Sunset*'s ads became more and more an integrated part of the package, particularly since the early 1920s when advertisement took on a decidedly new look and stressed results rather than the object.[33] Products such as "Kelly Springfield Tires" allowed–as far as tires were concerned–uneventful trips from New York to San Francisco, and "Chevrolet" promised economical transportation for everybody to go everywhere. "Red Crown Gasoline," the motorist's "assurance of getting an all-refinery gasoline–with a continuous chain of boiling points," provided opportunity to view beautiful Lake Tahoe and other natural wonders throughout the West. If Lake Tahoe was not enough to instill wanderlust in readers, the adjacent magazine article about the design and creation of an early recreational vehicle, or auto home, as it was then called (December 1912), that enabled independent travel would further help shape readers' understanding of the American West.

    Sunset of the Woodhead, Field and Company years documented a broad picture of American Western life. It reflected the growth of its regional culture, established Western national and international politics,

and put Western education in the American landscape, at a time when education was still equated with Eastern private universities. But *Sunset*'s struggle to produce a regional magazine of national significance was not rewarded financially. The magazine's aim of being political, social, economic, and literary companion to Westerners was too much to fulfill in the long run. In addition, "moving pictures," the new rising industry in Hollywood, had a far-ranging and profound influence on the West, slowly reducing the influence of magazines like *Sunset* as "image makers" and chroniclers of the West.[34] In September 1928, the owners of *Sunset* announced that Laurence W. Lane of Des Moines, Iowa, had purchased *Sunset*[35] and the magazine would embark on yet another change in editorial policy: one that would take it into twenty-first century.

---

[33] Stephen Fox, *The Mirror Makers: A History of American Advertising and Its Creators*, 2nd ed. (Urbana: University of Illinois Press, 1997), 95.

[34] Nash, *The American West*, 136-37.

[35] "To the Stockholders of Sunset Magazine," 15 October 1928, DSJ Collection. Had the magazine enjoyed earlier profits under the new management (i.e., had the Depression not intervened), the outgoing stockholders might have realized up to $162,176 under the terms of the purchase agreement, taking into account a percentage of future profits and assuming current debt. The total payment, however, eventually worked out to about $60,000.

"Chefs of the West" presents the holiday goose in the German style (for both goose and presenter).
December 1948, p. 56.

"After use, the portable grill is rolled out, and open fire built in adobe brick recess ... Carmel Valley, California." One of a hundred variants on the barbecue theme.
May 1948, p. 36. (photo: Morley Baer)

Left: Men take over the cooking in the outdoor living space, perfect for hospitality.
May 1948, p. 25.

Outdoor living room in Sacramento, California, echoes many recurring features of the Western lifestyle as delineated by Sunset.
June 1938, p. 24.

Holidays

Holidays are played up big in Sunset; *the annual cycle of publication relies almost as much upon the procession of major (and other) festivities as it does on the gardening calendar. Food, crafts, and decorating ideas mark these events, culminating in the November and December issues.*

Right: "Snack table converted from ping pong table, foods duplicated on either side: meat balls in chafing dishes (picks in inverted cantaloup half); carrot, celery sticks; melon balls in watermelon rind bowls; frosted sheet cakes; punch in the coffee urns." Backyard catering for graduation party. May 1958, p. 129.

A great Western-theme holiday cover by Maynard Dixon. December 1904.

The Lane Family Defines A Vision of Western Living

The "Roaring Twenties" and the "Ballyhoo Years" are terms that remind us what the 1920s stood for: hope, wealth, optimism, to name but a few qualifiers. In spite of the fact that the 1920s had their downsides, they are generally considered a prosperous and happy era. Indeed, it was for many a very good time. More people were comfortably well-to-do, and American capitalism was in a hopeful phase. Business earnings were rising and opportunities were plentiful.[36] Toward the end of the 1920s more than 5 million automobiles were produced. But mass con-

sumerism was not confined to automobiles; ideas and news flourished as well. "It was now possible in the United States," remembered Frederick Lewis Allen, "for more people to enjoy the same good show at the same time than... at any previous time in history."[37]

In the spirit of the times, in 1928 an optimistic magazine executive from Des Moines, Iowa, sought financial backing from friends and purchased the ailing *Sunset* magazine from Woodhead, Field and Company. When Laurence W. Lane, embodying the American dream of the 1920s, became owner of the business, he and his wife, Ruth Bell Lane, were already visionaries for a Western magazine. Little did they know that the economic bubble would soon be punctured.

Larry Lane was well prepared to accept the responsibilities of a magazine. Born in 1890 in Horton, Kansas, Lane was educated at the University of Chicago and Drake University in Des Moines, Iowa. In 1913 he joined Meredith Publishing Company–publisher of *Successful Farming* and, later, *Better Homes and Gardens*–and remained with the company until 1928. At Meredith he worked in personnel, research, and sales, and was its advertising director by the time he left the company. He traveled extensively for the company and thus found ample opportunities to observe the Western landscapes.[38]

---

[36] John Kenneth Galbraith, *The Great Crash 1929* (1954; reprint, Boston: Houghton Mifflin Company, 1988), 2.

[37] Frederick Lewis Allen, *Only Yesterday: An Informal History of the Nineteen-Twenties* (1931; reprint, New York: Harper and Row, Publishers, 1964), 156.

[38] L. W. Lane, Jr., *The Sunset Story: "To Serve the Westerner...And No One Else"* (New York: Newcomen Society in North American, 1973), 16-17. Address delivered at the National Dinner of The Newcomen Society, San Francisco, Calif., 15 May 1969.

Ruth Bell Lane, too, who did not officially join the Lane Publishing Company until the 1940s, had the qualifications to make the magazine a success. Born in Lincoln, Nebraska, she attended Drake University, where her father, Hill McLeland Bell, was president. During her college years she was assistant editor of the student newspaper *Quax* and a member of the Literary Society. She graduated from Drake University in 1917 with an A.S. and a B.S. Soon after graduation she and Laurence were married. After raising two sons, Ruth officially joined the company as managing editor during the Second World War, later became vice president, and finally chaired Lane Publishing Company.[39]

Both Ruth and Larry were well grounded in Western traditions and understood the regional differences in the American landscape, in part because Mrs. Lane's parents had retired to Los Angeles, where they hosted visits of the Lane family during the 1920s. Their sons, Mel and Bill, remember as small boys the exciting train trips to and from their grandparents' home. The couple shared a clear vision of what *Sunset* should be and knew from the beginning that the magazine would need significant editorial changes. "Mr. Lane intends changing the policy of *Sunset*, making it more of a home and garden magazine but retaining the best features of the present magazine" read the stockholders in 1928.[40]

The "best features" to be retained were not specifically defined, but the magazine changed immediately, scarcely resembling its predecessor. During years of traveling the West for Meredith, Lane recognized the West's difference from other regions in the United States. The Sunbelt climate, the lack of water, the spacious, largely mountainous land, and cultural differences were so distinct that Lane was convinced a magazine addressing everyday people's needs exclusively in that region could be successful. Lane's extensive experience and expertise in *Better Homes and Gardens* and *Successful Farming*, combined with the less-than-successful concepts of the previous *Sunset* owners, made changes inevitable. Neil Morgan, the journalist, observed the obvious when he wrote that *Sunset* "divested itself of its involvement with the arts and the world of thought; it had tried, and it had failed."[41]

Lane borrowed editorial techniques from Meredith Publishing Company, and especially from *Successful Farming*, which was edited for both men and women, focusing on farming techniques in the Heartland with its many regional variances. He pursued his vision to make a regional family magazine that encouraged the rudimentary and underdeveloped interests of Westerners. So began the first evolutionary steps that over time transformed *Sunset: The West's Great National Magazine* into *Sunset: The Magazine of Western Living*, a title used to this day. In the last *Sunset* issued by Woodhead, Field and Company, the incoming owner announced the new concept of the magazine to the readers:

It is keyed to the prime interests of life in the West–indoors and out. It is pitched in the modern tempo. It's your editorial policy–as asked for in thousands of letters from readers over the past year. *Sunset* heartily endorses these wants. They are intelligent. They are progressive. They are intensely human. And so we know you will like the new spirit of *Sunset*. We think it will go far beyond any magazine printed in helping you get the most fun out of living in the West.

[39] Biographical Sketch–Ruth B. Lane," Vertical File, Cowles Library, Drake University, Des Moines, Iowa.

[40] "To the Stockholders of Sunset Magazine," Jordan Collection.

[41] Neil Morgan, *Westward Tilt: The American West Today* (New York: Random House, 1963), 17.

"Potted trees, pruned as globes and brilliantly lit with pin-point lights, lead guests along entry path to a pre-Christmas party." Holidays, hospitality, seasonal decorating: all favorite Sunset *topics. December 1968, p. 58.(photo: Glenn Christiansen)*

Next to Christmas, Thanksgiving is the most prominent holiday in Sunset's *calendar. October 1934, p. 30.*

Charming use of color during hard times. November 1934, p. 28.

Travel

Both the how-tos of travel and myriad destinations, near and far, have been the subjects of Sunset's *extensive pictorial treatment of travel. Anywhere that travel-minded Western families might go (even Teheran in the 1950s) has been depicted, roughly in proportion to how likely or easily locales were to be visited. In addition to the continental Western states (emphatically accessible by car), Hawaii and Mexico have been perennial favorites.*

Right top: "El Castillo, so called only for identification, dominated the Mayan ruins at Chichen-Itza. It's about 75 feet high and 180 feet square at the base." Mexican travel opportunities are a continuous presence.
November 1968, p. 32.

Right bottom: Anasazi ruins at Mesa Verde National Park.
June 1938, p. 6. (photo: Mesa Verde Co.)

Far right: "The granite castles need climbing, and many a secret cove awaits discovery. Here you plot a course among the Joshuas along the wall enclosing Hidden Valley." The West as a magnificent playground.
April 1958, p. 68.

The urban landscape of the New West.
May 1988, p. 116. (photo: Doug Wilson)

The new *Sunset* will cover the whole range of home-life and family interests with timely and practical suggestions on gardening, building, home-decorating and furnishing, cooking and home management, traveling, enjoying outdoor life and a host of other subjects of equal interest to men and women. (January 1929)

With the very first issue, Lane implemented the promise to attract both men and women readers and to emphasize the importance of family and home. That issue included excerpts from radio broadcasts by Herbert Hoover as part of his campaign for president, stressing family and home. Another article in that issue, "The House a Man Calls Home," drew attention to the importance of the man of the house as part of the family, also appealing to the male reader.

Lane limited *Sunset*'s target audience to the seven Far Western states, dropped articles on politics and economics altogether, thus choosing to focus on a wholesome Western American world of gardening, home improvement, travel, and cooking. Beginning with the first is-

sue in February 1929, *Sunset* became a magazine of service that could be welcomed in "any home of refinement."[42] Lane adopted a policy he learned from *Better Homes and Gardens* and designed articles for *Sunset* that helped readers to do something: to remodel a house, to decorate a room, to travel the countryside, or to plant a beautiful garden.[43] In its segments on gardening and cooking, Lane could draw on his experience from *Successful Farming*. *Successful Farming*, in an attempt to add more women to its readership, had implemented a cooking department to its lineup. The editorial segments on building, cooking, gardening, and traveling were directed toward concerns and interests specific to Westerners. To achieve his vision, Lane relied heavily on the talents of his senior editors, Genevieve A. Callahan and Lou Richardson, whom he had hired away from *Better Homes and Gardens*.

Following Lane's vision, in articles such as "A Trio of Attractive Sacramento Homes" (January 1930) and "From Carriage House to Cot-

[42] Charles William Mulhall, Jr., "Sunset: The History of a Successful Regional Magazine" (M.A. thesis, Stanford University, 1955), 26.

[43] Theodore Peterson, *Magazines in the Twentieth Century* (Urbana: University of Illinois Press, 1964), 383.

tage" (May 1936), *Sunset* featured Western homes along with floor plans and placed them in the historical context of the region. It suggested interior decoration ideas for "The Pictures on Your Wall" (August 1930) and for "Mailboxes That Are Different" (July 1936). Occasionally, *Sunset* displayed European leanings through such topics as Louis XVI furniture, which had little to do with the West but a lot to do with the cultural background of *Sunset*'s readership. Plenty of cooking ideas were featured in *Sunset* pages, from herbal cookery (April 1942) and pizza (May 1948) to shish kebab (February 1948) and chorizos (April 1954) to Hawaiian laulaus (April 1980) and marinated cheeses (January 1989). Travel articles were understood both by the Lanes and their advertisers to appeal to male readers. Every nook and corner of the Western region was visited, complctc with helpful hints and inviting photographs spread across the pages. It looked at what Alaska had to offer (March 1949) and addressed Westerners "who have yet to discover the [California] islands" (May 1951). It sampled the wilderness in the heart of Idaho (January 1951) and combed the beaches of Oahu (June 1956). In recent years, *Sunset* took its readers on desert walks in Arizona (May 1980) and helped them find gold in the Sierras (March 1989). Over time, *Sunset*'s understanding of the West grew to eventually encompass not only the Rocky Mountain states but Alaska and Hawaii in its 13-state target market.

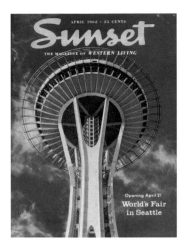

Seattle, a city much covered by Sunset, *makes a bid for world prominence through its Expo, Space Needle, and this April 1962* Sunset *cover; Bill Gates is elsewhere, learning about slide rules. (photo: Glenn Christiansen)*

New kinds of monthly editorials, too, appeared in the magazine. The magazine's editorial introduction, "Sunset Gold," emphasized such Western values as individuality, tradition, and generosity. Containing inspirational family-oriented messages that reflected the Lanes' Christian education at Drake University, "Sunset Gold" set the tone for what the magazine merited in living in the West. It addressed children's needs to experience the outdoors (February 1930), every Westerner's desire to relish nature's beautiful sunsets (November 1930), and the appreciation for hard-working men who helped make the West an attractive place to live (April 1936). Other regular monthly features were "Kitchen Cabinet," the creation of Ruth Lane in conjunction with Genevieve Callahan, which gave readers the opportunity to exchange culinary recipes, and "Tips for Tenderfeet," designed to encourage technically challenged Westerners to take their first steps in home improvement and gardening. Characteristic of the approach was the regular use of cartoon-like how-to illustrations demonstrating techniques for everything from building furniture to pruning trees to making sauces. As Bill Lane reminisced, "Reader participation became the holy grail of *Sunset* editorial policy."[44]

"The Casino, where varied amusements are provided for the summer visitors to Santa Cruz." June 1907, p. 176.

Sunset also recognized the growing contributions of Hollywood to cultural life in the West, before the town assumed national importance.[45] Acknowledging Hollywood as a maker of public opinion and popular culture in the West, the magazine began a short-lived column, "Headquarters Hollywood" (1936). In the column geared toward women, the magazine reported on the latest news and dernier cri in the world of fashion and makeup from Los Angeles.

Along with the new editorial policy, remnants of the old *Sunset* remained still visible in the early years of Lane Publishing Company, reinforcing the regional flavor of the magazine. In a series on personalities of the Old West, Leland Stanford, Charles Crocker, Mark Hopkins, and

"In Teheran's bazaar, you'll hear the din made by coppersmiths, smell the fragrance of all kinds of spices, and see the trunks bearing labels of American canned goods." Exotic travel was within reach of at least some Sunset readers. February 1958, p. 27. (photo: Robert Trimingham)

[44] Bill Lane to the author, January 23, 1998. The author acknowledges Bill Lane's guidance leading toward the preparation of this essay.

[45] Gerald D. Nash, *The American West Transformed: The Impact of the Second World War* (Bloomington: Indiana University Press, 1985), 178-79.

"Surprised diver gets a friendly pat from a curious sea otter" in Monterey Bay. November 1984, p. 92.

Sunset *has always drawn attention to Hawaii and the Pacific islands, as in this July 1916 cover.*

Collis Huntington were featured as "Makers of the West" (January 1934). When *Sunset* reported on contemporary Western personalities, as in the case of "Silver Key Pittman of Nevada" (May 1935), it confined its discussions to aspects of historical and socialite nature. And although Lane abandoned fiction, some of *Sunset*'s earlier stories were fiction in disguise, telling "good yarn[s]" about fishing, camping, and outdoor cooking (e.g., "Now You Tell One," July 1930). The magazine continued to feature Western heritage in the form of travel reports on Geronimo country (June 1956), Hopi snake dances (February 1962), and Navajo lifestyle (March 1963).

As much as *Sunset* portrayed itself as a Western magazine, marketing regionalism and making readers feel at home in a special place, *Sunset* needed Eastern capital in the form of advertisement revenue. Many major national advertisers such as Lucky Strike cigarettes, Gillette razor blades, Pontiac automobiles, and Shell gasoline joined California advertisers such as Southern Pacific Railroad, Golden State dairy products, and Standard Oil (of California) gasoline in appealing to the Western market. Perhaps vital to its success, *Sunset* had kept advertisement representative offices in New York, Chicago, and Boston long before it opened such an office in Los Angeles.

Ominously, events in the East almost overcame Larry and Ruth Lane's dream of a Western magazine when, in October 1929, the stock market crashed in New York and *Sunset*, like many other businesses, fell on hard times. Uncertainty and frugality widened among the population and unemployment spread.[46] Businesses, if they did not close as they found their trade fading, discharged employees and cut down on production and advertisements. The immediate impact of the Depression varied in the West, but it did eventually affect every sub-region and every industry of the relatively underdeveloped West.[47] To *Sunset* it meant lost revenue in advertisers as well as readers. Continuous financial support from friends in the East, loyal staff, and a readership still a bit better off than most of the West's population or infected with the "extravagant, *Sunset*-magazine dream of relocating in an easy oasis life"[48] helped *Sunset* to survive the Depression, as reflected by the magazine's gradual circulation growth through the Depression years.

One of its loyal business partners out West was Crown Zellerbach Company. Neighborly business relations between the two companies dated back to the beginning of *Sunset* in the late nineteenth century, a time when the fledgling new business owner Anthony Zellerbach found a reliable and respectable customer in the Southern Pacific Railroad. Both companies had offices on Sansome Street in San Francisco until the 1906 fire destroyed their businesses. The cordial relationship was maintained throughout the ownership changes at *Sunset* and paid off for the magazine in times of need. If Isedore Zellerbach's personal style (he was reputed to have been very generous to people in need) was any indication for the company's fiscal policy, it was not surprising that Crown Zellerbach repeatedly extended *Sunset*'s credit.[49] Finally, in 1952, *Sunset* made its last credit payment to Crown Zellerbach. Years later, Bill Lane

[46] Frederick Lewis Allen, *Since Yesterday: The Nineteen-Thirties in America* (New York: Harper and Brothers Publishers, 1940), 28.

[47] Gerald D. Nash, *The American West in the Twentieth Century: A Short History of an Urban Oasis* (Englewood Cliffs, NJ: Prentice-Hall, Inc., 1973), 139-40.

[48] Donald Worster, *Rivers of Empire: Water, Aridity and Growth of the American West* (New York: Pantheon Books, 1985), 229.

[49] *The Years of Paper: Isedore Zellerbach, 1866-1941* ([San Francisco]: Crown Zellerbach Corporation, 1941), 13.

joined Crown Zellerbach's board of directors.

In spite of the Depression, Lane continued to further refine the magazine and to streamline his vision of Western living. In 1932 *Sunset* began publishing separate editions of the magazine, tailored to the needs of the Pacific Northwest, central West, and the Desert West and Hawaii. At first, differences in the regional editions were editorial only, but regional advertising soon followed. By doing so, Lane not only acknowledged ecological and cultural diversity within the West but also implemented a marketing device that gave advertisers the opportunity to concentrate sales efforts in specific localities.[50] In 1936 Lane made *Sunset* an entirely staff-written magazine, permitting a more uniform style and better editorial control.[51] Both previous experience and continuous experimentation had convinced Lane that specialized employed writers could best convey the recurring ideas of Western living.[52]

If the Depression tested the survival of *Sunset*, the onset of World War II did not make the market for service magazines any easier. Federally enforced rationing of resources meant reduction in personal items such as home construction, cars, and gasoline, reducing many advertisements from manufacturers of building supplies, automobile makers, home appliances producers, or furniture makers.[53] Paper to print the magazine was equally difficult to come by, and *Sunset*'s cordial relation-

"A pair of river-runners wait in an eddy for companions to run Black Rock Rapid." Vigorous outdoor recreation under the Western sky (maybe under Western water as well).
March 1997, p. 38.(photo: Drew Thale)

Far left:"Dining alfresco: a long-billed curlew probes Morro Bay sands for a worm or crustacean meal." A quiet, almost contemplative form of environmental awareness.
February 1997, p. 36.(photo: David Weintraub)

Left: "At dusk, Point Bonita Lighthouse blinks its warning across an amethyst sea near the Golden Gate." The California coast remains a constant inspiration for native and visitor alike.
January 1997, p. 24.(photo: Andrew McKinney)

ship with (and its financial obligations to) Crown Zellerbach, the San Francisco distributor of print paper, was certainly beneficial. The scarcity of paper was one reason for Lane in December 1939 to increase the subscription price for states outside the West and then in April 1943 to discontinue "until further notice subscriptions new or renewals" to them. Yet despite all the war-related difficulties that created an obstacle course for a still struggling magazine, *Sunset* began to make "circulating" as well as "operating" profits in 1938 for the first time.[54]

Sunset used the Depression and war years not only to improve its fiscal situation but also to fine-tune its editorial content. Through direct reader contacts and company-sponsored surveys, the magazine learned

"Stop for lunch amid pristine majesty of Colorado River's Glen Canyon. Willows and tamarisks on far shore are typical growth shading many of the fine beaches and giving shelter to wildlife."
March 1958, p. 26.

[50] Peterson, *Magazines in the Twentieth Century*, 112.

[51] Mulhall, "*Sunset*," 42.

[52] Proctor Mellquist [Managing Editor of Sunset], "Sunset Is Unique as a Magazine," *Quill* 42 (February 1954): 13.

[53] Peterson, *Magazines in the Twentieth Century*, 386.

[54] Lane, *The Sunset Story*, 19.

Glacier National Park, part of a vast and expanding system dedicated to protection and enjoyment of the sportsman's paradise. June 1958, p. 65.

"Black Sea Bass (weight, 370 lbs.) caught by T. S. Manning on rod and reel." Might this be a subtle inducement for sportsmen to visit the West? January 1901, p. 77.

"Starry flounder was taken in about 12 feet of water near pier's end. Jackets keep out the chilly bay winds." Point Pinole, California. March 1978, p. 54.(photo: David Stubbs)

that recipes without sugar, inexpensive vacation destinations, or victory gardens helped readers to cope with war-related scarcities and to observe self-reliance.[55] But it was undoubtedly in the post–World War II era that *Sunset* took off as the magazine of Western living and saw its profits and popularity soar. Despite the growing acceptance of television, which in turn caused many families to take fewer magazines, magazines that catered to more specialized audiences thrived.[56]

Like no other region of the nation, the West had been economically and demographically transformed by the war. Americans' mobility and increased automobile ownership and usage, two simple factors in the West's population increase, were momentous *Sunset* trademark values almost from its inception in 1898. Population density was heretofore low and open spaces were still available. The mild climates, particularly along the Pacific Coast, and the natural beauties of the West were attractive prospects and longtime selling points of *Sunset*. Taken all together, the environment and job opportunities promised an attractive lifestyle, on which *Sunset* had capitalized all along.[57]

While increases in population and infrastructure took place throughout the West, the largest increases were registered in California. Huge aviation and shipbuilding plants and many smaller supplier establishments accounted for the vast influx of immigrants–and tight housing markets.[58] Its population growth was spectacular, increasing from 9 million in 1945 to 19 million in 1960. Indeed, in 1962 California overtook New York as the most populous state in the nation. More significantly for *Sunset*, this postwar immigration contributed to the development of suburban communities. There, the historical dream of "homesteading" continued in the form of assorted types of ranch houses for an upwardly mobile middle class.

Postwar United States gave magazines like *Sunset* a rich market, for the numbers of families owning or planning to own homes was immense. Years of rationing had developed a desire that needed to be appeased, and long hours of work to support war efforts provided ready cash to be spent. *Sunset*, practicing and preaching Western lifestyle for decades, was there for its readers with advice and suggestions on how improve their quality of life. It suggested home building and interior decorating, provided garden designs and patio layouts, exposed Westerners to new and often ethnic cuisines, and pointed to nearby and faraway travel spots. Later, in the face of "seam-splitting pressure of expanding population," *Sunset* helped interpret zoning laws and ordinances for those considering property in urbanized areas ("How to Look Into the Future," September 1960). Often it was on the forefront of picking up trends by promoting such lifestyle enhancements as air travel, garage-door openers, barbecues, recreational vehicles, and patios. To Larry Lane it was a Western dream come true. He was taking part in the development of distinct Western and California lifestyles.

This dream was even sweeter because *Sunset* was now a family-managed publication. Not only had Ruth Lane become managing editor of *Sunset* but the Lanes' two sons, Bill and Mel, joined the *Sunset* workforce in the late 1940s. After both graduated from Palo Alto High School and

[55] David E. Faville, *How Sunset Magazine Subscribers Evaluate the Magazines They Read: A Study of Magazine Preferences* (Stanford, CA: Graduate School of Business, 1940).

[56] James L. Baughman, *The Republic of Mass Culture: Journalism, Filmmaking, and Broadcasting in America since 1941*, 2nd ed. (Baltimore, ML: The Johns Hopkins University Press, 1997), 64.

[57] Nash, *The American West in the Twentieth Century*, 218.

[58] Nash, *The American West Transformed*, 62-63.

Stanford University and served in the U.S. Navy, they returned to San Francisco to become part of Lane Publishing Company. After brief stints in positions such as elevator operators, and training in the sales, circulation, production, and book departments, they rose quickly through the ranks, Bill in sales and editorial and Mel in production and business operations. In 1952 the operating management was turned over to Bill and Mel.

Earlier, Larry Lane had put his sons in charge of the book department; their challenge was to persuade their father to keep the Book Division with its large inventories. The elder Lane entertained thoughts of selling *Sunset* Books, which published 19 titles before the war. By the 1960s, after Mel had become publisher of *Sunset* Books, however, it sold 13 million books and by the 1980s had offered hundreds of titles, many in multiple editions, packed with expert advice. Its classic *Sunset Western Garden Book,* frequently updated (and completely revised and expanded most recently under Time Warner in 1995), is generally considered to be an indispensable reference work, "the bible" for Western gardeners.[59]

"Fiesta dancers. In Old Mexico costume, they're giving a special performance at the mission church of Tumacacori, now a national monument, south of Tucson." Exotic color, right here in the U.S. *February 1978, p. 77.(photo: Don Normark)*

Left: A very specialized example of cultural travel: the pipe organ tour. February 1978, p. 75.

Covering many of the magazine's topics in more detail and publishing monographs for corporations such as United Airlines, the book department furthered the company's reach for a wider audience.[60]

Bill and Mel, after military assignments in Hawaii, convinced their father of the islands' importance to the West and to *Sunset* and so rediscovered the Pacific Rim for the magazine. Subsequently, both Mel and Bill became involved in the Pacific Area Travel Association (PATA, now the Pacific Asia Travel Association), founded by a group of individuals that gathered in Hawaii in the early 1950s to promote travel and tourism in the Pacific Rim region. The Lanes' active interest in the Pacific was not only a natural continuation of *Sunset*'s role in promoting westward movement but also a realization "that the PATA region was bound to grow and be a source of advertisement revenues."[61] Bill Lane himself became such an expert in the affairs of the "West of the West" that in 1975 President Gerald Ford appointed him Ambassador-at-large and Commissioner General of Japan, and in 1985 President Ronald Reagan ap-

"Step dancers perform at Golden Gate Park this month." Holiday theme combines with domestic travel idea: San Francisco on St. Pat's. *March 1978, p. 88.(photo: Peter O. Whiteley)*

[59] Morgan, *Westward Tilt,* 17; "A Walking Tour of the Sunset Garden" [leaflet] (Menlo Park: Sunset Publishing Corporation, n.d.).

[60] Lane, *The Sunset Story,* 22.

[61] Chuck Y. Gee and Matt Lurie, eds., *The Story of the Pacific Asia Travel Association* (San Francisco: Pacific Asia Travel Association, 1993), 49-50.

Winter sports were available, if not as highly developed as nowadays.
December 1934, p. 47.
(Photograph by Ansel Adams.

Right: "Lone skier skims past snow-plastered firs and grand vistas down open slopes of 10,450-foot Rendezvous Mountain."
Prime Western skiing.
February 1978, p. 38.(photo: Keith Gunnar)

"Taos ski instructors teach their students how to be as well as how to ski."
December 1997, p. 30.

(photo: Ken Garllard)

pointed him Ambassador to Australia and Nauru.

Mel and Bill were also on hand when the same "suburban" flu that caught many Westerners hit Lane Publishing Company. After more than 50 years in "the City," *Sunset* in 1951 moved its headquarters upon land that was originally part of a grant to José Arguello, governor of Spanish California in 1815, in suburban Menlo Park.[62] The Lanes knew that their new headquarters needed to reflect the company's Western philosophy. They hired a prominent builder of early California ranch-style homes, Clifford May, to design what *Sunset* had preached for residential houses all along: open space, individuality, innovation, and tradition. May's design, shaped by the tradition of Spanish colonists and the innovation of modern Californians, reflected the company's desire for a special way of living.[63] *Sunset*'s residential- looking headquarters were revised to accommodate test kitchens, to provide for experimental gardens, and to serve as innovative office space. Architecture, design, and landscaping were so original and appealing to the public that the company offered daily "sightseeing tours" through its headquarters. The completed buildings offered spaciousness, social openness, indoor-outdoor living with privacy and protection.

Sunset remained a stoic defender of family values and middle-class merits, most directly reflected in its advertisement sections. *Sunset*'s advertisement policies have always been selective, particularly since the

magazine's owners began to endorse its advertising.[64] It abandoned tobacco advertisements early on and continued prohibition of liquor even after the Eighteenth Amendment was repealed. Nor did it accept ads for feminine personal products in an effort to avoid identification as a "women's magazine" (even though gender stereotypes from cooking to cleaning for women and home improvement and fishing for men were evident in its advertising). Restrictions for advertising categories had always been part of the Lanes' publishing business. "What might be common practice and very acceptable for other good media," Bill Lane once commented, "is 'just not our bag.'" [65]

But *Sunset* could afford the luxury of restricting advertisement. Es-

[62] "A Walking Tour of the Sunset Garden."

[63] *Sunset Western Ranch Houses* (San Francisco: Lane Publishing Company, 1946), 23.

[64] Mulhall, "Sunset," 73.

[65] Lane, *The Sunset Story*, 21-22.

pecially since changing printing techniques in the 1950s from rotary letterpress to offset lithography, ad production became more cost–effective and attracted many advertisers' interest in *Sunset* pages. By 1964, it had become one of the most successful magazines in the United States in volume of advertising and circulation, despite being regional. It had found an editorial balance that drew the desired readers, and thus continued the same formula with continuing evolution in style and focus. There was predictability to the editorial content that readers could expect from each issue: informative articles and familiar columns about gardening, traveling, home improvement, and cooking. Readability was paramount, with tables of contents on the first editorial page; departments always in the same relative place, and articles always continuous, without "continued on page x."

Sunset became such an icon of popular middle-class culture that it was subject to some biting ridicule (not unlike parodies of Martha Stewart today). In 1980 a mock magazine, Sunsect: The Magazine of Western Civilization, was featured in *New West* magazine. The cover photo pictured a family picnicking at a lakeshore in the backdrop of two towering nuclear reactors. "Toward evening," the cover is explained, "a towering cool engulfs the celebrants, and the entire scene is irradiated by a perfect California *Sunset*." Inside the magazine, Sunsect offered do-it-yourself advice on how "doors do double-duty as entrance [and] exit;" how to make an "under-counter recess" for used gum; and suggested that "slanted floors [will] make vacuuming a snap."[66] The spoof itself aside, it was a recognition of how deeply *Sunset* had become a part of segments of Western suburban society (and how difficult it was to maintain a successful Western magazine; *New West* is no longer in circulation).

Sunset, though apolitical for the most part, had looked favorably upon the environment for quite some time, which is not surprising. Highlighting the beauty of the environment in the West was long part of *Sunset*'s appeal to readers and was of great personal concern to the Lanes and their editors. In a few instances, however, particularly during *Sunset*'s formative years, the editors sent ambiguous messages to their readers. In one of its earlier issues, *Sunset* thanked "forward-looking men and women" for preserving trees along Redwood Highway: "Never to be sacrificed for progress" (November 1935). On the opposite page of the same issue, then, discussing "What the National Housing Act Means Here in the West," *Sunset* was enthusiastic about the Act's prospects to "stimulate our western lumber industry," and other industries such as transportation and publishing. Considering that the magazine experienced financial hardships and was searching for a way out of the Depression, it was not surprising that *Sunset* saw in the Housing Act a light at the end of the tunnel.

A notable issue among the magazine's environmental concerns was the DDT (dichloro-diphenyl-trichloro-ethane) controversy that was sparked by Rachel Carson's *Silent Spring* in 1962. In what has been considered the bible for modern environmentalists–*Silent Spring* sold over 100,000 copies within one year[67]–Carson was deeply worried by the widespread use of this and other chemicals. In fact, DDT was so universally used that it took on "the harmless aspect of the familiar."[68]

"The lip of the fall," Yosemite. May 1900, p. 24.(photo: Tibbitts)

"Pedestal Rock and soaring cliffs dwarf horsemen in the middle fork of The Maze." In terms of iconography as well as geology, it doesn't get any more Western than this. October 1968, p. 30. (photo: Philip Hyde)

"All she has to do is stay with this 2,000-pound bucking bull for 6 seconds. Rider is Amy Iverson, Byers, Colorado, 1976 bull-riding champion who still competes in this rough category." Of Westerners, for Westerners, by Westerners, male and female. June 1978, p. 85. (photo: Sue Levy)

[66] "Sunsect Magazine: A Parody," *The New West* (11 February 1980): 27-35.

[67] Jennifer Curtis and Tim Profeta, *After Silent Spring: The Unsolved Problems of Pesticide Use in the United States* (New York: Natural Resources Defense Council, 1993), 3.

[68] Rachel Carson, *Silent Spring* (Boston: Houghton Mifflin Company, 1962), 20.

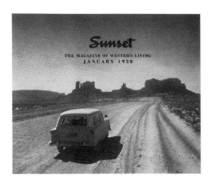

Family vacation on the road in Monument Valley: pure Sunset Southwest. January 1958, p. 37.

Right: "The Old Witch tree, among the ancient cypress along the famous Seventeen Mile Drive, at Monterey, is the symbol of the enchantment that holds this region of surpassing beauty." Monterey has long been noted for its natural splendor. February 1914, p. 298.

Far right: "Clipper now. She clips off the miles between California and Hawaii in about 19 hours." A great publicity shot for the successor to the westward-leading railroad. The Golden Gate as a backdrop hearkens to the original 1898 Sunset cover. May 1938, p. 11. (photo: Pan American)

"Introduced to his successor–the bronco and the motor car at Silver Peak, Nevada." Travel by either could be adventurous on the roads of the time. February 1902, p. 282.

Even *Sunset* rendered to its gardeners cautiously optimistic advice on "How to Use DDT" (October 1945). DDT (and other chemicals) was a poison, *Sunset* suggested, that "present[s] no hazard if properly handled and properly applied." Increasingly concerned about the health of its gardeners and gardens, however, *Sunset* eventually joined those who raised awareness about the use of the chemical. In "It's Time to Blow the Whistle on DDT" (August 1969), the magazine urged its readers to cease buying DDT immediately: "*Sunset* believes that we cannot afford to debate this question while using DDT any longer. The evidence against DDT as the cause of bird failure is such that we must agree with the biologists."

To back up its editorial position, *Sunset* thereafter refused to accept ads for garden pesticides containing DDT and other hydrocarbons, putting at risk its garden-product ad accounts, a significant source of revenue. Senator Gaylord Nelson read *Sunset*'s announcement of this policy into the *Congressional Record*. *Sunset* also ran many practical, rather than preachy, articles that impacted the (sub)urban environment and Western lifestyle. It featured articles such as "Riding a Bike to Work" (September 1983) and contributed pros and cons of moped use to the never-ending problem of urban congestion (December 1977).

Always supportive of the West's natural wonders, the Lanes increasingly realized that using the great outdoors–may it be in cities ("Wildlife Habitat on a Small City Lot," June 1979) or in the countryside ("Tin Can Clean-up in the Sierra," March 1961)–required a fine balance of multiple use and preservation. The urban West and the West of tourism, adventure, and national parks changed the way people related to the landscape. The editors acknowledged this and were committed in their own ways to protecting the quality of the environment in the American West. *Sunset* supplied information, reported on solutions, and always kept a balanced, if biased, viewpoint.[69] Through such articles as "Which Park for Your Vacation?" (April 1931), "When Is Yosemite Valley at Its Best?" (April 1956), or "How to Reach National Parks of the West Without a Car" (July 1979), *Sunset* provided entertainment and learning expe-

[69] Bill Lane, "Letter From Sunset," *Sunset* (November 1989): 230-31.

riences, and publicized parks as tourist destinations with appropriate words and pictures. It promised its readers the beauty of the West as well as its mythology and romance.[70]

In the decades since Larry and Ruth Lane began building their American dream and their sons continued and strengthened the legacy, *Sunset* had established a faithful readership and a solid reputation. The Lanes' real genius was to limit the magazine exclusively to a Western audience and to withstand the temptation to broaden to a wider patronage. *Sunset: Western Market Almanac*, the last market analysis to be produced under the Lane family, told not only a promotional success story for Western advertisers but paid tribute as well to *Sunset*'s efforts to capture a readership and a lifestyle and transpose them into a successful Western magazine.[71] When the Lane family decided to sell the magazine, *Sunset*'s reputation and success made it an attractive investment for other companies who wanted to break into the regional market. Among the many companies that courted the Lane family for its prized possession, Time Warner Inc. succeeded and now carries the responsibility to lead the magazine into the twenty-first century.

In the 62 years since Ruth and Larry Lane bought the small, financially troubled magazine largely for its name recognition, the family and dedicated staff transformed Sunset into a highly profitable regional magazine. With vision and tenacity, with a fine sense for "Westering," and with luck, they developed a magazine that not only chronicled the tastes and lifestyles of the West's more affluent society but at times even defined those tastes. As the writer Wallace Stegner once noted, "You can't look closely at Sunset without developing a considerable respect for the intelligence that goes into that operation."[72] Over six decades, the Lane family had made sure that operation not only served its readers immediate needs but also proved influential in shaping the modern West for the benefit of millions of Westerners beyond its readership.

Time Warner: Faithful to the Sunset Mission and Readership[73]

The August 1990 issue was *Sunset* magazine's first publication under the new ownership of Time Warner, a new entity created when mega-publisher Time Inc. had combined forces with Warner Communications earlier in the same watershed year. Before its merger with Warner, Time Inc. had built an impressive publishing empire. Time Inc., now a division of Time Warner, remains the United States' largest magazine publisher, carrying popular consumer publications such as *Time, Sports Illustrated,* and *People. Time*'s weekly circulation in the United States alone reaches 4 million copies weekly, while international circulation exceeds 1.4 million. But Time Inc. does not just publish magazines; it is also a leader in direct book marketing, and has been considered one of the world's most influential, broad-based information companies. Warner Communications, which had formerly lacked a distinct presence in the publishing business, was nevertheless an amazingly successful conglomeration of movie and broadcasting media companies. The merger of

A very early depiction of female motorists exploring the scenic West Coast in this February 1911 cover.

"Fall campers at secluded Jalama Beach have good opportunity to fish, or walk, or collect bounty of the heavy surf. Campsites are mostly right along the wide beachfront." Califonia coastal paradise remains accessible, if occasionally a bit crowded. November 1968, p. 67. (photo: Ken Niles, Jr.)

A (mobile) home on the range. February 1938, p. 6. (photo: Cy. Le Tour)

[70] Michael L. Johnson, *New Westers: The West in Contemporary American Culture* (Lawrence: University Press of Kansas, 1996), 360.

[71] *Sunset Western Market Almanac* (Menlo Park, CA: Lane Publishing Company, 1989).

[72] Wallace Stegner and Richard W. Etulain, *Conversations With Wallace Stegner on Western History and Literature,* rev. ed. (Salt Lake City: University of Utah Press, 1983), 127.

[73] The author would like to thank Steve Seabolt (CEO) and Jim Mitchell (CFO) for sharing their knowledge and opinions on Sunset magazine during an interview on 26 November 1997; and Lisa Anderson of *Sunset* Book Inc. for reviewing this article.

People

Sunset has always focused on individuals and groups of people, whether or not highlighting them as home owners or cooks. Here are just a few Western individuals whose interests have been featured.

"'We miss you, of course, but we're, oh, so proud of you!'" The June 1918 cover. (Artist: Matto Sandona)

Home improvement ideas from unlikely sources: "Hollywood. Humphrey Bogart, Warner Brothers star, on his outside stair." January 1938, p. 21.

these two giants into Time Warner Inc. created a media corporation that shapes the national and international news media, with major holdings in the regional magazine market.[74]

The Lanes saw in Time Warner, whose national magazines had long done well in the West, the "right home," that shared what they considered to be "the unique values of *Sunset* and the West."[75] With the acquisition of the Lane family's prospering book and magazine publishing businesses, Time Warner–already owner of *Southern Living* and other regional titles–became the country's largest regional magazine publisher. But the purchase of the company was more than just another magazine acquisition for the East Coast–based publishing giant. *Sunset* opened the door for Time Warner to a regional market in which it had been historically difficult to establish a truly Western publication. *Sunset*'s Pacific region ties were also of interest. Successful in both mirroring and anticipating the Western lifestyle, "*Sunset*'s unique heritage and your solid Western values" were reasons that attracted Time Warner to the purchase.[76]

Historically, Westerners have subscribed to more than their share of magazines, nearly all of which were published in the East. In this regional market, *Sunset* magazine is one of the few Western magazines that has prospered. Of its competitors of bygone days, Charles Lummis's *Land of Sunshine*, later renamed *Out West*, for instance, did not survive World War I. In more recent history, *Saturday Review* and the *New York Times* failed in their attempts to run a Western magazine or a regional edition from the East Coast. Learning well from others' mistakes, Time Warner retained the *Sunset* Menlo Park offices as headquarters and kept offices in Los Angeles and Seattle. To ensure the distinct sense of "Westering" that *Sunset* magazine radiated under the Lane family, Time Warner hired Bill and Mel Lane as consultants for a transitional period.

It was not surprising that, when Time Warner acquired the company, readers expressed concerns that the publishing company and especially its regional magazine might lose their appeal. Possibly because of different profit expectations of a large public corporation (compared with a family-owned business), Time Warner closed the small *Sunset* Films division operating out of an office in San Francisco. Some of *Sunset* Books' printing processes were moved to Eastern facilities and book promotions were combined with other Time Warner publications such as *Southern Living* and *Martha Stewart Living*. The Book Division reduced the number of titles while emphasizing home improvement and gardening, and leaving fewer titles in food and travel. Magazine readers shouldered more of the production cost as the magazine's newsstand and subscription prices increased significantly.[77]

Despite these changes, Time Warner has remained faithful to the successful editorial guidelines of the magazine. *Sunset* magazine continues to be a "formidable force in indoctrinating westerners in the regional mores of tossed salads, homemade patios, and automobile recre-

[74] Connie Bruck, *Master of the Game: Steve Ross and the Creation of Time Warner* (New York: Simon and Schuster, 1994), 64, 252. For a brief history of the Time Warner merger, see 246-81.

[75] Interoffice Memorandum, Bill and Mel Lane to Sunset employees and retirees, 27 March 1990.

[76] S. Christopher Meager III, remarks made to the staff of *Sunset*, 27 March 1990. Copy of transcript in possession of author.

[77] Newsstand issues increased by $1.00 to $2.50 (67 percent increase) when Time Warner took over. Newsstand issues cost currently $3.50.

[78] Earl Pomeroy, *Pacific Slope: A History of California, Oregon, Washington, Idaho, Utah, and Nevada* (New York: Alfred A. Knopf, 1965), 384.

ation."[78] Besides keeping the headquarters of the organization in the West, Time Warner retained *Sunset*'s successful and established formula by producing much of its magazine in-house with a full-time editorial staff and few contract articles. Editorial changes were also kept to a minimum. Its current CEO, Steve Seabolt, strongly believing in Western optimism, good education, and interest in the outdoors, confirmed in a *New York Times* article on February 2, 1996, that the magazine remains committed to the "four cornerstones" of *Sunset*: Western food, travel, home improvement, and gardening.

Still, the foundation of the magazine is its readership, a powerful predictor of magazine reading in itself.[79] *Sunset*'s target group remains home owners and first-time home buyers in the 13 Western states. In the early 1990s, subscribers to *Sunset* magazine were more often women than men (roughly a 75:25 ratio); probably the majority are Caucasian, and most likely to own their residence and to drive a car.[80] There is no indication that the readership profile has changed since. To the contrary, if current trends in Western suburban areas such as Las Vegas, Nevada; Phoenix, Arizona; Denver, Colorado; and Seattle, Washington, are an indication, an even greater number of readers own houses and cars–and presumably will subscribe to *Sunset*. Today's middle-aged *Sunset* readership remains overwhelmingly suburban, with a higher-than-average income and home value.[81]

Although the population in the West is increasingly heterogeneous, multicultural, multiethnic, and urban due to continuous (im)migration to the Sunbelt, *Sunset* continues to address only defined aspects of Western living. *Sunset*'s ability to merge "the real and the imaginary so that the boundary between the two becomes progressively vaguer" keeps the magazine attractive to many Western urbanites. It continues to offer information about travel, home improvement, gardening, and food to its readers, and as such helps Westerners to associate "suburbanization with their own cultivation of environmental amenities and an informal pace of life."[82] *Sunset* is successful, and has been for decades, at mixing the modern twentieth-century West with nineteenth-century Anglo-American Western dreams. The magazine remains largely apolitical and positive in tone, and none of the "current Weirdness in the West" such as the Unabomber and freemen should be expected to be discussed in the magazine any time soon.[83]

The new owners did make some editorial revisions in an attempt to broaden their target group and to reflect changing demographics, and presumably more changes can be anticipated. For instance, the logo was changed. On a more substantial level, *Sunset* tries to attract readers both from above and below that middle-aged group of readers, by expanding its editorials. "Watchful publishers, who see a growing market in a graying America..." try to appeal to this new constituency with a variety of special needs.[84] Thus, *Sunset* added more health food segments and

"Mrs. Clara Jensen's idea of happiness is to trail dangerous beasts to their lair and exterminate them. Here she is at the end of a perfect day. Stockmen and farmers send an S.O.S. to her when wildcats come round." Vestiges of frontier days persisting in the West's vast ranch lands.
June 1923, p. 63.

"Mrs. C. Brown Parker is the only woman, so far as known, who specializes in the dangerous occupation of mounting fish–dangerous because of the chemical solutions used." Not quite the traditional woman's occupation.
April 1926, p. 50.

A man and his beaver, "one of 26 adult, pen-raised beavers he keeps on his place near Concord, California"; the Western suburban yeoman in his element.
February 1958, p. 132.

[79] James L. Baughman, *The Republic of Mass Culture*, 2nd ed. (Baltimore: The Johns Hopkins University Press, 1997), 15.

[80] For demographics on *Sunset* readers, see Margaret L. Beck, ed., *Sunset Western Market Almanac, 1989-1990* (Menlo Park, CA: Sunset Magazine, 1989), 74-79; Katherine Grace Fry, "Old South, Agrarian Midwest and Frontier West: Discourses of Repression and Consumption in Southern Living, Midwest Living, and Sunset Magazines" (Ph.D. diss., Temple University, 1994), 227-28.

[81] "At Sunset, Another Day Is About to Dawn," *New York Times*, 10 February 1996.

[82] Richard White, "It's Your Own Misfortune and None of My Own:" *A New History of the American West* (Norman: University of Oklahoma Press, 1991), 546.

[83] Richard White, "The Current Weirdness in the West," *Western Historical Quarterly* 28 (Spring 1997), 5.

[84] Karen Hudes, "Not the Same Old Story," *Folio*, September 1997, 15.

Families

Families are the key, the unifying theme, to all Sunset *coverage, at least since 1929, and thus provide the subject or background for myriad illustrations and covers.*

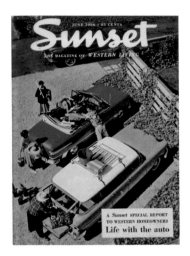

*June 1956 cover
(photo: Ernest Braun)*

*Right: "No wonder Mr. Gabrielson is such a smart gardener. When he's away from home working for Uncle Sam in the Department of Agriculture, his 'assistants' carry on his garden experiments."
May 1930, p. 16.*

*Far right: "Face-mounted outdoor easel makes for easy cleanup."
April 1990, p.125.
(photo: Peter O. Whiteley)*

*"Spring Nursery Shopping in Half Moon Bay"
April 1994 cover*

"Quick Cook" recipes. While *Sunset* had for decades emphasized fresh, regional foods, recipes now contain nutritional information as a matter of course. Herbal remedies, vitamin supplements, and fat-free foods, once the domain of health zealots, have now become part of mainstream America. Aging baby-boomers, as many *Sunset* readers are, want to preserve their quality of life. In its crossover to the "alternative approaches" of Western foods, *Sunset* found an opportunity to give greater attention to its readers' needs and interests.[85]

The current management also continues *Sunset*'s quiet efforts to become an environmentally aware magazine, pointing to the advancing limitations of the Western environment. Articles such as "Forests: Celebration of Light, Dilemmas Over Logging" (May 1992) or "Secrets of the Rain Forest" (November 1997) underline the detrimental impact of extractive industries on the environment. The photo spreads–continuing a *Sunset* tradition–are often as much wake-up calls on the deterioration of the environment as invitations to travel and see the grandeur of the West.

More physically active and lower-budget travel articles are also part of a plan to continue a broad appeal. To be sure, adventure travel was al-

ways a part of the magazine's lineup, but the term's meaning has changed with time. Traveling by car to Yellowstone in the 1930s was certainly an adventure, but *Sunset* has progressively emphasized rigorous activities such as white-water rafting and climbing, preferably in remote locations, as an increasing number of its readers pursue such demanding activities, and *Sunset*'s current plan affirms this direction. Travel articles tend to provide background information about destinations and suggestions regarding action sports geared to appeal to younger readers. Still, with its Western ambiance, *Sunset* reflects as much an attitude of regionalism as of specific demographics.[86]

Advertisements of stylish Cadillacs and Mercedes, exotic Hilton resorts, and healthy Quaker 100% Natural cereals continue to address that specific demographic group, but electric vehicles, too, have found their way into *Sunset*'s pages (Honda, September 1997). Appealing to adventure, tradition, innovation, and individualism, the ads often serve as a

[85] Lorraine Calvacca, "Publishers Heed Nature's Call," *Folio,* June 1997, 20-21.
[86] Karen Hudes, "Adventures in Travel Publishing," *Folio,* October 1997, 15.

continuum and natural extension to the text. Minorities, although still rare, begin to appear in advertisements.[87]

With its seat in the Silicon Valley, it is natural that *Sunset* would find ways to participate in the information highway. *Sunset* began publishing on-line in 1994 by providing garden articles to Virtual Garden, a Time Warner site on the Internet.[88] It added its *Western Garden Book* on CD-ROM with searchable interfaces to its lineup, and provided a Web site for its growing clientele of computer-literate readers with information on recent issues of its magazines and books. To accommodate the expanding demand for electronic presence, *Sunset*'s leadership has recently developed a new Web design with up-to-date information for its readers.

Readers themselves begin to internalize *Sunset* electronically. They link their personal home pages to *Sunset*, and advertise in their home pages specific articles dear to their causes and interests. College class syllabi mounted on home pages make *Sunset* publications required reading and provide hyperlinks to the magazine home page. Electronic *Sunset* chat rooms and bulletin boards fill the need for quick information on the Western lifestyle and link cyberspace gardeners as much to *Sunset* as to one another. Editors of *Sunset* use electronic resources, for example, by seeking on the Sierra Club home page John Muir quotes about San Joaquin wildflowers, a search rewarded immediately with a quote from *A Thousand-Mile Walk to the Gulf:*

> The valley of the San Joaquin is the floweriest place of world I ever walked, one vast, level, even flower-bed, a sheet of flowers, a smooth sea, ruffled a little in the middle by the tree fringing of the river and of smaller cross-streams here and there, from the mountains. (www.sierraclub.org/john_muir_exhibit/)

It is images like John Muir's of the San Joaquin valley, dreams of home ownership, and travel suggestions to places that signify Western values, combined with practical advice and how-to sections for gardeners and builders, that continue to make *Sunset* the successful magazine that it is. The editors successfully reach a readership that will identify with the region and its unique history of westward movement and open space. *Sunset*'s continuous efforts to anticipate its readers' practical needs and to promote American dreams of the wholesome frontier West promise the magazine a bright future in its second century. By purchasing the magazine, Time Warner recognized the regionalism that is deeply rooted west of the 100th meridian and acknowledged that the dream of "Western living" in the American West is vibrant and alive.

"Baby naps while parents and friend enjoy lunch among boulders along glacier-fed White River."
May 1978, p. 33.
(photo: Kieth Gunnar)

"A stop in the woods after a brisk walk, refresh with mugs of hot vegetable soup...."
April 1990, p. 166.
(photo: Norman A. Plate)

"This young daughter is already an active kitchen participant."
January 1997, p. 102.
(photo: Michael Johnson)

[87] For an analysis of under-representation of current non-White groups in magazines, see Fry, "Old South, Agrarian Midwest and Frontier West," 251; see also her chapter "Representation of Non-Whites," 129-152.

[88] *Sunset* also has created a Web site of its own, at http://www.Sunsetmagazine.com/. The URL for Sunset material on the Time Warner Pathfinder Virtual Gardener Web site, as of February 1998, is http:pathfinder.com/vg/Magazine-Rack/Sunset/.

SUNSET
DECEMBER

TEN CENTS A COPY
ONE DOLLAR A YEAR

NEW YORK: 349 Broadway
CHICAGO: 193 Clark Street
LONDON: 49 Leadenhall St.

SAN FRANCISCO
CALIFORNIA

Bibliography and Index

December 1904 cover by Maynard Dixon

1. Building and Remodeling

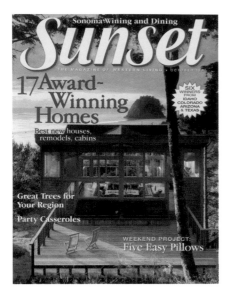

October 1997 cover (photo: Laurie Black)

Building and Remodeling

Domestic Architecture & Home Design have long been a mainstay of Sunset *Magazine, and civic or monumental architecture was an area of interest prior to the Depression. Coupled with a large number of practical articles on Home Improvement & Remodeling, the home–as structure, living space and aesthetic statement–is one of the Big Four areas of interest to* Sunset *readers. While truly opulent homes appear from time to time (particularly as part of the regional boosterism of the very early years), they are the exception to the rule. The emphasis has always been on creative approaches to ordinary, middle-class living-in witness whereof the procession of treatments for small lots, narrow lots, too-small living quarters, not enough storage, multiple uses of space, conversion of rooms to new functions and related means of intelligently overcoming limitations in scale and utility. Perhaps the key concept evident in the listing for home design and building is "attainable results." Despite the vagaries of the economy, of war, and of lesser demands on living styles,* Sunset *has long featured Recreational Homes–cabins, cottages, beach houses, weekend getaway houses–as a characteristic aspect of Western living.*

1. Building and Remodeling

46　Byers, Charles Alma, *Bungalows For Small Families*, 40, 5. (May.1918): p51-52.

47　Sanford, Sanchia, *What Can I Do With a Ten-Foot Lot*, 41, 4. (Oct.1918): p47.

48　Telling, George Palmer, *Colonial Bungalows*, 43, 1. (Jul.1919): p51-52.

49　Horner, Howard Brian, *The Colorful Houses of Clyde*, 43, 2. (Aug.1919): p51-52.

50　Byers, Charles Alma, *Build Me One Just Like It*, 44, 1. (Jan.1920): p6, 8.

51　Waldron, Gertrude Luckey, *Seven Rooms and Simplicity*, 44, 3. (Mar.1920): p64, 66.

52　Matson, Esther, *A House on Hill Crest*, 44, 5. (May.1920): p64, 66.

53　Bingham, Persis, *A Small House for a Warm Climate*, 44, 6. (Jun.1920): p64, 66.

54　*Here You Have a Choice of Floor Plans*, 45, 1. (Jul.1920): p68.

55　Brownfield, Marion, *Modernizing the Adobe*, 45, 4. (Oct.1920): p68, 70.

56　Byers, Charles Alma, *The Garage Part of a House*, 45, 5. (Nov.1920): p70, 72.

57　Ferguson, Lillian, *Variety in Bungalows*, 45, 6. (Dec.1920): p68,70.

58　Byers, Charles Alma, *A Cottage With a Cement Exterior*, 46, 1. (Jan.1921): p64.

59　Brownfield, Marion, *A Type of Spanish Renaissance*, 46, 2. (Feb.1921): p60, 62.

60　*When the Roof is Thatched*, 46, 3. (Mar.1921): p66, 68.

61　Byers, Charles Alma, *A Small House for a Warm Climate*, 46, 5. (May.1921): p70, 72.

62　Mills, Enos A., *A Home of Forest Fire Logs*, 46, 5. (May.1921): p66, 68.

63　Bingham, Persis, *Our New Architecture*, 46, 6. (Jun.1921): p66, 68.

64　Ferguson, Lillian, *Antiquity to Order*, 47, 5. (Nov.1921): p58, 60.

65　Brownfield, Marion, *Adapting the Spanish Patio to American Needs*, 47, 6. (Dec.1921): p58, 60, 62.

66　Byers, Charles Alma, *Mission and Pueblo Styles Combined*, 48, 2. (Feb.1922): p58, 59.

67　Davis, Herta Curme, *Making Their Own*, 48, 3. (Mar.1922): p60, 62-63.

68　*Where is a House More Electrified Than This*, 48, 3. (Mar.1922): p58, 60.

69　Keck, Maud M., *El Adobe Flores*, 48, 6. (Jun.1922): p60, 62, 64.

70　Brownfield, Marion, *The Fireplace*, 50, 2. (Feb.1923): p58-59, 62.

71　Bingham, Persis, *Cottage and Villa Types*, 50, 3. (Mar.1923): p66, 68.

72　Craig, Margaret, *A Spanish Casa*, 50, 5. (May.1923): p64, 66, 80.

73　Willard, Victor, *The Cities Of The Far West*, 50, 6. (Jun.1923): p8-13.

74　Mead, Elwood, *How To Build Up The Rural West*, 50, 6. (Jun.1923): p32-33, 108-112.

75　Maclay, Mira, *The Maybeck One-Room House*, 51, 1. (Jul.1923): p64, 66, 80-81.

76　Byers, Charles Alma, *The Heart of This House is the Patio*, 52, 3. (Mar.1924): p66, 68.

77　Bingham, Persis, *Duplex–Yet Different*, 53, 1. (Jul.1924): p64-65.

78　Bingham, Persis, *Living the Sunny Life*, 53, 3. (Sep.1924): p64,66.

79　Bingham, Persis, *A Patio Home*, 53, 6. (Dec.1924): p64, 66-67.

80　Maclay, Mira, *Reviving the Early California Type*, 55, 2. (Aug.1925): p64-65.

81　Simons, H. A., *Stucco in Its Variety*, 55, 3. (Sep.1925): p64-65.

82　Brownfield, Marion, *Round Rooms*, 55, 4. (Oct.1925): p65-66.

83　Barker, Frances T., *Camulos, A Ranch of Romance*, 55, 6. (Dec.1925): p65-66.

84　Maclay, Mira, *Villa Montalvo*, 56, 2. (Feb.1926): p14-16, 66.

85　L. F., *Homes Of Distinction*, 56, 2. (Feb.1926): p17.

86　Brownfield, Marion, *The Pueblo and Padre Influences on Stucco Homes*, 56, 6. (Jun.1926): p64-65, 83.

87　Hyers, Faith Holmes, *Where Simplicity Means Beauty*, 57, 6. (Dec.1926): p17, 56.

88　*The English Cottage in the Far West*, 57, 6. (Dec.1926): p50-51, 78.

89　Quisenberry, Francis, *Beauty Borrowed From The Painted Desert*, 58, 3. (Mar.1927): p13.

90　Byers, Charles Alma, *Porches for Outdoor Living*, 59, 1. (Jul.1927): p52-53, 76.

91　Marvin, George, *Building Against Time*, 59, 6. (Dec.1927): p28-30, 80-81.

92　Hicks, Cuthbert, *A Great Cathedral For The West*, 60, 4. (Apr.1928): p29, 60.

93　Maclay, Mira, *The Modified Swiss Chalet*, 60, 5. (May.1928): p50-51, 76.

94　Rhodes, Ruth, *A Homemade Homestead Home*, 60, 6. (Jun.1928): p26-27, 67-68.

95　Fordyce, Claude P., *Can You Build A Log Cabin?*, 61, 1. (Jul.1928): p18-19, 80.

96　Cassidy, Louise Lowber, *An Ancient Adobe Restored*, 61, 3. (Sep.1928): p54-55, 79.

97　*The California Home of Mr. and Mrs. Herbert Clark Hoover*, 61, 3. (Sep.1928): p56.

98　Ferguson, Lillian, *Palmdale, The Country Estate of O. L. Starr*, 61, 6. (Dec.1928): p40-43, 64.

99　Swett-Sommers, Naomi, *A Gray-Shingled Home In The West*, 62, 2. (Feb.1929): p15-18.

100　Mohler, Marjorie M., *The Lure of the Patio*, 62, 2. (Feb.1929): p32-33.

101　Ames, Katherine, *A New-World Chateau on a Twenty-Five Foot City Lot*, 62, 3. (Mar.1929): p17-19.

102　Hampton, Mary McDuffie, *Are Your Children Proud Of Their Home?*, 62, 3. (Mar.1929): p27-28.

103　Byers, Charles Alma, *Before You Build That New House*, 62, 3. (Mar.1929): p64-66.

104　Mohler, Marjorie M., *A Mediterranean Home In A Modern Setting*, 62, 4. (Apr.1929): p20-22.

105　Stanley, Neil, *A Dream City On The Pacific*, 62, 5. (May.1929): p14-15.

106　Officer, Gwynn, *A House For A Small Family*, 62, 6. (Jun.1929): p22-23.

107　Officer, Gwynn, *A Truly Livable City House*, 63, 1. (Jul.1929): p24-25.

108　Officer, Gwynn, *A Home In The Suburbs*, 63, 3. (Sep.1929): p28-29.

109　Taylor, Frank J., *A Boy's Dream Comes True*, 63, 4. (Oct.1929): p11-14.

110　Officer, Gwynn, *A Spanish House Designed for a Western Hillside*, 63, 4. (Oct.1929): p36-37.

111　Davis, Marion Lay, *A Little House of Brick*, 63, 5. (Nov.1929): p14-15.

112　Byers, Charles Alma, *Around The Christmas Fireside*, 63, 6. (Dec.1929): p23-25.

113　Harbinson, A. Marshall, *A Trio of Sacramento Homes*, 64, 1. (Jan.1930): p9-12.

114　Reimers, Frederick H., *On A Hillside In Piedmont*, 64, 5. (May.1930): p28-29.

115　Garren, William I., *First Steps In Home Planning*, 64, 6. (Jun.1930): p21-23, 57.

116　Garren, William I., *The Home You Build*, 65, 1. (Jul.1930): p22-24, 51.

117　Garren, William I., *Before Designing Your Western Home*, 65, 2. (Aug.1930): p15-18.

118　Garren, William I., *Through Western Windows*, 65, 3. (Sep.1930): p7-9.

119　Webber, Walter and Saulding, Sumner, *A Bungalow Built Around The Garden*, 65, 3. (Sep.1930): p26-27.

120　Gutterson, Henry H., *A Little Irish Cottage*, 65, 4. (Oct.1930): p24-25.

121　*A House in the Sun*, 65, 5. (Nov.1930): p20-21.

122　Garren, William I., *Getting More Beauty Into Western Homes*, 65, 6. (Dec.1930): p20-22, 45.

1. Building and Remodeling

1. Building and Remodeling

1. Building and Remodeling

1. Building and Remodeling

1. Building and Remodeling

1. Building and Remodeling

542 *Theatrical–Chaotic–The Most Interesting House We Saw*, 158, 4. (Apr.1977): p116-119.

543 *Is the Precut House a Bargain?*, 158, 5. (May.1977): p104-109.

544 *Owner-Built In Phoenix–Only $10+ Per Square Foot*, 159, 1. (Jul.1977): p74-75.

545 *The American Institute of Architects–Sunset Magazine Western Home Awards*, 159, 4. (Oct.1977): p98-113.

546 *Tall Pipes Of Water Heat And Cool Award-Winning House*, 159, 5. (Nov.1977): p112-115.

547 *Trade Winds Cool Honolulu Award–Winner; It's Multilevel on a Very Steep Site*, 160, 1. (Jan.1978): p58-59.

548 *Hawaii's Lovely 96-Year-Old Iolani*, 160, 2. (Feb.1978): p64-67.

549 *Three Award-Winning Weekend Places. They Are Geometric*, 160, 4. (Apr.1978): p116-121.

550 *The Adobes Of New Mexico*, 161, 1. (Jul.1978): p82-87.

551 *Thinking Small–Three Award-Winning Houses*, 161, 3. (Sep.1978): p80-83.

552 *Is The Manufactured House At Long Last On The Western Horizon?*, 161, 5. (Nov.1978): p98-109.

553 *Passive Solar: Yesterday Is Tomorrow*, 162, 2. (Feb.1979): p76-83.

554 *A White, Bright, Open Balcony House–Rustic "Barn" Exterior*, 163, 1. (Jul.1979): p70-73.

555 *Western Home Awards Winners–1979-1980*, 163, 4. (Oct.1979): p78-93.

556 *A Dozen Old Financial "Temples" Still on View In San Francisco's Downtown*, 163, 5. (Nov.1979): p22-24.

557 *Our First Alaska Home Design Award–Winner, Tight to the Elements*, 165, 3. (Sep.1980): p58-59.

558 *Almost Half Their Floor Plan Is Out-Of-Doors*, 165, 3. (Sep.1980): p64-65.

559 *1981-1982 Western Home Awards–Breakthroughs Are Needed*, 166, 2. (Feb.1981): p152-153.

560 *Successful Search For Studio Space*, 166, 2. (Feb.1981): p82-83.

561 *"Restfulness and Retreat, Rough and Rustic"–The Grand Park Hotels*, 166, 5. (May.1981): p92-97.

562 *Western Home Awards 1981-1982*, 167, 4. (Oct.1981): p74-89.

563 *California's Capitol Returns To Glory*, 168, 1. (Jan.1982): p44-47.

564 *The Earth-Sheltering Idea*, 168, 4. (Apr.1982): p120-126.

565 *Thinking Thin. Spacious Houses No Wider Than 20 Feet*, 168, 6. (May.1982): p114-115.

566 *Building Breakthroughs On The Way?*, 170, 4. (Apr.1983): p120-125.

567 *Bringing The Outdoors Indoors*, 170, 5. (May.1983): p114-117.

568 *Solar Sensible And Lively*, 170, 5. (May.1983): p168-169.

569 *Western Home Awards 1983-1984*, 171, 4. (Oct.1983): p84-101.

570 *Award-Winning And Owner-Built*, 171, 5. (Nov.1983): p116-119.

571 *Architectural Rubbernecking In San Francisco*, 172, 3. (Mar.1984): p88-91.

572 *They Added This To The Back of Their Ranch House?*, 174, 5. (May.1985): p134-137.

573 *Western Home Awards 1985-1986*, 175, 4. (Oct.1985): p100-117.

574 *Architectural "Tasting" in the Napa-Sonoma Wine Country*, 176, 4. (Apr.1986): p10-12, 14.

575 *Flair On A Budget*, 176, 5. (May.1986): p118-121.

576 *Moving The Kitchen Outdoors*, 177, 3. (Sep.1986): p80-85.

577 *The Best of Both Indoor and Outdoor Worlds: Multiuse Screened Porch*, 179, 1. (Jul.1987): p108-109.

578 *Western Home Awards 1987-1988*, 179, 4. (Oct.1987): p71-89.

579 *Big Scale and Bright, Architectural Lighting Makes a Bay Area Comeback*, 179, 6. (Dec.1987): p14-15.

580 *Squeezing In A Vest-Pocket "Victorian"*, 180, 4. (Apr.1988): p120-121.

581 *The Changing Western Home*, 180, 6. (Jun.1988): p102-103, 106.

582 *The Flexible Box*, 181, 4. (Oct.1988): p88-91.

583 *Think of it as a House With an Outdoor and Indoor Courtyard*, 182, 2. (Feb.1989): p112-114.

584 *Spend On The Design, Save On The Extras*, 182, 4. (Apr.1989): p148-150.

585 *Hawaiian H: Clean, Spacious, Economical*, 182, 5. (May.1989): p158-159.

586 *Bali In San Diego*, 182, 6. (Jun.1989): p128-130.

587 *1989-1990 Western Home Awards*, 183, 4. (Oct.1989): p87-138.

588 *Outside It Still Looks Like 1906*, 184, 3. (Mar.1990): p120-122.

589 *Mud-building 1990s-style*, 184, 4. (Apr.1990): p136-138.

590 NONE , *Gather Round The Fireplace...Outdoors*, 185, 3. (Sep.1990): p58-61.

591 *Inspired By Western Barns*, 185, 5. (Nov.1990): p86-91.

592 *Book Nooks*, 186, 2. (Feb.1991): p68-69.

593 *Floor Plans For Today's Kitchen*, 186, 2. (Feb.1991): p81-88.

594 *Inside It's Mostly One Grand Space*, 186, 3. (Mar.1991): p124-129.

595 *The Small-house, Tight-lot challenge*, 186, 6. (Jun.1991): p112-113, 116.

596 *Western Home Awards, 1991-1992*, 187, 4. (Oct.1991): p92-136.

597 *Remodeler's Secret: Thicken The Walls*, 187, 4. (Oct.1991): p138-140.

598 *Hillside House is Right for the Site; More Western Home Award Winners*, 187, 5. (Nov.1991): p116-120.

599 Gregory, Daniel P., *Far East Comes West*, 188, 2. (Feb.1992): p61-68.

600 Jaffe, Matthew, *Hollywood Palaces*, 188, 2. (Feb.1992): p76-79.

601 Gregory, Daniel P., *The Ranch House Rides Again*, 188, 3. (Mar.1992): p84-95.

602 Crosby, Bill, *Designs For Outdoor Living*, 188, 4. (Apr.1992): p105-113.

603 Gregory, Daniel P., *Patios Plus Walls Equal Privacy*, 188, 6. (Jun.1992): p86-89.

604 Fish, Peter, *Safety Versus History*, 189, 3. (Sep.1992): p80-83.

605 *Billboard Buildings In Los Angeles*, 189, 05. (Nov.1992): p84-87.

606 Whiteley, Peter O., *Best Owner-Built Deck*, 190, 2. (Feb.1993): p78-79.

607 Gregory, Daniel P. and Johnson, Elaine, *Designed For Dessert...And Efficiency*, 190, 3. (Mar.1993): p108-111.

608 Gregory, Daniel P. and Whiteley, Peter O., *Porches Are Still People Places*, 190, 5. (May.1993): p104-106, 108.

609 Fish, Peter and Gregory, Daniel P., *The Endangered Western Home*, 190, 5. (May.1993): p84-88, 90, 92-100, 102.

610 Gregory, Daniel P. and others, *1993-94 Western Home Awards*, 191, 4. (Oct.1993): p80-132.

611 Crosby, Bill and Chrisman, Kimberly, *Home Design Software*, 191, 5. (Nov.1993): p92-94, 97.

612 Jaffe, Matthew, *Eight Wonders Of Las Vegas*, 192, 2. (Feb.1994): p86-89.

613 Whiteley, Peter O., *Railings That Make The Decks*, 192, 3. (Mar.1994): p110-111, 113.

614 Crosby, Bill and Whiteley, Peter O., *Architects At Play*, 192, 4. (Apr.1994): p104-108.

615 Gregory, Daniel P. and others, *Out of the Ashes; Rebuilding The Oakland Hills*, 193, 3. (Sep.1994): p70-79.

616 Lorton, Steven R., *Making A Home In The Country*, 193, 3. (Sep.1994): p94-95, 96, 97.

617 Whiteley, Peter O., *Culinary Art*, 193, 5. (Nov.1994): p88-91.

618 *The Log Home Wins The West...Again*, 193, 07. (Jan.1995): p62-69.

1. Building and Remodeling

619 Whiteley, Peter O., *The New Adobes*, 194, 4. (Apr.1995): p100-106.

620 Gregory, Daniel P. and others, *Why We Still Love Bungalows*, 194, 5. (May.1995): p86-91.

621 Crosby, Bill and others, *Art Of The Addition*, 195, 3. (Sep.1995): p93-113.

622 *Western Home Awards*, 194, 04. (Oct.1995): p88-130.

623 Whiteley, Peter O., *Branch Office In The Backyard*, 196, 4. (Apr.1996): p122-124, 126, 128.

624 Whiteley, Peter O., *Garden Fireplaces*, 196, 6. (Jun.1996): p98-101.

625 Crosby, Bill and others, *Great Doors To The Outdoors*, 197, 1. (Jul.1996): p84-86, 88, 89.

626 Crosby, Bill and others, *Master Suites*, 197, 2. (Aug.1996): p85-90, 92, 94-96, 98-102.

627 *A Concrete Revival*, 198, 3. (Mar.1997): p110, 112-114.

628 Gregory, Daniel P. and others, *Dreaming Of Home*, 198, 4. (Apr.1997): p84-93.

629 Gregory, Daniel P., Whiteley, Peter O., and Bertelsen, Ann, *Western Home Awards, 1997-1998*, 199, 4. (Oct.1997): p92-94, 98-100, 102-123.

1.2 House Improvement & Remodeling

630 Cheney, May L., *New Science Of Home-Making*, 24, 3. (Mar.1910): p280-283.

631 Brownfield, Marion, *The Small Home Driveway*, 44, 4. (Apr.1920): p68, 70.

632 Hollis, Elaine, *Electrifying the Home*, 45, 4. (Oct.1920): p70, 72.

633 FitzGerald, Harold J., *The City Fire Menace*, 47, 5. (Nov.1921): p90-91.

634 *The Ups and Downs of Temperature*, 51, 1. (Jul.1923): p68-69, 74.

635 *The Kitchen Deluxe*, 51, 5. (Nov.1923): p68, 75-76.

636 *Lighting the Home*, 52, 1. (Jan.1924): p68-69.

637 Evens, Addie G., *Modernizing a Ranch House*, 52, 2. (Feb.1924): p67.

638 *The Bathroom Beautiful*, 53, 4. (Oct.1924): p68, 74-75.

639 *Controlling the Home Climate*, 54, 1. (Jan.1925): p68, 73 .

640 Maclay, Mira, *The Barn That Became A Studio*, 54, 2. (Feb.1925): p64-66.

641 Dillingham, J. O., *The Electrified Home*, 56, 2. (Feb.1926): p19.

642 Jakway, Bernard C., *Some Aspects Of Interior Decoration*, 56, 2. (Feb.1926): p30-32, 84-85.

643 *Choosing A Refrigerator*, 56, 4. (Apr.1926): p68, 76-77.

644 *Let There Be Light*, 57, 5. (Nov.1926): p70, 76-77.

645 *The Power Behind the Home*, 57, 4. (Apr.1927): p70-71.

646 *Windows of Personality*, 60, 2. (Feb.1928): p70-71.

647 *Awnings - New Style*, 61, 2. (Aug.1928): p72-73.

648 Gwynne, Herbert, *Solving the Country Bathroom Problem*, 62, 1. (Jan.1929): p45, 66.

649 Walker, John William, *You Can Paint Stucco*, 62, 2. (Feb.1929): p19, 57.

650 Hampton, Mary McDuffie, *The House A Man Calls Home*, 62, 2. (Feb.1929): p24-25.

651 Wileman, Edgar Harrison, *Does Your Home Picture Your Personality?*, 62, 5. (May.1929): p22-24.

652 O'Hara, Gerald J., *Where Do Your Children Play*, 62, 6. (Jun.1929): p27-29.

653 Wileman, Edgar Harrison, *Our Colorful Homes*, 62, 6. (Jun.1929): p30-31.

654 Wileman, Edgar Harrison, *Harmony Means Beauty*, 63, 1. (Jul.1929): p26-27.

655 Wileman, Edgar Harrison, *Period Styles In Furniture*, 63, 2. (Aug.1929): p24-26.

656 Wileman, Edgar Harrison, *These Modern Homes*, 63, 3. (Sep.1929): p26-27.

657 Harper, Jack Hasty John Eugene, *Flooring the Morrisons*, 63, 3. (Sep.1929): p32-34.

658 Wileman, Edgar Harrison, *The Spanish Style*, 63, 4. (Oct.1929): p25-27.

659 Hasty, John Eugene, *The Harpers Have a Heated Argument*, 63, 4. (Oct.1929): p31-33.

660 Wileman, Edgar Harrison, *Early English Furnishings*, 63, 5. (Nov.1929): p24-27.

661 Hasty, John Eugene, *The Harpers Move The Refrigerator*, 63, 5. (Nov.1929): p28-30.

662 Wileman, Edgar Harrison, *Furnishings Of A Georgian Type*, 64, 1. (Jan.1930): p20-22.

663 Hasty, John Eugene, *Auxiliary Heating Equipment*, 64, 1. (Jan.1930): p33-35.

664 Raker, Mary E., *Utilizing Desert Colors*, 64, 2. (Feb.1930): p24-25.

665 Willson, Roger, *Painting Old-Time Ironwork Furniture*, 64, 2. (Feb.1930): p26-28.

666 Wileman, Edgar Harrison, *Common Errors In Home Furnishing*, 64, 3. (Mar.1930): p27-28.

667 Wileman, Edgar Harrison, *For Tired Homes*, 64, 4. (Apr.1930): p26-28.

668 Wileman, Edgar Harrison, *When You Select A Rug*, 64, 5. (May.1930): p20-22.

669 Hasty, John Eugene, *Hot Water Heaters*, 64, 5. (May.1930): p30-31, 54-55.

670 Lewis, Martha, *How We Made Over Our Kitchen*, 64, 5. (May.1930): p40, 42.

671 Wileman, Edgar Harrison, *If You Need A New Chair*, 64, 6. (Jun.1930): p26-28.

672 Wileman, Edgar Harrison, *The Problem Of Storage*, 65, 1. (Jul.1930): p25-26.

673 Wileman, Edgar Harrison, *The Pictures On Your Walls*, 65, 2. (Aug.1930): p24-26.

674 Wileman, Edgar Harrison, *What About Bric-A-Brac*, 65, 3. (Sep.1930): p20-21.

675 Wileman, Edgar Harrison, *Electricity In Decorating*, 65, 4. (Oct.1930): p19-21.

676 Garren, William I., *Electricity Brings Light And Leisure*, 65, 4. (Oct.1930): p28-29, 42-43.

677 Wileman, Edgar Harrison, *We Furnish An All-Western Home*, 65, 5. (Nov.1930): p12-14.

678 Garren, William I., *What's New In Plumbing*, 65, 5. (Nov.1930): p28-29.

679 Garren, William I., *Keep Your Home From Depreciating In Value*, 66, 1. (Jan.1931): p15-16.

680 Ashby, N. B., *Two Old Fireplaces*, 66, 1. (Jan.1931): p17.

681 Wileman, Edgar Harrison, *Is Your Home Furnished To Scale?*, 66, 1. (Jan.1931): p25-26.

682 Wileman, Edgar Harrison, *Modernizing A Dark Ugly Living Room*, 66, 2. (Feb.1931): p20-21, 45.

683 Garren, William I., *Hardware For The Western Home*, 66, 2. (Feb.1931): p26-27.

684 Wileman, Edgar Harrison, *A Real Spring Cleaning*, 66, 3. (Mar.1931): p23-25.

685 Redfern, Curtis, *In Our Basement Living Room*, 66, 3. (Mar.1931): p26-27.

686 Garren, William I., *What Every Westerner Should Know About Heating*, 66, 3. (Mar.1931): p30.

687 Garren, William I., *Friendly Roofs Of Western Homes*, 66, 4. (Apr.1931): p17-18.

688 Wileman, Edgar Harrison, *Decorating After You Move*, 66, 4. (Apr.1931): p25-27.

689 Wileman, Edgar Harrison, *Bring The Outdoors In And The Indoors Out*, 66, 5. (May.1931): p25-26.

690 Powell, Tod, *How To Build A Barbecue*, 66, 06. (Jun.1931): p10-11.

1. Building and Remodeling

691 Wileman, Edgar Harrison, *Shift Your Furniture*, 67, 1. (Jul.1931): p24-25.

692 Mulvane, William R., *A Sea Wall*, 67, 2. (Aug.1931): p14-15.

693 Wileman, Edgar Harrison, *How To Choose The Correct Rug*, 67, 2. (Aug.1931): p24-25.

694 Garren, William I., *Garden Gates*, 67, 2. (Aug.1931): p26.

695 Wileman, Edgar Harrison, *Upholstery Fabrics*, 67, 3. (Sep.1931): p23-25.

696 Pyke, Albert M., Mrs., *A Combination Picnic Stove And Incinerator*, 67, 4. (Oct.1931): p18.

697 Wileman, Edgar Harrison, *Draperies For Western Homes*, 67, 4. (Oct.1931): p19-20.

698 Callahan, Genevieve A., *The Care Of Oak Floors*, 67, 4. (Oct.1931): p30-32.

699 Jenseth, P. I., Mrs. , *Our Old House*, 67, 5. (Nov.1931): p8.

700 Wileman, Edgar Harrison, *The Dining Room Ensemble*, 67, 5. (Nov.1931): p16-17.

701 Cooper, James F., *Our Home-Made Swimming Pool*, 68, 2. (Feb.1932): p14-15.

702 Wileman, Edgar Harrison, *Questions About Living Rooms*, 68, 4. (Apr.1932): p18.

703 Wileman, Edgar Harrison, *Furnishing The Small Colonial Home*, 68, 5. (May.1932): p21.

704 Wileman, Edgar Harrison, *Have You A New Home To Furnish*, 68, 6. (Jun.1932): p17-18.

705 Wileman, Edgar Harrison, *Furnishings For Western Homes*, 69, 2. (Aug.1932): p8.

706 Wileman, Edgar Harrison, *Sunset Decorator's Own Home*, 69, 3. (Sep.1932): p12-13.

707 Dodge, Natt N., *Back Yard Playgrounds*, 69, 4. (Oct.1932): p10-12.

708 Wileman, Edgar Harrison, *Where Do You Write Your Letters?*, 69, 4. (Oct.1932): p21.

709 Jackson, Eileen, *An Old San Diego Home Is Rejuvenated*, 69, 5. (Nov.1932): p15-16.

710 Wileman, Edgar Harrison, *How Do Your Pictures Hang?*, 69, 5. (Nov.1932): p17.

711 Shepherd, F. R., *How We Built Our Garden Stove*, 69, 5. (Nov.1932): p20-21.

712 Hurlbutt, Frances C., *How To Make Della Robbia Wreaths*, 69, 6. (Dec.1932): p11.

713 Stackable, Marion, *Our Little White Cot By The Sea*, 69, 6. (Dec.1932): p14, 35.

714 Zadach, Stanley, *Attracting Birds To Western Gardens*, 69, 6. (Dec.1932): p15-16.

715 Wileman, Edgar Harrison, *Four Windows That Are Dressed With Charm*, 69, 6. (Dec.1932): p17.

716 Stackable, Marion, *How We Built Our Garden Wall*, 70, 2. (Feb.1933): p10.

717 Wileman, Edgar Harrison, *Look At Your Rugs*, 70, 2. (Feb.1933): p15.

718 Weed, Howard, *Every Sunset Garden Deserves A Lily Pool*, 70, 3. (Mar.1933): p18-19.

719 Wileman, Edgar Harrison, *Spanish Furniture For California Homes*, 70, 4. (Apr.1933): p21.

720 Ross, Lindsley W., *Sun Dial*, 70, 6. (Jun.1933): p14-17.

721 Wileman, Edgar Harrison, *Furnishing The New Home On A Limited Budget*, 71, 1. (Jul.1933): p14-15.

722 Johnson, Arthur O., *Three Arbors For Sunset Gardens*, 71, 2. (Aug.1933): p16-17.

723 Hein, Herman E., *How To Build And Plant A Rock Wall*, 71, 3. (Sep.1933): p16-17.

724 Banks, H. C., *Charm House*, 71, 3. (Sep.1933): p18-19.

725 Wileman, Edgar Harrison, *We Furnish A Living Room In American Chippendale*, 71, 4. (Oct.1933): p16-17.

726 Edwards, Pauline K., *My Electric Refrigerator*, 71, 4. (Oct.1933): p20-21, 27, 30.

727 Cotton, Horace George, *An Outdoor Fireplace*, 71, 6. (Dec.1933): p16-17.

728 Wileman, Edgar Harrison, *Consider Linoleum For Your Western Home*, 72, 2. (Feb.1934): p14-15.

729 Forbes, J. Bert, *Ours Is A Year Round Rock Garden*, 72, 3. (Mar.1934): p7-9.

730 Callahan, Genevieve A., *Better Beds For Western Homes*, 72, 4. (Apr.1934): p18, 46-47.

731 Knight, Elsa Eloise, *What's New In Porch And Garden Furniture*, 72, 5. (May.1934): p12-13.

732 Cotton, Horace George, *Build A Barbecue For Your Sunset Garden*, 72, 5. (May.1934): p14-15.

733 Wileman, Edgar Harrison, *New Ideas For Western Homes*, 73, 1. (Jul.1934): p14-15.

734 Hoskins, James A., *Take Your Tool Kit Along*, 73, 1. (Jul.1934): p16-17.

735 *Are You An Arctic Explorer?*, 73, 3. (Sep.1934): p16-17, 36-37.

736 Berry, Alethe, *Transplanting The South Seas To The Home Aquarium*, 73, 4. (Oct.1934): p9-11.

737 Grady, Helen Bell, *Far Gleam The Lights Of Western Homes*, 73, 4. (Oct.1934): p12-13.

738 Conner, Doris, *Venetian Blinds Or Roll Shades–Which Shall It Be?*, 73, 4. (Oct.1934): p19, 42-43.

739 Conner, Doris, *A Western Decorator Talks About Children's Rooms*, 73, 6. (Dec.1934): p10-12, 38.

740 Muselwhite, Therine, *White Paint Does Wonders For The Tired Home*, 74, 1. (Jan.1935): p12-13.

741 Wileman, Edgar Harrison, *New Trends In Decorating Western Homes*, 74, 2. (Feb.1935): p12-13, 46-47.

742 Cobb, E. L., *When Your Fireplace Smokes*, 74, 2. (Feb.1935): p19.

743 Stark, Grace, *Denver Sends This Old Shutter Screen*, 74, 3. (Mar.1935): p17, 40-41.

744 Callahan, Genevieve A., *It's Fun To Wash*, 74, 3. (Mar.1935): p20-22, 42-43.

745 Asher, Mildred G., *Flood The Garden With Man-Made Moonlight*, 74, 4. (Apr.1935): p14-15, 69.

746 Burton, Mary June, *An Outdoor Living Room Of Abode Brick*, 74, 5. (May.1935): p20, 65-66.

747 Banghart, Edith H., *Rock Walls For West Of The Rockies*, 74, 5. (May.1935): p21, 72-73.

748 Head, Ethel M., *Let's Build More Comfort Into Our Sunset Homes*, 75, 2. (Aug.1935): p7-9.

749 Hindley, lia, *Good Times Are Coming*, 75, 3. (Sep.1935): p10-11.

750 Blake, Fred C., *Why Not Plant A Windbreak?*, 75, 3. (Sep.1935): p15, 48.

751 Cruise, Margaret, *How One Sunset Family Modernized An Old Dining Room*, 75, 3. (Sep.1935): p16, 41.

752 Wileman, Edgar Harrison, *Lighter Homes Are Brighter Homes*, 75, 6. (Dec.1935): p13, 36.

753 Gooch, J. A., *How To Build And Plant A Path*, 76, 1. (Jan.1936): p9.

754 *Garden Chair To Make*, 76, 2. (Feb.1936): p27.

755 *Home Work-Shopping*, 76, 4. (Apr.1936): p30-31.

756 *Improving The Home*, 76, 4. (Apr.1936): p36-36a.

757 *Build Ins & Build Ons*, 76, 6. (Jun.1936): p36-37.

758 *Living Rooms*, 77, 1. (Jul.1936): p20-21.

759 *Looking At Modern Lighting*, 77, 2. (Aug.1936): p28-29.

760 *The Barbecue Bar*, 77, 2. (Aug.1936): p30-31.

761 *Making The Garden Shrine*, 77, 3. (Sep.1936): p23.

1. Building and Remodeling

1. Building and Remodeling

1. Building and Remodeling

1. Building and Remodeling

1. Building and Remodeling

1. Building and Remodeling

1. Building and Remodeling

1. Building and Remodeling

1342 *Kitchen Models Of Efficiency*, 178, 2. (Feb.1987): p80-85.

1343 *Arizona Firebox Sculpture*, 178, 3. (Mar.1987): p128-129.

1344 *Vinyl-lined Pools: How Do They Look And Last?*, 178, 6. (Jun.1987): p150-151.

1345 *Why Wood Windows?*, 179, 2. (Aug.1987): p70-72, 74, 77.

1346 *They Put The Skeleton On The Outside*, 179, 2. (Aug.1987): p98-99.

1347 *The Outdoor Room Idea*, 179, 3. (Sep.1987): p68-71.

1348 *Only The Roof And Four Walls Remain*, 180, 1. (Jan.1988): p62-63.

1349 *1949 Flat-Top Enlarges Upward And Frontward*, 180, 3. (Mar.1988): p114-115.

1350 *Gravel: Good-Looking and Water Efficient, It Deserves More Respect*, 180, 4. (Apr.1988): p252-255.

1351 *The "Electronic House" At Last?*, 180, 05. (May.1988): p156-157.

1352 *Breaking Out Of The Box*, 180, 6. (Jun.1988): p90-91.

1353 *What About Asbestos in and Around Your House?*, 181, 3. (Sep.1988): p84-86, 88, 90.

1354 *The Cabinet Decision; It's the Biggest Decisions for Most Kitchen Remodelers*, 182, 1. (Jan.1989): p68-73.

1355 *No Longer An 'Afterthought' Kitchen*, 182, 3. (Mar.1989): p106-108.

1356 *The Back-Yard Beach*, 183, 1. (Jul.1989): p68-69.

1357 *Outdoor Lighting...Art And Technology*, 183, 1. (Jul.1989): p72-78, 80.

1358 *What's New in Outdoor Speakers?*, 183, 2. (Aug.1989): p76, 78, 79.

1359 *Sandstone And Cousins*, 183, 5. (Nov.1989): p102-104.

1360 *Time For A Fireplace Facelift?*, 184, 1. (Jan.1990): p56-59.

1361 *Finding Ways To Add A Family Room*, 184, 2. (Feb.1990): p82-86, 88.

1362 *Kitchen Glass*, 184, 3. (Mar.1990): p94-95.

1363 *Looking For Space? Think "Caboosing"*, 184, 4. (Apr.1990): p108-112, 114.

1364 *Between The Front Door And The Street*, 184, 5. (May.1990): p124-125.

1365 *Safer Pools*, 184, 5. (May.1990): p139-145.

1366 *After You Bring Home A Portable Spa*, 184, 6. (Jun.1990): p88-91.

1367 *It Was 'A Dog Run Of A Back Yard'*, 185, 3. (Sep.1990): p68-69.

1368 *Stairs For More Than Climbing*, 185, 04. (Oct.1990): p84-85.

1369 *Preparing For The Next Earthquake*, 185, 04. (Oct.1990): p163-177.

1370 *Inside The Western House*, 185, 04. (Oct.1990): p101-145.

1371 *The Apple Fence Idea*, 186, 1. (Jan.1991): p52-53.

1372 *Adding High Light With Clerestories*, 186, 1. (Jan.1991): p58-62.

1373 *How Do You Squeeze In A Home Workspace?*, 186, 3. (Mar.1991): p102-109.

1374 *Adding A Little, Gaining A Lot*, 186, 4. (Apr.1991): p98-106, 111.

1375 *Bricks As Garden Paving*, 187, 2. (Aug.1991): p48-51.

1376 *Inside The Western Home*, 187, 3. (Sep.1991): p95-96.

1377 *Mexico's Colors Come North To Tucson's Barrio Historico*, 187, 5. (Nov.1991): p128-132.

1378 Gregory, Daniel P., *Terra-Cotta...The Great Western Paving*, 188, 5. (May.1992): p128-129, 132.

1379 MacCaskey, Michael and others, *Capture A Little Water In Your Garden*, 189, 2. (Aug.1992): p90-93.

1380 Crosby, Bill, *Hunting Down Home Hazards*, 189, 3. (Sep.1992): p118-119.

1381 *Special Section: The West's Best Rooms*, 189, 04. (Oct.1992): p107-140.

1382 Whiteley, Peter O., *Choosing A Kitchen Sink*, 190, 1. (Jan.1993): p86-89, 92, 93.

1383 Whiteley, Peter O., *Basic Or Fanciful Baths For Birds*, 191, 2. (Aug.1993): p74-77.

1384 Crosby, Bill, *Space Planning 101*, 191, 3. (Sep.1993): p64-67.

1385 Anusasananan, Linda Lau, *A Food Writer Tears Up Her Kitchen*, 192, 2. (Feb.1994): p94-96.

1386 Crosby, Bill, *Ultimate Grills*, 192, 5. (May.1994): p124-128.

1387 Whiteley, Peter O., *Build A Garden Pond*, 192, 6. (Jun.1994): p116-120.

1388 Whiteley, Peter O., *At Home With Tiles*, 193, 2. (Aug.1994): p88-90.

1389 Gregory, Daniel P., *Winning Designs For Western Living*, 193, 4. (Oct.1994): p98-117.

1390 *The Cowboy Comes Home*, 194, 05. (Nov.1995): p90-91.

1391 Crosby, Bill, *Kitchen Remodels For Every Budget*, 196, 2. (Feb.1996): p72-79.

1392 Crosby, Bill, *Big Stoves*, 197, 3. (Sep.1996): p90-92, 94.

1393 *1996 Interior Design Awards*, 197, 04. (Oct.1996): p82-105.

1394 *The New Gas Fireplaces*, 197, 05. (Nov.1996): p100-102, 104, 105.

1395 *9 To 5 At Home*, 198, 1. (Jan.1997): p58-63, 66.

1396 *Screen Stars*, 198, 1. (Jan.1997): p82-83.

1397 *Redone To Perfection*, 198, 2. (Feb.1997): p98-102, 103, 106, 107.

1398 *Patio Furniture Goes Uptown*, 198, 3. (Mar.1997): p104-106, 108.

1399 Whiteley, Peter O., *Small Bath Success Stories*, 198, 4. (Apr.1997): p116-1118, 120, 21.

1400 *Open-Air Living*, 198, 6. (Jun.1997): p68-74.

1401 *Decks For Daydreaming*, 198, 6. (Jun.1997): p98-103.

1402 Whiteley, Peter O., *The Sunset Chair*, 199, 1. (Jul.1997): p74-76.

1403 Whiteley, Peter O., *Small Pools For Tight Lots*, 199, 1. (Jul.1997): p92-96.

1404 *Art Of The Addition*, 199, 2. (Aug.1997): p106-120.

1405 Bertelsen, Ann, *Playing with Color*, 199, 3. (Sep.1997): p76-80.

1406 Whiteley, Peter O., *Breaking the Mold*, 199, 3. (Sep.1997): p96-98.

1407 Bertelsen, Ann, *Harvest Tabletops*, 199, 5. (Nov.1997): p109-111.

1408 Whiteley, Peter O. and Bertelsen, Ann, *Fireplace Face-Lifts*, 199, 5. (Nov.1997): p116-122.

1409 Whiteley, Peter O., *First-Class Art*, 200, 1. (Jan.1998): p74-75.

1.3 Vacation Homes

1410 Carhart, Arthur Hawthorne, *Your Cabin of Logs*, 52, 1. (Jan.1924): p64, 66-67.

1411 Philbrook, Zay, *My Homestead Cabin*, 52, 5. (May.1924): p68-69.

1412 Eddy, Frank F., *Paradise In The Hills*, 59, 3. (Sep.1927): p32-33, 56-58.

1413 Powell, Tod, *Saturday Noon To Sunday Night*, 62, 3. (Mar.1929): p31-32.

1414 Officer, Gwynn, *A Cottage Of Charm*, 63, 2. (Aug.1929): p30-31, 59.

1415 Bingham, Persis, *Our Cottage Under The Trees*, 64, 1. (Jan.1930): p29-30.

1416 Deming, Dorothy, *Our Cabin In The Hills*, 64, 4. (Apr.1930): p13-14.

1417 Byers, Charles Alma, *Two Vacation Cottages*, 64, (May.1930). p17: .

1418 Biddle, Eunice, *A Miscellany Of Cabin Ideas*, 64, 6. (Jun.1930): p16-17.

1419 Byers, Charles Alma, *Cabin Ideas*, 66, 1. (Jan.1931): p8-11.

1420 Davis, Ronald G., *Building A Cabin Fireplace*, 66, 3. (Mar.1931): p16.

1421 Getsinger, Floyd R., *How We Built A Cabin Of Stone*, 1931, 5. (May.1931): p10-11.

1422 *Sixteen Cabin Ideas*, 68, 2. (Feb.1932): p9-11.

1423 Evans, S. H., *Mountain Cabins*, 69, 1. (Jul.1932): p9-10.

1424 Gaylord, Florence, *A Studio Home in Carmel*, 69, 4. (Oct.1932): p24-25.

1. Building and Remodeling

1425 Salmi, Hazel, *Our Cabin Built A Piece At A Time*, 70, 2. (Feb.1933): p16-17.

1426 Ives, Charlotte D., *Our Mountain Home At Lake Arrowhead*, 70, 3. (Mar.1933): p16-17.

1427 Wileman, Edgar Harrison, *Furnishing The Cabin Or Cottage*, 70, 3. (Mar.1933): p15, 30.

1428 Chamberlain, Percy, *Lazy Days In A Vacation Cabin*, 71, 1. (Jul.1933): p16, 31.

1429 Shaw, Howard I., *If You Are Planning To Build A Beach House*, 72, 4. (Apr.1934): p12-13.

1430 Shaw, Howard I., *A Two-Story Beach House*, 72, 5. (May.1934): p20.

1431 Hewetson, Angelo, *The Country Place Must Be Charming*, 72, 6. (Jun.1934): p36-37.

1432 Evans, Sumner L., *When An Engineer Builds His Cabin*, 73, 2. (Aug.1934): p12-13, 40.

1433 *Light and Water for Cabin Homes*, 74, 1. (Jan.1935): p30-32.

1434 *Weekend Homes for Woods-Loving Westerners*, 74, 1. (Jan.1935): p7-9.

1435 Benninghoff, Cornelia, *We Built A Fireplace Into Our Cabin*, 76, 1. (Jan.1936): p16-17.

1436 *From Carriage House To Cottage*, 76, 5. (May.1936): p34-35.

1437 *Beach Houses*, 78, 5. (May.1937): p24-25.

1438 *A Bungalow That Became a Beach House*, 80, 6. (Jun.1938): p18-19.

1439 *How Much For A Mountain Cabin*, 80, 1. (Jul.1938): p16-17.

1440 *A Weekend Cottage Grows Up*, 84, 3. (Mar.1940): p46-47.

1441 *Beach Latitude*, 84, 5. (May.1940): p28-29.

1442 *Adding Comfort To Cabins*, 84, 5. (May.1940): p26-27.

1443 *I Want To Live In My Lath House*, 85, 4. (Oct.1940): p21.

1444 *Sea Cots*, 86, 4. (Apr.1941): p48.

1445 *Your Own*, 88, 3. (Mar.1942): p12-13.

1446 *Close-Ups*, 88, 3. (Mar.1942): p16-17.

1447 *Cabin Garden*, 88, 4. (Apr.1942): p34-35.

1448 *You Might Call It A House*, 96, 3. (Mar.1946): p22-23.

1449 *Summer-Home Gardens*, 96, 6. (Jun.1946): p80-82.

1450 *Idea Cabin*, 97, 1. (Jul.1946): p24-27.

1451 *Western Vacation Homes*, 98, 2. (Feb.1947): p14-19.

1452 *Stone Cabin*, 98, 4. (Mar.1947): p24-28.

1453 *Cabins Are For Fun*, 98, 4. (Apr.1947): p24-25.

1454 *Adobe Sea House*, 99, 01. (Jul.1947): p30-31.

1455 *Glass Walls in Mountain Cabin?*, 101, 1. (Jul.1948): p30-31.

1456 *The Woodlands Are The Walls Of This Cabin House*, 104, 6. (Jun.1950): p34-37.

1457 *Designs For Cabin Living*, 105, 1. (Jul.1950): p30-33.

1458 *Tips On Closing A Cabin*, 105, 2. (Aug.1950): p46-50.

1459 *With This Camp Cabin You Add-A-Part Each Year*, 106, 6. (Jun.1951): p36-39.

1460 *Camp And Cabin Ideas For "That Place In The Country"*, 108, 3. (Mar.1952). p34-39.

1461 *Beach Houses*, 109, 1. (Jul.1952): p48-51.

1462 *Country Living … One Way to Develop a Foothill Retreat*, 109, 4. (Oct.1952): p164-167.

1463 *How Five Western Families Each Built A Cabin*, 118, 6. (Jun.1957): p69-75.

1464 *This Cabin Is Built Where The Weather Is Whimsical*, 119, 2. (Aug.1957): p50-51.

1465 *With Its Unusual Folded Roof…The Feeling Of A Mountain Lookout*, 120, 5. (May.1958): p80-81.

1466 *They Use It Weekends…The Year Round*, 121, 1. (Jul.1958): p52-55.

1467 *The Pre-Cut Or Pre-Fab Cabin…Bargain Or Not?*, 121, 1. (Jul.1958): p76-82.

1468 *For Weekends…The Year Around*, 122, 6. (Jun.1959): p78-79.

1469 *Mountain Living…The Exciting Ski Cabins You See In Squaw Valley*, 124, 2. (Feb.1960): p70-77.

1470 *Here are Ideas to Study… If you Dream of a Beach House*, 124, 3. (Mar.1960): p118-122.

1471 *Three Beach Cabins*, 124, 6. (Jun.1960): p98-103.

1472 *This Spacious Family Cabin Straddles A Sierra Foothill Stream*, 125, 5. (Nov.1960): p112-113.

1473 *Cabin Built From A Wine Tank*, 128, 2. (Feb.1962): p72, 73.

1474 *Vacation Houses: A Glass-Walled Hideaway…High In The Trees*, 128, 4. (Apr.1962): p100-103.

1475 *Tepee Cabin*, 130, 3. (Mar.1963): p112-113.

1476 *Vacation Houses*, 132, 5. (May.1964): p106-115.

1477 *Mountain Living Winter And Summer*, 134, 2. (Feb.1965): p64-71.

1478 *Ways To Finance A Vacation Home*, 134, 6. (Jun.1965): p146-148, 150.

1479 *They Live At The Beach Both Summer And Winter*, 135, 2. (Aug.1965): p56-57.

1480 *Look At What $5,000 Bought*, 136, 6. (Jun.1966): p94-95.

1481 *It Turns Like A Giant Lazy Susan*, 137, 2. (Aug.1966): p86.

1482 *Weekend Retreat*, 137, 4. (Oct.1966): p106-108.

1483 *4 Mountain Houses*, 138, 2. (Feb.1967): p86-93.

1484 *The House Stands Free Of The Beach*, 138, 4. (Apr.1967): p106-108.

1485 *The Narrow Beach Lot*, 139, 1. (Jul.1967): p58-63.

1486 *Sierra Cabin Stands Tall*, 140, 1. (Jan.1968): p44-45.

1487 *Breaking The Rules…And Breaking Through*, 140, 4. (Apr.1968): p88-95

1488 *How Do You Get Yourself A Cabin?*, 140, 5. (May.1968): p155-164.

1489 *Little Utah Cabin Sleeps Seven…And It Cost Just $7,500*, 142, 1. (Jan.1969): p56-57.

1490 *A Giant Window In The Woods*, 142, 2. (Feb.1969): p80-81.

1491 *Mountain Living Has A Long History In The West; Here are Six Pages of Cabin Ideas and Answers*, 150, 2. (Feb.1973): p62-67.

1492 *They Built Their Compromise Cabin in 3 Years For $4,400*, 154, 4. (Apr.1975): p128-129.

1493 *The Way to Go in 1976? - Build Small With No Frills*, 156, 5. (May.1976): p92-95.

1494 *Ways Vacation House Owners are Guarding Against Ripoffs*, 157, 1. (Jul.1976): p72-73.

1495 *A Big Surprise Behind This 1908 Cottage*, 175, 2. (Aug.1985): p80-81.

1496 *Award-Winning Cabins*, 181, 3. (Sep.1988): p70-73.

1497 *They Asked A Lot Of This Ski Cabin*, 186, 1. (Jan.1991): p72-74.

1498 *Compact But Airy, It Functions Like A Two-room Cabin*, 186, 5. (May.1991): p134-136.

2. Civic and Cultural Affairs

May 1994 cover (photo: Steve Smith)

Civic & Cultural Affairs

As Sunset *has redefined itself from time to time, it has variously emphasized major issues of the day. In the teens and twenties, there was substantial coverage of general issues, such as Politics & Government, Military affairs, the emergence of a Pacific or global awareness, and the American role in the world. These weighty issues were downplayed after 1929. In the early years,* Sunset's *coverage included both pedagogical matters (listed under Education), and the Arts & Literature as practiced in the West. Emphasis was on major nearby institutions of higher education, Stanford University in particular, hence a grouping of articles related to Stanford–about the University, by its officials or by members of the "Pioneer Class" of 1895. Up to the late 1920s, the magazine contained short stories, serial stories, drawings, and poems, so the inclusion of articles on, say, theater, visual arts or the social and moral aspects of motion pictures would not have seemed out of place. The arts continued thereafter to appear, but mainly in the form of cultural tourism: museums, festivals, theater series, concert series, adult learning programs, exhibits, and the like as travel destinations and attractions. These are listed as a subcategory of Travel. A group of articles highlight a community's efforts at defining or improving itself or that address issues of Community growth, including what we might think of as quality of life issues. Note, many Travel articles also focus on a community as destination.*

2.1 Arts & Literature

1500   Shoup, Paul, *An Old Story In Crumbling Walls*, 4, 6. (Apr.1900): p244-245.

1501   Aiken, Charles S., *A Young Sculptor And His 'Victory'*, 8, 5. (Mar.1902): p226.

1502   Burgess, Gelett, *'I Wonder Why!'*, 10, 3. (Jan.1903): p237-238.

1503   Miller, Joaquin, *At Vespers in Tokio*, 10, 6. (Apr.1903): p471-478.

1504   London, Jack, *The Faith of Men*, 11, 2. (Jun.1903): p114-121.

1505   Higgins, S. E. A., *"Passing Of The Nations"*, 11, 6. (Oct.1903): p537-543.

1506   Porter, Bruce, *Arthur Putnam's Animal Sculpture*, 14, 1. (Nov.1904): p54-58.

1507   The Ancient Mariner (sic), *Pictures that Tell Stories*, 16, 1. (Nov.1905): p62-64.

1508   Miller, Joaquin, *That Night in Nicaragua*, 16, 6. (Apr.1906): p553-563.

1509   Cheney, Sheldon, *Some California Book-Plates*, 18, 4. (Feb.1907): p332-336.

1510   Patchell, William T., *Poetry And Life*, 19, 2. (Jun.1907): p153-157.

1511   Austin, Mary, *Some Literary Myths*, 20, 1. (Nov.1907): p36-39.

1512   Holme, Garnet, *The Little Clay Cart*, 20, 2. (Dec.1907): p168-171.

1513   London, Jack, *That Spot*, 20, 4. (Feb.1908): p371-376.

1514   Bashford, Herbert, *Ascendency Of The American Drama*, 20, 5. (Mar.1908): p432-443.

1515   George, Grace, *Jonahs And Mascots Of The Stage*, 20, 5. (Mar.1908): p485-486.

1516   Cheney, Sheldon, *Notable Western Etchers*, 21, 8. (Dec.1908): p737-744.

1517   McClung, Littell, *New Plays That Win*, 22, 1. (Jan.1909): p47-49.

1518   McClung, Littell, *Cupid The Scene Shifter*, 22, 2. (Feb.1909): p188-192.

1519   McClung, Littell, *Hope For American Drama*, 22, 3. (Mar.1909): p300-305.

1520   McClung, Littell, *Real Drama Hits The Stage*, 22, 4. (Apr.1909): p373-379.

1521   London, Jack, *Make Westing*, 22, 4. (Apr.1909): p357-.

1522   McClung, Littell, *Exit Emotionalism - Enter Charm*, 22, 5. (May.1909): p493-501.

1523   McClung, Littell, *Seeking Plots And Players*, 22, 6. (Jun.1909): p624-629.

1524   Seares, Mabel Urmy, *The Spirit Of California Art*, 23, 3. (Sep.1909): p264-266.

1525   London, Jack, *The Whale Tooth*, 24, 1. (Jan.1910): p49-.

1526   Lewis, Sinclair, *Polly*, 24, 1. (Jan.1910): p3-8.

1527   Renaud, Ralph E., *Antigone Under The Californian Sky: Margaret Anglin's Impressive Portrayal Of The Classic Heroine In The Greek Theatre At Berkeley*, 25, 3. (Sep.1910): p331-336.

1528   McClung, Littell, *The Dawn of American Opera*, 25, 4. (Oct.1910): p423-429.

1529   McClung, Littell, *Natoma–A Real American Opera*, 26, 4. (Apr.1911): p437-440.

1530   Wright, Willard Huntington, *The Mission Play*, 29, 1. (Jul.1912): p93-100.

1531   *The Bohemian Grove Plays: An American Bayreuth*, 29, 5. (Nov.1912): p555-562.

1532   Register 25365, *The Star And The Stripes: When Berhardt Played to a Prison House*, 30, 5. (May.1913): p569-571.

1533   Lighton, William R., *By Way Of Illustration*, 31, 6. (Dec.1913): p1202-1203.

1534   Steele, Rufus M., *In The Sun Spot*, 34, 4. (Apr.1915): p691-699.

1535   Freeman, Lewis R., *The Passion Play Of Hiva-Oa*, 34, 4. (Apr.1915): p725-731.

1536   Steele, Rufus M., *The New Rialto*, 34, 5. (May.1915): p899-908.

1537   Maude, Cyril, *Pepys Of The Movies*, 35, 4. (Oct.1915): p732-737.

1538   Tolerton, Hill, *Christmas Trees*, 35, 6. (Dec.1915): p1063-1069.

1539   Field, Charles K., *On The New Rialto*, 36, 2. (Feb.1916): p23-26.

1540   Field, Charles K., *New Lights On An Old Roman*, 36, 6. (Jun.1916): p40-42, 97.

1541   Field, Charles K., *A Japanese Idol On The American Screen*, 37, 1. (Jul.1916): p22-25, 72-73.

1542   Field, Charles K., *A Little Mother Of The Movies*, 37, 3. (Sep.1916): p30-33, 68-69.

1543   *Open-Air Theatres*, 37, 4. (Oct.1916): p28-31.

1544   Lane, Rose Wilder, *Twinkle, Twinkle, Little Stars!*, 40, 1. (Jan.1918): p38-41, 70.

1545   Lane, Rose Wilder, *Mars In The Movies*, 40, 2. (Feb.1918): p39-42.

1546   Us Folks On The Film, *Earle Snell*, 40, 3. (Mar.1918): p43-46.

1547   Hall, Wilbur, *Drama Out Of Doors*, 45, 4. (Oct.1920): p29-32, 64-65.

1548   Gilbert, George, *The Great Adventure: Excursions in Dreamland by the Author of the Shanland Stories*, 46, 4. (Apr.1921): p20.

2. Civic and Cultural Affairs

1549 White, Stewart Edward, *They'll Only Have Themselves To Blame*, 48, 1. (Jan.1922): p40-42.

1550 Merrick, L. F., *The Rebirth Of The Movies*, 48, 4. (Apr.1922): p15, 83-85.

1551 *Mirrors Of Hollywood*, 51, 3. (Sep.1923): p31, 75-76.

1552 Place, Estelle M., *Erudition Among The Oranges*, 51, 3. (Sep.1923): p52, 97.

1553 Garbett, Arthur S., *Why You Like Jazz*, 52, 3. (Mar.1924): p21-23, 62-64.

1554 Goldsmith, L. C., *Grinding Out History*, 55, 1. (Jul.1925): p32-33, 59.

1555 Peterson, H. C., *Filming A Real Western*, 55, 5. (Nov.1925): p37.

1556 Cook, C. Clyde, *The Mission Play*, 57, 3. (Sep.1926): p34-35, 95-96.

1557 Lincoln, E. C., *Tony*, 57, 5. (Nov.1926): p27, 56.

1558 Partridge, Pauline, *Big Plays In The Little theatre*, 57, 6. (Dec.1926): p30-31, 58-62.

1559 Brewer, William A., Jr., *Helen Of California*, 59, 1. (Jul.1927): p19, 75.

1560 Lowry, Bert, *In The Days Of Variety*, 59, 3. (Sep.1927): p28-31, 78-79.

1561 Jopp, Fred Gilman, *The Miracle Man Of The Screen*, 59, 6. (Dec.1927): p32-33, 54-56.

1562 Woehlke, Walter V., *The Money Drunk Movies*, 60, 1. (Jan.1928): p12-14, 67-69, 78-79.

1563 Woehlke, Walter V., *What's Wrong With The Movies?*, 60, 2. (Feb.1928): p25.

1564 Woehlke, Walter V., *Better Movies!*, 60, 3. (Mar.1928): p14-16, 65-68.

1565 *We Visit Applied Arts Guild*, 69, 6. (Dec.1932): p8-10.

1566 Holt, Madora, *Songs Of Sunset's Yesterdays*, 74, 4. (Apr.1935): p18-19, 35.

1567 Hall, Wilbur, *Two Collections of Old Glass*, 74, 6. (Jun.1935): p18, 61.

1568 *With Pen And Ink And Paintbrush New Zealand's Leading Artist Does A Book On The American West*, 145, 5. (Nov.1970): p90-93.

1569 *In San Francisco and the East Bay, Artists Open Their Studios for October Visits*, 171, 4. (Oct.1983): p44-45.

1570 Whiteley, Peter O., *Sculpture That Keeps In The Sheep*, 188, 1. (Jan.1992): p72-75.

1571 MacPherson, Jena, *Walls Of History*, 189, 1. (Jul.1992): p66-69.

2.2 Community

1572 J. H. S., *A Society Day In The California Winter Season*, 5, 4. (Aug.1900): p173.

1573 *Saint Claire Club Of San Jose*, 7, 2-3. (Jun.1901): p70.

1574 Braden, H. Robert, *The Triennial Convention - A Retrospect*, 8, 2. (Dec.1901): p90-96.

1575 Burdette, Robert J., Mrs., *California Women's Clubs And Their Work*, 8, 4. (Feb.1902): p174-178.

1576 Winslow, Isabel Bates, *A National Assembly Of Women*, 8, 6. (Apr.1902): p265-266.

1577 Bramhall, Frank J., *At Fair Oaks On The American*, 8, 6. (Apr.1902): p256-261.

1578 Wells, Harry L., *In Blossom Land: A Springtime Sketch of San Jose and Santa Clara County, California*, 9, 1. (May.1902): p45-60.

1579 Burgess, Gelett, *On The Edge Of The World*, 9, 4. (Aug.1902): p233-234.

1580 Burdette, Robert J., Mrs., *'Why?'*, 10, 1. (Nov.1902): p33-36.

1581 Murray, Elizabeth, *California's Women's Clubs*, 10, 4. (Feb.1903): p342-350.

1582 Griswold, Mary Edith, *In Social Trinity*, 16, 5. (Mar.1903): p441-445.

1583 Griswold, Mary Edith, *Burning $600,000 Worth Of Bonds: The True Story Of The Earning Of A Merry Christmas*, 12, 2. (Dec.1903): p96-105.

1584 Dunbar, J. O., *Phoenix, Born Of Water*, 13, 4. (Aug.1904): p365-370.

1585 Menefee, E. L., *The Story Of Visalia*, 13, 4. (Aug.1904): p338-348.

1586 Merrick, Frank L., *In The Great Northwest*, 15, 1. (May.1905): p79-84.

1587 Steele, Rufus M., *Making San Francisco Beautiful*, 15, 2. (Jun.1905): p116-127.

1588 Dyer, Lilly O. Reichling, *Daughters Of The West*, 15, 2. (Jun.1905): p138-141.

1589 *The Great Northwest's Centennial Lewis & Clark Exposition*, 15, 3. (Jul.1905): p231-265.

1590 Casper, K. R., *The Bullfrog Bonanza*, 15, 4. (Aug.1905): p317-326.

1591 Dame, John B., *California's Venice*, 16, 1. (Nov.1905): p31-36.

1592 Locke, Kate Greenleaf, *A Realized Ideas*, 16, 1. (Nov.1905): p36-38.

1593 Dole, Arthur Macdonald, *How Los Angeles Grows*, 16, 2. (Dec.1905): p176-188.

1594 Emerson, Edwin, Jr., *Handling A Crisis: How Affairs In San Francisco Were Controlled By Men Who Knew Just What To Do*, 17, 2-3. (1906): p23-35.

1595 Harriman, E. H., *San Francisco's Experience*, 17, 2-3. (1906): p36-41.

1596 Collingwood, G. C., *The Story Of Houston*, 16, 3. (Jan.1906): p242-255.

1597 Sheriden, E. M., *Around San Buenaventura*, 16, 3. (Jan.1906): p289-297.

1598 Donovan, Percy Vincent, *The Western Ideal*, 16, 4. (Feb.1906): p379-381.

1599 Whittaker, Robert, *Is California Irreligious*, 16, 4. (Feb.1906): p382-385.

1600 Dame, John B., *Under Pasadena's Palms*, 16, 4. (Feb.1906): p360-365.

1601 Burrows, A., *Social Life Among Western Miners*, 16, 5. (Mar.1906): p434-435.

1602 Murdock, Charles A., *Berries & Character; Being the Story of a Summer Outing of the San Francisco Boys' and Girls' Aid Society*, 16, 5. (Mar.1906): p475-480.

1603 Hawson, Henry, *Blossoming Of The Desert*, 16, 6. (Apr.1906): p570-580.

1604 Magee, William A. and others, *San Francisco's Future*, 17, 5. (Sep.1906): p237-243.

1605 Hedrick, Harry, *The Newest Manhattan*, 17, 5. (Sep.1906): p258-262.

1606 Moon, A. W., *Astoria's Odd Festival*, 18, 1. (Nov.1906): p66-69.

1607 Cheney, Warren, *Commercial Berkeley*, 18, 1. (Nov.1906): p70-79.

1608 Strong, Elizabeth Haight, *San Francisco's Upbuilding*, 18, 2. (Dec.1906): p115-118.

1609 Aiken, Charles Sedgwick, *San Francisco - One Year After*, 18, 5. (Apr.1907): p500-528.

1610 *How Things Were Righted: San Francisco's Merchants And Men Of Affairs Tell Their Own Stories Of Rehabilitation, Growth And Adjustment*, 18, 5. (Apr.1907): p529-543.

1611 Leavitt, Bradford, *What San Francisco Stands For Today*, 18, 5. (Apr.1907): p545-550.

1612 Eldredge, George Granville, *The True San Francisco*, 18, 5. (Apr.1907): p551-554.

1613 Smith, Bertha H., *A City Of Ten-Acre Lots: Something About The Orange Grove Prosperity Of Ontario, California*, 19, 1. (May.1907): p65-69.

1614 Steele, Rufus M., *The Spread Of San Francisco: The New City, Under The Impetus Of Its Rapid Rebuilding, Is Moving South, Filling The Entire Peninsula, Being Helped Tremendously In Suburban Extension By The Bay Shore Railway Cut-Off*, 19, 2. (Jun.1907): p109-138.

1615 Judah, H. R., Jr., *At Santa Cruz By The Sea*, 19, 2. (Jun.1907): p171-177.

1616 Clarke, Francis H., *Coos Bay's North Bend*, 19, 2. (Jun.1907): p180-182.

1617 Sullivan, Knute, *Planning An Ideal City*, 19, 2. (Jun.1907): p183-185.

1618 Smith, Bertha H., *The Making Of Los Angeles*, 19, 3. (Jul.1907): p237-254.

2. Civic and Cultural Affairs

1619 Steele, Rufus M., *The Spread Of San Francisco: The Story Of The Enchanted Garden Down The Peninsula, And The Developments Which Make It Possible As A Home Site For City Toilers*, 19, 5. (Sep.1907): p437-452.

1620 Robinson, A. Warren, *A Pocket Empire*, 19, 5. (Sep.1907): p468-475.

1621 White, Lynn Townsend, *Oceanside's Example: How Willing Workers Built The First Permanent Church In San Francisco After The Big Fire*, 19, 6. (Oct.1907): p580-583.

1622 Baker, Joseph E., *Oakland And Roundabout*, 19, 6. (Oct.1907): p539-554.

1623 MacDonald, Donald, *In Pajaro Valley*, 20, 1. (Nov.1907): p64-65.

1624 Leavitt, Bradford, *San Francisco As It Is*, 20, 3. (Jan.1908): p291-293.

1625 *Two Years After: Facts And Figures That Tell The Story Of The Making Of San Francisco Since April, 1906*, 20, 6. (Apr.1908): p547-562.

1626 Holman, Frederick V., *Where Rose Is Queen: How The City Of Portland, Oregon, Decks Itself In Royal Array - The Annual Blossom Festival*, 21, 2. (Jun.1908): p105-109.

1627 Dezendorf, Alfred, *In The Ojai: The Valley Of The Swallow's Nest; It's Charm And Its Traditions*, 21, 3. (Jul.1908): p240-246.

1628 Wells, A. J., *The Joys Of Albany*, 21, 3. (Jul.1908).

1629 Wells, A. J., *Roseburg And The Umpqua Valley*, 21, 4. (Aug.1908).

1630 *A Prize-Winning Display: Alameda County's Permanent Exhibit Of The Varied Wealth Of Hills And Valleys And Waterfront*, 21, 6. (Oct.1908): p573-574.

1631 Walcott, Earle Ashley, *The Return Of San Francisco*, 21, 7. (Nov.1908): p621-642.

1632 *A Lake In A California Garden*, 21, 8. (Dec.1908): p800.

1633 Rucker, Colby, *Fighting An Unseen Foe: The Truth About A City's Battle To Check Asiatic Pestilence*, 22, 2. (Feb.1909): p113-123.

1634 Stearn, Edwin, *Clubdom In Oakland, California: Organizations That Dominate The City's Social Life*, 22, 2. (Feb.1909): p215-216.

1635 Woodhead, William, *The Material City: Some Details Of The Rehabilitation Of San Francisco's Business Houses*, 22, 4. (Apr.1909): p421-435.

1636 Steele, Rufus M., *The City That Is: San Francisco Three Years After*, 22, 4. (Apr.1909): p326-339.

1637 *The Music Of The People: The Story Of A Public Service Rendered By A Chain Of Piano Stores*, 22, 5. (May.1909): p562-563.

1638 *Booming Blooming Roses: Timely Facts Concerning The Rose Festival Of Portland, Oregon To Be Held June 7-12*, 22, 5. (May.1909): p509-510.

1639 Darling, Esther, *The Derby Of The North: Alaska*, 22, 5. (May.1909): p488-492.

1640 Goldsmith, Paul, *Before-And-After Photographs: Pictures Of Oakland That Tell The Story Of A City's Growth*, 22, 5. (May.1909): p560-561.

1641 Goldsmith, Paul, *'I'm One. Are You?': The Unique Plan By Which The Oakland Chamber Of Commerce Recruited Its Enthusiastic Membership*, 22, 6. (Jun.1909): p674-675.

1642 Goldsmith, Paul, *The Elks' Western Round-Up*, 23, 1. (Jul.1909): p60-66.

1643 Goldsmith, Paul, *For The Sake Of Her Guests: Oakland, California, City Of Homes, Churches And Schools, Rises To The Occasion Of Hospitality*, 23, 1. (Jul.1909): p106-107.

1644 Wells, A. J., *Down The Peninsula*, 23, 1. (Jul.1909): p102-105.

1645 Von Wiegand, Karl Heinrich, *Mystics, Babies And Bloom: Point Loma's Raja Yoga, Where Mrs. Tingley's People Live In Sunshine, And Grow In Joy And Wisdom*, 23, 2. (Aug.1909): p115-126.

1646 Brun, Hanna Otis, *France To San Francisco*, 23, 2. (Aug.1909): p169-172.

1647 Bond, E. M., *The Cowmen's Carnival*, 23, 2. (Aug.1909): p173-176.

1648 Otis, Harrison Gray, *Los Angeles - A Sketch*, 24, 1. (Jan.1910): p12-48.

1649 Colburn, Frona Waite, *Vintage Day*, 24, 2. (Feb.1910): p206-210.

1650 Bennett, Mark, *A New Way To Clear Land For Homes: The Work Of The Pittsburg Syndicate In The Sacramento Valley*, 24, 3. (Mar.1910): p359-362.

1651 Magee, William A., *San Francisco Four Years After*, 24, 4. (Apr.1910): p453-461.

1652 Coolidge, Herbert, *The Health Of The City*, 24, 4. (Apr.1910): p462-465.

1653 Lincoln, James Otis, Mrs. , *At St. Dorothy's Rest*, 24, 6. (Jun.1910): p689-692.

1654 Woodhead, William, *Los Angeles: The Most Rapidly Growing City In America*, 26, 1. (Jan.1911): p124.

1655 Griswold, F. H., *Home-Builders Displace Bonanza Farmers*, 26, 5. (May.1911): p578-579.

1656 Smith, Bertha H., *Beef A La Mode Californienne*, 27, 3. (Sep.1911): p282-286.

1657 Moore, Charles C., *San Francisco Knows How!*, 28, 1. (Jan.1912): p3-15.

1658 Irvine, Leigh H., *Alameda, The City Of Homes*, 28, 1. (Jan.1912): p113-116.

1659 Bennett, Addison, *Where The Home-Builder Can Find His Ideal*, 28, 1. (Jan.1912): p128.

1660 Walker, David H.,Jr., *Ontario, The City That Charms*, 28, 2. (Feb.1912): p253-254.

1661 Moore, Charles C., *San Francisco And The Exposition*, 28, 2. (Feb.1912): p196-199.

1662 Fisher, C. E., *Corvallis–A Mighty Good Place To Live*, 28, 5. (May.1912): p647.

1663 von Vieregg, G., *Santa Monica: The City Of Many Sides*, 28, 6. (Jun.1912): p773-774.

1664 Woehlke, Walter V., *Potlatch Town*, 29, 1. (Jul.1912): p5-16.

1665 Mattison, R. H., *Seattle The Indomitable*, 29, 1. (Jul.1912): p101-104.

1666 Ellis, Garton T., *Los Gatos: Gem City Of The Foothills*, 29, 2. (Aug.1912): p219-220.

1667 Hazenclever, Henry J., *Napa County*, 29, 2. (Aug.1912): p223-224.

1668 Fisher, C. E., *Why Oregonians Trek To Newport*, 29, 2. (Aug.1912): p227.

1669 Teck, Frank Carleton, *The Ultimate In Victoria*, 29, 2. (Aug.1912): p228-230.

1670 Wells, A. J., *An Oasis In The Desert*, 29, 3. (Sep.1912): p351-352.

1671 Laut, Agnes C., *Why Is Houston?*, 29, 5. (Nov.1912): p483-492.

1672 Lee, Rudolph, *Tucson, Arizona*, 29, 5. (Nov.1912): p598-599.

1673 Brotherton, R. H., *Philanthropy For Profit*, 29, 6. (Dec.1912): p664-666.

1674 Fawcett, Waldon, *Uncle Sam, Exhibitor*, 29, 6. (Dec.1912): p706-714.

1675 Young, John P., *The Metropolis*, 30, 1. (Jan.1913): p5-14.

1676 Drury, Wells, *Berkeley And The Calendar*, 30, 1. (Jan.1913): p66-72.

1677 Laut, Agnes C., *San Diego; First Port of Call*, 30, 2. (Feb.1913): p111-120.

1678 Drummond-Norie, W., *Los Gatos: A California Winter Paradise*, 30, 3. (Mar.1913): p74.

1679 Minton, Henry Collin, *Christian Citizenship*, 30, 6. (Jun.1913): p805-809.

1680 Clark, Walter E., *Alaska Makes Laws*, 31, 2. (Aug.1913): p322-327.

1681 Holt, Emerson, *Letting Down The Bars Into Tillamook County, Oregon*, 31, 3. (Sep.1913): p570-574.

1682 Hunt, George W. P., *The Making Of A State*, 31, 4. (Oct.1913): p681-683.

2. Civic and Cultural Affairs

1683 Clark, Walter E. and Lane, Franklin K., *Yesterday And Tomorrow In Alaska*, 32, 2. (Feb.1914): p299-315, 414.

1684 Steele, Rufus M., *Through The Golden Gate Of Romance*, 32, 3. (Mar.1914): p531-541.

1685 Lynch, Robert Newton, *Immigration*, 32, 3. (Mar.1914): p593-600.

1686 Woehlke, Walter V., *Staging The Big Show*, 33, 2. (Aug.1914): p336-346.

1687 Steele, Rufus M., *The Fourth Cry Of Eureka*, 33, 4. (Oct.1914): p714-726.

1688 Woehlke, Walter V., *Nueva Espana By The Silver Gate*, 33, 6. (Dec.1914): p1119-1132.

1689 Holt, Emerson, *Building a City on Health*, 34, 2. (Feb.1915): p356, 358.

1690 Woehlke, Walter V., *The Land Of Sunny Homes*, 34, 3. (Mar.1915): p463-472.

1691 Woehlke, Walter V., *Oregon And Its People*, 34, 4. (Apr.1915): p710-718.

1692 Spencer, Henry McDonald, *Democracy De Luxe*, 34, 5. (May.1915): p935-946.

1693 Woehlke, Walter V., *The Land Of Painted Hills*, 34, 6. (Jun.1915): p1099-1109.

1694 Dosch, Arno, *Beating Back To The City Hall*, 35, 4. (Oct.1915): p675-680.

1695 Adams, Edward F., *Australia, The Social Melting Pot*, 35, 6. (Dec.1915): p1071-1082.

1696 Morris, W. L., *The Town That Died A-Bornin'*, 36, 4. (Apr.1916): p41-42.

1697 Knowlton, Philip A., *The American Hyperboreans*, 37, 1. (Jul.1916): p33-35, 94-97.

1698 Barker, Ruth Laughlin, *Keeping The Oldest Capital Old*, 37, 3. (Sep.1916): p34-35.

1699 Vincent, Fred W., *Why The Country Church Is Dying*, 37, 4. (Oct.1916): p18.

1700 Fullerton, Aubrey, *Doukhobors And Their Utopia*, 38, 2. (Feb.1917): p31-32,66-68.

1701 Willard, Victor, *Go And Sin No More*, 38, 3. (Mar.1917): p11-12.

1702 Zerr, Gertrude A., *The People Who Stayed*, 38, 4. (Apr.1917): p22-24, 48-50.

1703 Kellogg, Charlotte, *California And France*, 40, 2. (Feb.1918): p29, 60.

1704 Driscoll, Marjorie Charles, *Making An Oasis*, 41, 1. (Jul.1918): p43.

1705 Hamby, William H., *To Rent Or To Buy?*, 42, 3. (Mar.1919): p20-21, 84-85.

1706 McMahon, Thomas J., *A Real Treasure Island*, 43, 3. (Sep.1919): p37-39.

1707 Stratton, George Frederic, *Alfalfa Widows*, 44, 2. (Feb.1920): p32-34, 74-78.

1708 Connor, Torrey, *The Boy*, 45, 5. (Nov.1920): p56-58.

1709 Morse, Franklin B., *Sufferin' Cats*, 46, 1. (Jan.1921): p77-79.

1710 Vincent, Fred W., *Running a Town Like a Home*, 46, 1. (Jan.1921): p36-37, 60.

1711 Gatlin, Lillian, *Adopting a Baby*, 46, 2. (Feb.1921): p83-86.

1712 Bechdolt, Frederick R., *Here's To Crime!*, 46, 3. (Mar.1921): p40-41, 90-94.

1713 Bechdolt, Frederick R., *What Are Your Children Doing?*, 46, 5. (May.1921): p45-47, 102.

1714 Bentinck, Richard, *The Slaughter Of The Innocents*, 47, 1. (Jul.1921): p36-38, 74-76.

1715 Bentinck, Richard, *Whose Is The Guilt?*, 47, 2. (Aug.1921): p36-38, 69.

1716 Woehlke, Walter V., *Is The Seattle Spirit Dead?*, 47, 3. (Sep.1921): p25-27, 88-90.

1717 Woehlke, Walter V., *The City Of Serene Indifference*, 47, 5. (Nov.1921): p24-28, 81-82.

1718 Considine, John L., *The Vigilantes Of The Comstock*, 48, 6. (Jun.1922): p16.

1719 Harding, Mabel T., *Religion With A Real Punch*, 50, 2. (Feb.1923): p15, 54.

1720 Collier, Lucy Wood, *Domestic Miracles*, 50, 4. (Apr.1923): p15-17, 86-87.

1721 Lucas, William Palmer, *How To Make The Child Grow*, 50, 5. (May.1923): p29, 81-82.

1722 Irwin, Will, *What Is The Western Spirit?*, 50, 6. (Jun.1923): p24-25.

1723 Thompson, W. F., *Strong Words From Alaska*, 51, 3. (Sep.1923): p15, 91-92.

1724 Considine, John L., *Justice In Early Nevada*, 51, 5. (Nov.1923): p23, 60.

1725 Woehlke, Walter V., *How Long. Los Angeles?*, 52, 4. (Apr.1924): p8-11, 100-102.

1726 Wooster, Ernest S., *They Shared Equally*, 53, 1. (Jul.1924): p21-2, , 80-82.

1727 Wooster, Ernest S., *Bread And Hyacinths*, 53, 2. (Aug.1924): p21-23, 59-60.

1728 Wooster, Ernest S., *The Colonists Win Through*, 53, 3. (Sep.1924): p30-33, 75-80.

1729 Willard, Victor, *The Rejuventation Of Hansen*, 53, 5. (Nov.1924): p28-29, 56-58.

1730 Amid, John, *Prospecting For Home*, 54, 4. (Apr.1925): p49-50, 60-62.

1731 Willard, Victor, *Gold And Sunshine*, 3, 32-35/91-92. (Sep.1925): .

1732 Partridge, Pauline, *This Club Teaches Tapestry Weaving And Kindness Too*, 55, 4. (Oct.1925): p35, 58-60.

1733 Loken, H. J., *A Melting Pot For Creeds*, 55, 6. (Dec.1925): p29.

1734 Johnson, Gladys E., *Divorce And The American Home*, 56, 2. (Feb.1926): p34-35, 86-90.

1735 Vollmer, August, *We Can Prevent Juvenile Crime!*, 56, 3. (Mar.1926): p32-33, 86-88.

1736 Downey, June E., *Is Modern Youth Going To The Devil?*, 56, 3. (Mar.1926): p34.

1737 Phillips, D. E., *The Jazz Age*, 56, 3. (Mar.1926): p35, 93-94.

1738 Partridge, Pauline, *The Home of the Fairies*, 56, 4. (Apr.1926): p38-39, 79.

1739 Conklin, Edmund S., *Youth Will Come Through*, 56, 4. (Apr.1926): p16-18, 83-84.

1740 Taylor, Frank J., *Palo Alto*, 56, 6. (Jun.1926): p32-33, 73.

1741 Franklin, T. J., *The Personality That Is Santa Barbara's*, 57, 1. (Jul.1926): p42-43.

1742 Hough, Donald, *Boosting For Jackson*, 57, 1. (Jul.1926): p43, 66.

1743 Gordon, James L., *I Am Quitting My Church–To Preach!*, 57, 6. (Dec.1926): p12-13, 85-89.

1744 Henderson, George C., *Light-Fingered*, 58, 1. (Jan.1927): p14-15, 69, 76-77.

1745 McFarland, Bates, *The Knots In The Purse-Strings*, 58, 2. (Feb.1927): p24-25, 78-79.

1746 Henderson, George C., *Caught With The Goods*, 58, 3. (Mar.1927): p40-41, 68-69.

1747 Hamby, William H., *No Red Lanterns For My Boy!*, 58, 4. (Apr.1927): p12-14, 98-99.

1748 Woehlke, Walter V., *Hurrah For Crime!*, 58, 4. (Apr.1927): p28 29, 62-64.

1749 McMurray, Orrin K., *Nip Crime In The Bud*, 59, 1. (Jul.1927): p12-15.

1750 Lane, D. R., *Fire Fighting With Tractors*, 59, 4. (Oct.1927): p27, 60.

1751 Leinard, A., *Woman And A Building*, 60, 1. (Jan.1928): p39, 60-61.

1752 Coonradt, Harry W., *Success In Sululand*, 60, 2. (Feb.1928): p38-39, 78-79.

1753 Henderson, George C., *The House Dectective Talks*, 60, 5. (May.1928): p30-32, 64-66.

1754 Newman, Louis I., *These "Wild" Youngsters*, 60, 6. (Jun.1928): p9-11, 71.

1755 Gould, O. C., *Robbing The Western Home-Owner*, 61, 4. (Oct.1928): p9-11, 70-71, 83.

1756 Schumann-Heink, Ernestine, *Why I Live In California*, 61, 4. (Oct.1928): p20-21, 73.

1757 Block, Eugene B., *Cupid's Battle Cry Of Freedom*, 61, 5. (Nov.1928): p24-26.

2. Civic and Cultural Affairs

1758 Kemper, Lucrecia, *There Is A Tide*, 61, 6. (Dec.1928): p16-17, 46-48.

1759 Schultz, Gladys Denny, *Getting Rid of the Glums*, 62, 2. (Feb.1929): p20, 45, 59.

1760 Shultz, Gladys Denny, *What is Your Mental Health Score?*, 62, 3. (Mar.1929): p39-40.

1761 Shultz, Gladys Denny, *Mental Health Problems in the Business World*, 62, 4. (Apr.1929): p38, 44.

1762 Shultz, Gladys Denny, *Mental Health Like Charity Begins at Home*, 62, 5. (May.1929): p33, 54.

1763 Shultz, Gladys Denny, *Setting Baby Feet on the Road to Mental Health*, 62, 6. (Jun.1929): p55-56.

1764 Shultz, Gladys Denny, *Mental Health Through the Years of Childhood*, 63, 1. (Jul.1929): p50, 53.

1765 Goodrich, Mary, *City Of The Magic Carpets*, 63, 2. (Aug.1929): p14-16, 63.

1766 Dockery, E. J., *Why The Train Stops Twenty Minutes At Boise, Idaho*, 63, 2. (Aug.1929): p22-23.

1767 Rowntree, Lester, *Homes In The Highlands*, 64, 5. (May.1930): p12-13.

1768 Berg, O. R., *Lighthouse Keeping is not Light Housekeeping*, 66, 3. (Mar.1931): p17-18.

1769 MacGibbon, Elizabeth Gregg, *A Sunshine Farm*, 67, 5. (Nov.1931): p9-11.

1770 Scheinert, Carleton A., *What Every Homeowner Should Know About Homestead Laws*, 75, 6. (Dec.1935): p33-35.

1771 *What's New In Western Living*, 77, 1. (Jul.1936): p15-19.

1772 *What's New In Western Living*, 79, 2. (Aug.1937): p17-19.

1773 *What's New In Western Living*, 79, 5. (Nov.1937): p15-17.

1774 *What's New In Western Living*, 80, 3. (Mar.1938): p15-17.

1775 *What's New In Western Living*, 81, 3. (Sep.1938): p11-13.

1776 *The ABC's Of Open Planning*, 85, 1. (Jul.1940): p12-16.

1777 *Eugene*, 86, 2. (Feb.1941): p22-23, 41.

1778 *Country Dreams*, 87, 3. (Sep.1941): p9.

1779 *For The Duration*, 89, 3. (Sep.1942): p8.

1780 *Victory Ideas*, 89, 3. (Sep.1942): p28.

1781 *Neighborhood Project*, 92, 6. (Jun.1944): p34-35.

1782 *Neighborhood Project*, 93, 1. (Jul.1944): p34-37.

1783 *Living Memorials*, 94, 4. (Apr.1945): p8.

1784 *Home Owners' Associations*, 114, 3. (Mar.1955): p99-100, 102, 104-105.

1785 *It's A Neighborhood Street Barbecue*, 120, 6. (Jun.1958): p68-70.

1786 *New Trees To Screen A Freeway*, 121, 4. (Oct.1958): p94, 96.

1787 *A California City Honors its Trees*, 124, 1. (Jan.1960): p116.

1788 *Gardening...As Therapy*, 125, 1. (Jul.1960): p96-98.

1789 *How To Look Into The Future*, 125, 3. (Sep.1960): p78-80.

1790 *"Green-Up Day" in Nichols Canyon... Homw Owners Plant to a Plan*, 126, 2. (Feb.1961): p84, 85.

1791 *Let Us Have Trees*, 127, 3. (Sep.1961): p50-57.

1792 *They Landscaped A Neglected Street*, 131, 3. (Sep.1963): p177, 179, 181.

1793 *Up In Flames On Twelfth Night*, 134, 1. (Jan.1965): p75.

1794 *How Mercer Island Got Its Kids' Forest Wonderland*, 134, 3. (Mar.1965): p96-99.

1795 *How San Mateo Got Its New Japanese Garden*, 137, 6. (Dec.1966): p178-179.

1796 *Two Newport Beach Neighbors Decide To Coordinate Their Front Landscaping*, 138, 5. (May.1967): p100-101.

1797 *The Mall Idea*, 139, 3. (Sep.1967): p70-75.

1798 *Where Are These People...And What Are They Doing?*, 141, 5. (Nov.1968): p88-93.

1799 *What To Do About Roadside Mess; Let Children Clean up After Parents*, 142, 5. (May.1969): p104-105.

1800 *Los Gatos Makes A Lively Comeback*, 143, 3. (Sep.1969): p36-40.

1801 *Their Fathers Built This Obstacle Course*, 143, 3. (Sep.1969): p76-77.

1802 *A Fresh Look At Yesterday's And Today's San Francisco*, 143, 4. (Oct.1969): p114-116.

1803 *Poles Down, Wires All Underground*, 144, 4. (Apr.1970): p124-126.

1804 *Students In San Jose Build A Park In A Month*, 145, 4. (Oct.1970): p86-87.

1805 *90 Serious People Armed With Shovels Plant At Almost 500 Trees-Per-Hour*, 146, 3. (Mar.1971): p138-139.

1806 *With Useful Land But Little Money, With Energy And 14 Weekend Days*, 147, 3. (Sep.1971): p68-69.

1807 *Mill Town Into Art Colony...Mendocino In The Seventies*, 148, 5. (May.1972): p106-109.

1808 *Seattle's Operation Triangle Turns Corner Islands Into Pocket Parks*, 149, 5. (Nov.1972): p138-139.

1809 *Changing San Francisco*, 150, 3. (Mar.1973): p74-83.

1810 *Sonoma Celebrates Its 150th Birthday This Year; Events Go May 27 to September 30*, 150, 6. (Jun.1973): p30-31.

1811 *If You Look In The Right Places, Downtown Palo Alto Can Surprise You*, 151, 5. (Nov.1973): p50-51.

1812 *How Does San Francisco Look To A City Planner? Photographs Now at De Young Show You*, 153, 5. (Nov.1974): p22-23.

1813 *April 19 Is Picnic Day At Davis*, 154, 4. (Apr.1975): p50-51.

1814 *The Community Garden Idea Keeps Picking Up Speed... Is Now the Time to Plan Yours?*, 155, 5. (Nov.1975): p88-91.

1815 *Old-Time Engines, Old-Time Fun - Gold Country Fair*, 157, 2. (Aug.1976): p20D.

1816 *The Got Together for a Day Of Serious Scarecrow Making*, 157, 2. (Aug.1976): p114-115.

1817 *They Parade And Perform Just For Fun.. Theirs Every Bit as Much as Yours*, 160, 1. (Jan.1978): p60-61.

1818 *$4,000 Pool Cost Is Now "Next To Nothing." Volunteer Action in San Jose in the Winter Pre-Season*, 166, 1. (Jan.1981): p60-61.

1819 *The Recycle Hassle; Things Are Looking Better*, 166, 2. (Feb.1981): p78-81.

1820 *Proposition 13 Keeps Bringing Surprises. This Summer Camp in Los Gatos is Run By Parents*, 166, 6. (Jun.1981): p92-93.

1821 *California Parks Need You. These Volunteers Show How to Pitch In*, 167, 1. (Jul.1981): p32-33.

1822 *Blisters And Boulders, Satisfaction And Achievement*, 167, 2. (Aug.1981): p62-63.

1823 *Four Families Get Together*, 167, 3. (Sep.1981): p174-175.

1824 *Gifts Of Time And Talent*, 177, 6. (Dec.1986): p210-212.

1825 *Letter From Sunset: Rebuilding After The Earthquake*, 185, 04. (Oct.1990): p260.

1826 Whiteley, Peter O., *In Five Days They Built Rainbow City*, 188, 1. (Jan.1992): p68-71.

1827 Crosby, Bill, *The Game That Won the West*, 189, 3. (Sep.1992): p85-87.

1828 Swezey, Lauren Bonar, *Sharing The Harvest*, 190, 3. (Mar.1993): p112-113.

1829 Crosby, Bill, *Rebuilding Los Angeles...One House At A Time*, 190, 4. (Apr.1993): p124-125.

1830 *Santa Cruz Gets Its Downtown Back*, 194, 04. (Oct.1995): p30-33.

2.3 Education

1831 Hoitt, Ira G., *Education In California*, 3, 1. (May.1899): p3-10.

2. Civic and Cultural Affairs

1832 Fitch, George Hamlin, *Mount Tamalpais Academy: A West Point For Boys*, 9, 3. (Jul.1902): p200-207.

1833 Wheeler, Benjamin Ide, *Outlook Of The University*, 9, 6. (Oct.1902): p358-364.

1834 Henderson, Victor, *The University Of California*, 9, 6. (Oct.1902): p364-372.

1835 O'Brien, Victor, *School Extension As Begun In San Francisco*, 10, 1. (Nov.1902): p76-78.

1836 Sephens, H. Morse, *University Extension In California And Elsewhere*, 10, 5. (Mar.1903): p439-446.

1837 Anderson, Leroy, *What Modern Farming Means: Should The California Polytechnic School Of San Luis Obispo Teach Agriculture?*, 10, 5. (Mar.1903): p456-458.

1838 Reid, Whitelaw, *Journalism As A Career*, 11, 4. (Aug.1903): p360-370.

1839 Donovan, Ellen, *Boy Farmers Of Napa*, 12, 1. (Nov.1903): p56-59.

1840 Aiken, Charles S., *The University Of Arizona*, 12, 1. (Nov.1903): p37.

1841 Landfield, Jerome B., *The Summer School At Berkeley*, 13, 1. (May.1904): p35-38.

1842 Lichtenstein, Joy, *San Francisco's Public Library*, 13, 2. (Jun.1904): p163-170.

1843 Overstreet, H. A., *Grown Folks At School: Interesting And Significant Results Of The Recent Summer Session, University Of California*, 14, 1. (Nov.1904): p14-22.

1844 Cheney, May L., *Schools Of California, First Paper*, 14, 2. (Dec.1904): p135-137.

1845 Cheney, May L., *California High Schools*, 14, 5. (Mar.1905): p532-535.

1846 Greene, Charles S., *The Public Library Outlook In California*, 15, 2. (Jun.1905): p173-176.

1847 Crittenden, William Clark, *A Rhodes Man at Oxford*, 15, 2. (Jun.1905): p142-148.

1848 Cheney, May L., *The University Summer Session*, 15, 3. (Jul.1905): p291-294.

1849 Burgess, Gelett, *Feminine Modernity*, 15, 6. (Oct.1905): p580-581.

1850 Williams, John A., *Treasures Of The Bancroft Library*, 16, 2. (Dec.1905): p145-157.

1851 Furlong, Robert, *A Notable Educational Exhibit*, 16, 3. (Jan.1906): p271-276.

1852 Hughes, Edward, *Farming In The Schools*, 16, 6. (Apr.1906): p589-591.

1853 Watson, William R., *Books That Go Traveling: How California's State Library Reaches Every County In The Great State*, 17, 6. (Oct.1906): p363-367.

1854 Taylor, Oscar N., *Trying Out Rugby*, 18, 1. (Nov.1906): p3-7.

1855 Brown, Elmer Ellsworth, *Uncle Sam As Schoolmaster*, 18, 3. (Jan.1907): p219-220.

1856 Cheney, May L., *'Common Schools For Common People' - A Protest*, 18, 5. (Mar.1907): p453-459.

1857 Cumming, Joseph M., *Theory Made Practice: The Story Of The Undertaking And Development Of The Mechanics' Institute Of San Francisco*, 19, 1. (May.1907): p43-50.

1858 Kenyon, Walter J., *The School Excursion: A Modern Movement That Must Prove A Telling Factor In Education*, 19, 1. (May.1907): p92-94.

1859 Shepard, Irwin, *The Teachers' Pilgrimage: Fiftieth Anniversary Convention Of The National Educational Association To Be Held At Los Angeles*, 19, 3. (Jul.1907): p273-279.

1860 Crittenden, William C., *The Invasion Of Oxford*, 19, 5. (Sep.1907): p406-413.

1861 Graupner, Elise W., *The Collegiate Alumnae And Their Work*, 21, 6. (Oct.1908): p515-517.

1862 Cheney, Warren, *How The University Helps*, 22, 3. (Mar.1909): p283-296.

1863 Jerome, Lucy Baker, *On The Army Farm: Where Fresh Air And Outdoor Work, Under The Inspiration Of Self-Sacrifice, Are Preparing Little Waifs Of The City Streets For Healthy, Useful Citizenship*, 23, 1. (Jul.1909): p46-51.

1864 Jones, William Carey, *Berkeley's Golden Jubilee: Fiftieth Anniversary Of The Beginnings Of The University Of California*, 24, 5. (May.1910): p538-542.

1865 Pritchett, Henry S., *The Spirit Of State Universities*, 24, 5. (May.1910): p543-552.

1866 Peixotto, Sidney S., *Making The All-Round Boy: The Story Of The Columbia Park Boys' Club*, 25, 1. (Jul.1910): p99-103.

1867 Perrin, Arch, *John And Jonathan At Oxford: How American Students Fail To Fulfil Cecil Rhodes' Dream Of A Broader Scholarship*, 25, 4. (Oct.1910): p387-401.

1868 Walker, John Brisben, *The 1915 Exposition And Education*, 28, 6. (Jun.1912): p751-758.

1869 Hume, Sam, *The Use And Abuse Of The Greek Theater*, 29, 2. (Aug.1912): p199-206.

1870 Dana, Marshall N., *Growing Things*, 30, 3. (Mar.1913): p281-285.

1871 Clarke, Warren T., *Sending College To The Farmer*, 30, 4. (Apr.1913): p383-389.

1872 Steele, Rufus M., *The University And Diversity Of Nevada*, 32, 5. (May.1914): p995-1008.

1873 Hailmann, W. N., *Is Montessori The Educational Columbus?*, 34, 6. (Jun.1915): p1110-1115.

1874 Knowles, Thomas C., *College Goes To The People*, 39, 4. (Oct.1917): p44-45.

1875 Thomason, Caroline Wasson, *A New Slant To Home Economics*, 41, 4. (Oct.1918): p43.

1876 Fitzgerald, Harold J., *The Ph.D. And The Burglar*, 43, 3. (Sep.1919): p40-43.

1877 Eddy, Elford, *The Boy Problem*, 45, 1. (Jul.1920): p40-42, 64.

1878 Hogg, Mildred, *Most Assuredly Yes!*, 49, 2. (Aug.1922): p11, 74-75.

1879 Houghton, Harriet, *The Hare And The Tortoise*, 49, 3. (Sep.1922): p42, 59.

1880 Pattee, George K., Mrs., *They Meet The Test*, 49, 4. (Oct.1922): p20-21.

1881 Rutherford, Jane, *The Parental Mind*, 50, 2. (Feb.1923): p48-49, 66-68.

1882 Collier, Lucy Wood, *The Teacher And Child Health*, 50, 5. (May.1923): p28, 54-56.

1883 Read, Edith L., *Are Parents Failures?*, 51, 1. (Jul.1923): p30-31, 77.

1884 Collier, Lucy Wood, *The Child, Its Bed And The School*, 51, 1. (Jul.1923): p33, 56-58.

1885 Stork, Victor E., *Clean Inside And Out*, 51, 5. (Nov.1923): p28-29.

1886 Collier, Lucy Wood, *Cleanliness As A Game*, 51, 5. (Nov.1923): p29, 62.

1887 *Teacher Versus Mother*, 52, 1. (Jan.1924): p31-32.

1888 Millberry, Guy S., *The Value Of Sound Teeth*, 52, 1. (Jan.1924): p38-39, 58-60.

1889 Collier, Lucy Wood, *Teaching Dental Hygiene In School*, 52, 1. (Jan.1924): p39.

1890 Bryan, Edith S., *Have You A School Nurse In Your City?*, 52, 2. (Feb.1924): p50-51.

1891 Collier, Lucy Wood, *The Growing Importance Of The Nurse*, 52, 2. (Feb.1924): p51, 76.

1892 Preston, Mary I., *Putting Pep Into The Schools*, 52, 3. (Mar.1924): p32-33, 62.

1893 Rowland, Leon, *Dugouts And Dormitories*, 52, 4. (Apr.1924): p21-22, 60-62.

1894 Morse, Franklin B., *Pets*, 52, 4. (Apr.1924): p35.

1895 Huntington, Thomas W., *How To Guard Against Cancer*, 54, 1. (Jan.1925): p42-43.

1896 Henderson, George C., *Learning Democracy In School*, 54, 2. (Feb.1925): p14-16, 81-82.

2. Civic and Cultural Affairs

1897 A Parent, *Are We Cheating Our Children?*, 57, 5. (Nov.1926): p12-13, 64-65.

1898 Leebrick, K. C., *Educating Hawaii*, 58, 1. (Jan.1927): p16-17, 64-65.

1899 Block, Eugene B., *The School, The Boy And The Job*, 58, 1. (Jan.1927): p30-31, 54-56.

1900 Marchand, Leslie A., *The Farthest North College*, 58, 2. (Feb.1927): p17, 65.

1901 Reinhardt, Aurelia Henry, *Why Is The Junior College?*, 59, 4. (Oct.1927): p12-13, 77.

1902 Savage, George W., *A New Note In American Education*, 59, 5. (Nov.1927): p16-17, 54-56.

1903 Davis, Marguerite Norris, *They Learn About Babies From Her*, 59, 5. (Nov.1927): p38-39, 56-58.

1904 Thompson, Avery W., *A Talking Tour*, 60, 1. (Jan.1928): p15, 54.

1905 Marchand, Leslie A., *Caribou at College*, 60, 2. (Feb.1928): p21, 56.

1906 Straton, John Roach and Shipley, Maynard, *What About Evolution?*, 60, 5. (May.1928): p12-15, 68, 81-83, 86-89.

1907 Terman, Lewis M. and Small, Sidney Herschel, *Testing For The "Crime Germ"*, 60, 5. (May.1928): p24-25, 54-56.

1908 Reynolds, Keld J., *A New Purpose In Education*, 62, 1. (Jan.1929): p18-19, 53-54.

1909 Hoskins, Joy, *When The Doctor Can't Come*, 75, 1. (Jul.1935): p14, 43.

1910 *What's New In Western Living*, 77, 4. (Oct.1936): p13-15.

1911 *Fire Safety in the Country*, 113, 4. (Oct.1954): p91-92, 94.

1912 *These Children Are Learning Their Land*, 131, 3. (Sep.1963): p94, 97.

1913 *Walk-Yourself Tour Of Berkeley's Changing Campus*, 139, 4. (Oct.1967): p52.

1914 *At Santa Cruz These College Students Go Out For Gardening*, 142, 3. (Mar.1969): p96-99.

1915 *College By College, A Public University In Oxford Style Is Evolving In Santa Cruz*, 149, 4. (Sep.1972): p60-63.

1916 *The Gift Of Time*, 155, 6. (Dec.1975): p62-63.

1917 *Creative Anachronism? Where To Go And Watch*, 157, 4. (Oct.1976): p62-63.

1918 *You Can Go Behind the Scenes... Fantastic Science Research World in the San Francisco Bay*, 157, 5. (Nov.1976): p100-101.

1919 *What Makes The Pac-8 The Pac-10? Arizona's Universities*, 161, 3. (Sep.1978): p84-87.

1920 *San Francisco's Lively Eight-Ring Science Circus*, 161, 5. (Nov.1978): p112-115.

1921 *Children Meet Up With Nature In Bay Area And Sacramento*, 164, 1. (Jan.1980): p32-33.

1922 *Stars On Your Ceiling*, 182, 1. (Jan.1989): p62-63.

1923 *Tortillas to Robots at San Jose's Youthful Museums*, 185, 6. (Dec.1990): p28-31.

1924 *Top 5 College Towns*, 189, 04. (Oct.1992): p86-97.

1925 Swezey, Lauren Bonar and Anusasananan, Linda Lau, *From Seed To Bread*, 191, 5. (Nov.1993): p88-91.

1926 Whiteley, Peter O., *An A+ For Her Deck*, 195, 2. (Aug.1995): p88-90.

1927 Phillips, Jeff, *A Stunning New View Of Monterey Bay*, 196, 3. (Mar.1996): p76-83.

2.4 History

1928 Aiken, Charles S., *California's Fiftieth Anniversary*, 5, 5. (Sep.1900): p250.

1929 Dixon, L. Maynard, *The Singing of the West*, 18, 2. (Dec.1902): p88-100.

1930 Stovall, Dennis H., *The Billiard Table That Made Kerbyville*, 11, 6. (Oct.1903): p543-544.

1931 McAdie, Alexander G., *When California Was New England*, 12, 6. (Apr.1904): p504-507.

1932 Stephens, H. Morse, *Far Western History: Something About The Pacific Coast Branch Of The American Historical Association And Its Work*, 14, 2. (Dec.1904): p172-175.

1933 Irwin, Will, *Out Of The Dead West*, 14, 2. (Dec.1904): p138-140.

1934 Eldredge, Zoeth S., *Save The Old Names: A Plea For The Preservation Of Early California Nomenclature*, 14, 4. (Feb.1905): p415-416.

1935 Thwaites, Reuben Gold, *Overland A Century Ago*, 15, 3. (Jul.1905): p212-224.

1936 Wheeler, Olin D., *On The Trail Of Lewis And Clark*, 16, 4. (Feb.1906): p343-348.

1937 Collingwood, G. C., *The City Of The Alamo*, 16, 6. (Apr.1906): p532-552.

1938 Coe, Charles Willard, *Oregon's Beginnings*, 17, 6. (Oct.1906): p381-384.

1939 Gordon, David E., *In Golden Trinity: Recollections Of A California Mountain County In '49, And The Outlook To-Day*, 20, 2. (Dec.1907): p157-163.

1940 North, Arthur W., *The Story Of Magdalena Bay*, 20, 5. (Mar.1908): p410-420.

1941 Aiken, Charles Sedgwick, *The Vision Of Cahuenga*, 22, 3. (Mar.1909): p251-266.

1942 *Discoveries And Inventions, A Hitherto Unpublished Lecture By Abraham Lincoln*, 22, 5. (May.1909): p463-474.

1943 Merriam, John C., *The True Story Of The Calaveras Skull*, 24, 2. (Feb.1910): p153-158.

1944 Leach, Frank A., *The History Of The American Cent*, 24, 3. (Mar.1910): p332-337.

1945 Dosch, Arno, *Oregon's Beginnings*, 24, 6. (Jun.1910): p641-645.

1946 Kroeber, A. L., *At The Bedrock Of History: Recent Remarkable Discovery Of Human Remains Over Three Hundred Years Old In The San Joaquin Valley Of California*, 25, 3. (Sep.1910): p255-260.

1947 Evans, Samuel M., *The Breath Of The Chinook*, 28, 5. (May.1912): p523-532.

1948 Woehlke, Walter V., *Unlocking British Columbia*, 29, 3. (Sep.1912): p235-241, 326-329.

1949 Cowan, John L., *The Oregon Trail*, 30, 2. (Feb.1913): p189-195.

1950 Black, Zenas E., *America's Unhorsed Knight - And His Lady*, 35, 6. (Dec.1915): p1138-1143.

1951 Chapman, Charles E., *The Cross And Buddha*, 43, 5. (Nov.1919): p43-44, 58-64.

1952 Chapman, Charles E., *The Treasure Galleons*, 46, 2. (Feb.1921): p31-33, 48-50.

1953 Shair, Charles Lugrin, *Old Barkerville is Doomed to Die*, 51, 2. (Aug.1923): p49, 77-78.

1954 Sutcliffe, Lester B., *When Silver Cliff Was Booming*, 51, 4. (Oct.1923): p52, 62.

1955 Considine, John L., *The Great Diamond Swindle*, 52, 2. (Feb.1924): p49, 56-58.

1956 Considine, John L., *How Zink Barnes Corrupted Pioche*, 54, 2. (Feb.1924): p40, 60.

1957 Brininstool, E. A., *Freighting Across The Plains*, 52, 3. (Mar.1924): p52, 92-94.

1958 Considine, John L., *The Privateer That Did Not Sail*, 52, 4. (Apr.1924): p27, 62-64.

1959 Jones, J. R., *Gold–Man's Greatest Game*, 52, 5. (May.1924): p12-14, 100-104.

1960 Jones, J. R., *Gold Camps And Lost Mines*, 53, 1. (Jul.1924): p8-11, 89-91.

1961 Bechdolt, Frederick R., *The Trappers' Fight For Empire*, 53, 2. (Aug.1924): p14-16, 74-75.

1962 Bechdolt, Frederick R., *The Finding Of The Wagon Pass*, 53, 9. (Sep.1924): p21-23, 54-56.

2. Civic and Cultural Affairs

1963   Bechdolt, Frederick R., *The First Wheels Across The Rockies*, 53, 5. (Nov.1924): p12-14.

1964   Considine, John L., *The Pistoleers Of Old Pioche*, 53, 6. (Dec.1924): p24-25.

1965   Considine, John L., *The Birth Of Old Pioche*, 54, 1. (Jan.1925): p29, 56-58.

1966   Considine, John L., *Tales Of The Old West*, 54, 6. (Jun.1925): p27, 58.

1967   Eberts, Jerome B., *The Gold Rush Deluxe*, 55, 2. (Aug.1925): p34-35.

1968   Scherer, James A. B., *The First Forty-Niner*, 55, 1. (Oct 1925): p24-27, 89-96.

1969   Considine, John L., *Boone Helm And The Stockman*, 55, 4. (Oct.1925): p49, 56.

1970   Graney, Eddie, *A Referee's Decision*, 55, 6. (Dec.1925): p22-25, 85-93.

1971   Eddie Graney, *A Referee's Decision*, 56, 1. (Jan.1926): p26-28.

1972   Farrington, Wallace R., *Hawaii's Anniversary*, 56, 1. (Jan.1926): p18-19, 84.

1973   Dunn, H. H., *The Pacific Slope–The Dawn Man's Nursery*, 56, 3. (Mar.1926): p26-29, 80-82.

1974   Considine, John L., *The Holdup At Verdi*, 57, 3. (Sep.1926): p15, 56.

1975   Lyman, Richard, Mrs. , *"Finder's Keepers"*, 57, 3. (Sep.1926): p22-23, 64.

1976   Emery, Christine, *Historic "Hacienda Grande"*, 57, 3. (Sep.1926): p50-51, 76-77.

1977   Peterson, H. C., *Re-Creating The Days Of '49*, 58, 2. (Feb.1927): p26-27, 82-84.

1978   Hough, Donald, *Lasts Of The Old West*, 58, 3. (Mar.1927): p28-29, 62-65.

1979   Scobee, Barry, *Where Are The Brands Of Yesteryear*, 58, 4. (Apr.1927): p20-22, 66-68.

1980   Charles, W. S., *When Joe Woods Cracked His Whip*, 58, 4. (Apr.1927): p23, 64.

1981   Frankish, Leonard John, *The First of the First Californians*, 59, 2. (Aug.1927): p24-25, 54.

1982   Macleod, R., *Picnicking With Royalty*, 59, 2. (Aug.1927): p29, 54.

1983   Ryder, David Warren, *Stage-Coach Days*, 59, 3. (Sep.1927): p16-17, 68-69.

1984   Rhodes, Eugene Manlove, *In Defense Of Pat Garrett*, 59, 3. (Sep.1927): p26-27, 85-91.

1985   Charles, W. S., *Auburn, Ghost City Of Oregon*, 59, 4. (Oct.1927): p31, 54-56.

1986   Loken, H. J., *Uncovering A Ghost City*, 59, 6. (Dec.1927): p24-25, 56-58.

1987   Considine, John L., *Gridley's Wager*, 60, 4. (Apr.1928): p38-39, 54-56.

1988   Heenan, David, Jr., *Hawaii's Sesqui*, 60, 6. (Jun.1928): p20-21, 80.

1989   Banning, William and Banning, George Hugh, *The Pony Express*, 61, 3. (Sep.1928): p13-15, 66.

1990   Richards, Kenneth F., *Shanghaied!*, 61, 3. (Sep.1928): p16-18, 58-60.

1991   Carr, Harry, *Lost Gold Of The Tejon*, 61, 3. (Sep.1928): p43, 66-69.

1992   Carhart, Arthur Hawthorne, *A Ghost Shows Life*, 61, 5. (Nov.1928): p38-39, 54.

1993   Jones, J. R., *Handlers Of Sixes*, 61, 6. (Dec.1928): p24-26, 48-51.

1994   Dickson, S. B., *Pilgrims Of The West*, 63, 5. (Nov.1929): p11-13.

1995   Dickson, S. B., *A Procession Of Christmas*, 63, 6. (Dec.1929): p13-14.

1996   Taylor, Katherine Ames, *Ringing 'Round The World*, 63, 6. (Dec.1929): p16-18.

1997   Swett-Sommers, Naomi, *Memories of Early Oregon Christmases*, 63, 6. (Dec.1929): p29-30.

1998   Dickson, S. B., *The Story Of The Big Four*, 64, 1. (Jan.1930): p16-17.

1999   Taylor, Frank J., *Promised Lands*, 67, 5. (Nov.1931): p6-7, 35.

2000   Taylor, Frank J., *Promised Lands*, 67, 6. (Dec.1931): p12-14.

2001   Taylor, Frank J., *Promised Lands*, 68, 5. (May.1932): p16-17, 38-39.

2002   Black, Marjorie H., *To Which Era Does Your Kitchen Range Belong?*, 71, 5. (Nov.1933): p20-22.

2003   Hall, Wilbur, *Collecting Branding Irons*, 74, 4. (Apr.1935): p16, 58-59.

2004   Hall, Wilbur, *A Famous Collection Of Old Stage Coaches*, 75, 1. (Jul.1935): p13, 30.

2005   Hall, Wilbur, *Her Hobby Is Collecting Bells*, 75, 2. (Aug.1935): p13, 32.

2006   Hall, Wilbur, *A Whaling Good Hobby*, 75, 4. (Oct.1935): p14-15.

2007   Hall, Wilbur, *His Hobby Is Guns*, 75, 5. (Nov.1935): p14-15.

2008   *What's New In Western Living*, 78, 5. (May.1937): p21-23.

2009   *What's New In Western Living*, 80, 4. (Apr.1938): p21-23.

2010   *40 Years Of Western Living 1898-1938*, 80, 5. (May.1938): p19-21.

2011   *Old Montgomery Street*, 80, 5. (May.1938): p28-29.

2012   *What's New In Western Living*, 82, 2. (Feb.1939): p15-17.

2013   *What's New In Western Living*, 82, 5. (May.1939): p21-23.

2014   *What's New In Western Living*, 83, 9. (Sep.1939): p13-15.

2015   *Rip Roaring Replica*, 84, 5. (May.1940): p20-21.

2016   *Quicksilver Town*, 85, 2. (Aug.1940): p44.

2017   *Before It's Too Late*, 86, 3. (Mar.1941): p10-11.

2018   *Before It's Too Late*, 86, 5. (May.1941): p22-23.

2019   *Southern Arizona Ghost Towns*, 99, 5. (Nov.1947): p12-13.

2020   *Bodie is Sleeping*, 101, 3. (Sep.1948): p16, 19.

2021   *Let's Take A Back Road Swing Through Utah's Colorful Past*, 110, 6. (Jun.1953): p22-25.

2022   *The West, Looking Ahead... From 60 Years' Experience*, 121, 5. (May.1958): p3-6.

2023   *Looking Ahead On Sunset's 75th Anniversary*, 150, 5. (May.1973): p104-111.

2024   *The Early Sunset 1898-1928*, 151, 5. (Nov.1973): p100-103.

2025   *Looking Back On Eight Lively Decades*, 160, 5. (May.1978): p120-125.

2026   *Rendezvousing With the Mountain Men*, 174, 6. (Jun.1985): p98-101.

2027   *What Was Christmas Like During The Gold Rush? Or When Los Angeles Belonged to Mexico?*, 177, 6. (Dec.1986): p10-14.

2028   Finnegan, Lora J., *Heed The Call Of The Sea In San Francisco*, 192, 3. (Mar.1994): p34-36.

2029   *The West Slept Here*, 194, 05. (Nov.1995): p64-71.

2.5   Military

2030   *Tracing A Terrible Trail*, 197, 04. (Oct.1996): p22-24, 26.

2031   Finley, John P., *Discharging A Philippine Army, Part One*, 9, 5. (Sep.1902): p292-308.

2032   Finley, John P., *Discharging A Philippine Army, Part Two*, 9, 6. (Oct.1902): p373-384.

2033   Finley, John P., *Discharging A Philippine Army, Part Three*, 10, 1. (Nov.1902): p15-25.

2034   Finley, John P., *Discharging A Philippine Army, Part Four*, 10, 2. (Dec.1902): p116-126.

2035   MacArthur, Arthur, *The Grand Army Of The Republic And Its Relation To American Institutions: A Tribute*, 11, 4. (Aug.1903): p314-315.

2036   Aiken, Charles S., *The Grand Army's Westward Ho*, 11, 4. (Aug.1903): p316-317.

2037   Smedberg, William R., *Little Stories Of War Time*, 11, 5. (Sep.1903): p476-480.

2038   White, Douglas, *Boy Blue Jackets Of Yerba Buena*, 11, 6. (Oct.1903): p517-525.

2. Civic and Cultural Affairs

2039 Weiss, R. A., *The Story Of Yerba Buena*, 11, 6. (Oct.1903): p526-528.

2040 Gibson, H. G., *The Mutiny Of The Ewing*, 12, 5. (Mar.1904): p422-426.

2041 Bronson-Howard, George, *Fighting For News In Manchuria*, 13, 3. (Jul.1904): p195-205.

2042 Hewson, Ernest Williams, *Kuropatkin In Japan*, 13, 3. (Jul.1904): p205-208.

2043 Gillette, Cassius E., *California's Army Camp*, 13, 4. (Aug.1904): p316-317.

2044 *California's Army Camp*, 13, 6. (Oct.1904): p508-538.

2045 Bramhall, Frank J., *The Pensacola, Sloop Of War*, 13, 6. (Oct.1904): p539-544.

2046 Raine, William MacLeod, *The Story Of Beecher's Island: How Fifty American Frontier Scouts Held Back Thousands Of Cheyenne And Sioux Indians For Nine Days*, 14, 2. (Dec.1904): p141-145.

2047 Redington, J. W., *When We Fought Chief Joseph*, 14, 4. (Feb.1905): p355-362.

2048 Archibald, James F. J., *The Railroad In War*, 16, 3. (Jan.1906): p160-266.

2049 McClintock, James H., *Fighting Apaches*, 18, 4. (Feb.1907): p340-343.

2050 Evans, H. A., *The Coming Of The Fleet*, 19, 6. (Oct.1907): p508-522.

2051 Evans, H. A., *The Pacific Fleet Of The Future*, 20, 4. (Feb.1908): p308-324.

2052 Evans, H. A., *Trade Follows The Flag: The Immediate Influence Of The American Battleship Fleet On The Commerce Of The Pacific*, 20, 5. (Mar.1908): p421-431.

2053 Evans, H. A., *Coming Of The Fleet*, 21, 1. (May.1908): p1-19.

2054 Capps, W. L., *Defense Of The American Navy*, 21, 1. (May.1908): p20-27.

2055 *$1,000,000 A Month: The Money That Must Go To The Navy Men And The Supplies Necessary To Keep Up The Fleet*, 21, 1. (May.1908): p28-30.

2056 Phelan, James D., *San Francisco's Greeting*, 21, 1. (May.1908): p30-37.

2057 Koike, Chozo, *'Kwangei!' Says Japan*, 21, 1. (May.1908): p37-39.

2058 Capps, W. L., *Defense Of The American Navy*, 21, 2. (Jun.1908): p163-172.

2059 Capps, W. L., *Defense Of The American Navy*, 21, 3. (Jul.1908): p252-254.

2060 Capps, W. L., *Defense Of The American Navy*, 21, 4. (Aug.1908): p311-316.

2061 Evans, H. A., *The Key To The Pacific: The Proposed Naval Station At Pearl Harbor, Hawaii, For Which Congress Has Appropriated $2,500,000, And Its Importance In Maintaining The Pacific Fleet*, 21, 4. (Aug.1908): p336-347.

2062 Evans, H. A., *Defense Of The Pacific: The Future Of Mare Island Navy Yard - Its Importance And Great Strategic Value For The Nation's West Coast - Patchwork Methods And Crazy-Quilt Results*, 22, 1. (Jan.1909): p15-24.

2063 Maus, Marion P., *The School Of War: The Maneuver Camp For Army Regulars And State Troops At Atascadero, California, And Obvious Reasons For Its Maintenance By The Government*, 22, 1. (Jan.1909): p25-39.

2064 Perkins, George C., *A Navy For The Pacific*, 23, 1. (Jul.1909): p32-36.

2065 Ashburn, Thomas Q., *Forts Under The Sea*, 23, 4. (Oct.1909): p327-336.

2066 Beck, Paul W., *Flying Men-O'-War*, 24, 3. (Mar.1910): p253-257.

2067 Evans, H. A., *Defense Of The Pacific*, 26, 1. (Jan.1911): p29-33.

2068 Ashburn, Thomas Q., *Using Uncle Sam's Soldiers To Fight Forest Fires*, 26, 2. (Feb.1911): p193-200.

2069 Beck, Paul W., *The Doves Of War*, 26, 3. (Mar.1911): p292-296.

2070 Smith, James F., *The Taking Of The Islands*, 27, 5. (Nov.1911): p503-514.

2071 Smith, James F., *The Philippines As I Saw them*, 27, 6. (Dec.1911): p617-632.

2072 Scott, Riley E., *Can The Panama Canal Be Destroyed From The Air?*, 32, 4. (Apr.1914): p774-784.

2073 Dunn, Arthur, *War On The West Coast*, 33, 1. (Jul.1914): p145-151.

2074 Kawakami, K. K., *Japan In The European War*, 33, 4. (Oct.1914): p665-667.

2075 Freeman, Lewis R., *Carrying The War Into The Pacific*, 33, 4. (Oct.1914): p668-676.

2076 Ridder, Herman, *Justice For Germany!*, 33, 5. (Nov.1914): p876-880.

2077 Beck, Paul W., *The Deadlock In France*, 33, 5. (Nov.1914): p880-884.

2078 Howell, James B., *Davids Of The Deep*, 33, 6. (Dec.1914): p1087-1088, 1196-1202.

2079 Jordan, David Starr, *The Ways To Peace*, 33, 6. (Dec.1914): p1103-1108.

2080 Abdullah, Achmed, *The Armed Yellow Fist*, 34, 1. (Jan.1915): p96-101.

2081 Evans, H. A., *Can The Pacific Coast Be Made Secure Against Invasion?*, 34, 2. (Feb.1915): p245-252.

2082 Pluschow, Gunther, *Flying Under Fire*, 34, 3. (Mar.1915): p449-454.

2083 Landfield, Jerome B., *The American Note And The Progress Of The War*, 35, 1. (Jul.1915): p60-63.

2084 Willard, Walter, *America, The Hyphen And The European War*, 35, 1. (Jul.1915): p64-66.

2085 Landfield, Jerome B., *Is International Law Extinct?*, 35, 2. (Aug.1915): p261-262, 366.

2086 Willard, Walter, *Shall We Fight Or Negotiate?*, 35, 2. (Aug.1915): p258-260, 364.

2087 Dosch, Arno, *The Blood-Offering Of British Columbia*, 35, 5. (Nov.1915): p881-890.

2088 Jordan, David Starr, *Enduring Peace*, 36, 1. (Jan.1916): p17-18.

2089 Dunn, Arthur, *Why Gild The Flintlock*, 36, 3. (Mar.1916): p16-18, 95-98.

2090 Reid, Frederick, *Mobilizing The Flintlock Army–An Object Lesson*, 36, 5. (May.1916): p16-18, 92-95.

2091 Dunn, Arthur, *Excuse Me!*, 36, 6. (Jun.1916): p32-33, 83-84.

2092 Carr, Harry, *Our Sociable War*, 37, 2. (Aug.1916): p46-49, 92-94.

2093 Vincent, Fred W., *Mobilization In The Northwest*, 37, 2. (Aug.1916): p94-95.

2094 Carr, Harry, *The Conquest Of Mexico*, 37, 3. (Sep.1916): p14-16, 64.

2095 Stokes, Charles, *Till The Boys Come Home*, 37, 3. (Sep.1916): p17.

2096 Jordan, David Starr, *What Of The Nation?*, 37, 4. (Oct.1916): p15.

2097 Carr, Harry, *Is Los Angeles Worth Defending?*, 38, 2. (Feb.1917): p9-12, 92.

2098 Hegger, Grace, *Sixteen Hands High*, 38, 6. (Jun.1917): p38-39, 68-69.

2099 Dunn, Arthur, *R.O.T.C.*, 39, 1. (Jul.1917): p30-31, 70-71, 89.

2100 Kyne, Peter B., *Officers And Gentlemen*, 39, 2. (Aug.1917): p9-11, 88-90.

2101 Partridge, Edward Bellamy, *Training Tars On Terra Firma*, 39, 5. (Nov.1917): p14-16, 82-83.

2102 Baily, Robin, *G-r-r-r-r-ah! The Grizzlies!*, 40, 1. (Jan.1918): p22-24.

2103 Stone, Harold Otho, *Give The Sailor A Chance!*, 40, 1. (Jan.1918): p25.

2104 Rader, Philips Dwight, *On Duty In The Air*, 40, 2. (Feb.1918): p11-13, 74.

2105 Yoell, Jean, *They Smile As They Fly*, 40, 2. (Feb.1918): p21-23.

2106 Rader, Philips Dwight, *How Wings Are Grown*, 40, 3. (Mar.1918): p14-16, 72-73.

2107 Baily, Robin, *The Athlete In This War*, 40, 3. (Mar.1918): p23-26, 66.

2108 Rader, Philips Dwight, *Zep Strafing*, 40, 4. (Apr.1918): p29-31, 68-69.

2109 Baily, Robin, *The Marines Tell It Themselves*, 40, 4. (Apr.1918): p43-45, 70-71.

2110 Rader, Philips Dwight, *Trick Flying*, 40, 5. (May.1918): p14-16.

2. Civic and Cultural Affairs

2111 Baily, Robin, *Songs Our Soldiers Sing*, 40, 5. (May.1918): p22-23.

2112 Player, Cyril Arthur, *The Frontier Trains For War*, 40, 6. (Jun.1918): p21-24.

2113 Hay, Ian and Baily, Robin, *When This Crush Arrives*, 40, 6. (Jun.1918): p24-25, 72.

2114 Gilbert, Hilda, *Mother's Boy*, 41, 1. (Jul.1918): p24-26, 56-57.

2115 Baily, Robin, *Uncle Sam's Trump Card*, 41, 1. (Jul.1918): p32-34.

2116 Whitaker, Herman, *The Eyes Of The Destroyers*, 41, 1. (Jul.1918): p34-36, 58-63.

2117 Cameron, John S., *The Sea Wolf's Prey*, 41, 2. (Aug.1918): p14-16, 66-67.

2118 Mitchell, Marion Otis, *Back Of The Front*, 41, 2. (Aug.1918): p33-37.

2119 Cameron, John S., *The Sea Wolf's Prey*, 41, 3. (Sep.1918): p20-23, 72-74.

2120 Baily, Robin, *The Bird-Man And The Rabbit's Foot*, 41, 3. (Sep.1918): p28-29.

2121 Crossman, Edward C., *John Browning's Gun Goes Marching On*, 41, 3. (Sep.1918): p36-38.

2122 Coover, George William, *Three Times And Out!*, 41, 4. (Oct.1918): p21-23, 65-66.

2123 Snell, Earl, *War And The Rah Rah Boy*, 41, 4. (Oct.1918): p24-26, 52.

2124 Cameron, John S., *The Sea Wolf's Prey*, 41, 4. (Oct.1918): p30-33, 69-72.

2125 Baily, Robin, *How May I Serve?*, 41, 4. (Oct.1918): p38-39.

2126 Reid, Mabel, *Angels Of Western War Camps*, 41, 4. (Oct.1918): p40-41.

2127 De Beaufort, J. M., *Beware Of The Dove!*, 41, 5. (Nov.1918): p14-16, 76-77.

2128 Cameron, John S., *The Sea Wolf's Prey*, 41, 5. (Nov.1918): p41-45.

2129 Smith, Alice Prescott, *The Battalion Of Life*, 41, 5. (Nov.1918): p30-33.

2130 Lane, Rose Wilder, *The Girls They Leave Behind*, 41, 5. (Nov.1918): p36-37.

2131 Whitaker, Herman, *Sub Vs. U*, 41, 6. (Dec.1918): p10-13, 73.

2132 Norton, Charles Philip, *Lumber Janes*, 41, 6. (Dec.1918): p32-33.

2133 Whitaker, Herman, *The Hun Harriers*, 42, 1. (Jan.1919): p23-25, 61.

2134 Waters, Crystal, *A Singing Girl In No-Man's Land*, 42, 1. (Jan.1919): p40-42.

2135 Partridge, Edward Bellamy, *La Guerre Est Finie!*, 42, 3. (Mar.1919): p30-32, 54.

2136 Trudgett, Robert D., *Hell Holes On Land And Sea*, 42, 5. (May.1919): p30-32.

2137 Braley, Berton, *Buddy Bosses The Boche*, 43, 1. (Jul.1919): p45-46.

2138 Griffin, R. A., *Say! Who Won The War?*, 43, 6. (Dec.1919): p19-22, 68-72.

2139 Griffin, R. A., *Say! Who Won The War?*, 44, 1. (Jan.1920): p41-44,66-68.

2140 Griffin, R. A., *Say! Who Won The War?*, 44, 2. (Feb.1920): p41-44, 58-62.

2141 FitzGerald, Harold J., *Blasting them Out Of The Rut*, 46, 4. (Apr.1921): p40-41, 66-68.

2142 FitzGerald, Harold J., *Hamstringing The Fleet*, 52, 2. (Feb.1924): p9-11, 89-92.

2143 Crary, Bess J., *Hobby Horse And Homer Pigeon*, 52, 5. (May.1924): p22-23,62.

2144 Squier, Emma-Lindsay, *A Little Bear Called Prunes*, 53, 1. (Jul.1924): p38-39.

2145 Lane, D. R., *Is Our Navy Fit To Fight?*, 54, 3. (Mar.1925): p10-11.

2146 Hughes, James Perley, *Making Sailors*, 59, 1. (Jul.1927): p26-28, 68.

2147 Barnes, Harry C., Jr., *Vacations On Uncle Sam*, 61, 1. (Jul.1928): p34-37.

2148 Spencer, G. K., *Squadrons West!*, 61, 6. (Dec.1928): p9-11, 52-53.

2149 O'Hargan, Roderick, *Wild Camels In Arizona?*, 62, 1. (Jan.1929): p30-32, 54-56, 59.

2150 *Your Boy*, 89, 4. (Oct.1942): p26-27.

2151 *Christmas Travel*, 93, 6. (Dec.1944): p2-4.

2.6 Politics & Government

2152 Landfield, Jerome B., *The Impending Conflict In The Orient*, 12, 4. (Feb.1904) p294-301.

2153 Peixotto, Edgar D., *Concerning National Conventions: The Part The West Has Played In The Great Assemblies That Name The Nation's President*, 13, 2. (Jun.1904): p115-119.

2154 Montgomery, Percy F., *The Department Of Commerce And Labor*, 13, 4. (Aug.1904): p300-304.

2155 Walcott, Earle Ashley, *Calamity's Opportunity*, 17, 4. (Aug.1906): p151-157.

2156 Walker, David H., *The Municipal Value Of Insurance*, 18, 4. (Feb.1907): p325-330.

2157 Bruncken, Ernest, *Helping Our Statesmen: How The Legislative Reference Bureau Has Been Developed And What It Means*, 19, 2. (Jun.1907): p159-167.

2158 Butler, Nicholas Murray, *An Aristocracy of Service*, 19, 6. (Oct.1907): p653-570.

2159 Belcher, Edward A., *Not War, But Peace*, 20, 3. (Jan.1908): p294-298.

2160 Stellmann, Louis J., *The Crisis In China*, 22, 2. (Feb.1909): p124-128.

2161 Park, Robert L., *Good Times Ahead For China*, 22, 2. (Feb.1909): p128-129.

2162 Richardson, D. S., *Does Japan Want War?*, 22, 2. (Feb.1909): p159-163.

2163 London, Jack, *If Japan Wakens China*, 23, 6. (Dec.1909): p597-601.

2164 Noguchi, Yone, *No Yellow Peril In China*, 25, 1. (Jul.1910): p14-16.

2165 Wall, Louise Herrick, *Moving To Amend*, 27, 4. (Oct.1911): p377-384.

2166 Jordan, David Starr, *Japan And The United States*, 28, 1. (Jan.1912): p59-63.

2167 Michelson, Miriam, *Vice And The Woman's Vote*, 30, 4. (Apr.1913): p345-348.

2168 Dutton, William J., *Immoral Legislation*, 33, 4. (Oct.1914): p688-690.

2169 Odell, S. W., *State Wide Prohibition In California*, 33, 4. (Oct.1914): p690-692.

2170 *When the Flag Came Down at Corregidor–A Prophecy*, 34, 1. (Jan.1915): p147-159.

2171 Freeman, Lewis R., *Shall We Keep The Philippines?*, 34, 3. (Mar.1915): p439-448.

2172 Brace, Alfred M., *Tsingtau And The Rising Sun*, 34, 4. (Apr.1915): p747-752.

2173 Kawakami, K. K., *The Chinese Policy Of Japan*, 34, 5. (May.1915): p920-924, 964.

2174 *Prison Reform and Sentimentality*, 35, 1. (Jul.1915): p104-106.

2175 *Pseudo Prison Reform*, 35, 1. (Jul.1915): p102-103.

2176 Smalley, George Herbert, *What Prohibition Did To Arizona*, 36, 1. (Jan.1916): p26-27.

2177 Jordan, David Starr, *What Of The Nation?*, 36, 2. (Feb.1916): p19-20.

2178 Hooper, S. Dike, *Skinning The Land Grant Bear*, 36, 2. (Feb.1916): p45-46, 82-84.

2179 Dosch, Arno, *California Next?*, 36, 3. (Mar.1916): p22-24, 59-63.

2180 Jordan, David Starr, *What Of The Nation?*, 36, 3. (Mar.1916): p25.

2181 Crow, Carl, *Dusting The Yellow Throne*, 36, 3. (Mar.1916): p26-27, 80-85.

2182 Crow, Carl, *Our Surrender Of The Pacific*, 36, 4. (Apr.1916): p13-15, 46-48.

2183 Jordan, David Starr, *What Of The Nation?*, 36, 4. (Apr.1916): p19.

2184 Jordan, David Starr, *What Of The Nation?*, 36, 5. (May.1916): p19.

2185 Jordan, David Starr, *What Of The Nation?*, 36, 6. (Jun.1916): p24.

2. Civic and Cultural Affairs

2186 Jordan, David Starr, *What Of The Nation?*, 37, 1. (Jul.1916): p21.

2187 Jordan, David Starr, *What Of The Nation?*, 37, 2. (Aug.1916): p27.

2188 Dosch, Arno, *Extinguishing The Red Light*, 37, 2. (Aug.1916): p38-40.

2189 Jordan, David Starr, *What Of The Nation?*, 37, 3. (Sep.1916): p13.

2190 Hodges, G. Charles, *Japanese Ambitions And Latin America*, 37, 4. (Oct.1916): p16-17, 82-85.

2191 Woehlke, Walter V., *The Second Battle Of Booze Run*, 37, 5. (Nov.1916): p9-11, 63-64.

2192 Jordan, David Starr, *What Of The Nation?*, 37, 5. (Nov.1916): p15.

2193 Jordan, David Starr, *What Of The Nation?*, 37, 6. (Dec.1916): p15-16, 39.

2194 Jordan, David Starr, *What Of The Nation?*, 38, 2. (Feb.1917): p19, 70.

2195 Jordan, David Starr, *What Of The Nation?*, 38, 3. (Mar.1917): p17, 88-90.

2196 *The Confessions Of A German-American*, 38, 4. (Apr.1917): p15-16, 94-95.

2197 Jordan, David Starr, *What Of The Nation?*, 38, 5. (May.1917): p27, 70.

2198 Spangler, Colin Irving, *Frame-Up Or Square Deal?*, 38, 5. (May.1917): p28-29, 90-92.

2199 Crow, Carl, *Chang, The Unchanging*, 39, 2. (Aug.1917): p12-13, 92.

2200 Landfield, Jerome B., *Siberia And The White Hope*, 39, 2. (Aug.1917): p32-33.

2201 Hodges, G. Charles, *The Gentled Bear*, 39, 4. (Oct.1917): p26, 77.

2202 Crow, Carl, *Getting-Rich-Quick Japan*, 39, 6. (Dec.1917): p32-33, 79.

2203 Crow, Carl, *We Complete The Chinese Wall*, 40, 1. (Jan.1918): p10-11, 72.

2204 Vincent, Fred W., *Making Their Own*, 40, 5. (May.1918): p25.

2205 Cornet, George, *This Is A Free Country Now*, 40, 6. (Jun.1918): p13-16.

2206 Monkhouse, Allan, *Bolshevik And Bolshvictim*, 41, 2. (Aug.1918): p11-13, 64-66.

2207 Hodges, G. Charles, *John Chinaman Breaks Through*, 41, 3. (Sep.1918): p24-25, 74-75.

2208 Woehlke, Walter V., *The Mooney Case*, 42, 1. (Jan.1919): p13-16, 66-67.

2209 Jordan, David Starr, *Problems Of The Peace Table*, 42, 1. (Jan.1919): p27-29.

2210 Woehlke, Walter V., *The Mooney Case*, 42, 2. (Feb.1919): p20-23, 69-70.

2211 Jordan, David Starr, *Problems Of The Peace Table*, 42, 2. (Feb.1919): p24-25, 62-64.

2212 Pelley, William Dudley, *When Brown Is Red*, 42, 2. (Feb.1919): p26-29.

2213 Woehlke, Walter V., *The Mooney Case*, 42, 3. (Mar.1919): p26-29, 70-73.

2214 Jordan, David Starr, *Problems Of The Peace Table*, 42, 3. (Mar.1919): p38-39, 82-84.

2215 Quire, Joseph H., *Upstairs And Down With The Solons*, 42, 3. (Mar.1919): p40-41, 52-54.

2216 Woehlke, Walter V., *Revolution In America*, 42, 4. (Apr.1919): p13-16, 64.

2217 Jordan, David Starr, *Problems Of The Peace Table*, 42, 4. (Apr.1919): p36-37.

2218 Woehlke. Walter V., *The Mooney Case*, 42, 4. (Apr.1919): p41-44, 90-93.

2219 Jordan, David Starr, *Problems Of The Peace Table*, 42, 5. (May.1919): p21-23.

2220 Woehlke, Walter V., *Poisoned Publicity*, 42, 5. (May.1919): p37-40, 82-86.

2221 Jordan, David Starr, *Problems Of The Peace Table*, 42, 6. (Jun.1919): p41-42, 76-78.

2222 Pelley, William Dudley, *Siberia, With The Lid Off*, 43, 1. (Jul.1919): p17-20, 85-87.

2223 Jordan, David Starr, *Problems Of The Peace Table*, 43, 1. (Jul.1919): p29-31.

2224 McMahon, Thomas J., *Japanning The Marshall Islands*, 43, 1. (Jul.1919): p31-33.

2225 Jordan, David Starr, *Problems Of The Peace Table*, 43, 2. (Aug.1919): p46-47, 78-82.

2226 Jordan, David Starr, *The New Fight For Democracy*, 43, 3. (Sep.1919): p23-24, 89-90.

2227 Johnson, Hiram W., *What Of The Nation?*, 43, 4. (Oct.1919): p15-16, 106-108.

2228 Pelley, William Dudley, *Korea And Japan's Boot*, 43, 4. (Oct.1919): p22-24, 52.

2229 Woehlke, Walter V., *When Will The Prices Go Down?*, 43, 4. (Oct.1919): p25-26, 88.

2230 Jordan, David Starr, *War And The League Of Nations*, 43, 4. (Oct.1919): p32-33.

2231 Johnson, Hiram W., *What Of The Nation?*, 43, 5. (Nov.1919): p12-13, 105-106.

2232 Hoover, Herbert, *Our Responsibility*, 43, 5. (Nov.1919): p14-16, 106.

2233 Pelley, William Dudley, *Siberia Back Of The Whiskers*, 43, 5. (Nov.1919): p17-19, 54-56.

2234 Ritchie, Robert Welles, *Britain In Revolution*, 43, 5. (Nov.1919): p25-26, 56-58.

2235 Jordan, David Starr, *Some Phases Of The Aftermath*, 43, 5. (Nov.1919): p41-42, 64-66.

2236 Johnson, Hiram W., *What Of The Nation?*, 43, 6. (Dec.1919): p15-16.

2237 Irwin, Will, *An Age Of Lies*, 43, 6. (Dec.1919): p23-25, 54-56.

2238 Jordan, David Starr, *When East Meets East*, 43, 6. (Dec.1919): p39-40.

2239 Johnson, Hiram W., *What Of The Nation?*, 44, 1. (Jan.1920): p23-24, 91-93.

2240 Dosch-Fleurot, Arno, *What The Reds Are After*, 44, 1. (Jan.1920): p25, 86-91.

2241 Taylor, Alonzo Englebert, *Hoover's Fifth Year*, 44, 1. (Jan.1920): p28-30, 80-86.

2242 Jordan, David Starr, *Pity The Poor Hermit!*, 44, 1. (Jan.1920): p48-50.

2243 Johnson, Hiram W., *What Of The Nation?*, 44, 2. (Feb.1920): p22-23, 72.

2244 Hoover, Herbert, *Unto The Least Of these*, 44, 2. (Feb.1920): p24, 109-110.

2245 Gregory, Thomas T. C., *Bolsheviks And Archdukes*, 44, 3. (Feb.1920): p25-28.

2246 Partridge, Edward Bellamy, *Unfair!*, 44, 2. (Feb.1920): p36-38, 80-82.

2247 Johnson, Hiram W., *What Of The Nation?*, 44, 3. (Mar.1920): p21-22.

2248 Johnson, Hiram W., *What Of The Nation?*, 44, 4. (Apr.1920): p17-18.

2249 Johnson, Hiram W., *What Of The Nation?*, 44, 5. (May.1920): p21-22.

2250 FitzGerald, Harold J., *Taking Your Name In Vain*, 44, 5. (May.1920): p38-40, 52-54.

2251 Johnson, Hiram W., *What Of The Nation?*, 44, 6. (Jun.1920): p21-22.

2252 Johnson, Hiram W., *What Of The Nation?*, 45, 1. (Jul.1920): p22-23.

2253 Pelley, William Dudley, *Behind The Dreadful Mask*, 45, 1. (Jul.1920): p32-34, 62-64.

2254 Johnson, Hiram W., *What Of The Nation?*, 45, 2. (Aug.1920): p23-24.

2255 Johnson, Hiram W., *What Of The Nation?*, 45, 3. (Sep.1920): p22-23.

2256 Millard, Bailey, *Paradoxes Of Prohibition*, 45, 6. (Dec.1920): p38-39, 75-78.

2257 Woehlke, Walter V., *The New Day In New Mexico*, 46, 6. (Jun.1921): p21-24, 54-56.

2258 FitzGerald, Harold J., *The Truth About Your Taxes*, 47, 5. (Nov.1921): p32-33, 76-81.

2259 Borah, William E., *Will Humanity Be Heard At Washington?*, 47, 6. (Dec.1921): p3.

2260 Borah, William E., *Why The Conference Must Act*, 48, 1. (Jan.1922): p18-19, 73-74.

2261 Borah, William E., *The Results Of Secrecy*, 48, 2. (Feb.1922): p30-31, 81.

2262 Martin, Anne, *Woman's Vote And Woman's Chains*, 48, 4. (Apr.1922): p12-14.

2263 Knappen, Theodore M., *The West At Washington*, 49, 1. (Jul.1922): p35-36.

2264 Stevens, Laird, *Distillitis*, 49, 4. (Oct.1922): p8-9, 50-52.

2265 Jordan, David Starr, *The Dark Stream Of World Politics*, 50, 6. (Jun.1923): p34-35, 117.

2266 Considine, John L., *Sack Senators of the Seventies*, 51, 1. (Jul.1923): p37-39, 62.

2267 Farrington, Wallace R., *Hawaii's Birthday*, 51, 3. (Sep.1923): p35.

2268 Whipple, Sidney B., *Is The Press Free In New Mexico?*, 51, 4. (Oct.1923): p17-19, 54.

2269 Dupuy, Ernest, *The "Biggity" Filipino*, 51, 5. (Nov.1923): p12-14, 52, 100-101.

2270 Caldwell, Worth W., *The Equality Colony*, 52, 2. (Feb.1924): p27-29.

2271 Eddy, Elford, *Hope For The Convict*, 52, 6. (Jun.1924): p20-21, 60.

2272 Shaw, Charles Lugrin, *Our Neighbor's Yellow Curse*, 53, 1. (Jul.1924): p36-37, 60.

2273 Sherman, Maybel, *Digesting The Immigrant*, 53, 3. (Sep.1924): p38-39.

2274 *Why I Quit The I.W.W.*, 53, 5. (Nov.1924): p15, 92-96.

2275 Knappen, Theodore M., *Every Odd Section*, 53, 6. (Dec.1924): p11-13, 54-56.

2276 Mavity, Nancy Barr, *Labor In The Saddle*, 54, 2. (Feb.1925): p11-13, 72-73.

2277 Lane, D. R., *Run Warfare Along The Pacific Coast*, 55, 4. (Oct.1925): p16-19, 60-62.

2278 Willard, Victor, *When A Governor Becomes A Czar*, 55, 4. (Oct.1925): p23, 56-57.

2279 Lane, D. R., *Law's Delays*, 55, 6. (Dec.1925): p14-17, 60-62.

2280 Willard, Victor, *Casting Out Fear*, 56, 6. (Jun.1926): p36-37, 81.

2281 Langerock, Hubert, *The Pocket Veto*, 57, 6. (Dec.1926): p93-95.

2282 Williams, E. T., *The Struggle In China*, 58, 6. (Jun.1927): p12-15, 88-89.

2283 Battu, Zoe A., *Pioneering For Peace In The Pacific*, 59, 2. (Aug.1927): p12-14, 75.

2284 Phillips, George W. and Older, Fremont, *The Death Penalty?*, 60, 1. (Jan.1928): p18-21, 76-77.

2285 Thurber, James G., *As Europe Sees Us*, 60, 3. (Mar.1928): p17.

2286 McNab, John L., *What Hoover Means To The West*, 61, 4. (Oct.1928): p12, 14, 70-71, 83.

2287 Atherton, Gertrude, *The West Will Support Smith*, 61, 4. (Oct.1928): p13, 15, 84.

2288 Hoover, Herbert, *Hoover Broadcasts on the Home*, 62, 2. (Feb.1929): p23.

2289 Welling, Blanche E., *Neighborly Chats With One Western Mother*, 67, 6. (Dec.1931): p16.

2290 Richardson, Lou, *What The National Housing Act Means Here In The West*, 73, 5. (Nov.1934): p9-11.

2291 Keyes, Frances Parkinson, *Working For The West At Washington, D. C.*, 74, 2. (Feb.1935): p9-11.

2292 Keyes, Frances Parkinson, *The Most Popular Member of the United States Senate Comes From Oregon*, 74, 3. (Mar.1935): p14-15, 36, 56-57.

2293 Keyes, Frances Parkinson, *Silver Key Pittman Of Nevada*, 74, 5. (May.1935): p16-18.

2294 *What's New In Western Living*, 83, 2. (Aug.1939): p13-15.

2295 Lane, Bill, *Letter From Sunset: The Pacific As Our Future*, 180, 05. (May.1988): p292.

2296 *Sunset's 90th Anniversary Special Report: Can The West Grow Wisely And Well?*, 180, 05. (May.1988): p110-117.

2.7 Stanford University

2297 Jordan, David Starr, *Mexico: A New Nation In An Old Country*, 2, 5. (Mar.1899): p82-89.

2298 Hartwell, Robert W., *Stanford University: The Larger University Has Found A Beginning*, 3, 1. (May.1899): p23.

2299 Jordan, David Starr, *The Kings River Canyon And The Alps Of The Great Divide*, 4, 6. (Apr.1900): p220-226.

2300 Rice, Archie, *Midwinter Football In California*, 8, 5. (Mar.1902): p203-206.

2301 Shinn, Charles Howard, *Down The San Mateo Peninsula*, 9, 4. (Aug.1902): p269-284.

2302 Simpson, Joseph Cairn, *Horses of California, Eighth Paper*, 9, 4. (Aug.1902): p235-250.

2303 Marrack, Cecil Mortimer, *Stanford University - The Real And The Ideal*, 10, 2. (Dec.1902): p90-104.

2304 Gardner, D. Charles, *Stanford's Memorial Church*, 10, 5. (Mar.1903): p409-415.

2305 Jordan, David Starr, *Jane Lathrop Stanford*, 14, 6. (Apr.1905): p632-633.

2306 Elliott, Orrin L., *The Situation at Stanford*, 17, 5. (Sep.1906): p293-294.

2307 Lanagan, James, *Rugby Vs. Intercollegiate*, 18, 1. (Nov.1906): p7-11.

2308 Jordan, David Starr, *The Stanford Jewels*, 18, 4. (Feb.1907): p303-304.

2309 Jordan, David Starr, *Save The Golden Trout*, 21, 2. (Jun.1908): p148-150.

2310 Jordan, David Starr, *Helping The Indians: What The Riverside Indian Conference Accomplished*, 22, 1. (Jan.1909): p57-61.

2311 Field, Charles K., *On The Wings Of To-Day: An Account Of The First International Aviation Meet In America, At Los Angeles, California*, 24, 3. (Mar.1910): p244-252.

2312 Field, Charles K., *Guests Of A Greater Chinatown*, 26, 5. (May.1911): p489-502.

2313 Field, Charles K., *The Return Of Yuan*, 27, 6. (Dec.1911): p697-701.

2314 Jordan, David Starr, *Japan And The United States*, 28, 1. (Jan.1912): p59-63.

2315 Jordan, David Starr, *A Man And His Mission*, 28, 2. (Feb.1912): p234-239.

2316 Smith, Everett W., *The New Stanford*, 31, 3. (Sep.1913): p494-500.

2317 Jordan, David Starr, *The Ways To Peace*, 33, 6. (Dec.1914): p1103-1108.

2318 Jordan, David Starr, *The Americans of the Hour in Europe*, 34, 6. (Jun.1915): p1175-1179.

2319 Peterson, H. C., *The Birthplace Of The Motion Picture*, 35, 5. (Nov.1915): p909-915.

2320 Jordan, David Starr, *Enduring Peace*, 36, 1. (Jan.1916): p17-18.

2321 Field, Charles K., *On The New Rialto*, 36, 1. (Jan.1916): p42-47.

2322 Field, Charles K., *On The New Rialto*, 36, 2. (Feb.1916): p23-26.

2323 Jordan, David Starr, *What Of The Nation?*, 36, 2. (Feb.1916): p19-20.

2324 Jordan, David Starr, *What Of The Nation?*, 36, 3. (Mar.1916): p25.

2325 Jordan, David Starr, *What Of The Nation?*, 36, 4. (Apr.1916): p19.

2326 Jordan, David Starr, *What Of The Nation?*, 36, 5. (May.1916): p19.

2327 Field, Charles K., *New Lights On An Old Roman*, 36, 6. (Jun.1916): p40-42, 97.

2328 Jordan, David Starr, *What Of The Nation?*, 36, 6. (Jun.1916): p24.

2329 Branner, John C., *Can We Keep The Canal Open?*, 36, 6. (Jun.1916): p13-15, 70-71.

2330 Field, Charles K., *A Japanese Idol On The American Screen*, 37, 1. (Jul.1916): p22-25, 72-73.

2331 Jordan, David Starr, *What Of The Nation?*, 37, 1. (Jul.1916): p21.

2332 Jordan, David Starr, *What Of The Nation?*, 37, 2. (Aug.1916): p27.

2333 Field, Charles K., *A Little Mother Of The Movies*, 37, 3. (Sep.1916): p30-33, 68-69.

2334 Jordan, David Starr, *What Of The Nation?*, 37, 3. (Sep.1916): p13.

2335 Jordan, David Starr, *What Of The Nation?*, 37, 4. (Oct.1916): p15.

2336 Jordan, David Starr, *What Of The Nation?*, 37, 5. (Nov.1916): p15.

2337 Jordan, David Starr, *What Of The Nation?*, 37, 6. (Dec.1916): p15-16, 39.

2338 Jordan, David Starr, *What Of The Nation?*, 38, 2. (Feb.1917): p19, 70.

2339 Jordan, David Starr, *What Of The Nation?*, 38, 3. (Mar.1917): p17, 88-90.

2340 Jordan, David Starr, *What Of The Nation?*, 38, 4. (Apr.1917): p17, 61.

2341 Jordan, David Starr, *What Of The Nation?*, 38, 5. (May.1917): p27, 70.

2342 Snell, Earl, *War And The Rah Rah Boy*, 41, 4. (Oct.1918): p24-26, 52.

2343 Jordan, David Starr, *Problems Of The Peace Table*, 42, 1. (Jan.1919): p27-29.

2344 Jordan, David Starr, *Problems Of The Peace Table*, 42, 2. (Feb.1919): p24-25, 62-64.

2345 Jordan, David Starr, *Problems Of The Peace Table*, 42, 3. (Mar.1919): p38-39, 82-84.

2346 Jordan, David Starr, *Problems Of The Peace Table*, 42, 4. (Apr.1919): p36-37.

2347 Jordan, David Starr, *Problems Of The Peace Table*, 42, 5. (May.1919): p21-23.

2348 Jordan, David Starr, *Problems Of The Peace Table*, 42, 6. (Jun.1919): p41-42, 76-78.

2349 Jordan, David Starr, *Problems Of The Peace Table*, 43, 1. (Jul.1919): p29-31.

2350 Jordan, David Starr, *Problems Of The Peace Table*, 43, 2. (Aug.1919): p46-47, 78-82.

2351 Jordan, David Starr, *The New Fight For Democracy*, 43, 3. (Sep.1919): p23-24, 89-90.

2352 Jordan, David Starr, *War And The League Of Nations*, 43, 4. (Oct.1919): p32-33.

2353 Hoover, Herbert, *Our Responsibility*, 43, 5. (Nov.1919): p14-16, 106.

2354 Jordan, David Starr, *Some Phases Of The Aftermath*, 43, 5. (Nov.1919): p41-42, 64-66.

2355 Jordan, David Starr, *When East Meets East*, 43, 6. (Dec.1919): p39-40.

2356 Taylor, Alonzo Englebert, *Hoover's Fifth Year*, 44, 1. (Jan.1920): p28-30, 80-86.

2357 Jordan, David Starr, *Pity The Poor Hermit!*, 44, 1. (Jan.1920): p48-50.

2358 Hoover, Herbert, *Unto The Least Of these*, 44, 2. (Feb.1920): p24, 109-110.

2359 Lane, Rose Wilder and Field, Charles K., *The Making Of Herbert Hoover*, 44, 4. (Apr.1920): p24-28, 121-134.

2360 Lane, Rose Wilder, *The Making Of Herbert Hoover*, 44, 5. (May.1920): p23-26, 96-116.

2361 Lane, Rose Wilder, *The Making Of Herbert Hoover*, 44, 6. (Jun.1920): p39-42, 68-70, 89-104.

2362 Lane, Rose Wilder, *The Making Of Herbert Hoover*, 45, 1. (Jul.1920): p43-46, 74-84.

2363 Lane, Rose Wilder, *The Making Of Herbert Hoover*, 45, 2. (Aug.1920): p42-44, 64-65, 72-80.

2364 Lane, Rose Wilder, *The Making Of Herbert Hoover*, 45, 3. (Sep.1920): p40-42, 52-58.

2365 Jordan, David Starr, *The Dark Stream Of World Politics*, 50, 6. (Jun.1923): p34-35, 117.

2366 Jordan, David Starr, *Evolution and Theology*, 52, 3. (Mar.1924): p15.

2367 Clarke, James R., *Touchdown!*, 55, 5. (Nov.1925): p12-15, 85-87.

2368 Wilbur, Ray Lyman and Taylor, Frank J., *What's Education For?*, 57, 6. (Dec.1926): p26-27, 54.

2370 Rowell, Chester H., *Herbert Hoover: then And Now*, 59, 5. (Nov.1927): p12-13, 84-86.

2371 *The California Home of Mr. and Mrs. Herbert Clark Hoover*, 61, 3. (Sep.1928): p56.

2372 McNab, John L., *What Hoover Means To The West*, 61, 4. (Oct.1928): p12, 14, 70-71, 83.

2373 Hoover, Herbert, *Hoover Broadcasts on the Home*, 62, 2. (Feb.1929): p23.

2374 Taylor, Frank J., *Broadening Horizons; An Interview with Dr. Ray Lyman Wilbur*, 62, 4. (Apr.1929): p17-19.

2375 Welling, Blanche E., *Neighborly Chats With One Western Mother*, 67, 6. (Dec.1931): p16.

2376 *At Stanford...8 Weeks Of Mozart*, 134, 6. (Jun.1965): p27-28.

2377 *Twentieth Century Music And Art...At Stanford*, 136, 6. (Jun.1966): p69-70.

2378 *Rodin Comes To The Bay Area*, 153, 5. (Nov.1974): p38-39.

April 1935 cover

Economic Matters

The agricultural wealth and potential of the West was one of the engines fueling the growth of the region in the early twentieth century, and this subject was covered from the outset in Sunset. *Agriculture served the Southern Pacific's aim of attracting interest in the West, while it also contributed mightily to the railroad's profits. The distinction between agriculture as a sector of the economy and agriculture as part of the charm or attraction of an area (i.e., as an aspect of tourism) was often blurred in language smacking of general boosterism. By about 1930, when the magazine started focusing on the practical, agricultural topics were de-emphasized or subsumed under discussion of food, gardening or travel. Highlighting Western Business & Industry similarly was a significant theme in the early years, and, similarly, it gave way in due course to more domestic concerns. In the vast reaches of the Western states, Transportation has played a key role in the development, settlement patterns, economy and culture of the region.* Sunset *chronicled many aspects of the growth and development of the transportation sector during its first three decades. Consonant with the later emphasis on recreational travel, in turn via rail, auto and airplane, transportation was subsumed under travel, and as such the travel section of this bibliography offer sadditional insight into transportation issues.*

3. The Economy

3.1 Agraculture

2379 Newman, R. R., *Irrigation–Past and Present*, 1, 5. (Sep.1898): p82.

2380 Sexton, Joseph, *Minor Industries Of California*, 1, 6. (Oct.1898): p102-103.

2381 *Minor Industries Of California*, 2, 1. (Nov.1898): p14-15.

2382 *Food Products Of California*, 2, 4. (Feb.1899): p75.

2383 Francis, Philip, *A Pacific Granary: Stockton, California*, 2, 5. (Mar.1899): p90-94.

2384 Downs, J. R., *Southeast California: A Valuable Section Of Mining Country And A Large Producer Of Forage Crops*, 2, 5. (Mar.1899): p111.

2385 *Important Producing Centers Of California: Fresno - Its Raisin Industry*, 2, 6. (Apr.1899): p127-128.

2386 *Food Products Of California*, 2, 6. (Apr.1899): p136.

2387 *Food Products of California*, 3, 3. (Jul.1899): p104.

2388 Buttner, L. N., *Port Costa: California's Grain Depot*, 4, 3. (Jan.1900): p104-106.

2389 Francis, Philip, *A Christmas Seed Time And A Spring Harvest In The Valley Of San Joaquin, California*, 4, 4. (Feb.1900): p126-161.

2390 Early, J. B., *Angora Goats In Oregon*, 5, 1. (May.1900): p35.

2391 *Red Pepper Money Makers*, 6, 1. (Nov.1900): p24.

2392 Lounsbury, H. E., *Dairying In Western Oregon*, 6, 2. (Dec.1900): p67-68.

2393 Wells, A. J., *Gold Mines Atop The Ground: The Olive-Growing Industry Of California And Its Promising Future*, 6, 3. (Jan.1901): p97-100.

2394 Allen, Charles H., *The Propaganda Of The Prune*, 6, 5. (Mar.1901): p164-169.

2395 Mayo, H. M., *High Land Rice Growing*, 6, 6. (Apr.1901): p191-198.

2397 Sain, Charles M., *Alfalfa In Nevada's Lovelock Valley*, 7, 2-3. (Jun.1901): p64-65.

2398 Bailey, L. H., *Stoneless Prunes, The Latest Wonder*, 7, 2-3. (Jun.1901): p81.

2399 Wells, A. J., *Growing Tannic Plants And Trees*, 7, 4. (Aug.1901): p101-102.

2400 Robinson, Ednah, *Seed Farms Of Santa Clara*, 7, 4. (Aug.1901): p106-111.

2401 Robinson, Ednah, *Oceano's Sweet Pea Farm*, 7, 5. (Sep.1901): p136-140.

2402 Shinn, Charles Howard, *Experimental Agriculture In California*, 8, 1. (Nov.1901): p15-19.

2403 Wells, A. J., *A Thanksgiving Ranch*, 8, 1. (Nov.1901): p22-24.

2404 Robinson, Ednah, *Carnations By The Sea*, 8, 2. (Dec.1901): p77-80.

2405 Knox, Jessie Juliet, *In A Garden Of Sleep: Onion Growing In The Santa Clara Valley*, 8, 3. (Jan.1902): p119-127.

2406 Wells, A. J., *A Western Valley Of The Nile*, 8, 5. (Mar.1902): p189-198.

2407 Green, Will S., *California's Inland Empire - The Sacramento Valley*, 8, 6. (Apr.1902): p231-250.

2408 Brown, Colvin B., *Millions In Potatoes*, 9, 1. (May.1902): p13-17.

2409 Thomas, Kate, *Wool Production Of California*, 9, 2. (Jun.1902): p95-96.

2410 Enderlein, Ella H., *Sugar Beets At Oxnard*, 9, 2. (Jun.1902): p113-117 .

2411 Wells, A. J., *The Land Of Opportunity: A Word To The Prospective Settler In California*, 9, 5. (Sep.1902): p332-335.

2412 Robinson, Ednah, *City Duck Farming*, 9, 6. (Oct.1902): p385-387.

2413 Cahill, Auguste M., *Celery For Commerce*, 10, 1. (Nov.1902): p53-56.

2414 Griffiths, David, *Range Improvement In Arizona*, 10, 1. (Nov.1902): p63-68.

2415 A Harvard Man, *Among Oregon Apples*, 10, 1. (Nov.1902): p70-71.

2416 *Rubber And How It Grows*, 10, 1. (Nov.1902): p41-43.

2417 Aiken, Charles S., *Thanksgiving Day Oranges*, 10, 3. (Dec.1902): p219-224.

2418 Honn, D. N., *A County That's An Empire: Study Of The Wonderful Mining, Agricultural And Horticultural Resources Of Shasta County, California*, 10, 3. (Jan.1903): p229-235.

2419 Ferry, Louis, *Eight Years On A Lemon Ranch*, 11, 2. (Jun.1903): p154-159.

2420 Wells, A. J., *The Bee Ranch In The Canyon*, 11, 3. (Jul.1903): p227-229.

2421 Smith, Bertha H., *Bees For Profit*, 11, 4. (Aug.1903): p334-340.

2422 Wells, A. J., *Concerning Sardines*, 11, 4. (Aug.1903): p379-380.

2423 Raine, William MacLeod, *Where Water Works Wonders*, 11, 5. (Sep.1903): p401-406.

2424 Basley, A.,Mrs., *My Chickens*, 11, 5. (Sep.1903): p412-417.

2425 Robinson, Ednah, *The Commerce Of Blossom Land*, 11, 5. (Sep.1903): p441-449.

2426 Smith, Bertha H., *Ten Thousand Squabs*, 11, 6. (Oct.1903): p545-546.

2427 Houghton, Emily, *Merinos Of Rag Gulch*, 12, 1. (Nov.1903): p29-34.

2428 Wickson, Edward J., *The National Irrigation Congress*, 12, 1. (Nov.1903): p60-64.

2429 Wright, Helen Ellsworth, *The Mission Of Hops*, 12, 3. (Jan.1904): p237-243.

2430 Marshall, Emma Seckle, *Hop Culture In Oregon*, 12, 3. (Jan.1904): p243-246.

2431 Cannon, J. S., *Something About Rubber*, 12, 3. (Jan.1904): p260-261.

2432 Wells, A. J., *California's Netherlands*, 12, 5. (Mar.1904): p 380-389.

2433 Cumming, Al M., *Where The Goose Honks High*, 12, 5. (Mar.1904): p404-410.

2434 Wells, A. J., *California's Netherlands, Second Paper*, 12, 6. (Apr.1904): p511-523.

2435 Whitney, J. Parker, *Oranges Of Sierra Foothills*, 12, 6. (Apr.1904): p543-553.

2436 Dickinson, C. A., *A Fig For A Fortune*, 13, 2. (Jun.1904): p149-153.

2437 Clarke, E. P., *California's Fruit Industry*, 13, 3. (Jul.1904): p239-242.

2438 Houghton, Edward T., *Forests Grown While You Wait*, 13, 4. (Aug.1904): p358-364.

2439 Howell, H. D., *Farming For Feathers*, 13, 5. (Sep.1904): p468-471.

2440 Marshall, Emma Seckle, *Dairying In Oregon*, 13, 6. (Oct.1904): p545-547.

2441 Dudley, M. E., *The Olive Industry In California*, 13, 6. (Oct.1904): p459-463.

2442 Kimball, Frank A., *How I Make Olive Oil*, 13, 6. (Oct.1904): p464-465.

2443 Chandler, Katherine, *How Almonds Are Grown*, 13, 6. (Oct.1904): p465-467.

2444 Marshall, Emma Seckle, *Cranberry Culture In The Northwest*, 14, 2. (Dec.1904): p170-171.

2445 Rogers, Alma A., *Oregon's Prune Product*, 14, 3. (Jan.1905): p259-262.

2446 Marshall, John, *Rice Of The Gulf*, 14, 3. (Jan.1905): p273-277.

2447 *Redeeming The Arid West: Important Results Of The Recent National Irrigation Congress At El Paso, Texas*, 14, 4. (Feb.1905): p325-338.

2448 Chandler, A. E., *The Reclamation Of Nevada*, 14, 4. (Feb.1905): p339-348.

2449 Hall, Sharlot M., *Ostrich Farming In Arizona*, 14, 6. (Apr.1905): p627-631.

2450 Kirk, Heatherwick, *A Lemon Propaganda*, 15, 2. (Jun.1905): p190-192.

2451 Ward, Elizabeth A., *Lemon Growing In California*, 15, 2. (Jun.1905): p192-198.

2452 Fox, Charles P., *The Empire of Kern*, 15, 2. (Jun.1905): p179-189.

2453 Wright, James L., *Rice In Texas*, 16, 6. (Apr.1906): p594-589.

2454 Marshall, Emma Seckle, *Oregon's Wool Industry*, 17, 4. (Aug.1906): p144-147.

2455 Whitney, J. Parker, *Educational Orange Growing*, 17, 4. (Aug.1906): p161-170.

2456 Wells, A. J., *Oranges Of The Foothills*, 17, 4. (Aug.1906): p171-173.

2457 Blanchard, C. J., *Redeeming The West: What The Great Klamath Project Means In Government Reclamation*, 17, 5. (Sep.1906): p206-214.

2458 McKay, G. L., *Oregon's Dairying*, 18, 1. (Nov.1906): p21-23.

2459 Stovall, Dennis H., *Oregon Angoras*, 18, 4. (Feb.1907): p309-312.

2460 Sheldon, Willard M., *Irrigation As A Social Factor*, 19, 2. (Jun.1907): p168-170.

2461 Marshall, Emma Seckle, *Oregon's Irrigon*, 19, 3. (Jul.1907): p233-236.

2462 Stovall, Dennis H., *Diversified Farming In Oregon*, 19, 4. (Aug.1907): p360-362.

2463 Blanchard, C. J., *Uncle Sam's New Farm: How Projected Work Of The Reclamation Service, Irrigating, And Redeeming The Desert, Will Add 6,468,000 Acres To The Nation's Crop-Producing Area*, 19, 5. (Sep.1907): p487-492.

2464 Smith, Bertha H., *A Sea Of Trees: The Story Of Old Sylmar, The Largest Olive Orchard In The World*, 19, 6. (Oct.1907): p571-576.

2465 Chapman, Arthur, *The War In The West: Tragedies Of Mountains And Prairies Resulting From Disputed Range Claims Between The Sheep And Cattle Men*, 20, 2. (Dec.1907): p103-109.

2466 Toles, Justin Kay, *Western Flax Culture*, 20, 4. (Feb.1908): p328-336.

2467 McAdie, Alexander G., *Frost, Snow And Dew*, 20, 4. (Feb.1908): p336-338.

2468 Dudley, M. E., *Among The Honey Makers*, 20, 5. (Mar.1908): p475-482.

2469 Paul, E. V. D., *Mountain Top Fruit: What Enterprise And Brains Are Doing In The Cañons And Forest Clearings Of Mendocino*, 21, 3. (Jul.1908): p231-234.

2470 Dunn, Allan, *Where The Land Owns The Water: The Successful Municipal Irrigation Districts Of Sunny Stanislaus*, 21, 4. (Aug.1908): .

2471 Aiken, Charles S., *The Surprise Of The Desert: That Country Of Cantaloupes And Corner Lots, Of Alfalfa And Ambition - Imperial - Where Runaway Water And Wide-Awake Men Are Busily Making The World's Greatest Oasis*, 21, 5. (Sep.1908): p375-398.

2472 Wells, A. J., *Twin Towns Of The Touchet: Dayton And Waitsburg, Two Capitals Of An Inland Empire - What The Whirligig Of Time Is Doing In The Old Bunchgrass Country Of Washington*, 21, 6. (Oct.1908): p561-568.

2473 Wells, A. J., *In Medford's Garden*, 21, 7. (Nov.1908): p677-683.

2474 Wells, A. J., *In The Klamath Country*, 22, 2. (Feb.1909): p210-214.

2475 Wells, A. J., *A Call To The Commuter: Washington County, Oregon*, 22, 3. (Mar.1909): p311-316.

2476 Wisner, Edward, *The American Holland: Natural Riches Reclaimed From The Mississippi In The Delta Lands Of The Great River*, 22, 3. (Mar.1909): p319-320.

2477 Wells, A. J., *On Umatilla Farms*, 22, 5. (May.1909): p551-556.

2478 Wells, A. J., *The Romance Of The Fresno Ranch*, 22, 5. (May.1909): p557-559.

2479 Littlepage, Louella Prouty, *The Useful Colorado*, 22, 6. (Jun.1909): p615-621.

2480 Walker, David H., *The Kern River As Farmer*, 22, 6. (Jun.1909): p684-686.

2481 Dunn, Allan, *The Little Kingdom Of Kerman*, 22, 6. (Jun.1909): p679-684.

2482 Wells, A. J., *The Garden Of Glenn*, 22, 6. (Jun.1909): p687-690.

2483 Burnham, Llewellyn, *'One Thousand Dollars Reward': How An Offer Seemed Easy Money Until The Contest Conditions Were Learned*, 23, 1. (Jul.1909): p108-109.

2484 Wells, A. J., *A Matter Of Manifest Destiny: The Place Of Colusa County In The Future Of The Sacramento Valley - Oranges And Alfalfa - Big Farms And Little Farms - Grapes, Olives And Figs - The County An Epitome Of The Valley*, 23, 1. (Jul.1909): p110-112.

2485 Wells, A. J., *Slicing The Great Ranches*, 23, 2. (Aug.1909): p219-221.

2486 Wells, A. J., *A Blossoming Desert: The Salt River Valley, The Glory Of Arizona, A Semi-Tropical Region With A Great Future*, 23, 2. (Aug.1909): p209-214.

2487 Sheridan, Sol N., *Beauty And The Beets: Ventury County, California, Where Scenery, Climate And Agriculture Combine To Make A World's Record*, 23, 2. (Aug.1909): p215-218.

2488 Goldsmith, Paul, *Putting Land Through The Wringer: How A Vast Acreage Of Marsh Near Pleasanton, California, Has Been Dried Out And Made Into Unexcelled Farming Land - Notable Example Of Advanced Hydraulic Engineering*, 23, 4. (Oct.1909): p433-434.

2489 Dasent, Bury Irwin, *Cherry Ripe! How Salem, Oregon, Is Being Made Famous As 'The Cherry City Of The World'*, 23, 5. (Nov.1909): p543-548.

2490 Wells, A. J., *Taproots Of Wealth: How Riches Are Rooted In Madera County, California*, 23, 5. (Nov.1909): p539-542.

2491 Wells, A. J., *A Valley County: Solano Farms And Orchards - A Solid Bit Of The Sacramento Valley With A Moist Margin*, 23, 6. (Dec.1909): p659-662.

2492 Bennett, Mark, *The Pittsburg Syndicate's Latest: Straight Facts About The Slicing Up Of The Sacramento Valley's Big Grain Farms*, 24, 1. (Jan.1910): p100-103.

2493 Husmann, George C., *Viticulture In California*, 24, 2. (Feb.1910): p132-137.

2494 Hall, Wilbur, *Just Like Dixie Land*, 24, 2. (Feb.1910): p173-175.

2495 Leake, Frank, *'Let The Dry Land Appear': How The Wet Prairies Built By The Mississippi River Are Being Made Into Phenomenal Farms*, 24, 2. (Feb.1910): p237-240.

2496 Cowan, John L., *Again The Busy Bee: How The Tiny Blastophaga Has Made Possible California's Growing Fig Industry*, 24, 3. (Mar.1910): p296-305.

2497 Steele, Rufus M., *What Pre-Cooling Means: Treatment Of California Fruit So It Will Reach Consumers Fresh From Tree Or Vine*, 24, 3. (Mar.1910): p339-343.

2498 Robertson, William, *Empire-Building Irrigation*, 24, 3. (Mar.1910): p351-354.

2499 Clark, Walter E., *Farming In Alaska*, 24, 5. (May.1910): p495-502.

2500 Coolidge, Dane, *With The Cherrycow Outfit*, 24, 5. (May.1910): p518-527.

2501 Atkinson, Reilly, *Busy Boise: The Story Of An Idaho City That Is Keeping Pace With The Progress Of Irrigation*, 24, 5. (May.1910): p593-596.

2502 Fay, Oliver H., *Fields And Factories: The Richly Productive County Of San Joaquin, California*, 24, 5. (May.1910): p587-590.

2503 Mosessohn, M., *Ambition And Apples: How The Bustling Young City Of Newberg, Oregon, Is Coming Of Age*, 24, 5. (May.1910): p591-592.

2504 Flicker, Andrew, *The Cost Of Living: A Transplanted Ohio Farmer's Solution Of The Problem*, 24, 6. (Jun.1910): p677-681.

2505 Mills, John Scott, *Burley And The Minidoka Project: How The Storage Of The Storm Waters Of The Snake River By The United States Government Is Building Up A Thriving Community In Idaho, With Burley As Its Distributing Center*, 24, 6. (Jun.1910): p707-708.

2506 Mills, John Scott, *How Water Backs Up Financially: Irrigation As An Asset - What The Town Of Gooding Has Accomplished In Sunny Southern Idaho*, 24, 6. (Jun.1910): p713-716.

2507 Coolidge, Dane, *The Cherrycow Horse-Changing*, 25, 1. (Jul.1910): p49-57.

2508 Mills, John Scott, *Merit In Irrigated Land: Richfield And Dietrich Tracts In Southern Idaho Attracting Settlers By Their Fertility*, 25, 1. (Jul.1910): p121-124.

3. The Economy

2509 Mosessohn, M., *In The Valley Of Content: Sheridan, Oregon - A City In The Making*, 25, 1. (Jul.1910): p112-114.

2510 Mills, John Scott, *Mount Hood's Front Yard: Mosier Hills, Oregon, On The Banks Of The Columbia, Renowned For The Excellence Of Its Orchard Products*, 25, 2. (Aug.1910): p229-230.

2511 Mills, John Scott, *Oregon's Garden Of Eden: Creswell And The Willamette Valley A Paradise For The Horticulturist, For The Agriculturist And For Others*, 25, 2. (Aug.1910): p231-232.

2512 Mills, John Scott, *A Western Oneida Community: American Falls, Idaho, Where Irrigation And Dry Farming Are Making Landowners Money Kings*, 25, 2. (Aug.1910): p237-241.

2513 Mills, John Scott, *Divided Wealth: Pioneer Holdings Being Segregated - Choice Fruit, Farm And Stock Lands In Caliapooia Valley Have Been Placed On The Market*, 25, 2. (Aug.1910): p235-236.

2514 Griffiths, David, *Vindicating The Prickly-Pear*, 25, 3. (Sep.1910): p273-276.

2515 Hall, Wilbur, *The Prize Farms Of Yuma*, 25, 3. (Sep.1910): p301-306.

2516 Mills, John Scott, *Twin Falls And Triple Opportunity*, 25, 3. (Sep.1910): p353-356.

2517 Barnes, William C., *Sheep Without A Shepherd*, 25, 4. (Oct.1910): p452-455.

2518 Mills, John Scott, *The Man With The Plow: Some Of The Things That He Is Doing At Rupert, Idaho, The Center Of Eighty Thousand Irrigated Acres*, 25, 4. (Oct.1910): p475-476.

2519 Wells, A. J., *In Apple Land: Pajaro Valley, Edenic Home Of A Million Apple-Laden Trees, And Another Million Coming Into Bearing*, 25, 4. (Oct.1910): p479-480.

2520 Mills, John Scott, *Riches Of An Inland Empire: Idaho Falls, Surrounded By Fertile Lands And Productive Mines, Is Growing In Population And Prestige*, 25, 4. (Oct.1910): p471-474.

2521 Mills, John Scott, *The Secret Of Success In Blackfoot*, 25, 5. (Nov.1910): p589-590.

2522 Wells, A. J., *Madera; A Pathway To Prosperity*, 25, 5. (Nov.1910): p593-594.

2523 Wilson, Bourdon, *The Surprise Of Modoc: Where Incoming Railroads Are Beating The Cowboys' Spurs Into The Pruning-knife And The Combined Harvester, Converting Vast Grazing Lands Into Fruitful Orchards And Fields*, 25, 5. (Nov.1910): p595-598.

2524 Mills, John Scott, *Where Farming Is A Science: Umatilla Project At Hermiston, Oregon, Offers Unexceptional Opportunities To The Man Of Limited Means*, 25, 5. (Nov.1910): p599-600.

2525 Wilson, Bourdon, *Imperial Valley The Ideal*, 25, 6. (Dec.1910): p710-711.

2526 Wilson, Bourdon, *The New Land Of Lassen*, 26, 1. (Jan.1911): p109-112.

2527 Mills, John Scott, *Ideal Farms Of The Inland Empire*, 26, 1. (Jan.1911): p113-116.

2528 Mills, John Scott, *From Garrison To Golconda*, 26, 1. (Jan.1911): p117-120.

2529 Ashley, A. S., *In The Land Of Plenty*, 26, 2. (Feb.1911): p237-240.

2530 Wells, A. J., *Fresno County, California*, 26, 2. (Feb.1911): p241-248.

2531 Parkhurst, Genevieve Yoell, *Yuba County, California*, 26, 2. (Feb.1911): p247-248.

2532 Mills, John Scott, *Riches of the Inland Empire*, 26, 2. (Feb.1911): p245-246.

2533 Woehlke, Walter V., *In The Orange Country*, 26, 3. (Mar.1911): p251-264.

2534 Mills, John Scott, *Wealth Along The Willamette*, 26, 3. (Mar.1911): p357-360.

2535 Jones, V. Vincent, *Layers Of Gold*, 26, 4. (Apr.1911): p395-400.

2536 Miller, O. H., *King Farmer*, 26, 5. (May.1911): p573-575.

2537 Wilson, Bourdon, *The Irrigation Of Glenn*, 26, 5. (May.1911): p580-581.

2538 Andrus, S. Glen, *The Nile Of The West*, 26, 5. (May.1911): p475-488, 571-572.

2539 Woehlke, Walter V., *Transplanting The Garden Of Eden*, 26, 6. (Jun.1911): p587-600.

2540 Andrews, H. L., *Grant's Pass, Oregon*, 26, 6. (Jun.1911): p684-687.

2541 Malboeuf, Charles A., *The Prince Of Pears–Doyen Du Comice*, 26, 6. (Jun.1911): p688-689.

2542 Wells, A. J., *San Joaquin County, California*, 26, 6. (Jun.1911): p693.

2543 Walker, David H., *Mission Chimes And Bumper Crops*, 26, 6. (Jun.1911): p697-698.

2544 Thacher, W. F. G., *St. Anthony, Idaho - On The Trail Of The Snake*, 27, 1. (Jul.1911): p108-109.

2545 Buckley, Louis W., *The Omaha Land Show*, 27, 1. (Jul.1911): p111-112.

2546 Mills, John Scott, *Silverton And Its Resources*, 27, 2. (Aug.1911): p223-224.

2547 Walker, David H.,Jr., *Madeline Meadows*, 27, 2. (Aug.1911): p225-226.

2548 Wells, A. J., *A Bit Of The Ideal*, 27, 3. (Sep.1911): p343-346.

2549 Levick, M. B., *Mines For Mendocino Farmers*, 27, 3. (Sep.1911): p347-348.

2550 Hope, Francis, *The Empire North Of The Bay*, 27, 3. (Sep.1911): p349-350.

2551 Levick, M. B., *Lindsay*, 27, 3. (Sep.1911): p351-352.

2552 Thacher, W. F. G., *Walla Walla–The Garden City Of Washington*, 27, 4. (Oct.1911): p457-460.

2553 Thacher, W. F. G., *Attalia–On The Columbia*, 27, 4. (Oct.1911): p461-462.

2554 Walker, David H.,Jr., *Palo Verde–Gem Of Valleys*, 27, 4. (Oct.1911): p463-464.

2555 Wilson, Bourdon, *The Fruit Lands Of Siskiyou*, 27, 4. (Oct.1911): p465-468.

2556 Mills, John Scott, *Kennewick And Its Environs*, 27, 4. (Oct.1911): p469-472.

2557 Woehlke, Walter V., *The Inland Emperors*, 27, 5. (Nov.1911): p475-488.

2558 Walker, David H.,Jr., *Where Fruit-Trees Play Hide-And-Seek*, 27, 5. (Nov.1911): p584.

2559 Wolf, August, *Marvels Of The Spokane Country*, 27, 5. (Nov.1911): p585-588.

2560 Mills, John Scott, *Sunnyside And Its Varied Resources*, 27, 5. (Nov.1911): p589-592.

2561 Thacher, W. F. G., *North Yakima And Yakima County*, 27, 5. (Nov.1911): p593-596.

2562 Mills, John Scott, *Endorsed By Uncle Sam*, 27, 5. (Nov.1911): p597-598.

2563 Thacher, W. F. G., *Weiser–Why And Wherefore*, 27, 6. (Dec.1911): p705-708.

2564 Levick, M. B., *Fortunes In Free Lands*, 27, 6. (Dec.1911): p711-712.

2565 Wilson, Bourdon, *The Riches Of San Benito*, 27, 6. (Dec.1911): p715-716.

2566 Thacher, W. F. G., *Buhl, Idaho–The Land That Beckons*, 27, 6. (Dec.1911): p717-718.

2567 Thacher, W. F. G., *Yamhill, Oregon*, 28, 1. (Jan.1912): p119-120.

2568 Thacher, W. F. G., *Montpelier And Bear Lake County, Idaho*, 28, 1. (Jan.1912): p123-124.

2569 Blanton, C. Peebles, *Nature's Golden Gift To Man*, 28, 1. (Jan.1912): p125-127.

2570 Levick, M. B., *Sacramento County–The Heart Of California*, 28, 2. (Feb.1912): p247-250.

2571 Woodhead, William, *A Missionary To The Oregon Farmers*, 28, 2. (Feb.1912): p255-256.

2572 Mills, John Scott, *Homes For The Homeseekers*, 28, 3. (Mar.1912): p380-383.

2573 Fisher, C. E., *Lebanon, Land Of Opportunity*, 28, 3. (Mar.1912): p386.

2574 Woehlke, Walter V., *The Land Of Before-And-After*, 28, 4. (Apr.1912): p391-400.

2575 Du Puy, William Atherton, *Uncle Sam's Cocoanuts*, 28, 4. (Apr.1912): p412-416.

2576 Levick, M. B., *Kern–A County Of Wonders*, 28, 4. (Apr.1912): p503-506.

2577 von Vieregg, G., *Imperial, The Valley Of Cotton, Cantaloupes And Contentment*, 28, 4. (Apr.1912): p507-508.

2578 von Vieregg, G., *Deming And The Mimbres Valley*, 28, 4. (Apr.1912): p509-510.

2579 Levick, M. B., *Secrets Of Sutter's Prosperity*, 28, 4. (Apr.1912): p511-512.

2580 Levick, M. B., *The Rich Resources Of Siskiyou County*, 28, 5. (May.1912): p635-638.

2581 Hartog, J. H., *A Chance For Everybody*, 28, 5. (May.1912): p639-640.

2582 Thacher, W. F. G., *The Potential Wealth Of Morrow County*, 28, 5. (May.1912): p643-644.

2583 Fisher, C. E., *You Will Want Your Orchard To Look Like Ours*, 28, 5. (May.1912): p649.

2584 Levick, M. B., *Sonoma–The County Of Fertile Valleys*, 28, 6. (Jun.1912): p767-770.

2585 Lee, Rudolph, *Dixon: A Town That Believes In Itself*, 28, 6. (Jun.1912): p775-776.

2586 Teck, Frank Carleton, *Realities Like Luring Dreams*, 29, 1. (Jul.1912): p108-110.

2587 Ellis, Garton T., *Nevada: The Banner Gold County*, 29, 1. (Jul.1912): p113-114.

2588 von Vieregg, G., *Santa Clara: The Delectable Valley*, 29, 2. (Aug.1912): p215-218.

2589 Wells, A. J., *The San Joaquin; An Irrigated Empire*, 29, 3. (Sep.1912): p331-334.

2590 Bedichek, R., *The Sunniest Corner Of The Sunshine State*, 29, 3. (Sep.1912): p335-336.

2591 Kendall, Isabelle Carpenter, *The Kittitas Valley–Washington*, 29, 3. (Sep.1912): p339-341.

2592 Levick, M. B., *Modoc County*, 29, 3. (Sep.1912): p347-348.

2593 Levick, M. B., *Yuba's Yield Of Bounty*, 29, 3. (Sep.1912): p349-350.

2594 Mills, John Scott, *Land That Is Worth While*, 29, 3. (Sep.1912): p353.

2595 Woehlke, Walter V., *The Garden Of Utah*, 29, 4. (Oct.1912): p359-368.

2596 Caine, Joseph E., *Utah–'The Center Of The Solid West'*, 29, 4. (Oct.1912): p463-466.

2597 Mills, John Scott, *Benton The Gateway City*, 29, 4. (Oct.1912): p467-468.

2598 Thacher, W. F. G., *Pullman*, 29, 4. (Oct.1912): p469-470.

2599 Thacher, W. F. G., *Zillah*, 29, 4. (Oct.1912): p471-472.

2600 Mills, John Scott, *Free Lands Of The Inland Empire*, 29, 4. (Oct.1912): p473-474.

2601 von Vieregg, G., *Land–The Lure Of Lassen*, 29, 4. (Oct.1912): p475-476.

2602 Norcross, Charles A., *Nevada: The Coming Potato Land*, 29, 5. (Nov.1912): p587-590.

2603 Mills, John Scott, *Rogue River Valley, Southern Oregon*, 29, 5. (Nov.1912): p591-594.

2604 Morrison, Robert A., *Kern County: Picturesque And Profitable*, 30, 1. (Jan.1913): p76-82.

2605 Maulsby, F. R., *San Simon: A Valley Of Opportunity*, 30, 1. (Jan.1913): p84.

2606 Fisher, C. E., *Where The Poor Man Sets Foot On The Ladder Of Prosperity*, 30, 1. (Jan.1913): p86-88.

2607 Mills, John Scott, *Logged-Off Lands For The Farmer*, 30, 1. (Jan.1913): p90-92.

2608 Ellis, Garton T., *Mariposa County: Yosemite And Apples*, 30, 1. (Jan.1913): p94-96.

2609 Fisher, C. E., *To Hunt And Fish And Farm*, 30, 1. (Jan.1913): p74.

2610 Ellis, Garton T., *The Farms Of Monterey County*, 30, 2. (Feb.1913): p74-76.

2611 Holt, Emerson, *Dixon Dairies And The Babies*, 30, 2. (Feb.1913): p78-80.

2612 Gower, Walter Mainhall, *Tulare: The County Of Versatility*, 30, 2. (Feb.1913): p82-88.

2613 Woehlke, Walter V., *The San Joaquin*, 30, 3. (Mar.1913): p219-229.

2614 Holt, Emerson, *Stanislaus, California–Kingdom Of The Small Farmer*, 30, 3. (Mar.1913): p66-70.

2615 Fisher, C. E., *Lodi, California–A Living And Plus*, 30, 3. (Mar.1913): p76-78.

2616 Foster, Charles E., *Mesa, Arizona–Gateway To The Roosevelt Dam*, 30, 3. (Mar.1913): p80-82.

2617 Laut, Agnes C., *Save The Citrus Groves!*, 30, 4. (Apr.1913): p325-334.

2618 Bradley, D. H., *Fresno County, California: Ten Acres And 3,862,390 Besides*, 30, 4. (Apr.1913): p66-72.

2619 Holt, Emerson, *Sacramento: A California County Of Superlative Fertility*, 30, 4. (Apr.1913): p74-80.

2620 Allen, M. E. L., *Casa Grande Valley: The Fruit Basket Of The Southwest*, 30, 5. (May.1913): p616.

2621 Egilbert, W. D., *Shasta, California: A Sovereignty In Itself*, 30, 6. (Jun.1913): p846-52.

2622 Cross, A. E., *Why The Turlock, California, District Is Different*, 30, 6. (Jun.1913): p858-860.

2623 Holt, Emerson, *Sonoma: The Valley Of The Moon*, 31, 1. (Jul.1913): p178-184.

2624 Day, W. H., *Ashland: An Oregon "Home" City*, 31, 1. (Jul.1913): p186.

2625 Bliven, B. O., *Coachella: The Valley Of The Date*, 31, 1. (Jul.1913): p188.

2626 Holt, Emerson, *San Joaquin–A Modern Californian El Dorado*, 31, 2. (Aug.1913): p378-384.

2627 Lighton, William R., *The Land Where Life Is Large*, 31, 3. (Sep.1913): p459-472.

2628 Maulsby, F. R., *Why They Came Back To Antelope Valley*, 31, 3. (Sep.1913): p576.

2629 Dunn, Arthur, *Kern's Getting There*, 31, 4. (Oct.1913): p782-788.

2630 Dunn, Arthur, *Monterey, The Magnificent*, 31, 5. (Nov.1913): p1010-1016.

2631 Dunn, Arthur, *Toulumne's New Golden Era*, 31, 6. (Dec.1913): p1254-1256.

2632 Fisher, C. E., *Coos Bay Coming Into Her Own*, 31, 6. (Dec.1913): p1258.

2633 Tarpey, M. F., *The Grape-Vine In California*, 32, 1. (Jan.1914): p202-208.

2634 Cole, W. Russell, *Smiling Sonoma County*, 32, 1. (Jan.1914): p210-214.

2635 Woehlke, Walter V., *The Rejuvenation Of San Fernando*, 32, 2. (Feb.1914): p357-365, 416.

2636 Holt, Emerson, *What Fresno County Raises Beside Raisins*, 32, 2. (Feb.1914): p426-430.

2637 Dunn, Arthur, *Cheer Up! Solano Cherries Are Ripe*, 32, 3. (Mar.1914): p656-660.

2638 Maulsby, F. R., *The Antelope Valley Breaks A Record*, 32, 3. (Mar.1914): p662.

2639 Holt, Emerson, *Twenty To Forty Acres And Success–Yolo*, 32, 4. (Apr.1914): p894-896.

2640 Hymer, Otis, *The Way They Do Things In Kern*, 32, 4. (Apr.1914): p898-900.

2641 Woehlke, Walter V., *In The Cream Of The Wheat Country*, 32, 5. (May.1914): p1050-1059.

2642 Holt, Emerson, *San Joaquin County–A Powerful Magnet For Opportunity Seekers*, 32, 5. (May.1914): p1118-1122.

2643 Dittmar, M. E., *The Olive: Shasta Country's Symbol Of Peace And Prosperity*, 33, 1. (Jul.1914): p170-174.

2644 Holt, Emerson, *The Enchanted Valley Of The Rogue*, 33, 2. (Aug.1914): p380-382.

3. The Economy

2645 Myers, John F., *The "Folly" Of The Great Gadsden Purchase*, 33, 5. (Nov.1914): p988-992.

2646 Willard, Walter, *When the Rainmaker Came to Kern*, 34, 1. (Jan.1915): p164-166, 168, 170.

2647 Willard, Walter, *The Story of Semple*, 34, 3. (Mar.1915): p406, 408.

2648 Holt, Emerson, *Nevada Homes for Industrious Farmers*, 34, 5. (May.1915): p1014, 1016.

2649 Woehlke, Walter V., *Stumps And Milking Stools*, 35, 1. (Jul.1915): p107-116.

2650 Woehlke, Walter V., *On The Trial Of The Wheat Gamblers*, 35, 2. (Aug.1915): p307-316.

2651 Holt, Emerson, *More Land Than Farmers*, 35, 2. (Aug.1915): p422-424.

2652 Willard, Walter, *The Fruits Of Cooperative Irrigation*, 35, 3. (Sep.1915): p620-624.

2653 Woehlke, Walter V., *The Pump In A Thirsty Land*, 35, 4. (Oct.1915): p713-721.

2654 Woehlke, Walter V., *What Ails The Big Red Apple?*, 35, 5. (Nov.1915): p916-925.

2655 Holt, Emerson, *Wanted–In the San Joaquin Valley, General Farmers*, 35, 5. (Nov.1915): p820, 822, 824.

2656 Fisher, Clarence E., *The Rice Fields of the Sacramento Valley*, 35, 6. (Dec.1915): p1024, 1026, 1028.

2657 Woehlke, Walter V., *The Taming Of The Rio Grande*, 36, 1. (Jan.1916): p39-41, 88-94.

2658 Fisher, Clarence E., *Sugar On The Farm*, 36, 1. (Jan.1916): p80-85.

2659 Woehlke, Walter V., *The Soul's Awakening And The Price Of Prunes*, 36, 5. (May.1916): p26-27, 75.

2660 Metzger, S. S., *A Day On The Ranch*, 37, 1. (Jul.1916): p47.

2661 Adams, Edward F., *Paternal Irrigation In Australia*, 37, 2. (Aug.1916): p34-35, 60-66.

2662 Woehlke, Walter V., *The Grape And Prohibition*, 37, 4. (Oct.1916): p9-11, 92-94.

2663 Barrows, David P., *Giving The New Settler A Lift*, 38, 3. (Mar.1917): p20-21.

2664 Hall, Wilbur, *Way Down Upon De Alamo Ribber (sic)*, 38, 6. (Jun.1917): p17-19, 46-54.

2665 Mead, Elwood, *Farming His Own*, 39, 3. (Sep.1917): p26-27, 67-70.

2666 Ferguson, Lillian, *It Beats The Dutch!*, 39, 4. (Oct.1917): p42-43, 60.

2667 Harris, A. H., *The Golden Fleece*, 39, 5. (Nov.1917): p33-35, 62-63.

2668 Bennett, Estelline, *Home Fires*, 41, 1. (Jul.1918): p30-31.

2669 Beebe, Ford I., *Homesteading On The Windswept*, 41, 2. (Aug.1918): p21-23, 54-59.

2670 Shirley, Edith, *When The Boys Come Home*, 41, 2. (Aug.1918): p28.

2671 Hughes, Agnes Lockhart, *Pigs Is More Than Pigs!*, 42, 1. (Jan.1919): p31-32.

2672 Anstruther, Eleanor, *The Newlyweds And Their Goat*, 42, 1. (Jan.1919): p25-26.

2673 Hall, Wilbur, *Cultivated Weeds*, 42, 5. (May.1919): p41-43, 58.

2674 Beebe, Ford I., *Society Of The Windswept*, 42, 6. (Jun.1919): p17-20, 82-91.

2675 Dickie, Francis J., *The T-Bone Of Tomorrow*, 43, 6. (Dec.1919): p41-42, 92.

2676 Stratton, George Frederic, *When The Drouth Came*, 45, 2. (Aug.1920): p36-38, 50.

2677 Bordwell, Georgia Graves, *Who Says White Folks Won't Work?*, 45, 6. (Dec.1920): p28-31, 101-104.

2678 Bordwell, Georgia Graves, *Nothing Down But Hard Work*, 46, 1. (Jan.1921): p21-23, 46.

2679 FitzGerald, Harold J., *Easy Come, Easy Go*, 46, 3. (Mar.1921): p26-27, 64-65, 94-95.

2680 Woehlke, Walter V., *What Cotton Did For Arizona*, 47, 1. (Jul.1921): p21-23, 62-64.

2681 Perry, Austin D., *How I Acquired My Little Farm*, 47, 4. (Oct.1921): p42-43.

2682 Dukeman, A., *How I Acquired My Little Farm*, 47, 5. (Nov.1921): p29, 66-68.

2683 Woehlke, Walter V., *The Courage Of The West*, 47, 6. (Dec.1921): p22-26, 70-72.

2684 Worley, Guy, *How I Acquired My Little Farm*, 47, 6. (Dec.1921): p41, 57.

2685 Lewis, William Corodon, *How I Acquired My Little Farm*, 48, 1. (Jan.1922): p51, 68.

2686 Griffiths, Julia B., *How I Acquired My Little Farm*, 48, 2. (Feb.1922): p36, 66.

2687 Tracy, Ray Palmer, *Lambs, Ewes And Devils*, 48, 3. (Mar.1922): p16-19, 68-69.

2688 Kay, Myrtle, *The Homestead On Cedar Mesa*, 49, 1. (Jul.1922): p16-18, 56-58.

2689 Kay, Myrtle, *The Homestead On Cedar Mesa*, 49, 2. (Aug.1922): p17-20.

2690 Kay, Myrtle, *The Homestead On Cedar Mesa*, 49, 3. (Sep.1922): p21-23, 50-52.

2691 Woehlke, Walter V., *Alien Enemies*, 49, 4. (Oct.1922): p16-18,58.

2692 Woehlke, Walter V., *The Bugs' World Conquest*, 49, 6. (Dec.1922): p15-16, 83-88.

2693 Woehlke, Walter V., *Asiatic Parasites In Our Forests*, 50, 1. (Jan.1923): p30-31, 67.

2694 Tracy, Ray Palmer, *The Romantic Cow*, 51, 2. (Aug.1923): p17-19, 54-56.

2695 James, Will, *Bronco Twisters*, 51, 3. (Sep.1923): p24-26.

2696 James, Will, *Bronco Twisters II*, 51, 4. (Oct.1923): p23-25, 56.

2697 The Homesteader's Wife, *On A Grazing Homestead*, 51, 5. (Nov.1923): p17-18, 60-62.

2698 James, Will, *Bronco Busters III*, 51, 5. (Nov.1923): p26-27, 62.

2699 James, Will, *Desert Range Riding*, 51, 6. (Dec.1923): p20-22, 54-56.

2700 Taylor, Alonzo Englebert, *Your Inelastic Appetite*, 52, 2. (Feb.1924): p20-21, 58-60.

2701 Woehlke, Walter V., *Has Federal Reclamation Failed?*, 53, 1. (Jul.1924): p14-15.

2702 Reid, Margaret Redington, *Back To The Land*, 53, 2. (Aug.1924): p32-34, 60-61.

2703 Reid, Margaret Redington, *Back To The Land*, 53, 3. (Sep.1924): p40-41, 58.

2704 Reid, Margaret Redington, *Back To The Land*, 53, 4. (Oct.1924): p49-50.

2705 James, Will, *When Wages Are Low*, 54, 1. (Jan.1925): p9-12, 75-77.

2706 Farrington, Wallace R., *The Economic Development Of Hawaii*, 58, 1. (Jan.1927): p12-13, 68.

2707 Metzger, Berta, *Ukulele Cowboys*, 58, 1. (Jan.1927): p22-23, 77.

2708 Montgomery, Martha, *Lord Of The Plains*, 58, 4. (Apr.1927): p39, 65.

2709 Tims, L. B., *Snake Farmers*, 59, 1. (Jul.1927): p25, 67.

2710 Thompson, Herbert Cooper, *Fresh Fruit!*, 59, 1. (Jul.1927): p38-39, 58-60.

2711 Webber, Herbert J., *California's Oldest Orange Tree*, 59, 3. (Sep.1927): p21, 79-80.

2712 White, Tom, *Pioneering In Pines*, 59, 4. (Oct.1927): p38-39, 69.

2713 Lisle, Charles J., *Toppermost Crops*, 60, 4. (Apr.1928): p12-15.

2714 Block, Eugene B., *Grapes Crushed While You Wait!*, 60, 4. (Apr.1928): p22-24, 64.

2715 Dye, Homer, Jr., *Us Sheepherders*, 61, 3. (Sep.1928): p32-33, 58.

2716 DuPerrier, Edmund A., *An Aviator Sows Good Seed*, 63, 5. (Nov.1929): p22-23.

3. The Economy

2717 Adams, Bertha Snow, *A Holly Grower Of The Northwest*, 64, 1. (Jan.1930): p28, 60.

2718 Brockman, C. Frank, *Western Christmas Trees*, 67, 6. (Dec.1931): p7-9.

2719 Watters, E. R., *Our Rose-Covered Fence*, 68, 6. (Jun.1932): p14.

2720 Dodge, Natt N., *Your Cranberry Jelly Grows In Washington*, 75, 5. (Nov.1935): p16-17.

2721 *What's New In Western Living*, 82, 3. (Mar.1939): p17-19.

2722 *Vegetables*, 85, 2. (Aug.1940): p40-41.

2723 *Replacing the Bee*, 85, 5. (Nov.1940): p48-49.

2724 *Pro & Con*, 88, 3. (Mar.1942): p44.

2725 *RFD*, 88, 4. (Apr.1942): p8-9.

2726 *Rabbits*, 89, 6. (Dec.1942): p38-39.

2727 *Make Room For Fruit*, 90, 1. (Jan.1943): p12-13.

2728 *Fall Preferred*, 92, 4. (Oct.1943): p54-57.

2729 *Flowering Fruit Trees*, 94, 1. (Jan.1945): p16-17.

2730 *How Deep Is An Acre?*, 95, 1. (Jul.1945): p8-9.

2731 *Homesteads?*, 95, 3. (Sep.1945): p8-11.

2732 *How To Prune Bearing Fruit Trees*, 96, 2. (Feb.1946): p60-63.

2733 *Water Supply from Dams*, 105, 1. (Jul.1950): p84, 87.

2734 *Sheep in Flocks of Two to Twenty*, 105, 5. (Nov.1950): p116-118.

2735 *Which Apple And Which Plum?*, 110, 3. (Mar.1953): p186-188.

2736 *Cane, Pineapples, Coffee, Macadamias, Papaya*, 149, 1. (Jul.1972): p62-65.

2737 *Chickens In Suburbia? Why Not?*, 152, 3. (Mar.1974): p66-73.

2738 *To Fruiful Watsonville... Apples, Olallies, Plus, More. They're Freshest, Prices Best When You Pick Your Own*, 157, 1. (Jul.1976): p30-31.

2739 *California Farmers Invite You Into Their Fields and Orchards on Seven "Farm-Trails" Tours*, 161, 1. (Jul.1978): p26-28.

2740 *It's A Different Livestock Show Backstage At The Cow Palace; You Can Make a Self-Guided Tour*, 161, 4. (Oct.1978): p38-40.

2741 *Berry Picking's Picking Up*, 166, 6. (Jun.1981): p96-97.

2742 *Agricultural Adventuring In California's Central Valley*, 169, 1. (Jul.1982): p58-67.

2743 *Bringing Home The Harvest*, 199, 2. (Aug.1997): p72-75.

3.2 Business & Industry

2744 *A Great California Industry*, 1, 3. (Jul.1898): p42-43.

2745 *Minor Industries Of California*, 2, 2. (Dec.1898): p27.

2746 Langwith, J. A., *Golconda, Nevada, Its Mineral Wealth And Promising Future*, 2, 3. (Jan.1899): p57.

2747 Yale, Charles G., *Gold Mining In California*, 3, 4. (Aug.1899): p116-124.

2748 Mitchell, E. A., *Sugar Making: A Bay Shore Industry At Crockett, CAL.*, 3, 4. (Aug.1899): p129-130.

2749 *Opportunities in the Philippines*, 3, 5. (Sep.1899): p154-155.

2750 Kirkland, J. B., *Gold Mining In Southern Oregon*, 4, 3. (Jan.1900): p103.

2751 Hook, J. W., *Minor Industries Of California*, 5, 3. (Jul.1900): p137-138.

2752 O'Neill, Edmond, *Petroleum In California*, 6, 6. (Apr.1901): p177-184.

2753 Hodgson, Balm M., *An Oregon Treasure Bed*, 7, 1. (May.1901): p29.

2754 Griswold, Mary Edith, *'Living Water': The Romance Of The New Almaden Quicksilver Mines*, 9, 3. (Jul.1902): p173-180.

2755 Sinnard, L. G., *Buried Treasure Of The Santa Lucia*, 10, 3. (Jan.1903): p208-214.

2756 Walcott, Earle Ashley, *Laying The Trans-Pacific Cable*, 10, 4. (Feb.1903): p252-264.

2757 O'Neill, Edmond, *The Texas Petroleum Fields*, 10, 5. (Mar.1903): p379-386.

2758 Dunham, Sam C., *Tonopah And Its Gold*, 11, 1. (May.1903): p6-18.

2759 O'Ryan, J. F., *How The Thornycroft Heir Was Discovered: A Story Of The Beaumont, Texas, Oil Fields*, 11, 6. (Oct.1903): p567-568.

2760 Wells, A. J., *Benicia - California's Future Manchester*, 12, 1. (Nov.1903): p42-51.

2761 Pittock, G. W., *Story Of The Pearce Mines*, 12, 2. (Dec.1903): p169-171.

2762 Wells, A. J., *The Story Of A Copper Mine*, 13, 1. (May.1904): p57-64.

2763 O'Brien, James F., *Nevada's Latest Bonanza*, 13, 4. (Aug.1904): p305-311.

2764 Street, Arthur I., *Another 'Go West' Period*, 14, 3. (Jan.1905): p205-217.

2765 Walker, David H., *San Francisco As A Money Center*, 15, 2. (Jun.1905): p128-134.

2766 Street, Arthur I., *Seeking Trade Across The Pacific*, 15, 5. (Sep.1905): p407-415.

2767 Stickney, Mary E., *Luck and Chance in Mining*, 15, 6. (Oct.1905): p585-589.

2768 Flood, T. Redmond, *A Little Story of Sulphur*, 16, 1. (Nov.1905): p41-45.

2769 Tinsley, John F., *Under The Sea To Alaska*, 16, 5. (Mar.1906): p454-458.

2770 Casper, K. R., *Silver State Gold Surprises*, 16, 5. (Mar.1906): p436-440.

2771 Stovall, Dennis H., *Mining In Southern Oregon*, 17, 4. (Aug.1906): p139-144.

2772 Pixley, Frank, *The Door Of Japan*, 17, 4. (Aug.1906): p158-160.

2773 Niles, Edith L., *Oregon's Manufactures*, 17, 5. (Sep.1906): p273-276.

2774 Douglas, Clara E., *Those Nevada Bonanzas*, 17, 5. (Sep.1906): p262-265.

2775 Wright, Hamilton, *Philippine Prospects*, 18, 1. (Nov.1906): p42-49.

2776 Casper, K. R., *The Gold Of Fairview*, 18, 3. (Jan.1907): p247-254.

2777 Denison, Adna A., *Oakland's Awakening*, 18, 5. (Mar.1907): p466-477.

2778 Gaston, Joseph, *Oregon's Inland Empire*, 18, 5. (Mar.1907): p479-489.

2779 Steele, Rufus M., *The Spread Of San Francisco: The Wonderful Impetus To Manufacturing On The Peninsula Resulting From The Making Of Bay Shore Factory Sites*, 19, 3. (Jul.1907): p263-272.

2780 Wright, E. W., *The Pacific Northwest*, 19, 4. (Aug.1907): p300-332.

2781 Chapman, C. C., *A Goal For Young Men*, 19, 4. (Aug.1907): p349-359.

2782 Cowgill, W. C., *About Baker City*, 19, 5. (Sep.1907): p481-485.

2783 Yandell, C. B., *Seattle And Its Millionaires*, 20, 1. (Nov.1907): p23-32.

2784 Steele, Rufus M., *A Tenderfoot In Greenstone: The Strange Things To Be Seen In A Big New Copper District Among The Saguaros Of The Arizona Desert Country*, 20, 3. (Jan.1908): p271-280.

2785 Bailey, E. G., *The Other Side Of It: The Question Of 'What Is Wrong With The System?' Discussed From The View-Point Of A Western Laboring Man*, 20, 5. (Mar.1908): p472-474.

2786 Carroll, J. M., *The Truth About Nevada*, 21, 1. (May.1908): p51-63.

2787 Newberry, Perry H., *Where Cleanliness Is First*, 21, 2. (Jun.1908): .

2788 Goldsmith, Paul, *Banks That Mean Prosperity: New Structures In The Center Of Oakland, California That Tell Of The City's Wonderful Growth*, 21, 3. (Jul.1908): .

2789 Cradlebaugh, J. H., *Rawhide And Its Gold: The Newest Record Breaker Among The Wonderful Treasure Towns Of Nevada*, 21, 3. (Jul.1908): p224-230.

2790 Wells, A. J., *At Grant's Pass*, 21, 3. (Jul.1908): .

2791 Wells, A. J., *Yamhill - Garden And Empire*, 21, 5. (Sep.1908): .

2792 Dunn, Allan, *In Contra Costa Land*, 21, 5. (Sep.1908): .

2793 Wells, A. J., *Olympia, Washington*, 21, 5. (Sep.1908): .

2794 *'The Line Is Busy': How The Pacific Telephone And Telegraph Company Has Rebuilt Its Great San Francisco System*, 21, 6. (Oct.1908): p575-576.

2795 Aiken, Charles S., *On The Trail Of Skookum John*, 21, 6. (Oct.1908): p479-494.

2796 Hayes, J. P., *Health Of The Hills: What Pure Water And Salubrious Climate Mean, Physically And Commercially, To Baker City, Oregon*, 21, 6. (Oct.1908): p569-572.

2797 Dunn, Allan, *The Kingdom Of Kern: A California County Rich In Many Things - A Principality Of Mineral, Agricultural, Climatic And Scenic Wealth*, 21, 8. (Dec.1908): p793-796.

2798 Wells, A. J., *Oregon's Lincoln County*, 21, 8. (Dec.1908): p797-799.

2799 Wells, A. J., *The Promise Of Vancouver*, 22, 1. (Jan.1909): p97-104.

2800 Walker, David H., *Four Rivers Of Wealth: Mines And Meadows, Ditches And Dairies In Shasta County, California*, 22, 1. (Jan.1909): p105-107.

2801 Coolidge, Dane, *Arizona The Next Star: Mountains, Desert And Border Awaiting Statehood*, 22, 3. (Mar.1909): p228-242.

2802 Magee, William A., *The City In Figures: Substantial Foundation Upon Which The Spirit Of San Francisco Has Rebuilt A Metropolis - Mortgage Indebtedness Relatively Lower Than That Of Other Great Cities - Status Of Real Estate To-Day*, 22, 4. (Apr.1909): p405-408.

2803 Castle, N. H., *Alaska From The Inside*, 22, 5. (May.1909): p475-487.

2804 Steirly, Georgia A., *The Hidden Wealth Of San Benito*, 22, 6. (Jun.1909): p671-673.

2805 Wells, A. J., *The San Diego Region*, 22, 6. (Jun.1909): p676-678.

2806 Bryce, James, *"And Then, What Next?"*, 22, 6. (Jun.1909): p589-592.

2807 Steirly, Georgia A., *The Land Of The Jumping Frog: Calaveras, One Of The Five Mother Lode Counties Of California*, 23, 2. (Aug.1909): p222-224.

2808 Parkhurst, Genevieve Yoell, *On Both Sides Of The Top-Soil: Prolific Placer County, California*, 23, 3. (Sep.1909): p321-324.

2809 Walker, David H., *The Cradle Of Men-O'-War: How The Vast Plant Of The Union Iron Works At San Francisco Launches Famous Ships Upon The Pacific*, 23, 4. (Oct.1909): p431-433.

2810 Millard, Bailey, *In The Puget Sound Country*, 23, 5. (Nov.1909): p436-451.

2811 McGraw, John H., *Concerning Washington*, 23, 5. (Nov.1909): p452-455.

2812 Allen, Charles Sedgwick, *Farming For Gold: The New Game That Dredgers Are Playing - Net Profits Of Ten Thousand An Acre*, 23, 6. (Dec.1909): p651-656.

2813 *Oranges And Iron Fingers: The Time-Honored Custom Of Wrapping Fruit By Hand Revolutionized By A Mechanical Invention*, 24, 1. (Jan.1910): p113-114.

2814 Wells, A. J., *An Orange Empire: San Bernardino County, Where Gold Grows On Trees*, 24, 1. (Jan.1910): p105-112.

2815 Parkhurst, Genevieve Yoell, *Inyo Invites*, 24, 6. (Jun.1910): p709-712.

2816 Woehlke, Walter V., *California's Black Gold: The Romance Of the Oil Gushers*, 25, 2. (Aug.1910): p173-187.

2817 Brown, Frank L., *California's Greatest Industry: How Oil Has Supplanted Gold Twice Over In The Production Records Of The State*, 25, 2. (Aug.1910): p242.

2818 Segur, I. E., *From Crude To Refining: The Scope Of The Sunset Monarch Oil Company*, 25, 2. (Aug.1910): p243.

2819 Wells, A. J., *Oakland's Industrial Development*, 25, 3. (Sep.1910): p357-360.

2820 Lafler, Henry Anderson, *Borax*, 26, 4. (Apr.1911): p418-423.

2821 Schartz, Sidney L., *The Opportunity In Western Securities*, 26, 4. (Apr.1911): p451-453.

2822 Parkhurst, Genevieve Yoell, *Kern County And Its Resources*, 26, 4. (Apr.1911): p461-464.

2823 Booth, Willis H., *A Word To Conservative Investors*, 26, 5. (May.1911): p547-548.

2824 Field, Charles K., *Guests Of A Greater Chinatown*, 26, 5. (May.1911): p489-502.

2825 Peirce, Cyrus, *California Securities And Their Growth In Popularity*, 26, 6. (Jun.1911): p660-662.

2826 Graves, J. A., *California As A Field For Investment*, 27, 2. (Aug.1911): p199-201.

2827 Mills, John Scott, *Grant County's Rich Acres*, 27, 2. (Aug.1911): p217-218.

2828 Mills, John Scott, *At The Falls Of The Williamette*, 27, 2. (Aug.1911): p221-222.

2829 Adams, Edward F., *California District Irrigation Bonds*, 27, 3. (Sep.1911): p324-327.

2830 Ferris, J. E., *The Pacific Northwest*, 27, 5. (Nov.1911): p566-568.

2831 Williamson, R., *The Evolution Of Printing*, 27, 5. (Nov.1911): p578-580.

2832 McIntire, Warren, *The Valley Of Opportunity*, 27, 6. (Dec.1911): p713-714.

2833 Thacher, W. F. G., *Carlton–In Western Oregon*, 28, 1. (Jan.1912): p121-122.

2834 Evans, Samuel M., *Kings Of The Golden River*, 28, 2. (Feb.1912): p131-144.

2835 Thacher, W. F. G., *Tacoma*, 28, 2. (Feb.1912): p241-246.

2836 Woehlke, Walter V., *Angels In Overalls*, 28, 3. (Mar.1912): p261-272.

2837 Thacher, W. F. G., *Kelso–On The Cowlitz River*, 28, 5. (May.1912): p645-646.

2838 Clark, Walter E., *Alaska: A Condition And A Program*, 29, 1. (Jul.1912): p27-36.

2839 Walker, David H., *Treasure Island–Tuolumne*, 29, 2. (Aug.1912): p221-222.

2840 Powell, E. Alexander, *The Valley Of Heart's Delight*, 29, 2. (Aug.1912): p119-125, 211-214.

2841 Teck, Frank Carleton, *An Emerald Elysium*, 29, 3. (Sep.1912): p343-345.

2842 Woehlke, Walter V., *The Club As An Industrial Weapon*, 29, 5. (Nov.1912): p577-583.

2843 Farbar, Jerome H., *Investment In The Greatest State*, 29, 5. (Nov.1912): p584-585.

2844 Briggs, H. W., *The Effect Of Population On Security Values An Important Factor Of The Desirability Of The Pacific Coast As An Investment Field*, 30, 1. (Jan.1913): p110-112.

2845 Davidson, G. A., *Why San Diego Investments Are Good*, 30, 2. (Feb.1913): p52.

2846 Kerchoff, William G., *Opportunities For Investors In The San Joaquin Valley*, 30, 3. (Mar.1913): p50.

2847 Willard, Walter, *Moving The Factory Back To The Land*, 30, 3. (Mar.1913): p299-304.

2848 Straus, S. W., *The Great American Investment Field*, 30, 4. (Apr.1913): p50.

2849 McClelland, L. L., *Irrigation And Irrigation Securities*, 30, 5. (May.1913): p632.

2850 Britton, John A., *Public Utility Securities As An Investment*, 30, 6. (Jun.1913): p676.

3. The Economy

2851 Woehlke, Walter V., *Live Wires*, 31, 2. (Aug.1913): p267-280.

2852 Fisher, C. E., *Madera, Transformed By Water And Electricity*, 31, 2. (Aug.1913): p386-388.

2853 Street, Arthur I., *When The Canal "Starts Something"*, 31, 5. (Nov.1913): p940-946.

2854 Woehlke, Walter V., *Smoke-Stacks On The Pacific*, 31, 6. (Dec.1913): p1161-1171.

2855 Black, Zenas E., *Southwesterly By The Lone Star*, 32, 3. (Mar.1914): p576-584.

2856 Street, Arthur I., *The Battle Of The Pacific*, 33, 3. (Sep.1914): p471-484.

2857 Lane, Franklin K., *Our Paternal Uncle*, 33, 3. (Sep.1914): p512-518.

2858 Street, Arthur I., *The Battle Of The Pacific*, 33, 5. (Nov.1914): p898-912.

2859 Dreier, Thomas, *Give Us This Day Our Daily Work*, 33, 5. (Nov.1914): p943-950.

2860 Freeman, Lewis R., *Pacific Coast To The Front*, 33, 6. (Dec.1914): p1109-1119.

2861 Dunn, Arthur, *The Golden Goddess*, 34, 6. (Jun.1915): p1142-1150.

2862 Dunn, Arthur, *The Battle Of The Money Kings*, 35, 1. (Jul.1915): p124-132.

2863 Dunn, Arthur, *Rainbows*, 35, 2. (Aug.1915): p339-346.

2864 Dunn, Arthur, *Gardens Of Gold*, 35, 3. (Sep.1915): p515-521.

2865 Groff, Frances A., *Sugar On The Candy*, 35, 4. (Oct.1915): p745-751.

2866 Dosch, Arno, *Self-Help For The Hobo*, 36, 1. (Jan.1916): p19-21, 97-98.

2867 Woehlke, Walter V., *Mobilizing Western Metals*, 37, 2. (Aug.1916): p28-30, 85-87.

2868 Biermann, Francis J., *The Gem Of Prophecy*, 37, 4. (Oct.1916): p27, 67-68.

2869 Stanton, George A., *A Real Christmas*, 37, 6. (Dec.1916): p17, 92.

2870 Willard, Walter, *Give Us This Day Our Daily Ship*, 37, 6. (Dec.1916): p40-42, 78-79.

2871 Woehlke, Walter V., *The I. W. W. And The Golden Rule*, 38, 2. (Feb.1917): p16-18, 62-65.

2872 Woehlke, Walter V., *Golden Bubbles*, 38, 3. (Mar.1917): p24-26, 65-68.

2873 Woehlke, Walter V., *From Henry George To 'Gene Schmitz*, 38, 4. (Apr.1917): p7-10, 93.

2874 Jordan, David Starr, *What Of The Nation?*, 38, 4. (Apr.1917): p17, 61.

2875 Woehlke, Walter V., *The Boycott Loses Out*, 38, 5. (May.1917): p10-12, 83-85.

2876 Sprague, J. R., *Pity The Poor Storekeeper!*, 38, 5. (May.1917): p34-35, 47.

2877 Woehlke, Walter V., *Who Killed Cock Robin?*, 38, 6. (Jun.1917): p10-12, 95-96.

2878 Woehlke, Walter V., *What Can Your Boy Do?*, 39, 1. (Jul.1917): p17-18, 95.

2879 Hodges, G. Charles, *Our Chinese Wall*, 39, 1. (Jul.1917): p34, 65-68.

2880 Coleman, B. S., *I. W. W. And The Law*, 39, 1. (Jul.1917): p35, 68.

2881 Woehlke, Walter V., *Pin Pricks And Gnat Bites*, 39, 2. (Aug.1917): p14-16, 91.

2882 Van Inwegen, Mildred, *A Girl's-Eye View Of Whaling*, 39, 2. (Aug.1917): p20-22, 52.

2883 Hall, Wilbur, *Ship Craftsmen Of The Pacific*, 39, 3. (Sep.1917): p11-13, 86-88.

2884 Woehlke, Walter V., *The Red Rebels Declare War*, 39, 3. (Sep.1917): p20-21, 75-77.

2885 Hodges, G. Charles, *A Little Brown War-Baby*, 39, 3. (Sep.1917): p92-94.

2886 Hall, Wilbur, *Making Winged Motors*, 39, 4. (Oct.1917): p24-25, 78.

2887 Woehlke, Walter V., *The Unions' Mailed Fist*, 39, 4. (Oct.1917): p28-29, 80-81.

2888 Woehlke, Walter V., *The Striker And Low Justice*, 39, 5. (Nov.1917): p11-13, 73, 82.

2889 Woehlke, Walter V., *The Unions And Democracy*, 39, 6. (Dec.1917): p14-16, 80.

2890 Woehlke, Walter V., *Bolsheviks Of The West*, 40, 1. (Jan.1918): p14-16, 70-72.

2891 Woehlke, Walter V., *The Square Deal Pays*, 40, 2. (Feb.1918): p15-16, 73-74.

2892 Roosevelt, Theodore, *Slackers Behind The Lines*, 40, 3. (Mar.1918): p10.

2893 Woehlke, Walter V., *The Shipyard Hold-up*, 40, 3. (Mar.1918): p11-13, 71-72.

2894 Willard, Victor, *KC1 Answers Here!*, 40, 4. (Apr.1918): p10-13, 52.

2895 Woehlke, Walter V., *America's First Defeat*, 40, 4. (Apr.1918): p14-16, 72-74.

2896 Woehlke, Walter V., *Wages And Output*, 30, 5. (May.1918): p11-13, 56.

2897 Markley, Arthur, *What The Workers Think*, 40, 5. (May.1918): p13, 90-92.

2898 Vincent, Fred W., *WIng-Bones Of Victory*, 40, 6. (Jun.1918): p30-32, 68-70.

2899 Allen, Frederick Lewis, *Convoying The Ship Of State*, 40, 6. (Jun.1918): p33-35.

2900 Woehlke, Walter V., *The Wooden Span*, 40, 6. (Jun.1918): p36-38, 60-64.

2901 Underwood, John J., *Because He Wanted To*, 41, 2. (Aug.1918): p44-45.

2902 Vincent, Fred W., *The Southern Nigger In The Northwest Woodpile*, 41, 2. (Aug.1918): p41-43, 62-63.

2903 Hall, Wilbur, *Midnight Oil And An Oiler*, 41, 3. (Sep.1918): p39-40.

2904 Underwood, John J., *Reindeer To The Rescue*, 41, 3. (Sep.1918): p34-36.

2905 Philbrook, Zay, *My Wyoming Timber Claim*, 41, 6. (Dec.1918): p22-23.

2906 Pelley, William Dudley, *Hustling The Far East*, 42, 3. (Mar.1919): p13-15, 85.

2907 Sprague, J. R., *The Easiest Way*, 42, 3. (Mar.1919): p44-45, 56-60.

2908 Hall, Wilbur, *Johnny Comes Marching Home–To What?*, 42, 4. (Apr.1919): p23-25, 88-90.

2909 Sprague, J. R., *Is Yours A One-Man Business?*, 42, 6. (Jun.1919): p39-40, 58-60.

2910 FitzGerald, Harold J., *Charge It, Please!*, 44, 3. (Mar.1920): p42-44, 96-106.

2911 Woehlke, Walter V., *King Kilowatt*, 44, 6. (Jun.1920): p33-35, 81-84.

2912 Blackiston, A. H., *Desdemona The Fair*, 44, 6. (Jun.1920): p45-46.

2913 Woehlke, Walter V., *What Is Industrial Democracy?*, 45, 1. (Jul.1920): p35-36, 56-58.

2914 Woehlke, Walter V., *Copper, Prunes And Plebiscites*, 46, 2. (Feb.1921): p20-22, 80-82.

2915 Bechdolt, Frederick R., *The Hydra's Heads*, 46, 4. (Apr.1921): p24-26, 86.

2916 Seymour, Robert T., *Cripple Creek Dies*, 46, 5. (May.1921): p41-43.

2917 Millard, Bailey, *Have You An Agreeable Voice?*, 47, 1. (Jul.1921): p44-45, 56.

2918 Woehlke, Walter V., *The Corn Belt In California*, 47, 2. (Aug.1921): p29-32, 70.

2919 Woehlke, Walter V., *Oregon Enters The Race*, 47, 4. (Oct.1921): p22-26, 50.

2920 Willard, Victor, *Harnessing The Colorado*, 47, 5. (Nov.1921): p36-37.

2921 FitzGerald, Harold J., *Room At The Top*, 48, 1. (Jan.1922): p43-45.

2922 Woehlke, Walter V., *Taming Of The Snake*, 48, 2. (Feb.1922): p25-27, 75-76.

2923 Woehlke, Walter V., *Utah And Europe*, 48, 3. (Mar.1922): p9-11, 57, 70, 72.

2924 Woehlke, Walter V., *Real Forestry At Last*, 48, 4. (Apr.1922): p17-19.

2925 Jackson, Joseph Henry, *Making The Ether Talk*, 48, 6. (Jun.1922): p41-42.

2926 Willoughby, Barrett, *Twenty-five Per Cent A Month*, 49, 3. (Sep.1922): p9-11, 79-81.

2927 FitzGerald, Harold J., *Inventions, Patents And Pitfalls*, 49, 5. (Nov.1922): p20-22, 75-76.

2928 Hall, Wilbur, *Cheating Chance*, 49, 6. (Dec.1922): p9-11, 74-76.

2929 Spencer, M. Lyle, *Going Up!*, 49, 6. (Dec.1922): p24-25, 68-72.

2930 Lane, D. R., *Hard Scrapping*, 49, 6. (Dec.1922): p40-41.

2931 Freeman, Lewis R., *Unity And The Colorado*, 50, 3. (Mar.1923): p17-20, 58-60.

2932 Wilson, Paul N., *All Within The Law*, 50, 5. (May.1923): p32-33, 56.

2933 *1898-1923*, 50, 6. (Jun.1923): p14-15.

2934 Woehlke, Walter V., *The Prospector Leaves The Stage*, 50, 6. (Jun.1923): p48-49, 116-117.

2935 Greeley, W. B., *The Westward Ho Of The Sawmill*, 50, 6. (Jun.1923): p56-58, 96-107.

2936 Hackers, John Gilbert, *If You Had To–*, 51, 2. (Aug.1923): p21-22.

2937 Freeman, Lewis R., *Near Sights Of Dam Sites*, 51, 3. (Sep.1923): p21-23, 84-90.

2938 Lanphere, Leland, *Suckers Old And New*, 52, 1. (Jan.1924): p44-45, 56.

2939 Mason, Francis H., *Mining Luck*, 52, 2. (Feb.1924): p24, 79-80.

2940 Woehlke, Walter V., *Fight Or Pay Tribute?*, 52, 5. (May.1924): p11.

2941 Rosette, Breese, *The Miner Quits*, 52, 5. (May.1924): p49, 62-64.

2942 Macfarlane, Peter Clark, *A Sawmill In Heaven*, 52, 6. (Jun.1924): p8-10, 56-58.

2943 Jones, J. R., *The Prospector*, 52, 6. (Jun.1924): p12-14, 93-96.

2944 Eberts, Jerome B., *The Gold Rush De Luxe*, 55, 2. (Aug.1924): p34-35.

2945 Bechdolt, Frederick R., *The Rocky Mountain Fur Company* , 53, 4. (Oct.1924): p9-12, 76-78.

2946 Woehlke, Walter V., *After The Great Drouth*, 53, 6. (Dec.1924): p41-43, 92-93.

2947 Mavity, Nancy Barr, *More Wool Or More Men?*, 54, 1. (Jan.1925): p21-24, 54-56.

2948 Wilkinson, Jessie, *Tulips - Made In America*, 54, 4. (Apr.1925): p22-23.

2949 One Who Is Rolling, *Change Jobs Every Year*, 54, 4. (Apr.1925): p12, 77-79, 92-93.

2950 Eberts, Jerome B., *Free Gold In The Cassiar!*, 54, 6. (Jun.1925): p32-33, 79, 81-82.

2951 Jackson, Joseph Henry, *Back Where The Wave Begins*, 55, 3. (Sep.1925): p22-23, 83, 94-96.

2952 Thurston, Lorrin A., *Hawaii–What It Means To America*, 56, 1. (Jan.1926): p34-36, 81.

2953 Vandeventer, Edward A., *When Boulder Dam Is Built*, 56, 2. (Feb.1926): p25-27, 56-58, 86.

2954 Woehlke, Walter V., *Can I Double My Money Quick?*, 56, 5. (May.1926): p33-35.

2955 Stevens, James, *The New Northwest*, 56, 6. (Jun.1926): p12-15, 84-85.

2956 Holbrook, Stewart H., *The Logging Camp Loses Its Soul*, 56, 6. (Jun.1926): p19 21, 62.

2957 Swindell, George M., *The Magic Spell Of "High-Grade!"*, 56, 6. (Jun.1926): p34-35, 82-83.

2958 Block, Eugene B., *Send For The Doctor!*, 57, 2. (Aug.1926): p28-29, 54-58.

2959 Jones, Idwal, *The Rush To Windy Weepah*, 58, 6. (Jun.1927): p28-29, 79-82.

2960 Henderson, George C., *You're Bound To Lose!*, 59, 2. (Aug.1927): p26-28.

2961 Woehlke, Walter V., *The Great Julian "Pete" Swindle*, 59, 3. (Sep.1927): p12-15, 69, 80-81.

2962 Woehlke, Walter V., *The Great Julian "Pete" Swindle*, 59, 4. (Oct.1927): p16-19, 78-82.

2963 Woehlke, Walter V., *The Great Julian "Pete" Swindle*, 59, 5. (Nov.1927): p18-20, 66-68, 81-83.

2964 Marvin, George, *De-Bunking Banking*, 60, 2. (Feb.1928): p11-15, 65.

2965 Hastings, Cristel, *This Gold Rush Business*, 60, 5. (May.1928): p19, 78.

2966 Robertson, R. E., *Alaska As Is!*, 61, 4. (Oct.1928): p22-25, 62-64.

2967 Gallagher, T. A., *The Women's Bank*, 62, 1. (Jan.1929): p24-26, 50-53.

2968 Garren, William I., *What It Costs To Build A House*, 66, 5. (May.1931): p24.

2969 O'Hara, Gerald J., *Sitting Pretty In The Next Depression*, 67, 4. (Oct.1931): p8-11.

2970 Welling, Blanche E., *Neighborly Chats With One Western Mother*, 67, 5. (Nov.1931): p22.

2971 *What's New In Western Living*, 77, 3. (Sep.1936): p13-17.

2972 *What's New in Western Living*, 83, 1. (Jul.1939): p15.

2973 *What's New In Western Living*, 83, 1. (Jul.1939): p13-15.

2974 *Spider Farm*, 88, 3. (Mar.1942): p9.

2975 *Cork*, 91, 4. (Oct.1943): p58-59.

2976 *The Age Of Nuclear Power Is Here, And Even Experts Disagree About What's Ahead*, 153, 2. (Aug.1974): p30-31.

3.3 Transportation

2977 *Sunset Limited*, 1, 6. (Oct.1898): p92-101.

2978 *The Evolution Of The Tourist Car*, 2, 1. (Nov.1898): p6-9.

2979 Boardman, William, *Coaching In California*, 2, 5. (Mar.1899): p97-98.

2980 Sequoia, *From Tide To Tide On Sunset Limited*, 4, 2. (Dec.1899): p43-45.

2981 Miramont, *Within The Limited Freight*, 4, 5. (Mar.1900): p183-193.

2982 Williams, H. F., *Early Mail Service And Chronological History Of San Francisco Postoffices*, 5, 2. (Jun.1900): p89-90.

2983 *A Day On The Inside Track*, 5, 4. (Aug.1900): p166-168.

2984 Rainey, Edward, *A Day's Coaching At Santa Barbara*, 5, 4. (Aug.1900): p177-179.

2985 *A Hundred Miles Awheel By The Golden Gate*, 5, 4. (Aug.1900): p190-195.

2986 Shoup, Paul, *The Closing Of The Gap*, 5, 5. (Sep.1900): p239-249.

2987 *Half Round The World With Grand Opera*, 6, 1. (Nov.1900): p1-16.

2988 Simpson, Joseph Cairn, *Horses Of California*, 6, 3. (Jan.1901): p86-97.

2989 Wells, A. J., *San Francisco And Its Opportunity*, 7, 2-3. (Jun.1901): p84-86.

2990 Shoup, Paul, *The Evolution Of A Railroad*, 7, 6. (Oct.1901): p166-175.

2991 Aiken, Charles S., *Ten 'Cross Continent Meteors*, 9, 1. (May.1902): p6-9.

2992 Millard, Bailey, *Going To Sea By Rail*, 12, 3. (Jan.1904): p195-203.

2993 Aiken, Charles S., *Crossing Great Salt Lake*, 12, 3. (Jan.1904): p204-211.

2994 Eastwood, Carlin Pratt, *'The Dutch Flat Swindle': A Reminiscent Story Of The Building Of The First Overland Railway*, 12, 3. (Jan.1904): p212-222.

2995 Charlton, Robert, *The Story Of A Great Tunnel*, 13, 3. (Jul.1904): p219-224.

2996 Eames, Ninetta, *Over Trail And Track*, 13, 3. (Jul.1904): p225-238.

2997 Abbott, James W., *The Government And The Highways*, 13, 5. (Sep.1904): p425-428.

2998 Holder, Charles F., *The San Pedro Breakwater*, 13, 6. (Oct.1904): p473-477.

2999 Alberger, W. R., *San Francisco's Transportation Club*, 14, 4. (Feb.1905): p350-353.

3000 Hoffman, Elwyn, *The Old Dutch Flat Road*, 14, 4. (Feb.1905): p373-376.

3001 Harrison, E. S., *From Reindeer To Railway*, 14, 5. (Mar.1905): p469-480.

3002 Evans, Wallace Dana, *American Railway Building In China*, 15, 4. (Aug.1905): p367-368.

3. The Economy

3003 *Upbuilding The West: New Railway Projects And Improvements That Help Keep The Country Growing*, 18, 4. (Feb.1907): p348-350.

3004 Bailey, W. F., *Overland By Butterfield Stage*, 18, 5. (Mar.1907): p446-452.

3005 *Upbuilding The West: New Railway Projects And Improvements That Help Keep The Country Growing*, 18, 5. (Apr.1907): p584.

3006 *Upbuilding The West: New Railway Projects And Improvements That Help Keep The Country Growing*, 19, 1. (May.1907): p54-56.

3007 *Upbuilding The West: New Railway Projects And Improvements That Help Keep The Country Growing*, 19, 3. (Jul.1907): p281-282.

3008 *Upbuilding the West: New Railway Projects And Improvements That Help Keep The Country Growing*, 19, 6. (Oct.1907): p584-586.

3009 Athearn, F. G., *A Human Block System: Something About The Unique Railway Clubs Of The Southern Pacific System*, 20, 1. (Nov.1907): p60-63.

3010 *Upbuilding The West: New Railway Projects And Improvements That Help Keep The Country Growing*, 20, 2. (Dec.1907): p178-179.

3011 *Upbuilding The West: New Railway Projects And Improvements That Help Keep The Country Growing*, 20, 3. (Jan.1908): p281-282.

3012 Steele, Rufus M., *Expanding A National Highway*, 20, 6. (Apr.1908): p576-591.

3013 Daggett, Charles D., *Making Good Roads*, 20, 6. (Apr.1908): p598-601.

3014 Goldsmith, Paul, *The Movement For Good Roads*, 21, 1. (May.1908): .

3015 Citizens League, The, *Opening An Empire: New Railroads In Baker County, Oregon, Tapping Eagle And Pine Valleys, And Cornucopia And Other Rich Agricultural Timber, Mining And Stock Raising Districts*, 21, 4. (Aug.1908): .

3016 Steele, Rufus M., *Expediting Overland Freight*, 21, 6. (Oct.1908): p533-541.

3017 Goldsmith, Paul, *Smoothing The Way: The Movement For Good Roads In Alameda County, California*, 21, 7. (Nov.1908): p684-685.

3018 *Relation Of The Railroads To The Trans-Mississippi Territory*, 21, 8. (Dec.1908): p730-736.

3019 *At Berkeley's Front Door: The New Depot Of The Southern Pacific In The University City*, 22, 1. (Jan.1909): p108-109.

3020 Scott, J. H., *Build Better Roads*, 22, 2. (Feb.1909): p185-187.

3021 Jenkins, D. C., *Alaskan Road Building*, 22, 5. (May.1909): p541-543.

3022 Field, Charles K., *On The Wings Of To-Day: An Account Of The First International Aviation Meet In America, At Los Angeles, California*, 24, 3. (Mar.1910): p244-252.

3023 Hand, Pitt P., *Western Men Who Would Fly*, 24, 3. (Mar.1910): p258-269.

3024 Pillsbury, Arthur C., *From One Air-craft To Another*, 24, 3. (Mar.1910): p343-346.

3025 Willey, Day Allen, *Building The M. R.*, 24, 6. (Jun.1910): p635-640.

3026 Buck, H. A., *One Hundred And Fifty-five Million Dollars To Enter New York: The Crowning Achievement Of The Pennsylvania Railroad's Ten-year Struggle To Cross The Hudson River Into New York City*, 25, 5. (Nov.1910): p601-604.

3027 Smith, Katherine Louise, *Alaska's Reindeer Express*, 25, 6. (Dec.1910): p701-705.

3028 Kyne, Peter B., *Worm's-Eye Views Of Flying Men*, 26, 3. (Mar.1911): p281-291.

3029 Saville, Frank, *The Biggest Job In The World*, 26, 6. (Jun.1911): p601-611.

3030 Lanning, MacClellan, *Wooleyport Harbor*, 26, 6. (Jun.1911): p690-692.

3031 Knowland, Joseph R., *When The Canal Is Opened*, 28, 1. (Jan.1912): p94-96.

3032 Springer, Thomas Grant and Campbell, Fleta, *The Water-way Of Wonder*, 28, 5. (May.1912): p544-550.

3033 Putnam, George Palmer, *The Dream Of The Centuries*, 29, 3. (Sep.1912): p247-254.

3034 Putnam, George Palmer, *The Canal Today*, 29, 4. (Oct.1912): p383-394.

3035 Steele, Rufus M., *Alma Mater On Wheels*, 29, 4. (Oct.1912): p448-454.

3036 Black, Zenas E., *Honk And Bronc*, 29, 5. (Nov.1912): p531-537.

3037 Thomas, E. C., *Transformation And The Trolley*, 29, 5. (Nov.1912): p596-597.

3038 Steele, Rufus M., *The Modern Tower Of Aben Habuz*, 30, 2. (Feb.1913): p175-181.

3039 Edwards, Paul, *Richmond: Fastest Growing Of Western Seaports*, 30, 2. (Feb.1913): p66-72.

3040 Steele, Rufus M., *Forty Miles Of Dinner De Luxe*, 30, 6. (Jun.1913): p790-795.

3041 Steele, Rufus M., *The Personal Conductor*, 31, 3. (Sep.1913): p518-521.

3042 Steele, Rufus M., *The Red Car Of Empire*, 31, 4. (Oct.1913): p710-717.

3043 Hastings, Milo, *The Continuous House*, 32, 1. (Jan.1914): p111-116.

3044 Cloud, D., *Language Of The Lights*, 32, 3. (Mar.1914): p626-631.

3045 Willard, Walter, *The Pacific Coast And Dissolution*, 32, 4. (Apr.1914): p871-874.

3046 Steele, Rufus M., *The Road To Tomorrow*, 32, 5. (May.1914): p1035-1039.

3047 Steele, Rufus M., *The Man Who Makes 'All Aboard' Possible*, 32, 6. (Jun.1914): p1280-1287.

3048 Hopkins, Ernest J., *The Seamen's Act–Blessing Or Boomerang*, 35, 3. (Sep.1915): p478-480.

3049 Morris, Clyde L., *Blasting the Cascade Barrier*, 36, 4. (Apr.1916): p68, 70.

3050 Steele, Rufus M., *The Man On The Smoky End*, 36, 5. (May.1916): p20-22.

3051 Branner, John C., *Can We Keep The Canal Open?*, 36, 6. (Jun.1916): p13-15, 70-71.

3052 Brooks, James W., *Road Building East and West*, 37, 4. (Oct.1916): p70,72,74,76.

3053 Underwood, John J., *Uncle Sam's Own Railroad*, 37, 5. (Nov.1916): p23.

3054 Campbell, Lindsay, *Wooden Walls vs. Steel Sharks*, 38, 6. (Jun.1917): p7-9, 94-95.

3055 Crow, Carl, *Can The Flag Come Back?*, 39, 3. (Sep.1917): p14-16, 88-90.

3056 Steele, Rufus M., *Steadying Our Wings*, 39, 4. (Oct.1917): p13-16.

3057 Crow, Carl, *Uncle Ben And The Caterpillar*, 39, 5. (Nov.1917): p21-24, 70-71.

3058 Hodges, G. Charles, *The Pacific's Key To Panama*, 39, 5. (Nov.1917): p36-37.

3059 Woehlke, Walter V., *Admiral Of The Merchant Fleet*, 41, 5. (Nov.1918): p27-29, 52-54.

3060 Stott, Josephine, *Man's Best Friend–But A Devil With The Women*, 41, 6. (Dec.1918): p39-40.

3061 Thompson, L. G., *The New Transportation*, 42, 3. (Mar.1919): p74-78.

3062 Hamby, William H., *Back To The Sea*, 42, 4. (Apr.1919): p32-35, 62.

3063 Hamby, William H., *Somewhere Safe To Sea*, 42, 5. (May.1919): p24-26, 58.

3064 Hamby, William H., *What Will He Do With them?*, 42, 6. (Jun.1919): p24-26, 56.

3065 Klepper, Milton R., *Sailing Across The Siskiyous*, 43, 3. (Sep.1919): p43, 74-78.

3066 Haines, F., *The Golden Fleet*, 44, 4. (Apr.1920): p29.

3067 Fitzgerald, Harold J., *Auto Bloodhounds*, 46, 1. (Jan.1921): p33-35, 52.

3. The Economy

3068 Millard, Bailey, *Traffic Perils And The Law*, 46, 4. (Apr.1921): p33-34, 72-76.

3069 Willard, Victor, *Who Owns The Highways*, 48, 4. (Apr.1922): p31, 66-68.

3070 Willard, Victor, *Highways, Trucks And Taxes*, 48, 5. (May.1922): p9-11, 68-69.

3071 Willard, Victor, *What Destroys The Highways?*, 48, 6. (Jun.1922): p9-11, 84-86.

3072 Willard, Victor, *Who Shall Pay The Piper?*, 49, 1. (Jul.1922): p9-11, 74-75.

3073 Willard, Victor, *Using The Highways For Profit*, 49, 2. (Aug.1922): p34-35, 73-74.

3074 Bement, Austin F., *The Closed Desert Gate*, 50, 2. (Feb.1923): p9-10, 70-71.

3075 Peterson, Preston G., *Utah's Right Of Way*, 50, 2. (Feb.1923): p11, 84.

3076 Considine, John L., *Eleven Days To Saint Joe!*, 51, 4. (Oct.1923): p36, 80-81.

3077 Allan, Scotty, *The Bravest Dogs In The World*, 54, 4. (Apr.1925): p8-9, 63, 75-76.

3078 Schick, Murray, *Riding The Rainbow Trail*, 54, 5. (May.1925): p10-11, 88.

3079 *Do You Give The Tramp A Ride?*, 54, 5. (May.1925): p15, 79.

3080 Moses, Stanford E., *Travel By Air!*, 55, 2. (Aug.1925): p20-23, 60.

3081 McGaffey, Ernest, *What Federal Aid Means To The West*, 56, 3. (Mar.1926): p37, 94-95.

3082 Woehlke, Walter V., *Traffic Jams*, 56, 3. (Mar.1926): p38-41, 92-93.

3083 Lewis, W. B., *Are Mountain Roads Safer Than Highways?*, 57, 1. (Jul.1926): p15, 68.

3084 Reade, Charles and Lane, D. R., *Pull Up By The Side Of The Road*, 57, 6. (Dec.1926): p14-16, 65-66.

3085 Lane, D. R., *Flying With The Western Air Mails*, 58, 5. (May.1927): p12-14, 54-56.

3086 Lane, D. R., *Business Takes The Air*, 58, 6. (Jun.1927): p30-31, 54-56.

3087 Cribbins, Walter W., *Their Names Shall Live!*, 59, 5. (Nov.1927): p14-15, 95-96.

3088 Richardson, J. Frederick, *First In The Air*, 59, 6. (Dec.1927): p12-13, 66-69, 81.

3089 Gardner, Erle Stanley, *West Goes East*, 60, 1. (Jan.1928): p28-31.

3090 Coleman, Dobry Chryse, *The Jinx Ship*, 60, 1. (Jan.1928): p35, 75-76.

3091 McAllister, Paul R., *Honestly, Officer–*, 61, 2. (Aug.1928): p36-39.

3092 Calvin, Jack, *Romance And A Sailing Ship*, 61, 3. (Sep.1928): p40-42, 70-73, 83.

3093 Calvin, Jack, *Romance And A Sailing Ship*, 61, 4. (Oct.1928): p34-36, 56-58.

3094 Rogers, Bogart, *Are You A Pilot?*, 61, 5. (Nov.1928): p30-33, 73.

3095 Powell, Tod, *The Romance Of Western Road Building*, 62, 4. (Apr.1929): p11-14.

3096 Taylor, Katherine Ames, *Riding High*, 63, 2. (Aug.1929): p19-21.

3097 Vincent, Fred W., *Map Making In The Modern Manner*, 63, 3. (Sep.1929): p23-25.

3098 Bailey, Almira, *A Home On The Rolling Deep*, 64, 4. (Apr.1930): p24.

3099 Osgood, Elizabeth J., *An Old Rum Runner Becomes Our Cabin Cruiser*, 75, 2. (Aug.1935): p17, 20-22.

3100 Hall, Wilbur, *Hobby Horses That Lead to Rancho Juan Y Lolita*, 75, 3. (Sep.1935): p19, 35-36.

3101 *What's New In Western Living*, 76, 2. (Feb.1936): p13-15.

3102 *What's New In Western Living*, 77, 5. (Nov.1936): p13-15.

3103 *Going Homes*, 78, 2. (Feb.1937): p24-25.

3104 *What's New In Western Living*, 82, 4. (Apr.1939): p19-21.

3105 *Auto Insurance*, 107, 2. (Aug.1951): p63-65.

3106 *Coast-To-Coast Air Detour*, 107, 5. (Nov.1951): p22-24.

3107 *Still Steaming On Western Rails...*, 114, 2. (Feb.1955): p14-16.

3108 *Life With The Auto*, 116, 6. (Jun.1956): p73-89.

3109 *A Christmas Gift to the Auto-Explorer... Why Not A Carrier Rack For The Car?*, 117, 6. (Dec.1956): p36-39.

3110 *The Trailer Is Also A Houseboat*, 122, 5. (May.1959): p77, 78, 80, 82.

3111 *Scenic Rail Trips In The West*, 125, 2. (Aug.1960): p31, 34, 36.

3112 *For Skippers Who Keep Their Boats At Home*, 125, 4. (Oct.1960): p82-85.

3113 *California Steamboat On Mark Twain's Rivers*, 126, 4. (Apr.1961): p54-60.

3114 *The Boats Are Rolling. Are You Tempted?*, 126, 6. (Jun.1961): p94-99.

3115 *You Can Go On Board San Francisco's Floating Ship Museum October 5*, 131, 4. (Oct.1963): p18-21.

3116 *For Travelers East, Here Are Three Rides Behind Steam*, 135, 2. (Aug.1965): p20-21.

3117 *What Steam Is Left In The West? These 10 Cheerful Excursion Short Hauls*, 140, 5. (May.1968): p92-93.

3118 *BART 1971...Advance Looks Are Possible Now*, 142, 6. (Jun.1969): p45, 46, 49.

3119 *How Safe Is Your Camper?*, 148, 3. (Mar.1972): p92-94.

3120 *On August 2, 1873, The First Cable Car Made Its First Official Hill Climb -This August San Francisco Will Celebrate*, 151, 2. (Aug.1973): p26-27.

3121 *Your BART Under The Bay To Discover Today's Oakland*, 153, 3. (Sep.1974): p80-82.

3122 *BART On Weeknights*, 157, 6. (Dec.1976): p30-32.

3123 *Away from Interstate 5*, 158, 6. (Jun.1977): p80-89.

3124 *The Moped Decision*, 159, 6. (Dec.1977): p86-87.

3125 *Can You Better A Package's Chances In The Mails?*, 163, 6. (Dec.1979): p88-90.

3126 *California's Rip-Roaring Railroad Past*, 166, 5. (May.1981): p108-109.

3127 *Still Steaming-All Over The West*, 169, 2. (Aug.1982): p48-53.

3128 *"Where Should we pull off?" Here Are Our Answers For I-80 Travelers To The Sierra*, 170, 5. (May.1983): p54-56.

3129 *Riding A Bike To Work*, 171, 3. (Sep.1983): p94-98.

3130 *Welcome To the Laboratory Of Western Driving*, 187, 1. (Jul.1991): p46-53.

3131 *Coping With Busy Airports*, 189, 5. (Nov.1992): p74-83.

4. Food and Entertaining

July 1979 cover (photo: Glenn Christiansen)

Food & Entertaining

Just as there were the "Big Four" railroad tycoons of nineteenth-century California, Sunset has long had its own Big Four: Food, Garden, Home and Travel, and of these, Food has taken up the largest share, in terms of overall number of words and number of specific identifiable units (whether articles, columns or individual recipes). At least since 1929, every issue of Sunset has had a large number of food-related items, and as such it would be nearly impossible to include every item in the present volume, and we have made no effort to do so. There are still well over 1,000 articles listed. A review of this listing should provide a wide range of thoughts about home kitchen technology, available ingredients, cultural borrowings, and concerns with diet or convenience through the years. Hospitality, in the form of Parties & Entertaining, is a frequent theme. Holidays have always been emphasized, and in this category we chose to include all aspects of home holiday preparation, from seasonal foods, to thematic table arrangements and home decorations, to Christmas trees, to pumpkin carving, and so on. Consciously foreign-inspired cookery is a separate category, International Cookery. One of the commonly recurring types of articles is dedicated to a particular food, often including discussion of available varieties as well as cooking techniques; these are grouped under the heading, Specific Ingredients & Foods.

4. Food and Entertaining

4. Food and Entertaining

4. Food and Entertaining

4. Food and Entertaining

4. Food and Entertaining

4. Food and Entertaining

3664 *Super Nachos*, 187, 2. (Aug.1991): p46-47.

3665 *A Pacific Clambake is Quicker, Simpler... Don't Forget The Salsa*, 187, 2. (Aug.1991): p56-57.

3666 *They're 'Pasta Pictures'*, 187, 3. (Sep.1991): p166-167.

3667 Johnson, Elaine and Hale, Christine Weber, *Coffee Reconquers The West*, 188, 2. (Feb.1992): p70-75.

3668 Anusasananan, Linda Lau and Lipman, Karyn I., *Light And Healthy*, 188, 2. (Feb.1992): p85-88.

3669 Johnson, Elaine, *Tropical Treasures: Desserts From Hawaii*, 188, 3. (Mar.1992): p142-144.

3670 Johnson, Elaine, *Hawaii's Treasures Of The Deep*, 188, 4. (Apr.1992): p98-103.

3671 Bateson, Betsy Reynolds and Freschet, Paula Smith, *The Wonderful World Of Watermelons*, 189, 2. (Aug.1992): p72-75.

3672 *School Lunches For A Week*, 189, 04. (Oct.1992): p162-164.

3673 Anusasananan, Linda Lau, *The Best Barbecued Steak?*, 190, 2. (Feb.1993): p72-73.

3674 Lipman, Karyn I., *Margarita Champions... with Choices*, 190, 2. (Feb.1993): p76-77.

3675 Crosby, Bill, *Stalking The West's Best Burgers*, 190, 2. (Feb.1993): p80.

3676 Anusasananan, Linda Lau, *Western Classics: Recipes From Sunset's Best Of The West*, 190, 3. (Mar.1993): p114-120.

3677 Anusasananan, Linda Lau, *Cowboy Cooking*, 190, 5. (May.1993): p72-79.

3678 Johnson, Elaine, *Nine Decades Of Great Western Breads*, 190, 5. (May.1993): p152-156, 158.

3679 Anusasananan, Linda Lau, *Secrets Of Wine Country Cooks*, 191, 2. (Aug.1993): p78-84, 86.

3680 Hale, Christine Weber, *It's Center Stage For Vegetable Casseroles*, 191, 4. (Oct.1993): p152-155.

3681 Bateson, Betsy Reynolds, *How To Make Bread Machines Work For You*, 191, 4. (Oct.1993): p162, 164, 166.

3682 Johnson, Elaine, *Gingerbread Masterpieces*, 191, 6. (Dec.1993): p80-81.

3683 Johnson, Elaine, *The Bread Rush*, 192, 1. (Jan.1994): p64-69.

3684 Bateson, Betsy Reynolds, *Revolution In Your Salad Bowl*, 192, 4. (Apr.1994): p100-103.

3685 Swezey, Lauren Bonar, *Salads From Your Summer Garden*, 192, 5. (May.1994): p64-65, 68, 70.

3686 Anusasananan, Linda Lau, *The Farmers' Market Frenzy*, 192, 6. (Jun.1994): p98-106.

3687 Anusasananan, Linda Lau, *Rotisserie Revival*, 193, 1. (Jul.1994): p72-75.

3688 Hale, Christine Weber, *Fresher, Lighter Jams*, 193, 1. (Jul.1994): p112-114.

3689 Bateson, Betsy Reynolds, *Fresh From The West*, 193, 2. (Aug.1994): p82-86.

3690 Hale, Christine Weber, *Spiced And Iced*, 193, 2. (Aug.1994): p118-120.

3691 *Eat Smart*, 193, 07. (Jan.1995): p92-95.

3692 Fish, Peter and Johnson, Elaine, *Celebrating Strawberries*, 194, 5. (May.1995): p92-97, 100.

3693 Anusasananan, Linda Lau and McPherson, Jena, *Yakima Valley Barbecue*, 194, 6. (Jun.1995): p92-96.

3694 Anusasananan, Linda Lau, *Great Dishes For A Low-fat Summer*, 194, 6. (Jun.1995): p133-156.

3695 Johnson, Elaine, *Great Western Picnics*, 195, 1. (Jul.1995): p80-85.

3696 DiVecchio, Jerry Anne, *65 Years Of Kitchen Cabinet*, 195, 3. (Sep.1995): p124-128.

3697 *California's Heritage Wine*, 194, 04. (Oct.1995): p76-82.

3698 Anusasananan, Linda Lau, *Lasagne, Any Way You Want It*, 196, 2. (Feb.1996): p108-111.

3699 Hale, Christine Weber, *Oh, So Smooth*, 196, 6. (Jun.1996): p126-128, 130, 131.

3700 Hale, Christine Weber, *Grilled Chicken As You Like It*, 197, 1. (Jul.1996): p70-74.

3701 Anusasananan, Linda Lau, *Low-fat Summer Classics*, 197, 1. (Jul.1996): p99-122.

3702 Lansing, David, *California's Other Wine Country*, 197, 3. (Sep.1996): p20-22, 24-27.

3703 *Beer... And The Foods That Love It*, 197, 04. (Oct.1996): p76-79.

3704 *Gifts In Glass*, 197, 06. (Dec.1996): p78-83.

3705 *A Wine For All Seasons*, 197, 06. (Dec.1996): p88-89, 92-93.

3706 *Star Of The Table*, 197, 06. (Dec.1996): p118-120.

3707 *Quick, Light, & Healthy; Flavors of the Southwest*, 198, 1. (Jan.1997): p95-110.

3708 *Some Like It Hot!*, 198, 2. (Feb.1997): p86-89.

3709 *When Time Is Short, Think Thin*, 198, 2. (Feb.1997): p124-128.

3710 *O Pioneers!*, 199, 2. (Aug.1997): p84-86, 91-95.

3711 Baker, Andrew, *Reinventing the Casserole*, 199, 4. (Oct.1997): p136-141.

3712 Anusasananan, Linda Lau and Baker, Andrew, *Irresistible Sweets*, 199, 5. (Nov.1997): p144-150.

3713 Anusasananan, Linda Lau, *Two Cooks Create a Southwest Supper*, 199, 6. (Dec.1997): p80-85.

3714 Anusasananan, Linda Lau, *Native American Holiday Feast*, 199, 6. (Dec.1997): p88-93.

3715 Anusasananan, Linda Lau, *Just Like Mom Made - Almost*, 200, 1. (Jan.1998): p98-115.

4.2 Holidays

3716 Merriman, Effie W., *Christmas At Santa Monica*, 6, 2. (Dec.1900): p53-54.

3717 Dixon, L. Maynard, *Christmas in the Range*, 12, 2. (Dec.1903): p106-113.

3718 Grinnell, Elizabeth, *The Thanksgiving Turkey*, 14, 1. (Nov.1904): p10-12.

3719 Bramhall, Frank J., *A California Christmas*, 18, 2. (Dec.1906): p167-170.

3720 *Desserts for the Holiday*, 51, 5. (Nov.1923): p70, 72-75.

3721 Shreve, Dorothy, *Pasadena's Christmas Trees*, 55, 6. (Dec.1925): p30.

3722 *Holiday Candies and Cakes*, 57, 6. (Dec.1926): p72, 77.

3723 Bernoudy, Jane, *An Alaskan Christmas*, 63, 6. (Dec.1929): p31-34.

3724 Rowntree, Lester, *For Yuletide Decorations*, 65, 6. (Dec.1930): p9-11.

3725 Moss, Doris Hudson, *Loveliest Of All Are Thanksgiving Tables*, 67, 5. (Nov.1931): p20-21.

3726 Moss, Doris Hudson, *Christmas Comes To Our House*, 67, 6. (Dec.1931): p22-23.

3727 Boyd, Eunice Mays, *Christmas In Alaska*, 69, 5. (Nov.1932): p6-8.

3728 Murphy, Marjorie C., *Christmas Decorations*, 69, 6. (Dec.1932): p12-13.

3729 Moss, Doris Hudson, *Holiday Entertaining*, 71, 6. (Dec.1933): p12-13.

3730 Starbuck, Helen E., *Really Decorate Your Christmas Tree*, 75, 6. (Dec.1935): p7.

3731 *What's New In Western Living*, 77, 6. (Dec.1936): p13-15.

3732 *Festivity Foods*, 79, 6. (Dec.1937): p26.

3733 *What's New In Western Living*, 79, 6. (Dec.1937): p13-15.

3734 *Festivity Fashions*, 79, 6. (Dec.1937): p28.

3735 *She Makes Christmas Magic*, 81, 6. (Dec.1938): p16-17.

3736 *Cut Outs For Christmas*, 81, 6. (Dec.1938): p20-21.

3737 *Ingenuity*, 83, 6. (Dec.1939): p10-11.

3738 *Good Doors, Good Cheer*, 83, 6. (Dec.1939): p12-13.

3739 *Ideas That Come But Once A Year*, 85, 6. (Dec.1940): p16-17.

3740 *Decorations*, 85, 6. (Dec.1940): p22-23.

4. Food and Entertaining

4. Food and Entertaining

4. Food and Entertaining

4.3 International Cookery

4. Food and Entertaining

4. Food and Entertaining

4056 *The Dutch Honor History With Mashed Potatoes*, 153, 4. (Oct.1974): p152–153.

4057 *Wake Them up to a Fragrant Butterfly or a Grand Warm Heart*, 154, 2. (Feb.1975): p102-103.

4058 *This Easter Morning Bread Is Italian; It's Round, Flat, Handsome Inside and out*, 154, 3. (Mar.1975): p142-144.

4059 *The Turkish Kebab Way... Lamb or Veal on Skewers or in a Paper Wrap*, 154, 5. (May.1975): p132-133.

4060 *A Big Tea*, 154, 6. (Jun.1975): p136-138.

4061 *Mexican Cooks In Los Angeles Share Their Secrets*, 155, 1. (Jul.1975): p50-55.

4062 *What's Roulade? This One is A Delicious Stuffed Veal Roll*, 155, 2. (Aug.1975): p54-55.

4063 *How Brazilians Barbecue Meat Over Charcoal; The Idea is Easy, The Result if Delicious*, 155, 2. (Aug.1975): p98-99.

4064 *Low Cost And Colorful–Middle East Cooking*, 155, 3. (Sep.1975): p62-68.

4065 *Steam Cooking As The Chinese Do It In Szechwan; It's Easy, It's Delicious. You Can Work a Day Ahead. Here are 5 Dishes as Openers, Chicken or Pork*, 155, 4. (Oct.1975): p140-141.

4066 *Maybe Mexico's, Maybe Ours–Nachos are a Delicious Border Mystery*, 156, 1. (Jan.1976): p48-49.

4067 *Hot Knife-And-Fork Soups From Spain, Mexico, Colombia*, 156, 1. (Jan.1976): p78-81.

4068 *The Other French Cuisine–The French Family Meal*, 156, 4. (Apr.1976): p90-97.

4069 *China's Pine Cone Fish*, 156, 5. (May.1976): p182-183.

4070 *How The Basques Bake Sheepherder's Bread; We Give you the Baking Champion's Easy-to-Follow Recipe*, 156, 6. (Jun.1976): p66-67.

4071 *Le Pique-Nique–Two Great Ones For August*, 157, 2. (Aug.1976): p48-49.

4072 *Outdoor Cooking Ideas From The Middle East*, 157, 3. (Sep.1976): p68-69.

4073 *Fun With Fo-Kah-Cha*, 157, 3. (Sep.1976): p126-127.

4074 *Moroccan One-Pots–They're Delicious Stews*, 157, 5. (Nov.1976): p178-182.

4075 *Knishes–Plump And Delicious Pastry Pillows*, 158, 1. (Jan.1977): p78-79.

4076 *The Curry Mystery*, 158, 2. (Feb.1977): p78-81.

4077 *All About Choy... Growing, Cooking, Shopping for Chinese Greens*, 158, 3. (Mar.1977): p102-103.

4078 *Your Own French Country Picnic*, 159, 1. (Jul.1977): p102-103.

4079 *One-Soup And Two-Soup Dinners From Nigeria*, 160, 2. (Feb.1978): p72-73.

4080 *Cioppino - San Francisco, L.A., Seattle Versions*, 160, 3. (Mar.1978): p84-87.

4081 *Neapolitan Gravy*, 160, 3. (Mar.1978): p162-163.

4082 *Come For A Japanese Picnic*, 160, 6. (Jun.1978): p112-114.

4083 *Mexico Dinner In The Hollywood Hills*, 161, 1. (Jul.1978): p78-79.

4084 *Come to Morocco at Our House. We're Having a Couscous Party*, 161, 4. (Oct.1978): p96-99.

4085 *Here's a Different Chinese Dinner... Six Plates Of Cold Tidbits*, 162, 1. (Jan.1979): p60-61.

4086 *Fish-In-A-Fish. The Outside One Is Crust*, 162, 6. (Jun.1979): p84-85.

4087 *Chinese Sesame Buns Have A Pocket for a Spicy Surprise*, 162, 6. (Jun.1979): p88-89.

4088 *Play It Cool? Here's One Way–Japan's Icy-Cold Noodle Soups*, 163, 1. (Jul.1979): p68-69.

4089 *Dip In–As The Greeks Do*, 163, 2. (Aug.1979): p118-120.

4090 *Dim Sum–Chinese Appetizers Make A Meal*, 164, 2. (Feb.1980): p68-71.

4091 *Make-Ahead Mediterranean Picnic; It can Wait for a Sunny Day*, 164, 2. (Feb.1980): p80-81 .

4092 *For Breakfast–Tortilla Eye-Openers*, 164, 2. (Feb.1980): p126-127.

4093 *Taking Liberties With Armenian Cracker Bread*, 164, 3. (Mar.1980): p86-87.

4094 *Bread From Portugal To Hawaii To You*, 164, 4. (Apr.1980): p104-105.

4095 *It's A Tamale Pie That Is Really And Truly Mexican*, 164, 5. (May.1980): p104-105.

4096 *The Simple French Meal*, 165, 3. (Sep.1980): p48-55.

4097 *Welcome 1981 With Spicy Paella*, 166, 1. (Jan.1981): p52-53.

4098 *Was Gnocchi An Accident Or Not?*, 166, 3. (Mar.1981): p140-141, 144.

4099 *Java Comes To Marin–Indonesian Buffet*, 166, 6. (Jun.1981): p168-169.

4100 *All Cold. All Make-Ahead. All Italian Buffet*, 167, 1. (Jul.1981): p74-75.

4101 *Burrito Barbecue*, 167, 2. (Aug.1981): p60-61.

4102 *Country French Cake*, 167, 4. (Oct.1981): p90-91.

4103 *Quenelles Easy? Yes... If You Let the Food Processor do Most of the Work*, 168, 2. (Feb.1982): p152-153.

4104 *Tortilla Cones, Bowls, Lids*, 168, 5. (May.1982): p112-113.

4105 *A Surprise With Every Bite... Tart, Sweet, Hot, Cool, Here are Four Main-Dish Salads From Thailand*, 169, 2. (Aug.1982): p112-113.

4106 *California Hacienda Dinner*, 169, 3. (Sep.1982): p78-79.

4107 *Gelateria At Home*, 169, 3. (Sep.1982): p86-87.

4108 *Italian Won Ton? Chinese Tortellini? You Combine Italian Fillings with Chinese Wrappers You Buy*, 170, 1. (Jan.1983): p50-51.

4109 *Sushi For The Brave, Sushi For The Timid*, 170, 2. (Feb.1983): p96-97.

4110 *Soup Surprises From Thailand*, 170, 3. (Mar.1983): p104-105.

4111 *Rotolo Italiano*, 170, 3. (Mar.1983): p196-197.

4112 *Caribbean Spice Barbecue*, 170, 5. (May.1983): p200-201.

4113 *From The Tip Of Mexico, Yucatan's Surprising Tropical Tastes*, 170, 6. (Jun.1983): p96-99.

4114 *It's Chinese Steeping; Takes The Trickiness Out Of Poaching*, 170, 6. (Jun.1983): p166-167.

4115 *Striped With Pesto, A Stunning Cheese Torta*, 171, 1. (Jul.1983): p76-77.

4116 *Garnachas Doesn't Mean Crisp Bean Boats. But It Could*, 171, 4. (Oct.1983): p196-197.

4117 *French Farm Cooks Have A Secret. It's Confit*, 172, 1. (Jan.1984): p62-63.

4118 *Italian Farm Women Draw It Out Of Stone Ovens... "Mother Loaf"*, 172, 2. (Feb.1984): p84-85.

4119 *Meet The Cooks And Foods Of Southeast Asia*, 172, 4. (Apr.1984): p126-136.

4120 *It's Pashka, Western-Style*, 172, 4. (Apr.1984): p204-205.

4121 *Surprise Salads From Mexico City*, 173, 5. (May.1984): p112-113.

4122 *Knife-And-Fork Soups From Colombia*, 172, 6. (Jun.1984): p104-105.

4123 *Italian Splashes–They Are Super-Fruity*, 173, 1. (Jul.1984): p84-85.

4124 *Don't Be Surprised if you Eat a Dozen... Tiny Green Corn Tamales Are A Mexican Summer Treat*, 173, 1. (Jul.1984): p88-89.

4125 *This Fondue Is Mexican–And It's Barbecued* , 173, 3. (Sep.1984): p76-77.

4126 *Hoppers? They're Kind Of An Edible Brunch Bowl*, 174, 1. (Jan.1985): p116-117.

4127 *There's Buried Treasure In This Mediterranean Bread... Green and Black Olives*, 174, 3. (Mar.1985): p116-117.

4128 *These Are Add-On Soups From Vietnam*, 174, 3. (Mar.1985): p176-178.

4. Food and Entertaining

4. Food and Entertaining

4.5 Specific Ingredients & Foods

4. Food and Entertaining

4. Food and Entertaining

4453 *Peaches And Cream–Old Friends Together*, 171, 2. (Aug.1983): p108-109.

4454 *The Red Pears Are Here*, 171, 3. (Sep.1983): p86-87.

4455 *Should They Reserve Space In The Vegetable Hall Of Fame For Snap Peas?*, 171, 4. (Oct.1983): p108-109.

4456 *The Pumpkin Clan Gathers In The Fall*, 171, 4. (Oct.1983): p110-113.

4457 *Are You Ready For Two Turkey Innovations? Under-the-Skin Dressing. And Butterlying*, 171, 5. (Nov.1983): p112-113.

4458 *These Are The Semiprecious Nuts*, 172, 2. (Feb.1984): p88-91.

4459 *Beef-In-A-Barrel Barbecue*, 172, 5. (May.1984): p120-121.

4460 *The Crunch Pears*, 173, 3. (Sep.1984): p72-75.

4461 *Boneless Beef Bargains*, 173, 3. (Sep.1984): p122-124.

4462 *Why Not A Purple Pepper? Or Golden… as Well as Green Red*, 173, 4. (Oct.1984): p106-107.

4463 *Adventures With The Faraway Nuts*, 173, 5. (Nov.1984): p282-284.

4464 *The Tropical Fruits Are Here*, 174, 4. (Apr.1985): p138-143.

4465 *This Spring Feast Is Easy To Tote*, 174, 4. (Apr.1985): p204-207.

4466 *Picklers, Salad-Makers, Lemon, Armenian–Your Cucumber Choices*, 174, 5. (May.1985): p300-301.

4467 *Sunset's Guide To Summer Fruit*, 175, 1. (Jul.1985): p68-77.

4468 *Melon Marvels*, 175, 2. (Aug.1985): p66-67.

4469 *It's Exhausting, Tricky, Chancy - Noodle Stretching*, 175, 2. (Aug.1985): p130-132.

4470 *Really Small Chickens*, 175, 3. (Sep.1985): p138-140.

4471 *Fresh-From-The-Grower Citrus*, 175, 5. (Nov.1985): p10-12.

4472 *Blue Corn–New Mexico's Gift To Cooks*, 176, 2. (Feb.1986): p86-87.

4473 *Basil Isn't Bashful*, 177, 2. (Aug.1986): p70-72.

4474 *What About All The New Mushrooms?*, 177, 4. (Oct.1986): p78-81.

4475 *Oats: Cookies, Breads, More*, 178, 2. (Feb.1987): p134-136.

4476 *Choose-The-Color Chili*, 178, 3. (Mar.1987): p86-87.

4477 NONE , *Out Of The Stream And Into The Frying Pan… Fresh Trout*, 179, 2. (Aug.1987): p116-117.

4478 *Oystering and Musseling Around Point Reyes*, 180, 2. (Feb.1988): p14-15.

4479 *Lamb And Springtime Companions*, 180, 4. (Apr.1988): p204-205.

4480 *Something Wondrous Happens When you Cook European Plums*, 183, 3. (Sep.1989): p112-115.

4481 *Game Birds In A Festive Fall Dinner*, 183, 4. (Oct.1989): p168-173.

4482 *'Come For An Oyster Tasting'*, 184, 2. (Feb.1990): p156-158.

4483 *Summer Fruit Pies… Readers Share Their Favorites*, 184, 6. (Jun.1990): p82-86.

4484 *Overnight Sensations*, 185, 1. (Jul.1990): p64-65.

4485 *Rhubarb's A Winner*, 186, 2. (Feb.1991): p70-71.

4486 *Tropical Treats*, 186, 5. (May.1991): p174-175.

4487 DiVecchio, Jerry Anne, *From Chile To Your Market…And Table*, 188, 1. (Jan.1992): p76-78.

4488 Anusasananan, Linda Lau, *Red Greens*, 188, 5. (May.1992): p158-159.

4489 Lipman, Karyn I., *Smoked And More, It's Peppered Salmon*, 189, 1. (Jul.1992): p104-105.

4490 Fish, Peter and Johnson, Elaine, *Raspberry Heaven*, 189, 2. (Aug.1992): p110-112.

4491 *What's So Great About Olive Oil?*, 189, 04. (Oct.1992): p98-103.

4492 Finnegan, Lora J. and Anusasananan, Linda Lau, *Crayfish Or Crawfish?*, 190, 4. (Apr.1993): p132-138.

4493 Anusasananan, Linda Lau and Johnson, Elaine, *Sweet Cherry Surprises*, 191, 1. (Jul.1993): p106-108.

4494 Swezey, Lauren Bonar, *The Crinkly, Colorful Crispheads*, 191, 2. (Aug.1993): p58-59.

4495 Anusasananan, Linda Lau, *Chile Crazy In New Mexico*, 191, 3. (Sep.1993): p56-63.

4496 Bateson, Betsy Reynolds, *Lamb Grilled, Baked, Or Stir-fried*, 194, 4. (Apr.1995): p156-160.

4497 Bateson, Betsy Reynolds, *Mastering The Mango*, 194, 5. (May.1995): p130-132, 134.

4498 Hale, Christine Weber, *Who Grew That Fish On Your Plate?*, 1995, 2. (Aug.1995): p72-82.

4499 Johnson, Elaine, *Melon Mania*, 195, 2. (Aug.1995): p84-87.

4500 Johnson, Elaine and Swezey, Lauren Bonar, *Heirloom Tomatoes*, 195, 3. (Sep.1995): p80-84, 86.

4501 *Smoked Salmon Reigns*, 194, 06. (Dec.1995): p80-82.

4502 Jaffe, Matthew, *Empire Of The Orange*, 196, 2. (Feb.1996): p64-71.

4503 Fish, Peter, *A Crab Lover's Guide*, 196, 2. (Feb.1996): p81-86.

4504 Bateson, Betsy Reynolds, *The Mushroom Boom*, 196, 3. (Mar.1996): p122-126.

4505 Anusasananan, Linda Lau, *Aaahhh - Artichokes*, 196, 4. (Apr.1996): p106-110.

4506 Hale, Christine Weber, *The Wild Bunch*, 196, 5. (May.1996): p146-149.

4507 Fish, Peter and Bateson, Betsy Reynolds, *The Taste Of Summer*, 196, 6. (Jun.1996): p86-89.

4508 Anusasananan, Linda Lau, *Prize Salmon*, 197, 2. (Aug.1996): p114-119.

4509 Johnson, Elaine, *Not Just Any Eggplant*, 197, 2. (Aug.1996): p120-123.

4510 Anusasananan, Linda Lau and Swezey, Lauren Bonar, *Garlic Revival*, 197, 3. (Sep.1996): p80-84.

4511 Hale, Christine Weber, *Succulent Tomatoes, Rich Soups*, 197, 3. (Sep.1996): p120-121.

4512 *An American Original*, 197, 04. (Oct.1996): p116-116B.

4513 *A Treasury of Western Nuts*, 197, 05. (Nov.1996): p82-87.

4514 *A Passion For Beans*, 198, 3. (Mar.1997): p120-122, 124, 125.

4515 *The Sweet Side Of Meyer Lemons*, 198, 3. (Mar.1997): p130-132.

4516 *Thick, Sizzling and Juicy… It's Steak Season*, 198, 6. (Jun.1997): p82-84, 89.

4517 *Strawberry Dazzler*, 198, 6. (Jun.1997): p76-77.

4518 *Heaven On A Half-Shell*, 199, 2. (Aug.1997): p96-99.

4519 *A Summer Salmon Feast*, 199, 2. (Aug.1997): p136-143.

4520 Johnson, Elaine, *The Whole Tomato Story: A party for the Season*, 199, 3. (Sep.1997): p116-120.

4521 Hale, Christine Weber, *The Whole Tomato Story: 10 Fresh and Fast Tomato Ideas*, 199, 3. (Sep.1997): p122-123.

4522 Hale, Christine Weber, *The Whole Tomato Story: Cooking up the Classics*, 199, 3. (Sep.1997): p124, 126.

5. Gardening

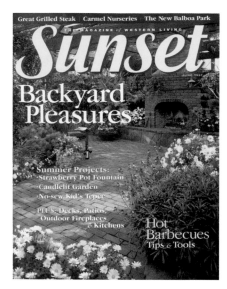

July 1997 cover (Photo: Stephen Simpson)

Gardening

Gardening is another of Sunset*'s Big Four. With a broad approach ranging from exotic garden designs, to Victory Gardens, to formal flower beds, to patio (or even apartment) plants,* Sunset *has emphasized growing themes without pause for almost 70 years. Its regular monthly garden-related columns also provide a wealth of seasonal and problem-solving information for the Western gardener. While many articles treat general techniques or principles, there are distinct specific threads, including Fruit&Vegetable Gardening, Flower Gardening and Container & Indoor Gardening, which we have listed separately. It is worth noting, in particular, how the idea of home-grown produce has persisted through the years, whether as a form of domestic economy, war effort, or health-conscious lifestyle. There is much cross-fertilization between the gardening focus demonstrated here and landscaping (which tends more toward grounds management and design issues).*

5.1 General Gardening

4523 Connor, J. Torrey, *California Winter Gardens*, 10, 4. (Feb.1903): p270-274.

4524 Burbank, Luther, *How This 'Miracle' Came To Be*, 12, 1. (Nov.1903): p35-36.

4525 Wickson, Edward J., *California's Garden Calendar*, 14, 4. (Feb.1905): p414-415.

4526 Wickson, Edward J., *California's Garden Calendar*, 14, 6. (Apr.1905): p625-627.

4527 Wickson, Edward J., *California's Garden Calendar*, 15, 3. (Jul.1905): p284-286.

4528 Gabard, Louis, *My Town Lot Income*, 18, 4. (Feb.1907): p343-347.

4529 Smith, Bertha H., *Antitoxin For Cost-Of-Livingitis*, 25, 2. (Aug.1910): p159-165.

4530 Robinson, A. D., *A Palace Of Lath*, 28, 3. (Mar.1912): p283-284.

4531 Chandler, Harley P., *Making School Gardens In Winter*, 38, 3. (Mar.1917): p32-33.

4532 Brownfield, Marion, *How Will You Have Your Roses?*, 45, 2. (Aug.1920): p66, 68.

4533 Carhart, Arthur Hawthorne, *Gardens of Distinction*, 52, 6. (Jun.1924): p66, 68-69.

4534 Hood, Juliette Mairon, *Gardens in the Bret Harte Country*, 55, 4. (Oct.1925): p64-65.

4535 Place, Estelle M., *Water Gardens in City Lots*, 55, 5. (Nov.1925): p65-66.

4536 Diener, Richard and Small, Sidney Herschel, *How Does Your Garden Grow?*, 58, 3. (Mar.1927): p14-17, 81-84.

4537 Davies, Ada Hilton, *Poet's Tree*, 60, 2. (Feb.1928): p37, 79.

4538 Carhart, Arthur Hawthorne, *Are You Satisfied With Your Garden?*, 62, 2. (Feb.1929): p21-22.

4539 Carhart, Arthur Hawthorne, *The Western Garden Must Be Livable*, 62, 3. (Mar.1929): p24-26.

4540 Sawtelle, Mary Martin, *Desert Gardens Of Delight*, 62, 4. (Mar.1929): p14-16.

4541 Carhart, Arthur Hawthorne, *The Right Use Of Color In The Garden*, 62, 4. (Apr.1929): p28-29.

4542 Sommers, Naomi Swett, *Water Gardens For Western Homes*, 62, 5. (May.1929): p19-21.

4543 Hasty, John Eugene, *I Quit Golf To Fight Gophers*, 62, 6. (Jun.1929): p19-21.

4544 Sawtelle, Mary Martin, *Do You Know these Desert Plants?*, 63, 7. (Jul.1929): p21-23.

4545 Hasty, John Eugene, *Aiding Arid Gardens*, 63, 1. (Jul.1929): p29-30.

4546 Moss, Doris Hudson, *A Bouquet Of Ideas*, 63, 3. (Sep.1929): p11-13.

4547 Woodman, A. M., *Trees And Shrubs For Western Gardens*, 63, 3. (Sep.1929): p30-31, 60.

4548 Taylor, Katherine Ames, *In The Shadow Of The Arctic Circle*, 63, 3. (Sep.1929): p18-20.

4549 Marsh, Warner Lincoln, *What to Plant in Gardens by the Sea*, 63, 4. (Oct.1929): p34-35.

4550 de Forest, Lockwood and de Forest, Elizabeth, *Christmas In A Santa Barbara Garden*, 63, 6. (Dec.1929): p20-21.

4551 Gabrielson, Ira N., *My Portland Garden At Christmas Time*, 63, 6. (Dec.1929): p22.

4552 Mitchell, Sydney B., *For Color In Your Garden*, 64, 1. (Jan.1930): p23-25.

4553 Carhart, Arthur Hawthorne, *We Planned A Garden We Can Use*, 64, 1. (Jan.1930): p26-27.

4554 McLaren, John, *A Year Round Garden Calendar*, 54, 2. (Feb.1930): p21-23.

4555 DuPerrier, Edmund A., *An Introduction To Flora*, 64, 3. (Mar.1930): p23-25.

4556 Mitchell, Sydney B., *Plant Flowering Fruit Trees*, 64, 3. (Mar.1930): p32-34.

4557 Reid, Mary Redington, *Water Gardens*, 64, 4. (Apr.1930): p15-17.

4558 Breeden, Marshall, *His Garden Lesson*, 64, 4. (Apr.1930): p19-20.

4559 Gabrielson, Ira N., *The Northwest Garden Needs Drainage*, 64, 5. (May.1930): p15-16.

4560 Dickson, H. K., *In The Valley Of The Sun*, 64, 5. (May.1930): p27.

4561 Finney, Marian MacLean, *Gardening In The Land Of Little Rain*, 64, 6. (Jun.1930): p13-15.

4562 Trask, Edna Betts, *How to Build the The Cactus Garden*, 65, 1. (Jul.1930): p15-17.

4563 Mitchell, Sydney B., *Plant A Carpet Of Pansies*, 65, 2. (Aug.1930): p19-20.

4564 Hasty, John Eugene, *I Am The Hero Of The Hoe!*, 65, 2. (Aug.1930): p29-31.

4565 Goodrich, Mary, *Little Gardens With Personality*, 65, 3. (Sep.1930): p15-17.

4566 Trask, Edna Betts, *What To Plant For Winter Bloom*, 65, 4. (Oct.1930): p14-16.

4567 Weed, Howard, *Can Westerners Grow Peonies?*, 65, 4. (Oct.1930): p26.

4568 Mitchell, Sydney B., *Phlox Are Easy To Grow*, 65, 4. (Oct.1930): p30-31.

5. Gardening

4569 Prather, Richard L., *Why A Million Westerners Plant Gardens*, 65, 5. (Nov.1930): p9-11.

4570 Bohl, Joe, *This Is My Garden!*, 65, 5. (Nov.1930): p22–24.

4571 Hasty, John Eugene, *A Garden Tenderfoot Interviews An Old-Timer*, 65, 5. (Nov.1930): p25-27, 62-63.

4572 Gooch, J. A., *Plant these Shrubs And Vines*, 66, 1. (Jan.1931): p27.

4573 Mitchell, Sydney B., *Annuals For Rock Gardens*, 66, 2. (Feb.1931): p14-15, 56.

4574 Reid, Margaret Redington, *Vines For Valley Homes*, 66, 2. (Feb.1931): p23-24, 46-47.

4575 Gooch, J. A., *If You Live At An Altitude Of 5000 Feet*, 66, 2. (Feb.1931): p25.

4576 Mitchell, Sydney B., *For Lazy Gardners*, 66, 3. (Mar.1931): p20-22.

4577 Delius, Louise E., *Do You Know Echeverias?*, 66, 3. (Mar.1931): p31, 60-61.

4578 Gooch, J. A., *If You Live In The Desert*, 66, 4. (Apr.1931): p22.

4579 Mitchell, Sydney B., *Thirteen Lucky Rock Plants*, 66, 4. (Apr.1931): p23-24.

4580 McIntyre, C. F., *Our Garden Seven Thousand Feet High*, 66, 5. (May.1931): p12-14.

4581 Mitchell, Sydney B., *Perennials For Western Gardens*, 66, 5. (May.1931): p22-23, 52-53.

4582 Gooch, J. A., *Less Common Shrubs And Vines For The Bay Region*, 66, 5. (May.1931): p29.

4583 Deming, Harriet N., *Notes From Our Foothill Garden*, 66, 6. (Jun.1931): p16-18.

4584 Nidever, Vernon N., *Bird Of Paradise*, 67, 1. (Jul.1931): p18.

4585 Mitchell, Sydney B., *Delphinium Data For Westerners*, 67, 1. (Jul.1931): p19-22.

4586 Toy, Marian Q., *My Little Garden Studio*, 67, 1. (Jul.1931): p26.

4587 Rothe, Lewis, *Garden Models For Model Gardens*, 67, 2. (Aug.1931): p20-21.

4588 Garren, William I., *Garden Architecture*, 67, 3. (Sep.1931): p18.

4589 Rothe, Lewis, *Garden Models For Model Gardens*, 67, 3. (Sep.1931): p28-29.

4590 Gooch, J. A., *A Planting List For Monterey And Vicinity*, 67, 4. (Oct.1931): p21.

4591 Mitchell, Sydney B., *Rules For Growing Rhododendrons*, 67, 5. (Nov.1931): p13-15.

4592 Cuthbertson, Frank G., *Grow Better Sweet Peas*, 67, 5. (Nov.1931): p18-19.

4593 Gooch, J. A., *Special Plants For Special Places*, 67, 6. (Dec.1931): p18-19.

4594 Mitchell, Sydney B., *Armchair Gardening*, 68, 1. (Jan.1932): p18-20.

4595 Mitchell, Sydney B., *12 Less Common Perennials For Western Gardens*, 68, 3. (Mar.1932): p14-17.

4596 Chegwidden, Maude, *When It's Springtime In The Rockies*, 68, 4. (Apr.1932): p14.

4597 Mitchell, Sydney B., *Shade Loving Plants For Western Gardens*, 68, 4. (Apr.1932): p15-17, 48.

4598 Sherrard, Drew, *Gardening Beside A Lake*, 68, 6. (Jun.1932): p15.

4599 Rothe, Lewis, *Garden Models for Model Gardens*, 68, 6. (Jun.1932): p32-33.

4600 Denholm, David, *Plant Stocks Now For Winter Bloom*, 69, 3. (Sep.1932): p9-10.

4601 Mark, Frederick A., *How To Transplant Your Trees And Shrubs*, 69, 4. (Oct.1932): p16.

4602 Mitchell, Sydney B., *Plant these Annuals Now*, 69, 5. (Nov.1932): p12-13, 39.

4603 Mitchell, Sydney B., *Deciduous Flowering Shrubs For Sunset Gardens*, 70, 1. (Jan.1933): p5-7, 32.

4604 Blake, Herbert H., *This Is My Way Of Starting Seeds*, 70, 1. (Jan.1933): p10-11, 33.

4605 Cornell, Ralph, *Good Taste In Western Gardens*, 70, 2. (Feb.1933): p8-9, 32-33.

4606 Mitchell, Sydney B., *Evergreen Shrubs For Sunset Land*, 70, 2. (Feb.1933): p13-14, 33.

4607 Mitchell, Sydney B., *Dwarf Shrubs Suitable For Sunset Rock Gardens*, 70, 3. (Mar.1933): p12-14.

4608 Greeves-Carpenter, C. F., *Care Of Ornamental Trees On The Pacific Coast*, 70, 4. (Apr.1933): p14-16.

4609 Mitchell, Sydney B., *Color In The Western Garden*, 70, 5. (May.1933): p19-20, 37.

4610 Crowl, D., *Try Growing Delphinium From Seed*, 71, 1. (Jul.1933): p12-13.

4611 Mitchell, Sydney B., *Flax And Sage*, 71, 2. (Aug.1933): p14-15.

4612 Murphey, Edith V. A., *Build A Glass Garden To Hold A Few Wild Westerners*, 71, 3. (Sep.1933): p21-22.

4613 Mitchell, Sydney B., *Plant Hunting Expedition*, 71, 4. (Oct.1933): p12-14, 33.

4614 Ketner, H. O., *The Easy Way To Improve Garden Soil*, 71, 4. (Oct.1933): p15, 38-39.

4615 Schaeffer, Clara M., *A Pruning Guide For Sunset Gardeners*, 71, 4. (Oct.1933): p18-19.

4616 Scheinert, Carleton A., *A Few Of Our Most Popular Types Of Cactus*, 71, 6. (Dec.1933): p18-19.

4617 Holmes, Harry L., *The Way To Prune Fruit Trees*, 71, 6. (Dec.1933): p20.

4618 Mitchell, Sydney B., *New Annuals For Western Gardens*, 72, 1. (Jan.1934): p10-11, 30.

4619 Gray, Whitley, *A Prince In Tatters*, 72, 2. (Feb.1934): p6-7.

4620 Sherrard, Drew, *What The Portland Garden Club Is Doing*, 72, 2. (Feb.1934): p10-11.

4621 Rothe, Lewis, *An English Nook For A Sunset Garden*, 72, 2. (Feb.1934): p12-13.

4622 Morse, Norman Donald, *Growing Tigridias This Year*, 72, 2. (Feb.1934): p16.

4623 Mitchell, Sydney B., *New Perennials For Sunset Gardens*, 72, 2. (Feb.1934): p17-18.

4624 Boyle, Catherine J., *Cinerarias For The Pacific Coast*, 72, 2. (Feb.1934): p19.

4625 Mitchell, Sydney B., *New Shrubs For Sunset Gardens*, 72, 3. (Mar.1934): p14-15, 46-47.

4626 Cowan, Harry, Mrs. , *My Way Of Growing Asters*, 72, 3. (Mar.1934): p16.

4627 King, Helen W., *The California Garden Club Federation*, 72, 4. (Apr.1934): p14, 51-52.

4628 Bristol, Edith, *A Garden in Your Heart*, 72, 5. (May.1934): p22, 61.

4629 McCully, Anderson, *Plant them With A Pinch Of Patience*, 72, 6. (Jun.1934): p7-9.

4630 Mitchell, Sydney B., *A Cutting Garden*, 73, 1. (Jul.1934): p12-13.

4631 Egan, Urges Leslie, *Let's Learn To Identify Our Western Ferns*, 73, 2. (Aug.1934): p14-15.

4632 Olsson, Marie, *Views & News Of Valley Gardens*, 73, 2. (Aug.1934): p17, 47.

4633 *When Hollywood Stars Come Down to Earth*, 73, 2. (Aug.1934): p9-11.

4634 Lammerts, W. E., *Rust-Proof Snapdragons*, 73, 3. (Sep.1934): p18-19.

4635 Shults, Grace A., *Cyclamen*, 73, 4. (Oct.1934): p14-15.

4636 Mitchell, Sydney B., *Sunset Garden Talks*, 73, 4. (Oct.1934): p17-18, 56.

4637 Home, Mary Tracy, *Try these Fruits In Your Frost Pockets*, 73, 4. (Oct.1934): p20-21.

4638 Martin, R. Sanford, *A Lesson In Pruning Western Shrubs*, 73, 5. (Nov.1934): p14-15.

4639 Mitchell, Sydney B., *Talks About Perennials*, 73, 5. (Nov.1934): p18, 55.

5. Gardening

4640 Lambert, A. B., *What 10,000 Westerners Have Asked Me About Gardening*, 73, 6. (Dec.1934): p14-15, 55.

4641 Mitchell, Sydney B., *Try Growing Trees And Shrubs From Seeds And Cuttings*, 73, 6. (Dec.1934): p16, 56.

4642 Bohl, Joe, *All-American Selections For Your 1935 Bouquets*, 74, 1. (Jan.1935): p14-15.

4643 Hein, Herman E., *Try Succulents On That Sun-Baked Hillside*, 74, 2. (Feb.1935): p14.

4644 Mitchell, Sydney B., *The Story Of My Own Sunset Garden*, 74, 2. (Feb.1935): p16-17.

4645 Laughlin, Ruth, *Patio Gardens Of Santa Fe*, 74, 3. (Mar.1935): p9-11.

4646 Mitchell, Sydney B., *Why I Chose These Trees for My Sunset Garden*, 74, 3. (Mar.1935): p18-19, 65.

4647 Mitchell, Sydney B., *Every Western Garden Calls For Flowering Trees*, 74, 4. (Apr.1935): p11, 66-68.

4648 Starker, Carl, *Brooms Sweep My Garden*, 74, 4. (Apr.1935): p17, 69.

4649 Powell, Lawrence Clark, *Robinson Jeffers And His Garden*, 74, 5. (May.1935): p11, 66-67.

4650 Mitchell, Sydney B., *I Choose these Deciduous Shrubs For Sunset Gardens*, 74, 5. (May.1935): p14-15, 71-72.

4651 Chegwidden, Maude, *I Had To Learn About High Altitude Gardening*, 74, 6. (Jun.1935): p20-21.

4652 Keeney, Ben E., *A Rock Garden*, 74, 6. (Jun.1935): p22.

4653 Gooch, J. A., *Summer Care Of Sunset Gardens*, 75, 1. (Jul.1935): p10-11, 27-29.

4654 Mitchell, Sydney B., *Garden Page*, 75, 1. (Jul.1935): p12, 28-29.

4655 McCully, Anderson, *What To Plant Around A Rock Garden Pool*, 75, 1. (Jul.1935): p16-17.

4656 Davidson, W. Cox, *Some Of You Will Plant Perennials This Month*, 75, 2. (Aug.1935): p11-12.

4657 Mitchell, Sydney B., *Shrubs That Thrive On My Rocky Slope*, 75, 2. (Aug.1935): p14-15.

4658 Davidson, W. Cox, *Color In The Western Garden*, 75, 2. (Aug.1935): p30-31.

4659 Frye, Else M., *Six Tried And True Alpines For Sunset Gardens*, 75, 3. (Sep.1935): p12-13.

4660 Grant, Marian W., *Pelargoniums for Pacific Coast Gardens*, 75, 5. (Nov.1935): p12-13.

4661 Mitchell, Sydney B., *Talks About Autumn Color*, 75, 5. (Nov.1935): p18-19, 36-37.

4662 Mitchell, Sydney B., *More Comfort In The Garden*, 76, 1. (Jan.1936): p13-14, 37-38.

4663 *What's New In Western Living*, 76, 4. (Apr.1936): p21-23.

4664 *How to Grow Espalier Fruit Trees*, 76, 5. (May.1936): p60-61.

4665 *What's New In Western Living*, 78, 6. (Jun.1937): p19-21.

4666 *Time To Take A Garden Tour*, 78, 6. (Jun.1937): p22-23.

4667 *Gunning For Garden Gangsters*, 78, 7. (Jul.1937): p26-27.

4668 *Color For Your Garden*, 79, 2. (Aug.1937): p26.

4669 Mitchell, Sydney B., *Plant These Easy Evergreens*, 80, 2. (Feb.1938): p42, 44-45.

4670 *Sunset Selections For Western Rock Gardens*, 80, 2. (Feb.1938): p20-21.

4671 Mitchell, Sydney B., *A Friend's Fine Small Garden*, 80, 3. (Mar.1938): p48, 50.

4672 *A Gardening Family*, 81, 5. (Nov.1938): p20-21.

4673 *All-American Winners*, 82, 1. (Jan.1939): p16-17.

4674 *Garden Time*, 82, 6. (Jun.1939): p26-27.

4675 *Cacti Aren't Just Prickly!*, 83, 3. (Sep.1939): p20-21.

4676 *What's New In Western Living*, 83, 5. (Nov.1939): p11-13.

4677 *Western Garden Primer*, 84, 1. (Jan.1940): p10-11.

4678 *Vegetables*, 84, 1. (Jan.1940): p22.

4679 *Fruits*, 84, 1. (Jan.1940): p23.

4680 *All-Americans*, 84, 1. (Jan.1940): p13.

4681 *Color*, 84, 1. (Jan.1940): p14-15.

4682 *Greenhouses*, 84, 1. (Jan.1940): p18-20.

4683 *Trees*, 84, 1. (Jan.1940): p21.

4684 *Mixed Border*, 84, 1. (Jan.1940): p16-17.

4685 *Fragrance*, 84, 2. (Feb.1940): p48.

4686 *How To Grow Montbretias*, 84, 3. (Mar.1940): p54-55.

4687 *A Spring Garden At Christmas*, 85, 3. (Sep.1940): p9.

4688 *Miracle Drugs?*, 85, 3. (Sep.1940): p36-37, 39.

4689 *Pelargonium Cuttings*, 85, 3. (Sep.1940): p40.

4690 *Next Year's Garden Is October's Problem*, 85, 4. (Oct.1940): p14-17.

4691 *I Like The Old-Favorite Perennials*, 85, 4. (Oct.1940): p20.

4692 *I Want Lots of Daffodils*, 85, 4. (Oct.1940): p18.

4693 *I Want Lots of Dafodils*, 85, 4. (Oct.1940): p18.

4694 *Wild Flowers*, 85, 5. (Nov.1940): p51.

4695 *Sunset's 1941 All-Westerns*, 86, 1. (Jan.1941): p10-11.

4696 *Gardens Can Be Mirrors*, 86, 1. (Jan.1941): p16-17.

4697 *Carmel Biblical Garden*, 86, 1. (Jan.1941): p22-23, 43.

4698 *Herb Garden*, 86, 2. (Feb.1941): p48.

4699 *For Summer Bloom Sow Now*, 86, 3. (Mar.1941): p20-21.

4700 *Box Gardens*, 86, 4. (Apr.1941): p64-65.

4701 *Chameleon*, 87, 4. (Oct.1941): p19.

4702 *Tree Gardeners*, 87, 6. (Dec.1941): p10-11.

4703 *Gardens 1942...*, 88, 1. (Jan.1942): p8-9.

4704 *If Plants Could Choose Their Favorite Garden Spots*, 88, 1. (Jan.1942): p16-17.

4705 *Chemists to the Rescue*, 88, 5. (May.1942): p50.

4706 *Victory*, 88, 5. (May.1942): p51.

4707 *Vegetables*, 88, 6. (Jun.1942): p42.

4708 *Gardening For Victory*, 89, 1. (Jul.1942): p34-35.

4709 *Fall Planting*, 89, 3. (Sep.1942): p14-15.

4710 *How To Be An Efficient Gardener*, 89, 4. (Oct.1942): p10-11.

4711 *How To Be A Color Gardener*, 89, 4. (Oct.1942): p14-15.

4712 *How To Be A Bulb Gardener*, 89, 4. (Oct.1942): p16-17.

4713 *How to be a Better Putterer*, 89, 4. (Oct.1942): p12-13.

4714 *Color Expert*, 89, 5. (Nov.1942): p48-49.

4715 *Pruning*, 89, 6. (Dec.1942): p42-43.

4716 *Fall And Winter Vegetables*, 91, 1. (Jan.1943): p14-17.

4717 *Planning Vegetable Variety*, 90, 1. (Jan.1943): p10-11.

4718 *Shrubby Perennials*, 90, 1. (Jan.1943): p40.

4719 *England's Campaign*, 90, 2. (Feb.1943): p12-13.

4720 *How To Make Your Own Planting Equipment*, 90, 2. (Feb.1943): p16-17.

4721 *Big Three*, 90, 2. (Feb.1943): p42-43.

4722 *Spring Failures And How To Avoid them*, 90, 3. (Mar.1943): p36-39.

4723 *How Much Is A Little?*, 90, 4. (Apr.1943): p8-9.

4724 *War Garden Strategy*, 90, 4. (Apr.1943): p36-39.

4725 *Garden Temperatures*, 90, 5. (May.1943): p8-11.

4726 *Practical Pointers For Victory Gardeners*, 90, 5. (May.1943): p55-57.

4727 *Vegetable Tips*, 91, 1. (Jul.1943): p50-51.

4728 *Fall and Winter Vegetables*, 91, 1. (Jul.1943): p14-17.

4729 *Beneficial Bacteria*, 91, 1. (Jul.1943): p52-53.

5. Gardening

5. Gardening

5. Gardening

4901 *The Weed Invasion Is On*, 128, 5. (May.1962): p238-239.

4902 *June In Your Garden: We've Had Good Rains... But Irrigation is Still the First Concern*, 128, 6. (Jun.1962): p182-185.

4903 *How To Make Softwood Cuttings*, 128, 6. (Jun.1962): p186-187.

4904 *A New Way To Wet Things Down... You Put Sprinkler Heads in Ordinary Plastic Hose*, 129, 1. (Jul.1962): p148-150.

4905 *The Rewarding Art Of The Espalier*, 129, 1. (Jul.1962): p160-162.

4906 *How To Grow Sound And Tasty Fruit On A Handsome, Healthy Tree*, 129, 2. (Aug.1962): p70-72.

4907 *Budding Is Like Grafting, Only Easier...And You Have Nothing To Lose*, 129, 2. (Aug.1962): p136-137.

4908 *Autumn's The Time To Plant*, 129, 4. (Oct.1962): p232-234.

4909 *Greenhouses*, 129, 5. (Nov.1962): p240-241.

4910 *Hard To Find But Worth It*, 129, 5. (Nov.1962): p262-264.

4911 *All These Red-Berried Christmas Hollies Do Well In Western Gardens*, 129, 6. (Dec.1962): p168-169.

4912 *For The Observant Gardener...The Beauties Of Tree Bark*, 130, 1. (Jan.1963): p66-67.

4913 *Quick Bonsai...By Air-Layering*, 130, 1. (Jan.1963): p146-147.

4914 *The Azalea Color Wave*, 130, 4. (Apr.1963): p92-97.

4915 *How To Multiply Succulents... With Cuttings It's Easy and Most Rewarding*, 130, 5. (May.1963): p272-276.

4916 *For Successful Color...Five Successful Border Plans*, 130, 5. (May.1963): p262-264.

4917 *Native Ferns*, 130, 6. (Jun.1963): p204-206, 208.

4918 *The Folklore Of Steer Manure*, 130, 6. (Jun.1963): p214-218.

4919 *For A Cool Look On Your Terrace*, 130, 6. (Jun.1963): p234-235.

4920 *Perennials In California... Plant Now... Or Plant Soon*, 131, 4. (Oct.1963): p102-105.

4921 *Spring Planting In The Fall...In California*, 131, 4. (Oct.1963): p260-264.

4922 *If You Plan To Grow Natives*, 131, 4. (Oct.1963): p266, 268, 270.

4923 *It's Easy To Become Infatuated With Pines*, 131, 5. (Nov.1963): p88-93.

4924 *A First Anniversary...And A Look At The Year's Selections*, 131, 5. (Nov.1963): p264, 266, 268, 270.

4925 *Gift To A Gardener: Shears Or A Saw*, 131, 6. (Dec.1963): p180-182, 184.

4926 *Flowering Cherry*, 132, 1. (Jan.1964): p118-119.

4927 *Getting To Know The Junipers*, 132, 2. (Feb.1964): p174, 177, 178, 180.

4928 *The Art Of Growing Plants As Standards*, 132, 3. (Mar.1964): p86-93.

4929 *Is This Your Year For Tomatoes?*, 132, 3. (Mar.1964): p102-105.

4930 *Usually It's Wise To Choose A Small Maple*, 132, 3. (Mar.1964): p232-233.

4931 *Pruning Primer*, 132, 4. (Apr.1964): p246-248, 253.

4932 *You Don't Just Grow A Rhododendron You Live With It*, 132, 5. (May.1964): p120-125.

4933 *Here Are 20 Outstanding Annuals; 10 Are new Ones, 10 Are Old-Timers*, 132, 5. (May.1964): p264-265.

4934 *Your Own Underground X-Ray*, 133, 2. (Aug.1964): p66-67.

4935 *How To Enjoy Spring In Midwinter*, 133, 3. (Sep.1964): p182, 185, 186,188 .

4936 *Now's The Very Best Time To Plant Perennials*, 133, 4. (Oct.1964): p262-263.

4937 *The Making of a Garden is Much Easier if You Just Rent Power*, 133, 5. (Nov.1964): p108-113.

4938 *Bare-Root Planting*, 134, 1. (Jan.1965): p130-131.

4939 *Early Apricot To Late Cherry*, 134, 2. (Feb.1965): p82-87.

4940 *Idea Collecting In Specialty Nurseries*, 134, 2. (Feb.1965): p184-186.

4941 *An Apple Wall And A Pear Wall*, 134, 2. (Feb.1965): p190.

4942 *We In California Live In A Treasure-House Of Ferns*, 134, 3. (Mar.1965): p102-107.

4943 *Form Chart: A Knowing Look At 50 Annuals New This Year*, 134, 3. (Mar.1965): p236-237.

4944 *Palms Yes? Or Palms No?*, 134, 4. (Apr.1965): p100-105.

4945 *Man Versus Gopher In The Western United States*, 134, 6. (Jun.1965): p102-107.

4946 *If You Are Sure They Are Burls, You Can Ignore Them*, 135, 1. (Jul.1965): p158.

4947 *Mulching Just Makes Your Gardening Easier*, 135, 1. (Jul.1965): p167.

4948 *New Idea-Gardens You Can Visit In San Francisco's Golden Gate Park*, 135, 3. (Sep.1965): p74-77.

4949 *For Color Come Winter, Plant these Annuals Now*, 135, 4. (Oct.1965): p250-251.

4950 *Airy, Delicate Japanese Marvels*, 135, 5. (Nov.1965): p92-95.

4951 *Here You See A Garden Gamble Paying Off*, 135, 5. (Nov.1965): p230-231.

4952 *Christmas Aralia...At Home...As A Gift*, 135, 6. (Dec.1965): p62-63.

4953 *The All-America Annuals For 1966 Are Stunners*, 136, 1. (Jan.1966): p122-123.

4954 *The Elegant Oriental Magnolias*, 136, 2. (Feb.1966): p72-75.

4955 *Vines And Shrubs On Trellises, Arches, Posts, Pyramids*, 136, 4. (Apr.1966): p102-103.

4956 *Gardening On A Deck, Terrace Or Even A Roof*, 136, 4. (Apr.1966): p236-238, 240.

4957 *The Colorful Bottlebrushes Are A California Answer*, 136, 5. (May.1966): p262-264, 266.

4958 *Garden Walking By Strawberry Creek Just Minutes From Berkeley's Noisy Streets*, 136, 5. (May.1966): p250-251.

4959 *Choosing A Eucalyptus*, 136, 6. (Jun.1966): p96-106.

4960 *What To Spray At...And What To Spray With*, 136, 6. (Jun.1966): p230, 232, 234.

4961 *One Of The Plants You Can Build A Garden Around*, 136, 6. (Jun.1966): p238-239.

4962 *Character Pruning*, 137, 2. (Aug.1966): p60-61.

4963 *If The Deer Are Breakfasting On Your Favorite Garden Plants*, 137, 3. (Sep.1966): p74-77.

4964 *If Gardeners' Talk Is Greek To You*, 137, 4. (Oct.1966): p268-271.

4965 *Are Those Flowers Real*, 137, 5. (Nov.1966): p80-81.

4966 *If You Only Know Old Snowball, Meet The Other Viburnums*, 137, 5. (Nov.1966): p233-234.

4967 *It's The Conifer That Grows Every Which Way*, 137, 5. (Nov.1966): p238-240.

4968 *Day And Night Bloomers...And Dazzlers All*, 138, 3. (Mar.1967): p98-101.

4969 *The Story Of A Baseball Garden...April's Opening To October's World Series*, 138, 4. (Apr.1967): p90-91.

4970 *The Rhododendron Color Explosion*, 138, 5. (May.1967): p94-97.

4971 *It's Australia Come To California...An Almost All-Eucalyptus Garden*, 138, 6. (Jun.1967): p190, 193.

4972 *Ways To Tie Your Vines*, 138, 6. (Jun.1967): p194-195.

4973 *October's The Month To Plant For 1968 Flower Color*, 139, 4. (Oct.1967): p224, 226, 229.

4974 *The Trees Are Good-Looking All Year...And The Handsome Fruit Ripens In November*, 139, 5. (Nov.1967): p212-213.

4975 *Gift Ideas...To Please A Weeder, And Even To Start A Non-Weeder Off On Weeding*, 139, 6. (Dec.1967): p162-164.

5. Gardening

4976 *Thanks To Acacia, California's Spring Starts In January*, 140, 1. (Jan.1968): p46-47.

4977 *It's Not A True Plum...But It's The Most In The Pink*, 140, 3. (Mar.1968): p70-71.

4978 *What Can A Gardener Do Between Now And October? A Great Deal; Here is Proof*, 140, 4. (Apr.1968): p104-108, 111.

4979 *Too Good Looking To Be True? That's the Way It is With Clematis*, 140, 5. (May.1968): p246-247.

4980 *The Plants You Usually Can't Get In Nurseries*, 141, 1. (Jul.1968): p138-142.

4981 *Handsome Hang-Ups*, 141, 3. (Sep.1968): p66-67.

4982 *Succulent Garden...Bold Shapes, Interesting Close-Ups*, 141, 5. (Nov.1968): p244-247.

4983 *An Easy And Different Approach To Grafting*, 142, 1. (Jan.1969): p114-115.

4984 *How Much Can A Gardener Accomplish Between Spring And Fall*, 142, 4. (Apr.1969): p86-91.

4985 *Old Garden Tools Get A Fresh Start*, 142, 4. (Apr.1969): p118-123.

4986 *April In Northwest Gardens*, 142, 4. (Apr.1969): p222-225.

4987 *Here Are Color Ideas For Your Rock Garden*, 142, 4. (Apr.1969): p242-244.

4988 *Eye-Catchers When In Bloom...Landscape Performers Later On*, 142, 5. (May.1969): p218-219.

4989 *Child Gardeners...How To Encourage Success, Discourage Dropping Out*, 142, 6. (Jun.1969): p200-201.

4990 *Tepee, Stepladder, Shelf, Wire, Old Boards*, 142, 6. (Jun.1969): p210.

4991 *It's Time To Blow The Whistle On DDT*, 143, 2. (Aug.1969): p58-59.

4992 *Life With Birds*, 143, 3. (Sep.1969): p62-71.

4993 *A New Idea Center For Gardeners In San Francisco's Golden Gate Park*, 143, 5. (Nov.1969): p94-97.

4994 *It's Good Looking And Well Behaved. It's Nandina*, 143, 6. (Dec.1969): p166-167.

4995 *Apple Fences*, 144, 1. (Jan.1970): p58-59.

4996 *How Two Boys In Pasadena Grow Jungly Plants With Long Names*, 144, 1. (Jan.1970): p122-123.

4997 *Early Bulbs; Put Them in Special Pots... Then Bring Them Indoors*, 144, 2. (Feb.1970): p74-75.

4998 *10-Page Introduction To The Joys Of California Gardening*, 144, 3. (Mar.1970): p84-93.

4999 *The Gardener's Achievement in a Single Season*, 144, 4. (Apr.1970): p114-120.

5000 *The Youngest Gardener Was 5, The Oldest 16*, 144, 4. (Apr.1970): p218-219.

5001 *Giant Corn, Giant Pumpkins, Giant Sunflowers*, 144, 5. (May.1970): p220-221.

5002 *Baby's Tears...A Smothering Green Wave?*, 145, 1. (Jul.1970): p144-145.

5003 *The Theory and Practice of Scarecrowing*, 145, 2. (Aug.1970): p130-131.

5004 *Summer Is The Time To See These Historic Trees In Sunset's Garden*, 145, 2. (Aug.1970): p132-133.

5005 *October Is A Great Month To Put Spring Color In The Ground*, 145, 4. (Oct.1970): p90-91.

5006 *This Spring-Flowering Marvel Is The Happy Result Of Autumn Planting*, 145, 4. (Oct.1970): p194-195.

5007 *If You Play It Right, Up To Eleven Months Of Azalea Bloom*, 145, 5. (Nov.1970): p80-83.

5008 *What Does An Ecologically Defensive Gardener Really Want For Christmas*, 145, 6. (Dec.1970): p66-67.

5009 *A Really Useful Gardener Gift... A Pruning Saw*, 145, 6. (Dec.1970): p172-173.

5010 *If You Have Prunings That Need Chomping Up*, 146, 1. (Jan.1971): p50-53.

5011 *Clivia Is Happy Indoors Or Outdoors, Almost Anywhere Except In The Sun*, 146, 2. (Feb.1971): p72-73.

5012 *Big Container Plants Add Interest To Indoor Spaces, Soften Outdoor House Lines*, 146, 2. (Feb.1971): p162-163.

5013 *What's Ahead For An Atrium Owner*, 146, 2. (Feb.1971): p164-165.

5014 *Is Organic Gardening Success Easy? No, But It's Possible. Here is Picture Evidence*, 146, 3. (Mar.1971): p216-217, 224-225.

5015 *Garden Contest Winners*, 146, 4. (Apr.1971): p102-110.

5016 *The Young Garden Prizewinners Of 1970*, 146, 4. (Apr.1971): p262-263.

5017 *Organic Leftovers As Soil Improvers*, 146, 6. (Jun.1971): p218-220.

5018 *Summer And Spring Show, And A Water View*, 147, 1. (Jul.1971): p142-143.

5019 *Strawberry Marvels; Maybe the Best You've Ever Tasted... Ready in January and They'll Keep Coming for Months*, 147, 3. (Sep.1971): p54-55.

5020 *With Chicken Wire And Hay Hook*, 147, 4. (Oct.1971): p240-241.

5021 *Great Plants From Scattered Bird Seed Grow...Unless You Plan It Otherwise*, 148, 1. (Jan.1972): p126-127.

5022 *Garden Contest Winners*, 148, 3. (Mar.1972): p66-73.

5023 *Sedums Are Great If You Don't Give them Too Much Room*, 148, 3. (Mar.1972): p218-219.

5024 *Gardening At School? It's A Kick*, 148, 4. (Apr.1972): p98-101.

5025 *The Happy Season Begins. Its Time To Plant Color*, 148, 4. (Apr.1972): p106-109.

5026 *If You Garden On The Coast, Here Are Plants That Can Take Wind, Spray, Sand*, 149, 3. (Sep.1972): p180-181.

5027 *His Garden Took Just Eight Weekends To Build; Cost Less Than $900*, 149, 4. (Oct.1972): p268-270.

5028 *Love That Rainwater*, 150, 1. (Jan.1973): p86-87.

5029 *Spring Starts In January In California Thanks To Acacias; Here is the Month-By-Month Parade of the Yellow Bloomers*, 150, 1. (Jan.1973): p126-128, 130.

5030 *We Are Trying To Clear Up The Great Daphne Mystery*, 150, 2. (Feb.1973): p68-69.

5031 *The Great Freeze Of 1972: What Did It Do to Your Garden? What Can You Do This Spring?*, 150, 3. (Mar.1973): p84-87.

5032 *The One Perfect Digging Tool?*, 150, 3. (Mar.1973): p216-217, 220.

5033 *This Garden Was Young In 1898; It Puts on a Grand Color Show in 1973*, 150, 5. (May.1973): p130-131.

5034 *A Garden That Grows*, 151, 2. (Aug.1973): p134-135.

5035 *Head Start Planting Time*, 151, 3. (Sep.1973): p68-71.

5036 *Now's The Time To Consider Alliums; The Grand Performance Comes Next Spring*, 151, 4. (Oct.1973): p222-224.

5037 *How To Make Your Garden More Bird-Livable*, 151, 5. (Nov.1973): p94-97.

5038 *The One Thing Every Gardener Needs*, 151, 6. (Dec.1973): p70-71.

5039 *Something For Practically Nothing; That's What You Get With Piece Root Grafting*, 152, 1. (Jan.1974): p102-103.

5040 *Sprouts Grow In Your Kitchen*, 152, 2. (Feb.1974): p64-67.

5041 *How To Be A New Englander In The West*, 152, 2. (Feb.1974): p152-153.

5042 *In Most Of The West In April Anything Goes*, 152, 4. (Apr.1974): p100-101.

5043 *The Bees Are Fascinating And Not Really Very Hazardous; They're Honey Productive; They're Yours*, 152, 4. (Apr.1974): p218-220.

5044 *Tricky To Grow Rhododendrons Will Behave Themselves If You Soil Build Correctly... And Use a Mound*, 152, 5. (May.1974): p214-215.

5045 *They Did Over The Garden For A Summer Wedding*, 152, 6. (Jun.1974): p84-87.

5046 *From The Woods Of France*, 153, 3. (Sep.1974): p64-65.

5. Gardening

5047 *South Africa Comes To California*, 153, 3. (Sep.1974): p68-69.

5048 *She Plants In Rocks, Driftwood, And Old Stumps, As Well as in Pots and In Mother Earth. Her Garden Is Shady and Woodsy - It Happened Fast*, 153, 4. (Oct.1974): p218-219.

5049 *The Now And Future Garden Gift...Potted Bulbs*, 153, 6. (Dec.1974): p66-67.

5050 *The Ficus (Fig) Trees–Indoors And Out*, 154, 1. (Jan.1975): p104-107.

5051 *Handsaws, Sawbucks For Pruning Or Logging*, 154, 2. (Feb.1975): p138-139.

5052 *Is A Greenhouse For You?*, 154, 3. (Mar.1975): p204-206.

5053 *Treat Your Nursery In May Like A Delicatessen*, 154, 5. (May.1975): p84-85.

5054 *Lollipop Trees* , 154, 6. (Jun.1975): p68-71.

5055 *The Plant Damagers–And What You Can Do*, 154, 6. (Jun.1975): p72-77.

5056 *The Earth's Tallest Trees Right At Your House*, 156, 2. (Feb.1976): p72-75.

5057 *Boston Ferns, Like Children, Need You. Here We Summarize 25 Success Stories*, 156, 2. (Feb.1976): p76-77.

5058 *How Wet Is Your Soil*, 156, 3. (Mar.1976): p194-196.

5059 *The Impatiens Breakthrough*, 156, 4. (Apr.1976): p102-103.

5060 *Here's Last-Minute Help for Garden Procrastinators*, 156, 6. (Jun.1976): p68-69.

5061 *Successful Mountain Gardeners Share Some Secrets and a Reminder... With June There's Reason to Rush Vegetable Planting*, 156, 6. (Jun.1976): p186-187.

5062 *The Bromeliads–Curiouser And Curiouser*, 157, 1. (Jul.1976): p66-69.

5063 *Gardens That Go Without Watering*, 157, 4. (Oct.1976): p78-85.

5064 *Why California Ceanothus Are Such Great Californians*, 157, 5. (Nov.1976): p96-99.

5065 *Christmas Bonsai*, 157, 6. (Dec.1976): p62-65.

5066 *House Plant Paraphernalia As Gifts*, 157, 6. (Dec.1976): p176-177.

5067 *Cactus? Spiny And Sometimes Spectacular*, 158, 1. (Jan.1977): p50-53.

5068 *Have You Discovered Spur Apples? The Trees are Smaller and the Apples Grow Close Together*, 158, 1. (Jan.1977): p96-97.

5069 *Spring Jumps The Gun In Orange County*, 158, 2. (Feb.1977): p72-75.

5070 *A Revolution In Greenhouses*, 158, 3. (Mar.1977): p96-99.

5071 *Frugality With Garden Water - Here is a Summing up of Experience in Super-Dry Marin County In 1976*, 158, 3. (Mar.1977): p240B.

5072 *Garden Contest Winners Of 1976–A Sampler*, 158, 4. (Apr.1977): p112-113.

5073 *Water-Short Gardening... Here are Some Guidelines for Plants*, 158, 4. (Apr.1977): p126-129.

5074 *Gray Water Put To Work In Your Garden?*, 158, 5. (May.1977): p268-269.

5075 *Carrots, to Topiary, to Impatiens*, 159, 1. (Jul.1977): p72-73.

5076 *Water-Frugal Garden In Pasadena... Way Ahead of His Time*, 159, 1. (Jul.1977): p76-77.

5077 *Gray Water–The Hazards And The Hope*, 159, 3. (Sep.1977): p168-169.

5078 *Garden In The Sky In San Francisco*, 159, 3. (Sep.1977): p86-87.

5079 *If You'd Like To Make Wine, What About A Vineyard?*, 159, 4. (Oct.1977): p273-275.

5080 *Drought Discoveries*, 159, 5. (Nov.1977): p96-97.

5081 *Gift Ideas For The Water Miser*, 159, 6. (Dec.1977): p78-79.

5082 *A Gift Plant to Treasure... A Lacy, Ruffly, Billowy, or Variegated Maidenhair Fern*, 159, 6. (Dec.1977): p178-180.

5083 *Some Tomatoes are Just Right for Pots*, 160, 3. (Mar.1978): p100-101.

5084 *The Rhododendron-Azalea Extravaganza*, 160, 4. (Apr.1978): p124-125.

5085 *Carpeting Ground Covers*, 160, 4. (Apr.1978): p294-297.

5086 *Pay our Garden a Visit In May*, 160, 5. (May.1978): p126-129.

5087 *Bedding Plants–Special Care Brings Better Bloom*, 160, 5. (May.1978): p266-267.

5088 *The Right Way To Start Eucalyptus*, 160, 6. (Jun.1978): p110-111.

5089 *Tomatoes In The Home Stretch - Here's How to Bring In Winners*, 161, 1. (Jul.1978): p186-187.

5090 *Cuttings Are Free And Almost Foolproof*, 161, 2. (Aug.1978): p78-79.

5091 *Not At All Venerable Bonsai–The Fuchsia*, 161, 3. (Sep.1978): p76-77.

5092 *For Covering the Ground With Little Trouble, It's Hard To Beat Dwarf Coyote Brush*, 161, 3. (Sep.1978): p182-183.

5093 *Pittosporums–Utility Infielders*, 161, 4. (Oct.1978): p232-234.

5094 *It's A Bonsai Party*, 161, 5. (Nov.1978): p122-123.

5095 *The Can't-Do-Without Garden Tool*, 162, 1. (Jan.1979): p132-133.

5096 *The Mild Winter "Privilege Plants"*, 162, 2. (Feb.1979): p86-91.

5097 *Plants To Walk Over And Walk On For Garden Paths*, 162, 2. (Feb.1979): p204-205.

5098 *Color Around The Seasons Around The West*, 162, 3. (Mar.1979): p76-83.

5099 *Tillers The Toilers*, 162, 3. (Mar.1979): p206-208.

5100 *Water Gardening; It's Cool, Colorful, Not Wasteful*, 162, 4. (Apr.1979): p110-113.

5101 *Ideas From Garden Contest Winners Five 1978 Contest Winners; Top Prize Goes to a City-Lot-Size Palm Garden*, 162, 4. (Apr.1979): p118-120.

5102 *Eppi-I-Fill-Ums? They Are Flower Factories*, 162, 5. (May.1979): p108-109.

5103 *Boulder, Colorado, Garden Suits Its Mountain Climate, Needs Little Water*, 162, 5. (May.1979): p292-293.

5104 *Playing A Leafy Color Game In The Shade–With Coleus*, 162, 6. (Jun.1979): p86-87.

5105 *How to Get Tangerines, Lemons, Gapefruit, Limes From Your Healthy Citrus Tree? Tree Budding*, 163, 3. (Sep.1979): p188-189.

5106 *Sunshiny Color In Your Garden This Winter? Why Not?*, 163, 4. (Oct.1979): p94-95.

5107 *Old Is New–Bulbs In A Pot Of "Bulb Mix"*, 163, 5. (Nov.1979): p264B-264C.

5108 *Plant Mezzanine: A Hanging Garden Over Their Kitchen*, 164, 1. (Jan.1980): p52-53.

5109 *Coral trees–Midwinter Standouts*, 164, 2. (Feb.1980): p72-75.

5110 *Which Sprayer For You?*, 164, 2. (Feb.1980): p166-167.

5111 *These Spectacular Magnolias–Only In The Mid-Winter West*, 164, 3. (Mar.1980): p92-93.

5112 *What's New With Whirring Weeders?*, 164, 3. (Mar.1980): p198-199.

5113 *Which Tomatoes are Best? Which Tomatoes Are Losers?*, 164, 5. (May.1980): p94-101.

5114 *Gardening Under a Roomy Tent You Make With Whadecloth or Plastic Over PVC Pipe*, 164, 5. (May.1980): p268-269.

5115 *Bright Garden Color All The Year Round At Disneyland*, 164, 5. (May.1980): p106-109.

5116 *150 Knowing Fuchsia Growers Tell Us Which are Best for Hanging Baskets*, 165, 2. (Aug.1980): p150-151.

5117 *What's He Doing With Those Snapdragons?*, 165, 4. (Oct.1980): p100-101.

5118 *It's Perennial Division Time. We Show How*, 165, 5. (Nov.1980): p232-233.

5119 *Which Garden Ladder?*, 166, 1. (Jan.1981): p54-55.

5. Gardening

5193 *Green And Water-Efficient Near Sacramento*, 181, 2. (Aug.1988): p124-125 .

5194 *When You Really Need A 2-Man Post-Hole Auger*, 181, 2. (Aug.1988): p62-63.

5195 *The Unthirsty 100*, 181, 4. (Oct.1988): p74-83.

5196 *Are Jays the Gardener's Friend or Foe? Our Readers Speak Out*, 182, 3. (Mar.1989): p192, 194, 196-197.

5197 *Questions And Answers About Water And Gardens*, 182, 5. (May.1989): p126 129.

5198 *Color In A Dry Year?*, 182, 5. (May.1989): p234-235.

5199 *Shrubs That Pass For Trees*, 182, 6. (Jun.1989): p84-85.

5200 *Living Tapestry In Santa Fe*, 182, 6. (Jun.1989): p90-91.

5201 *What Can an Automatic Controller Do for Your Irrigation System*, 182, 6. (Jun.1989): p228-230.

5202 *Foxgloves' New Faces*, 183, 3. (Sep.1989): p60-61.

5203 *Sweet Peas Bring Smiles*, 193, 4. (Oct.1989): p76-77.

5204 NONE , *Watch Out, New England!*, 183, 5. (Nov.1989): p88-91.

5205 *The Easy-going Alstroemerias*, 184, 3. (Mar.1990): p98-99.

5206 *Water-wise, "Friendly" Carmel Gardens*, 184, 4. (Apr.1990): p98-101.

5207 *What Else Would You Call them?*, 184, 4. (Apr.1990): p104-105.

5208 NONE , *80 Little Things and One Great Big Thing You Can Do to Save Water in the Garden*, 184, 5. (May.1990): p234-235.

5209 *Saving Your Big Trees*, 185, 1. (Jul.1990): p68-71.

5210 *Little Water, Big Effect: Secrets of Mediterranean-Style Gardens*, 185, 1. (Jul.1990): p74-75.

5211 *Garden Discoveries In The Russian River Wine Country*, 185, 1. (Jul.1990): p168-169.

5212 *Who Says Dry Is Drab?*, 185, 3. (Sep.1990): p64-67.

5213 *Put Everything to Use: The Art Of Garden Recycling*, 185, 3. (Sep.1990): p120-123.

5214 *A Lot More Garden Color With A Lot Less Water*, 185, 04. (Oct.1990): p192-193.

5215 *Spring Indoors...With Bulbs You Plant Now*, 185, 5. (Nov.1990): p92-93.

5216 *Time To Start Composting?*, 185, 6. (Dec.1990): p132-133.

5217 *Tomato Adventures Start In February*, 186, 2. (Feb.1991): p76-79.

5218 *Secrets Of Sunset's Test Garden*, 96-99, 186. (Mar.1991): p3.

5219 *After The Big Freeze*, 186, 3. (Mar.1991): p152-154.

5220 *Dealing With The Drought*, 186, 4. (Apr.1991): p156-159.

5221 *Butterfly Gardening*, 186, 6. (Jun.1991): p92-95.

5222 *Drought Survival: What About Watering Your Plants In Containers*, 186, 6. (Jun.1991): p134-135.

5223 *Raised Beds Are Problem Solvers*, 187, 3. (Sep.1991): p140-143.

5224 *Living With Native Plants*, 187, 4. (Oct.1991). p68-73.

5225 MacCaskey, Michael, *It's Glory Time For Ceanothus*, 188, (Mar.1992). p68-71: .

5226 Ocone, Lynn, *Look What Our Nurseries Have Given Us*, 188, 4. (Apr.1992): p72-75, 78-80.

5227 MacCaskey, Michael, *So You Want To Control Pests Naturally*, 188, 4. (Apr.1992): p115-120.

5228 Swezey, Lauren Bonar, *Chefs In The Garden*, 188, 6. (Jun.1992): p80-82.

5229 MacCausland, Jim, *Your Garden's Most Amazing Visitors*, 189, 1. (Jul.1992): p70-74.

5230 Lincowski, Emely and Ocone, Lynn, *The New California Gardens and Garden Makers*, 189, 3. (Sep.1992): p68-73.

5231 Swezey, Lauren Bonar, *The Best Tomato*, 190, 2. (Feb.1993): p70-71.

5232 MacCaskey, Michael, *Perennials Come Back–Stronger Than Ever*, 190, 5. (May.1993): p52-55, 58, 60, 62.

5233 Ocone, Lynn, *Colorado Country Gardens*, 190, 6. (Jun.1993): p90-95.

5234 Ocone, Lynn, *Pretty Small Gardens*, 191, 1. (Jul.1993): p70-75 .

5235 MacCaskey, Michael and others, *The Miracle Of Fall Planting*, 191, 3. (Sep.1993): p44-49.

5236 Murray, Elizabeth, *Paint A Little Monet In Your Garden; Monet Comes West*, 192, 3. (Mar.1994): p90-93.

5237 *How To Be A Really Smart Nursery Shopper*, 192, 4. (Apr.1994): p72-75, 77, 80.

5238 Whiteley, Peter O., *Avant Gardens*, 193, 1. (Jul.1994): p76-79, 82.

5239 Swezey, Lauren Bonar, *Snip-And-stuff Topiaries*, 193, 6. (Dec.1994): p90-91.

5240 *What's Your Garden Climate*, 193, 08. (Feb.1995): p80-87.

5241 Deming, Harriet M., *Notes From Our Foothill Garden*, 66, 06. (Jun.1995): p16-18.

5242 Swezey, Lauren Bonar, *Garden Inspirations And Renovations*, 195, 1. (Jul.1995): p74-79.

5243 Swezey, Lauren Bonar, *Great Gardens With Great Ideas For Fall Planting*, 195, 3. (Sep.1995): p52-56, 58.

5244 Cohoon, Sharon, *It's Gloating Time!*, 196, 1. (Jan.1996): p64-69.

5245 Brenzel, Kathleen Norris, *First Gardens*, 196, 3. (Mar.1996): p84-92.

5246 Swezey, Lauren Bonar, *A Garden For The Senses*, 197, 1. (Jul.1996): p50-51.

5247 Swezey, Lauren Bonar, *A Passion For Heathers*, 197, 2. (Aug.1996): p56-58.

5248 Cohoon, Sharon, McCausland, Jim, and Swezey, Lauren Bonar, *Secrets Of The Garden Masters*, 197, 3. (Sep.1996): p72-79.

5249 *A Tale Of Two Lilies*, 197, 04. (Oct.1996): p56-58, 60.

5250 *Flower Discoveries*, 197, 04. (Oct.1996): p64-65.

5251 *Taming Wildflowers*, 197, 05. (Nov.1996): p64-66, 68, 70.

5252 *The New Western Garden*, 198, 2. (Feb.1997): p80-85.

5253 *1997 Western Garden Design Awards*, 198, 3. (Mar.1997): p64-89.

5254 McCausland, Jim and Swezey, Lauren Bonar, *Superstars Of The Summer Garden*, 198, 4. (Apr.1997): p62-70.

5255 McCausland, Jim and Swezey, Lauren Bonar, *All-Seasoning Gardens*, 198, 5. (May.1997): p68-72, 74, 76.

5256 Cohoon, Sharon, *The New Organic Garden*, 198, 5. (May.1997): p94-97.

5257 *A Little Water Music*, 198, 6. (Jun.1997): p78-80.

5258 *A Bit Of England In Napa*, 198, 6. (Jun.1997): p94-97.

5259 Cohoon, Sharon, *No Time To Garden?*, 199, 1. (Jul.1997): p54-56.

5260 *Heavenly Oregon Nurseries*, 199, 2. (Aug.1997): p64-69.

5261 Anusasananan, Linda Lau, McCausland, Jim, and Swezey, Lauren Bonar, *Apple Eden*, 199, 3. (Sep.1997): p83-91.

5262 Swezey, Lauren Bonar, *Outsmarting Bambi*, 199, 5. (Nov.1997): p78-82.

5263 Lorton, Steven R., *Gifts for the Well-Dressed Gardener*, 199, 6. (Dec.1997): p68-71.

5264 Williamson, Joseph F. and Lorton, Steven R., *Western Plants that Won the World*, 200, 1. (Jan.1998): p76-82.

5.2 Flower Gardening

5265 Wells, Harry L., *A Sky-Seeking Rose*, 9, 3. (Jul.1902): p211-213.

5266 Metcalfe, Gertrude, *Among Portland's Roses*, 13, 3. (Jul.1904): p213-218.

5267 Lawson, William A., *Christmas Camellias*, 14, 2. (Dec.1904): p165-166.

5268 Otis, Debora, *Where Roses Grow On Trees*, 14, 3. (Jan.1905): p230-234.

5. Gardening

5269 Aiken, Ednah, *A Sponsor To Lilies*, 16, 4. (Feb.1906): p328-335.

5270 Saunders, Charles Francis, *A City Wild-Flower Park*, 38, 5. (May.1917): p34.

5271 Loken, H. J., *Gilding The Gladiolus*, 58, 3. (Mar.1927): p27, 73.

5272 Gast, Ross H., *Around the Year with Gladiolus*, 62, 2. (Feb.1929): p34, 48-49.

5273 Mitchell, Sydney B., *Along the Primrose Path in Western Gardens*, 62, 3. (Mar.1929): p33-34.

5274 McCully, Anderson, *The Land Of Lillies*, 62, 4. (Apr.1929): p15-16.

5275 Mitchell, Sydney B., *Chrysanthemums For Coast Gardens*, 62, 5. (May.1929): p25-26.

5276 Scarborough, Opal, *Some of the New Roses*, 62, 5. (May.1929): p34-35.

5277 Mitchell, Sydney B., *Irises and Irises*, 62, 6. (Jun.1929): p33-35.

5278 Mitchell, Sydney B., *Daffodils*, 63, 4. (Oct.1929): p28-30.

5279 Mitchell, Sydney B., *Western Tulip Truths*, 63, 5. (Nov.1929): p31-33.

5280 Mitchell, Sydney B., *The "Glad" Game*, 64, 2. (Feb.1930): p34-36.

5281 Benscoe, Matt O., *The Night Blooming Cereus*, 64, 4. (Apr.1930): p23, 69.

5282 Mitchell, Sydney B., *Poppies For Pacific Gardens*, 64, 4. (Apr.1930): p29-30.

5283 Mitchell, Sydney B., *A Flower Family Worth Cultivating*, 64, 5. (May.1930): p25-26.

5284 Bartell, Louis, *Twenty Years To Find A Rose*, 64, 6. (Jun.1930): p24-25.

5285 Mitchell, Sydney B., *Why I Like The Wallflower*, 64, 6. (Jun.1930): p29-30, 79.

5286 Mitchell, Sydney B., *We Learn About Lupines*, 65, 1. (Jul.1930): p27-28.

5287 Mitchell, Sydney B., *Fuchsias Are In Fashion*, 65, 3. (Sep.1930): p29-30, 57.

5288 Trask, Edna Betts, *Grow Poinsettias–The Christmas Flower*, 65, 6. (Dec.1930): p23-24.

5289 Browne, Ashley C., *How to Grow Camellias in Coast Gardens*, 66, 1. (Jan.1931): p20-21.

5290 Mitchell, Sydney B., *Rose Rules For Amateurs*, 66, 1. (Jan.1931): p28-29.

5291 Schuchard, Otto F., *How I Grow Giant Chysanthemums*, 66, 4. (Apr.1931): p19-20.

5292 Goodrich, Mary, *When It's Iris Time In Sunset Land*, 66, 5. (May.1931): p15.

5293 Dodge, Natt N., *The Lily Grower Of Haller Lake*, 66, 06. (Jun.1931): p38-41.

5294 Mitchell, Sydney B., *South African Flowers For Western Gardens*, 67, 2. (Aug.1931): p27-28.

5295 Mitchell, Sydney B., *Western Dahlia Growing*, 67, 3. (Sep.1931): p16-17.

5296 Mitchell, Sydney B., *Growing Western Lilies*, 67, 4. (Oct.1931): p12-14.

5297 Mitchell, Sydney B., *Geraniums*, 68, 5. (May.1932): p11-12, 45.

5298 Morse, Norman Donald, *How To Grow Tree Peonies On The Pacific Coast*, 69, 2. (Aug.1932): p6-7.

5299 Mitchell, Sydney B., *Half A Dozen Bulbs To Plant This Month In Western Gardens*, 69, 3. (Sep.1932): p14-15, 37.

5300 Howes, Helen, *Autumn Bouquets from Western Woods*, 69, 4. (Oct.1932): p13, 35.

5301 Mitchell, Sydney B., *Bulbs For October Planting*, 69, 4. (Oct.1932): p14-15, 47.

5302 Hilscher, Helen Yates, *Growing Violas for Variety*, 69, 4. (Oct.1932): p48-49.

5303 Lester, Francis E., *Choose Your Roses Thoughtfully*, 69, 6. (Dec.1932): p18-19.

5304 Studerus, Anita, *You Can Grow Orchids In Your Own Sunset Garden*, 70, 4. (Apr.1933): p17, 35.

5305 Weed, Howard, *You Can Have Iris The Year Round In Sunset Land*, 70, 5. (May.1933): p16-17.

5306 Mitchell, Sydney B., *Garden Blues*, 70, 6. (Jun.1933): p38-41.

5307 Mitchell, Sydney B., *Trials Of A Sunset Gardener*, 71, 3. (Sep.1933): p12-14.

5308 Lester, Francis E., *Wild Roses*, 71, 5. (Nov.1933): p12-13.

5309 Mitchell, Sydney B., *Daffodils, Tulips, And Difficult Plants In California*, 71, 5. (Nov.1933): p16-17, 41.

5310 Williamson, Emma, *Growing Lilies In Sunset Gardens*, 71, 5. (Nov.1933): p18.

5311 Brook, Rosamond, *My Method Of Growing Gladiolus* , 72, 1. (Jan.1934): p12-13.

5312 Howell, E. M., *Growing Carnations from Seed*, 72, 1. (Jan.1934): p13.

5313 Williamson, Emma, *Plant Primulas Now To Bloom Next Spring*, 72, 4. (Apr.1934): p15-16.

5314 Mitchell, Sydney B., *Trials Of A Sunset Gardener*, 72, 6. (Jun.1934): p16-17.

5315 Cronenwett, Clare, *The Bouquet Of The Month*, 73, 4. (Oct.1934): p8.

5316 Mitchell, Sydney B., *My Experiences In Growing And Breeding Irises*, 74, 6. (Jun.1935): p16-17, 23.

5317 Cash, Gwen, *The Head Gardener Gives Away His Chrysanthemum*, 75, 2. (Aug.1935): p10, 26-27.

5318 Swezy, Olive, *Winter Bloom in Bay Region Gardens*, 75, 3. (Sep.1935): p14, 48.

5319 Mitchell, Sydney B., *Tiny Bulb Flowers This Year*, 75, 3. (Sep.1935): p17-18.

5320 Mitchell, Sydney B., *Gophers Don't Like Daffodils, But I Do*, 75, 4. (Oct.1935): p18-19.

5321 *Flowers And Flower Gardens*, 76, 2. (Feb.1936): p20-25.

5322 *What's New In Western Living*, 76, 6. (Jun.1936): p21-25.

5323 *What's New In Western Living*, 78, 1. (Jan.1937): p13-15.

5324 *What's New In Western Living*, 80, 2. (Feb.1938): p13-15.

5325 *Flowers At The Fair*, 82, 1. (Jan.1939): p24-25.

5326 *2 Rows Of Roses*, 82, 2. (Feb.1939): p26-27.

5327 *Fuchsias*, 82, 4. (Apr.1939): p30-31.

5328 *It's Iris Time*, 82, 5. (May.1939): p30-31.

5329 *What's New In The West*, 83, 4. (Oct.1939): p13-15.

5330 *How to Grow Daylilies*, 83, 5. (Nov.1939): p46-48.

5331 *Camellias Are Capricious*, 84, 1. (Jan.1940): p36-37.

5332 *Begonia Experts*, 84, 5. (May.1940): p 66-67.

5333 *Irises*, 85, 1. (Jul.1940): p46-47.

5334 *I Never Knew There Were So Many Bulbs*, 85, 4. (Oct.1940): p19.

5335 *Flower of Antiquity*, 85, 5. (Nov.1940): p50.

5336 *Here Are 1942's Best For The West*, 88, 1. (Jan.1942): p10-11.

5337 *Rose Appraisal*, 88, 1. (Jan.1942): p36, 42.

5338 *Pedigree of the Marigolds*, 88, 1. (Jan.1942): p12-13.

5339 *Irises*, 88, 6. (Jun.1942): p44-45.

5340 *Food For The Eye*, 90, 1. (Jan.1943): p16-17.

5341 *Success With Glads*, 90, 1. (Jan.1943): p41.

5342 *Your New Daffodils*, 91, 2. (Aug.1943): p12-13.

5343 *Roses*, 91, 6. (Dec.1943): p16-17.

5344 *Fuchsias*, 92, 4. (Apr.1944): p14-15.

5345 *Hibiscus Aren't Particular*, 92, 4. (Apr.1944): p50-51.

5346 *Iris Varieties*, 93, 1. (Jul.1944): p42-43.

5347 *Orchid House*, 94, 4. (Apr.1945): p44-45.

5348 *Bulb Planting Arrangements*, 95, 3. (Sep.1945): p48-49.

5349 *Home Orchid Culture*, 95, 4. (Oct.1945): p20-21.

5350 *Grow More Camellias*, 95, 5. (Nov.1945): p22-23.

5351 *What Is The Ideal Rose?*, 96, 1. (Jan.1946): p48-51.

5352 *Graft Camellias*, 96, 2. (Feb.1946): p54-55.

5. Gardening

5353 *Geraniums*, 96, 3. (Mar.1946): p64-65.

5354 *Orchid Guide*, 96, 3. (Mar.1946): p76-77.

5355 *Camellia Pests And Diseases*, 96, 3. (Mar.1946): p82-85.

5356 *Orchid Guide*, 96, 4. (Apr.1946): p72-75.

5357 *Lilacs*, 96, 4. (Apr.1946): p76-79.

5358 *Chrysanthemum Varieties*, 98, 2. (Feb.1947): p76-79.

5359 *What Causes Mass Flowering?*, 98, 3. (Mar.1947): p56-58.

5360 *Bloom Control*, 99, 3. (Sep.1947): p66-67.

5361 *Different Daffodils*, 99, 4. (Oct.1947): p30-31.

5362 *Sunset And Caltech Join In Research Program To Aid Western Flower Gardeners*, 99, 5. (Nov.1947): p22-23.

5363 *Lilies for Western Gardens*, 99, 5. (Nov.1947): p112-114, 116-118, 121.

5364 *Camellia Selector*, 100, 1. (Jan.1948): p24-26.

5365 *Rose Survey*, 100, 1. (Jan.1948): p30-31.

5366 *The Climactic Response Of Dwarf Marigolds*, 100, 3. (Mar.1948): p26-27.

5367 *The Strange Behavior of Camellias*, 100, 5. (May.1948): p142-144.

5368 *New Roses...An Appraisal*, 102, 1. (Jan.1949): p44-45.

5369 *Camellia Introductions–1949*, 102, 2. (Feb.1949): p24-25.

5370 *Start Your Chrysanthemum Parade Now*, 102, 3. (Mar.1949): p34-35.

5371 *New Lilies Made To Order While You Wait*, 103, 5. (Nov.1949): p32-37.

5372 *From The Flower Introduction Of 1949 And 1950, We Select these As Outstanding*, 104, 1. (Jan.1950): p28-30.

5373 *New Camellias*, 104, 2. (Feb.1950): p84-86.

5374 *Roses For 1951*, 106, 1. (Jan.1951): p78.

5375 *10 Solid Camellia Favorites*, 106, 2. (Feb.1951): p30-31.

5376 *Color and More Color*, 106, 3. (Mar.1951): p128-132.

5377 *Eleven Most Popular Orchids...And How To Grow them*, 106, 4. (Apr.1951): p152-153.

5378 *The Stately Bearded Iris*, 106, 5. (May.1951): p166-169.

5379 *Nine Jasmines*, 106, 6. (Jun.1951): p113-115.

5380 *Blue in the Garden*, 107, 1. (Jul.1951): p96-99.

5381 *How to Time and Place Your Daffodils*, 107, 4. (Oct.1951): p167-170, 173.

5382 *Fuchsias Are Tractable*, 108, 6. (Jun.1952): p134-136.

5383 *Little Bulbs That Laugh At Winter*, 109, 3. (Sep.1952): p138-140.

5384 *Old-Fashioned Roses*, 109, 5. (Nov.1952): p165-169.

5385 *Meet The Chrysanthemum Family*, 109, 5. (Nov.1952): p176-181.

5386 *Look What's Happened To The California Poppy*, 110, 2. (Feb.1953): p155-156.

5387 *Fuchsia Report: Seven Tested Varieties And Twenty-Two Interesting Newcomers*, 110, 5. (May.1953): p194-196.

5388 *Learn To Know The Lilies*, 111, 1. (Jul.1953)· p106-110.

5389 *How To Grow And Train Dwarf Camellias*, 112, 2. (Feb.1954): p56-58.

5390 *Iris*, 112, 4. (Apr.1954): p236-240.

5391 *Which Roses For Western Climates?*, 114, 1. (Jan.1955): p92-94.

5392 *Bulb Magic*, 115, 4. (Oct.1955): p210-212.

5393 *Ways To Display Your Orchid Collection*, 116, 1. (Jan.1956): p78-79, 81, 83.

5394 *You Can Have Iris The Year Around*, 118, 5. (May.1957): p63-67.

5395 *Foliage Geraniums; If you Garden in California, you Can Grow These Treasures...*, 118, 6. (Jun.1957): p170-171, 173.

5396 *Is Your Favorite Fuchsia Here?*, 119, 1. (Jul.1957): p46-49.

5397 *For Wisteria Beauty, You Need a Careful Eye and Sharp Pruning Shears*, 120, 3. (Mar.1958): p70-71.

5398 *What's Wrong With My Begonias? Here are Signals of Distress... And What to Do About Them*, 120, 6. (Jun.1958): p168-169.

5399 *Late Summer Sun Lover...Globe Thistle*, 121, 2. (Aug.1958): p115.

5400 *Now's The Time To Plant Spring Color*, 121, 4. (Oct.1958): p66-69.

5401 *Right Now Is The Time To Go See And Study Chrysanthemums*, 123, 5. (Nov.1959): p90-93.

5402 *Why We In The West Like Camellias*, 124, 3. (Mar.1960): p110-117.

5403 *10 Years Of The All-Americas*, 126, 2. (Feb.1961): p76-79.

5404 *Little Bulbs*, 127, 4. (Oct.1961): p96-99.

5405 *How Do You Like Your Daffodils*, 127, 5. (Nov.1961): p82-85.

5406 *How To Live With And Love Your Roses*, 128, 1. (Jan.1962): p72-73.

5407 *Geranium Surprises*, 128, 3. (Mar.1962): p84-89.

5408 *Crocus Surprises*, 129, 3. (Sep.1962): p74-77.

5409 *A New Look At Lilies*, 129, 5. (Nov.1962): p102-107.

5410 *How To Grow Happy Begonias*, 131, 1. (Jul.1963): p154-155.

5411 *How To Grow Fuchsias As Shrubs*, 131, 2. (Aug.1963): p158-159.

5412 *9 New Hybrid Teas*, 132, 1. (Jan.1964): p62-64.

5413 *From The Blue Danube To Waltz Time*, 132, 2. (Feb.1964): p68-69.

5414 *It's About Time To Prune Your Fuchsias*, 132, 3. (Mar.1964): p226, 228.

5415 *How Does Disneyland Do It?*, 132, 6. (Jun.1964): p224-225.

5416 *The New Lantanas Are Colorful And They Thrive On Neglect*, 133, 3. (Sep.1964): p178, 179, 181.

5417 *The True Bulbs*, 133, 4. (Oct.1964): p94-99.

5418 *November is the Month to Choose and to Plant Lily Hybrids*, 133, 5. (Nov.1964): p238-241.

5419 *For 1965, A Dozen New Hybrid Teas, Nine Floribunds, One Grandiflora, And A Structural Rose*, 134, 1. (Jan.1965): p60-62.

5420 *To Start A Camellia Off Right, Refill The Planting Hole Like This*, 134, 1. (Jan.1965): p126-127.

5421 *Nothing Else Really Splashes Like Petunias*, 134, 4. (Apr.1965): p264-265.

5422 *The Stunning Chinese Hibiscus*, 134, 5. (May.1965): p104-107.

5423 *These Strangers Are All Happy Here*, 135, 3. (Sep.1965): p182-183.

5424 *Plant Wisteria This Month For Bloom Year After Year In March And April*, 136, 1. (Jan.1966): p58-59.

5425 *The Colorful Cousins*, 136, 3. (Mar.1966): p96-97.

5426 *The "East Meets West" Flower Show*, 136, 3. (Mar.1966): p222.

5427 *Begonias*, 137, 1. (Jul.1966): p148-149.

5428 *Most Jasmines Are Fragrant; All Are Easy To Grow*, 137, 1. (Jul.1966): p150-151.

5429 *Here's What You Should Do To Have Showcase Dahlias In August*, 137, 2. (Aug.1966): p126-127.

5430 *Sunset's Guide To The September Bulbs*, 137, 3. (Sep.1966): p190, 192, 194.

5431 *For The Great Spring Show*, 137, 4. (Oct.1966): p102-105.

5432 *1967 Roses*, 138, 1. (Jan.1967): p130-132.

5433 *The Stunning Japonicas*, 138, 2. (Feb.1967): p82-85.

5434 *Iris Color Show*, 139, 3. (Sep.1967): p68-69, 158-159.

5435 *Little Bulbs: You Grow Them Just for the Fun of It*, 139, 4. (Oct.1967): p90-91.

5436 *Here's A Refreshing Way To Say Merry Christmas...Flowering Plants Brought Indoors*, 139, 6. (Dec.1967): p64-65.

5437 *The New 1968 Roses...Ready And Waiting*, 140, 1. (Jan.1968): p94-95.

5. Gardening

5. Gardening

6. Landscaping and Outdoor Building

April 1946 cover (photo: Sam Oppee)

Landscaping

Treating the Western home(stead) as an organic unity, Sunset has given much attention to issues of landscaping around the home (and, to a lesser extent, elsewhere) and integration of living spaces between the indoors and outdoors, a characteristic feature of Western living (at least in the more temperate parts). This theme integrates with parallel developments in outdoor cookery and outdoor living long emphasized by the magazine, so we find, variously, outdoor barbecues and fireplaces, garden buildings, lanais, patios, decks and other open spaces connected in some manner to the home, but redefining the boundary of where the house ends and the outdoors begins, and thus reinventing living space. Likewise, we will find much overlap or blurring of edges among the landscaping, gardening, domestic architecture and even food categories. The reader may further pursue this concept by looking in the index under "Outdoor Living."

6. Landscaping and Outdoor Building

5719 Festner, F. Julius, *We Build A Home In The Desert*, 70, 3. (Mar.1933): p20-21, 41.

5720 Cuthbertson, Frank G., *Good Lawns in the West*, 70, 3. (Mar.1933): p38-41.

5721 Cornell, Ralph, *Making the Ordinary City Lot Into a Modern Garden*, 70, 4. (Apr.1933): p24-25.

5722 *Landscaping a City Ranch House*, 73, 4. (Oct.1934): p16, 57.

5723 McCully, Anderson, *Woodsy Effects In Western Gardens*, 73, 5. (Nov.1934): p12-13.

5724 Little, Evelyn Steel, *When A Creek Cuts Through Your Yard*, 74, 1. (Jan.1935): p10-11, 47.

5725 Redfern, Curtis, *What Every Westerner Should Know About Rock Gardens*, 74, 2. (Feb.1935): p15, 58-59.

5726 Burke, H. E., *Control Insects That Destroy Western Trees*, 75, 6. (Dec.1935): p16-17.

5727 *Water Terraces*, 77, 1. (Jul.1936): p22-23.

5728 *Yard Of Ideas*, 77, 2. (Aug.1936): p26-27.

5729 *What's New In Western Living*, 78, 2. (Feb.1937): p13-15.

5730 *Garden Pools*, 78, 7. (Jul.1937): p20-21.

5731 *Screen Fences*, 79, 5. (Nov.1937): p20-21.

5732 Mitchell, Sydney B., *Roadsides Need Good Gardening, Too!*, 81, 1. (Jan.1938): p42-43.

5733 *How To Plant A Retaining Wall*, 80, 6. (Jun.1938): p22-23.

5734 *Rooftrees & Treestones For Western Patios*, 81, 4. (Oct.1938): p18.

5735 *Garden Sculpture*, 82, 4. (Apr.1939): p22.

5736 *Come Into the Garden*, 82, 6. (Jun.1939): p36-37.

5737 *Two Borders In One Back Yard Garden*, 84, 2. (Feb.1940): p16.

5738 *Foundation Borders*, 84, 2. (Feb.1940): p17.

5739 *Outdoor Rooms*, 84, 3. (Mar.1940): p27.

5740 Shellhorn, Ruth Patricia, *Balance in Garden Design*, 84, 3. (Mar.1940): p62.

5741 *Patio*, 84, 4. (Apr.1940): p24-27.

5742 *Scale And Proportion In Garden Design*, 84, 4. (Apr.1940): p64.

5743 *Steps*, 85, 3. (Sep.1940): p14-15.

5744 *How To Plant An Outdoor Living Room*, 86, 1. (Jan.1941): p12-13.

5745 *Tender?*, 86, 1. (Jan.1941): p42.

5746 *Lawn Substitutes*, 86, 3. (Mar.1941): p54-55.

5747 *Salad And Cut Flower Garden*, 86, 3. (Mar.1941): p56.

5748 *Color And Backgrounds*, 86, 4. (Apr.1941): p26-27.

5749 *Why Not More Exterior Decoration?*, 86, 5. (May.1941): p27-29.

5750 *Exterior Decoration*, 86, 6. (Jun.1941): p24-25.

5751 *Shade*, 87, 2. (Aug.1941): p16-17.

5752 *October's Challenge*, 87, 4. (Oct.1941): p12-18.

5753 *Water, Water Everywhere*, 87, 4. (Oct.1941): p22.

5754 *How To Plant A Welcome*, 88, 2. (Feb.1942): p16-17.

5755 *Garden Fences*, 88, 3. (Mar.1942): p36.

5756 *Thomas Church*, 88, 5. (May.1942): p14-15.

5757 *How To Build A Backyard Golf Course*, 88, 5. (May.1942): p42-43.

5758 *Walls...A Part Of Your Garden*, 89, 2. (Aug.1942): p12-13.

5759 *Gardening With Brick*, 89, 3. (Sep.1942): p10-13.

5760 *How To Be A Food Gardener*, 89, 4. (Oct.1942): p18-19.

5761 *Subtropicals In The West*, 90, 1. (Jan.1943): p14-15.

5762 *Hillside Oven*, 90, 1. (Jan.1943): p36-37.

5763 *Greenhouses*, 90, 4. (Apr.1943): p34-35.

5764 *Flattened Contours*, 90, 5. (May.1943): p50-51.

5765 *Ground-Covers*, 90, 5. (May.1943): p52-53.

5766 *Before And After*, 91, 4. (Oct.1943): p18-21.

5767 *Dirt Gardening*, 92, 4. (Apr.1944): p52-54.

5768 *Design is Permanent*, 92, 4. (Apr.1944): p42.

5769 *How to Build a Pool*, 92, 6. (Jun.1944): p42-43.

5770 *Pools For Garden and Terrace*, 92, 6. (Jun.1944): p14-15.

5771 *Planting A House*, 93, 4. (Oct.1944): p16-17.

5772 *How Much Of Your Lot Belongs To The Public?*, 94, 1. (Jan.1945): p10-13.

5773 *Why Prune?*, 94, 2. (Feb.1945): p44-45.

5774 *Concentrated Garden*, 94, 3. (Mar.1945): p46.

5775 *New Ways With Old Favorites*, 94, 4. (Apr.1945): p18-19.

5776 *What Is Western Gardening?*, 94, 5. (May.1945): p12-15.

5777 *What About the Landscape Architect?*, 94, 5. (May.1945): p44.

5778 *Gardening On A Hill*, 94, 6. (Jun.1945): p14-15.

5779 *Native Shrubs*, 94, 6. (Jun.1945): p54-55.

5780 *Patios Can be Pools*, 94, 6. (Jun.1945): p38-39.

5781 *Steps*, 94, 6. (Jun.1945): p50-51.

5782 *Retaining Walls*, 94, 6. (Jun.1945): p52-53.

5783 *Dry Walls*, 94, 6. (Jun.1945): p48-49.

5784 *Lath Construction*, 95, 1. (Jul.1945): p38-43.

5785 *Too Windy? Too Cold?*, 95, 5. (Nov.1945): p20-21.

5786 *Good Ideas From Sunset Homes*, 96, 1. (Jan.1946): p40-41.

5787 *Landplanning Knits House and Site Together*, 96, 5. (May.1946): p20-21.

5788 *Hillside Planning...And Engineering*, 96, 6. (Jun.1946): p22-25.

5789 *Try the Easy Way*, 96, 6. (Jun.1946): p26.

5790 *A Garden To Be Lived In*, 97, 1. (Jul.1946): p22-23.

5791 *All-Citrus Garden*, 97, 2. (Aug.1946): p58-61.

5792 *Landscapes For Living*, 97, 5. (Nov.1946): p24-25.

5793 *Paving Materials In Combination*, 98, 3. (Mar.1947): p18-21.

5794 *Quick Effects in Gardens*, 98, 3. (Mar.1947): p108, 110, 111.

5795 *Back Yards For Gardeners...And For Loafers*, 98, 4. (Apr.1947): p34-36.

5796 *Wind Control In Western Gardens*, 98, 5. (May.1947): p24-25.

5797 *Idea Garden*, 98, 6. (Jun.1947): p32-34.

5798 *Fire In The Garden*, 98, 6. (Jun.1947): p36-38.

5799 *Garden Planning Clinic*, 98, 6. (Jun.1947): p52-53.

5800 *Flame Lighting The Garden*, 99, 1. (Jul.1947): p48-49.

5801 *Building A Tear Drop Pool*, 99, 2. (Aug.1947): p48-51.

5802 *When The Yard Belongs To Johnny And Mary*, 99, 3. (Sep.1947): p19-21.

5803 *Building A Garden On A Windswept Hillside*, 99, 4. (Oct.1947): p32-34.

5804 *Mosaics...And Their Use In Western Homes And Gardens*, 99, 4. (Oct.1947): p38-42.

5805 *Landscaping Is Not The Word*, 100, 1. (Jan.1948): p11.

5806 *Planning Garden Space On A Hillside*, 100, 1. (Jan.1948): p12-13.

5807 *Planning Life On A 55-Foot Lot*, 100, 1. (Jan.1948): p16-19.

5808 *How to Choose the Right Tree*, 100, 2. (Feb.1948): p88-91.

5809 *Changing Levels Poses A Few Problems*, 100, 2. (Feb.1948): p24-25.

5810 *How To Use Concrete In The Garden*, 100, 3. (Mar.1948): p30-40.

6. Landscaping and Outdoor Building

5811 *Ground Covers*, 100, 4. (Apr.1948): p120, 123-124.

5812 *Sculpture In Western Gardens?*, 100, 4. (Apr.1948): p38-39.

5813 *Yes...You Can Landscape Your Own Home...*, 100, 5. (May.1948): p26-31.

5814 *There's A Fence For Every Lot*, 100, 5. (May.1948): p32-35.

5815 *Automatic Weather In The Greenhouse...As You Like It*, 101, 1. (Jul.1948): p32-35.

5816 *How To Prune Trees*, 101, 3. (Sep.1948): p108-111.

5817 *Natives As Garden Shrubs*, 101, 4. (Oct.1948): p34-37.

5818 *Going To Buy A Tractor?*, 101, 6. (Dec.1948): p24-25.

5819 *It's Called Foundation Planting*, 102, 1. (Jan.1949): p26-31.

5820 *Knowledge Of Garden Costs Can Solve Some Of The Puzzles Of Garden Planning*, 102, 2. (Feb.1949): p26-29.

5821 *Take Full Advantage Of Your Garden Shows*, 102, 3. (Mar.1949): p24-25.

5822 *To Help You Choose The Right Plant For The Right Place*, 102, 4. (Apr.1949): p30-33.

5823 *New Tools For The Gardener*, 103, 2. (Aug.1949): p24-25.

5824 *How And What To Plant On Slopes*, 103, 2. (Aug.1949): p82-88.

5825 *Look At What The Pine Family Offers You*, 103, 6. (Dec.1949): p30-36.

5826 *The Best Trees For Your Street*, 104, 1. (Jan.1950): p32-37.

5827 *Trees Are Forms To Build With*, 104, 3. (Mar.1950): p42-44.

5828 *A Dramatic New Idea In Gardening*, 104, 4. (Apr.1950): p44-47.

5829 *Gophers Can Be Licked!*, 104, 5. (May.1950): p52-55.

5830 *Hedgerows and Fences for Country Places*, 104, 6. (Jun.1950): p112, 115-116.

5831 *Fish Ponds For Sport And Food*, 105, 2. (Aug.1950): p83-85.

5832 *Have You Tried Gardening In Boxes*, 105, 3. (Sep.1950): p108-111.

5833 *Nine Ground Covers*, 105, 5. (Nov.1950): p126-127.

5834 *We Nominate For All-West Garden Fame*, 106, 1. (Jan.1951): p20-27.

5835 *The Growing Importance Of The Garden In Western Living*, 106, 2. (Feb.1951): p26-29.

5836 *Multi-Purpose Garden Panels*, 106, 3. (Mar.1951): p40-43.

5837 *How Gardeners Fool themselves*, 106, 4. (Apr.1951): p38-41.

5838 *Shade Vs. Sun In California Gardens*, 106, 5. (May.1951): p40-43.

5839 *On A Sloping Lot...Ways To Gain Extra Garden And Living Space*, 106, 5. (May.1951): p70-71.

5840 *Gray Is A Color, Too*, 107, 2. (Aug.1951): p110-111.

5841 *When Gardener Turns To Plumbing Gadgeteer*, 107, 3. (Sep.1951): p38-39.

5842 *What Are Your Choices In Garden Paving?*, 108, 1. (Jan.1952): p30-33.

5843 *Which Trees For Spring Color?*, 108, 2. (Feb.1952): p30-35.

5844 *Country Living: What Can You Do About Erosion?*, 108, 2. (Feb.1952): p127-130.

5845 *Trees Of Our Southwest Deserts*, 108, 3. (Mar.1952): p20-23.

5846 *Which Deciduous Vines for Your California Climate?*, 108, 3. (Mar.1952): p142, 144-146.

5847 *Western Creation: The Garden Living Room*, 108, 6 . (Jun.1952): p44-47.

5848 *Which Fruit Tree Espalier?*, 108, 6. (Jun.1952): p140-142.

5849 *Water Cooling*, 109, 1. (Jul.1952): p42-45.

5850 *In The Winter Garden... Set a Stage for Portable Plants*, 109, 3. (Sep.1952): p46 [not 36]-49.

5851 *Succulents Solve Tough Problems– Beautifully*, 109, 3. (Sep.1952): p54-55.

5852 *Sixteen Decorative Ferns*, 109, 3. (Sep.1952): p152-155.

5853 *Which Trees For Autumn Color?*, 109, 4. (Oct.1952): p48-49.

5854 *In January...It's Time To Take A Fresh Look At Your Garden*, 110, 1. (Jan.1953): p25-29.

5855 *Trees Out Of Leaf Have A Beauty Of Their Own*, 110, 2. (Feb.1953): p44-45.

5856 *Your Own Redwood Forest*, 110, 2. (Feb.1953): p149-153.

5857 *Irrigation With a Sprinkler System*, 110, 3. (Mar.1953): p181-185.

5858 *Why Can't I Enjoy The Beauty Of My Garden At Night?*, 110, 6. (Jun.1953): p68-73.

5859 *Eighteen Ground Covers and Where to Use Them*, 110, 6. (Jun.1953): p80-81.

5860 *Lawns*, 111, 3. (Sep.1953): p50-53.

5861 *Pebble Blocks*, 111, 4. (Oct.1953): p54-57.

5862 *Installing A Sprinkler System*, 11, 4. (Oct.1953): p70-75.

5863 *A Fresh Look At Western Garden Trees*, 111, 5. (Nov.1953): p67-73.

5864 *In Planning Your Country Place, The First Requirement Is A Good Water Supply*, 111, 3. (Nov.1953): p86-93.

5865 *When You Plant A Tree*, 111, 5. (Nov.1953): p240-245.

5866 *Which Pine Will Fit Your Garden?*, 111, 6. (Dec.1953): p56-61.

5867 *The Right Flower In The Right Place*, 112, 1. (Jan.1954): p28-31.

5868 *How Westerners Use Vines*, 112, 3. (Mar.1954): p60-65.

5869 *Ferns Are Luxuriant The Year Round*, 112, 4. (Apr.1954): p68-69.

5870 *How The Japanese Combine Stone, Water, And Planting...*, 112, 5. (May.1954): p68-69.

5871 *The Outdoor Room*, 112, 6. (Jun.1954): p60-69.

5872 *Succulents*, 112, 6. (Jun.1954): p210-214, 219.

5873 *When You Garden With Raised Beds*, 113, 1. (Jul.1954): p44-45.

5874 *Ground Covers*, 113, 1. (Jul.1954): p46-47.

5875 *How To Furnish Your Patio With Portable Plants*, 113, 2. (Aug.1954): p46-49.

5876 *Small Trees For The Small Garden*, 113, 2. (Aug.1954): p140-144.

5877 *'Doing Over' Your Streetside Garden*, 113, 3. (Sep.1954): p48-49.

5878 *Where Your Garden Meets The Street*, 113, 5. (Nov.1954): p50-51.

5879 *How To Use Trees For Privacy, Sun Control, And Wind Protection*, 113, 5. (Nov.1954): p60-65.

5880 *How To Use The Ferns*, 113, 5. (Nov.1954): p192-196.

5881 *The Case For...And Against...The 'Living Fence' Hedgerows*, 113, 6. (Dec.1954): p150-152.

5882 *Hedges...What They Are...How To Use them*, 114, 1. (Jan.1955): p30-32.

5883 *Rose Pruning*, 114, 2. (Feb.1955): p56-57.

5884 *An Orchard In A Small Garden*, 114, 2. (Feb.1955): p148-152.

5885 *How To Choose A Magnolia For Your Garden*, 114, 3. (Mar.1955): p56-59.

5886 *Within The Patio Itself...A Planting Bed*, 114, 3. (Mar.1955): p221-222.

5887 *How To Keep Western Lawns Green The Whole Year Long...*, 114, 4. (Apr.1955): p216-219.

5888 *What About Citrus in the Small Gardens*, 114, 4. (Apr.1955): p82-85.

5889 *The Trees, The Garden, The Hillside...All Are Part Of This House*, 114, 5. (May.1955): p86-88.

5890 *Landscaping The New Subdivision House*, 114, 5. (May.1955): p63-82.

5891 *Palms For the Small Garden*, 114, 5. (May.1955): p232-237.

5892 *How To Make The Most Of Your Portable Sprinkler*, 114, 6. (Jun.1955): p70-73.

6. Landscaping and Outdoor Building

5893 *Awful Truth: The Grass Must Be Cut*, 115, 1. (Jul.1955): p126-129.

5894 *Hillside Landscaping*, 115, 2. (Aug.1955): p50-55.

5895 *After Your Garden Is Well-Established, Add The Glory Of Lilies...*, 115, 2. (Aug.1955): p136-138.

5896 *Yesterday's Houses Often Look Better...*, 115, 3. (Sep.1955): p58-63.

5897 *Color Through The Seasons*, 115, 4. (Oct.1955): p58-62.

5898 *Four Different Approaches to the Small Garden*, 115, 4. (Oct.1955): p72-76, 79.

5899 *A Real Garden...For A Doll House*, 115, 6. (Dec.1955): p130-131.

5900 *If Your Live in a New Hillside Subdivision... Here Are 8 Ways To Think Through Your Landscaping Problems*, 116, 1. (Jan.1956): p34-37.

5901 *These Garden Steps invite you to Pause... Enjoy the Plants Nearby*, 116, 2. (Feb.1956): p64-65.

5902 *Landscaping With Grape Vines: now is the Time to Plan... And to Plant*, 116, 2. (Feb.1956): p48-51.

5903 *When You Plant Against A Wall*, 116, 2. (Feb.1956): p154-156, 158, 160.

5904 *How To Use Flowers As Color Accents*, 116, 4. (Apr.1956): p66-71.

5905 *Here Are Picture Panels And Colorful Fence Inserts*, 116, 5. (May.1956): p64-67.

5906 *The Efficient Garden Builder*, 116, 6. (Jun.1956): p113-116.

5907 *Green Vines Overhead, A Leafy Green Roof For Your Terrace*, 116, 6. (Jun.1956): p208-209, 212, 214, 217, 218, 220, 222, 223.

5908 *How To Decorate Your Garden With The Magic Of Light*, 117, 1. (Jul.1956): p60-69.

5909 *How To Bring The Sight And Sound Of Water Into Your Garden*, 117, 2. (Aug.1956): p54-61.

5910 *How To Make A Slope Work For You*, 117, 3. (Sep.1956): p79, 81, 83.

5911 *Sword Leafed Plants...Even Smog Doesn't Bother them*, 117, 3. (Sep.1956): p178-181.

5912 *Walk-In Gardens In The Heart Of San Francisco*, 117, 4. (Oct.1956): p224-225.

5913 *The Fun Of Color Gardening*, 118, 1. (Jan.1957): p25-33.

5914 *New Idea Catching on In The West...Gardening With Gravel*, 118, 2. (Feb.1957): p62-66, 69.

5915 *What "Landscaping" Has Meant To One Western Family*, 118, 6. (Jun.1957): p77-81.

5916 *You Can Cast This Circular Fountain Yourself*, 119, 1. (Jul.1957): p44-45.

5917 *Here's One Successful Answer To The "Look-Alike" Problem In Subdivisions*, 119, 3. (Sep.1957): p64-66.

5918 *The New Look In Old Favorites*, 119, 3. (Sep.1957): p156-159.

5919 *From Acorn To Mighty Oak*, 119, 4. (Oct.1957): p68-70, 72.

5920 *Japan's Family Gardens*, 120, 3. (Mar.1958): p80-95.

5921 *Utah's New Kind Of Garden...Using Native Stone And Plants*, 120, 5. (May.1958): p94-96.

5922 *Clay Color In The Garden*, 121, 2. (Aug.1958): p54-55.

5923 *Even If Only A Trickle...Water Is August's Best Garden Cooler*, 121, 2. (Aug.1958): p58-59.

5924 *They Started With A Five-Year Plan...And Did The Garden Installation On Their Own*, 121, 4. (Oct.1958): p60-63.

5925 *How To Fit Roses Into Your Landscape Scheme*, 122, 1. (Jan.1959): p40-42.

5926 *At The Desert's Edge...A Special Lesson In Western Outdoor Living*, 122, 2. (Feb.1959): p68-71.

5927 *Success Story From Sacramento*, 122, 3. (Mar.1959): p88-96, 98.

5928 *How Western And Japanese Landscape Designers See Eye To Eye*, 122, 5. (May.1959): p106-111.

5929 *What Will Make An Artist Out Of An Ordinary Gardener? A Japanese Maple...*, 122, 5. (May.1959): p112-113.

5930 *How To Make A Chemical Attack On Weeds*, 122, 6. (Jun.1959): p168, 170, 172, 174.

5931 *Lawn Misery: What To Do About Fungus...Before It Strikes Or Afterwards*, 123, 1. (Jul.1959): p136-138.

5932 *Convertible Garden...Container Plants On Gravel*, 123, 2. (Aug.1959): p46-48.

5933 *Crabgrass Showdown*, 123, 2. (Aug.1959): p110-116.

5934 *Three Unusual Landscape Plans For Subdivision-Size Lots*, 123, 3. (Sep.1959): p56-59.

5935 *The Raised Bed Idea*, 124, 4. (Apr.1960): p118-123.

5936 *An Emphatic Color Scheme...With Everything In Great Scale*, 124, 5. (May.1960): p128-131.

5937 *Now's The Time To Go Idea Collecting*, 124, 6. (Jun.1960): p92-97.

5938 *Which Trees For Autumn Color*, 125, 5. (Nov.1960): p102-106.

5939 *Three Unusual Small Gardens*, 126, 3. (Mar.1961): p87-93.

5940 *Landscaping With Succulents*, 126, 6. (Jun.1961): p88-91.

5941 *Made In A Single Day*, 127, 2. (Aug.1961): p66-67.

5942 *Lanai Luxury... On A Subdivision Lot*, 127, 4. (Oct.1961): p90-93.

5943 *The Garden In A Small Space*, 128, 3. (Mar.1962): p98-101.

5944 *Choosing A Vine: Here are Questions Your Should Ask*, 128, 4. (Apr.1962): p202-206.

5945 *Gardens In The Japanese Manner*, 128, 5. (May.1962): p118-123.

5946 *Plants That Can Take It*, 128, 5. (May.1962): p240-242, 244, 248.

5947 *Oaks From Your Own Acorns*, 129, 3. (Sep.1962): p174.

5948 *A Spacious New Garden Surrounds The Old House*, 129, 5. (Nov.1962): p114-118, 120.

5949 *Getting Rid Of A Stump: Here are Ideas From Sunset Readers*, 130, 1. (Jan.1963): p132-133.

5950 *Have Some Fun With Garden Rock*, 130, 2. (Feb.1963): p184, 186, 187.

5951 *A Different Way To Train Your Pine*, 130, 3. (Mar.1963): p252.

5952 *A Hobby Gardener Enjoys Himself In Topanga Canyon*, 130, 4. (Apr.1963): p278-279.

5953 *A Garden Of Ideas In Outdoor Living*, 130, 5. (May.1963): p100-105.

5954 *Where Auto Meets Garden*, 130, 6. (Jun.1963): p94-99.

5955 *Why Not Chess In The Garden*, 131, 1. (Jul.1963): p74-76.

5956 *Is A Perfect Lawn Possible?*, 131, 3. (Sep.1963): p72-77.

5957 *Leafy Arbors*, 132, 4. (Apr.1964): p98-103.

5958 *The Giant Grasses*, 132, 5. (May.1964): p128-134, 136.

5959 *Landscaping With Cactus*, 132, 6. (Jun.1964): p228-230, 232.

5960 *A Cool Green Carpet Under The Trees*, 133, 1. (Jul.1964): p150-151.

5961 *Plant A Forest In Your Garden*, 133, 1. (Jul.1964): p152-153.

5962 *A Garden Lives Its Second Life*, 133, 3. (Sep.1964): p62-63.

5963 *Ferns Set The Rich Tone You See Here*, 134, 3. (Mar.1965): p254-255.

5964 *Green Walls: You Have Many Splendid Choices*, 134, 5. (May.1965): p248, 250, 252.

5965 *This Garden Is Just Four Months Old*, 134, 5. (May.1965): p270-271.

5966 *New Way To Move Big Young Trees*, 135, 2. (Aug.1965): p142-143.

5967 *This Garden Without A Lawn Offers Variety Instead*, 135, 2. (Aug.1965): p64, 65, 67.

5968 *Among Deciduous Trees, The Birches Are The West's Most Popular*, 135, 4. (Oct.1965): p98-101.

6. Landscaping and Outdoor Building

6. Landscaping and Outdoor Building

6041 *Oasis Garden In San Jose*, 162, 1. (Jan.1979): p56-57.

6042 *Landscaping With Ferns in L. A. Here Are 13 Good Choices: Ground Covers, Trees, "Fountains"*, 162, 3. (Mar.1979): p212-214.

6043 *Did They Build In A Dry Creek Bed? No. It Just Looks That Way*, 163, 1. (Jul.1979): p170-171.

6044 *August Is A Big Month For Dichondra*, 163, 2. (Aug.1979): p160-161.

6045 *How To Make A Stone "Sink" In Your Garden*, 163, 4. (Oct.1979): p100-101.

6046 *The Acorn Game. You Grow Your Own Oaks*, 163, 4. (Oct.1979): p224-226.

6047 *Grape-Leafy Gazebo Roof is Also Grape Abundant*, 164, 1. (Jan.1980): p56-57.

6048 *Back-Yard Parcourse In Berkeley*, 164, 4. (Apr.1980): p106-107.

6049 *New Pool And Mounding Garden... New Pathways, New Gates, a New Deck*, 164, 6. (Jun.1980): p194-195.

6050 *Theater In The Garden; Audience On The Steps*, 165, 2. (Aug.1980): p66-67.

6051 *Trees Gentle The Los Altos Street Scene And Parking Scene*, 165, 3. (Sep.1980): p166-167.

6052 *Artistry In Paving–18 Examples*, 165, 4. (Oct.1980): p86-91.

6053 *Planting Out The Power Pole*, 165, 4. (Oct.1980): p242-243.

6054 *Long, Slim Lot Seems Spacious. It's Open On Changing Levels*, 166, 3. (Mar.1981): p194-195.

6055 *Drip–It's Time Has Come*, 166, 5. (May.1981): p117-124.

6056 *All-Drip Garden*, 166, 6. (Jun.1981): p90-91.

6057 *Getting-Away Places*, 166, 6. (Jun.1981): p106-110.

6058 *Five Foggers Turn Small Denver Garden Into A Cool Party Place*, 167, 3. (Sep.1981): p76-77.

6059 *Berm It–For Noise Control, Privacy, Outdoor Living Space*, 167, 5. (Nov.1981): p262-263.

6060 *Which Spreader? Wheel It Or Crank It? Big Lawn Or Not?*, 168, 2. (Feb.1982): p204-205.

6061 *Dining Deck, Shade Arbor, Fish Pond... Garden Rooms Fit Together Like Puzzle Pieces*, 168, 3. (Mar.1982): p234-235.

6062 *For Shade And Good Looks, Adding On A Vine Arbor*, 168, 5. (May.1982): p266-268.

6063 *For Watering Lots Of Pots, Drip Could Be The Answer*, 168, 6. (Jun.1982): p94-97.

6064 *Garden Flip-Flop Gives Them a More Formal Entry, Privacy, Shade, Work Space*, 169, 1. (Jul.1982): p112-113.

6065 *Filoli–Groomed Gardens, Stately Home*, 169, 2. (Aug.1982): p56-57.

6066 *Demolish Your Own Concrete Or Asphalt Paving?*, 169, 3. (Sep.1982): p196-198.

6067 *Getting Tough With An Old Stump*, 169, 5. (Nov.1982): p246-247.

6068 *Gardening in Tight Quarters... Lessons from San Francisco*, 169, 5. (Nov.1982): p92-99.

6069 *He Couldn't Touch It With A Ten-Foot Pole, So He Rented A Scaffold*, 170, 1. (Jan.1983): p56-57.

6070 *Landscape Lessons from Australia*, 170, 2. (Feb.1983): p90-95.

6071 *The Red and the White: These are the Deciduous Oaks*, 170, 2. (Feb.1983): p196-197.

6072 *Over the Bridge, Through the Forest*, 171, 2. (Aug.1983): p148-149.

6073 *Do You Really Know How To Plant A Tree?*, 171, 4. (Oct.1983): p264-265.

6074 *How To Prevent Storm Damage To Trees*, 171, 5. (Nov.1983): p130-133.

6075 *Candle-Lighting The Garden*, 173, 2. (Aug.1984): p78-79.

6076 *Just Old-Fashioned Hose-End Sprinklers*, 175, 2. (Aug.1985): p76-78.

6077 *When Old Faithful Appears In Your Lawn*, 176, 6. (Jun.1986): p240-243.

6078 *How Much Water Does Your Lawn Really Need?*, 178, 6. (Jun.1987): p213-219.

6079 *Changing From Sprinklers To Drip*, 179, 2. (Aug.1987): p148-149.

6080 *The Perfect Lawn Grass?*, 179, 3. (Sep.1987): p74-77.

6081 *Landscaping For A Water-Sensible Future*, 180, 05. (May.1988): p144-147.

6082 *Drip Irrigation: Choosing And Installing A System*, 181, 1. (Jul.1988): p68-76.

6083 *Where's The Drip?*, 183, 2. (Aug.1989): p58-59.

6084 *What About The New Liquid Lawn Fertilizers?*, 193, 5. (Nov.1989): p204-205.

6085 *Landscaping With Native Plants*, 184, 3. (Mar.1990): p90-93.

6086 NONE , *Time to Ask Serious Questions About Lawns And Water*, 184, 6. (Jun.1990): p175-180.

6087 *If You Have Room For Only One Tree; Japanese Maples*, 185, 5. (Nov.1990): p100-103.

6088 *Taking The Mystery Out Of Drip Irrigation*, 187, 1. (Jul.1991): p94-98.

6089 *Still More Ways To Save Water...And Your Plants*, 197, 2. (Aug.1991): p90-91.

6090 *Colorful And Unthirsty Garden...Thanks To Concrete*, 187, 3. (Sep.1991): p66-69.

6091 Ocone, Lynn, *Straight Talk About Drip*, 189, 1. (Jul.1992): p52-55.

6092 Ocone, Lynn, *A House Where Saguaros And Sofa Meet*, 190, 4. (Apr.1993): p128-131.

6093 Whiteley, Peter O., *The Art Of Rock Walls*, 193, 3. (Sep.1994): p88-90 .

6094 *Gettin To Know The Other Magnolias*, 193, 08. (Feb.1995): p62-67.

6095 *In This Country Garden The Design Starts With A Rolling Meadow*, 114, 3. (Mar.1995): p76-78.

6096 *Landscaping For Wildfire Safety*, 194, 04. (Oct.1995): p66-68.

6097 *Ground Covers For The '90s*, 194, 05. (Nov.1995): p52-55.

6098 Whiteley, Peter O., *Gravel Leads The Way*, 196, 5. (May.1996): p114, 115, 118, 119, 122, 123.

6099 *A Backyard Fantasy*, 198, 6. (Jun.1997): p90-92.

6100 McCausland, Jim and Walheim, Lance, *Smart Trees for Fall Planting*, 199, 4. (Oct.1997): p64-67, 70, 72.

7. The Outdoors

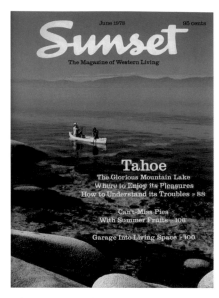

July 1978 cover (photo: Norman A. Plate)

The Outdoors

Sunset *has long woven a thread of concern with the natural environment into its pages. Many articles describe aspects of nature and wildlife in the Western States and the interaction of humans with the environment. At certain times, concern with Environmental Issues & Interests has been strongly expressed, as with long-term emphasis on and promotion of National Parks and the perils of development in sensitive areas (e.g., "A Close and Concerned Look at Tahoe" of June 1978).*

To a large extent, this concern was expressed more subtly in the general subject of Outdoor Recreation & Leisure Activities, as well as in travel. Certainly, much of Sunset's *recreation and travel coverage dealt with enjoying the West's (relatively) unspoiled natural environment. We have grouped articles that focus particularly on that environment, but it is important to note that there is a great deal of overlap with other sections. The distinction between recreation, defined as activities, and travel, defined as description of places or journeys, becomes almost moot: is, say, "Tuolumne Rafting, Camping, Exploring" (April 1984) about rafting and camping (i.e., recreation) or about a certain river and its environs (i.e., a travel destination), including a well-known national park?* Sunset *has long supported not only extant national parks, but their creation as well.*

7. The Outdoors

6151 Stevens-Walter, Carrie, *Arbor Day In Santa Clara Valley*, 11, 2. (Jun.1903): p185-189.

6152 Fitch, George Hamlin, *Some Glimpses Of Lake Tahoe*, 11, 3. (Jul.1903): p214-218.

6153 Grinnel, Elizabeth, *Joys And Sorrows In A Banana Leaf: Being The Story Of An Oriole's Nest In June*, 11, 3. (Jul.1903): p223-226.

6154 Smith, Bertha H., *Face Rocks Of Nature*, 11, 3. (Jul.1903): p234-239.

6155 Powell, Sherman, *The Black Tail Deer Of The Mackenzie River Country, Oregon*, 11, 3. (Jul.1903): p244-248.

6156 LeConte, Helen Gompertz, *The Sierra Club In The Kings River Canyon*, 11, 3. (Jul.1903): p250-262.

6157 Grinnel, Elizabeth, *The Linnet, California's One Criminal*, 11, 4. (Aug.1903): p330-333.

6158 MacDonald, Donald, *Vancouver's Pinnacles*, 11, 4. (Aug.1903): p345-349.

6159 Allen, Charles H., *The World Beneath The Wave*, 11, 4. (Aug.1903): p382-383.

6160 Grinnel, Elizabeth, *Home For Thanksgiving*, 12, 1. (Nov.1903): p18-20.

6161 Gill, John, *From Tillamook To Clatsop*, 12, 1. (Nov.1903): p38-41.

6162 Peixotto, Edgar D., *Protecting California Fish And Game*, 12, 1. (Nov.1903): p67-71.

6163 Miller, Dorothy, *The Artist In Kern River Canyon*, 12, 2. (Dec.1903): p129-134.

6164 Miller, Lischen M., *The Valley Of Mystery*, 12, 2. (Dec.1903): p154-160.

6165 Grinnel, Elizabeth, *Tourist Robins And Waxwings*, 12, 3. (Jan.1904): p224-226.

6166 Boyd, Edward McFarland, *Hawaii's Volcano-Made Scenery*, 12, 3. (Jan.1904): p247-257.

6167 Honn, D. N., *All About Shasta*, 13, 1. (May.1904): p80-87.

6168 Emerson, Otto, *The Singer Of The Fields*, 13, 2. (Jun.1904): p129-130.

6169 *Billions of Blossoms: The Flower Festival Among The Prune Trees Of California's Santa Clara Valley*, 13, 2. (Jun.1904): p171-175.

6170 Treat, Archibald, *Up Mount Tallac*, 13, 3. (Jul.1904): p208-212.

6171 Grinnel, Elizabeth, *Autumn Days Among The Birds*, 13, 5. (Sep.1904): p436-438.

6172 Eastwood, Alice, *California Alpine Flowers*, 13, 5. (Sep.1904): p439-440.

6173 Grinnel, Elizabeth, *The Turtle Dove*, 14, 1. (Nov.1904): p43-45.

6174 Purdy, Carl, *Floral Butterflies*, 14, 1. (Nov.1904): p59-61.

6175 Stevens-Walter, Carrie, *In The Mt. Hamilton Hills*, 14, 1. (Nov.1904): p62-64.

6176 Harrison, William Greer, *Outdoor Life In California*, 14, 2. (Dec.1904): p151-154.

6177 Jepson, W. L., *Where Ducks Dine*, 14, 4. (Feb.1905): p409-411.

6178 McAdie, Alexander G., *Weighing The World And The Air*, 14, 5. (Mar.1905): p528-531.

6179 Hussey, Ethel Fountain, *Chasing The Hidden Sun: How Lick Observatory Scientists Will See The Total Solar Eclipse Next August - The William H. Crocker Expeditions To Spain, Egypt, And Labrador*, 14, 6. (Apr.1905): p555-564.

6180 Bade, William Frederic, *Forests Of The Tuolumne*, 14, 6. (Apr.1905): p597-603.

6181 Sterling, E. A., *The American Forest Congress*, 14, 6. (Apr.1905): p604-606.

6182 Tinsley, John F., *Tree Telegraphy*, 14, 6. (Apr.1905): p613-617.

6183 Grinnell, Elizabeth, *The Valley Quail*, 15, 1. (May.1905): p86-88.

6184 Marshall, Emma Seckle, *Mining In Oregon*, 15, 3. (Jul.1905): p273-275.

6185 Carpenter, Geo E., *Bird Life On The Great Salt Lake*, 15, 5. (Sep.1905): p455-457.

6186 Wickson, Edward J., *An Irrigation Pilgrimage*, 15, 6. (Oct.1905): p530-537.

6187 Grant, Roland Dwight, *Columbia's Crags & Castles*, 15, 6. (Oct.1905): p539-545.

6188 Schley, Edna Rowell, *Where Nature Stores Her Jewels*, 15, 6. (Oct.1905): p546-555.

6189 Gross, William B., *Kunzite The Precious*, 15, 6. (Oct.1905): p556-559.

6190 Coe, Marie, *A New Polar Explorer*, 15, 6. (Oct.1905): p561-566.

6191 McAdie, Alexander G., *The Los Angeles Rain-Making*, 15, 6. (Oct.1905): p575-577.

6192 Perkins, E. T., *Redeeming the West*, 16, 1. (Nov.1905): p2-25.

6193 Burgess, Gelett, *The Rights Of Animals*, 16, 1. (Nov.1905): p65-66.

6194 Ellison, O. C., *In The Sea Of Pearls*, 16, 2. (Dec.1905): p165-175.

6195 McAdie, Alexander G., *The Scientific Side Of It*, 17, 2-3. (1906): p42-44.

6196 Wells, A. J., *Helping The Sierra Sequoias*, 16, 3. (Jan.1906): p280-283.

6197 Yale, Charles G., *California's Treasure Bed*, 16, 5. (Mar.1906): p418-430.

6198 Stevens-Walter, Carrie, *Rivers Of Buried Gold*, 16, 5. (Mar.1906): p431-434.

6199 LeConte, Joseph N., *In The Highest Sierra*, 17, 5. (Sep.1906): p215-226.

6200 Gilbert F. Bailey, *Sierra Sky-Line Guardians*, 17, 5. (Sep.1906): p227-229.

6201 Swingle, G. K., *Chaining The Sacramento*, 17, 6. (Oct.1906): p353-355.

6202 White, G. A., *Oregon's Outlook*, 18, 1. (Nov.1906): p12-17.

6203 Crowell, Bertha C., *White Sands Of New Mexico*, 18, 1. (Nov.1906): p30-32.

6204 Grinnel, Elizabeth, *A Christmas Greeting*, 18, 2. (Dec.1906): p102-103.

6205 Wells, A. J., *Capturing The Colorado*, 18, 5. (Mar.1907): p391-404.

6206 Watson, C. B., *In The Siskiyous*, 18, 5. (Apr.1907): p566-571.

6207 Sterling, E. A., *The Use Of Forest Reserves*, 19, 1. (May.1907): p10-17.

6208 Cowgill, W. C., *Around Eagle Chief: The Wonderland Scenic And Sportsman Country Of Three Big Counties Of Oregon*, 19, 1. (May.1907): p37-42.

6209 Sullivan, Knute, *Some Water Facts*, 19, 1. (May.1907): p74-76.

6210 Louderback, George Davis, *Where Mammoths Roved: Recent Remarkable Discoveries In Carson, Nevada, State Prison - Footprints That Make Geologists Wonder - Theory Of Their Human Origin*, 19, 3. (Jul.1907): p204-216.

6211 Chandler, Katherine, *Sierra Wild Flowers*, 19, 4. (Aug.1907): p333-335.

6212 Finley, William L., *Feathered Foragers*, 19, 4. (Aug.1907): p382-387.

6213 Sheldon, Edmund P., *Millions In Trees: The Forest Wealth Of The Pacific Northwest*, 19, 4. (Aug.1907): p388-392.

6214 Glover, Alfred K., *Good-Bye, Abalone!*, 19, 6. (Oct.1907): p577-578.

6215 Finley, William L., *Birds About An Oregon Pond*, 20, 2. (Dec.1907): p129-135.

6216 O'Hara, P. J., *Harnessing Streams*, 20, 5. (Mar.1908): p452-454.

6217 Grinnel, Elizabeth, *Garden Tragedies*, 20, 5. (Mar.1908): p455-458.

6218 Jordan, David Starr, *Save The Golden Trout*, 21, 2. (Jun.1908): p148-150.

6219 Smith, S. H., *In Calaveras Long Ago*, 21, 3. (Jul.1908): p235-237.

6220 Barnum, Charles Pete, *How I Trap Wild Horses*, 21, 4. (Aug.1908): p285-305.

6221 Payne, H. T., *Game Birds Of The Pacific, First Paper*, 21, 4. (Aug.1908): p326-335.

6222 *Turning The Merced River To Gold*, 21, 4. (Aug.1908): .

7. The Outdoors

6223 Payne, H. T., *Game Birds Of The Pacific, Second Paper*, 21, 5. (Sep.1908): p442-451.

6224 Merriam, John C., *Death Trap Of The Ages: A Pathetic Page From The Prehistoric Past*, 21, 6. (Oct.1908): p465-475.

6225 Matteson, Sumner W., *Saving The Buffalo*, 21, 6. (Oct.1908): p498-503.

6226 Payne, H. T., *Game Birds Of The Pacific, Third Paper*, 21, 6. (Oct.1908): p507-514.

6227 Payne, H. T., *Game Birds Of The Pacific, Fourth Paper*, 21, 7. (Nov.1908): p643-651.

6228 Payne, H. T., *Game Birds Of The Pacific, Fifth Paper*, 21, 8. (Dec.1908): p767-774.

6229 McAdie, Alexander G., *Frost, Snow And Dew*, 22, 1. (Jan.1909): p40-46.

6230 Payne, H. T., *Game Birds Of The Pacific, Sixth Paper*, 22, 1. (Jan.1909): p65-73.

6231 McAdie, Alexander G., *In Galileo's Footsteps*, 22, 2. (Feb.1909): p133-143.

6232 Cornell, F. D., *Hickory's Younger Brother: Widespread Movement For Eucalyptus Forests While You Wait That Promises To Renew The Nation's Fast Disappearing Supply Of Hardwood Timber*, 22, 3. (Mar.1909): p274-282.

6233 Farewell, George E., *Heroism On The Alsek*, 22, 5. (May.1909): p531-536.

6234 Young, John P., *The Hetch-Hetchy Problem*, 22, 6. (Jun.1909): p599-606.

6235 *Open-Air Sleeping*, 23, 2. (Aug.1909): p200-204.

6236 Miller, Joaquin, *Oregon's Marble Halls*, 23, 3. (Sep.1909): p227-235.

6237 Cornell, F. D., *Utility Of The Eucalyptus*, 23, 3. (Sep.1909): p254-258.

6238 Aust, George F., *Sport Vs. Slaughter*, 23, 5. (Nov.1909): p523-524.

6239 Heinly, Burt A., *Water For Millions: Building The Great Aqueduct That Is To Supply Los Angeles*, 23, 6. (Dec.1909): p631-638.

6240 Walker, T. B., *Forests For The Future*, 24, 1. (Jan.1910): p59-65.

6241 Campbell, W. W., *The Coming Of Halley's Comet*, 24, 4. (Apr.1910): p365-371.

6242 See, T. J. J., *Is Venus Inhabited?*, 24, 4. (Apr.1910): p399-404.

6243 Schmidt, Karl, *Wayside Bloom In The Siskiyou*, 24, 6. (Jun.1910): p647-649.

6244 Hoxiem, George L., *How Fire Helps Forestry*, 25, 2. (Aug.1910): p145-151.

6245 Jones, Clayton M., *Greater Than Gold: 'White Coal' Mines Of The Sierra And Their Treasure Beds Of Energy - The Story Of Big Bend*, 25, 4. (Oct.1910): p406-414.

6246 McAdie, Alexander G., *Frost, Snow And Dew*, 25, 4. (Oct.1910): p463-465.

6247 French, Harold, *Forecasting Storms: The Weather Bureau's Businesslike Helpfulness To Western Fruit-growers And Seafarers*, 25, 5. (Nov.1910): p529-532.

6248 Wilson, Bourdon, *Sierra The Golden*, 25, 6. (Dec.1910): p716-717.

6249 Stovall, Dennis H., *Power Of A Million Horses*, 26, 3. (Mar.1911): p325-328.

6250 Griswold, F. H., *The Orland Project*, 27, 1. (Jul.1911): p110-111.

6251 Thacher, W. F. G., *The Sutherlin Valley*, 27, 2. (Aug.1911): p219-220.

6252 Olmstead, F. E., *How Forestry Uses Fire*, 27, 3. (Sep.1911): p276-281.

6253 Park, W. L., *Federal Reclamation Of Wet Lands*, 27, 3. (Sep.1911): p328-335.

6254 Willard, Walter, *Saving The World's Most Valuable Water*, 28, 3. (Mar.1912): p373-375.

6255 Levick, M. B., *Tucson, Old And New*, 28, 3. (Mar.1912): p384-385.

6256 Parker, Walter, *The Doom Of The Frogs*, 30, 2. (Feb.1913): p204-206.

6257 Saunders, Charles Francis, *Speaking Of The Weather*, 30, 3. (Mar.1913): p266-270.

6258 Teck, Frank Carleton, *How The Rich Naas Valley In British Columbia Was At Last Pried Open*, 30, 5. (May.1913): p608-614.

6259 Hoak, E. K., *Yuma: Where Guesswork Has Been Eliminated*, 30, 5. (May.1913): p618.

6260 Jackson, H. C., *Play Ball At Midnight*, 30, 6. (Jun.1913): p812-815.

6261 Dawson, William Leon, *The Christmas Bird Census At Santa Barbara*, 31, 6. (Dec.1913): p1185-1190.

6262 Woehlke, Walter V., *Idaho And The Green Snake*, 32, 4. (Apr.1914): p763-773.

6263 Lane, Franklin K., *Uncle Sam, Contractor And Builder Of Western Homes*, 32, 5. (May.1914): p1016-1022.

6264 Woehlke, Walter V., *The Great Valley*, 34, 2. (Feb.1915): p285-296.

6265 Dean, William Harper, *Our National Parks–A Seven Reel Feature*, 36, 6. (Jun.1916): p19-23, 69-70.

6266 Gross, Carl W., *The Star-Spangled Sockeye*, 28, 3. (Mar.1917): p36, 94.

6267 Cradlebaugh, R. B., *Well, Of All Things!*, 41, 6. (Dec.1918): p24-25, 66.

6268 Curtin, Walter R., *The Stream Gauger*, 43, 5. (Nov.1919): p38, 72.

6269 White, Stewart Edward, *Woodsmen, Spare Those Trees!*, 44, 3. (Mar.1920): p23-26, 108-116.

6270 Becker, F. E., *Famine In The Wild*, 44, 3. (Mar.1920): p31-32, 118-122.

6271 Graves, Henry S., *The Torch In The Timber*, 44, 4. (Apr.1920): p37-40, 80-90.

6272 De Vis-Norton, L. W., *Mauna Loa On A Spree*, 44, 5. (May.1920): p48-49.

6273 White, Stewart Edward, *Getting At The Truth*, 44, 5. (May.1920): p62, 80-82.

6274 Redington, Paul G., *What Is The Truth?*, 44, 6. (Jun.1920): p56-58.

6275 *Slaughtering the Forest Patriarchs*, 45, 2. (Aug.1920): p20.

6276 *You Can Help Preserve the Sequoia Groves*, 45, 2. (Aug.1920): p21.

6277 Condon, Frank, *Fifty! Fifty!*, 45, 3. (Sep.1920): p38-39, 74-78.

6278 DeWitt, Harry, *Fire Eagles*, 45, 3. (Sep.1920): p104-105.

6279 Stellmann, Louis J., *The Official Upsetter*, 45, 4. (Oct.1920): p50-54.

6280 *Help Preserve God's Greatest Free Cathedral (editorial)*, 46, 6. (Jun.1921): p12, 14.

6281 Waugh, Lena Sanford, *Snowed In*, 47, 3. (Sep.1921): p42-43.

6282 Mills, Enos A., *Being Nice To Skunks*, 48, 1. (Jan.1922): p49-50.

6283 Saunders, Charles Francis, *The Paradox Of The Desert*, 48, 5. (May.1922): p17-19.

6284 McKee, Thomas Heron, *Brighty, Free Citizen*, 49, 2. (Aug.1922): p42, 70-71.

6285 Mills, Enos A., *Wild Animal Homesteads*, 50, 1. (Jan.1923): p45-47, 58.

6286 Renfro, Alfred, *Far West Firs Are Reforesting France*, 50, 5. (May.1923): p30.

6287 Merrick, L. F., *The Power of the Far West*, 50, 6. (Jun.1923): p66, 120.

6288 Porter, Langley, *Do You Sleep Enough?*, 51, 1. (Jul.1923): p32-33.

6289 Woehlke, Walter V., *Warren Harding's Bequest*, 51, 4. (Oct.1923): p9-11, 104-105.

6290 O'Byrne, Will, *Overcrowding The Ranges*, 51, 4. (Oct.1923): p27-28, 58-60.

6291 Collier, Lucy Wood, *Water And Your Health*, 51, 4. (Oct.1923): p29, 56.

6292 Scheffer, Theodore H., *Saving The Beaver*, 51, 6. (Dec.1923): p51.

6293 Fassett, Clara, *Housekeeping on the Farallones*, 51, 6. (Dec.1923): p66-67.

6294 Mills, Enos A., *Little Blue*, 52, 1. (Jan.1924): p47-48, 60.

7. The Outdoors

6295 Jordan, David Starr, *Evolution and Theology*, 52, 3. (Mar.1924): p15.

6296 Willard, Victor, *Lifting The Stump Mortgage*, 52, 4. (Apr.1924): p52, 107-109.

6297 Leopold, Aldo, *Pioneers And Gullies*, 52, 5. (May.1924): p15-16, 91-95.

6298 Finley, William L. and Finley, Irene, *The Crime Of The Lower Klamath*, 53, 4. (Oct.1924): p36-40, 56-58.

6299 Metcalf, Vernon, *The Antelope's Comeback*, 53, 6. (Dec.1924): p14-16.

6300 Stevens, Donald Kenneth, *The Last Stand Of The Lobos*, 54, 1. (Jan.1925): p14-16, 52.

6301 Stevens, Donald Kenneth, *The Last Stand Of The Lobos*, 54, 2. (Feb.1925): p23-25, 54.

6302 Leopold, Aldo, *Conserving The Covered Wagon*, 54, 3. (Mar.1925): p21, 56.

6303 Merrick, L. F., *Who Is The Worst Game Hog?*, 55, 4. (Oct.1925): p12-13, 80-82.

6304 *Southern California Needs Colorado River Water*, 56, 3. (Mar.1926): p50, 98.

6305 Woehlke, Walter V., *Gasoline And Trout*, 56, 4. (Apr.1926): p19-21, 86.

6306 Watkins, A., *Beefsteak Or Soup-meat?*, 56, 4. (Apr.1926): p25, 73.

6307 Murphy, Ralph, *Arizona's Side Of The Question*, 56, 4. (Apr.1926): p34.

6308 Goldsmith, Louis C., *The Air Patrol*, 59, 3. (Sep.1927): p40-41, 60-62.

6309 Belden, Charles J., *Prong-Horn Antelope*, 59, 4. (Oct.1927): p32-33, 56-58.

6310 Skinner, C. Kay, *Five Thousand Fish In A Bucket*, 59, 5. (Nov.1927): p21, 77-78.

6311 Notson, Robert C., *Horses! Horses!*, 59, 5. (Nov.1927): p29, 79-81.

6312 Greeley, W. B., *What Shall We Do With Our Mountains?*, 59, 6. (Dec.1927): p14-15, 81-85.

6313 Boyer, Warren E., *Shopping In Sky Draperies*, 60, 2. (Feb.1928): p64-65.

6314 Skinner, C. Kay, *The City Which Owns A Glacier*, 60, 3. (Mar.1928): p31, 77.

6315 Boyer, Warren E., *The Thunder Bird*, 60, 6. (Jun.1928): p19.

6316 Munson, Edward L., *What Price California Climate?*, 60, 6. (Jun.1928): p28-32.

6317 Carhart, Arthur Hawthorne and Young, Stanley P., *Senor Yip-Yap*, 61, 6. (Dec.1928): p28-30.

6318 Taylor, Frank J., *The Flowers Are Winning*, 62, 2. (Feb.1929): p26-27.

6319 Purdy, Carl, *What I Learned About Wild Plants*, 63, 4. (Oct.1929): p22-24.

6320 Dufresne, Frank, *A Wild Westerner Rises To Real Fame*, 64, 2. (Feb.1930): p16-17.

6321 Hasty, John Eugene, *A Burning Question*, 64, 2. (Feb.1930): p29-31.

6322 Overholt, Alma, *The Catalina Aviaries*, 64, 3. (Mar.1930): p18-20.

6323 Finney, Marian MacLean, *Let's Save Our Oak Trees*, 64, 5. (May.1930): p23-24.

6324 O'Hara, Gerald J., *Health Rays*, 65, 1. (Jul.1930): p11-14.

6325 Prather, Richard L., *The Birds In My Garden*, 65, 2. (Aug.1930): p21-23.

6326 Hasty, John Eugene, *The Really Big Game Of The Year*, 66, 4. (Apr.1931): p14-15.

6327 Fischer, Caroline, *Some Of The Common Shells On Our Western Beaches*, 67, 1. (Jul.1931): p13-15.

6328 Christal, M., *Attractive Aviary*, 67, 2. (Aug.1931): p13.

6329 Garside, F. E., *Let's Make A Rain Gauge*, 75, 4. (Oct.1935): p16-17.

6330 *What's New In Western Living*, 76, 5. (May.1936): p21-23.

6331 *What's New In Western Living*, 79, 3. (Sep.1937): p17-19.

6332 *What's New In Western Living*, 79, 4. (Oct.1937): p17-19.

6333 *What's New In Western Living*, 81, 4. (Oct.1938): p11-13.

6334 *What's New In Western Living*, 81, 6. (Dec.1938): p13-15.

6335 *An Outdoor Aviary*, 84, 1. (Jan.1940): p40-42.

6336 *Amateurs Assist Science*, 84, 4. (Apr.1940): p30-31.

6337 *Native Explorers*, 84, 4. (Apr.1940): p37.

6338 *How To Identify Birds By Beaks*, 85, 2. (Aug.1940): p19.

6339 *Bird's Eye View*, 85, 4. (Oct.1940): p46-47.

6340 *Earthworms*, 88, 1. (Jan.1942): p38-39.

6341 *No Improvements*, 88, 2. (Feb.1942): p8-9.

6342 *Sugar On The Wing*, 89, 1. (Jul.1942): p10-11.

6343 *Feathered Travelers*, 90, 1. (Jan.1943): p5-7.

6344 *Birdhouses*, 90, 3. (Mar.1943): p6-7.

6345 *Birds In Your Garden*, 90, 4. (Apr.1943): p6-7.

6346 *Gophers, Moles*, 90, 4. (Apr.1943): p40-43.

6347 *Wild Country*, 92, 5. (May.1944): p2-3, 5-6.

6348 *Pests*, 92, 5. (May.1944): p59-61.

6349 *More about DDT*, 95, 6. (Dec.1945): p84-85.

6350 *Rivers Of Oregon Part I*, 96, 5. (May.1946): p10-15.

6351 *Rivers Of Oregon Part II*, 96, 6. (Jun.1946): p6-8.

6352 *Feather River*, 97, 1. (Jul.1946): p14-17.

6353 *The Land Of Second Growth*, 99, 2. (Aug.1947): p16-19.

6354 *Steelhead Or Rainbow?*, 101, 2. (Aug.1948): p20-21.

6355 *Pacific Waves–Packages Of Power*, 101, 4. (Oct.1948): p22-27.

6356 *Joshua Tree National Monument*, 104, 2. (Feb.1950): p12-13.

6357 *The Vanishing Western Frontiers*, 104, 2. (Feb.1950): p19-23.

6358 *Birds...*, 105, 4. (Oct.1950): p120-125.

6359 *This 2,000-Year-Old Redwood Forest Soon May Disappear*, 108, 6. (Jun.1952): p14-16.

6360 *The Shy And Busy Beaver*, 110, 4. (Apr.1953): p41-43.

6361 *Get to Know the Hawks*, 111, 3. (Sep.1953): p36, 39.

6362 *The Desert's Critters*, 112, 2. (Feb.1954): p33-37.

6363 *Living Space...For Your Dog*, 112, 6. (Jun.1954): p95-106.

6364 *How To Look At Nature*, 113, 2. (Aug.1954): p38-43.

6365 *Which Gull Is That?*, 114, 1. (Jan.1955): p16-20.

6366 *The Story Of Western Trout*, 114, 4. (Apr.1955): p58-63.

6367 *Up The River Of The West...From The Pacific Through The High Cascades*, 116, 6. (Jun.1956): p62-69.

6368 *The Trees That Captured California*, 117, 2. (Aug.1956): p44-49.

6369 *Exploring The Night Sky*, 117, 2. (Aug.1956): p74, 76, 78.

6370 *The Wonderful Wild Trees Of The West*, 117, 5. (Nov.1956): p60-69.

6371 *The West Is Earthquake Country*, 118, 6. (Jun.1957): p82-84, 87, 88, 91.

6372 *In Arizona's Desert...The Mighty Saguaros*, 122, 4. (Apr.1959): p88-89.

6373 *You Watch A Million Salmon Swim Home*, 123, 4. (Oct.1959): p16-18.

6374 *Have You Looked At The Sky Today?...Here's An Autumn Guide To The Pacific Flyway*, 123, 5. (Nov.1959): p74-81.

6375 *Poison Oak: The West's Worst Plant Pest? "Leaflets Three, Let it Be"*, 124, 6. (Jun.1960): p43-48.

6376 *The Independent Rascals That we Mistakenly Call Blue Jays*, 125, 2. (Aug.1960): p74-76.

6377 *The Spiders in Western Gardens*, 125, 3. (Sep.1960): p168, 170, 173.

6378 *The Truth About Scorpions*, 126, 2. (Feb.1961): p59, 60, 63.

7. The Outdoors

7. The Outdoors

6457 McCausland, Jim, *A Wonderful Wildflower Year?*, 190, 4. (Apr.1993): p116-123.

6458 Finnegan, Lora J., *Please Don't Feed The Bears*, 190, 6. (Jun.1993): p96-98.

6459 Crosby, Bill, *War In Our Forests*, 191, 1. (Jul.1993): p62-69.

6460 Phillips, Jeff, *Saving Sequoias*, 191, 2. (Aug.1993): p66-73.

6461 Jaffe, Matthew, *Nature On The Move*, 191, 5. (Nov.1993): p73-85.

6462 McCausland, Jim, *Saguaro Country*, 192, 2. (Feb.1994): p78-85.

6463 Fish, Peter, *Chaparral*, 192, 4. (Apr.1994): p92-99.

6464 Phillips, Jeff and Hale, Christine Weber, *Splendors Of The Rice Fields*, 193, 4. (Oct.1994): p86-91.

6465 Marks, Ben, *Painting To Save The Land*, 193, 5. (Nov.1994): p92-95.

6466 *California Desert*, 193, 08. (Jan.1995): p54-61.

6467 Fish, Peter, *It's Our Fault*, 194, 6. (Jun.1995): p80-87.

6468 Jaffe, Matthew, *The Joys Of Mud In Morro Bay*, 194, 6. (Jun.1995): p38-40, 42.

6469 Phillips, Jeff, *The Crisis In Our Forests*, 195, 1. (Jul.1995): p87-90, 92.

6470 *The New Lumber*, 194, 05. (Nov.1995): p72-76.

6471 Finnegan, Lora J., *Where Eagles Gather*, 196, 2. (Feb.1996): p24-25, 28.

6472 *The Art Of Recycling*, 198, 2. (Feb.1997): p76-77.

6473 Whiteley, Peter O., *Splashdown*, 1997, 198. (May.1997): p122-123, 126, 127.

7.2 National Parks

6474 *Yosemite*, 1, 1. (May.1898): p3-8.

6475 Keith, Eliza D., *Wawona And The Mariposa Big Trees*, 2, 5. (Mar.1899): p102-105.

6476 *Our Nation's Playground*, 2, 6. (Apr.1899): p124.

6477 LeConte, Joseph N., *Yosemite*, 2, 6. (Apr.1899): p118-120.

6478 Bailey, Charles A., *The Vantage Point Of Yosemite*, 2, 6. (Apr.1899): p121-123.

6479 The Scene Shifter, *The Hidden Cabin Of The Yosemite Valley*, 2, 6. (Apr.1899): p125-126.

6480 LeConte, Joseph N., *King's River Canyon*, 3, 1. (May.1899): p17-22.

6481 Street, W. J., *Fishing In The Yosemite National Park*, 4, 6. (Apr.1900): p231-235.

6482 Gompertz, Helen M., *A Closer Acquaintance With Yosemite*, 5, 1. (May.1900): p23-28.

6483 May, William B., *Red Letter Day In The Yosemite*, 5, 1. (May.1900): p29-31.

6484 LeConte, Joseph N., *My Trip To Kings River Canyon*, 5, 6. (Oct.1900): p275-285.

6485 Jorgensen, Chris, *My Studio In The Yosemite*, 6, 4. (Feb.1901): p113-114.

6486 Lukens, T. P., *Giant's Causeway Of Yosemite*, 6, 5. (Mar.1901): p145-146.

6487 Hodgson, Caspar W., *Crater Lake By Night And Day*, 9, 1. (May.1902): p68-73.

6488 Connell, Irene, *On Glacier Point*, 11, 3. (Jul.1903): p276-277.

6489 Best, H. C., *Impressions Of Yosemite*, 13, 2. (Jun.1904): p105-110.

6490 Miller, Joaquin, *The Sea Of Silence*, 13, 5. (Scp.1904): p394-404.

6491 Everett, Wallace W., *Touring To Yosemite*, 14, 3. (Jan.1905): p281-283.

6492 Greene, Charles S., *A Yearn For Yosemite*, 15, 1. (May.1905): p27-32.

6493 Truman, Ben C., *Falls Of The Yosemite*, 21, 2. (Jun.1908): p111-119.

6494 Clark, Galen, *Yosemite - Past And Present*, 22, 4. (Apr.1909): p394-396.

6495 North, Arthur W., *Alone In The Yellowstone*, 27, 2. (Aug.1911): p131-140.

6496 Evans, Samuel M., *Forty Gallons Of Gasoline To Forty Miles Of Water*, 27, 4. (Oct.1911): p393-399.

6497 Hicks, Harry H., *Crater Lake In Mid-Winter*, 28, 3. (Mar.1912): p299-304.

6498 Kendall, Carpenter, *Motoring On Mount Rainier*, 31, 2. (Aug.1913): p304-309.

6499 Daniels, Mark, *The War With Switzerland*, 35, 1. (Jul.1915): p81-92.

6500 Holway, Ruliff S., *When Lassen Wakes*, 35, 2. (Aug.1915): p263-269.

6501 Grover, Con L., *Soaring Across Tioga Pass*, 37, 1. (Jul.1916): p74,76,78,80-82.

6502 Laing, Hamilton M., *On Barking Betsy To The Mountain*, 37, 3. (Sep.1916): p21-23, 72.

6503 Drury, Aubrey, *Crater Lake National Park*, 38, 4. (Apr.1917): p92.

6504 Howell, Lindsay, *Two Miles High On Highgear*, 39, (Aug.1917). p74-81: .

6505 Loomis, Metta M., *Girls Will Be Guides!*, 39, 3. (Sep.1917): p30, 66.

6506 Saunders, Charles Francis, *In The Heart Of The Giant Forest*, 39, 3. (Sep.1917): p41-43, 71-72.

6507 Saunders, Charles Francis, *Lodging With Montezuma*, 40, 3. (Mar.1918): p41-43.

6508 Laing, Hamilton M., *Barking Betsy And The Chilled Volcano*, 41, 2. (Aug.1918): p24-27.

6509 Burrund, Leland J., *Filming The Phantom*, 43, 5. (Nov.1919): p3.

6510 Benson, Stella, *Upstarts*, 45, 6. (Dec.1920): p105-106.

6511 *Pulse of the Pacific*, 46, 2. (Feb.1921): p14-16.

6512 Tracy, Ray Palmer, *Roughneck Pioneers*, 48, 2. (Feb.1922): p32-35, 66.

6513 Freeman, Lewis R., *Skiing Through Yellowstone*, 48, 6. (Jun.1922): p12-15, 66-71.

6514 Grimes, Oliver J., *In Nature's Own Studio*, 52, 4. (Apr.1924): p12-13.

6515 Wells, John W., *The Cavern Of The Bats*, 52, 5. (May.1924): p20-21, 77-79.

6516 Carhart, Arthur Hawthorne, *A Western Gnomeland*, 53, 1. (Jul.1924): p12-13, 79.

6517 Freeman, Lewis R., *Hell And High Water*, 53, 2. (Aug.1924): p9-13, 57-59.

6518 Freeman, Lewis R., *Hell and High Water*, 53, 3. (Sep.1924): p24-27, 62-63.

6519 Freeman, Lewis R., *Hell And High Water*, Hell And High Water, 4. (Oct.1924): p16-19, 52-56.

6520 Edwards, Allison, *Where Nature Stages Her Variety Show*, 55, 2. (Aug.1925): p14-15, 92.

6521 Boyer, Warren E., *Motor-Lassoing The Gabled Rockies Of Colorado*, 56, 3. (Mar.1926): p20-21, 62.

6522 Steele, Rufus M., *The Celestial Circuit*, 56, 5. (May.1926): p24-26, 92-94.

6523 Vinton, George M., *Crater Lake*, 56, 6. (Jun.1926): p26.

6524 Henry, James J., *Where Creed Is Least*, 57, 4. (Oct.1926): p21, 54.

6525 Fordyce, Claude P., *Afoot Through The Grand Canyon*, 58, 5. (May.1927): p23, 78-79.

6526 Ewing, Paul A., *The Monument Tour*, 58, 5. (May.1927): p32-33, 65-66.

6527 Ewing, Paul A., *Let's Go!*, 59, 2. (Aug.1927): p16-19.

6528 Taylor, Frank J., *The Story Of Utah's Dixie*, 62, 3. (Mar.1929): p20-23.

6529 Taylor, Frank J., *Something Besides Scenery In Yosemite*, 62, 6. (Jun.1929): p11-13, 70-71.

6530 Taylor, Frank J., *Speaking Of Vacations*, 64, 4. (Apr.1930): p9-12.

6531 Taylor, Frank J., *On The Trail Of A Thrill*, 64, 5. (May.1930): p9-11.

6532 Burns, Colette Wagner, *Plan Now To Visit Death Valley*, 65, 5. (Nov.1930): p15-17.

6533 Lubcke, Charles, *A Sunset Family Visits The Grand Canyon*, 66, 1. (Jan.1931): p18-19.

7. The Outdoors

6534 Taylor, Frank J., *Which Park For Your Vacation?*, 66, 4. (Apr.1931): p10-13.

6535 Freeland, E. D., *Explorers Underground*, 66, 5. (May.1931): p16-17, 50.

6536 Taylor, Frank J., *Two Weeks To Roam Away From Home*, 68, 4. (Apr.1932): p8-11.

6537 Vare, Carl, *A Little Patch Of Heaven*, 70, 2. (Feb.1933): p12, 27.

6538 Ellis, Ralph Webster, *A Sunset Family Visits Zion National Park*, 75, 1. (Jul.1935): p15.

6539 *What's New In Western Living*, 78, 4. (Apr.1937): p23-25.

6540 *What's New In Western Living*, 81, 5. (Nov.1938): p13-15.

6541 *Destination: Our Land*, 94, 5. (May.1945): p2-4, 6.

6542 *How About The Vacationland You Own?*, 96, 6. (Jun.1946): p19-21.

6543 *Sequoia-Kings Canyon*, 97, 2. (Aug.1946): p6-9.

6544 *Winter In The Desert*, 97, 5. (Nov.1946): p6-12.

6545 *Hiking, Comfort, And Fish–*, 100, 5. (May.1948): p6-10.

6546 *Discovery Trips On The Olympic Peninsula*, 103, 1. (Jul.1949): p18-21.

6547 *Trout Waters of West Yellowstone*, 103, 2. (Aug.1949): p11-13.

6548 *Death Valley–Via Trona*, 103, 6. (Dec.1949): p16-17.

6549 *A Swing Around Mount Rainier*, 105, 2. (Aug.1950): p25-29.

6550 *Montezuma Castle To Tuzigoot And Flagstaff*, 109, 6. (Dec.1952): p14-16.

6551 *The Expected...And The Unexpected...In Death Valley*, 110, 1. (Jan.1953): p12-16.

6552 *Spring Trip To The Desert...In Search Of Sun...And Wild Flowers*, 110, 3. (Mar.1953): p16-18.

6553 *Between Yellowstone And Glacier*, 110, 6. (Jun.1953): p44-49.

6554 *Utah's Fabled Color Country*, 111, 2. (Aug.1953): p34-39.

6555 *Jackson Hole And The Grand Tetons...*, 112, 4. (Apr.1954): p54-59.

6556 *Arizona's Canyon Maze*, 113, 1. (Jul.1954): p30-33.

6557 *Across The Highest Sierra Pass*, 113, 2. (Aug.1954): p34-37.

6558 *Lassen...Right After Labor Day Is The Best Time To Go*, 113, 3. (Sep.1954): p42-47.

6559 *If You Drive Toward Texas*, 114, 2. (Feb.1955): p26, 29.

6560 *Family Vacation In Olympic Park... The Rain Forest, The Ocean, and The Snowy Olympics*, 114, 6. (Jun.1955): p48-56.

6561 *From Pele's Pig Pen To Maker Of Mists...Exploring The Wasteland Of Haleakala*, 115, 3. (Sep.1955): p14-24.

6562 *The Unknown Grand Canyon*, 115, 4. (Oct.1955): p45-53.

6563 *When Is Yosemite Valley At Its Best?*, 117, 4. (Oct.1956): p46-53.

6564 *Pinnacles...At Its Best Right Now*, 118, 4. (Apr.1957): p16, 19, 20, 22.

6565 *Springtime Adventure in the Desert... There's Still Room to Wander in the Capitol Reef Country*, 118, 4. (Apr.1957): p56-59.

6566 *For The Rocks...And The Wildflowers...And The Clean Spring Desert Air*, 120, 4. (Apr.1958): p68-73.

6567 *When We Found Glacier, We Stopped Looking...*, 120, 6. (Jun.1958): p60-67.

6568 *A Lazy Day On The Snake*, 121, 1. (Jul.1958): p35-36, 37, 40.

6569 *Teewinot And Grand Teton...Close Enough To Touch*, 123, 1. (Jul.1959): p26-32.

6570 *Into Death Valley ... Over Jubilee Pass*, 124, 1. (Jan.1960): p39-40.

6571 *A Flawless Winter World...Along The Generals' Highway*, 124, 2. (Feb.1960): p42-53.

6572 *If Your Summer Travels Take You To Mid-America*, 124, 5. (May.1960): p77, 78, 80, 83,84.

6573 *Kolob*, 124, 6. (Jun.1960): p82-91.

6574 *A Walk Through Wildflowers*, 125, 1. (Jul.1960): p32-38.

6575 *Uncrowded Wilderness...Caribou Peak Wild Area*, 125, 3. (Sep.1960): p22, 25, 26.

6576 *Autumn In The Black Canyon Of The Gunnison: Reds And Yellows, Bold And Bright*, 125, 4. (Oct.1960): p28-30, 32.

6577 *The Castle That Walter Scott Built*, 125, 5. (Nov.1960): p42, 44, 46.

6578 *In Spring Dress... The Arizona Desert Park Called Organ Pipe*, 126, 3. (Mar.1961): p38, 39, 41, 43, 44, 46, 48, 50.

6579 *The Valley Of Color*, 128, 3. (Mar.1962): p74-83.

6580 *Sequoia*, 128, 5. (May.1962): p94-106.

6581 *Christmas At The Bottom Of The Grand Canyon*, 129, 6. (Dec.1962): p22-24.

6582 *The Grand Old Park. It is Still Full of Surprises*, 130, 6. (Jun.1963): p76-91.

6583 *"See One Big Tree... And You Want To See Another"*, 131, 1. (Jul.1963): p30-32.

6584 *By Lake Launch And Open Air Bus*, 132, 5. (May.1964): p100-105.

6585 *The Grand Canyon*, 133, 4. (Oct.1964): p76-89.

6586 *A Sunny Winter Holiday At Furnace Creek*, 134, 2. (Feb.1965): p42, 44.

6587 *In Utah...An Early Look At Our Newest National Park*, 134, 4. (Apr.1965): p32, 36, 39.

6588 *Our Wilderness Alps*, 134, 6. (Jun.1965): p84-97.

6589 *An Autumn Walk Through The Smith River Redwoods*, 135, 5. (Nov.1965): p20.

6590 *The Winter Animal Show Is Now Under Way In Snowy Yellowstone*, 135, 6. (Dec.1965): p31-32.

6591 *At Last A Redwood National Park Is In The Making; What Sort of Park Will it Be?*, 136, 3. (Mar.1966): p44-46, 51.

6592 *Tomorrow The Tourists Will Come Flooding; Today You Can Have it Almost to Yourself*, 137, 3. (Sep.1966): p26-28.

6593 *A Visit To The West's First National Seashore*, 138, 2. (Feb.1967): p48, 50, 52, 54.

6594 *Unlocking The Canyon Country*, 138, 5. (May.1967): p82-91.

6595 *Alaska Adventure...A Visit To Glacier Bay*, 139, 1. (Jul.1967): p30, 32, 35.

6596 *The Great Wildlife Park Is Alaska's McKinley*, 140, 6. (Jun.1968): p62-71.

6597 *The New Redwood National Park Is Not The Victory It May Yet Become*, 142, 5. (May.1969): p90-91.

6598 *The Olympic Wilderness*, 142, 6. (Jun.1969): p64-75.

6599 *Death Valley*, 143, 5. (Nov.1969): p78-89.

6600 *Winter Holiday In Yosemite*, 143, 6. (Dec.1969): p58-61.

6601 *From Low To High Desert In Rock-Ribbed Joshua Tree*, 4, 2. (Feb.1970): p66-73.

6602 *Down, Down To Havasu*, 144, 5. (May.1970): p80-83.

6603 *North Cascades National Park*, 145, 1. (Jul.1970): p48-57.

6604 *Hawaii's Seven Pools*, 146, 1. (Jan.1971): p40-45.

6605 *Arches*, 146, 5. (May.1971): p92-95.

6606 *North To Canada's Grand Mountain Parks*, 146, 6. (Jun.1971): p75-79.

6607 *Fire Rivers And Fire Falls In Hawaii*, 147, 3. (Sep.1971): p50-53.

6608 *Utah's New Park Is Ready For Exploring*, 150, 4. (Apr.1973): p90-95.

6609 *The Other Rim*, 151, 3. (Sep.1973): p54-57.

6610 *Idaho's First National Park?*, 153, 1. (Jul.1974): p46-51.

6611 *'Up-Country' Maui On The Side Of Haleakala*, 154, 2. (Feb.1975): p66-69.

6612 *Autumn Yosemite*, 157, 4. (Oct.1976): p66-69.

7. The Outdoors

6613 *Fun in the Snow Near Yosemite's South Entrance... Among the Giant Sequoias, On a Little Rail Car*, 158, 3. (Mar.1977): p46-47.

6614 *It's A Great Year And Month To Discover Death Valley*, 160, 1. (Jan.1978): p54-57.

6615 *Uncrowded Is The Winter Word For Lassen*, 161, 6. (Dec.1978): p20-21.

6616 *Ways To Reach National Parks Of The West Without Using Your Car*, 163, 1. (Jul.1979): p74-75.

6617 *Again You Can Drive The Chain Of Craters In Hawaii Volcanos park*, 163, 4. (Oct.1979): p96-99.

6618 *Magnificent Mineral King*, 167, 2. (Aug.1981): p26-28.

6619 *Sequoia Winter Magic*, 167, 6. (Dec.1981): p82-85.

6620 *The Channel Islands–Our Newest National Park*, 168, 2. (Feb.1982): p68-73.

6621 *Tuolomne Rafting, Camping, Exploring*, 172, 4. (Apr.1984): p58-62.

6622 *The Olympic Peninsula*, 172, 6. (Jun.1984): p98-103.

6623 *Yellowstone Winter... Magic, Uncrowded*, 174, 1. (Jan.1985): p56-59.

6624 *Yosemite–Still Magnificent*, 174, 5. (May.1985): p108-129.

6625 *Rafting, Hiking, Fishing in and Around Yosemite's River - The Merced*, 178, 5. (May.1987): p14-16.

6626 *Yosemite In Winter*, 180, 1. (Jan.1988): p12-16.

6627 *Where Wildflowers and Geology Flourish... Pinnacles National Monument*, 180, 3. (Mar.1988): p12-16.

6628 *Miracle On the North Coast?*, 181, 2. (Aug.1988): p48-53.

6629 *Yellowstone A Year Later*, 182, 5. (May.1989): p108-120, 122.

6630 *All's Quiet At Lassen*, 183, 2. (Aug.1989): p16-17, 19, 21.

6631 *Grand Canyon In Winter*, 183, 5. (Nov.1989): p26-28, 32, 33.

6632 *The Presidio*, 183, 5. (Nov.1989): p78-85.

6633 *Death Valley Biking*, 184, 2. (Feb.1990): p21, 25, 27.

6634 *Backcountry Yosemite*, 184, 5. (May.1990): p98-114.

6635 *117 Miles Of Twists, Turns, Red-rock Splendor*, 184, 6. (Jun.1990): p76-79.

6636 Finnegan, Lora J., *Winter Treasures Of Yellowstone Country*, 193, 5. (Nov.1994): p28-32.

6637 *Geology Lessons In Death Valley*, 193, 08. (Feb.1995): p30-35.

6638 Lorton, Steven R., *The Loneliest National Parks*, 195, 1. (Jul.1995): p66-73.

6639 Finnegan, Lora J., *Can We Save Our National Parks?*, 196, 6. (Jun.1996): p74-80.

6640 Jaffe, Matthew, *Forgotten Islands*, 197, 1. (Jul.1996): p58-63.

6641 *Desert Duet In Zion And Bryce*, 197, 05. (Nov.1996): p22-24, 26, 28.

6642 *Utah's Grand New Monument*, 198, 2. (Feb.1997): p20-22, 25, 26.

6643 Finnegan, Lora J., *The Hidden Point Reyes*, 198, 4. (Apr.1997): p24-26, 27, 28.

7.3 Outdoor Recreation & Leisure Activities

6644 *Sportsmen's Targets*, 1, 4. (Aug.1898): p53-56.

6645 *The French Opera House And The Carnival Balls*, 2, 3. (Jan.1899): p45.

6646 Powell, Sherman, *Game Of Southern Arizona*, 2, 5. (Mar.1899): p109-111.

6647 Powell, Sherman, *A Sportsman in Old Mexico*, 3, 1. (May.1899): p20-22.

6648 Keller, Clara D., *A Horseback Ride In The Mountains*, 3, 3. (Jul.1899): p102-104.

6649 The Hunter, *Big Game Hunting In Oregon And The Trout Wonders Of Pelican Bay*, 3, 4. (Aug.1899): p125-128.

6650 Hodgson, Caspar W., *Where To Go Skating In California*, 4, 5. (Mar.1900): p199-200.

6651 Hodgson, Caspar W., *Camping Among Sequoias*, 5, 1. (May.1900): p36.

6652 Treat, Archibald, *Trolling On Tahoe*, 5, 2. (Jun.1900): p63-68.

6653 Street, W. J., *Trout Fishing On The Upper Sacramento*, 5, 2. (Jun.1900): p80-83.

6654 Coon, H. I., *A Fishing Trip In The Big Basin, Santa Cruz Mountains*, 5, 2. (Jun.1900): p86-88.

6655 Treat, Archibald, *Fly Fishing Near Tahoe*, 5, 3. (Jul.1900): p125-132.

6656 Powell, Sherman, *Bear Hunting In Oregon*, 5, 3. (Jul.1900): p134-136.

6657 Higgins, C. W., *A Day's Golfing At Del Monte*, 5, 4. (Aug.1900): p159-161.

6658 Gilmour, John Hamilton, *A Day's Mid-Winter Mountain Climbing*, 5, (Aug.1900). p169-173: .

6659 Earll, F. A., *A Day's Dove Shooting In California*, 5, 4. (Aug.1900): p174-177.

6660 Raymond, I. H., *A December's Day Tennis At Santa Cruz*, 5, 4. (Aug.1900): p180.

6661 J. C., *An Early Spring Day At The Santa Monica Polo Grounds*, 5, 4. (Aug.1900): p200.

6662 Simpson, Joseph Cairn, *Horses of California, First Paper*, 6, 1. (Nov.1900): p25-34.

6663 Holder, Charles F., *Rod, Reel And Gaff In Southern California*, 6, 3. (Jan.1901): p73-83.

6664 Powell, Sherman, *Hunting The Pheasant In Oregon*, 6, 5. (Mar.1901): p161-163.

6665 Simpson, Joseph Cairn, *Horses of California*, 6, 3. (Mar.1901): p149-160.

6666 Coon, H. I., *Fishing On The Truckee*, 7, 1. (May.1901): p24-28.

6667 Simpson, Joseph Cairn, *Horses of California*, 7, 1. (May.1901): p9-23.

6668 *California Winter Recreations*, 7, 6. (Oct.1901): p157-165.

6669 Simpson, Joseph Cairn, *Horses of California*, 8, 1. (Nov.1901): p25-42.

6670 Simpson, Joseph Cairn, *Horses of California*, 8, 3. (Jan.1902): p129-142.

6671 Inkersley, Arthur, *Yachting On San Francisco Bay*, 8, 5. (Mar.1902): p207-216.

6672 Cumming, Al M., *Trout Fishing In The Sierras*, 8, 6. (Apr.1902): p251-255.

6673 Chandler, Katherine, *Housekeeping In The Summer Camp*, 9, 1. (May.1902): p20-25.

6674 Simpson, Joseph Cairn, *Horses of California, Seventh Paper*, 9, 1. (May.1902): p29-40.

6675 Rutter, Cloudsley, *Down The Sacramento In A Skiff*, 9, 2. (Jun.1902): p118-126.

6676 Buck, Charles G., *After Trout On The Rogue*, 9, 2. (Jun.1902): p128-130.

6677 Simpson, Joseph Cairn, *Horses of California, Eighth Paper*, 9, 4. (Aug.1902): p235-250.

6678 Hodgson, Caspar W., *Hunting Mazamas In The Cascades*, 9, 5. (Sep.1902): p313-318.

6679 Coon, H. I., *Championship Fly Casting*, 9, 6. (Oct.1902): p407-411.

6680 Whitney, J. Parker, *Salmon Fishing Off Monterey*, 10, 1. (Nov.1902): p5-14.

6681 Cumming, Al M., *California Duck Hunting*, 10, 2. (Dec.1902): p132-138.

6682 Simpson, Joseph Cairn, *Horses of California, Ninth Paper*, 10, 4. (Feb.1903): p306-320.

6683 Cumming, Al M. and Church, A. S., *Striped Bass Fishing*, 11, 1. (May.1903): p76-82.

6684 Parsons, Edward T., *We Go A Fishing In The High Sierra*, 11, 2. (Jun.1903): p137-141.

6685 Fulton, C. W., *My Tussle With A Black Bass*, 11, 2. (Jun.1903): p162-165.

6686 Powell, Sherman, *A Bear Tip*, 11, 4. (Aug.1903): p309-313.

6687 Burgess, Gelett, *The Royal Game Of Chess*, 11, 4. (Aug.1903): p357-359.

7. The Outdoors

6688 Simpson, Joseph Cairn, *Horses Of California*, 11, 5. (Sep.1903): p429-440.

6689 Henderson, Victor, *Up Mount Whitney With The Sierra Club*, 11, 6. (Oct.1903): p505-515.

6690 Fitch, George Hamlin, *How To Climb Shasta*, 11, 6. (Oct.1903): p529-536.

6691 James, George Wharton, *Camping With Le Conte*, 11, 6. (Oct.1903): p563-566.

6692 Cumming, Al M., *Rod And Reel At Weber [sic] Lake*, 12, 1. (Nov.1903): p14-17.

6693 Inkersley, Arthur, *Golf At Del Monte*, 12, 4. (Feb.1904): p335-339.

6694 Cavill, O. C. H. and Cavill, Arthur R. C., *Swimming In Midwinter*, 12, 5. (Mar.1904): p462-463.

6695 Simpson, Joseph Cairn, *Horses of California, Eleventh Paper*, 12, 5. (Mar.1904): p427-446.

6696 Jones, Isaak Walton, *Trout Fishing Time*, 12, 6. (Apr.1904): p508-509.

6697 Hamilton, John W., *The Bishop's Fish Story*, 13, 1. (May.1904): p3-13.

6698 Parsons, E. T., *Alpine Angling*, 13, 2. (Jun.1904): p111-114.

6699 Powell, Sherman, *Hunting Elk In Oregon*, 13, 4. (Aug.1904): p320-324.

6700 Rogers, James E., *A Vacation Republic: How A Boys' Club Mixed Sociology And Sport In A Summer Outing In The Santa Cruz Mountains*, 13, 5. (Sep.1904): p430-433.

6701 Kollmyer, W. B., *Where The Trout Leaps Quickest*, 13, 5. (Sep.1904): p459-463.

6702 Simpson, Joseph Cairn, *Horses of California*, 14, 1. (Nov.1904): p65-78.

6703 Hopps, H. R., *After Ducks With Camera And Gun*, 14, 2. (Dec.1904): p176-178.

6704 Rainey, Edward, *Beats The World At Tennis*, 14, 2. (Dec.1904): p182-183.

6705 Simpson, Joseph Cairn, *Horses of California, Thirteenth Paper*, 14, 3. (Jan.1905): p241-254.

6706 Cumming, Al M., *Rod And Gun Between Sun And Sun*, 14, 4. (Feb.1905): p406-408.

6707 Simpson, Joseph Cairn, *Horses of California, Fourteenth Paper*, 14, 5. (Mar.1905): p499-512.

6708 Vachell, Guy, *After Truckee Rainbows*, 15, 1. (May.1905): p19-24.

6709 Bramhall, Frank J., *In California's Lake Country*, 15, 1. (May.1905): p46-55.

6710 Reed, Charles Wesley, *Summer In Sierra Snow Land*, 15, 3. (Jul.1905): p277-284.

6711 Garnett, E. M., *Intercollegiate Boating On The Pacific Coast*, 15, 4. (Aug.1905): p332-337.

6712 Greene, Charles S., *Camping For Two*, 15, 4. (Aug.1905): p356-358.

6713 Winterburn, Rosa V., *Up Castle Crags*, 15, 4. (Aug.1905): p369-374.

6714 Sutton, May G., *How I Play Tennis*, 15, 4. (Aug.1905): p327-331.

6715 Stewart, Charlotte, *In The Mt. Diablo Country*, 16, 1. (Nov.1905): p27-31.

6716 Glascock, Roglan, *How We Climbed Rainier*, 16, 1. (Nov.1905): p49-55.

6717 Parsons, E. T., *An Unexpected Afternoon With The True Speckled Trout*, 17, 2-3. (1906): p71-74.

6718 Adams, Frank, *Up Whitney By Lone Pine Trail*, 17, 2-3. (1906): p74-80.

6719 Willets, Gilson, *A Tenderfoot In Texas*, 16, 3. (Jan.1906): p227-238.

6720 Smith, Thomas B., *Western Boys Beat The World*, 16, 5. (Mar.1906): p466-471.

6721 Dunn, Allan, *The Transpacific Yacht Race*, 16, 6. (Apr.1906): p532-531.

6722 Sherman, W. B., *An Oregon Deer Hunt*, 17, 4. (Aug.1906): p148-149.

6723 Graupner, A. E., *A Storied Turnpike*, 17, 5. (Sep.1906): p269-273.

6724 Emerson, Edwin, Jr., *San Francisco At Play*, 17, 6. (Oct.1906): p319-328.

6725 Williams, C. H., *Paddling Down The Willamette*, 18, 3. (Jan.1907): p242-246.

6726 Cumming, Al M., *Angling On The Klamath*, 18, 5. (Apr.1907): p577-583.

6727 Chandler, Katherine, *Nature's Drug Store: Timely Tips To Campers About Helpful And Harmful Shrubs And Plants*, 19, 1. (May.1907): p51-53.

6728 Kruttschnitt, John, *Deer Hunting In The Siskiyous*, 19, 4. (Aug.1907): p336-337.

6729 North, Arthur W., *Hunting The Big-Horn*, 19, 6. (Oct.1907): p523-532.

6730 Veitchm, Tom, *Mirthful Ripples: An Idyl Of Angling And The Things That Happen And Some That Don't*, 21, 3. (Jul.1908): p220-223.

6731 Wentworth, George A., *On The Paper Mill*, 21, 6. (Oct.1908): p504-506.

6732 Unmack, William, *Rugby, 1908*, 21, 7. (Nov.1908): p662-664.

6733 Stearn, Edwin, *A Sea Park In A City's Heart: The Unique Jewel Of Oakland's Park System*, 22, 1. (Jan.1909): p109-110.

6734 Wells, A. J., *'Siskiyou The Golden': A Land Of Mountain Meadows And Farms, Of Mineral Springs And Health Resorts*, 22, 2. (Feb.1909): p207-209.

6735 Doten, Samuel B., *Fly-Fishing For Rainbows*, 23, 2. (Aug.1909): p195-198.

6736 Schultz, James Willard, *In Wild Turkey Land*, 23, 5. (Nov.1909): p514-518.

6737 Lewis, Sinclair, *A San Francisco Pleasure Cure*, 24, 4. (Apr.1910): p432-439.

6738 Chandler, Katherine, *California's Topsy-Turvy Calendar*, 25, 1. (Jul.1910): p104-107.

6739 Adams, Samuel Hopkins, *Tenderfooting For Mountain Sheep*, 25, 1. (Jul.1910): p25-34.

6740 Beach, Everett C., *The Playground Movement In California*, 26, 5. (May.1911): p521-526.

6741 Kyne, Peter B., *Sunshine & Seabreeze, Inc.*, 27, 1. (Jul.1911): p3-18.

6742 Gilmour, John Hamilton, *Magic Wrought By Men And Money*, 27, 1. (Jul.1911): p113-114.

6743 Chandler, Katherine, *The Pleasant Duty Of Del Monte*, 27, 4. (Oct.1911): p425-427.

6744 Goodwin, Orton E., *The Spirit Of The Round-Up*, 27, 6. (Dec.1911): p639-642.

6745 Fisher, C. E., *Bayocean*, 28, 5. (May.1912): p641-642.

6746 Comings, A. V., *Motor-Boating On Puget Sound*, 29, 1. (Jul.1912): p53-59.

6747 Kyne, Peter B., *Two Mules And A Motorist*, 29, 2. (Aug.1912): p159-171.

6748 Bartlett, William A., *In The Horseman's Paradise*, 29, 3. (Sep.1912): p256-260.

6749 Hardy, Lowell, *A Crab's-eye View*, 29, 3. (Sep.1912): p298-305.

6750 McGroarty, John S., *At The Sign Of The Poinsettia*, 29, 6. (Dec.1912): p619-626, 715.

6751 Freeman, Lewis R., *The King Of Sports; Polo in California*, 30, 2. (Feb.1913): p135-141.

6752 Bradley, Arthur Z., *Motoring For Trout*, 30, 5. (May.1913): p541-547.

6753 Powell, E. Alexander, *The Coast Of Enchanted Summer*, 30, 6. (Jun.1913): p735-748, 832.

6754 Cooper, F. J., *Cast That Fly*, 30, 6. (Jun.1913): p810-811.

6755 Steele, Rufus M., *In A Friendly Outdoors*, 33, 1. (Jul.1914): p50-64.

6756 Graham, Thomas F., *Putting Over The Next Big League*, 33, 2. (Aug.1914): p269-275.

6757 Smith, Bertha H., *Sandyland!*, 33, 2. (Aug.1914): p291-305.

6758 Field, Charles K., *On The New Rialto*, 36, 1. (Jan.1916): p42-47.

6759 Laing, Hamilton M., *Bucking the Dust Trail : Adventures on a Gas Cart in the Western Sagebrush*, 36, 5. (May.1916): p76,78,80,82,84,86,88.

6760 Foster, Maximilian, *Eight Days*, 36, 6. (Jun.1916): p29-31, 94-95.

7. The Outdoors

6761 Peck, Leland W., *Practical Hints for the Motor Camping*, 36, 6. (Jun.1916): p74,76,78,80,82-83.

6762 Evans, Billy, *Nuggets In The National Game*, 37, 1. (Jul.1916): p44-46.

6763 Arnold, Frank R., *When Hyrum Dances*, 37, 3. (Sep.1916): p35-36.

6764 Hall, Wilbur, *A Complete Vacation For $7.50*, 37, 3. (Sep.1916): p36, 88.

6765 Wynne, Roy, *Polo's Winter Capital*, 38, 2. (Feb.1917): p37-39, 87-89.

6766 Laing, Hamilton M., *Indian Fishin'*, 38, 5. (May.1917): p20-21, 47-48.

6767 Baily, Robin, *A Manufactory Of Champions*, 38, 6. (Jun.1917): p34-35, 90.

6768 Laing, Hamilton M., *Nights Out*, 39, 2. (Aug.1917): p23-24, 54-60.

6769 Wilson, Kathryne, *Over The Top*, 39, 3. (Sep.1917): p38-40, 73-74.

6770 Pope, Saxton, *Hunting With The Long Bow*, 39, 4. (Oct.1917): p36-37, 79.

6771 Forster, Charles Hancock, *Obeying The Scout Law*, 40, 5. (May.1918): p24.

6772 Howard, Randall R., *Chautauqua Invades The West*, 40, 5. (May.1918): p49-50.

6773 Hough, Emerson, *Get Outdoors!*, 41, 3. (Sep.1918): p14-16, 50.

6774 Hildebrand, Joel H., *The Babe On Burro-Back*, 41, 3. (Sep.1918): p26-27.

6775 Klouchek, Charles E., *Crowing On Rooster Rock*, 41, 4. (Oct.1918): p42.

6776 White, Stewart Edward, *How To Be A Good Shot*, 43, 3. (Sep.1919): p19-22, 72-74.

6777 Laing, Hamilton M., *Those Heathen Chinees*, 43, 4. (Oct.1919): p41-43, 68-72.

6778 Chase, J. Smeaton, *A Little Brown Tent On The Desert*, 43, 4. (Oct.1919): p43-45.

6779 Burrund, Leland J., *Look Pleasant, Please!*, 44, 1. (Jan.1920): p4.

6780 Burrund, Leland J., *Playing Round With The Wind Goddess*, 44, 2. (Feb.1920): p4.

6781 Irwin, Wallace, *Two Schools Of Fishers*, 45, 5. (Nov.1920): p24-27.

6782 FitzGerald, Harold J., *Your Diversions*, 46, 2. (Feb.1921): p26-27, 65-66.

6783 Kofeldt, Walter W., *Your Taste In Movies*, 46, 3. (Mar.1921): p23-25, 52-56.

6784 Percy, E. N., *Regular Campers*, 47, 1. (Jul.1921): p91-94.

6785 Bentinck, Richard, *Isador Sits In* , 47, 6. (Dec.1921): p32-34, 66-70.

6786 Freeman, Lewis R., *The Yellowstone And A Tin Boat*, 49, 2. (Aug.1922): p30-32, 56-59.

6787 Tracy, Ray Palmer, *Bed And Board In The Open*, 51, 1. (Jul.1923): p17-19.

6788 Baldwin, Asa C., *Bearding Saint Elias*, 51, 2. (Aug.1923): p8-10, 60-62.

6789 Sanford, T. F., *A Tenderfoot Wedding Tour*, 51, 4. (Oct.1923): p88-93.

6790 Nash, J. B., *Where Can Your Children Play?*, 51, 6. (Dec.1923): p26-27, 58.

6791 Stoltz, Herbert F., *Outdoor Games For Health*, 51, 6. (Dec.1923): p27.

6792 White, Stewart Edward, *Outguessed*, 52, 5. (May.1924): p8-10, 104-106.

6793 Gwynne, Hilda, *Can Women Fish?*, 53, 1. (Jul.1924): p16, 84-86.

6794 Kenyon A. Joyce, *The Persistent Bear*, 53, 4. (Oct.1924): p43.

6795 Davis, Marguerite, *Are You A Hoot Owl?*, 53, 6. (Dec.1924): p49, 76-78.

6796 White, Stewart Edward, *Stalkers And Fakers*, 54, 3. (Mar.1925): p9, 52-54.

6797 Lockwood, Frank C., *Co-Eds A-Horseback*, 54, 5. (May.1925): p41.

6798 Elford, E. J., *The Art Of Flycasting*, 54, 6. (Jun.1925): p12, 83-85.

6799 *More Fish For Western Anglers*, 54, 6. (Jun.1925): p13, 87.

6800 Foster, Maximilian, *My First Steelhead*, 54, 6. (Jun.1925): p19, 52, 54.

6801 Mulvane, William R., *Tenting On The New Camp Ground*, 55, 1. (Jul.1925): p12-13, 58.

6802 Scherck, G., *University Of Washington Cradle Of Rowing Coaches*, 55, 1. (Jul.1925): p20-21, 54.

6803 Edwards, Allison, *Camping In Comfort*, 55, 1. (Jul.1925): p38-39.

6804 Powell, Tod, *Hunting Thrills*, 55, 4. (Oct.1925): p14-15, 79-80.

6805 Eddie Graney, *A Referee's Decision*, 55, 5. (Nov.1925): p16-19, 80-84.

6806 Edwards, Allison, *Where Youth Meets Age*, 55, 5. (Nov.1925): p34-36.

6807 Yost, Harold H., *Rough Riders Of The Surf*, 56, 1. (Jan.1926): p12-13, 82.

6808 Andrews, Walter, *My Radio*, 56, 1. (Jan.1926): p38-39, 62.

6809 Grey, Zane, *The Log Of The Gladiator*, 56, 4. (Apr.1926): p9-11, 56-62.

6810 Powell, Tod and Lane, D. R., *Mostly About Trout*, 56, 4. (Apr.1926): p26-29, 88.

6811 Lane, D. R., *Camping De Luxe*, 57, 1. (Jul.1926): p9-11, 82-83.

6812 Harriman, E. E., *Cold Nights*, 57, 1. (Jul.1926): p29, 64.

6813 Burke, Carleton F., *Goal!*, 57, 2. (Aug.1926): p12-13, 76.

6814 Dunn, H. H., *Summer Beneath The Mainsail*, 57, 2. (Aug.1926): p14-17.

6815 Grey, R. C., *The Thrill Of The Season*, 57, 2. (Aug.1926): p21, 60-62.

6816 Peak, Mayme Ober, *Riding The Bucking Bounding Main!*, 57, 2. (Aug.1926): p22-23, 76.

6817 Head Wrangler, *Rope Your Own!*, 57, 3. (Sep.1926): p12-14.

6818 Brininstool, E. A., *Another Redskin Bit The Dust*, 57, 3. (Sep.1926): p28-29, 54.

6819 Dohlman, Billy, *Let them Ride!*, 57, 4. (Oct.1926): p22-23, 80-82.

6820 Small, Sidney Herschel, *She Knew Them All!*, 57, 4. (Oct.1926): p30-31, 65-66.

6821 Woehlke, Walter V., *The Football Business*, 57, 5. (Nov.1926): p14-15.

6822 Boone, Andrew R., *White Elephants And Others*, 57, 5. (Nov.1926): p22-23, 56.

6823 Hough, Donald, *Horses Are Funny People!*, 58, 2. (Feb.1927): p18-19, 66-68.

6824 Jopp, Fred Gilman, *At The Drop Of The Flag*, 58, 2. (Feb.1927): p38-39, 69, 76-77.

6825 Block, Eugene B., *Lion-Hunting For A Living*, 58, 4. (Apr.1927): p15, 65-66.

6826 O'Hara, Gerald J., *Champions Of The Far West*, 58, 4. (Apr.1927): p26-27, 88-92.

6827 Schwab, Peter J., *Camping Is An Art!*, 58, 5. (May.1927): p20-22, 80-83.

6828 Frisbie, Robert Dean, *Armchair Yachting*, 58, 5. (May.1927): p24-25, 66-68.

6829 Monroe, Anne Shannon, *Why I Enjoy Mountain Climbing*, 58, 5. (May.1927): p26-27, 68, 76-77.

6830 Sutherland, Donald W., *Drive Right In!*, 59, 1. (Jul.1927): p20-21, 68, 83-84.

6831 Hutchinson, Wallace, *Dollar-A-Day Vacation*, 59, 1. (Jul.1927): p36-37, 62-63.

6832 Cosulich, Bernice, *Mr. Wright Builds A Boat*, 59, 2. (Aug.1927): p15, 66-67.

6833 Calvin, Jack, *Vacation With A Dash Of Salt*, 59, 2. (Aug.1927): p30-31, 56-58.

6834 Grey, R. C., *The Conquest Of The Broadbill*, 59, 2. (Aug.1927): p32-34, 58.

6835 McCann, Leo P., *Ride'Em Cowboy*, 59, 3. (Sep.1927): p18-20, 62.

6836 Stubblefield, Blaine, *If You Had To Fly*, 59, 4. (Oct.1927): p14-15, 87-89.

6837 Dye, Homer, Jr., *They Ride'Em At The 4W*, 59, 5. (Nov.1927): p32-33.

6838 Guise, Merle Howard, *Stranglin' Cats*, 60, 3. (Mar.1928): p32-35, 78.

6839 Raine, William MacLeod, *The Dude Rides Circle*, 60, 4. (Apr.1928): p16-17, 56-60.

7. The Outdoors

6840 Northey, Neil Wayne, *That Indispensable Throw-Rope*, 60, 4. (Apr.1928): p25, 62.

6841 Sibley, Hi, *The Man Behind The Magic*, 60, 4. (Apr.1928): p30-31.

6842 Skinner, C. Kay, *A Life-Saving Mountain Memorial*, 60, 5. (May.1928): p33, 54.

6843 Lash, G. H., *Trail Riding–It's Ups And Downs*, 60, 6. (Jun.1928): p38-40.

6844 Porter, Rebecca N., *Say It With Tents*, 61, 1. (Jul.1928): p38-39, 64-67.

6845 Long, John D., *Pack Up Your Troubles*, 61, 2. (Aug.1928): p9-11, 56-58.

6846 Willard, Walter, *In Person!*, 61, 2. (Aug.1928): p12-15, 64-68.

6847 Von Tempski, Armine, *We Run A Dude-Ranch–In Hawaii!*, 61, 3. (Sep.1928): p20-23.

6848 Sibley, Hi, *Marionettes*, 61, 5. (Nov.1928): p28-29, 56.

6849 Ayre, Robert, *The Sierras Go Over The Top*, 61, 6. (Dec.1928): p22-23, 46.

6850 Hughes, James Perley, *A City For Children*, 62, 1. (Jan.1929): p14-16, 47.

6851 Powell, Tod, *At Home In The Open*, 62, 2. (Feb.1929): p11-13.

6852 O'Hara, Gerald J., *Good News For Golfers*, 62, 3. (Mar.1929): p11-13.

6853 Thompson, Jim, *Camping Out With the Fellows*, 62, 4. (Apr.1929): p49-50.

6854 Powell, Tod, *What To Do For Fishin' Fever*, 62, 5. (May.1929): p17-18.

6855 Powell, Tod, *The Blue Water Is Calling*, 62, 6. (Jun.1929): p14-15.

6856 Powell, Tod, *The Knights Of The Diamond Hitch*, 63, 1. (Jul.1929): p11-13.

6857 Taylor, Frank J., *Beyond The Trail's End*, 63, 2. (Aug.1929): p10-13.

6858 Brewer, Wheaton H., *Where Rainbow Trout Have "It"*, 63, 2. (Aug.1929): p28-29.

6859 Powell, Tod, *Greet The Feathered Throng*, 63, 5. (Nov.1929): p17-19.

6860 Hiestand, O. O., *My Haywire Apartments*, 64, 3. (Mar.1930): p9-11.

6861 Ish, Roy V., *Now You Tell One!*, 64, 4. (Apr.1930): p18.

6862 Hawkins, Florence, *Landing A Job With Fish Flies*, 64, 5. (May.1930): p14.

6863 Kreider, Claude M., *Take A Pack Train To Paradise*, 65, 1. (Jul.1930): p7-10.

6864 Ferree, J. E., *Now You Tell One!*, 65, 1. (Jul.1930): p21.

6865 Powell, Tod, *You And Your Camera*, 65, 2. (Aug.1930): p7-10.

6866 Toevs, Mary Lois, *A Dog's Finishing School*, 65, 2. (Aug.1930): p34-35, 47.

6867 Powell, Tod, *From Marsh To Platter*, 65, 5. (Nov.1930): p18-19.

6868 Powell, Tod, *Holiday Fun In The Mountains*, 65, 6. (Dec.1930): p15-18.

6869 Bemus, Frank, *Now You Tell One!*, 66, 1. (Jan.1931): p22.

6870 Hansen, Alice D., *And So I Went Deer Hunting*, 66, 2. (Feb.1931): p10-13.

6871 Cuenin, J. P., *For the Amateur Fisherman*, 66, 5. (May.1931): p20-21.

6872 Cuenin, J. P., *Steelhead Are Running In Western Rivers*, 67, 2. (Aug.1931): p22-23.

6873 Sullivan, J. Stephen, *It's Fun To Hunt Fossils*, 68, 1. (Jan.1932): p13-15.

6874 Dumont, Henry, *Five Perfect Days*, 68, 1. (Jan.1932): p21.

6875 Cuenin, J. P., *Outdoor Life In The West*, 68, 4. (Apr.1932): p21.

6876 Taylor, Frank J., *All Roads Lead To The Olympics*, 69, 1. (Jul.1932): p6-7.

6877 Cuenin, J. P., *Outdoor Life In The West*, 69, 1. (Jul.1932): p10.

6878 Corwin, Doris, *And So We Went Duck Hunting*, 69, 4. (Oct.1932): p19-20.

6879 Cuenin, J. P., *Winter Care Of Fishing Tackle*, 69, 1. (Jan.1933): p8.

6880 Cuenin, J. P., *How to Select Fishing Tackle*, 70, 4. (Apr.1933): p20.

6881 Cuenin, J. P., *Early Season Trout Fishing*, 70, 5. (May.1933): p21, 33.

6882 Cuenin, J. P., *Black Bass Fishing*, 70, 6. (Jun.1933): p24.

6883 Cuenin, J. P., *Mid-Season Trout Fishing*, 71, 2. (Aug.1933): p20.

6884 Philbrook, Leonora, *Camping In The Sierra National Forest*, 72, 2. (Feb.1934): p21-22.

6885 Ide, Leta Foster, *Camping With a Little Fresh Heir*, 72, 5. (May.1934): p24, 38-40.

6886 Kemper, Lucrecia, *Plan The Children's Vacation*, 72, 6. (Jun.1934): p12-13, 49.

6887 Moss, Doris Hudson, *Ye Who Enter Here Leave All Boiled Shirts Behind*, 73, 1. (Jul.1934): p9-11.

6888 Minton, Ruth, *Knapsacking Over The Muir Trail*, 74, 2. (Feb.1935): p20.

6889 Larsh, Elisabeth, *Try These On Your Mountain Boots*, 74, 6. (Jun.1935): p11-13, 56-57.

6890 Cowie, Alice, *They Laughed When We Started Up Mt. Whitney*, 75, 2. (Aug.1935): p16.

6891 Iversen, Helga, *Fish Are Biting–Let's Make Camp!*, 75, 2. (Aug.1935): p19-20.

6892 Holt, Madora, *Help Yourself To The World*, 75, 6. (Dec.1935): p12.

6893 Hall, Wilbur, *Francis Farquhar Collects Mountain Peaks*, 76, 1. (Jan.1936): p7-8.

6894 *Home Work-Shopping*, 76, 6. (Jun.1936): p31-33.

6895 *Pack Trips & Hike Trails*, 77, 1. (Jul.1936): p29-30.

6896 *Christmas Gifts From Western Shops*, 77, 6. (Dec.1936): p16-17.

6897 *What's New In Western Living*, 78, 7. (Jul.1937): p15-17.

6898 *Mountain Moments*, 79, 2. (Aug.1937): p20-21.

6899 *Garden Games*, 80, 2. (Feb.1938): p16-17.

6900 *What's New In Western Living*, 80, 6. (Jun.1938): p15-17.

6901 *What's New In Western Living*, 80, 1. (Jul.1938): p13-15.

6902 *Hobby Horses*, 81, 6. (Dec.1938): p22-23.

6903 *What's New In Western Living*, 82, 6. (Jun.1939): p21-23.

6904 *What's New In Western Living*, 83, 6. (Dec.1939): p7-9.

6905 *White Sun*, 85, 6. (Dec.1940): p4-8.

6906 *Marlin*, 85, 6. (Dec.1940): p12.

6907 *The West Rides Again*, 86, 5. (May.1941): p4.

6908 *Ranches West*, 86, 5. (May.1941): p6-8.

6909 *Why Camp The Hard Way?*, 86, 6. (Jun.1941): p28-29, 38-41.

6910 *Flashing Silver*, 87, 2. (Aug.1941): p14-15.

6911 *How And What To Read In Bed*, 87, 6. (Dec.1941): p18-19.

6912 *Rainbow Trail*, 88, 6. (Jun.1942): p14-15.

6913 *Backyard Summer Resorts*, 89, 1. (Jul.1942): p12-13.

6914 *Build Your Own Games*, 89, 2. (Aug.1942): p16.

6915 *Fly Tying*, 89, 5. (Nov.1942): p50.

6916 *Fly Tying*, 91, 1. (Jul.1943): p42-43.

6917 *Pacific Crest Trail*, 93, 1. (Jul.1944): p2-8.

6918 *Snow Camp*, 96, 2. (Feb.1946): p6-7.

6919 *Fish In Your Own Back Yard?*, 96, 4. (Apr.1946): p22-23.

6920 *For Picnics...*, 96, 5. (May.1946): p48-49.

6921 *Tips For Outdoor Living*, 96, 6. (Jun.1946): p10-11.

6922 *The Trinity Country*, 96, 6. (Jun.1946): p12-16.

6923 *The McKenzie Of Oregon*, 97, 1. (Jul.1946): p18-19.

6924 *Winter's Wonderland*, 97, 6. (Dec.1946): p6-10.

6925 *Sierra Pack Trip*, 98, 4. (Apr.1947): p19-23.

6926 *Mountain Heart Of Idaho*, 99, 3. (Sep.1947): p12-15.

6927 *Along The Deep Blue Western Edge*, 100, 2. (Feb.1948): p20-23.

7. The Outdoors

6928 *Down The White Waters Of The West*, 100, 3. (Mar.1948): p19-23.

6929 *At The Edge Of The Snow*, 100, 5. (May.1948): p19-21.

6930 *Base Camp Building*, 100, 5. (May.1948): p56-61.

6931 *Fishermen Rediscover Humboldt Bay*, 100, 6. (Jun.1948): p16-19.

6932 *Mountain Camping...By Easy Stages*, 101, 1. (Jul.1948): p8-11.

6933 *Beginner's Trout Outfit*, 101, 1. (Jul.1948): p16-19.

6934 *Mt. Adams Recreation Area*, 101, 2. (Aug.1948): p10-13.

6935 *A Gold Country For Sportsmen*, 101, 3. (Sep.1948): p24-29.

6936 *Steelhead Fly Tackle*, 101, 4. (Oct.1948): p20-21.

6937 *To Fisherman's Wives*, 101, 5. (Nov.1948): p20-23.

6938 *Western Skiing*, 102, 1. (Jan.1949): p10-12, 13.

6939 *Fishing In The Desert*, 102, 2. (Feb.1949): p14-16.

6940 *Charter A Yacht–*, 102, 5. (May.1949): p14-15.

6941 *Northwest Passages For Charter Boat Sailors*, 102, 6. (Jun.1949): p10-12.

6942 *Climb The Rogue River Riffles By Mail Boat*, 102, 6. (Jun.1949): p18-21.

6943 *How To Use The Weather For Greater Comfort In Camp*, 103, 1. (Jul.1949): p30-32.

6944 *Don't Forget List For Campers*, 103, 2. (Aug.1949): p46-51.

6945 *White Mountains*, 103, 3. (Sep.1949): p8-13.

6946 *See The Pacific The Fishermen Know*, 103, 3. (Sep.1949): p24-29.

6947 *Family Trips To The Snow*, 103, 6. (Dec.1949): p6-11.

6948 *Camping Can Be Comfortable*, 104, 6. (Jun.1950): p29-33.

6949 *Weekend For Golden Trout*, 105, 1. (Jul.1950): p14-19.

6950 *Boat Trip For A Summer Evening*, 105, 3. (Sep.1950): p12-16.

6951 *Winter Fishing*, 106, 2. (Feb.1951): p10-11.

6952 *The Friendly Wilderness Of The Northern Cascades*, 106, 5. (May.1951): p25-33.

6953 *Cascade Crest Trail...*, 106, 5. (May.1951): p34-39.

6954 *Swimming In The Surf*, 106, 6. (Jun.1951): p19-20.

6955 *Camping...In Solid Comfort*, 106, 6. (Jun.1951): p25-28.

6956 *Comfort On The Beach*, 106, 6. (Jun.1951): p44-46.

6957 *Checklist Of Southern California Beaches*, 107, 2. (Aug.1951): p25-27.

6958 *A Unique Beach World*, 107, 2. (Aug.1951): p31-35.

6959 *Fishing The Cattails Of The Colorado*, 107, 6. (Dec.1951): p16-20.

6960 *Fishing with a Tire Iron*, 108, 04. (Apr.1952): p22-23.

6961 *Up The McKenzie...Into Oregon's Cascades*, 108, 5. (May.1952): p42-47.

6962 *Cow Country Rodeos*, 109, 1. (Jul.1952): p22-24.

6963 *When You Take Your Family To The Snow*, 110, 2. (Feb.1953): p22-27.

6964 *Grand Coulee Country*, 110, 3. (Mar.1953): p38-45.

6965 *Western Camper's Planning Guide*, 110, 5. (May.1953): p48-55.

6966 *High Sierra*, 110, 6. (Jun.1953): p50-57.

6967 *Climbing, Building, Splashing, Swinging*, 111, 1. (Jul.1953): p40-43.

6968 *The Fun...And The Problems...Of Owning Your Own Horse*, 111, 4. (Oct.1953): p64-67.

6969 *The "Passive Wisdom" Of The Western Burro*, 111, 6. (Dec.1953): p154-156.

6970 *Desert Camping...*, 112, 2. (Feb.1954): p26-29.

6971 *Fishing At Noyo Harbor*, 112, 3. (Mar.1954): p37-38.

6972 *Water Exploring The West...*, 112, 3. (Mar.1954): p48-53.

6973 *The Yolla Bolly Wilderness*, 112, 5. (May.1954): p37-40.

6974 *For Two Weeks...How To Really 'Get Away From It All'*, 112, 5. (May.1954): p52-59.

6975 *For High Adventure...The Undiscovered Mount Rainier*, 112, 6. (Jun.1954): p50-57.

6976 *He-Devil, She-Devil, And All The Little Devils*, 113, 2. (Aug.1954): p30-33.

6977 *It's Time To Go Clam Hunting*, 113, 4. (Oct.1954): p68-72.

6978 *Here Are Record Cutthroat*, 113, 5. (Nov.1954): p19-20.

6979 *For Families Who Like Comfort...And Like To Keep Moving*, 113, 5. (Nov.1954): p24-32.

6980 *Let's Pick Up The Family...And Head For Snow*, 114, 1. (Jan.1955): p22-27.

6981 *Camping In The Snow*, 114, 2. (Feb.1955): p19-24.

6982 *March Is The Month To Fish The Cool Waters Of Lake Mojave*, 114, 3. (Mar.1955): p20-26.

6983 *Rodeo: The West's Own Wild And Wonderful Spectator Sport*, 114, 5. (May.1955): p60-62.

6984 *Why So Many Westerners Like...The Dude Ranch Idea...*, 115, 1. (Jul.1955): p38-43.

6985 *A Volcanic Wonderland Of Black Glass Cliffs, Explosion Pits, Featherweight Boulders*, 115, 2. (Aug.1955): p16-20.

6986 *Combing The Beaches On Puget Sound*, 115, 2. (Aug.1955): p40-41.

6987 *Bird 'Shooting'...In Your Garden*, 116, 3. (Mar.1956): p33, 35, 36.

6988 *Family Sailing In The West*, 116, 3. (Mar.1956): p52-59.

6989 *Family Adventure...The River Run*, 116, 4. (Apr.1956): p56-63.

6990 *Fishing And Hunting At Homer*, 116, 5. (May.1956): p22, 24.

6991 *Deep Under The Siskiyous*, 116, 5. (May.1956): p27, 29, 30.

6992 *In The Far Northwest Corner Of Washington State...You'll Find The Driftwood Coast*, 116, 5. (May.1956): p60-63.

6993 *Ever Watch A Sea Otter?*, 116, 6. (Jun.1956): p42, 44, 46.

6994 *What Will Tempt A Western Trout?*, 116, 6. (Jun.1956): p70-72.

6995 *The Steelhead Are Coming*, 117, 5. (Nov.1956): p42, 45-46.

6996 *Come and Cut Your Own Christmas Tree*, 117, 6. (Dec.1956): p52-54.

6997 *Water Holiday...On Your Own Outboard Cruiser*, 118, 4. (Apr.1957): p49-55.

6998 *Here's A Tent That Rides "Piggy-Back" On Top Of Your Car*, 119, 1. (Jul.1957): p52-56, 59.

6999 *Have You Ever Tried Water Skis?*, 119, 1. (Jul.1957): p16, 18, 21, 22, 24.

7000 *Have You Tried Field Archery?*, 119, 4. (Oct.1957): p62-63.

7001 *How To Fiber-Glass Your Boat Hull*, 119, 4. (Oct.1957): p19-21.

7002 *How To Choose Binoculars*, 120, 2. (Feb.1958): p38, 40, 42.

7003 *Rockhounding*, 120, 3. (Mar.1958): p64-69.

7004 *Western Sailors Start Young*, 121, 2. (Aug.1958): p22-24, 26.

7005 *A Walk In California's Hills...On A Sunny Day In March*, 122, 3. (Mar.1959): p80-81.

7006 *Private Flying In The West*, 122, 4. (Apr.1959): p82-87.

7007 *Camping With A Small Foreign Car*, 122, 5. (May.1959): p45, 46, 48.

7008 *If The Burro Doesn't Have A Good Time, You Won't Either*, 126, 4. (Apr.1961): p78-83.

7009 *Which Backpack Is Right For You*, 126, 5. (May.1961): p50, 53, 54, 56.

7010 *How To Behave Around Bears*, 127, 1. (Jul.1961): p50-55.

7. The Outdoors

7. The Outdoors

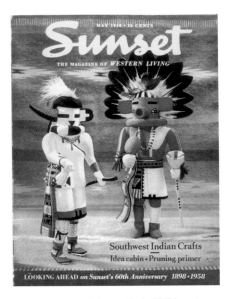

May 1958 cover (photo: Clyde Childress)

People

Granted Sunset*'s emphasis on home, garden, food and travel, it has always included articles that discuss individuals and groups of people. Whereas Biography was a frequent topic only in the early years, awareness and issues of Ethnicity & Nationality, particularly of Native Americans, have been continuing themes–themes which have, at times, painfully reflected regional concerns over difficult issues of immigration, assimilation and race. And while* Sunset *strove not to be identified as a "women's magazine," there are numerous articles that are specifically about or addressed to Women and their particular interests and needs, as perceived at the time of publication. We may today find the identification and treatment of some of these interests and needs stereotypical or even offensive, but they reflect their times–and if we look a bit closer, we may find on balance that* Sunset*'s treatment of household duties, time management and gender roles are often precursors of what we would recognize as modern, more liberated, attitudes. Certainly the magazine's appeal to its mixed readership has always countered the division of interests by gender.*

Additional coverage of issues related to women, most notably women's suffrage, may be found under Politics & Government.

8. People

8.1 Biography

7212 *Collis Potter Huntington*, 5, 4. (Aug.1900): p196-199.

7213 Aiken, Charles Sedgwick, *Dr. Joseph LeConte - A Tribute*, 7, 2-3. (Jun.1901): p82.

7214 Wickson, Edward J., *Luther Burbank: The Man, His Methods, And His Achievements*, 8, 2. (Dec.1901): p56-68.

7215 Wickson, Edward J., *Luther Burbank: Man, Methods And Achievements*, 8, 4. (Feb.1902): p145-156.

7216 Wickson, Edward J., *Luther Burbank: Man, Methods, And Achievements*, 8, 6. (Apr.1902): p277-285.

7217 Wickson, Edward J., *Luther Burbank: Man, Methods, And Achievements*, 9, 2. (Jun.1902): p101-112.

7218 Vore, Elizabeth, *Famous California Women*, 9, 2. (Jun.1902): p136-138.

7219 Longhead, Flora Haines, *Ina Coolbrith*, 9, 3. (Jul.1902): p217-219.

7220 Cahill, Edward F., *Harte's Protest Against 'Respectability'*, 9, 4. (Aug.1902): p222-224.

7221 Aiken, Charles Sedgwick, *Harte's Tribute To Dickens*, 9, 4. (Aug.1902): p225-230.

7222 Morrow, W. C., *An Estimate Of Bret Harte*, 9, 4. (Aug.1902): p230-232.

7223 Drury, Wells, *The Problem John Mackay Solved*, 10, 4. (Feb.1903): p264-269.

7224 Davis, Sam, *The Governor Of Nevada*, 11, 1. (May.1903): p19-20.

7225 Ackerman, Carl E., *President Roosevelt In California*, 11, 2. (Jun.1903): p103-113.

7226 Ackerman, Carl E., *President Roosevelt In The High Sierra*, 11, 3. (Jul.1903): p205-212.

7227 Hofmeyr, Adrian, *Cecil Rhodes - The Man*, 11, 6. (Oct.1903): p569-573.

7228 Yerington, J. A., *Stories Of Hank Monk*, 12, 1. (Nov.1903): p24-28.

7229 Hus, H. T. A., *The Work Of Hugo De Vries*, 13, 1. (May.1904): p39-42.

7230 Tompkins, Eufina C., *Story Of Two California Artists*, 13, 2. (Jun.1904): p131-136.

7231 Griswold, Mary Edith, *In Memory Of Le Conte*, 13, 4. (Aug.1904): p314-315.

7232 Waterhouse, Alfred J., *California In The Cabinet: Stories And Facts Concerning Secretary Metcalf, Of The Department Of Commerce And Labor*, 13, 4. (Aug.1904): p294-300.

7233 Stovall, Dennis H., *A Woman Placer Piper*, 13, 5. (Sep.1904): p434-435.

7234 Jordan, David Starr, *Jane Lathrop Stanford*, 14, 6. (Apr.1905): p632-633.

7235 Wickson, Edward J., *The Real Luther Burbank*, 15, 1. (May.1905): p3-15.

7236 Chandler, Katherine, *Sacajawea*, 15, 2. (Jun.1905): p135-137.

7237 Stephens, H. Morse, *The Oregon Expedition's Historian*, 15, 3. (Jul.1905): p224-228.

7238 Emerson, Edwin, *When West Met East*, 15, 6. (Oct.1905): p515-530.

7239 Buckham, John Wright, *Frederick Billings*, 16, 5. (Mar.1906): p487-491.

7240 Spearman, Frank H., *The Strategy Of George McCloud*, 17, 4. (Aug.1906): p174-177.

7241 Canfield, Chauncey L., *In Bret-Harte Land*, 19, 1. (May.1907): p77-91.

7242 Hervey, John L., *Joseph Cairn Simpson - A Tribute*, 20, 2. (Dec.1907): p164-167.

7243 Wickson, Edward J., *Luther Burbank And His New Environment*, 21, 2. (Jun.1908): p151-162.

7244 Smith, Bertha H., *Where Fighting Bob Evans Won His Latest Victory*, 21, 5. (Sep.1908): p410-420.

7245 Pratt, Samuel W., *The Making Of Whitman*, 23, 2. (Aug.1909): p185-188.

7246 Smith, Donald E., *Don Gaspar De Portol·*, 23, 4. (Oct.1909): p337-351.

7247 Noguchi, Yone, *Prince Ito At Oiso*, 24, 2. (Feb.1910): p123-127.

7248 Williams, Michael, *Horace Fletcher's Philosophy*, 24, 3. (Mar.1910): p284-290.

7249 Whitaker, Herman, *Diaz, Maker Of Mexico*, 24, 5. (May.1910): p480-494.

7250 Hyde, Henry M., *The Great Cartwright Grubstake*, 25, 1. (Jul.1910): p11-14.

7251 MacPherson, Robert, *A Captain Of The Oil Industry*, 25, 2. (Aug.1910): p244.

7252 Simpson, William, *Fremont And The Bear Flag*, 25, 3. (Sep.1910): p283-292.

7253 Whyte, W. Farmer, *More Tales Of Tusitala*, 25, 5. (Nov.1910): p497-507.

7254 Shoup, Paul, *In Memoriam–Charles Sedgwick Aiken*, 26, 2. (Feb.1911): p173-175.

7255 Michael, M. F., *Thomas Bard McFarland*, 26, 2. (Feb.1911): p201-204.

7256 Smith, Bertha H., *What Women Are Doing In The West*, 26, 3. (Mar.1911): p316-324.

7257 Smith, Bertha H., *What Women Are Doing In The West*, 26, 4. (Apr.1911): p407-415.

7258 Groff, Frances A., *The Emperor Of Imperial Valley*, 26, 5. (May.1911): p527-531.

7259 Groff, Frances A., *Paloma And Karla Schramm*, 26, 5. (May.1911): p531-533.

7260 Groff, Frances A., *A Pioneer Palette*, 26, 5. (May.1911): p533-536.

7261 Groff, Frances A., *The Encyclopedia Of Kern County*, 26, 6. (Jun.1911): p633-635.

7262 Dole, Arthur MacDonald, *A Man's Campaign For A Campus*, 26, 6. (Jun.1911): p635-636.

7263 Groff, Frances A., *A Militant Editor-General*, 26, 6. (Jun.1911): p637-639.

7264 Smith, Bertha H., *What Women Are Doing In The West*, 26, 6. (Jun.1911): p640-647.

7265 Groff, Frances A., *A Priest Of The People*, 27, 1. (Jul.1911): p58-60.

7266 Hand, Pitt P., *Physician To The World*, 27, 1. (Jul.1911): p60-62.

7267 Smith, Bertha H., *Elise P. Buckingham*, 27, 1. (Jul.1911): p44-52.

7268 Smith, Bertha H., *Emma A. Summers*, 27, 1. (Jul.1911): p49-52.

7269 Douglas, Clara E., *The Father Of Tonopah*, 27, 2. (Aug.1911): p165-167.

7270 Groff, Frances A., *The Sage Of Hood's Canal*, 27, 2. (Aug.1911): p170-172.

7271 McGuiness, J. Holmes, *The Other Side Of E. H. Harriman*, 27, 2. (Aug.1911): p196-198.

7272 Groff, Frances A., *A Woman Pathfinder*, 27, 2. (Aug.1911): p162-165.

7273 Groff, Frances A., *The Mother Of Clubs*, 27, 2. (Aug.1911): p167-170.

7274 Groff, Frances A., *A Sixteen-Million-Dollar Timber Cruiser*, 27, 3. (Sep.1911): p301-304.

7275 Maclay, Mira, *A Troubadour Tourist*, 27, 3. (Sep.1911): p306-308.

7276 Greening, Clara M., *Policewoman Number One*, 27, 3. (Sep.1911): p304-306.

7277 London, Jack, *Navigating Four Horses North of the Bay*, 27, 3. (Sep.1911): p233-246.

7278 Fletcher, Montelle R., *An Eveless Eden*, 27, 4. (Oct.1911): p419-424.

7279 Groff, Frances A., *"Stonewall" Boschke*, 27, 4. (Oct.1911): p407-410.

7280 Groff, Frances A., *Unanimous Melvin*, 27, 4. (Oct.1911): p410-413.

7281 Coolidge, Herbert, *An Educator In Politics*, 27, 4. (Oct.1911): p413-415.

7282 Groff, Frances A., *A Mistress Of Mechanigraphics*, 27, 4. (Oct.1911): p415-418.

7283 Stern, Samuel S., *A Sphinx Of The Northwest*, 27, 5. (Nov.1911): p544-546.

7284 Groff, Frances A., *A Pedigreed Reformer*, 27, 5. (Nov.1911): p547-549.

8. People

8. People

7363 De Witt, L. Harry, *A Brace Of Champions*, 31, 6. (Dec.1913): p1217-1219.

7364 Sabin, Edwin L., *An Aviator On Earth*, 31, 6. (Dec.1913): p1219-1221.

7365 Bland, Henry Meade, *The Padre Of The Rains*, 32, 1. (Jan.1914): p170-172.

7366 Botts, Ebert, *A Queen Without A Queendom*, 32, 1. (Jan.1914): p167-170.

7367 Hess, Pauline, *A Youthful And Useful Octogenerian*, 32, 2. (Feb.1914): p398-400.

7368 Underwood, John J., *A Man Of Quiet Force*, 32, 2. (Feb.1914): p402-405.

7369 Barnhill, O. H., *Oregon's Account With Banker Beckman*, 32, 3. (Mar.1914): p632-634.

7370 Greening, Clara M., *A Famous Model*, 32, 3. (Mar.1914): p636-638.

7371 Smith, Bertha H., *A Perpetual Leading Lady*, 32, 3. (Mar.1914): p634-636.

7372 Doyle, Grace, *An Economist Of Time*, 32, 4. (Apr.1914): p864-866.

7373 Hess, Pauline, *A Patriot In Two Wars*, 32, 4. (Apr.1914): p866-868.

7374 Ross, William Edward, *Maker Of Good Roads By Better Men*, 32, 4. (Apr.1914): p868-870.

7375 Dunn, Arthur, *An Interested Westerner*, 32, 5. (May.1914): p1095-1097.

7376 R. S., *A Horseless Horseman*, 32, 5. (May.1914): p1097-1101.

7377 Doyle, Grace, *The Lady With The Eagle Eye*, 32, 5. (May.1914): p1101-1102.

7378 Flint, Edward P., *My Recollections Of Vigilante Days*, 32, 6. (Jun.1914): p1219-1227.

7379 Carson, Todd, *The Birdman Who Mastered The Tehachapi*, 32, 6. (Jun.1914): p1325-1327.

7380 French, Harold, *The Builder Of California's Navy*, 32, 6. (Jun.1914): p1321-1323.

7381 Smith, Bertha H., *A Nervy Movie Lady*, 32, 6. (Jun.1914): p1323-1325.

7382 Barnhill, O. H., *The Man Who Put Oregon On The Map*, 33, 7. (Jul.1914): p116-118.

7383 Anderson, Buell D., *A California Conservationist*, 33, 1. (Jul.1914): p118-120.

7384 James, Rita Bell, *The General Of A Bug Army*, 33, 1. (Jul.1914): p122-124.

7385 Greening, Clara M., *A Daughter Of The Dons*, 33, 1. (Jul.1914): p120-122.

7386 Bland, Henry Meade, *John Barleycorn At The Plow*, 33, 2. (Aug.1914): p347-349.

7387 Smith, F. Gordon, *An Empire-Builder In Canada*, 33, 2. (Aug.1914): p353-354.

7388 French, Harold, *The Psalmist Of The Sierra*, 33, 2. (Aug.1914): p355-357.

7389 Bethell, Laura, *A Guardian At The Gate*, 33, 2. (Aug.1914): p349-353.

7390 Aiken, Ednah, *Two California Songbirds In Europe*, 33, 3. (Sep.1914): p531-536.

7391 Curtis, Edwin Emmet, *A Practical Idealist*, 33, 3. (Sep.1914): p558-560.

7392 Jackson, H. C., *The Gentleman From Alaska*, 33, 3. (Sep.1914): p564-568.

7393 Dunn, Arthur, *The Man They Swear By*, 33, 3. (Sep.1914): p568-572.

7394 Smith, Bertha H., *A Lady Garage Man*, 33, 3. (Sep.1914): p560-564.

7395 Barnhill, O. H., *A Lumberjack And His Millions*, 33, 4. (Oct.1914): p753-755.

7396 Jeffreys, Alfred, *Nemesis And The Bad Angels*, 33, 4. (Oct.1914): p757-760.

7397 W. V. W., *The Farm Woman's Moses*, 33, 4. (Oct.1914): p755-757.

7398 Parker, Sir Gilbert, *The War Maker*, 33, 5. (Nov.1914): p869-875.

7399 Scott, Riley E., *The Enemy Of The Smoke Nuisance*, 33, 5. (Nov.1914): p976-978.

7400 White, Lucy G., *An Educator Of Parents*, 33, 5. (Nov.1914): p978-981.

7401 Steele, Rufus M., *A Giant Sitting Down*, 33, 6. (Dec.1914): p1184-1186.

7402 Hurja, Emil E., *A Pessimist On The Gridiron*, 33, 6. (Dec.1914): p1186-1188.

7403 Dreier, Thomas, *The Hostess Of The Inn*, 33, 6. (Dec.1914): p1188-1190.

7404 Taylor, Marian, *A Poet-Laureate Hostess*, 34, 1. (Jan.1915): p135-138.

7405 Jordan, David Starr, *The Americans of the Hour in Europe*, 34, 6. (Jun.1915): p1175-1179.

7406 Groff, Frances A., *The Senator From California*, 35, 1. (Jul.1915): p156-159.

7407 French, Harold, *Driver Of A 58-In-Hand*, 35, 1. (Jul.1915): p159-161.

7408 Newell, Bernice E., *A Paver To Success*, 35, 1. (Jul.1915): p161-164.

7409 Whitney, O. F., *The Mormon President*, 35, 2. (Aug.1915): p356-358.

7410 Prosser, W. T., *A Crusader Against The National Ash Heap*, 35, 2. (Aug.1915): p362.

7411 Greening, Clara M., *The Leader Of The Point Loma Theosophists*, 35, 2. (Aug.1915): p360.

7412 Peterson, H. C., *Vioget, First Painter And Prophet Of San Francisco*, 35, 3. (Sep.1915): p523-524.

7413 Groff, Frances A., *Thomas Burke*, 35, 3. (Sep.1915): p546.

7414 Dickie, F. J., *J. K. Cornwall*, 35, 3. (Sep.1915): p550.

7415 Dunn, Arthur, *Charles Collins Teague*, 35, 3. (Sep.1915): p554.

7416 M. B. R., *Zelia Nuttall*, 35, 3. (Sep.1915): p544.

7417 Orr, Gertrude, *D. M. Rolph*, 35, 3. (Sep.1915): p548.

7418 Hoard, Dean, *Edith McCarl Hickey*, 35, 3. (Sep.1915): p552.

7419 Bede, Elbert, *Opal Whiteley*, 35, 3. (Sep.1915): p556.

7420 Grimes, O. J., *Interesting Westerners [John M. Browning]*, 35, 5. (Nov.1915): p960.

7421 Stellman, Louis J., *Interesting Westerners [Bernard R. Maybeck]*, 35, 5. (Nov.1915): p951-952.

7422 Dosch, Arno, *The Mystery Of John Muir's Money*, 36, 2. (Feb.1916): p20-22, 61-64.

7423 Sanchez, Nellie Van De Grift, *Grafting Romance On A Rose-Tree*, 36, 4. (Apr.1916): p40.

7424 Armstrong, Amy, *Homesteading Without A Chaperon*, 36, 6. (Jun.1916): p25-26, 95-97.

7425 Yard, Robert Sterling, *Director Of The Nation's Playgrounds*, 37, 3. (Sep.1916): p27.

7426 Stellmann, Louis J., *Jack London, Super-Boy*, 38, 2. (Feb.1917): p42, 81.

7427 Lane, Rose Wilder, *Life And Jack London*, 39, 4. (Oct.1917): p17-20, 72-73.

7428 Lane, Rose Wilder, *Life And Jack London*, 39, 5. (Nov.1917): p29-32, 64-66.

7429 Lane, Rose Wilder, *Life And Jack London*, 39, 6. (Dec.1917): p21-23, 60-68.

7430 Baily, Robin, *"Notonecta" Ross*, 39, 6. (Dec.1917): p42-43, 72.

7431 Lane, Rose Wilder, *Life And Jack London*, 40, 1. (Jan.1918): p34-37, 62-64.

7432 Lane, Rose Wilder, *Life And Jack London*, 40, 2. (Feb.1918): p30-34, 67-68.

7433 Lane, Rose Wilder, *Life And Jack London*, 40, 3. (Mar.1918): p27-30, 64-66.

7434 Roe, Vingie E., *Vingie E. Roe*, 40, 3. (Mar.1918): p21.

7435 Lane, Rose Wilder, *How I Became A Great Actress*, 40, 4. (Apr.1918): p35-38.

7436 Lane, Rose Wilder, *Life And Jack London*, 40, 4. (Apr.1918): p21-25, 60-62.

7437 Lane, Rose Wilder, *Life And Jack London*, 40, 5. (May.1918): p28-32, 60-72.

8. People

7438 Hall, Wilbur, *Exposing Yourself To Success*, 40, 5. (May.1918): p39-41.

7439 Hall, Wilbur, *How Doheny Did It*, 41, 1. (Jul.1918): p21-23.

7440 Lane, Rose Wilder, *Rose Wilder Lane*, 41, 5. (Nov.1918): p26.

7441 Cooley, Winnifred Harper, *How Bold Is Anne!*, 41, 5. (Nov.1918): p39-40, 73-75.

7442 Lummis, Charles F., *T.R., Westerner*, 42, 4. (Apr.1919): p17-19, 74-82.

7443 Thomas, Horace E., *The Man Who Never Worried*, 42, 6. (Jun.1919): p33-36, 64-68.

7444 Irwin, Will, *Hiram Johnson*, 43, 4. (Oct.1919): p13-14.

7445 Hall, Wilbur, *Leaping The Barrier*, 43, 4. (Oct.1919): p37-38, 76.

7446 Hamby, William H., *Lifted By Loyalty*, 43, 5. (Nov.1919): p45, 66-68.

7447 Woehlke, Walter V., *The Captain Courageous*, 44, 3. (Mar.1920): p38-39, 106-108.

7448 Lane, Rose Wilder and Field, Charles K., *The Making Of Herbert Hoover*, 44, 4. (Apr.1920): p24-28, 121-134.

7449 Filofey, F., *Asia's Man On Horseback*, 44, 4. (Apr.1920): p30-32, 110-112.

7450 Davis, Meredith, *Love, Faith And Life*, 44, 4. (Apr.1920): p62-66.

7451 Lane, Rose Wilder, *The Making Of Herbert Hoover*, 44, 5. (May.1920): p23-26, 96-116.

7452 Lane, Rose Wilder, *The Making Of Herbert Hoover*, 44, 6. (Jun.1920): p39-42, 68-70, 89-104.

7453 Thompson, Herbert Cooper, *Mexico's New Strong Man*, 45, 1. (Jul.1920): p23-24.

7454 Lane, Rose Wilder, *The Making Of Herbert Hoover*, 45, 1. (Jul.1920): p43-46, 74-84.

7455 Lane, Rose Wilder, *The Making Of Herbert Hoover*, 45, 2. (Aug.1920): p42-44, 64-65, 72-80.

7456 Lane, Rose Wilder, *The Making Of Herbert Hoover*, 45, 3. (Sep.1920): p40-42, 52-58.

7457 Clark, Badger, *That Was The Life!*, 45, 5. (Nov.1920): p31-32, 62.

7458 Woehlke, Walter V., *Be Sure You're Right, then Stick!*, 45, 6. (Dec.1920): p27, 78-88.

7459 Crowell, Merle, *He Understood Men*, 46, 6. (Jun.1921): p33-35, 60-62.

7460 Prince, Arnold, *Does Bad Luck Pursue You?*, 47, 5. (Nov.1921): p44-45, 65-66.

7461 Peck, Leland W., *Will You Pay The Price*, 47, 6. (Dec.1921): p30-31,64-65.

7462 FitzGerald, Harold J., *The Man Who Could Not Be Scared*, 48, 3. (Mar.1922): p34-35, 48.

7463 Jacobson, Pauline, *The Whip Of Discontent*, 48, 4. (Apr.1922): p29-30, 56-58.

7464 Wilson, Paul N., *Is Your Salary High Enough?*, 48, 5. (May.1922): p23-25, 56.

7465 Mulroy, Martin, *Fame And Fortune In Six Months*, 48, 5. (May.1922): p38-39.

7466 Matteson, Herman Howard, *How Much Of A Coward Are You?*, 48, 6. (Jun.1922): p36-39.

7467 Jones, Robert E., *Is Marriage A Handicap?*, 49, 1. (Jul.1922): p15, 68.

7468 Freeman, Lewis R., *Calamity Jane And Yankee Jim*, 49, 1. (Jul.1922): p22-25, 52-54.

7469 Wilson, Paul N., *Does Your Job Fit You?*, 49, 2. (Aug.1922): p28-29, 56.

7470 Wilson, Paul N., *Tackle Today's Problems Now*, 49, 4. (Oct.1922): p22-23, 52-54.

7471 Ritchie, Robert Welles, *Making Friends For America*, 49, 6. (Dec.1922): p22-23, 78-80.

7472 Small, Sidney Herschel, *Graduated Into Romance*, 49, 6. (Dec.1922): p34, 90-91.

7473 Hall, Wilbur, *Cheating Chance*, 50, 1. (Jan.1923): p16-19.

7474 Lindsey, Ben B., *The Passing Of Enos Mills*, 50, 1. (Jan.1923): p44.

7475 Hall, Wilbur, *Cheating Chance*, 50, 2. (Feb.1923): p16-18, 64.

7476 Hall, Wilbur, *Cheating Chance*, 50, 3. (Mar.1923): p21-23.

7477 Bemis, Samuel Flagg, *David Thompson, Explorer*, 50, 3. (Mar.1923): p28-29.

7478 Blythe, Samuel G., *On Becoming Western*, 50, 6. (Jun.1923): p23, 112-113.

7479 *Mirrors Of Hollywood*, 51, 1. (Jul.1923): p29, 77-78.

7480 Eddy, Elford, *Has Your Job A Future?*, 51, 1. (Jul.1923): p40, 81-82.

7481 *Mirrors Of Hollywood*, 51, 2. (Aug.1923): p15, 58.

7482 Willard, Victor, *Making Good After Fifty*, 51, 2. (Aug.1923): p39, 90-91.

7483 Hall, Wilbur, *See Mrs. Pierce!*, 51, 5. (Nov.1923): p24-25, 77-79.

7484 Jopp, Fred Gilman, *The Laughing Gas Station*, 51, 6. (Dec.1923): p28-29, 56.

7485 Rossiter, Harriet, *What Will You Do At Seventy-Six?*, 52, 4. (Apr.1924): p32-34, 78-81.

7486 Bechdolt, Frederick R., *"For To Admire And For To See"*, 53, 4. (Oct.1924): p41-42.

7487 Carr, Donald, *Making The Golden Rule Pay*, 53, 4. (Oct.1924): p44, 76.

7488 Jopp, Fred Gilman, *Photographing The Invisible*, 53, 5. (Nov.1924): p21-22, 62.

7489 Barnes, Will, *Ranger Shinn*, 53, 6. (Dec.1924): p32, 60-62.

7490 Jacobson, Pauline, *He Prospered Through Giving*, 53, 6. (Dec.1924): p52, 56-58.

7491 Ballard, F. L., *Making A Million A Year*, 54, 1. (Jan.1925): p43-44.

7492 Eddy, Elford, *Stick, Dig And Save*, 54, 4. (Apr.1925): p13-14, 84-87.

7493 Loomis, Charles Battell, Jr., *The Work Eater*, 54, 5. (May.1925): p16-17, 78.

7494 Eddy, Elford, *The Carpenter Who Went To Night School*, 54, 6. (Jun.1925): p17, 60-61.

7495 Boone, Andrew R., *Gaze At The Stars–And Grow!*, 55, 1. (Jul.1925): p30-31, 54.

7496 Willard, Victor, *Making $5 Grow To Millions*, 55, 2. (Aug.1925): p30-31, 56.

7497 Scherer, James A. B., *The First Forty-Niner*, 55, 3. (Sep.1925): p14-16, 86-91.

7498 Woehlke, Walter V., *The Champion Borrower Of them All*, 55, 3. (Sep.1925): p17-19, 58.

7499 Woehlke, Walter V., *The Champion Borrower Of them All*, 55, 4. (Oct.1925): p28-31, 62-63, 73-74.

7500 Woehlke, Walter V., *The Champion Borrower Of them All*, 55, 5. (Nov.1925): p23-27, 62, 76.

7501 Woehlke, Walter V., *The Champion Borrower Of them All*, 55, 6. (Dec.1925): p34-37, 100-101.

7502 Willard, Victor, *Bringing The Light To Main Street*, 56, 1. (Jan.1926): p37, 62.

7503 Woehlke, Walter V., *The Champion Borrower Of them All*, 56, 1. (Jan.1926): p45-47, 75.

7504 Woehlke, Walter V., *The Champion Borrower Of them All*, 56, 2. (Feb.1926): p41-43, 73.

7505 Vandeventer, Edward A., *Death Valley Scotty*, 56, 3. (Mar.1926): p22-25, 72-73.

7506 Eddy, Elford, *Forget The Clock*, 56, 4. (Apr.1926): p30.

7507 Peak, Mayme Ober, *From Immigrant Lad To Empire-Builder*, 56, 6. (Jun.1926): p16-18, 62.

7508 Vandeventer, Edward A., *Boring Through The Backbone Of The American Continent*, 56, 6. (Jun.1926): p27-29, 58-60.

7509 Block, Eugene B., *A Man-Sized Job*, 57, 1. (Jul.1926): p24-25, 56-58.

7510 Lampman, Ben Hur, *Who Was Mary Homsley?*, 57, 3. (Sep.1926): p27.

7511 McPherson, Aimee Semple, *Foursquare!*, 58, 2. (Feb.1927): p14-16, 80-82.

7512 Rhodes, Eugene Manlove, *He'll Make A Hand!*, 58, 6. (Jun.1927): p23, 89-91.

8. People

7513 Steele, Rufus M., *Jones Of Zion*, 58, 6. (Jun.1927): p32-33, 76-77.

7514 Cook, C. Clyde, *A Portia Of The West*, 59, 1. (Jul.1927): p43, 63.

7515 Pielkovo, Ruth, *The Making Of An Artist*, 59, 3. (Sep.1927): p39, 54-56.

7516 Rowell, Chester H., *Herbert Hoover: then And Now*, 59, 5. (Nov.1927): p12-13, 84-86.

7517 Brewer, W. A., Jr., *What Manner Of Man Is "Pop" Warner?*, 59, 5. (Nov.1927): p26-28.

7518 Block, Eugene B., *Humanizing Figures*, 59, 6. (Dec.1927): p31, 77-78.

7519 Quest, Mark, *Be Pleasant When You're Angry*, 60, 2. (Feb.1928): p32-33, 77-78.

7520 Bogert, George Dudley, *The Man Who Saved San Francisco*, 60, 5. (May.1928): p38-39, 62.

7521 Kessler, Sidney H., *Mayor Jimmie Rolph–An Institution*, 60, 6. (Jun.1928): p16-18, 54.

7522 Monroe, Anne Shannon, *The World I Saw*, 61, 1. (Jul.1928): p9-13, 68-71, 81.

7523 Monroe, Anne Shannon, *The World I Saw*, 61, 2. (Aug.1928): p16-19, 58-59, 68-70.

7524 Monroe, Anne Shannon, *The World I Saw*, 61, 3. (Sep.1928): p28-31, 69-70.

7525 Monroe, Anne Shannon, *The World I Saw*, 61, 4. (Oct.1928): p30-32, 67-68.

7526 Vivian, C. H., *What Kind Of A Boy Was Doug?*, 61, 4. (Oct.1928): p38-39, 60-62.

7527 Stern, Max, *The Amazing Mr. Marvin*, 61, 5. (Nov.1928): p22-23, 54.

7528 Tarkington, Elizabeth Murray, *The Story Of Sam Platt*, 61, 5. (Nov.1928): p27, 70-72.

7529 Monroe, Anne Shannon, *The World I Saw*, 61, 5. (Nov.1928): p34-36, 58-69.

7530 Kessler, Sidney H., *Belasco Looks Backward*, 61, 6. (Dec.1928): p18-21, 57.

7531 Roth, Charles B., *The Old Maxwell Manor*, 62, 1. (Jan.1929): p28-29, 54.

7532 Vasper, Norman L., *Ernest Bloch, Composer*, 62, 2. (Feb.1929): p35, 67.

7533 Mallon, Walter, *A Poet In A Raccoon Coat*, 62, 3. (Mar.1929): p38, 61.

7534 Johnson, Willard, *A Municipal Mother*, 62, 4. (Apr.1929): p25, 68.

7535 Davis, Marion Lay, *Tall Tells*, 62, 5. (May.1929): p16, 72-73.

7536 Johnson, Willard, *Earl Cummings*, 62, 6. (Jun.1929): p18, 67.

7537 Johnson, Willard, *A Trouper And Wrangler*, 63, 1. (Jul.1929): p19-20.

7538 Smith, Darwin J., *A Diamond Jubilee*, 63, 2. (Aug.1929): p27.

7539 Harris, Mable Arundel, *A Recorder of Pioneer Tales*, 63, 2. (Aug.1929): p14.

7540 Dickson, S. B., *Ambrose Bierce*, 63, 4. (Oct.1929): p15-16.

7541 Dickson, S. B., *James Lick*, 63, 5. (Nov.1929): p20-21.

7542 Hasty, John Eugene, *John Henry Nash, Printer*, 63, 6. (Dec.1929): p26-27, 57.

7543 Jackson, Stewart, *The Star Gazer Of Ukiah*, 65, 2. (Aug.1930): p27-28.

7544 Howard, Paul, *Captain Dobbsie*, 65, 3. (Sep.1930): p13-14.

7545 Little, Evelyn Steel, *Tree Planting Is His Hobby*, 65, 4. (Oct.1930): p17-18.

7546 Taylor, Frank J., *Promised Lands*, 68, 1. (Jan.1932): p8-10.

7547 Taylor, Frank J., *Promised Lands*, 68, 2. (Feb.1932): p12-14.

7548 Taylor, Frank J., *Promised Lands*, 68, 3. (Mar.1932): p12-13.

7549 *Jack London's "Dream Ranch", Today a State Park*, 178, 2. (Feb.1987): p10-11.

7550 Phillips, Jeff, *Royal Hawaii*, 190, 1. (Jan.1993): p68-73.

7551 Phillips, Jeff, *Buckaroo Bards*, 192, 1. (Jan.1994): p74-76.

8.2 Ethnicity & Nationality

7552 The Scene Shifter, *An Evening In Chinatown*, 3, 3. (Jul.1899): p98-101.

7553 Connell, Irene, *The Garden Of The Willow Pattern Plate*, 8, 2. (Dec.1901): p69-74.

7554 Wood, Williard, *A New Year's Celebration In Chinatown*, 11, 1. (May.1903): p59-64.

7555 Vaughan, Mary, *Daruma*, 14, 1. (Nov.1904): p84-85.

7556 Spinello, Marius J., *Italians Of California*, 14, 3. (Jan.1905): p256-258.

7557 Emerson, Edwin, Jr., *Japan's Brightest New Year*, 16, 3. (Jan.1906): p267-270.

7558 Taffinder, Will G., *Happy As A Peon*, 18, 4. (Feb.1907): p357-359.

7559 Aiken, Charles S., *San Francisco's Japanese*, 20, 1. (Nov.1907): p3-12.

7560 Saito, Shiuichiro, *Bushido Stories; Studies Of Japanese Rural Life*, 21, 8. (Dec.1908): p745-751.

7561 Dunlop, E. M., *Evolution Of The Young Maori Party*, 23, 6. (Dec.1909): p584-595.

7562 Harvey-Elder, Churchill, *Looking Ahead In Hawaii: The Japanese And The Census - A Suggestion For Government*, 24, 2. (Feb.1910): p183-184.

7563 Stellmann, Louis J., *Yellow Journals: San Francisco's Oriental Newspapers*, 24, 2. (Feb.1910): p197-201.

7564 MacLeod, Campbell, *Lagniappe*, 24, 4. (Apr.1910): p395-398.

7565 Noguchi, Yone, *Isamu And Others: Paternal Pointers Concerning Baby San And His Koishikawa Playmates*, 25, 5. (Nov.1910): p534-539.

7566 Noguchi, Yone, *The Japanese Temple Of Silence*, 26, 4. (Apr.1911): p377-384.

7567 Clausen, Walter Bertin, *The Chung Hwa Republic*, 28, 2. (Feb.1912): p157-162.

7568 Scott, Winfield, *Old Wine In New Bottles*, 30, 5. (May.1913): p519-526.

7569 Dunn, Arthur, *Keeping The Coast Clear*, 31, 1. (Jul.1913): p122-127.

7570 Lynch, Robert Newton, *Immigration*, 31, 6. (Dec.1913): p1144-1149.

7571 Lynch, Robert Newton, *Immigration*, 33, 1. (Jul.1914): p97-105.

7572 Das, Taraknath, *The Attitude Of India*, 33, 4. (Oct.1914): p772-778.

7573 Hodges, G. Charles, *Honorable Gentlemen's Agreement*, 38, 6. (Jun.1917): p24-25, 69-70.

7574 McMahon, Thomas J., *The Hiding Place Of Thunder*, 41, 3. (Sep.1918): p33-34.

7575 McMahon, Thomas J., *Post Bellum Papua*, 41, 4. (Oct.1918): p37-38.

7576 Kyne, Peter B., *Fathering A War Veteran*, 43, 4. (Oct.1919): p17-19, 54-68.

7577 Woehlke, Walter V., *Food First*, 45, 4. (Oct.1920): p35-38, 76-80.

7578 Irwin, Wallace, *Hashimura Togo, Westerner*, 45, 6. (Dec.1920): p22-23, 54-55.

7579 Irwin, Wallace, *Hashimura Togo, Westerner*, 46, 1. (Jan.1921): p28-30.

7580 Irwin, Wallace, *Hashimura Togo, Westerner*, 46, 2. (Feb.1921): p23-25.

7581 Irwin, Wallace, *Hashimura Togo, Westerner*, 46, 3. (Mar.1921): p32-34.

7582 Allen, Riley H., *Americans All–In Hawaii!*, 56, 1. (Jan.1926): p24-25, 86-88.

7583 Coonradt, Harry W., *When A Midget Goes A-Wooing*, 56, 1. (Jan.1926): p29, 98.

7584 Block, Eugene B., *Happy New Year–In Prison*, 59, 2. (Aug.1927): p35, 65-66.

7585 *Basques In The West*, 124, 5. (May.1960): p122-127.

7586 *It's Bomb Day In Marysville March 12*, 138, 3. (Mar.1967): p50.

7587 *Behind The Scenes In San Francisco's Chinatown*, 139, 1. (Jul.1967): p28-29.

7588 *San Francisco's Changing Chinatown*, 156, 2. (Feb.1976): p58-65.

7589 *Basques In The West*, 156, 6. (Jun.1976): p62-65.

7590 *Irish Month In The Bay Area*, 160, 3. (Mar.1978): p88-91.

7591 *There's Still Some Italy Left In North Beach*, 177, 5. (Nov.1986): p12-14, 16.

7592 *Lively Times In Latino San Francisco*, 183, 4. (Oct.1989): p32-33, 34-37.

8.3 Native Americans

7593 Mayo, H. M., *Bullitt's Cave: A Mystery Of The Kickapoo Raids In Texas*, 3, 4. (Aug.1899): p132-133.

7594 James, George Wharton, *Among The Mono Basket Makers*, 6, 4. (Feb.1901): p106-112.

7595 Barton, C. W., *Riverside's New Indian School*, 7, 6. (Oct.1901): p153-156.

7596 James, George Wharton, *Basket Makers Of California At Work*, 8, 1. (Nov.1901): p2-14.

7597 Wilson, Bourdon, *How The Fox Became Cunning - An Indian Myth*, 8, 6. (Apr.1902): p286.

7598 Clum, John P., *Fighting Geronimo: A Story Of The Apache Indian Campaign Of 1876*, 11, 1. (May.1903): p36-41.

7599 Sharp, J. H., *Indian Anecdotes*, 11, 2. (Jun.1903): p122.

7600 James, George Wharton, *Palomas Apaches And Their Baskets*, 11, 2. (Jun.1903): p146-153.

7601 Wilson, Bourdon, *The Legend Of Coyote Hill*, 11, 5. (Sep.1903): p461-462.

7602 Miller, Joaquin, *The Story And Glory Of Shasta*, 11, 6. (Oct.1903): p498-504.

7603 Shackelford, R. S., *The Wasco Sally Bag*, 12, 3. (Jan.1904): p258-259.

7604 Chandler, Katherine, *The Story Of The Pleiades*, 13, 2. (Jun.1904): p154-156.

7605 Gage, A. Clifford, *Pueblo Santa Clara*, 13, 3. (Jul.1904): p270-276.

7606 Davis, Mary A., *A Legend Of San Jacinto*, 13, 6. (Oct.1904): p469-473.

7607 Maxwell, Laura W., *Wahpauta: Basket-Maker*, 14, 6. (Apr.1905): p582-584.

7608 Davis, Sam, *The Nevada Piutes*, 15, 5. (Sep.1905): p458-460.

7609 Lockwood, Lillie LeGrand, *Good Bye, Totem*, 16, 4. (Feb.1906): p336-341.

7610 Inkersley, Arthur, *Chilliwac's Passion Play*, 18, 5. (Apr.1907): p572-576.

7611 Wells, A. J., *Helping The Indian: Result Of Paternalism As Shown At The Walker Lake Reservation*, 19, 1. (May.1907): p95-96.

7612 Davis, L. Clare, *Long Ago In San Joaquin*, 19, 6. (Oct.1907): p533-538.

7613 Jordan, David Starr, *Helping The Indians: What The Riverside Indian Conference Accomplished*, 22, 1. (Jan.1909): p57-61.

7614 Saunders, Charles Francis, *In Happy Zuni*, 22, 4. (Apr.1909): p379-388.

7615 Foreman, Grant, *Lo The Rich Indian*, 22, 6. (Jun.1909): p647-650.

7616 Coolidge, Dane, *The Yaquis In Exile*, 23, 2. (Sep.1909): p299-302.

7617 London, Jack, *The Wit of Porportuk*, 24, 2. (Feb.1910): p159-172.

7618 Murray, Robert Hammond, *Mexico And The Yaquis*, 24, 6. (Jun.1910): p619-628.

7619 Valentine, Robert G., *Making Good Indians*, 24, 6. (Jun.1910): p598-611.

7620 Stellmann, Louis J., *Ishi, The Lonely*, 28, 1. (Jan.1912): p107-110.

7621 Prince, L. Bradford, *New Mexico, The New State*, 28, 6. (Jun.1912): p683-695.

7622 Laut, Agnes C., *Why Go Abroad?: Wandering Amount the Cavemen*, 30, 2. (Feb.1913): p156-164.

7623 Laut, Agnes C., *Why Go Abroad?*, 30, 3. (Mar.1913): p243-249.

7624 Steele, Rufus M., *The Cave Of Captain Jack*, 30, 5. (May.1913): p565-568.

7625 Gates, Eleanor, *Motoring To Mass At Pala*, 31, 4. (Oct.1913): p730-736.

7626 Geddes, Alice Spencer, *Recorder Of The Red Man's Music*, 32, 1. (Jan.1914): p165-167.

7627 Steele, Rufus M., *The Son Who Showed His Father*, 34, 3. (Mar.1915): p473-485.

7628 Read, Roland and Wright, Allen H., *Camera Scalps*, 34, 6. (Jun.1915): p1159-1164.

7629 Larson, Emma Mauritz, *On The War-Work Path*, 42, 2. (Feb.1919): p42-43.

7630 Moon, Carl, *An Aboriginal Thanksgiving*, 43, 5. (Nov.1919): p35-37, 52.

7631 Brown, Estelle Aubrey, *The Three Rs On The Reservation*, 46, 6. (Jun.1921): p38-39, 74.

7632 Brown, Estelle Aubrey, *The Three Rs On The Reservation*, 47, 1. (Jul.1921): p40-41, 54-56.

7633 Brown, Estelle Aubrey, *The Three Rs On The Reservation*, 47, 2. (Aug.1921): p39-42.

7634 Schultz, James Willard, *The Case Of The Hopi*, 47, 4. (Oct.1921): p20-22.

7635 White, Stewart Edward, *Our Treatment Of The Indians*, 49, 5. (Nov.1922): p16.

7636 Schultz, James Willard, *America's Red Armenians*, 49, 5. (Nov.1922): p17-19, 70-74.

7637 Kelly, M. Clyde, *The Indian And His Master*, 49, 6. (Dec.1922): p17-18, 66.

7638 Collier, John, *Plundering The Pueblo Indians*, 50, 1. (Jan.1923): p21-25, 56.

7639 Collier, John, *The Pueblos' Last Stand*, 50, 2. (Feb.1923): p19-22, 65-66.

7640 Collier, John, *Our Indian Policy*, 50, 3. (Mar.1923): p13-15, 89-93.

7641 Ward, Alice May, *Red Tragedies*, 50, 4. (Apr.1923): p22-23, 80-81.

7642 Atwood, Stella M., *The S.O.S. Of The Pimas*, 50, 4. (Apr.1923): p24.

7643 Woehlke, Walter V., *The Filipino And The Indian*, 50, 4. (Apr.1923): p25, 87-88.

7644 Collier, John, *No Trespassing*, 50, 5. (May.1923): p14-15, 58-60.

7645 Scott, Hugh L., *The Paiute Uprising*, 50, 6. (Jun.1923): p38-39, 118.

7646 Woehlke, Walter V., *Let 'Em Die!*, 51, 1. (Jul.1923): p14-15.

7647 Woehlke, Walter V., *Poisoning The Navajos With Oil*, 51, 2. (Aug.1923): p11, 91-92.

7648 Collier, John, *The Pueblos' Land Problem*, 51, 5. (Nov.1923): p15, 101.

7649 Woehlke, Walter V., *Hope For The Blackfeet*, 51, 6. (Dec.1923): p9-11, 97-101.

7650 Collier, John, *The Fate Of The Navajos*, 52, 1. (Jan.1924): p11-13, 60-62, 73-74.

7651 Lummis, Charles F., *Is The Snake Dance A Fake?*, 52, 52. (Jan.1924): p1.

7652 Wickersham, James, *The Oldest And Rarest Lincoln Statue*, 52, 2. (Feb.1924): p35.

7653 Collier, John, *The Red Slaves Of Oklahoma*, 52, 3. (Mar.1924): p9-11, 94-100.

7654 Collier, John, *The Accursed System*, 52, 6. (Jun.1924): p15-16, 80-82.

7655 Collier, John, *Persecuting The Pueblos*, 53, 1. (Jul.1924): p50, 92-93.

7656 Arnold, Frank P., *Gloomy Gray Or Bright Red?*, 53, 5. (Nov.1924): p34, 63.

7657 Willoughby, Barrett, *The Passing Alaskan*, 56, 5. (May.1926): p27-29, 58-60.

7658 Campbell, Lindsay, *The Apache Trail*, 56, 5. (May.1926): p36-37, 54.

7659 Von Blon, John L., *The Last Of The First Americans*, 57, 4. (Oct.1926): p16-17, 56-58.

7660 Swinnerton, Louise Scher, *Making War On Evil Thoughts*, 58, 1. (Jan.1927): p36-37.

7661 Kopta, Anna Phelps, *Housekeeping In Hopiland*, 58, 3. (Mar.1927): p34-35, 60-62.

7662 Hughes, George, *The First Sequoyah*, 59, 3. (Sep.1927): p25, 64-66.

7663 Boyer, Warren E., *Cliff Cave Customs*, 61, 4. (Oct.1928): p37, 60.

7664 Woehlke, Walter V., *Starving The Nation's Wards*, 61, 5. (Nov.1928): p11-14, 69-70.

7665 Sperling, Freda, *Better Homes Among The Klamath Indians*, 64, 6. (Jun.1930): p18-20.

7666 *What's New In Western Living*, 81, 2. (Aug.1938): p11-13.

7667 *Coupeville Races*, 87, 1. (Jul.1941): p8.

8. People

7668 *Alaska Totems*, 87, 2. (Aug.1941): p11.

7669 *Pictographs and Petroglyphs*, 91, 1. (Jul.1943): p8-9.

7670 *Indians, Canyons, And Desert Color*, 97, 2. (Aug.1946): p10-12, 14.

7671 *Navajo-Hopi Rugs*, 98, 1. (Jan.1947): p42-43.

7672 *Chinook Salmon*, 98, 4. (Apr.1947): p16.

7673 *Indian Country*, 100, 6. (Jun.1948): p22-27.

7674 *Southwest Indian Christmas Dance*, 107, 6. (Dec.1951): p15.

7675 *Monument Valley: Heart Of The Navajo Country*, 110, 4. (Apr.1953): p48-53.

7676 *Air Trip To Eskimo Villages*, 110, 4. (Apr.1953): p29-32.

7677 *Camping, Fishing, Resorts In Colville Indian Reservation*, 110, 6. (Jun.1953): p40-43.

7678 *In Arizona's Ancient Land Of The Papagos...*, 111, 5. (Nov.1953): p46-49.

7679 *How To Buy A Navajo Rug*, 111, 6. (Dec.1953): p22-26.

7680 *How To Read A Totem Pole*, 113, 4. (Oct.1954): p35-38.

7681 *Indian Country*, 113, 4. (Oct.1954): p46-53.

7682 *A Visit To New Mexico's Indian Country*, 117, 5. (Nov.1956): p30-33.

7683 *A Visit With The Apaches*, 118, 5. (May.1957): p32, 34-36, 38.

7684 *The Hopi Craftsman's Show*, 119, 1. (Jul.1957): p38.

7685 *In The Southwest Indian Country...Shopping For Rugs, Pottery, Basketry, Jewelry*, 120, 5. (May.1958): p68-75.

7686 *Back Road Cruise Through The Papago Country*, 127, 4. (Oct.1961): p24, 26, 28, 30, 33.

7687 *The Smoki Will Dance On August 4*, 129, 2. (Aug.1962): p38.

7688 *Navajo Country*, 131, 3. (Sep.1963): p60-71.

7689 *Pictographs Along The Columbia*, 132, 3. (Mar.1964): p24-26.

7690 *Exploring New Mexico's Ancient City Ruins*, 133, 3. (Sep.1964): p52-59.

7691 *A Visit To The Living Pueblos*, 135, 3. (Sep.1965): p64-71.

7692 *Meet The Kachinas*, 140, 2. (Feb.1968): p58-63.

7693 *The Indians Are Coming*, 141, 1. (Jul.1968): p42-45.

7694 *The Navajo Canyon Of History*, 143, 1. (Jul.1969): p52-57.

7695 *At The Indian Fair...Navajos, Apaches, Hopis, Papagos*, 144, 3. (Mar.1970): p74-79.

7696 *Southwest Indian Art In 1972*, 148, 4. (Apr.1972): p86-95.

7697 *Totem Art Of The Northwest Coast; Where to See the Poles... a 1973 Report*, 150, 5. (May.1973): p120-129.

7698 *Powwows In 1978–Montana To Oregon To Arizona*, 160, 5. (May.1978): p106-113.

7699 *Indian Doings In Sacramento In September*, 163, 3. (Sep.1979): p76-77.

7700 *Handsome Coiled Baskets Of The Papagos–Still Plentiful, Prices Within Reason*, 164, 3. (Mar.1980): p78-79.

7701 *Hopi Kachinas Throng To California*, 164, 6. (Jun.1980): p92-93.

7702 *Eskimo Art In And From Alaska*, 166, 3. (Mar.1981): p86-89.

7703 *The Anasazi Puzzle–Mystery In New Mexico*, 166, 5. (May.1981): p100-103.

7704 *Before Video Games, There Was Motowu*, 171, 2. (Aug.1983): p64-65.

7705 *Splendid New Showcases For Southwest Indian Art*, 174, 2. (Feb.1985): p78-81.

7706 Whiteley, Peter O., *Native American Ornaments, Deck Your Tree With History*, 191, 6. (Dec.1993): p82-84.

7707 Fleming, Jeanie Puleston, *Pueblo Pottery: Renaissance of an Ancient Art*, 192, 3. (Mar.1994): p84-89.

7708 Jaffe, Matthew, *Ancient West*, 194, 5. (May.1995): p78-85.

8.4 Women

7709 Griswold, Mary Edith, *The Mountain Girl's Dresses*, 11, 3. (Jul.1903): p222.

7710 Stoddard, Florence Jackson, *How To Do Without Servants*, 11, 5. (Sep.1903): p452-453.

7711 Chandler, Katherine, *A Lesson In Loving: Study Of The Work Accomplished By The Visiting Nurses' Home, Of San Francisco*, 13, 3. (Jul.1904): p264-269.

7712 De Constant, Baron D'Estournelles, *Western Women Through French Eyes*, 29, 5. (Nov.1912): p527-530.

7713 Michelson, Miriam, *The Terrible Consequences Of Clothing*, 34, 2. (Feb.1915): p253-262.

7714 Tipton, Alice Stevens, *Women's Work In New Mexico*, 37, 5. (Nov.1916): p34, 92-93.

7715 *Two Girls and "Preparedness"*, 37, 5. (Nov.1916): p78,80.

7716 Holaday, May, *The Lure Of The West For Women*, 38, 3. (Mar.1917): p61.

7717 Austin, Mary, *Woman And Her War Loot*, 42, 2. (Feb.1919): p13-16.

7718 Anstruther, Eleanor, *My Experiment In Motherhood*, 42, 2. (Feb.1919): p43-45, 64.

7719 Wilson, Woodrow, Mrs., *The Splendid Years*, 44, 1. (Jan.1920): p34-36, 62-64.

7720 Heizer, Kate L., *Via The Homesteading Route*, 46, 3. (Mar.1921): p36-37, 52.

7721 Wierman, Frances, *The Green-Eyed Mother*, 47, 4. (Oct.1921): p90-91.

7722 A Bewildered Husband, *The End Of The Trail*, 50, 3. (Mar.1923): p30-33.

7723 A Bewildered Husband, *The End Of The Trail*, 50, 4. (Apr.1923): p40-43, 82-86.

7724 Barrett, Lilian, *Can The American Woman Love?*, 51, 3. (Sep.1923): p32-34, 62.

7725 Williams, Mary O'Brien, *How I Saved Our Crop*, 54, 1. (Jan.1925): p37, 62.

7726 Burks, Barbara and Burks, Frances, *Motherhood Plus A Career*, 54, 2. (Feb.1925): p49-50.

7727 Cassidy, Louise Lowber, *At Home At Large*, 55, 1. (Jul.1925): p34-35, 88.

7728 Taylor, Katherine Haviland, *How I Control A Bad Disposition*, 55, 2. (Aug.1925): p24-25.

7729 Davies, A. Hilton, *Wohelo In The West*, 55, 4. (Oct.1925): p32-34, 76-77.

7730 Dohlman, Billy, *King, Son Of Gold-Dust*, 55, 5. (Nov.1925): p30-33.

7731 Dohlman, Billy, *More About King*, 55, 6. (Dec.1925): p26-28.

7732 Dare, *The Western Girl's Summer Day*, 57, 1. (Jul.1926): p52.

7733 Dare, *Western Midsummer Modes*, 57, 2. (Aug.1926): p48-49.

7734 Dare, *Smart Togs For The Chic Co-Ed*, 57, 3. (Sep.1926): p48-49.

7735 Humphrey, Adele, *What's The Matter With Parents?*, 57, 4. (Oct.1926): p14-15, 86-90.

7736 Dare, *The First Breath Of Autumn*, 57, 4. (Oct.1926): p42-43.

7737 Dare, *Hats For Every Type*, 57, 5. (Nov.1926): p44-45.

7738 Dare, *Smart Holiday Apparel*, 57, 6. (Dec.1926): p42-43.

7739 Dare, *Midwinter Modes*, 58, 1. (Jan.1927): p48-49.

7740 deFleur, Marise, *Beauty and the Business Woman*, 58, 3. (Mar.1927): p74-75.

7741 Block, Eugene B., *A Court Without Trials*, 60, 3. (Mar.1928): p39, 54-58.

7742 Allen, Winifred, *Globetrotting Working Girls*, 61, 1. (Jul.1928): p28-29, 67-68.

7743 Chappell, Dorothea Havens, *The Ease Of Western Housekeeping*, 61, 5. (Nov.1928): p16-17, 72-73.

7744 Hill, Janet Raitt and Biddle, Helen, *Do Your Children Enjoy The Outdoors?*, 66, 2. (Feb.1931): p22.

7745 Moss, Doris Hudson, *Why I Believe in Electrical Equipment*, 68, 3. (Mar.1932): p26, 28, 30.

9. Travel

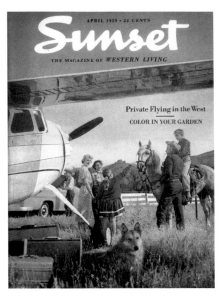

April 1959 cover (photo: Martin Litton)

Travel

From its inception through the most recent issue, Sunset *has consistently focused on Touring and Vacation Destinations, another of the Big Four. While its emphasis has always been primarily on travel destinations within the Western States, the coverage has been international from the beginning, hence Foreign Travel. We may have forgotten that Automobile Travel as a pastime is as much an invention as the vehicles themselves. Before World War I, and until much later in some parts of the West, roads did not invite long-distance recreational travel, but* Sunset *presented a world of exploration opportunity for motorists, both male and female. The choice and features of the many travel destinations in the pages of* Sunset *tell us much about tastes and interests of the times, but also provide a series of snapshots (both literally and in text) about regions, towns, parks, wildernesses, Cultural Travel & Events, countries and specific roads at various moments through the century.* Sunset *has always highlighted the Spanish heritage of the American Southwest and treated Mexico as an important travel destination. In this sense, it has long drawn the Western U.S. closer to, rather than away from, its Hispanic legacy. A substantial body of travel and cultural-historical addresses our Spanish Borderlands, as we have called this section, which helped to formulate a general consciousness of Spanish or Mexican influences and styles in Western living.*

9. Travel

7794 Woehlke, Walter V., *The Puget Sound Country*, 32, 6. (Jun.1914): p1228-1243.

7795 Powell, E. Alexander, *Autobirds Of Passage*, 32, 6. (Jun.1914): p1257-1267.

7796 Powell, E. Alexander, *Autobirds Of Passage*, 33, 1. (Jul.1914): p65-75.

7797 Powell, E. Alexander, *Autobirds Of Passage*, 33, 2. (Aug.1914): p318-327.

7798 Powell, E. Alexander, *Autobirds Of Passage*, 33, 3. (Sep.1914): p519-530.

7799 Powell, E. Alexander, *Autobirds Of Passage*, 33, 4. (Oct.1914): p739-748.

7800 Powell, E. Alexander, *Autobirds Of Passage*, 33, 5. (Nov.1914): p924-934.

7801 Powell, E. Alexander, *Autobirds Of Passage*, 33, 6. (Dec.1914): p1145-1155.

7802 Hillman, J. Constantine, *The Gasoline Nursery in the Sierra*, 34, 2. (Feb.1915): p360, 362, 364, 366, 368, 370.

7803 Peck, L. W., *The Pacific Highway*, 35, 1. (Jul.1915): p184, 188, 190, 192.

7804 Howard, Randall R., *Through The Columbia River Gorge By Auto*, 35, 8. (Aug.1915): p303-306.

7805 Grover, Con L., *Sierran Roads And Passes*, 35, 4. (Oct.1915): p668-674.

7806 Willard, Walter, *Blazing The Motor Trail To Whitney*, 35, 5. (Nov.1915): p861-868.

7807 Laing, Hamilton M., *The Transcontinental Game*, 38, 1. (Feb.1917): p72,74,76,78,80.

7808 Hall, Wilbur, *A Free Car And The Open Road*, 39, 1. (Jul.1917): p22-26, 86-87.

7809 *Main Traveled Roads in the Sunset Country*, 39, 1. (Jul.1917): p42-43,82,85,88.

7810 Smith, Bertha H., *Motor-Shopping On The Highways*, 39, 2. (Aug.1917): p39-40, 82.

7811 Steele, Rufus M., *On The Warpath For Fun*, 40, 2. (Feb.1918): p49-52, 68.

7812 Gurney, Vivian, *An Auto-Burro Honeymoon*, 43, 1. (Jul.1919): p40-42, 66-70.

7813 Laing, Hamilton M., *A Motorcyclist On Horseback*, 45, 2. (Aug.1920): p27-29, 62-63.

7814 Buker, Horace Edward, *A Little Rough In Spots*, 46, 6. (Jun.1921): p40-42, 64.

7815 Saunders, Charles Francis, *Two Motor Vagabonds In Oregon*, 49, 3. (Sep.1922): p38-40.

7816 Waugh, Lena Sanford, *Motor Vagabonds*, 50, 5. (May.1923): p22-23, 58.

7817 *Motor Routes From The Mississippi To The Rockies And The Pacific Coast*, 50, 6. (Jun.1923): p36-37.

7818 Younger, Maud, *Alone Across The Continent*, 52, 5. (May.1924): p43, 106-109.

7819 Younger, Maud, *Alone Across The Continent*, 52, 6. (Jun.1924): p25-27, 60.

7820 Woehlke, Walter V., *Transcontinental Motor Trails Of The Far West*, 54, 3. (Mar.1925): p24-25, 77-78.

7821 Knight, C. P., *About Road Hogs And Gentlemen*, 54, 3. (Mar.1925): p49-50, 60-62.

7822 Woehlke, Walter V., *Transcontinental Motor Trails Of The Far West–II. Overland Routes*, 54, 4. (Apr.1925): p24-25.

7823 *New Joys For Motorists*, 54, 5. (May.1925): p23.

7824 Woehlke, Walter V., *Transcontinental Motor Trails Of The Far West–III. Northwestern Highways*, 54, 5. (May.1925): p24-25.

7825 Edmondson, R. E., *'Cross Continent By Motor*, 54, 5. (May.1925): p33-34, 96-104.

7826 Woehlke, Walter V., *Transcontinental Motor Trails Of The Far West–IV. Pacific Slope Highways*, 54, 6. (Jun.1925): p22-23, 61.

7827 King, Ray McIntyre, *The Family Takes A Vacation!*, 55, 2. (Aug.1925): p32-33, 58-59.

7828 Kneen, Beryl D. and Kneen, O. H., *Motoring Through The Land Of Glaciers*, 56, 3. (Mar.1926): p14-15, 58-59.

7829 Fordyce, Claude P., *Auto Rambles*, 57, 1. (Jul.1926): p16-19, 80-82.

7830 Mavity, Nancy Barr, *The Woman At The Wheel*, 58, 4. (Apr.1927): p30-31, 62.

7831 Ewing, Paul A., *Emphatic Arizona*, 61, 1. (Jul.1928): p30-33.

7832 Thornton, Sibyl, *From A Motoring Mother*, 67, 5. (Nov.1931): p25.

7833 Prather, R. L., *Around The West In Forty-Seven Days*, 68, 3. (Mar.1932): p7-9.

7834 *578 Miles Of U.S. 395*, 98, 3. (Mar.1947): p15-17.

7835 *Detour! Gold Country*, 99, 1. (Jul.1947): p13-17.

7836 *A Connecting Link In California's History*, 101, 1. (Jul.1948): p14-15.

7837 *California Highway 89*, 101, 1. (Jul.1948): p22-25.

7838 *Notes On A B.C. Road Map*, 101, 3. (Sep.1948): p10-13.

7839 *Mexico's Highway South*, 101, 4. (Oct.1948): p2-12.

7840 *Criss-Crossing Highway 101*, 101, 5. (Nov.1948): p24-29.

7841 *Alaska Highway*, 102, 4. (Apr.1949): p6, 8-15.

7842 *Spring Samples Of Summer Vacations*, 102, 4. (Apr.1949): p19-23.

7843 *Why October Is A Favored Travel Month*, 103, 4. (Oct.1949): p24-29.

7844 *Three Flags Highway–The Back Country Freeway*, 104, 3. (Mar.1950): p26-29.

7845 *Sierra Sample Via Kit Carson Highway*, 107, 2. (Aug.1951): p19.

7846 *Auto Exploring Along The Golden Forks Of The Yuba*, 107, 3. (Sep.1951): p32-37.

7847 *The Ocean Roadways To The Golden Gate*, 107, 4. (Oct.1951): p16-21.

7848 *Driving The Pages Of Western History*, 107, 4. (Oct.1951): p22-25.

7849 *Exploring The Coachella Valley*, 108, 1. (Jan.1952): p10-11.

7850 *Campsites and Resorts in San Diego County's Borrego Valley*, 108, 2. (Feb.1952): p15-17.

7851 *Side-Road Exploring From U.S. 95...Nevada's Ghost Town Highway*, 108, 3. (Mar.1952): p14-16.

7852 *Ten Weekend Trips To Spring*, 108, 3. (Mar.1952): p30-33.

7853 *Off The Tourist-Beaten Track, The West Still Offers Discovery*, 108, 4. (Apr.1952): p40-47.

7854 *Now Is The Time To Dip Into The Sespe*, 108, 4. (Apr.1952): p16-17.

7855 *From Monterey South To Morro Bay*, 108, 5. (May.1952): p22-23.

7856 *Mt. Diablo's Ghost Towns*, 108, 6. (Jun.1952): p25-26.

7857 *How To Fit California's Northeast Corner Into Your Next North-South Trip*, 108, 6. (Jun.1952): p38-43.

7858 *Traveling With Children : It's a Sort of Capsule Course in Child Care*, 109, 1. (Jul.1952): p29-30,32.

7859 *Auto Exploring On Maui, Hawaii's Valley Isle*, 109, 1. (Jul.1952): p14-16.

7860 *Is Your Car's Cooling System In Shape For A Mountain Trip?*, 109, 2. (Aug.1952): p16, 19.

7861 *After 100 Years, It's Still Surprise Valley*, 109, 2. (Aug.1952): p20-23.

7862 *Lake Mead: One Surprise After Another*, 109, 3. (Sep.1952): p14-16.

7863 *By Highway And Ferry Around Hood Canal*, 109, 4. (Oct.1952): p14-18.

7864 *The Mountains In San Diego's Back Yard*, 109, 5. (Nov.1952): p14-16.

7865 *El Salvador; It's Wonderful Once You Get There*, 109, 6. (Dec.1952): p22-25.

7866 *Along The Apache Trail To Arizona's Tonto Basin*, 110, 2. (Feb.1953): p12-13.

7867 *By Ferry And Auto Along British Columbia's Coast*, 110, 4. (Apr.1953): p18-21.

7868 *Down The Mountainous Length Of Idaho On Twisting U.S. 95*, 110, 5. (May.1953): p22-26.

9. Travel

9.2 Cultural Travel & Events

9. Travel

7942 Collier, D. C., *What An Exposition Is For*, 31, 1. (Jul.1913): p145-150.

7943 Calder, A. Stirling, *Sculpture At The Exposition*, 32, 3. (Mar.1914): p610-615.

7944 McGroarty, John S., *A Pageant Of Transportation*, 33, 4. (Oct.1914): p749-752.

7945 Steele, Rufus M., *A Matter Of Millions*, 34, 1. (Jan.1915): p80-87.

7946 Whitaker, Herman, *In A Blaze Of Glory*, 34, 3. (Mar.1915): p511-518.

7947 Groff, Frances A., *Lovely Women At The Exposition*, 34, 5. (May.1915): p876-889.

7948 Groff, Frances A., *Exposition Moths*, 35, 1. (Jul.1915): p133-148.

7949 Hudson, Charles Bradford, *Monterey On The Etching Plate*, 35, 2. (Aug.1915): p298-302.

7950 Williams, Michael, *Western Art At The Exposition*, 35, 2. (Aug.1915): p317-326.

7951 Harding, Mabel T., *Madame Butterfly At Home*, 35, 2. (Aug.1915): p352-355.

7952 Stellmann, Louis J., *A Pageant In The Wilderness*, 35, 5. (Nov.1915): p907-908.

7953 Clark, Franklin S., *Seats Down Front!*, 54, 4. (Apr.1925): p33, 54.

7954 Dexter, John, *Music Hath Charms*, 59, 1. (Jul.1927): p35, 60-62.

7955 *The West Gives a Party*, 82, 1. (Jan.1939): p6-9.

7956 *Shakespeare Under The Stars…From July 21 Until September 2 in Ashland, Oregon*, 129, 1. (Jul.1962): p30-33.

7957 *While Nobody Was Looking, The West Has Launched An Art Museum Boom*, 137, 5. (Nov.1966): p90, 92, 94.

7958 *One Of The World's Outstanding Displays Of 20th Century Sculpture; Where? UCLA*, 138, 2. (Feb.1967): p96.

7959 *Little Ferndale Will Get Lively This Month*, 138, 5. (May.1967): p48-50.

7960 *Monterey's Tenth Jazz Festival*, 139, 3. (Sep.1967): p42-44.

7961 *The Lively California Design Show Gives You A Look At Tomorrow*, 140, 4. (Apr.1968): p96-97.

7962 *Art Surpises At Half Moon Bay*, 146, 1. (Jan.1971): p25-26.

7963 *Opera, Ballet, Jazz, Or Symphony In A San Francisco Forest; Reserve a Picnic Table if you Like. Come Early. It's Free*, 146, 6. (Jun.1971): p84-85.

7964 *Every Weekend This Summer in California's Mother Lode; Melodramas, Musicals, Straw Hats, and Stovepipes*, 146, 6. (Jun.1971): p98-101.

7965 *A Grand Musical Experience In Carmel Starting July 16*, 147, 1. (Jul.1971): p27-28.

7966 *Bufano*, 147, 6. (Dec.1971): p32, 35.

7967 *Baroque And Classical Street Music…Now In San Francisco*, 148, 5. (May.1972): p50-51.

7968 *Barnsdall Park Comes To Life For The Annual Outdoor Art Show*, 148, 6. (Jun.1972): p46-47.

7969 *It's Open-Air Shakespeare Season In Marin*, 149, 1. (Jul.1972): p34-35.

7970 *On View Now In Pasadena…America's Folk Craft Tradition*, 149, 6. (Dec.1972): p58-59.

7971 *Street Art Explosion In Los Angeles*, 150, 4. (Apr.1973): p110-113.

7972 *Stopover For Shakespeare In Oregon's Ashland*, 150, 6. (Jun.1973): p70-74.

7973 *African Spirit…Real African Vibrations. Coming To San Francisco Legion Of Honor*, 151, 1. (Jul.1973): p34-35.

7974 *Oakland Opens A Grand New-Old Performance Arts Hall That Takes You Back to the 1930's; For For Music - Go For a Tour*, 151, 4. (Oct.1973): p28-29.

7975 *It's Tapestry Discovery Month In San Francisco*, 153, 1. (Jul.1974): p32-33.

7976 *The Most Complete Look Ever at What Bufano Was Up To*, 154, 2. (Feb.1975): p38-39.

7977 *The Big Fair In Sacramento*, 155, 3. (Sep.1975): p30-31.

7978 *Jack London's Old Stamping Ground In His Centennial Year*, 156, 1. (Jan.1976): p26-27.

7979 *Inside The New Blue Whale In Los Angeles…A Bicentennial Look At Tomorrow*, 156, 3. (Mar.1976): p74-76.

7980 *Hoedowns, Jamborees, Folk Music Festivals In Over The West, from Now to Autumn*, 156, 4. (Apr.1976): p54-56.

7981 *On The Trail Of Sam Spade In San Francisco*, 157, 5. (Nov.1976): p54-56.

7982 *Opera in the West, 1977*, 158, 2. (Feb.1977): p60-65.

7983 *Artists Put Their Colorful Stamp On Santa Cruz*, 159, 2. (Aug.1977): p36-38.

7984 *For Visitors to Los Angles, The Movie Experience*, 159, 3. (Sep.1977): p64-71.

7985 *"Roaring, Soaring, Exulting, Trembling"*, 160, 2. (Feb.1978): p74-75.

7986 *'A Museum Should Not Be Shut Off From Life'*, 160, 6. (Jun.1978): p46-48.

7987 *L. A. Jazz–Out-Of-Doors, Free*, 160, 6. (Jun.1978): p102-103.

7988 *High In Utah–Hiking, Theater, Art, Music*, 161, 1. (Jul.1978): p70-75.

7989 *Away from the Casinos, There is Another Reno–From Jazz To Baroque Music To Opera*, 162, 2. (Feb.1979): p60, 62, 64.

7990 *Pasadena's Impressionist Collection, Splendid And Growing*, 162, 5. (May.1979): p110-113.

7991 *Shakespeare Busting Out In the West Out of Doors*, 163, 1. (Jul.1979): p32-34.

7992 *Carillon Concerts: They Are Fun and Free. Eight Places in the West Have Hem*, 163, 5. (Nov.1979): p38-42.

7993 *Old Books, Rare Books, Musty or Mint; In the L. A. Area, in Santa Barbara, in S. F., the Browsing is Good*, 164, 2. (Feb.1980): p46-48.

7994 *Public Art Walk In Six Blocks Of San Francisco's Downtown*, 164, 3. (Mar.1980): p46-48.

7995 *Unfolding In San Francisco–A Grand Music-Art District*, 165, 3. (Sep.1980): p60-63.

7996 *Salt Lake City's New Triple Play*, 166, 2. (Feb.1981): p42-43.

7997 *Sculpture Hard-Edged To Beguiling–In Oakland Now*, 169, 2. (Aug.1982): p26-27.

7998 *San Francisco's Sidewalk Vaudeville… Where and When to Watch*, 169, 4. (Sep.1982): p76-77.

7999 *San Jose's Best Kept Secret? Art Where you Wouldn't Expect it*, 169, 4. (Oct.1982): p92-93.

8000 *San Francisco's 'Off Geary' Theaters*, 169, 5. (Nov.1982): p34-40.

8001 *A Treasure-Trove Of Folk Art In Santa Fe*, 170, 1. (Jan.1983): p40-43.

8002 *Hiss The Villian, Cheer The Hero; It's Time for Melodrama in the West*, 171, 1. (Jul.1983): p68-71.

8003 *The Crafts And Crafts People Of Oregon*, 171, 2. (Aug.1983): p56-61.

8004 *Indoor-Outdoor Art Strolling In Sacramento's Capitol District*, 173, 3. (Sep.1984): p32-34.

8005 *The Caravan Is Coming*, 175, 2. (Aug.1985): p12-14.

8006 *Cartoon California*, 181, 5. (Nov.1988): p12-13, 16, 18.

8007 *Film Festivals All Around The West*, 184, 1. (Jan.1990): p21, 23.

8008 *Mozart On Main Street*, 186, 2. (Feb.1991): p15-17.

8009 MacCaskey, Michael, *Behind The Scenes At The Rose Parade*, 190, 1. (Jan.1993): p74-79.

8010 Crosby, Bill, *L. A.'s New Iron Age*, 196, 6. (Jun.1996): p90-92.

9.3 Foreign Travel

8011 Savay, Arif, *The Commercial Awakening Of Russia*, 12, 1. (Nov.1903): p72-73.

8012 Cuthbert, Herbert, *An Undiscovered City: Facts Worth Knowing Concerning Victoria, Capital Of British Columbia*, 14, 1. (Nov.1904): p46-50.

8013 Landfield, Jerome B., *Prospecting In Siberia*, 14, 3. (Jan.1905): p226-229.

8014 Everett, Wallace W., *Automobiling Up The Rhine*, 14, 5. (Mar.1905): p517-520.

8015 Gilmour, John Hamilton, *Idling In Tahiti*, 14, 5. (Mar.1905): p465-468.

9. Travel

8016 Harada, Jiro, *Japan's Mission In The World*, 14, 6. (Apr.1905): p609-612.

8017 Beecher, Amourette M., *China The Silent*, 15, 5. (Sep.1905): p436-439.

8018 Young, John P., *Reminders Of California*, 19, 4. (Aug.1907): p338-340.

8019 Triggs, Oscar L., *Modern Fiji*, 21, 7. (Nov.1908): p594-610.

8020 Hewson, Ernest Williams, *Pu-Yi's Walled Garden*, 23, 3. (Sep.1909): p282-287.

8021 Smith, James F., *The Philippines As I Saw them*, 25, 2. (Aug.1910): p126-138, 223-225.

8022 Smith, James F., *The Philippines As I Saw Them*, 26, 2. (Feb.1911): p141-155.

8023 Laut, Agnes C., *Why Go Abroad?*, 29, 6. (Dec.1912): p667-671.

8024 Wilson, John Fleming, *Out Of Doors In Panama*, 30, 5. (May.1913): p527-531.

8025 Mitchell, Edmund, *Filming In The South Seas*, 31, 5. (Nov.1913): p954-963.

8026 Freeman, Lewis R., *Tropical Landfalls*, 33, 3. (Sep.1914): p494-504.

8027 Williams, Daniel R., *Watchful Waiting For The Philippines*, 35, 6. (Dec.1915): p1083-1086.

8028 Partridge, Edward Bellamy, *Pressing Forward With The Press*, 42, 5. (May.1919): p33-35, 66-78.

8029 Partridge, Edward Bellamy, *Under Suspicion In Paris*, 43, 2. (Aug.1919): p25-28, 72-76.

8030 Partridge, Edward Bellamy, *All Aboard For Belgium*, 43, 4. (Oct.1919): p27-29, 84-88.

8031 Partridge, Edward Bellamy, *The Horn-Rimmed Test*, 43, 5. (Nov.1919): p32-34, 108-111.

8032 Irwin, Wallace, *The Cruise Of The Lucky Thirteen*, 45, 4. (Oct.1920): p22-26, 65-66.

8033 McMahon, Thomas J., *Phosphate And Frigate-Birds*, 46, 3. (Mar.1921): p38-39, 56.

8034 Cannon, E. B., *Go Further West!*, 46, 4. (Apr.1921): p35-36, 64-65.

8035 Russell, John, *Aussie Discovered*, 46, 5. (May.1921): p16-18, 65.

8036 McGregor, Angus, *On The Love Path*, 47, 3. (Sep.1921): p20-23, 56-57.

8037 Barrett, Lilian, *The Kangaroo Sizes Us Up*, 49, 4. (Oct.1922): p10-11, 87-91.

8038 Chauvel, Charlie, *An Aussie's Landing*, 52, 6. (Jun.1924): p50.

8039 Mavity, Nancy Barr, *Exploring Life On The Other Side*, 53, 5. (Nov.1924): p8-9.

8040 Mavity, Nancy Barr, *Imperturbable New Zealand*, 53, 5. (Nov.1924): p9-11, 86-92.

8041 Mavity, Nancy Barr, *Misunderstood Australia*, 53, 6. (Dec.1924): p17-19, 62-63.

8042 Mavity, Nancy Barr, *The Yen Beats The Gun*, 54, 3. (Mar.1925): p14-16, 85-86.

8043 Mavity, Nancy Barr, *Barmaiding In Australia*, 54, 4. (Apr.1925): p15-17, 80-82.

8044 Mavity, Nancy Barr, *The Dutch Win, America Loses*, 54, 5. (May.1925): p20-22, 60-62.

8045 Mavity, Nancy Barr, *Seeing Singapore After Dark*, 54, 6. (Jun.1925): p4950, 62-63.

8046 Mavity, Nancy Barr, *Nights In Hong Kong*, 55, 1. (Jul.1925): p22-25, 56.

8047 Lebeau, Francois, *Steaming Through The Panama Canal*, 55, 2. (Aug.1925): p36-37, 67.

8048 Smith, Wallace, *The Passenger List*, 56, 5. (May.1926): p16-17.

8049 Taylor, Katherine Haviland, *The Hidden Heart Of Havana*, 56, 5. (May.1926): p18-19, 87-91.

8050 Foster, Harry L., *A Tropical Tramp In The South Seas*, 58, 3. (Mar.1927): p24-26, 54-58.

8051 Foster, Harry L., *Touring The Tongas*, 58, 4. (Apr.1927): p36-38, 92-96.

8052 Foster, Harry L., *In The Land Of Long Pig*, 58, 5. (May.1927): p34-35, 90-99.

8053 Foster, Harry L., *Overland Through Fiji*, 58, 6. (Jun.1927): p34-35, 56-60.

8054 Foster, Harry L., *Progress In Polynesia*, 59, 1. (Jul.1927): p40-42, 56-58.

8055 Barret, Dorothy, *Sketches In Havana And Panama*, 59, 2. (Aug.1927): p36-37, 64.

8056 Hampton, Mary McDuffie, *My Eleven Leaps to Romance*, 63, 5. (Nov.1929): p36-39.

8057 Tipton, Edna Sibley, *A Tale Of Two Cities*, 64, 2. (Feb.1930): p18-20.

8058 Robson, Barbara Reid, *Eating And Shopping Through Europe*, 64, 5. (May.1930): p18-19, 68-69.

8059 Leighton, Ardith, *Japan*, 66, 2. (Feb.1931): p16-18.

8060 Ribbink, Edward Van Lier, *The Other "Golden State"*, 66, 4. (Apr.1931): p21, 51-53.

8061 Mitchell, Sydney B., *Garden-Touring Through Europe*, 66, 06. (Jun.1931): p24-25, 51-52.

8062 Kay, Lenore, *Vacation Cruises From Sunset Ports*, 72, 4. (Apr.1934): p9-11.

8063 *Pan American Highway*, 91, 4. (Oct.1943): p6-9.

8064 *Oceania*, 92, 6. (Jun.1944): p2-6.

8065 *Travel-Military Style*, 94, 1. (Jan.1945): p2-6.

8066 *Guatemala*, 95, 3. (Sep.1945): p2-4, 6.

8067 *When You Go To South America*, 97, 6. (Dec.1946): p11-15.

8068 *An Artist In Guatemala*, 100, 3. (Mar.1948): p6-16.

8069 *Antigua And Atitlan, Guatemala*, 100, 5. (May.1948): p12-16.

8070 *An Adventure On Little-Known Rails*, 100, 6. (Jun.1948): p8-10.

8071 *Guatemala: Notes On A Marimba*, 100, 6. (Jun.1948): p20-21.

8072 *Journey Through Africa*, 101, 6. (Dec.1948): p6-11.

8073 *Through Western Peru*, 101, 6. (Dec.1948): p16-19.

8074 *Continuing Our Report On The Pan American Highway*, 101, 5. (Dec.1948): p6-11.

8075 *By Freighter To South America*, 102, 3. (Mar.1949): p16-23.

8076 *Cities Of South America*, 104, 1. (Jan.1950): p12-15.

8077 *Around South America By Freighter*, 104, 1. (Jan.1950): p16-19.

8078 *Wandering Through Sweden*, 104, 3. (Mar.1950): p16-20.

8079 *Guatemala: Impressions Of An Artist*, 104, 4. (Apr.1950): p6-8.

8080 *Vancouver Island–Old England, Wilderness, Quiet Shores*, 104, 4. (Apr.1950): p30-33.

8081 *Impressions Of Bali*, 105, 3. (Sep.1950): p21-23.

8082 *How Far Are The Far Corners?*, 105, 5. (Nov.1950): p20-28.

8083 *Europe*, 107, 1. (Jul.1951): p19-24.

8084 *Ecuador–Small And Spectacular*, 107, 4. (Oct.1951): p31-32.

8085 *If You Spend This Christmas In Europe*, 107, 5. (Nov.1951): p12-14.

8086 *Around La Paz in a Taxi*, 108, 2. (Feb.1952): p18-21.

8087 *Is Japan Ready for Travelers?*, 109, 4. (Oct.1952): p27-30.

8088 *Guide To The South Pacific*, 111, 5. (Nov.1953): p26-33.

8089 *Europe's Countryside Is Rich With Discovery*, 111, 5. (Dec.1953): p14-25.

8090 *Back Road Driving In...Switzerland And Austria*, 112, 1. (Jan.1954): p19-32.

8091 *Spring Garden Tour In England And Holland*, 112, 2. (Feb.1954): p16-24.

8092 *Norway's Twisting, Gravel Roads*, 112, 5. (May.1954): p32-34.

8093 *Japan...Much Closer Than You Think*, 112, 6. (Jun.1954): p36-47.

8094 *4000 Miles Down The Nile*, 113, 4. (Oct.1954): p28-29.

8095 *Include A Visit To Turkey*, 113, 6. (Dec.1954): p14-18.

8096 *Guatemala...*, 114, 2. (Feb.1955): p33-36.

9. Travel

8097 *Your Health Abroad*, 114, 4. (Apr.1955): p38, 40, 42.

8098 *Australia Is Only 33 Hours Away*, 114, 5. (May.1955): p47-53.

8099 *South Seas Adventure...The Fijis*, 115, 2. (Aug.1955): p28-30.

8100 *For College-Age Westerners Who Are Planning A European Tour*, 116, 1. (Jan.1956): p26-27.

8101 *The Fascination Of Hong Kong*, 116, 2. (Feb.1956): p25, 26, 27, 30.

8102 *African Safari...What's It Like?*, 116, 3. (Mar.1956): p28, 31.

8103 *Inexpensive Holiday...In Portugal*, 116, 6. (Jun.1956): p48, 51, 52, 54.

8104 *October Is A Fine Time To Visit The Okanogan*, 117, 4. (Oct.1956): p28-30, 32, 24, 36.

8105 *From the West Coast to the South Seas... Tahiti, Samoa, Fiji... Here's The Once-In-A-Lifetime Holiday*, 117, 5. (Nov.1956): p50-55.

8106 *Amazon Adventure - By Freighter*, 118, 1. (Jan.1957): p8, 13.

8107 *Vancouver Island*, 118, 6. (Jun.1957): p57-65.

8108 *Looping The Big Bend Country...And The Watery Kootenays*, 119, 2. (Aug.1957): p44-49.

8109 *A Skyful Of Mountain Peaks*, 119, 4. (Oct.1957): p23-24, 27.

8110 *Western Families Go Camping in Europe*, 120, 3. (Mar.1958): p14-16.

8111 *Opening April 17th In Brussels...The First World's Fair Since Pre-War*, 120, 4. (Apr.1958): p74-75.

8112 *Singapore: In the Orient, It's Strangely Like Home*, 121, 5. (Nov.1958): p18-20.

8113 *Spring In England's West Country*, 122, 3. (Mar.1959): p60, 62, 64, 66.

8114 *Sunny Corsica...Uncrowded And Unforgettable*, 122, 4. (Apr.1959): p40, 43, 44, 36, 48.

8115 *Here Is A Road For Adventurers Only*, 122, 5. (May.1959): p28-30, 32.

8116 *In Panama's Highland Valleys*, 124, 1. (Jan.1960): p41, 43, 44.

8117 *Afloat on a Lotus Lake: House-boat Holiday in the Vale of Kashmir*, 124, 1. (Jan.1960): p34,36.

8118 *You...Behind The Iron Curtain*, 124, 2. (Feb.1960): p35, 37, 38, 41.

8119 *Andalusia...It Can Be Downright Intoxicating*, 124, 4. (Apr.1960): p54-56, 58, 61.

8120 *Incomparable Iguassu*, 124, 6. (Jun.1960): p54-58, 60, 63, 64, 67.

8121 *The Carefree Of The Windward Islands*, 125, 4. (Oct.1960): p52, 54, 57, 58, 60.

8122 *Three Faces Of Buenos Aires*, 125, 5. (Nov.1960): p24-26, 28, 30, 33.

8123 *Island-Exploring The South Pacific*, 126, 2. (Feb.1961): p66-75.

8124 *If you Visit Australia: Fun And Fossicking Along The Great Barrier Reef*, 126, 6. (Jun.1961): p36-3845.

8125 *How's Puerto Rico In The Summer Off-Season?*, 127, 2. (Aug.1961): p18, 21, 23, 27.

8126 *Shopping Your Way Through Scandinavia*, 127, 3. (Sep.1961): p37-41.

8127 *The Shining Andean Lakes*, 127, 5. (Nov.1961): p36, 37, 40, 42, 45, 46, 49, 51, 52, 55, 56 .

8128 *A Disarming Indifference To Tourists*, 127, 6. (Dec.1961): p34-38.

8129 *The Wonderful Walk Over The Milford Track*, 128, 2. (Feb.1962): p20, 22, 24, 26, 28, 30, 33.

8130 *Jungle Adventure In Guatemala*, 128, 3. (Mar.1962): p64-69.

8131 *Discovery Trip For Visitors To Britain: On The Isles Of Scilly*, 128, 4. (Apr.1962): p34-36, 39-40, 44, 47, 4848.

8132 *When A Californian Goes Garden Walking In Australia*, 128, 6. (Jun.1962): p90-93.

8133 *Jumping-Off Point For The Strait Of Magellan*, 130, 1. (Jan.1963): p24, 26.

8134 *Trinidad Is One Colorful Surprise After Another*, 130, 2. (Feb.1963): p30, 32, 34.

8135 *The Little "Hells" Around Beppu... On Japan's Inland Sea*, 131, 4. (Oct.1963): p110-111.

8136 *Stopping Off In The Middle Of The Middle East*, 131, 6. (Dec.1963): p26-28.

8137 *Across Europe With Sign Language*, 132, 2. (Feb.1964): p64-65.

8138 *Three-Mile April Walk In The Heart Of London*, 132, 4. (Apr.1964): p54, 55, 57.

8139 *You And Your Camera In Places Where Lions Climb Trees*, 133, 5. (Nov.1964): p65, 66, 68, 71.

8140 *To The Highest Waterfall In All The World*, 135, 3. (Sep.1965): p24, 26, 28, 30, 32, 34.

8141 *The Surprises Of Tijuana*, 136, 1. (Jan.1966): p44-57.

8142 *To Madeira And The Canaries*, 136, 2. (Feb.1966): p26, 29, 30, 34.

8143 *Guam Is A Surprise Bonus For Cross-Pacific Travelers*, 136, 4. (Apr.1966): p30-32, 34, 38.

8144 *Victoria*, 137, 2. (Aug.1966): p40-53.

8145 *Micronesia*, 147, 4. (Oct.1971): p42-44.

8146 *Tahiti Adventure*, 148, 1. (Jan.1972): p38-43.

8147 *Now You Can Loop The Top Of Baja*, 158, 4. (Apr.1977): p122-125.

8148 *Eating In Tokyo*, 161, 2. (Aug.1978): p62-67.

8149 *The Caribbean Question*, 162, 3. (Mar.1979): p88-91.

8150 *How Expensive Is Japan? Some Comparisons*, 164, 5. (May.1980): p62-64.

9.4 Spanish Borderlands

8151 May, William B., *Chronicles Of A Highway: El Nuevo Camino Real*, 2, 1. (Nov.1898): p2-6.

8152 May, William B., *Chronicles Of A Highway: El Nuevo Camino Real, Second Paper*, 2, 2. (Dec.1898): p20-25.

8153 May, William B., *Chronicles Of A Highway: El Nuevo Camino Real, Third Paper*, 2, 4. (Feb.1899): p68-73.

8154 Jordan, David Starr, *Mexico: A New Nation In An Old Country*, 2, 5. (Mar.1899): p82-89.

8155 May, William B., *Chronicles Of A Highway: El Nuevo Camino Real, Fourth Paper*, 2, 5. (Mar.1899): p105-108.

8156 Webster, F. S., *From Benson To Bocoachi*, 2, 5. (Mar.1899): p94-96.

8157 May, William B., *Chronicles Of A Highway: El Nuevo Camino Real, Fifth Paper*, 2, 6. (Apr.1899): p133-136.

8158 May, William B., *Chronicles Of A Highway: El Nuevo Camino Real, Sixth Paper*, 3, 1. (May.1899): p11-15.

8159 May, William B., *Chronicles Of A Highway: El Nuevo Camino Real, Seventh Paper*, 3, 3. (Jul.1899): p105-107.

8160 May, William B., *Chronicles Of A Highway: El Nuevo Camino Real, Eighth Paper*, 3, 6. (Oct.1899): p173-180.

8161 Webster, F. S., *The Magdalena Fiesta*, 4, 2. (Dec.1899): p39-43.

8162 Mayo, H. M., *Cuba And The Way There*, 4, 3. (Jan.1900): p94-98.

8163 Hoover, E. A., *A Trip Up Popocatapetl And Down Again*, 4, 3. (Jan.1900): p107-109.

8164 The Pioneer, *Fourth Of July, 1836*, 5, 3. (Jul.1900): p138-139.

8165 Knightly, Margaret T., *A Day of Reminiscences In Santa Barbara*, 5, 4. (Aug.1900): p157-159.

8166 Jones, Philip M., *Mission San Antonio - A Plea For Its Restoration And Preservation*, 5, 6. (Oct.1900): p301-303.

8167 Smythe, William E., *An International Wedding: The Tale Of A Trip On The Borders Of Two Republics*, 5, 6. (Oct.1900): p286-300.

8168 Scott, C. A., *San Antonio Texas In 1867*, 6, 2. (Dec.1900): p59-66.

8169 Kirk, Henry S., *The Missions Of Monterey*, 6, 4. (Feb.1901): p115-119.

9. Travel

8170 Stein, Evaleen, *A December Morning At Santa Barbara Mission*, 7, 4. (Aug.1901): p90-98.

8171 Connor, J. Torrey, *Christmas In Mexico, The City Of Delights*, 8, 2. (Dec.1901): p49-53.

8172 Van Dyke, T. S., *Fresh Fields For Rod And Gun - Sonora, Mexico*, 8, 3. (Jan.1902): p106-111.

8173 *Guaymas On The Gulf*, 8, 3. (Jan.1902): p111-112.

8174 Connor, J. Torrey, *La Fiesta De Los Angeles*, 8, 6. (Apr.1902): p267.

8175 Henry, Sarah, *San Francisco's Mission Dolores*, 9, 3. (Jul.1902): p181-189.

8176 Hoover, E. A., *Mexico Of Long Ago*, 9, 5. (Sep.1902): p339-341.

8177 Coney, Alejandro K., *Mexico Of Today*, 9, 5. (Sep.1902): p342-345.

8178 Knox, Jessie Juliet, *At Mission Santa Clara*, 9, 6. (Oct.1902): p391-396.

8179 Shoup, Paul, *The Mission Of San Juan Bautista*, 10, 5. (Mar.1903): p435-438.

8180 Enderlein, Ella H., *Camulos And Ramona*, 11, 1. (May.1903): p44-47.

8181 Maurer, Margaret Fenn, *Old Santa Barbara And Its Mission*, 11, 2. (Jun.1903): p181-184.

8182 Isaacs, J. D., *Spanish Art In Texas*, 11, 4. (Aug.1903): p384-387.

8183 Loud, Emily S., *Mission Days At Sonoma*, 11, 5. (Sep.1903): p481-483.

8184 Piatt, W. J., *Mexico's Antique Pottery*, 12, 3. (Jan.1904): p262-266.

8185 Bell, Mary, *The Romance Of The Spanish Grants: Rancho El Sur*, 13, 4. (Aug.1904): p332-337.

8186 Powers, Laura Bride, *A Mission Centennial*, 13, 5. (Sep.1904): p418-419.

8187 Ellison, O. C., *About Baja California*, 14, 1. (Nov.1904): p37-42.

8188 Keatinge, Alice M., *Texas Missions Today*, 14, 6. (Apr.1905): p591-595.

8189 James, Vinton L., *West Texas, Present and Past*, 15, 5. (Sep.1905): p483-487.

8190 Coolidge, Dane, *The Passing Of The Cowboy*, 16, 3. (Jan.1906): p239-242.

8191 Stoddard, Charles Warren, *Old Mission Idyls, Part One*, 17, 2-3. (Jun.1906): p81-93.

8192 Stoddard, Charles Warren, *Old Mission Idyls, Part Two*, 17, 4. (Aug.1906): p178-192.

8193 Stoddard, Charles Warren, *Old Mission Idyls, Part Three*, 17, 5. (Sep.1906): p244-255.

8194 North, Arthur, *On The Road To Guadalajara*, 17, 6. (Oct.1906): p329-342.

8195 Tisdale, Lieuella, *Young Mexico*, 17, 6. (Oct.1906): p343-347.

8196 Stoddard, Charles Warren, *Old Mission Idyls, Part Four*, 17, 6. (Oct.1906): p368-375.

8197 North, Arthur, *The Mother Of California*, 18, 1. (Nov.1906): p33-41.

8198 North, Arthur, *The Mother Of California*, 18, 2. (Dec.1906): p145-155.

8199 Stoddard, Charles Warren, *Old Mission Idyls: The Mission of a Mission (Part Five)*, 18, 3. (Dec.1906): p109-114.

8200 North, Arthur, *The Mother Of California*, 18, 3. (Jan.1907): p177-188.

8201 Stoddard, Charles Warren, *Old Mission Idyls: From a Mission Garden - A Revery and a Retrospect (Part Six)*, 18, 3. (Jan.1907): p189-195.

8202 Saunders, Charles Francis, *San Juan Capistrano*, 18, 4. (Feb.1907): p306-309.

8203 Truesdell, Amelia Woodward, *A Fiesta At San Miguel*, 18, 4. (Feb.1907): p313-319.

8204 Coolidge, Dane, *In Cuernavaca*, 18, 4. (Feb.1907): p337-339.

8205 Danenbaum, Roby, *In Mexico To-Day*, 20, 1. (Nov.1907): p13-22.

8206 Guyer, George Vest, *In Guadalajara*, 20, 1. (Nov.1907): p51-59.

8207 Aiken, Charles Sedgwick, *The Land Of Tomorrow*, 22, 6. (Jun.1909): p568-583.

8208 Peixotto, Ernest C., *Christmas Mission Bells*, 23, 6. (Dec.1909): p553-558.

8209 Gonzales, Gaspar Estrada, *Mexico As It Is, First Paper*, 24, 1. (Jan.1910): p73-79.

8210 Gonzales, Gaspar Estrada, *Mexico As It Is, Second Paper*, 24, 3. (Mar.1910): p291-295.

8211 Hornaday, W. D., *Reclaiming A Land Of Romance*, 24, 4. (Apr.1910): p404-409.

8212 Gonzales, Gaspar Estrada, *Mexico As It Is, Third Paper*, 24, 4. (Apr.1910): p426-431.

8213 Gonzales, Gaspar Estrada, *Mexico As It Is, Fourth Paper*, 25, 1. (Jul.1910): p83-98.

8214 Murray, Robert Hammond, *Growling At Mexico*, 25, 2. (Aug.1910): p205-212.

8215 Wilson, Bourdon, *Hermosillo, The New Dixie Land*, 26, 1. (Jan.1911): p105-108.

8216 Madison, Elizabeth Syle, *Hacienda De La Guerra*, 26, 1. (Jan.1911): p37-47.

8217 Whitaker, Herman, *Mexico And Her Common Man*, 26, 2. (Feb.1911): p217-222.

8218 Kyne, Peter B., *The Gringo As Insurrecto*, 27, 3. (Sep.1911): p257-267.

8219 Gates, Eleanor, *Motoring Among The Missions*, 28, 3. (Mar.1912): p305-314.

8220 Gates, Eleanor, *Motoring Among The Missions*, 28, 4. (Apr.1912): p438-445.

8221 Gates, Eleanor, *Motoring Among The Missions*, 28, 6. (Jun.1912): p703-709.

8222 Laut, Agnes C., *Why Go Abroad?: The Mission in the Arizona Desert*, 30, 1. (Jan.1913): p27-32.

8223 Powell, E. Alexander, *Is There Any Hope For Mexico?*, 31, 2. (Aug.1913): p297-303.

8224 Whitaker, Herman, *Villa And His People*, 33, 2. (Aug.1914): p251-257, 358-366.

8225 Barrett, John, *The Pacific Coast And Pan-America*, 33, 4. (Oct.1914): p660-664.

8226 Barrows, David P., *The Dove In The Bull Ring*, 35, 5. (Nov.1915): p857-860.

8227 Bradley, Arthur Z., *Motoring After Missions*, 36, 1. (Jan.1916): p64-68, 78-79.

8228 Reid, Frederick, *Must We Clean Up Mexico?*, 36, 2. (Feb.1916): p27-28, 81.

8229 Connor, Torrey, *Si, Senor!*, 38, 3. (Mar.1917): p34-35, 91-92.

8230 Adams, Eleanor, *The Penitent Brothers*, 38, 4. (Apr.1917): p26-28, 88.

8231 Carr, Harry, *The Kingdom Of Cantu*, 38, 4. (Apr.1917): p33-34, 65-67.

8232 Reighard, J. Gamble, *Do We Know Our ABC's?*, 40, 6. (Jun.1918): p44-45, 73.

8233 Murray, Robert Hammond, *Gringo-Baiting*, 41, 1. (Jul.1918): p11-13, 50-52.

8234 Saunders, Charles Francis, *With Pancho On A Pilgrimage*, 43, 5. (Nov.1919): p22-24, 107.

8235 Thompson, Herbert Cooper, *Understanding Mexicans*, 43, 6. (Dec.1919): p31-33, 82-86.

8236 Thompson, Herbert Cooper, *Is Mexico Hopeless?*, 44, 5. (May.1920): p33-36, 72-74.

8237 Dunn, H. H., *Mexico's Pedagogic Medicine*, 52, 1. (Jan.1924): p21-23, 58.

8238 Hamby, William H., *In Search Of Senoritas*, 52, 3. (Mar.1924): p24-26, 78-79.

8239 Dunn, H. H., *Will Thirteen Be A Lucky Number?*, 54, 2. (Feb.1925): p9-10, 52-54.

8240 MacDowell, Syl, *Castles Of Mud*, 56, 2. (Feb.1926): p23, 72.

8241 Raley, Helen, *Guardians Of Our Border*, 57, 5. (Nov.1926): p30-31, 62-63.

8242 Lyman, Helen, *The Charm Of Spain In The Far West*, 58, 3. (Mar.1927): p22-23, 76.

8243 Echternach, A. V., *Spanish Or Californian?*, 58, 5. (May.1927): p15, 87-88.

8244 Obregon, Alvaro and Willard, Victor, *Hooking Up With Mexico*, 59, 1. (Jul.1927): p22-24.

8245 Ewing, Paul A., *The Borderland Missions*, 59, 4. (Oct.1927): p24-26, 54.

9. Travel

8246 Yates, Helen Eva, *Take A New Way To Old Mexico*, 65, 3. (Sep.1930): p10-12.

8247 Morhardt, J. E., Jr., *We Drove Down Through Lower California*, 67, 3. (Sep.1931): p10-12.

8248 *Down To Mexico*, 79, 5. (Nov.1937): p22-23.

8249 *Shopping Through Mexico*, 93, 4. (Oct.1944): p24-30.

8250 *Handmade In Mexico*, 93, 5. (Nov.1944): p2.

8251 *Report From Mexico*, 94, 3. (Mar.1945): p2-9.

8252 *Mexico - With Guide*, 94, 6. (Jun.1945): p2-4, 6.

8253 *Baja California*, 102, 2. (Feb.1949): p19-21.

8254 *Trailer Trek Through Mexico*, 103, 6. (Dec.1949): p14-15.

8255 *High Road To Mexico*, 105, 4. (Oct.1950): p12-16.

8256 *Mexico's West Coast Ready For Tourist Boom*, 105, 4. (Oct.1950): p30-35.

8257 *Discover Southern Arizona*, 106, 1. (Jan.1951): p8-12.

8258 *Mexico's Colorado Back Country*, 107, 4. (Oct.1951): p34-37.

8259 *Exploring, Camping, And Fishing...On The Sea Of Cortez*, 107, 4. (Oct.1951): p38-43.

8260 *Camping on the Beach in Lower California*, 107, 5. (Nov.1951): p26, 29.

8261 *New Paving South Of Mexico City*, 107, 6. (Dec.1951): p10-13.

8262 *San Diego To Yuma*, 108, 1. (Jan.1952): p16-18.

8263 *Loreto: Below-The-Border Discovery*, 109, 5. (Nov.1952): p19-22.

8264 *Tropical Relaxing In Manzanillo On Mexico's West Coast*, 110, 1. (Jan.1953): p18-22.

8265 *Arizona's Mexican Neighbor...Gay And Friendly Sonora*, 110, 2. (Feb.1953): p32-37.

8266 *Across Mexico To Veracruz*, 111, 3. (Sep.1953): p19-24.

8267 *Mexico's New West Coast Highway Is Ready For The Family Car*, 111, 4. (Oct.1953): p48-53.

8268 *Mexico City*, 112, 2. (Feb.1954): p38-43.

8269 *Easter In Mexico*, 112, 4. (Apr.1954): p39-41.

8270 *You Can Forget Traffic Along The Coronado Trail*, 113, 2. (Sep.1954): p20-28.

8271 *Not Tahiti...But Mexico*, 113, 3. (Sep.1954): p37-40.

8272 *Eight Ways To Sample The Colorful Heart Of Old Mexico*, 113, 5. (Nov.1954): p42-49.

8273 *You Miss So Much...If You Hurry Through Northern Sonora*, 113, 6. (Dec.1954): p20-24.

8274 *Why Fisherman Go to Guaymas*, 114, 3. (Mar.1955): p29, 31-32, 34.

8275 *At The Pan Am Highway's End*, 115, 4. (Oct.1955): p38-43.

8276 *Three Ways To Discover Mexico's Own California*, 115, 5. (Nov.1955): p46-53.

8277 *383 Highway Miles Below Arizona's Border Is The Ancient, Sleepy City Of Alamos*, 116, 2. (Feb.1956): p44-47.

8278 *Shopping In Mexico Is Fun*, 117, 6. (Dec.1956): p20-21.

8279 *Deep In Mexico...A Wonderful Loop You Can Drive In 2 Days*, 118, 3. (Mar.1957): p14-16, 18.

8280 *1000 Miles Of Tropical Discovery*, 119, 3. (Sep.1957): p44-51.

8281 *If You are in Southern California or Arizona Before Christmas... One-Day Christmas Shopping Just Below the Border*, 119, 6. (Dec.1957): p14-16.

8282 *For Its People And For Its Crafts...Viva Oaxaca...There Is No Other*, 120, 2. (Feb.1958): p48-53.

8283 *How's The High Road To Mexico City?*, 122, 2. (Feb.1959): p52-57.

8284 *Just Below The Border...The Devil's Highway*, 122, 4. (Apr.1959): p26-28, 30, 32.

8285 *The Arizona Valley Is A Soft Sea Of Grass*, 123, 3. (Sep.1959): p34-35.

8286 *Mexico's Adventuresome National Highway 180...Now Open To Yucatan*, 125, 6. (Dec.1960): p26-28, 30, 32, 34, 37.

8287 *Sunny Sonora, Mexico*, 126, 1. (Jan.1961): p48-63.

8288 *In The Plaza Of San Juan Bautista You Step Back Into California's Past*, 126, 5. (May.1961): p88-95.

8289 *Mexico City*, 131, 2. (Aug.1963): p42-57.

8290 *Puerto Vallarta Is Changing...Perhaps You Should Hurry*, 132, 1. (Jan.1964): p25, 26, 28, 30.

8291 *Rail Adventure Trip Across Mexico's Sierra Madre*, 132, 3. (Mar.1964): p34, 36, 38.

8292 *Shopping For Mexico's Folk Art And Homewares*, 133, 5. (Nov.1964): p80-87.

8293 *Eating Out Is A Pleasure In Guadalajara*, 137, 4. (Oct.1966): p180, 182, 184.

8294 *Guadalajara*, 137, 4. (Oct.1966): p78-91.

8295 *The Mexican Eating In Tucson And Nogales Is Good, And It's Different... Chimichangas, Burros, Gorditas, Tostadas de Harina*, 138, 1. (Jan.1967): p58-61.

8296 *By Car Into Next-Door Mexico...Arizona's Friendly Neighbor, Sonora*, 140, 3. (Mar.1968): p60-69.

8297 *The Bottom Of Baja*, 142, 3. (Mar.1969): p76-85.

8298 *Shopping Tour Guadalajara To Mexico City And Back To Guadalajara*, 145, 4. (Oct.1970): p64-75.

8299 *Poking Around In The Mission Village Of San Juan Capistrano*, 146, 6. (Jun.1971): p46-48.

8300 *Just Below Arizona A Mission Chain 150 Years Older Than California*, 148, 1. (Jan.1972): p30-31.

8301 *A Mixture Of Yesterday And Today*, 148, 4. (Apr.1972): p62-64.

8302 *Pick Your Mexico-Pacific Beach Holiday*, 149, 5. (Nov.1972): p88-97.

8303 *The Baja News For 1973... It Now Is Easy To Get To Bahia Concepcion; A New Car Ferry is One Big Reason*, 150, 2. (Feb.1973): p76-79.

8304 *On Mexico's Tropical West Coast.. Change Comes to Old Manzanillo*, 151, 4. (Oct.1973): p50-52.

8305 *Your Own Discovery Of Mexico's Yucatan*, 151, 5. (Nov.1973): p74-83.

8306 *Should You Try The New Baja Road This Year?*, 153, 3. (Sep.1974): p36-38, 40, 42, 44, 46.

8307 *Again A Comeback For The Grand Old Mission Inn*, 154, 3. (Mar.1975): p42-43.

8308 *Oaxaca*, 156, 3. (Mar.1976): p80-85.

8309 *Spanish America In Today's New Mexico*, 158, 5. (May.1977): p94-99.

8310 *Christmas Ideas From New Mexico*, 161, 6. (Dec.1978): p74-75.

8311 *What's Sonora? It's Mucho*, 163, 5. (Nov.1979): p82-91.

8312 *Early Christmas Comes Back At The 21 California Missions*, 165, 6. (Dec.1980): p52-57.

8313 *Folklorico—Mexico's Folk Ballet*, 167, 2. (Aug.1981): p64-65.

8314 *Mexico's Michoacan*, 167, 5. (Nov.1981): p92-101.

8315 *The New Tijuana*, 170, 2. (Feb.1983): p76-81.

8316 *Puebla, Mexico's Colonial Treasure House*, 186, 2. (Feb.1991): p60-67.

8317 Finnegan, Lora J., *Mission Alert*, 189, 2. (Aug.1992): p64-71.

8318 Fish, Peter, *Unraveling The Mysteries Of The Maya*, 193, 5. (Nov.1994): p82-87.

8319 *Beyond Former Glory*, 197, 05. (Nov.1996): p90-92, 94.

8320 Jaffe, Matthew, *Colors of Oaxaca*, 199, 4. (Oct.1997): p78-83.

8321 Jaffe, Matthew, *Cabo Grows Up*, 199, 5. (Nov.1997): p24, 28-32.

9. Travel

9.5 Touring & Vacation Destinations

8322 A Peep At The South, 1, 1. (May.1898): p12.

8323 *Summer Holidays Among The Hills*, 1, 2. (Jun.1898): p18-25.

8324 *What Constitutes A State*, 1, 2. (Jun.1898): p27-31.

8325 *A Vacation Department Store*, 1, 3. (Jul.1898): p37-41.

8326 *An Outing At Eagle Lake, Texas*, 1, 3. (Jul.1898): p43.

8327 *Lake County, California*, 1, 3. (Jul.1898): p44-45.

8328 Mayo, H. H., *New Orleans*, 1, 4. (Aug.1898): p59-61.

8329 *Some Possibilities Of A Pleasure Tour In Southern California*, 1, 5. (Sep.1898): p69-73.

8330 Mayo, H. H., *New Orleans*, 1, 5. (Sep.1898): p75-77.

8331 *El Camino Real*, 1, 6. (Oct.1898): p87-88.

8332 *The Carnival - Its History*, 2, 3. (Jan.1899): p36-40.

8333 *A Calendar Of The Carnival Organizations*, 2, 3. (Jan.1899): p40-41.

8334 *A Mardi Gras Day*, 2, 3. (Jan.1899): p42-44.

8335 *On To Washington*, 2, 3. (Jan.1899): p54-56.

8336 Zuehl, O. W., *Kinney County, Texas*, 2, 3. (Jan.1899): p59.

8337 *N.E.A. A Visitors Souvenir Guide To California*, 3, 2. (Jun.1899): p33-89.

8338 Braden, H. Robert, *Some Of The Sights Of San Francisco*, 3, 3. (Jul.1899): p91-96.

8339 Fassett, J. Sloat, *A Trans-Pacific Voyage To The 'Land Of Aloha' And Beyond*, 3, 5. (Sep.1899): p146-152.

8340 Sexton, Ella, *Lake Tahoe And Mountain Resorts*, 3, 5. (Sep.1899): p158-159.

8341 Coulter, Maud Dougherty, *Across Nevada*, 3, 5. (Sep.1899): p160-162.

8342 Connell, Irene, *The Garden Of California*, 3, 6. (Oct.1899): p188-190.

8343 Kellogg, Vernon L., *A Stanford Party In The Kings River Canyon*, 4, 1. (Nov.1899): p16-18.

8344 Schenck, D. B., *Whittier, California: A Hillside City Of Quaker Origin And Cosmopolitan Environments. An Account Of Its Advantageous Situation And Manifold Products*, 4, 1. (Nov.1899): p23-25.

8345 Booth, S. F., *Fresno County: Its Resources And Possibilities*, 4, 1. (Nov.1899): p6-15.

8346 Kinney, Abbott, *Sanitary Santa Monica*, 4, 3. (Jan.1900): p98-102.

8347 Van Dyke, T. S., *The Head Of The San Joaquin Valley*, 4, 4. (Feb.1900): p162-163.

8348 Kirkland, J. B., *Southern Oregon*, 4, 6. (Apr.1900): p235-236.

8349 Riggs, W., *Orange County, California*, 4, 6. (Apr.1900): p237-242.

8350 McAdie, Alexander G., *San Francisco-The Convention City*, 5, 1. (May.1900): p8-16.

8351 Keith, Eliza D., *San Francisco As A Summer Resort*, 5, 2. (Jun.1900): p69-73.

8352 Powell, Sherman, *Through Sacramento Canyon To Pelican Bay*, 5, 2. (Jun.1900): p74-77.

8353 Meyers, Mrs. Susan E. Bittle, *A Trip To The Sierras, The Painted Rocks And Millwood*, 5, 2. (Jun.1900): p78-79.

8354 *The Pan-American Exposition*, 5, 2. (Jun.1900): p83-85.

8355 Fulton, R. L., *Camp Life On A Great Cattle Range In Northern Nevada*, 5, 3. (Jul.1900): p112-118.

8356 Clarke, Arthur F., *A Day Of Street Fair Amid Orange Groves*, 5, 4. (Aug.1900): p161-163.

8357 Robinson, Martha Ingersoll, *A Day's Possibilities In 'The San Diego Bay Region'*, 5, 4. (Aug.1900): p163-166.

8358 Coope, J. F., *Santa Cruz - The City Of Mountain And Shore*, 5, 5. (Sep.1900): p226-238.

8359 *California As A Summer Resort*, 7, 2-3. (1901): p37-63.

8360 *Seeing California - How, When And Why*, 6, 4. (Feb.1901): p123.

8361 Pierson, Charles H., *The Pan-American Exposition At Buffalo*, 6, 4. (Feb.1901): p126.

8362 Gremke, Elesa M., *To Tehipite Through Silver Canyon*, 6, 5. (Mar.1901): p135-141.

8363 *Forest, Fish And Game At Chicago: A Study Of The Recent Novel International Exposition*, 6, 6. (Apr.1901): p187-189.

8364 Neiswender, W. H., *Summer Outing In The Cascades*, 7, 2-3. (Jun.1901): p71-80.

8365 Kirk, Henry S., *A Day In San Buenaventura*, 7, 2-3. (Jun.1901): p66-69.

8366 Shinn, Charles Howard, *A Study Of San Luis Obispo County, California*, 7, 5. (Sep.1901): p118-134.

8367 *Pasadena's Flower Festival*, 8, 2. (Dec.1901): p97.

8368 Clarke, Alla Aldrich, *In Orange Land - Riverside*, 8, 3. (Jan.1902): p113-118.

8369 Bell, Mary, *With The Mardi Gras Maskers*, 8, 4. (Feb.1902): p179-184.

8370 Robinson, Ednah, *From A Globe Trotter's Journal*, 8, 5. (Mar.1902): p223-226.

8371 Barr, Jas. A., *Feasting On County Products*, 9, 1. (May.1902): p44-60.

8372 Cantine, R. S., *Loma Linda Impressions*, 9, 2. (Jun.1902): p141.

8373 Walcott, Earle Ashley, *San Francisco: The Gateway Of The Orient*, 9, 3. (Jul.1902): p152-162.

8374 *San Francisco In Carnival Colors: An Electric Canopy Of Light*, 9, 3. (Jul.1902): p214-216.

8375 Hocking, T. C., *Sunny Stanislaus: The Gateway County Of The Great San Joaquin Valley Of California*, 9, 4. (Aug.1902): p251-264.

8376 Shinn, Charles Howard, *Down The San Mateo Peninsula*, 9, 4. (Aug.1902): p269-284.

8377 MacDonald, Donald, *El Paso De Robles*, 9, 5. (Sep.1902): p319-324.

8378 White, Kathryn, *The East And The West*, 10, 1. (Nov.1902): p72-73.

8379 Dezendorf, Alfred, *In Sunshine And Surf*, 10, 2. (Dec.1902): p150-153.

8380 Klein, John C., *Where Water Is Life*, 10, 2. (Dec.1902): p155-158.

8381 Mayo, H. M., *New Orleans Of The Present*, 10, 3. (Jan.1903): p179-186.

8382 Hodgson, Caspar W., *Up Oregon's Rogue River*, 10, 3. (Jan.1903): p198-203.

8383 Armstrong, F. W., *Where Words Have Wings: What A Visitor To Santa Catalina Island Saw And Heard Of The Practical Workings Of Wireless Telegraphy*, 10, 3. (Jan.1903): p225-227.

8384 Robinson, Ednah, *New Orleans, City Of Eternal Youth*, 10, 3. (Jan.1903): p172-178.

8385 Grinnell, Elizabeth, *New Year's Rose Tourney*, 10, 4. (Feb.1903): p285-289.

8386 Sayres, Carroll, *Amid Foothill Riches: Placer County, California*, 10, 4. (Feb.1903): p322-332.

8387 Mitchell, Edmund, *Winter At Palm Springs*, 10, 4. (Feb.1903): p351-353.

8388 Peixotto, Ernest C., *Italy's Message To California*, 10, 5. (Mar.1903): p367-377.

8389 Goff, E. F., *In The Orange Grove City: A Few Facts Concerning The Past And Present And The Unparalleled Progress Of Riverside, California*, 10, 5. (Mar.1903): p388-403.

8390 Taylor, Arthur A., *Santa Cruz By The Sea*, 10, 5. (Mar.1903): p419-433.

8391 Walcott, Earle Ashley, *Our Share In Oriental Commerce*, 10, 6. (Apr.1903): p479-492.

9. Travel

8392 Jaynes, Allan B., *Tucson Of Today*, 10, 6. (Apr.1903): p527-537.

8393 Curtis, Martin, *A Morning In Berkeley*, 11, 1. (May.1903): p69.

8394 Keatinge, Mary Alice, *Two Girls In A Buggy: The Story Of A Three-Hundred-Mile Drive Through California Valleys*, 11, 4. (Aug.1903): p318-329.

8395 O'Brien, Frederick, *The Land Of The Lotus - Capitola*, 11, 4. (Aug.1903): p340-344.

8396 McCormick, E. O., *The Search For Nature's Best*, 11, 6. (Oct.1903): p558-562.

8397 Jenks, W. R. L., *Los Gatos, Gem Of The Foothills*, 12, 2. (Dec.1903): p135-142.

8398 Chapman, J. Wilbur, D.D., *Six Weeks In California*, 12, 3. (Jan.1904): p275-276.

8399 Coulter, Arthur D., *A Summer In Siberia*, 12, 4. (Feb.1904): p301-314.

8400 Harmon, James Phineas, Esq., *Why I Moved West: A Typical Story Of Santa Cruz, California, The City Of The Holy Cross*, 12, 4. (Feb.1904): p316-330.

8401 Grinnell, Elizabeth, *Pasadena's Rose Tournament*, 12, 4. (Feb.1904): p331-334.

8402 Shaw, A. D., *Concerning San Benito*, 12, 4. (Feb.1904): p350-363.

8403 Pugsley, Cornelius Amory, *Financiers At The Golden Gate*, 12, 5. (Mar.1904): p400-403.

8404 Sinnard, L. G., *The Garden Of The Bishop: A Study Of The Characteristics Of San Luis Obispo County, California*, 12, 5. (Mar.1904): p448-461.

8405 Hoffman, Elwyn, *California At St. Louis*, 12, 6. (Apr.1904): p481-484.

8406 Hayward, Florence, *Abroad For St. Louis*, 12, 6. (Apr.1904): p484-487.

8407 Dezendorf, Alfred, *Oregon's Coming Exposition*, 12, 6. (Apr.1904): p489-498.

8408 Sinnard, L. G., *The Garden Of The Bishop: A Study Of The Characteristics Of San Luis Obispo County, California - The Coast Region*, 12, 6. (Apr.1904): p525-541.

8409 Ocheltree, G. B., *In The Klamath Country: The Story Of A Summer Vacation In The Wonderland Of Southern Oregon*, 13, 1. (May.1904): p14-25.

8410 Oakley, Isabella G., *Santa Barbara Of Today*, 13, 1. (May.1904): p43-53.

8411 Jaynes, Allan B., *Like A Mirage Miracle: A Study Of The Development Of Tucson, Arizona*, 13, 1. (May.1904): p68-77.

8412 Dezendorf, Alfred, *Five Days On Peaceful Waters*, 13, 2. (Jun.1904): p120-128.

8413 Eldredge, George Granville, *On Vacation Values*, 13, 3. (Jul.1904): p254-255.

8414 Day, James R., *A California Vacation*, 13, 4. (Aug.1904): p249.

8415 Smith, S. H., *All About Angels: Being The Narrative Of A Summer Venture Into The Bret Harte Region Of The Sierra Nevada Mountains Of California*, 13, 4. (Aug.1904): p350-357.

8416 Austin, Mary, *Over The Kearsarge Trail*, 13, 4. (Aug.1904): p375-377.

8417 Odell, Anna Avis, *Ho, For Tahoe!*, 13, 4. (Aug.1904): p378-379.

8418 MacCallum, John Bruce, *The Nest By The Sea*, 13, 5. (Sep.1904): p456-458.

8419 Jay, Alfred, *Sights At St. Louis*, 13, 5. (Sep.1904): p405-411.

8420 Waterhouse, Alfred J., *Two Pilgrimages Westward: Plans For Greeting Knights Templar And Odd Fellows In San Francisco During September*, 13, 5. (Sep.1904): p413-417.

8421 Cradlebaugh, J. H., *Oregon's Capital City*, 13, 5. (Sep.1904): p420-424.

8422 Staats, William R., *About Oneonta*, 13, 5. (Sep.1904): p453-455.

8423 Kellogg, W. W., *A Sierra Empire: Something About The Orchards, Fields And Mines Of Plumas County, California*, 13, 6. (Oct.1904): p549-553.

8424 Stabler, Marguerite, *Between Two Rivers: A Description Of Sutter County, California*, 13, 6. (Oct.1904): p478-484.

8425 Fitch, George Hamlin, *Through Western Eyes: Notes Of A Trip To Chicago, New York And Washington, And The St. Louis Exposition*, 13, 6. (Oct.1904): p588-594.

8426 Hutchings, Emily Grant, *Getting About At St. Louis*, 14, 1. (Nov.1904): p30-32.

8427 Peters, Clay, *Reno Of The Silver State*, 14, 1. (Nov.1904): p78-83.

8428 Coolidge, Dane, *The Rodeo At Pinal*, 14, 3. (Jan.1905): p263-271.

8429 Unger, Frederic William, *China, The New West*, 14, 3. (Jan.1905): p218-226.

8430 Kirk, Heatherwick, *Another Treasure Island*, 14, 3. (Jan.1905): p235-240.

8431 Wakeman-Curtis, M. L., *Voyaging From The Golden Gate*, 14, 4. (Feb.1905): p377-390.

8432 King, I. Manning, *Three Times Little Rhody: Facts And Pictures That Tell Of The Natural Marvels And Industrial Resources Of Monterey County, California*, 14, 4. (Feb.1905): p392-403.

8433 Robinson, Ednah, *An American Lourdes: The Lesson And The Story Of Saint Roch, Or The Campo Santo, Of New Orleans*, 14, 4. (Feb.1905): p417-419.

8434 Merrick, Frank L., *Oregon's Great Centennial: Lewis And Clark Exposition Far Advanced - How It Looks Four Months Before Opening Day*, 14, 5. (Mar.1905): p439-448.

8435 Harris, W. N., *California At St. Louis*, 14, 5. (Mar.1905): p489-498.

8436 Armes, William Dallam, *The Story Of Colton Hall*, 14, 5. (Mar.1905): p521-525.

8437 Fraser, Julia, *With Lewis And Clark: The Approaching Exposition At Portland, Oregon; A Centennial Tribute To The Expansion theories Of Jefferson*, 14, 6. (Apr.1905): p576-581.

8438 Casper, K. R., *Ho, For Tonopah!*, 14, 6. (Apr.1905): p620-624.

8439 Smith, S. H., *In Bret Harte's Country*, 15, 1. (May.1905): p33-38.

8440 Coe, Marie, *New York To Paris By Rail*, 15, 4. (Aug.1905): p361-366.

8441 Murphy, Agnes J., *On The World's Highway*, 15, 5. (Sep.1905): p417-418.

8442 Aiken, Charles S., *San Francisco's Plight And Prospect*, 17, 2-3. (1906): p13-22.

8443 MacDonald, Donald, *Portland Points The Way*, 17, 2-3. (1906): p50-70.

8444 Harriman, E. H., *San Francisco*, 17, 1. (Jun.1906): p1-3.

8445 Gilmour, John Hamilton, *Midsummer Oregon*, 17, 4. (Aug.1906): p124-138.

8446 Landfield, Jerome B., *The Sunny Side Of Yuma*, 17, 5. (Sep.1906): p266-268.

8447 Thorpe, W. B., *California's Capital County*, 17, 5. (Sep.1906): p280-290.

8448 Wells, A. J., *Through Many Zones*, 18, 2. (Dec.1906): p134-137.

8449 Harris, Elmer B., *The New West: A Social Study Of Life In Nevada Towns Today*, 18, 4. (Feb.1907): p296-298.

8450 Merrick, Frank L., *The Great Northwest Next: Some Facts About The Alaska-Yukon-Pacific Exposition To Be Held In Seattle In 1909 - Superb Site On The Shores Of Lake Washington*, 18, 5. (Mar.1907): p421-429.

8451 Dunn, Allan, *The Sailing Of The Snark*, 19, 1. (May.1907): p2-9.

8452 Merrick, Frank L., *The Northwest's Exposition*, 19, 5. (Sep.1907): p416-420.

8453 Phillips, Blaine, *In The Twin Falls Country*, 19, 5. (Sep.1907): p476-480.

8454 Truesdell, Amelia Woodward, *At Mowry's Hacienda: Life To-Day At A Mountain Mine In Southern Arizona*, 20, 2. (Dec.1907): p172-176.

8455 Holder, Charles F. and others, *In Winter's Outdoor Land*, 20, 3. (Jan.1908): p210-256.

8456 Gilmour, John Hamilton, *On Clatsop Plains*, 20, 3. (Jan.1908): p283-290.

9. Travel

8457 Steele, James King, *Fairmont Hotel*, 21, 2. (May.1908): .

8458 *Lake Tahoe To-Day*, 21, 1. (May.1908): p81-82.

8459 Cutter, Charles Edward, *Tacoma Beautiful*, 21, 1. (May.1908): .

8460 Wells, A. J., *A Story Of Beginnings: Turlock, California, And How And Why Men Are Making Homes There*, 21, 1. (May.1908): .

8461 *The Woodward: One More Luxurious Home For Los Angeles Tourists*, 21, 2. (Jun.1908): .

8462 Wells, A. J., *In Here-We-Rest Land: Something About Ashland, Oregon, For Residence, For Comfort And For Profit*, 21, 2. (Jun.1908): .

8463 Citizens League, The, *More About Baker City*, 21, 2. (Jun.1908): .

8464 Brooks, Joseph T., *San Jose And The Santa Clara Valley*, 21, 2. (Jun.1908): .

8465 *The Return Of The City: San Francisco Firms Occupy Finer Quarters In The Old Localities*, 21, 7. (Nov.1908): p686.

8466 Hewson, Ernest Williams, *Where Chinese Kings Lie Buried*, 22, 2. (Feb.1909): p130-132.

8467 Walker, David H., *The Romance Of Monterey*, 22, 3. (Mar.1909): p316-318.

8468 Raymond, William H., *Uncle Sam's Next Big Show: Everything Ready To Open The Big Alaska-Yukon-Pacific Exposition At Seattle On June 1st* , 22, 5. (May.1909): p449-462.

8469 Wells, A. J., *Beauty And Bounty Of Monterey*, 22, 6. (Jun.1909): p667-670.

8470 Pike, LeRoy F., *Nevada's Latest Stampede*, 23, 1. (Jul.1909): p67-70.

8471 Gilmour, John Hamilton, *A Midsummer Idyl Of Santa Cruz*, 23, 1. (Jul.1909): p70-76.

8472 Truman, Ben C., *Tahoe, Where Sky And Water Meet*, 23, 1. (Jul.1909): p77-79.

8473 Law, Herbert E., *A California Chamonix*, 23, 1. (Jul.1909): p79-80.

8474 Newman, Elizabeth Murray, *Here's Drinking Your Health! How Some Of Lake County's Fame Is Writ In Water - A Land Of Wealth As Well As Health*, 23, 1. (Jul.1909): p97-101.

8475 Young, Lucien, *The Birthplace Of Lincoln*, 23, 2. (Aug.1909): p136-137.

8476 Struble, Wallace R., *Metropolis, Jr.: How Albany Qualifies For Second Place In Oregon - The Coming Manufacturing, Jobbing, And Central Trade Center Of The Great Willamette Valley*, 23, 5. (Nov.1909): p549-550.

8477 Parkhurst, Genevieve Yoell, *The Merits Of Mendocino: A California County Of Forests And Streams, Bordering On The Ocean*, 23, 6. (Dec.1909): p663-666.

8478 Arnold, Zachary, *Southern Hospitality: Where The Stranger That Is Within The Gates Of Southern California Finds Welcome*, 24, 1. (Jan.1910): p115-116.

8479 Parkhurst, Genevieve Yoell, *A Land Of Milk And Honey: How Sutter County, California, With Its Thriving Dairies And Busy Hives, Realizes The Description Of The Promised Land*, 24, 2. (Feb.1910): p225-227.

8480 Purcell, M., *In The Klamath Country*, 24, 2. (Feb.1910): p228.

8481 Parkhurst, Genevieve Yoell, *Living Up To Its Name: How The County Of El Dorado Continues To Justify The Title That Lured The Argonauts*, 24, 2. (Feb.1910): p229-232.

8482 Wells, A. J., *A Rose Of The Desert: Modern City Of Tucson, Arizona* , 24, 2. (Feb.1910): p233-236.

8483 Parkhurst, Genevieve Yoell, *An Opened Door: How Plumas County, California, Is Becoming Known To Enterprising Investors*, 24, 2. (Feb.1910): p241-242.

8484 Le Conte, Cardine, *A Californian's Return*, 24, 2. (Feb.1910): p211-216.

8485 Wells, A. J., *'Over Against The Coast': Modest Contra Costa, Rich In Virtues*, 24, 3. (Mar.1910): p347-350.

8486 Coonan, J. F., *Uncle Sam's Most Western City: Remarkable Resources Of Humboldt County, California, And Prosperity Of Its City, Eureka*, 24, 3. (Mar.1910): p355-358.

8487 Chetwood, John, *The Coolest Summer City*, 24, 4. (Apr.1910): p440-443.

8488 Conley, Fred G., *Concerning Cottage Grove: Something About The Sunny South Of The Willamette Valley, Oregon*, 24, 4. (Apr.1910): p467-470.

8489 Parkhurst, Genevieve Yoell, *The Lure O' Lassen*, 24, 4. (Apr.1910): p471-474.

8490 Farnsworth, Olin H., *The Meaning Of Monterey*, 24, 5. (May.1910): p583-586.

8491 Jackson, A. C., *Telling Oregon Truths*, 24, 6. (Jun.1910): p650-659.

8492 Giltner, E. C., *The Metropolitan Handicap: Portland, Oregon, In The Race For Supremacy On The Pacific Coast*, 24, 6. (Jun.1910): p701-704.

8493 Mills, John Scott, *At The Foot Of Mt. Ashland*, 24, 6. (Jun.1910): p705-706.

8494 Wells, A. J., *A Little Section Of Paradise: Napa County, California*, 25, 1. (Jul.1910): p109-111.

8495 Mosessohn, M., *Boasting A Blue Ribbon: Why Benton County, Oregon, Is A Prize-winning Subdivision Of The Famed Willamette Valley - The Claims Of Corvallis*, 25, 1. (Jul.1910): p115-116.

8496 Cowgill, W. C., *Enterprising Elgin: A Growing Oregon Town In The Center Of A Great Agricultural District*, 25, 1. (Jul.1910): p117-118.

8497 Mills, John Scott, *A Gateway To The Future: The Promise Of Pocatello, Idaho*, 25, 1. (Jul.1910): p119-120.

8498 Parkhurst, Genevieve Yoell, *In the High Sierra of Inyo County*, 25, 2. (Aug.1910): p233-234.

8499 Sloan, Richard E., *The Forty-Seventh Star: Some Straight Facts Concerning Arizona And Her Outlook In The Family Of States*, 25, 3. (Sep.1910): p267-272.

8500 Shouse, Jean Paul, *The Great Valley Of The Sacramento: A Thousand Square Miles Of Fertility*, 25, 3. (Sep.1910): p349-352.

8501 Squier, H. G., *The Vale Of Sacramento: Attractive Colonization Work Of The Sacramento Valley Irrigation Company*, 25, 3. (Sep.1910): p361-362.

8502 Freeman, Dan Curtis, *Eugene, The Well-Born*, 25, 3. (Sep.1910): p363-366.

8503 North, Arthur W., *The Spirit Of Idaho*, 25, 4. (Oct.1910): p368-379.

8504 Mills, John Scott, *Golden Harvests For Miner And Farmer: Hailey, Idaho, A Rich Mineral District With Remarkable Resources In Agriculture And Room For Thousands Of Settlers' Families* , 25, 4. (Oct.1910): p477-478.

8505 Woehlke, Walter V., *Where Rolls The Oregon*, 25, 5. (Nov.1910): p482-496.

8506 Malboeuf, Charles A., *Oregon's Wonder City: Medford, Supported By Five Hundred Square Miles Of Rich Territory, Is A Beehive Of Business Activity*, 25, 5. (Nov.1910): p585-588.

8507 Wilson, Bourdon, *The Treasures Of Tucson*, 25, 5. (Nov.1910): p591-592.

8508 Gillett, James N., *What California Offers*, 25, 6. (Dec.1910): p621-623.

8509 Denison, A. A., *Oakland, The City That Charms*, 25, 6. (Dec.1910): p712-715.

8510 Walker, David H., *San Francisco The Hospitable*, 25, 6. (Dec.1910): p718-722.

8511 Woehlke, Walter V., *San Diego, The City Of Dreams Come True*, 26, 2. (Feb.1911): p127-140.

8512 Saunders, Charles Francis, *Winter On The Isle Of Summer*, 26, 2. (Feb.1911): p205-209.

8513 Watson, C. B., *In The Heart Of Oregon*, 26, 3. (Mar.1911): p312-315.

8514 Choate, Rufus, *San Diego, California*, 26, 4. (Apr.1911): p465-468.

8515 Parkhurst, Genevieve Yoell, *El Dorado 'The Golden' County*, 26, 4. (Apr.1911): p469-470.

8516 Mills, John Scott, *Twenty-Six Miles Of Delight*, 26, 4. (Apr.1911): p471-472.

8517 Fitch, George Hamlin, *On Horseback To Mount Rose*, 26, 6. (Jun.1911): p612-615.

8518 Chandler, Katherine, *Tavern Of The Big Water*, 26, 6. (Jun.1911): p657-659.

9. Travel

8519 Parkhurst, Genevieve Yoell, *The Land Of The Golden Feather River*, 27, 1. (Jul.1911): p106-107.

8520 Saunders, Charles Francis, *What We Went To The Desert To See*, 27, 1. (Jul.1911): p66-68.

8521 Wells, A. J., *Monterey County, California*, 27, 1. (Jul.1911): p102-105.

8522 Freeman, Dan Curtis, *Enjoying Outdoorsland At Eugene, Oregon*, 27, 2. (Aug.1911): p213-216.

8523 Woehlke, Walter V., *Astoria The Amphibious*, 27, 2. (Aug.1911): p117-130.

8524 Snell, Earle, *Motoring In The Sierra*, 27, 3. (Sep.1911): p286-291.

8525 Evans, Samuel M., *Eden of the Cooled-Off Caldron*, 27, 4. (Oct.1911): p355-368.

8526 Gates, Eleanor, *Pasadena–Paradise Regained*, 27, 6. (Dec.1911): p603.

8527 Steele, Rufus M., *Eating And Sleeping The Stranger*, 28, 1. (Jan.1912): p101-106.

8528 Smith, Bertha H., *The Charm Of Coronado*, 28, 3. (Mar.1912): p362-364.

8529 Fisher, C. E., *Where Pleasure And Profit Abound*, 29, 3. (Sep.1912): p342.

8530 Thompson, Joe D., *The Columbia River Road*, 29, 6. (Dec.1912): p693-698.

8531 Laut, Agnes C., *Why Go Abroad?*, 30, 4. (Apr.1913): p397-403.

8532 McGaffey, Ernest, *The Island Of Discovery*, 30, 5. (May.1913): p495-508.

8533 Egilbert, W. D., *Trinity–A California Treasure-Trove*, 30, 6. (Jun.1913): p854.

8534 Powell, E. Alexander, *The Land Of Magic Names*, 31, 1. (Jul.1913): p67-80.

8535 Powell, E. Alexander, *Arizona*, 31, 4. (Oct.1913): p667-680.

8536 Powell, E. Alexander, *Chopping A Path To Tomorrow*, 31, 5. (Nov.1913): p895-907.

8537 Powell, E. Alexander, *The Land Of The Turquoise Sky*, 32, 1. (Jan.1914): p67-79.

8538 Maulsby, F. R., *Tucson, Arizona, In A New Dress*, 32, 1. (Jan.1914): p216-218.

8539 Hymer, Otis, *Kern County Starts Something–A Rodeo Home Coming*, 32, 3. (Mar.1914): p664-666.

8540 Howard, Randall R., *The Port Of The Columbia*, 32, 4. (Apr.1914): p833-842.

8541 Underwood, John J., *That Land Up There*, 34, 5. (May.1915): p890-898.

8542 Moss, Herbert C., *Motoring Among The American Fjords*, 34, 6. (Jun.1915): p1124-1134.

8543 North, Arthur W., *The Cut-Off*, 35, 6. (Dec.1915): p1095-1104.

8544 Gillmore, Inez Haynes, *The Californiacs*, 36, 2. (Feb.1916): p13-15, 52-60.

8545 Woehlke, Walter V., *Through Apache Lands*, 37, 1. (Jul.1916): p13-16, 82.

8546 Mayhew, Katherine P., *In Aloha Land*, 37, 2. (Aug.1916): p17-20, 69-74.

8547 O'Neil, Charles I., *Motor-Touring As A Family Affair*, 37, 4. (Oct.1916): p76-77.

8548 Laing, Hamilton M., *Chugging About The Sound Country*, 37, 5. (Nov.1916): p16-19, 72-77.

8549 Crowell, Elsinore Robinson, *Little Ovens*, 37, 5. (Nov.1916): p39-40, 66-68.

8550 Laing, Hamilton M., *Chugging Over And Through Colorado*, 37, 6. (Dec.1916): p24-25, 72-78.

8551 Daniels, Mark, *The Box Canyon*, 38, 3. (Mar.1917): p19.

8552 Shepardson, Lucia, *Butterfly Trees*, 38, 3. (Mar.1917): p27.

8553 Clemens, Mildred Leo, *Trailing Mark Twain Through Hawaii*, 38, 5. (May.1917): p7-9, 95-98.

8554 Laing, Hamilton M., *By Motor and Muscle to Mt. Hood*, 39, 1. (Jul.1917): p72,74,76,78,80.

8555 Laing, Hamilton M., *By Motor And Mule To The Marble Halls*, 39, 5. (Nov.1917): p74-80.

8556 Terrill, Lucy Stone, *New York–At Last!*, 40, 3. (Mar.1918): p47, 70.

8557 Bois, Jules, *The Vision In The West*, 41, 1. (Jul.1918): p16, 65-66.

8558 Partridge, Edward Bellamy, *On The King's Carpet*, 42, 6. (Jun.1919): p30-33, 78-82.

8559 Partridge, Edward Bellamy, *Hunting The Dove Round The Adriatic*, 43, 1. (Jul.1919): p37-39, 80-85.

8560 Partridge, Edward Bellamy, *Lafayette, We Are Home!*, 43, 6. (Dec.1919): p26-28, 72-82.

8561 Laing, Hamilton M., *When Spring Calls From The Hilltops*, 44, 4. (Apr.1920): p42-44, 97-98.

8562 White, Stewart Edward, *Wizard's River*, 44, 6. (Jun.1920): p23-25.

8563 Laing, Hamilton M., *On The Skyline Trail*, 45, 3. (Sep.1920): p32-34, 65.

8564 Bennett, James W., *Night Sounds In Shanghai*, 45, 5. (Nov.1920): p101-107.

8565 White, Stewart Edward, *My Helper Falls Down*, 46, 4. (Apr.1921): p21-23, 60-62.

8566 Hinrichs, H. Stanley, *The San Juan Country*, 46, 5. (May.1921): p23-27.

8567 Tracy, Ray Palmer, *On The Sunrise Sheep Trail*, 46, 5. (May.1921): p35-37, 58-60, 103.

8568 Waugh, Lena Sanford, *Birds Of Passage*, 46, 5. (May.1921): p43-44, 58.

8569 Freeman, Lewis R., *Down The Columbia*, 47, 1. (Jul.1921): p25-27, 57-62.

8570 Freeman, Lewis R., *Down The Columbia*, 47, 1. (Aug.1921): p25-28, 65-68.

8571 Freeman, Lewis R., *Down The Columbia*, 47, 3. (Sep.1921): p34-36, 50-56.

8572 Freeman, Lewis R., *Down The Columbia*, 47, 4. (Oct.1921): p31-33, 76-78.

8573 Freeman, Lewis R., *Down The Columbia*, 47, 5. (Nov.1921): p34-35, 50-57.

8574 Woehlke, Walter V., *The Dividends Of Hospitality*, 48, 1. (Jan.1922): p23-27.

8575 Chapman, Charles E., *China's Lost Chance*, 48, 2. (Feb.1922): p28-29, 66.

8576 Freeman, Lewis R., *River Adventures*, 49, 3. (Sep.1922): p17-20, 54-59.

8577 George, W. L., *On The Road To Canaan*, 49, 5. (Nov.1922): p9-11, 52-54.

8578 Freeman, Lewis R., *Exploring The Colorado Delta*, 50, 4. (Apr.1923): p11-14, 100-105.

8579 Freeman, Lewis R., *Boating In The Bowels Of The Earth*, 50, 5. (May.1923): p17-20, 84-94.

8580 Lincke, C. J., *Alaska's Pullman Trail*, 50, 5. (May.1923): p24-25.

8581 Freeman, Lewis R., *Bucking Rapids In The Inferno*, 50, 6. (Jun.1923): p40-43, 76-78.

8582 Freeman, Lewis R., *The End Of The Water Trail*, 51, 1. (Jul.1923): p23-25, 83-90.

8583 Willard, Victor, *Round The World In The Air*, 52, 6. (Jun.1924): p38-39.

8584 Woehlke, Walter V., *Let's Go Northwest*, 52, 6. (Jun.1924): p40-41, 82-84.

8585 Pentz, Linden B., *To Alaska In A Sixteen-Foot Boat*, 55, 1. (Jul.1925): p36, 79-81.

8586 Pentz, Mabel Trafton, *Oh Yes,–But!*, 55, 1. (Jul.1925): p37, 78-79.

8587 *The Etiquette of Travel*, 55, 2. (Aug.1925): p68-69.

8588 Barret, Dorothy, *For To Admire And For To See*, 55, 2. (Aug.1925): p12-13, 91.

8589 Irwin, Inez Haynes, *The Californiacs*, 55, 3. (Sep.1925): p24-27, 83-85.

8590 Adams, Roxana M., *The Isles Of Wonder*, 56, 1. (Jan.1926): p14-15.

8591 Calvin, Jack, *The Last Of The Windjammers*, 58, 5. (May.1927): p19, 64.

8592 Gardner, Erle Stanley, *Landlubbing To Alaska*, 58, 6. (Jun.1927): p20-22, 66-67.

9. Travel

8593 Russell, C. P., *Sierra Nevada*, 60, 1. (Jan.1928): p36-38.

8594 Stevens, James, *Idaho*, 60, 3. (Mar.1928): p22-25, 54.

8595 Hemphill, Josephine, *Catalina–Isle Of Magic Beauty*, 60, 4. (Apr.1928): p37, 62.

8596 Ewing, Paul A., *Land Of The Ohgees*, 60, 5. (May.1928): p16-18, 80.

8597 Johnson, Lamont, *Adventuring At Lost Cabin*, 60, 5. (May.1928): p29, 79-80.

8598 Carhart, Arthur Hawthorne, *Odd Sights In Ouray*, 60, 6. (Jun.1928): p15, 68-70.

8599 Bankson, Russell Arden, *Romance Trails*, 61, 1. (Jul.1928): p20-22, 62-64.

8600 Warren, Herbert Otis, *So This Is Where They Lived*, 61, 2. (Aug.1928): p40-43, 60.

8601 Burn, June, *Sky-Blue Water*, 61, 2. (Aug.1928): p24-27, 60-62.

8602 Ewing, Paul A., *Nevada Discovered!*, 61, 2. (Aug.1928): p28-30, 73.

8603 Geggie, James Cole, *California's Araby*, 61, 6. (Dec.1928): p31, 46.

8604 Yost, Harold H., *Hawaiian Sketches*, 61, 6. (Dec.1928): p44-45.

8605 Overholt, Alma, *Death Valley From The Air*, 62, 1. (Jan.1929): p34-36.

8606 Hall, Wilbur, *The Scenery Salters*, 62, 1. (Jan.1929): p11-13, 47-48.

8607 Allen, Edward Frank, *A New Yorker Looks At The West*, 62, 5. (May.1929): p11-13.

8608 Gordon, Gilbert, *To Mark Twain's Shrine*, 62, 6. (Jun.1929): p16-17.

8609 Burnett, Frederick J., *Gateway To The Land Of Gold*, 62, 6. (Jun.1929): p24-26.

8610 Mace, Viola, *The Lure Of The Sierra*, 63, 1. (Jul.1929): p16-18.

8611 Yates, Helen Eva, *Feeding the Family on Vacation*, 63, 1. (Jul.1929): p40-41, 56-57.

8612 Robson, Barbara Reid, *Round-The-World Trip*, 63, 4. (Oct.1929): p17-19.

8613 Davis, Marion Lay, *The Battle Cry Of Beauty*, 63, 4. (Oct.1929): p20-21.

8614 Bailey, Almira, *The Land Of Living Christmas Trees*, 63, 6. (Dec.1929): p9-12.

8615 Sanchez, Louis A., *Summer Homes For All*, 64, 2. (Feb.1930): p9-11.

8616 Mead, Dorothy Irving, *Hang Your Vacation Hat On A Totem Pole*, 64, 4. (Apr.1930): p21-22.

8617 Bean, Margaret, *A New Trail For Balloon Tire Pilgrims*, 64, 6. (Jun.1930): p9-12.

8618 Mannix, Frank J., *Visiting Our Neighbors To The West*, 65, 8. (Aug.1930): p11-14.

8619 Chappell, J. F. and Chappell, D. H., *Lassoing The United States In One Vacation*, 65, 4. (Oct.1930): p9-13.

8620 McGrew, Wilhelmina, *Christmas Comes By Pack Train*, 65, 6. (Dec.1930): p12-14, 42-43.

8621 Wilson, Carol Green, *Where West Meets East*, 66, 3. (Mar.1931): p10-13.

8622 Burton, Mildred, *We Visit The Site Of Hoover Dam*, 66, 06. (Jun.1931): p12-14.

8623 Bean, Margaret, *Vacation Geography*, 67, 1. (Jul.1931): p10-12.

8624 Reed, Edwin T., *Oregon Preserves The Beauty Of Her Trails*, 67, 2. (Aug.1931): p16-18.

8625 Marsh, Olive Vincent, *El Paseo De Los Angeles*, 67, 3. (Sep.1931): p26-27.

8626 Sterrett, Jack, *Vacationing In Alaska*, 68, 2. (Feb.1932): p6-8.

8627 Hudson, Chris, *Our Vacation Train Crossed The Cascades*, 68, 5. (May.1932): p6-8.

8628 White, Ruth Taylor, *Hawaii–Of Thee I Sing*, 68, 6. (Jun.1932): p8-10, 42.

8629 Bean, Margaret, *Vacationing In The Inland Empire*, 69, 3. (Sep.1932): p6-8.

8630 Morhardt, J. E., Jr., *Let's Go To The Desert*, 69, 4. (Oct.1932): p7-9.

8631 Dodge, Natt N., *Trails To Two Cities*, 70, 5. (May.1933): p22-24.

8632 Minton, Paul, *We Liked Our Scotch Holiday*, 72, 2. (Feb.1934): p20.

8633 *What's New In Western Living*, 77, 1. (Jul.1936): p15-19.

8634 *What's New In Western Living*, 78, 3. (Mar.1937): p19-21.

8635 *Around The World In Southern California*, 78, 6. (Jun.1937): p26-27.

8636 *Sailing South!*, 79, 5. (Nov.1937): p28.

8637 *What's New In Western Living*, 82, 1. (Jan.1939): p13-15.

8638 *Western Summers*, 86, 2. (Feb.1941): p14-19.

8639 *Puget Sound*, 89, 2. (Aug.1942): p4-5.

8640 *Telegraph Creek*, 90, 5. (May.1943): p4-5.

8641 *Air Age*, 91, 5. (Nov.1943): p6-9.

8642 *War Travel*, 94, 4. (Mar.1945): p2-8.

8643 *Travels Off the Beaten Path*, 95, 4. (Oct.1945): p2, 4-8.

8644 *Marble Canyon*, 96, 3. (Mar.1946): p8-10.

8645 *The Forests Of Oregon*, 97, 1. (Jul.1946): p9-11.

8646 *The Forests Of Washington*, 97, 1. (Jul.1946): p12-13.

8647 *The Redwood Coast Between 101 And 1*, 97, 4. (Oct.1946): p6-9, 10, 12, 14, 16.

8648 *Winter On The Oregon Coast*, 98, 1. (Jan.1947): p12-14.

8649 *The Pleasures Of Western Meandering*, 98, 5. (May.1947): p17-21.

8650 *Your Winter Sun Rooms*, 99, 5. (Nov.1947): p16-21.

8651 *Through The Northern Diggin's* , 100, 4. (Apr.1948): p20-23.

8652 *San Diego's Ocean, Mountain, And Desert*, 101, 6. (Dec.1948): p20-21.

8653 *Along the Rim of the Desert*, 102, 2. (Feb.1949): p6-9.

8654 *What Does Alaska Offer?*, 102, 3. (Mar.1949): p6-13.

8655 *West Of The Crest Of The Cascades*, 102, 5. (May.1949): p19-22.

8656 *Western Vacation Guide*, 102, 5. (May.1949): p26-31.

8657 *La Push On The Quillayute River*, 103, 1. (Jul.1949): p6-8.

8658 *The Coastal Lakes Of Oregon*, 103, 1. (Jul.1949): p14-17.

8659 *Summer Vacations In Arizona?*, 103, 2. (Aug.1949): p6-10.

8660 *In The Hidden Valley Of The Kern*, 103, 2. (Aug.1949): p19-23.

8661 *Exploring California's Mattole River Country*, 103, 5. (Nov.1949): p12-21.

8662 *Three Deserts For Winter Exploring* , 104, 1. (Jan.1950): p20-23.

8663 *Seattle To Nome By Air*, 104, 4. (Apr.1950): p16-20.

8664 *The Klamath Country–For A Day, A Week, Or A Lifetime*, 104, 5. (May.1950): p32-35.

8665 *Ways To Sample Oregon's Skyline Trail*, 105, 1. (Jul.1950): p26-29.

8666 *Desolation Valley*, 105, 2. (Aug.1950): p19-22.

8667 *Along The Route Of The Mormon Pioneers*, 105, 3. (Sep.1950): p6-10.

8668 *Lake Chelan*, 105, 3. (Sep.1950): p24.

8669 *Astoria Loop*, 105, 3. (Sep.1950): p30.

8670 *Trips To The Snow*, 105, 6. (Dec.1950): p8-10.

8671 *California's Deserts*, 105, 6. (Dec.1950): p12-24.

8672 *Inexpensive Six-Day Voyage*, 106, 1. (Jan.1951): p16-19.

8673 *The Three Twisting Eels*, 106, 3. (Mar.1951): p28-31.

8674 *Side Trips Into Oregon History*, 106, 4. (Apr.1951): p21.

8675 *How Will You Have Your Alaska?*, 106, 4. (Apr.1951): p33-37.

8676 *California Close-Up*, 106, 6. (Jun.1951): p33-35.

8677 *Sampling The Wilderness Heart Of Idaho*, 107, 1. (Jul.1951): p29-33.

8678 *Exploring The Northern Gold Country*, 107, 3. (Sep.1951): p19-22.

8679 *What's Tahoe Like In The Fall?*, 107, 3. (Sep.1951): p25-26.

9. Travel

8680 *To The Westerners Who Have Yet To Discover "The Islands"*, 107, 5. (Nov.1951): p30-35.

8681 *Exploring The Desert Around Salton Sea*, 108, 2. (Feb.1952): p26-29.

8682 *San Juans...Treasure Islands Of The Northwest*, 109, 1. (Jul.1952): p36-41.

8683 *Idaho's Mountain-Filled Panhandle*, 109, 2. (Aug.1952): p24-29.

8684 *Oregon's 'Lost' Corner...Antelope, Trout, Jackrabbits, Silence*, 109, 2. (Aug.1952): p30-35.

8685 *In September It's Indian Summer... and It's Uncrowded... East of the High Sierra*, 109, 4. (Sep.1952): p38-43.

8686 *October...In The Shasta Country*, 109, 4. (Oct.1952): p20, 22-24.

8687 *Arizona Holiday*, 109, 4. (Oct.1952): p40-45.

8688 *On The North Shore Of Great Salt Lake*, 109, 5. (Nov.1952): p24-27.

8689 *A Winter Vacation In The Sun*, 109, 5. (Nov.1952): p37-43.

8690 *The Land Of The Three Sisters...*, 111, 1. (Jul.1953): p32-36.

8691 *From Vancouver To The Horse Heaven Hills...On The Washington Side Of The Columbia*, 111, 2. (Aug.1953): p14-16.

8692 *Gold Mines And Ghost Towns...In Oregon's Blue Mountains*, 111, 3. (Sep.1953): p14-15.

8693 *September...The Time To Visit California's Peaceful Vine-Growing Valleys And Hills*, 111, 3. (Sep.1953): p40-45.

8694 *The Cariboo Country*, 111, 4. (Oct.1953): p29-32.

8695 *The Mojave's Red Rock Canyon*, 111, 6. (Dec.1953): p34-36.

8696 *Off The Main Tourist Trail, Kauai Is Cool, Green, Uncrowded*, 112, 1. (Jan.1954): p24-27.

8697 *Point Lobos: One Of The West's Most Exciting Headlands*, 112, 4. (Apr.1954): p19-20.

8698 *This Cool Country May Upset Your Preconceived Notions About Nevada*, 113, 2. (Aug.1954): p22-28.

8699 *Skyway To Fall Color*, 113, 4. (Oct.1954): p19.

8700 *The Oahu Most Tourists Miss*, 113, 5. (Nov.1954): p35-40.

8701 *Hawaii's Undiscovered Island*, 113, 6. (Dec.1954): p30-39.

8702 *The Sun Is Shining In Wickenburg...*, 114, 1. (Jan.1955): p12-15.

8703 *The Wild Wasteland Of Anza And Borrego*, 114, 2. (Feb.1955): p38-43.

8704 *Hawaii's Lovely, Peaceful Kona Coast ...*, 114, 3. (Mar.1955): p46-51.

8705 *The Pleasantly Unspoiled Coastal Country South Of Carmel...*, 114, 4. (Apr.1955): p20-26.

8706 *Between Hot Valley And Hotter Desert...A Cool Green Mountain Retreat*, 114, 5. (May.1955): p24-31.

8707 *Along The Mendocino Coast For A Hundred Crooked Miles*, 114, 5. (May.1955): p56-59.

8708 *Into the Uinta Wilderness*, 114, 5. (May.1955): p18, 21, 23.

8709 *Lakes Basin*, 114, 6. (Jun.1955): p20-22.

8710 *The Fish Are Big And Hungry*, 115, 1. (Jul.1955): p24-30.

8711 *The Trinity Alps...A Pocket-Size Sierra Flanked By A Pocket-Size Mother Lode*, 115, 2. (Aug.1955): p36-39.

8712 *Nevada's Vast Desert Lake*, 115, 5. (Nov.1955): p38-44.

8713 *If December Finds You In Arizona...*, 115, 6. (Dec.1955): p18-21.

8714 *Here Are January Desert Trips*, 116, 2. (Jan.1956): p16, 19.

8715 *The "Ramona Country" At San Diego's Back Door*, 116, 3. (Mar.1956): p22-2, 27.

8716 *California's Clear Lake Country In April... Before the Summer Crowds Arrive*, 116, 4. (Apr.1956): p26-30.

8717 *If You Are Looking For Some Great Mountains To Get Lost In...*, 116, 5. (May.1956): p54-59.

8718 *The Land Of Geronimo, Wyatt Earp, Pete Kitchen, And Johnny Ringo*, 116, 6. (Jun.1956): p24-26, 29, 30, 32.

8719 *Man-Made Lakes In Central California's Foothill Country*, 117, 1. (Jul.1956): p26-28, 30, 33, 34, 36.

8720 *High And Cool*, 117, 1. (Jul.1956): p40-47.

8721 *At The Foot Of St. Helens*, 117, 2. (Aug.1956): p24, 26, 28, 28.

8722 *The Hawaii Few Tourists Get To Know... Dramatic Kokee and Na Pali*, 117, 2. (Aug.1956): p32-34, 36, 38, 1.

8723 *Ever Look For Fossils? There is Good Hunting in Oregon's Hilly John Day Country...*, 117, 3. (Sep.1956): p28-30, 32, 34, 37.

8724 *Exploring California's Fabled Mother Lode And Northern Mines*, 117, 3. (Sep.1956): p45-55.

8725 *What Lies Behind The Barren Inyos?*, 117, 5. (Nov.1956): p22-24, 26.

8726 *Beachcombing On Oahu*, 117, 6. (Dec.1956): p8-9.

8727 *For All Who Long For An Island Holiday*, 118, 2. (Feb.1957): p46-51.

8728 *Here Are The Lighthouses*, 118, 3. (Mar.1957): p50-57.

8729 *Here is Why Our Markets Outlast the Seasons*, 118, 3. (Mar.1957): p58-59.

8730 *Alaska's Land Of Steaming Volcanoes*, 118, 4. (Apr.1957): p24, 27, 28, 30, 33.

8731 *After 100 Years...There's Still An Unknown Coast*, 118, 5. (May.1957): p24-26, 28, 30, 31.

8732 Challacombe, J. R., *John Muir's Walk In The Sky*, 118, 5. (May.1957): p53-59.

8733 *California's Cascades...If You Like Your Wilderness Friendly...*, 119, 1. (Jul.1957): p40-43.

8734 *Why Not An October Vacation? It's Still Summer In Arizona*, 119, 4. (Oct.1957): p30-32, 34, 37.

8735 *Owens Valley–Superheated In Summer, But Cool And Pleasant Now*, 119, 5. (Nov.1957): p18-20, 22, 24.

8736 *San Francisco*, 119, 5. (Nov.1957): p51-61.

8737 *Your Ship Twists And Turns For A Thousand Spectacular Miles*, 120, 4. (Apr.1958): p42-44, 46, 48.

8738 *A Visit To Puna...Three Years After The Eruption*, 120, 5. (May.1958): p38-44.

8739 *Cool, Sparkling, And Peaceful...For 230 Winding Miles*, 120, 6. (Jun.1958): p22-24, 27, 28, 29.

8740 *Into The Rugged Heartland Of California's Trinity Alps*, 121, 1. (Jul.1958): p46-51.

8741 *Skyscraper Country*, 121, 2. (Aug.1958): p42-47.

8742 *One Surprise After Another*, 121, 3. (Sep.1958): p50-55.

8743 *Into The Needles Country By Jeep Tour*, 121, 4. (Oct.1958): p28-32.

8744 *Old Virginia City*, 121, 4. (Oct.1958): p50-58.

8745 *Just 67 Miles South Of The Border...You Come To The Fabulous Gulf*, 121, 5. (Nov.1958): p58-69.

8746 *Southern California's Ocean And Desert...For A Family Christmas Vacation*, 122, 6. (Dec.1958): p14-18, 20.

8747 *The Dream Vacation*, 122, 1. (Jan.1959): p34-38.

8748 *The Rose Parade: Going Early...On The Great Day In Pasadena...*, 122, 1. (Jan.1959): p14-16.

8749 *The Delta*, 122, 3. (Mar.1959): p70-79.

8750 *The Water World Of Seattle*, 122, 5. (May.1959): p84-101.

8751 *Where Uncle Billy Holcomb Struck Gold*, 122, 6. (Jun.1959): p40, 43, 44, 46.

8752 *The Wilderness Home Of The Golden Trout*, 122, 6. (Jun.1959): p60-67.

8753 *The Walking Mountains Of Siskiyou County*, 123, 1. (Jul.1959): p46-51.

8754 *Exploring Arizona's Rim Country*, 123, 2. (Aug.1959): p34-39.

8755 *The North Coast Wine Country*, 123, 3. (Sep.1959): p48-55.

8756 *From La Paz To Cabo San Lucas...Exploring The Tip Of Baja California*, 123, 5. (Nov.1959): p18-24.

9. Travel

8757 *The Lovely, Unspoiled Country North And South Of Hana Town*, 123, 6. (Dec.1959): p14-22.

8758 *The Heart Of Old Los Angeles*, 124, 1. (Jan.1960): p29, 32, 32.

8759 *This month Sunset Takes You to the historic old Monterey Peninsula*, 124, 1. (Jan.1960): p46-61.

8760 *Winter Olympics; The Big Show at Squaw Opens February 18*, 124, 2. (Feb.1960): p25-32.

8761 *The Fishing Village of Astoria*, 124, 3. (Mar.1960): p76,78,81.

8762 *Now's The Time To Visit The West's Sunniest, Warmest Desert*, 124, 3. (Mar.1960): p24-26, 28, 30, 32.

8763 *The Great Central Valley*, 124, 3. (Mar.1960): p82-100.

8764 *White Sails And Water Skis...In The Desert*, 124, 4. (Apr.1960): p22-29.

8765 *Exploring The Mojave In April... For Westerners Who Like Their Desert Fresh and Friendly*, 124, 4. (Apr.1960): p96-105.

8766 *Come Exploring And Shopping In The Pacific Northwest; The Beaver, the Bear, the Raven, and the Killer Whale*, 124, 5. (May.1960): p112-115.

8767 *The Fjords And Glaciers Along Alaska's Gulf Coast*, 124, 5. (May.1960): p24, 27, 28.

8768 *Cruising The Peaceful Willamette*, 124, 6. (Jun.1960): p20-22, 24.

8769 *The Ferryboat Islands*, 125, 1. (Jul.1960): p46-55.

8770 *The Unmarked Shore...In Washington's Lonely Northwest Corner*, 125, 2. (Aug.1960): p52-55.

8771 *The Wonderful Outdoor World Of San Diego*, 125, 3. (Sep.1960): p48-67.

8772 *Autumn In The Northern Redwoods*, 125, 4. (Oct.1960): p62-71.

8773 *Autumn Color Cruise...Along The Swift Trail*, 125, 5. (Nov.1960): p48-50, 52.

8774 *Kilauea: Still Smoking...But Much More Friendly*, 126, 1. (Jan.1961): p34, 36, 38.

8775 *The West's First World's Fair In 22 Years*, 126, 4. (Apr.1961): p49-51.

8776 *An Open Road Invites You Into The Silent World Of Moses Coulee*, 126, 4. (Apr.1961): p84-87.

8777 *The Bitterroots Of Idaho-Montana*, 126, 5. (May.1961): p42-44, 46, 48.

8778 *Exploring Oregon's Delightful Willamette Valley; It's a Great Big Rural Park*, 126, 6. (Jun.1961): p74-87.

8779 *You Hike From Lake To Lake*, 127, 1. (Jul.1961): p22-24.

8780 *You Get A Top-Of-The-World Feeling*, 127, 1. (Jul.1961): p37, 38, 40, 43, 44.

8781 *Santa Barbara; For a Fiesta Visit This Month, or a Family Vacation any Month in the Year*, 127, 2. (Aug.1961): p50-65.

8782 *Today You Can Visit Hawaii's Mystery Place*, 127, 3. (Sep.1961): p30-32, 35.

8783 *Gold Rush Town; An Autumn Visit to Historic Old Nevada City*, 127, 5. (Nov.1961): p66-71.

8784 *Gift Ideas For Travelers*, 127, 6. (Dec.1961): p30-32.

8785 *Midwinter Family Holiday In Palm Springs*, 128, 1. (Jan.1962): p52-65.

8786 *Poking Around In New Chinatown*, 128, 2. (Feb.1962): p52, 55.

8787 *Oregon's Great Snowy Mountain*, 128, 2. (Feb.1962): p56-61.

8788 *They Are Almost Empty Of Humankind*, 128, 3. (Mar.1962): p27-28, 30.

8789 *The Last Year To See Unspoiled Glen Canyon*, 128, 4. (Apr.1962): p58-61, 62, 65.

8790 *World's Fair In Seattle*, 128, 4. (Apr.1962): p78-91.

8791 *The White-Water Cruise Trip Up Hell's Canyon*, 128, 5. (May.1962): p58, 60, 62.

8792 *There Are 52 Lakes On Trinity Divide*, 128, 6. (Jun.1962): p34-36, 38, 40.

8793 *The Friendly Wilderness*, 128, 6. (Jun.1962): p72-77.

8794 *How To Make The Most Of Your World's Fair Visit*, 128, 6. (Jun.1962): p78-87.

8795 *Vancouver*, 129, 2. (Aug.1962): p50-65.

8796 *Homeward Bound From Pendleton's Round-Up...Why Not Explore The Blues?*, 129, 3. (Sep.1962): p18, 19, 21.

8797 *"On A Clear Day, You Can See Catalina"*, 129, 3. (Sep.1962): p56-65.

8798 *Autumn Loop Out of Taos*, 129, 3. (Sep.1962): p29-30.

8799 *Here Come The Canoes From Molokai*, 129, 4. (Oct.1962): p50-52.

8800 *Mendocino*, 129, 4. (Oct.1962): p74-81.

8801 *November In The Verde Valley*, 129, 5. (Nov.1962): p18-20, 22, 24.

8802 *For December Visitors To The Gold Country*, 129, 6. (Dec.1962): p42-44, 46.

8803 *Honolulu*, 130, 1. (Jan.1963): p50-65.

8804 *Last High Water Winter At Lake Mead?*, 130, 2. (Feb.1963): p38-40.

8805 *Touring The Redwood Country By Rail Car*, 130, 3. (Mar.1963): p24-27.

8806 *Oregon Still Has 106 Covered Bridges*, 130, 4. (Apr.1963): p34-38.

8807 *Where Animals Can Really Get To Know Children*, 130, 5. (May.1963): p36-38, 40, 42.

8808 *Poking Around In Owens Valley*, 130, 5. (May.1963): p92-99.

8809 *If You Like Your Mountains All To Yourself...Consider Idaho's Seven Devils*, 130, 6. (Jun.1963): p40, 43, 44.

8810 *Camper's Discovery*, 131, 1. (Jul.1963): p50-55.

8811 *Seafair: August Fun And Foolery In Seattle*, 131, 2. (Aug.1963): p18-23.

8812 *Forest Walking And Forest Camping*, 131, 3. (Sep.1963): p19-20.

8813 *It's Round-Up Time This Month In Pendleton*, 131, 3. (Sep.1963): p28, 31, 33.

8814 *The Surprises Of Baja*, 131, 5. (Nov.1963): p74-87.

8815 *Phoenix: An Escape-To-The-Sun Holiday in the Arizona Desert*, 132, 1. (Jan.1964): p42-57.

8816 *The Whipples Are Almost Untouched*, 132, 2. (Feb.1964): p34-40.

8817 *The Waves Of Spring Color In Antelope Valley*, 132, 4. (Apr.1964): p82-89.

8818 *If You Plan To See The New York Fair...And You Don't Want To Drive*, 132, 5. (May.1964): p44-46, 48, 51-54, 58.

8819 *The Wild Ride Down The Middle Fork Of Idaho's Salmon*, 132, 6. (Jun.1964): p36-38, 40.

8820 *June is a Fine Month to Visit Portland... The River City*, 132, 6. (Jun.1964): p74-91.

8821 *Afoot Or On Horseback*, 133, 1. (Jul.1964): p30, 32, 35.

8822 *By Boat Into The Cascade Wilderness*, 133, 2. (Aug.1964): p18-20.

8823 *Spend A Wonderful Day At Mission Bay*, 133, 2. (Aug.1964): p44-51.

8824 *The Klamath Offers Some Easy Drifting*, 133, 3. (Sep.1964): p30-32, 35.

8825 *Maps Of The West And The World As Gifts For Campers, Fishermen, Trip Planners, And Armchair Geographers*, 133, 6. (Dec.1964): p52-53.

8826 *Lahaina*, 134, 1. (Jan.1965): p40-55.

8827 *Along The Arizona-California Water Border...You Can Explore The Desert By Boat*, 134, 3. (Mar.1965): p34-36, 39, 40, 43.

8828 *A Two-Hour Walk Through The Heart Of Downtown L.A.*, 134, 3. (Mar.1965): p84-95.

8829 *What This Is Is Picnic Country*, 134, 4. (Apr.1965): p46, 48, 50.

8830 *The Mormon City*, 134, 4. (Apr.1965): p76-91.

8831 *Sometimes It's Peaceful And Then Again... Sometimes It's Not*, 134, 5. (May.1965): p30-32.

8832 *Marin-On-The-Bay*, 134, 5. (May.1965): p86-97.

8833 *By Boat On Lewis And Clark's Water Highway*, 134, 6. (Jun.1965): p34-38.

9. Travel

8834 *To Big Bald Rock And Plunging Feather Falls*, 135, 1. (Jul.1965): p30, 32, 35.

8835 *The Salt-Water Highways Of Puget Sound*, 135, 2. (Aug.1965): p42-51.

8836 *Porpoises Do An Aerial Hula At Sea Life Park*, 135, 4. (Oct.1965): p20, 22, 24.

8837 *Old Tombstone*, 135, 5. (Nov.1965): p80-85.

8838 *Pismo*, 136, 2. (Feb.1966): p62-67.

8839 *At Mammoth In The Spring*, 136, 3. (Mar.1966): p86-95.

8840 *1966 In Alaska's Southeastern*, 136, 4. (Apr.1966): p78-97.

8841 *Up And Down Oregon's Rogue*, 136, 6. (Jun.1966): p76-85.

8842 *Mile-High Prescott*, 137, 1. (Jul.1966): p40-45.

8843 *250 Things To See And Do In And Around Los Angeles*, 137, 1. (Jul.1966): p61-68.

8844 *The Fine Wild Forest Of Nisene Marks*, 137, 2. (Aug.1966): p20, 21, 22, 25.

8845 *In California's Lonely Corner*, 137, 3. (Sep.1966): p42-45.

8846 *Shopping, Sampling, And Sightseeing Along San Francisco's Unpretentious Clement*, 137, 4. (Oct.1966): p32-34.

8847 *Kohala*, 137, 5. (Nov.1966): p64-71.

8848 *Game Gifts For Young Travelers*, 137, 6. (Dec.1966): p46, 48, 50.

8849 *Into Utah's Treasure Mountains*, 138, 1. (Jan.1967): p22-25.

8850 *Tucson Sun Country*, 138, 1. (Jan.1967): p46-57.

8851 *Changing Sun Valley*, 138, 2. (Feb.1967): p74-81.

8852 *The Quiet Boonville Country...And Boontling*, 138, 3. (Mar.1967): p30-34.

8853 *So Big And So Empty*, 138, 3. (Mar.1967): p84-91.

8854 *Following The Santa Monicas As They March Out To Sea*, 138, 4. (Apr.1967): p78-85.

8855 *After 700 Road Curves, There's Old Mineral King...Your Destination Or Jumping-Off Place*, 138, 6. (Jun.1967): p42-44, 46, 48, 50, 52.

8856 *Idaho's Lake Country*, 138, 6. (Jun.1967): p58-63.

8857 *Coos Bay*, 139, 2. (Aug.1967): p26-28.

8858 *A Classic Cascades Wilderness Walk*, 139, 2. (Aug.1967): p31-32.

8859 *It's Apple Time*, 139, 3. (Sep.1967): p50-57.

8860 *The Aspens Turn To Gold This Month Along Arizona's Coronado Trail*, 139, 4. (Oct.1967): p42-44, 47, 48.

8861 *Stopover In Stockton...To Explore The Delightful Haggin Museum*, 139, 5. (Nov.1967): p44.

8862 *The Changing North Face Of San Francisco*, 139, 5. (Nov.1967): p64-79.

8863 *Lee Canyon And Its Ski Slopes Are Just Around The Corner From Las Vegas*, 140, 1. (Jan.1968): p24-25.

8864 *The Grand Pali*, 140, 1. (Jan.1968): p36-39.

8865 *Midwinter Visit To Jackson Hole*, 140, 2. (Feb.1968): p28-30.

8866 *The Waterfall Walks Above Los Angeles*, 140, 2. (Feb.1968): p50-53.

8867 *A Grand Spring In Utah...On Your Own Or With A Group Into Lonely, Beautiful Escalante Canyon*, 140, 3. (Mar.1968): p38-40.

8868 *On The Idaho-Utah Border*, 140, 5. (May.1968): p68, 70.

8869 *The Good Life At The Beach In Los Angeles... It Gets Better as Summer Advances*, 141, 1. (Jul.1968): p34, 37, 38, 40.

8870 *Park-In-The-Bay*, 141, 2. (Aug.1968): p22-23.

8871 *Between Los Angeles And San Francisco...Stop For A Walk Through San Luis Obispo*, 141, 2. (Aug.1968): p26-27.

8872 *Seattle's Great Performing Park*, 141, 2. (Aug.1968): p40-51.

8873 *Over Labor Day Weekend...The Lively Action At Fort Bragg*, 141, 3. (Sep.1968): p22-24.

8874 *La Jolla And The Water's Edge*, 141, 3. (Sep.1968): p52-57.

8875 *Indian Summer In The Sawtooths*, 141, 3. (Sep.1968): p58-61.

8876 *Utah Adventure... A Look Into The Maze*, 141, 4. (Oct.1968): p28-33.

8877 *Grand Coulee And The Grand Coulee Country*, 141, 4. (Oct.1968): p70-77.

8878 *A Gingerbread Walk On Mission Hill In Santa Cruz*, 141, 5. (Nov.1968): p28, 31.

8879 *Gold Rush Town*, 141, 5. (Nov.1968): p78-83.

8880 *Snow Shenanigans In Idaho On January's Last Weekend*, 142, 1. (Jan.1969): p34-35.

8881 *The Big Island*, 142, 1. (Jan.1969): p42-55.

8882 *To Cold Colorado...For The Joys Of Powder Skiing*, 142, 2. (Feb.1969): p62-69.

8883 *This Year From West Coast Ports...More Than 200 Cruises*, 142, 3. (Mar.1969): p48-50.

8884 *What's New At Mission Bay*, 142, 4. (Apr.1969): p56-58, 60.

8885 *North To Kamloops...For Possibly The Best Trout Fishing You've Ever Known*, 142, 5. (May.1969): p54-59.

8886 *Weaverville; Why This Old Town is Worth a Stopover... Even a Detour*, 143, 1. (Jul.1969): p36-39.

8887 *San Diego: To Celebrate A 200th Anniversary...A Spirited Fiesta In Old Town*, 143, 1. (Jul.1969): p66-69.

8888 *Unlocking the Secrets Graven on Mojave Rocks*, 143, 1. (Jul.1969): p108-109.

8889 *Up B.C. 101...Along The Sunshine Coast*, 143, 2. (Aug.1969): p24-25.

8890 *Away From The Crowds...In Klamath Country*, 143, 2. (Aug.1969): p28, 31.

8891 *Sampling The Marble Peak Trail*, 143, 5. (Nov.1969): p24-26.

8892 *The Old Inns On Highway 49*, 143, 5. (Nov.1969): p30-32.

8893 *For Christmas Shopping...Or Just For A Visit...Here Is The New Japan Center In San Francisco*, 143, 6. (Dec.1969): p44-46.

8894 *In Between Storms, Why Not A Winter's Day At The Beach?*, 144, 1. (Jan.1970): p28-29.

8895 *Why Wait For Hawaii?*, 144, 1. (Jan.1970): p46-55.

8896 *In Arizona's Southwest Corner, Consider A Stopover In Sunny Yuma*, 144, 3. (Mar.1970): p42-44.

8897 *When The Winter's Over...But Before The Summer Crowds...A Great Time To Visit Coloma*, 144, 5. (May.1970): p62-63.

8898 *Where To Find Bargains In Paris For Your Kitchen*, 144, 6. (Jun.1970): p86-87.

8899 *Claremont Offers Three Easy Walks To See Its Treasure Of Trees*, 144, 6. (Jun.1970): p44-46.

8900 *Santa Fe...The Southwest's Most Historic City*, 144, 6. (Jun.1970): p72-77.

8901 *Trinity Lake In Summer Is Hard To Resist*, 145, 1. (Jul.1970): p30-31.

8902 *Into The Apache Country...For The Camping, The Fishing, The Apaches*, 145, 2. (Aug.1970): p26-28.

8903 *San Diego's Lively Waterfront*, 145, 2. (Aug.1970): p42-49.

8904 *Between Reno And Vegas...Ghosts*, 145, 3. (Sep.1970): p28-29.

8905 *Shopping Excursion Into The Gold Country*, 145, 6. (Dec.1970): p28-29.

8906 *To The Marin Headlands For A Winter Picnic*, 146, 1. (Jan.1971): p54-55.

8907 *Can You Squeeze In A Weekend Cruise Between Two Work Weeks?*, 146, 3. (Mar.1971): p42-44.

8908 *In The California, Arizona, Sonora Low Desert, Spring Signals The Time To Camp*, 146, 3. (Mar.1971): p70-75.

8909 *Is 1971 Your Year To Discover Or Rediscover The Railroad Adventure?*, 146, 5. (May.1971): p100-105.

9. Travel

8910 *An Hour And A Half North Of San Francisco Is Tomales Bay... Art, Beaches, Birds, Picnicking,* 146, 5. (May.1971): p60-63.

8911 *San Francisco's Union Street,* 146, 5. (May.1971): p112-115.

8912 *Exploring The Border Islands,* 147, 1. (Jul.1971): p44-51.

8913 *There's A New Wet Walk In San Francisco,* 147, 2. (Aug.1971): p30-31.

8914 *If You Plan To Cross Nevada In Sweltering August, Here's The Great Place To Cool Off,* 147, 2. (Aug.1971): p44-47.

8915 *Detour 85 Miles Northwest Of L.A. To See Horses, Flowers, History...Danes,* 147, 2. (Aug.1971): p60-61.

8916 *A Rather Large Vessel In Long Beach Invites You To Come Aboard,* 147, 3. (Sep.1971): p38-39.

8917 *Old Cannery Row Is An Ever-Changing Show,* 147, 4. (Oct.1971): p94-95.

8918 *Bolinas,* 147, 4. (Oct.1971): p104-106.

8919 *The Palm Springs Back Country,* 147, 5. (Nov.1971): p74-79.

8920 *At Taos The Ski Slopes Are Really Steep And The Powder Lasts Into May,* 148, 1. (Jan.1972): p56-57.

8921 *On A Windy Cliff Top Outside the Golden Gate,* 148, 2. (Feb.1972): p48-50.

8922 *Alaska's Kenai And Midnight Sun,* 148, 6. (Jun.1972): p70-75.

8923 *The Willamette...Oregon's River Parkway,* 149, 1. (Jul.1972): p54-59.

8924 *What's New With Old Monterey,* 149, 4. (Oct.1972): p86-89.

8925 *Hawaii's Undiscovered City Is Downtown Honolulu,* 150, 1. (Jan.1973): p42-49.

8926 *San Diego's Grand Park,* 151, 1. (Jul.1973): p54-59.

8927 *Utah's Uintas,* 151, 1. (Jul.1973): p60-62.

8928 *One Great September Treat At Eureka Is Exploring The Margin Of Humboldt Bay,* 151, 3. (Sep.1973): p30-31.

8929 *What Is Alcatraz Really Like? You Can See for Yourself,* 151, 5. (Nov.1973): p52.

8930 *Old Lahaina In 1974,* 152, 1. (Jan.1974): p34-35.

8931 *A Walk For Gardeners Right In Tropical Waikiki,* 152, 2. (Feb.1974): p60-63.

8932 *Nest Building, Courtship Dances, Hatchings, Yours To Watch In March At The Audubon Ranch,* 152, 3. (Mar.1974): p38-39.

8933 *A Weekend Guide On How To Get To And Then Around San Francisco Without A Car,* 152, 4. (Apr.1974): p84-87.

8934 *Expo '74 Is Opening: Where to Go? Where to Stay? How to Get Around in Spokane?,* 152, 5. (May.1974): p88-89.

8935 *What's Expo '74 Like? Should You Go To Spokane?,* 152, 6. (Jun.1974): p74-81.

8936 *Using Sunset Boulevard For Los Angeles Discovery; You Tour and Detour. Here is a Report,* 153, 2. (Aug.1974): p46-51.

8937 *How Is Bike Touring In Hawaii? Good, Especially if You Hand-Pick Your Routes,* 153, 4. (Oct.1974): p36-42.

8938 *How Did Santa Barbara Get That Way?,* 154, 1. (Jan.1975): p36-43.

8939 *What's The News At Big Sur? Some Bad, Much Good,* 154, 4. (Apr.1975): p38-40, 42.

8940 *For Visitors to Hawaii's Kona Coast: The Choice in Beaches is Better in 1975,* 154, 5. (May.1975): p48-50.

8941 *Music Goes With Picnicking In The California Wine Country May Through September,* 154, 5. (May.1975): p88-89.

8942 *Comeback for Old Main Street? It's Possible. Here is How Santa Cruz Made Over Its Tired Old Pacific Avenue,* 154, 5. (May.1975): p168-169.

8943 *The Steep Tides Of Puget Sound Reveal Treasures,* 154, 6. (Jun.1975): p56-63.

8944 *Taos–It's Spain, Frontier America, Pueblo,* 155, 1. (Jul.1975): p64-67.

8945 *California's Lonely Corner,* 155, 2. (Aug.1975): p42-47.

8946 *Surprise World's Fair–Okinawa's Expo '75,* 155, 3. (Sep.1975): p46-51.

8947 *The Friendly Inns Of The Mendocino-Sonoma Coast,* 155, 4. (Oct.1975): p34-38.

8948 *It's A Good Year To Get To Know The California Coast,* 155, 4. (Oct.1975): p90-91.

8949 *The Changing Face Of Downtown L.A.,* 155, 5. (Nov.1975): p74-79.

8950 *A Different Hawaii Vacation If you Have a Kitchen,* 155, 5. (Nov.1975): p82-85.

8951 *Folk Art Gifts from Around the World,* 155, 6. (Dec.1975): p58-59.

8952 *San Francisco's Polk Street–Colorful, and in Places is Just Outrageous,* 155, 6. (Dec.1975): p22-23.

8953 *Should You Consider A Bicentennial Trip East?,* 156, 1. (Jan.1976): p54-58.

8954 *It's The Turnoff Not Enough People Make–To Salty Old Moss Landing,* 156, 2. (Feb.1976): p38-39.

8955 *Ice, Fiords, Fish, Totems, History,* 156, 5. (May.1976): p84-91.

8956 *Much Is Happening On The Oakland Estuary,* 156, 6. (Jun.1976): p42-43.

8957 *The Pleasures Of Dining In The Delta... Crayfish, 'Fishermen''s Breakfast," Waterside Views,* 157, 2. (Aug.1976): p20B-20C.

8958 *Come On A Walk In Reviving Old Newport Beach... New Shops, Boagyards, Restaurants, Fish Markets,* 157, 2. (Aug.1976): p26-28.

8959 *Dancing, Feasting, Song, Games in Late September At Indian Grinding Rock Near Volcano,* 157, 3. (Sep.1976): p80-81.

8960 *North of San Francisco, Sonoma's Uncrowded Coast Is A September Pleasure,* 157, 3. (Sep.1976): p34-36.

8961 *Between L. A. and S. F., a Detour Into Some New Wine Country,* 157, 3. (Sep.1976): p70-73.

8962 *October Up In Nevada City,* 157, 4. (Oct.1976): p38-40.

8963 *The Marin Headlands... Here is How to Explore Them Afoot or With your Car,* 157, 5. (Nov.1976): p30-32.

8964 *The One-Day Train Trip,* 158, 1. (Jan.1977): p26-27.

8965 *Eureka's Waterfront Is Coming Back To Life,* 158, 1. (Jan.1977): p28D-30.

8966 *The Changing Heart Of Downtown Tucson,* 158, 1. (Jan.1977): p36-39.

8967 *The Other Oahu,* 158, 3. (Mar.1977): p78-83.

8968 *The Rediscovery Of Capitola,* 158, 4. (Apr.1977): p72-74.

8969 *Carquinez Strait - Instead of Just Zipping Across, Why Not Consider Some Poking Around?,* 158, 5. (May.1977): p64-65.

8970 *Oregon's Astonishing Lava Lands,* 159, 2. (Aug.1977): p64-67.

8971 *The Quiet Coast South Of Big Sur... Where Cambria is the Big City,* 159, 4. (Oct.1977): p40-41.

8972 *Is This The Year To Discover Molokai?,* 159, 4. (Oct.1977): p122-125.

8973 *November is a Good Month to Sample The Four Valley Of The Moon Parks,* 159, 5. (Nov.1977): p42-43.

8974 *San Jose–Nowheresville In Renaissance,* 159, 5. (Nov.1977): p98-105.

8975 *Bountiful Coachella Valley for a Midwinter Holiday,* 159, 6. (Dec.1977): p82-85.

8976 *The Superb Winter Beaches,* 160, 1. (Jan.1978): p30-32.

8977 *Apres-Ski Today In Ramshackle Old Truckee,* 160, 2. (Feb.1978): p44-46.

8978 *Walking in Wildflowers,* 160, 4. (Apr.1978): p110-113.

8979 *"Beautiful Hidden Valley Round As A Cup",* 160, 5. (May.1978): p38-40.

8980 *For Views Of Three Bridges–And Close-Ups Of Feisty Little Point Richmond,* 161, 3. (Sep.1978): p40-41.

8981 *130 Small California Wineries You Can Visit,* 161, 3. (Sep.1978): p68-75.

8982 *The Mono Country Is Pleasantly Lonesome In October,* 161, 4. (Oct.1978): p86-91.

9. Travel

8983 *Colorado's Steamboat Springs Is Unhurried, Uncrowded Still, But the Crowds are Coming*, 161, 5. (Nov.1978): p26-27.

8984 *European Charms (and Goods and Foods) Of Saratoga And Los Gatos*, 162, 1. (Jan.1979): p28-29.

8985 *Kauai's Beautiful Rain-Shine Coast*, 162, 1. (Jan.1979): p44-51.

8986 *February is Steinbeck Month In Steinbeck Country*, 162, 2. (Feb.1979): p44-45.

8987 *Are National Historic Districts Coming Soon for Downtown Los Angeles?*, 162, 2. (Feb.1979): p94-96.

8988 *Carmel Valley Love Affair–April In Its Time*, 162, 4. (Apr.1979): p54-56.

8989 *From Alaska's Skagway Over The Top To The Yukon and Dawson*, 162, 5. (May.1979): p102-107.

8990 *There Is Another Coronado*, 162, 6. (Jun.1979): p78-83.

8991 *Marin's Quiet Campuses In Summer… Lute Concerts, Hiking, Biking, Dance, Swimming, Theater, Historic Trees, Picnics*, 163, 2. (Aug.1979): p54-55.

8992 *On San Francisco's North Waterfront, an Extravaganza That is Literally Everchanging*, 163, 3. (Sep.1979): p84-85.

8993 *October Is The Great Month To See The Beautiful Arabians*, 163, 4. (Oct.1979): p44-45.

8994 *High Colorado–Within Ski-Reach Without Your Car*, 164, 1. (Jan.1980): p44-47.

8995 *Salton Sea–For The Birds, Baths, Bubbling Pots, Desert Touring*, 164, 3. (Mar.1980): p58-60, 62.

8996 *Imaginative and Daring Urban Park-Mall is Changing Downtown Vancouver*, 163, 3. (Mar.1980): p72-75.

8997 *Exploring Portland By Bus*, 164, 5. (May.1980): p112-117.

8998 *Santa Cruz Beach–Too Popular*, 165, 1. (Jul.1980): p36-38.

8999 *The Great Detour–Whidbey Island*, 165, 1. (Jul.1980): p64-67.

9000 *Harvest Hoopla–July To October*, 165, 1. (Jul.1980): p82-84.

9001 *August Adventures On The Feather*, 165, 2. (Aug.1980): p34-36.

9002 *New Tower Looks Down On L.A.'s Changing Little Tokyo*, 165, 2. (Aug.1980): p54-57.

9003 *Ghosts In The Bay Area? Here Is A Guide To Four*, 165, 3. (Sep.1980): p32-34.

9004 *'Bed And Breakfast' and Other Small Inns are Catching on in California CitiesI*, 165, 4. (Oct.1980): p38-40.

9005 *Desert Walks An Hour Or Less From Phoenix To Tucson*, 165, 5. (Nov.1980): p88-95.

9006 *San Diego's Lively Embarcadero*, 166, 3. (Mar.1981): p70-73.

9007 *Discovering The Sunset District*, 166, 4. (Apr.1981): p46-48.

9008 *Rogue Oregon 1981*, 166, 6. (Jun.1981): p84-89.

9009 *A Day In Downtown Oakland*, 167, 1. (Jul.1981): p58-61.

9010 *Secret Sausalito*, 167, 3. (Sep.1981): p38-40.

9011 *Vallejo Offers New Reasons For A Stopover… Lively Waterfont, Whaleboat Races, History Walk*, 167, 4. (Oct.1981): p38-40.

9012 *Up In Nevada City, A Gold Country Renaissance*, 167, 4. (Oct.1981): p94-95.

9013 *Dining With The Basques Near Reno*, 167, 5. (Nov.1981): p38-40.

9014 *Hawaii's Cowboy Country*, 168, 3. (Mar.1982): p84-89.

9015 *South Of Market: No-Nonsense San Francisco*, 168, 4. (Apr.1982): p98-103.

9016 *Majestic Sierra Buttes, Poky Sierra City… Time for a Discovery Trip*, 168, 6. (Jun.1982): p44-46.

9017 *Sandstone And Shakespeare In Southwest Utah*, 168, 6. (Jun.1982): p78-83.

9018 *The Country Inns And Little Wineries Of Amador*, 169, 3. (Sep.1982): p32-37.

9019 *Glory Season In The West's Aspen Country*, 169, 3. (Sep.1982): p70-73.

9020 *Paso Robles to Santa Barbara, Cattle Country Becomes Wine Country*, 169, 4. (Oct.1982): p34-39.

9021 *Mendocino Winter*, 169, 6. (Dec.1982): p22-24.

9022 *Bed And Breakfast In Monterey, Carmel, Pacific Grove, And Santa Cruz*, 170, 1. (Jan.1983): p32-34.

9023 *A Parade Of Spontaneous Street the-ater…And A Good Place To Shop. That's Haight Street Today*, 170, 3. (Mar.1983): p60-62.

9024 *Anza Borrego*, 170, 3. (Mar.1983): p96-101.

9025 *Colorado's San Juan Country*, 170, 6. (Jun.1983): p104-108.

9026 *Humboldt Bay Makes A Comeback*, 171, 1. (Jul.1983): p40-42.

9027 *Baja Sur*, 171, 5. (Nov.1983): p104-111.

9028 *Christmas In And Around Union Square*, 171, 6. (Dec.1983): p70-73.

9029 *Magnificent Sand Seas Of The West*, 172, 1. (Jan.1984): p46-57.

9030 *Livelier Than Ever, San Diego's Balboa Park*, 172, 2. (Feb.1984): p72-83.

9031 *Tropical Discovery On Kauai*, 172, 2. (Feb.1984): p86-87.

9032 *California History Comes Alive At 13 State Parks… Watch or Join in*, 172, 6. (Jun.1984): p52-54.

9033 *Cannon That Were Never Fired In Anger and other Defenders of San Francisco Bay*, 173, 1. (Jul.1984): p42-46.

9034 *Surprises In And Around Los Angeles*, 173, 1. (Jul.1984): p108-134.

9035 *It's Gravenstein Month In Gravenstein Country*, 173, 2. (Aug.1984): p34-36, 38.

9036 *Quiet Catalina*, 173, 3. (Sep.1984): p60-65.

9037 *Good-By To the Dowager Downtown; This is the New Denver*, 173, 4. (Oct.1984): p96-99.

9038 *History, Art, Music… Free December Discoveries in San Francisco's Financial District*, 173, 6. (Dec.1984): p10-11.

9039 *Inns Of Tahoe*, 173, 6. (Dec.1984): p58, 61.

9040 *Urban Hiking In San Francisco's Marina District*, 174, 2. (Feb.1985): p12-14, 16.

9041 *Come Visit Us At Sunset's "Laboratory of Western Living"*, 174, 3. (Mar.1985): p143-146.

9042 *Primate See, Primate Do*, 174, 5. (May.1985): p10-12.

9043 NONE , *Mellow Living Among Majestic Mountains*, 174, 6. (Jun.1985): p10-12.

9044 *Lively Old Monterey*, 175, 1. (Jul.1985): p10-12.

9045 *Tiburon–A Ferry Trip From San Francisco*, 175, 1. (Jul.1985): p78-81.

9046 *Northwest Island-Hopping By Ferry*, 175, 2. (Aug.1985): p58-63.

9047 *Crush Time In Livermore Valley*, 175, 3. (Sep.1985): p38-42.

9048 *Best Month On The San Mateo Coast?*, 175, 4. (Oct.1985): p12-16.

9049 *Van Ness… San Francisco's Old 'Auto Row' Offers New Reasons to Get Out of Your Car*, 176, 1. (Jan.1986): p68-71.

9050 *Dolphins And Friends At Home In Vallejo*, 176, 6. (Jun.1986): p14-16.

9051 *California's Accessible Alps - The Trinities*, 177, 2. (Aug.1986): p52-55.

9052 *Beach, Dune, and Bluff Hiking on the Wild Sonoma - Mendocino Beaches*, 177, 4. (Oct.1986): p10-11.

9053 *The Wide-Open Spaces Of Marin*, 178, 3. (Mar.1987): p12-13.

9054 *Western Mountains And Bluegrass Music… They go Together Like Banjo and Fiddle*, 178, 6. (Jun.1987): p10-12.

9055 *In Utah's Northeastern Corner, a Hidden, Hay-Scented Valley*, 179, 1. (Jul.1987): p10-13.

9. Travel

April 1993 cover (photo: Norman A. Plate)

Workshop & Craft Projects

One of Sunset*'s long-held editorial precepts–a primary way it has defined itself apart from other publications–is its determination to appeal to both male and female readers. It has done so in part by balancing its practical, "how-to" materials among traditionally female, male and shared interests and hobbies, all revolving around the home and grounds. So we find a juxtaposition of woodworking, pottery, flower arranging, table decorating and many other suggestions, unlike any other large-circulation magazine. These homely arts dovetail nicely–and consciously–with other major coverage, such as outdoor building, cookery and holiday hospitality. This is one of the defining qualities that has truly made* Sunset *a family magazine. As projects, crafts and hobbies have been treated as closely related concepts, this section includes a smattering of hobbies and interests that may seem slightly out of place, e.g., keeping birds as pets, until we recognize the characteristic* Sunset *touch, which, in our example, transforms fanciers of birds into builders of aviaries that become part of the home, whether indoors or outdoors.*

10. Workshop & Craft Projects

10. Workshop & Craft Projects

9271 *Rubbings Are Easy*, 133, 2. (Aug.1964): p58-59.

9272 *The Magi With Gifts In Your Entry Window*, 133, 6. (Dec.1964): p64-65.

9273 *Christmas Decorating With Fruit*, 133, 6. (Dec.1964): p70.

9274 *A Stableful Of Christmas Ponies*, 133, 6. (Dec.1964): p75, 76, 79.

9275 *This Year Our Doll House Is Four Stories Tall*, 135, 5. (Nov.1965): p78-79.

9276 *The Christmas Ball*, 135, 6. (Dec.1965): p56-59.

9277 *Your Gingerbread Boys Can Carol, Cavort, Kick High, Or Just Yawn*, 135, 6. (Dec.1965): p60-61.

9278 *The Wraps*, 135, 6. (Dec.1965): p66-67.

9279 *The Christmas Trees You Make Yourself*, 137, 6. (Dec.1966): p54-61.

9280 *The Magic You Make With Papier-MachÈ*, 137, 6. (Dec.1966): p74-75.

9281 *Pop Goes The Pop-uppet*, 137, 6. (Dec.1966): p80, 83, 84.

9282 *The Fine Art Of Napkin Folding*, 139, 4. (Oct.1967): p98-99.

9283 *The Idea For Our Doll House This Year Comes From Across The Pacific*, 139, 5. (Nov.1967): p80-81.

9284 *Why Not A Package As Much Fun As What's Inside?*, 139, 6. (Dec.1967): p58-59.

9285 *How To Make Marbled Candles, Ice-Mold Candles, Waffle Candles*, 139, 6. (Dec.1967): p80, 82, 85, 86.

9286 *The Art Of Measuring Without a Rule*, 140, 3. (Mar.1968): p80-81.

9287 *The Zoo At Home*, 141, 2. (Aug.1968): p60-62, 65.

9288 *You Can Do Much With Caning Besides Sitting On It*, 141, 4. (Oct.1968): p94-97.

9289 *The Reach-Into Dollhouse*, 141, 5. (Nov.1968): p102-103.

9290 *The Surprises You Hang On The Tree Are All Yours*, 141, 6. (Dec.1968): p64-67.

9291 *Built In One Busy Weekend By Three Energetic Adults For Something Under $75*, 142, 3. (Mar.1969): p94-95.

9292 *If You Don't Have A Real Goat...The Riders Can Take Turns Being Goat*, 143, 2. (Aug.1969): p46-47.

9293 *Bright Idea From Portugal...Sunshade, Windscreen, Privacy Screen*, 143, 2. (Aug.1969): p54-55.

9294 *Rooms Stack Up To Make A Doll's Habitat*, 143, 5. (Nov.1969): p98-99.

9295 *Start Him Off On A Home Weather Station*, 143, 6. (Dec.1969): p34-38.

9296 *For A Quick Getaway There's A Slide Tunnel And A Fireman's Pole*, 144, 1. (Jan.1970): p60-61.

9297 *Not All Wild Pets Like Captivity, But Some Do If You Treat them Right*, 145, 1. (Jul.1970): p150-151.

9298 *The Super Bean Bag*, 145, 2. (Aug.1970): p50-51.

9299 *The Bull, The Rooster, The Giraffe, The Raccoon, The Who's-It...Halloween Comes In A Walking Paper Bag*, 145, 4. (Oct.1970): p88-89.

9300 *Christmas Snowflakes In The Window*, 145, 6. (Dec.1970): p52-55.

9301 *For The Rolling Seventies A Doll House Trailer*, 145, 6. (Dec.1970): p56-57.

9302 *Stitches In Burlap*, 145, 6. (Dec.1970): p68-69.

9303 *Young Sculptors At The Beach*, 146, 3. (Mar.1971): p86-87.

9304 *It Mustn't Topple...Or Look Like It Might*, 147, 1. (Jul.1971): p52-53.

9305 *A Hat For The Seventies*, 147, 2. (Aug.1971): p48-49.

9306 *Built In A Day...Ready To Use In A Week...Your Own Pueblo Oven*, 147, 2. (Aug.1971): p50-53.

9307 *Woodworker's Discovery...Japanese Tools*, 147, 3. (Sep.1971): p56-59.

9308 *Look Who Will Be Knocking At Your Door*, 147, 4. (Oct.1971): p98-99.

9309 *Interesting Things Sometimes Happen To Old Utility Poles*, 147, 5. (Nov.1971): p84-87.

9310 *Silkscreening*, 147, 5. (Nov.1971): p98-101.

9311 *Make One, Two, Or A Dozen All Different*, 147, 6. (Dec.1971): p54-57.

9312 *Elegance Right Out Of The Scrap Bin...Christmas Candle Lights*, 147, 6. (Dec.1971): p58-59.

9313 *Gonfalons*, 147, 6. (Dec.1971): p70-73.

9314 *For Bikers And Walkers To Carry A Book Or Their Lunch*, 148, 4. (Apr.1972): p102-103.

9315 *It's Your Clock And It Works*, 148, 5. (May.1972): p104-105.

9316 *Pacific Wraparounds*, 149, 1. (Jul.1972): p70-73.

9317 *Snail, Mouse, Or Two-Gun Hombre. Here Are Translations In Stitchery*, 149, 2. (Aug.1972): p60-61.

9318 *Which Way Is The Wind Blowing Right Now?*, 149, 5. (Nov.1972): p110-111.

9319 *Christmas Cheerfulness With Painted-On Colors*, 149, 6. (Dec.1972): p52-53.

9320 *Noodle Gluing*, 149, 6. (Dec.1972): p76-77.

9321 *If You Were Good At Mud Pies, Maybe You're Ready For Pot Making*, 149, 6. (Dec.1972): p170-171.

9322 *The Ancient Basket Art Isn't All That Difficult*, 150, 1. (Jan.1973): p56-57.

9323 *Wither Quilting?*, 150, 2. (Feb.1973): p70-73.

9324 *You Handweave A Collar Without A Loom*, 150, 5. (May.1973): p182-184.

9325 *For Tool-Using Gardeners, Three Tool-Carrying Aprons*, 151, 1. (Jul.1973): p100-102, 104.

9326 *Multi-Candles Are Magical*, 151, 6. (Dec.1973): p58-61.

9327 *He Or She May Secretly Want One. Here Is A Look At Some Western Hat Gift Options*, 151, 6. (Dec.1973): p72-73.

9328 *An Easter Basket That Grows Its Own Grass*, 152, 4. (Apr.1974): p96-87.

9329 *Stand By As The Sun Takes Charge*, 153, 2. (Aug.1974): p60-61.

9330 *Making A Dog Or Pig Will Take You Two Days*, 153, 5. (Nov.1974): p96-99.

9331 *Soapbox Racer - You Give The Parts*, 153, 6. (Dec.1974): p70-71.

9332 *Just Sugar On A Balloon*, 153, 6. (Dec.1974): p86-87.

9333 *There's A Very Easy Way To Make A Life Mask*, 154, 1. (Jan.1975): p44-45.

9334 *In YourEaster Bonnet With The Green Salad On It*, 154, 3. (Mar.1975): p84-85.

9335 *They Made Their Own Beach Towels*, 155, 1. (Jul.1975): p58-59.

9336 *Between You And The Sun*, 155, 2. (Aug.1975): p56-57.

9337 *Half-Barrel Fountains Make Water Music*, 155, 2. (Aug.1975): p60-61.

9338 *See-Through Tables Built By Home Craftsmen*, 155, 4. (Oct.1975): p84-85.

9339 *Small Wine Racks for Storage, Display*, 155, 6. (Dec.1975): p56-57.

9340 *You–The Mad Christmas Hatter*, 155, 6. (Dec.1975): p64-65.

9341 *Snowflakes And Starflakes*, 155, 6. (Dec.1975): p66-66.

9342 *Leafy Eggs For Easter*, 156, 4. (Apr.1976): p88-89.

9343 *The Family Portrait Cards... It's Easy With Just a n Instant Camera, Maybe a Tripod, and an Early Start*, 157, 5. (Nov.1976): p90-91.

9344 *Glue-And-Slice Wood Ornaments*, 157, 6. (Dec.1976): p62-65.

9345 *The Christmas Hit–Animal Slippers*, 157, 6. (Dec.1976): p76-79.

9346 *The Log Cabin Renaissance Continues*, 157, 6. (Dec.1976): p80-81.

9347 *Slides Into Posters*, 158, 1. (Jan.1977): p54-56.

9348 *Four Beds From The Lumberyard. You Assemble*, 158, 5. (May.1977): p176-180.

9349 *Good for 50 or More Years of Weather, Picnics and Initial Carving*, 158, 6. (Jun.1977): p94-95.

10. Workshop & Craft Projects

Right: Sunset's all-time best-known and best-selling book; this is the 40th Anniversary edition (1995).

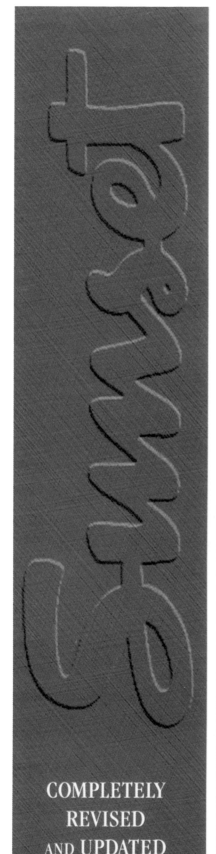

Sunset

Western

Garden BOOK

ANNIVERSARY 40th EDITION

COMPLETELY
REVISED
AND UPDATED

Books

1932–1940

B001 *The Sunset Camp and Cabin Book*. San Francisco, Calif.: Lane Pub. Co., 1932.

B002 *Sunset Garden Book; All Year Gardening in the West*. San Francisco, Calif.: Lane Pub. Co., 1932.

B003 *Sunset Garden Book: All Year Gardening in the West*. San Francisco, Calif.: Sunset Magazine, 1933.

B004 *Sunset All-Western Cook Book; Recipes Included for Favorite Regional and Foreign Dishes Peculiar to the West, How to Select, Prepare, Cook, and Serve All Typically Western Food Products*. Genevieve Anne Callahan. San Francisco, Calif.: Sunset Magazine, 1933.

B005 *Sunset's All-Western Garden Guide*. Allison M. Woodman. 1st ed. San Francisco, Calif.: Sunset Magazine, 1933.

B006 *Sunset's Grubstake Cook Book*. Charles M. Mugler. San Francisco, Calif.: Sunset Magazine, 1934.

B007 *Sunset All-Western Cook Book: How to Select, Prepare, Cook, and Serve All Typically Western Food Products : Recipes Included for Favorite Regional and Foreign Dishes Peculiar to the West*. Genevieve Anne Callahan. 2d ed. San Francisco, Calif.: Lane Pub. Co., 1935.

B008 *Sunset's Favorite Company Dinners*. Genevieve Anne Callahan. [5th ed.]. San Francisco, Calif.: Sunset Magazine, 1935.

B009 *Sunset's Garden Handbook / Compiled and Edited by Richard Merrifield*. Richard Merrifield. 1st ed. San Francisco, Calif.: Sunset Magazine, 1935.

B010 *Sunset All-Western Cook Book: How to Select, Prepare, Cook, and Serve All Typically Western Food Products : Recipes Included for Favorite Regional and Foreign Dishes Peculiar to the West*. Genevieve Anne Callahan. 3d ed. San Francisco, Calif.: Lane Pub. Co., 1936.

B011 *Sunset's All-Western Garden Guide*. Allison M. Woodman. San Francisco, Calif.: Sunset Magazine, 1936.

B012 *Sunset's Hostess Handbook for Western Homes*. San Francisco, Calif.: Sunset Magazine, 1937.

B013 *Sunset's Salad Book With Hors D'OEuvres and Canapes*. Genevieve A. Callahan. 1st ed. San Francisco, Calif.: Sunset Magazine, Lane Pub. Co., 1937.

B014 *Sunset's Kitchen Cabinet Cook Book*. San Francisco, Calif.: Sunset Magazine, Lane Pub. Co., 1938.

B015 *Sunset's New Kitchen Cabinet Cook Book*. San Francisco, Calif.: Sunset Magazine, 1938.

B016 *Sunset Salad Book, With Hors D'Oeuvres and Canapes*. Genevieve A. Callahan. San Francisco, Calif.: Sunset Magazine, 1938.

B017 *Sunset's Cabin Plan Book*. Ralph P Dillon. 1st ed. San Francisco, Calif.: Sunsent Magazine, 1938.

B018 *Sunset's Western Hostess Guide*. Virginia Rich. San Francisco, Calif.: Sunset Magazine, 1938.

B020 *Sunset's Barbecue Book*. George A. Sanderson and Virginia Rich. San Francisco, Calif.: Sunset Magazine, 1938.

B021 *Sunset's Dessert Book*. Shirley Douglass and Norman Gordon. San Francisco, Calif.: Sunset Magazine, 1939.

B022 *Sunset's Complete Garden Book*. Richard Merrifield. 1940. San Francisco, Calif.: Lane Pub. Co., 1939.

B023 *Sunset's Barbecue Book*. George A. Sanderson and Virginia Rich. San Francisco, Calif.: Sunset Magazine, 1939.

B024 *Famous Recipes by Famous People*. Herbert Cerwin. San Francisco, Calif.: Sunset Magazine in cooperation with Hotel del Monte, 1940.

B025 *How to Grow Sweet Peas*. Norvell Gillespie. San Francisco, Calif.: Sunset Magazine, 1940.

B026 *Sunset's Popular Flower Book*. Norvell Gillespie. San Francisco, Calif.: Sunset Magazine, Lane Pub. Co., 1940.

B027 *Sunset's Host and Hostess Book*. Helen Kroeger Muhs. San Francisco, Calif.: Lane Pub. Co., 1940.

1941–1950

B028 *Sunset's Meat Menu Book*. Shirley Douglass. San Francisco, Calif.: Sunset Magazine, Lane Pub. Co., 1941.

B029 *The Visual Garden Manual*. Elsa Uppman. San Francisco, Calif.: Lane Pub. Co., 1941.

B030 *Sunset's Household Handbook*. Helen C. Wright. San Francisco, Calif.: Lane Pub. Co., 1941.

B031 *Sunset's Flower Arrangement Book*. Nell True Welch and Rudolph Schaeffer. San Francisco, Calif.: Lane, 1942.

B032 *Sunset's Vegetable Garden Book*. San Francisco, Calif.: Lane Pub. Co., 1943.

B033 *Sunset's Kitchen Cabinet Recipes*. San Francisco, Calif.: Lane Pub. Co., 1944.

B034 *Sunset Flower Garden Book*. Richard Merrifield. San Francisco, Calif.: Lane Pub. Co., 1945.

B035 *Sunset Barbecue Book*. George A. Sanderson and Virginia Rich. Revised and enlarged July, 1945. San Francisco, Calif.: Lane Pub. Co., 1945.

B036 *Sunset Barbecue Book*. San Francisco, Calif.: Lane Pub. Co., 1946.

B037 *Sunset Homes for Western Living, From Five Years of Sunset*. San Francisco, Calif.: Lane Pub. Co., 1946.

B038 *Sunset Salad Book, With Hors D'Oeuvres and Canapes*. Emily Chase. San Francisco, Calif.: Lane Pub. Co., 1946.

B039 *Sunset Craft Manual*. Elise Mannel. San Francisco, Calif.: Lane Pub. Co., 1946.

B040 *Sunset Western Ranch Houses*. Cliff May. San Francisco, Calif.: Lane Pub. Co., 1946.

B041 *Sunset Flower Garden Book*. Rev. and enl. San Francisco, Calif.: Lane Pub. Co., 1947.

B042 *Sunset Flower Garden Book*. Rev. and enl. San Francisco, Calif.: Lane Pub. Co., 1947.

B043 *Sunset Home for Western Living: From Five Years of Sunset*. San Francisco, Calif.: Lane Pub. Co., 1947.

B044 *Sunset All-Western Foods Cook Book: Typical Western Foods : How to Pick the Best of the Offerings ; How to Cook and Serve Them Most Attractively*. Genevieve Anne Callahan. San Francisco, Calif.: Lane Pub. Co., 1947.

B045 *Sunset Flower Garden Book*. Rev. and enl. San Francisco, Calif.: Lane Pub. Co., 1948.

B046 *Sunset Craft Manual*. Elise Mannel. San Francisco, Calif.: Lane Pub. Co., 1948.

B047 *Sunset Cook Book of Favorite Recipes*. Emily Chase. San Francisco, Calif.: Lane Pub. Co., 1949.

B048 *Sunset Barbecue Book*. 3d ed. Menlo Park, Calif.: Lane Pub. Co., 1950.

B049 *Sunset Ideas for Landscaping Your Home*. San Francisco, Calif.: Lane Pub. Co., 1950.

B050 *Sunset Vegetable Garden Book*. Rev. and enl. 2d ed. Menlo Park, Calif.: Lane Pub. Co., 1950.

B051 *Sunset Salad Book With Hors D'Oeuvres and Canapes*. Emily Chase. Menlo Park, Calif.: Lane Pub. Co., 1950.

1951–1960

B052 *Chefs of the West*. 1st ed. Menlo Park, Calif.: Lane Pub. Co., 1951.

B053 *How to Build Fences and Gates*. Menlo Park, Calif.: Lane Book Co, 1951.

B054 *How to Plan and Build Your Fireplace*. [1st ed.]. San Francisco, Calif.: Lane Pub. Co., 1951.

B055 *Sunset Ideas for Building Plant Shelters and Garden Work Centers*. Menlo Park, Calif.: Lane Pub. Co., 1951.

B056 *Sunset Planting Ideas for Your Northwest Garden*. [1st ed.]. San Francisco, Calif.: Lane Pub. Co., 1951.

B057 *Sunset Planting Ideas for Your Southern California Garden*. [1st ed.]. San Francisco, Calif.: Lane Pub. Co., 1951.

Books

B058 *Wood Carving Book*. Doris Aller. [1st ed.]. Menlo Park, Calif: Lane Pub. Co., 1951.

B059 *How to Grow African Violets*. Carolyn Kenny Rector. [lst ed.]. San Francisco, Calif.: Land Pub. Co, 1951.

B060 *Cooking With a Foreign Accent a Collection of International Recipes for Everyday Kitchen Use, Each One Tested in the Sunset Magazine Kitchen*. 1st ed. Menlo Park, Calif.: Lane Pub. Co., 1952.

B061 *How to Build Walls, Walks, Patio Floors*. [1st ed.]. Menlo Park, Calif.: Lane Pub. Co., 1952.

B062 *Ideas for Bookcases & Bookshelves*. Menlo Park, Calif.: Lane Pub. Co., 1952.

B063 *Patio Book*. [1st ed.]. Menlo Park, Calif.: Lane Book Co, 1952.

B064 *The Portable Garden*. [1st ed.]. Menlo Park, Calif.: Lane Pub. Co., 1952.

B065 *Sunset Homes for Western Living; From Five Years of Sunset*. Menlo Park, Calif.: Lane Pub. Co., 1952.

B066 *Sunset Ideas for Cabins and Beach Houses*. [1st ed.]. Menlo Park, Calif.: Lane Pub. Co., 1952.

B067 *Leather Craft Book*. Doris Aller. Menlo Park, Calif.: Lane Pub. Co., 1952.

B068 *Sunset Salad Book, With Hors D'Oeuvres and Canapes*. Emily Chase. Menlo Park, Calif: Lane Pub. Co., 1952.

B069 *Colorado River and Lake Mead: Boating, Fishing, Exploring*. Clarence Elmer Erickson. 1st ed. Menlo Park, Calif.: Lane Pub Co., 1952. (Sunset sportsman's atlas).

B070 *San Francisco Bay and Delta Area: Boating, Fishing, Hunting*. Clarence Elmer Erickson. [1st ed.] Menlo Park, Calif.: Lane Pub. Co., 1952.

B071 *Sunset Pruning Handbook*. Roy L. Hudson. 1st ed. Menlo Park, Calif.: Lane Books, 1952.

B072 *The Visual Garden Manual*. Elsa Uppman. Menlo Park, Calif.: Lane Pub. Co., 1952.

B073 *How to Build Outdoor Furniture*. [1st ed.]. Menlo Park, Calif.: Lane Pub. Co., 1953.

B074 *Outdoor Building Book; Five Complete Sunset Books in One Volume to Cover Your Basic Outdoor Building Needs*. [1st ed.]. Menlo Park, Calif.: Lane Pub. Co., 1953.

B075 *Sunset Ideas for Hillside Homes*. 1st ed. Menlo Park, Calif.: Lane Pub. Co., 1953.

B076 *Handmade Rugs*. Doris Aller. 1st ed. Menlo Park, Calif: Lane Pub. Co., 1953. (Sunset craft books).

B077 *How to Fish the Pacific Coast, a Manual for Salt Water Fishermen*. Raymond Cannon. [1st ed.]. Menlo Park, Calif.: Lane Pub. Co., 1953.

B078 *Puget Sound and Northwest Waterways; Boating, Fishing, Hunting*. James W. Cutter. [1st ed.] Menlo Park, Calif.: Lane Pub. Co., 1953.

B079 *Southern California Coast: Boating, Fishing, Beaches*. Clarence Elmer Erickson. [1st ed.] Menlo Park, Calif.: Lane Pub. Co., 1953.

B080 *How to Grow Fuchsias*. Frances Howard. [1st ed.]. Menlo Park, Calif.: Lane Pub. Co., 1953.

B081 *Introduction to Western Birds*. Lillian Grace Paca. [1st ed.]. Menlo Park, Calif.: Lane Pub. Co., 1953.

B082 *African Violet Variety List*. Carolyn Kenny Rector. Menlo Park, Calif.: Lane Pub. Co., 1953.

B083 *Sunset Ceramics Book*. Herbert H Sanders. [1st ed.] Menlo Park, Calif., Lane Pub. Co. Menlo Park, Calif.: Lane Pub. Co., 1953.

B084 *Sunset Western Garden Book*. 1st ed. Menlo Park, Calif.: Lane Pub. Co., 1954.

B085 *Sunset Western Sea Food Cookbook*. Menlo Park, Calif., : Lane Pub. Co., 1954.

B086 *Tables You Can Build*. [1st ed.]. Menlo Park, Calif.: Lane Pub. Co., 1954.

B087 *Pacific Area Travel Handbook*. Pacific Area Travel Association. Menlo Park, Calif.: Lane Pub. Co., 1954.

B088 *Discovery Trips in California; Byways of the Highways. 66 Travel Articles Reprinted From Sunset Magazine*. 1st ed. Menlo Park, Calif.: Lane Pub. Co., 1955.

B089 *Discovery Trips in Mexico*. 1st ed. Menlo Park, Calif.: Lane Pub. Co., 1955.

B090 *How to Install and Care for Your Lawn*. 1st ed. Menlo Park, Calif.: Lane Pub. Co., 1955.

B091 *Ideas for Western Kitchens*. [1st ed.]. Menlo Park, Calif.: Lane Pub. Co., 1955.

B092 *Sunset Seasonal Garden Guide and Record Book*. [1st ed.]. Menlo Park, Calif.: Lane Pub. Co., 1955.

B093 *Western Campsite Directory*. Menlo Park, Calif.: Lane Books, 1955.

B094 *How to Grow Roses*. John Paul Edwards. 1st ed. Menlo Park, Calif.: Lane Pub. Co., 1955. (A Sunset book).

B095 *The High Sierra Hiking, Camping, Fishing*. Clarence Elmer Erickson. Menlo Park, Calif.: Lane Pub. Co., 1955.

B096 *San Francisco Bay and Delta Area: Boating, Fishing, Hunting*. Clarence Elmer Erickson. 2d ed. Menlo Park, Calif.: Lane Pub. Co., 1955.

B097 *Pacific Area Travel Handbook*. Pacific Area Travel Association. [2d ed.]. Menlo Park, Calif.: Lane Pub. Co., 1955.

B098 *African Violet Variety List*. Carolyn Kenny Rector. [Rev. ed.]. Menlo Park, Calif.: Lane Pub. Co., 1955. (A Sunset book).

B099 *Discovery Trips in Arizona*. [1st ed.]. Menlo Park, Calif.: Lane Pub. Co., 1956.

B100 *Discovery Trips in Oregon*. 1st ed. Menlo Park, Calif.: Lane Pub. Co., 1956.

B101 *Discovery Trips in Washington*. [1st ed.]. Menlo Park, Calif.: Lane Pub. Co., 1956.

B102 *How to Build Patio Roofs*. 1st ed. Menlo Park, Calif.: Lane Book Co, 1956.

B103 *Landscaping for Western Living*. 1st ed. Menlo Park, Calif.: Lane Book Co, 1956.

B104 *New Homes for Western Living*. [1st ed.]. Menlo Park, Calif.: Lane Pub. Co., 1956.

B105 *Sunset Ideas for Hillside Homes; Ideas Compiled From Sunset Magazine*. [2d ed.]. Menlo Park, Calif.: Lane Pub. Co., 1956. (Hillside homes).

B106 *Pacific Area Travel Handbook, 1957 Revision*. Pacific Area Travel Association. 4th. Menlo Park, Calif.: Lane Pub. Co., 1956.

B107 *How to Grow African Violets*. Carolyn K. Rector. [2d ed.]. Menlo Park, Calif.: Lane Pub. Co., 1956.

B108 *Cooking Bold and Fearless: Recipes by Chefs of the West*. 1st ed. Menlo Park, Calif.: Lane Pub. Co., 1957.

B109 *Gold Rush Country; Guide to California's Mother Lode & Northern Mines*. [1st ed.]. Menlo Park, Calif.: Lane Pub. Co., 1957.

B110 *How to Grow Camellias, Including a 600-Variety Encyclopedia*. [1st ed.]. Menlo Park, Calif.: Lane Pub. Co., 1957.

B111 *Ideas for Christmas Decorating*. Menlo Park, Calif.: Lane Pub. Co., 1957.

B112 *Sunset Barbecue Cook Book*. [3d ed.]. Menlo Park, Calif.: Lane Pub. Co., 1957.

B113 *Sunset Ideas for Family Camping*. Menlo Park, Calif.: Lane Pub. Co., 1957.

B114 *Sunset Salad Book, With Hors D'Oeuvres and Canapes*. Emily Chase. Menlo Park, Calif.: Lane Pub. Co., 1957.

B115 *This Is California; Photographs*. Karl Obert. [1st ed.]. Menlo Park, Calif.: Lane Pub. Co., 1957.

Books

B116 *Hawaii; a Sunset Discovery Book*. Pacific Area Travel Association. Menlo Park, Calif.: Lane Pub. Co., 1957.

B117 *Beautiful Canada, With Canadian Rocky Mountain National Parks*. Menlo Park, Calif.: Lane Pub. Co., 1958.

B118 *British Columbia: With Canadian Rocky Mountain National Parks*. Menlo Park, Calif.: Lane Pub. Co., 1958.

B119 *Cooking With a Foreign Accent*. [2d ed.]. Menlo Park, Calif.: Lane Pub. Co., 1958.

B120 *Cooking With Casseroles*. Menlo Park, Calif.: Lane Pub. Co., 1958.

B121 *How to Build Fences and Gates*. 2d ed. Menlo Park, Calif.: Lane Book Co., 1958.

B122 *Landscaping for Modern Living*. Menlo Park, Calif.: Lane Pub. Co., 1958.

B123 *Sunset Ideas for Color in Your Garden; Selected Articles*. 1st ed. Menlo Park, Calif.: Lane Pub. Co., 1958.

B124 *Sunset Ideas for Remodeling Your Home*. [1st ed.]. Menlo Park, Calif.: Lane Pub. Co., 1958.

B125 *Sunset Ideas for Storage in Your Home*. [1st ed.]. Menlo Park, Calif.: Lane Pub. Co., 1958.

B126 *Western Campsite Directory*. [Completely rev. ed.]. Menlo Park, Calif.: Lane Pub. Co., 1958.

B127 *Western Ranch Houses by Cliff May*. Cliff May. [1st ed.]. Menlo Park, Calif.: Lane Pub. Co., 1958.

B128 *Breakfasts & Brunches*. Menlo Park, Calif.: Sunset, 1959.

B129 *Cooking Charts; Quick Guides to Basic Herbs, Cooking Spices, Baking Spices, Flavorings, Vegetables, Barbecuing*. Menlo Park, Calif.: Lane Pub. Co., 1959.

B130 *Gardening in Containers*. [1st ed.]. Menlo Park, Calif.: Lane Books, 1959.

B131 *Mexico*. 2d ed. Menlo Park, Calif.: Lane Pub. Co., 1959.

B132 *Northern California*. [1st ed.]. Menlo Park, Calif.: Lane Pub. Co., 1959.

B133 *Southern California*. [1st ed.]. Menlo Park, Calif.: Lane Pub. Co., 1959.

B134 *Swimming Pools*. [1st ed.]. Menlo Park, Calif.: Lane Pub. Co., 1959.

B135 *Sunset Mosaics*. Doris Aller and Diane Lee Aller. [1st ed.]. Menlo Park, Calif.: Lane Book Co., 1959. (Sunset craft books).

B136 *National Parks in California*. Dorr Graves Yeager. Menlo Park, Calif.: Lane Pub. Co., 1959.

B137 *Cabins and Vacation Houses*. Menlo Park, Calif.: Lane Book Co, 1960.

B138 *Children's Rooms and Play Yards*. Menlo Park, Calif.: Lane Book Co, 1960.

B139 *Garden & Patio Building Book; Five Complete Sunset Books in One Volume to Cover Your Basic Outdoor Building Needs*. Menlo Park, Calif.: Lane Books, 1960.

B140 *Garden Work Centers*. [1st ed.]. Menlo Park, Calif.: Lane Book Co, 1960.

B141 *Gold Rush Country: Guide to California's Mother Lode & Northern Mines*. Menlo Park, Calif.: Lane Books, 1960.

B142 *Hawaii*. [2d ed.]. Menlo Park, Calif.: Lane Book Co., 1960. (A Sunset discovery book).

B143 *The Sunset Cook Book; Food With a Gourmet Touch*. Menlo Park, Calif.: Lane Book Co, 1960.

B144 *Sunset Lawn and Ground Cover Book*. 2d ed. Menlo Park, Calif.: Lane Book Co., 1960.

B145 *Western Campsite Directory*. 2d rev. Menlo Park, Calif.: Lane Book Co., 1960.

B146 *Rodeo Days*. Elizabeth Clemons. [1st ed.]. Menlo Park, Calif.: Lane Book Co, 1960. (A Sunset junior book).

B147 *How to Grow Roses*. John Paul Edwards. 2d ed. Menlo Park, Calif.: Lane Book Co., 1960.

B148 *San Francisco Bay and Delta Area: Boating, Fishing, Hunting*. Clarence Elmer Erickson. Menlo Park, Calif.: Lane Book Co., 1960.

B149 *Young Ranchers at Oak Valley*. Lucille M. 1908-1963 Nixon. [1st ed.]. Menlo Park, Calif.: Lane Book Co., 1960. (A Sunset junior book).

B150 *Crystal & Mineral Collecting*. William B. Sanborn. 1st ed. Menlo Park, Calif.: Lane Book Co., 1960. (A Sunset book).

B151 *There Stand the Giants; the Story of the Redwood Trees*. Harriett E. Weaver. Menlo Park, Calif.: Lane Book Co, 1960.

B152 *Ducks, Geese, and Swans*. Herbert H. Wong. [1st ed.]. Menlo Park, Calif.: Lane Book Co, 1960.

1961–1970

B153 *Food Freezing Charts; Useful for the Largest or the Smallest Freezer*. Menlo Park, Calif.: Lane Books, 1961.

B154 *How to Cool Your House*. [1st ed.]. Menlo Park, Calif.: Lane Book Co, 1961.

B155 *Ideas for Entryways and Front Gardens*. [1st ed.]. Menlo Park, Calif.: Lane Book Co, 1961.

B156 *Official Guide to Pacific Northwest and Century 21 Exposition*. Menlo Park, Calif.: Lane Book Co., 1961.

B157 *Patio Book*. Rev.(i.e.2d). Menlo Park, Calif.: Lane Books, 1961.

B158 *Sunset Ideas for Building Barbecues*. 1st ed. Menlo Park, Calif.: Lane Book Co., 1961.

B159 *Sunset Ideas for Hillside Homes*. 2d ed. Menlo Park, Calif.: Lane Pub. Co., 1961.

B160 *Sunset Western Garden Book*. Rev. [i. e., 2d]. Menlo Park, Calif.: Lane Book Co, 1961.

B161 *Things to Make for Children: Toys, Togs, Party Fun*. Menlo Park, Calif.: Lane Book Co., 1961. (A Sunset book).

B162 *Vegetable Gardening*. Menlo Park, Calif.: Lane Books, 1961.

B163 *Aluminum: the Story of an Industry*. Bart Benedict.1st ed., Menlo Park, Calif.: Lane Book Co., 1961. (A Sunset Junior book).

B164 *State Parks of California*. John Robinson and Alfred Calais. Menlo Park, Calif.: Lane Book Co., 1961.

B165 *Western Butterflies*. Arthur Clayton Smith. [1st ed.]. Menlo Park, Calif.: Lane Book Co., 1961.

B166 *The Spice Islands Cook Book*. Spice Islands Company. 1st ed. Menlo Park, Calif.: Lane Books, 1961.

B167 *Arizona*. [2d ed.]. Menlo Park, Calif.: Lane Book Co, 1962.

B168 *Furniture You Can Build*. [1st ed.]. Menlo Park, Calif.: Lane Book Co, 1962.

B169 *Garden Art & Decoration*. [1st ed.]. Menlo Park, Calif.: Lane Book Co, 1962.

B170 *How to Build Walls, Walks, Patio Floors*. Menlo Park, Calif.: Lane Book Co., 1962. (A Sunset book).

B171 *How to Grow and Use Annuals*. Menlo Park, Calif.: Lane Book Co., 1962.

B172 *How to Grow and Use Bulbs*. 1st ed. Menlo Park, Calif.: Lane Book Co, 1962.

B173 *How to Grow and Use Camellias*. [2d ed.]. Menlo Park, Calif.: Lane Book Co, 1962.

B174 *How to Plan and Build Your Fireplace*. [2d ed.]. Menlo Park, Calif.: Lane Book Co, 1962.

B175 *Sunset Barbecue Cook Book*. Menlo Park, Calif.: Lane Book Co, 1962.

B176 *Sunset Family Camping*. [2d ed.]. Menlo Park, Calif.: Lane Book Co, 1962.

B177 *Sunset Ideas for Family Camping*. 2d ed. Menlo Park, Calif.: Lane Pub. Co., 1962.

B178 *Sunset Modern Kitchens*. [2d ed.]. Menlo Park, Calif.: Lane Book Co, 1962.

B179 *Sunset Salad Book*. Menlo Park, Calif.: Lane Book Co, 1962.

B180 *Swimming Pools*. [2d ed.]. Menlo Park, Calif.: Lane Book Co, 1962.

B181 *Western Campsite Directory*. Menlo Park, Calif.: Lane Pub. Co., 1962.

Books

B182 *The Art of Flower Preservation*. Geneal Condon. [1st ed.]. Menlo Park, Calif.: Lane Book Co, 1962.

B183 *The Dinner Party Cook Book*. Dorothy Krell. 1st ed. Menlo Park, Calif.: Lane Book Co., 1962.

B184 *How to Grow African Violets*. Carolyn K. Rector. [3d ed.]. Menlo Park, Calif.: Lane Book Co, 1962.

B185 *California State Parks*. John Robinson. Menlo Park, Calif: Lane Books, 1962.

B186 *Sunset Ceramics Book*. Herbert H. Sanders. [1st ed.]. Menlo Park, Calif.: Lane Pub. Co., 1962. (Sunset craft books).

B187 *Logging; the Story of an Industry*. Arthur Samuel Taylor and Jack Sutton. Menlo Park, Calif.: Lane Book Co., 1962. (A Sunset junior book).

B188 *Alaska*. [1st ed.]. Menlo Park, Calif.: Lane Book Co., 1963. (A Sunset discovery book).

B189 *Basic Gardening Illustrated*. Menlo Park, Calif.: Lane Book Co., 1963.

B190 *Beautiful California*. 1st ed. Menlo Park, Calif.: Lane Book Co., 1963.

B191 *Garden Plans*. 1st ed. Menlo Park, Calif.: Lane Book Co., 1963.

B192 *Gold Rush Country; Guide to California's Mother Lode and Northern Mines*. [2d ed.]. Menlo Park, Calif.: Lane Book Co, 1963.

B193 *How to Build Decks for Outdoor Living*. Menlo Park, Calif.: Lane Book Co, 1963.

B194 *Interior Art & Decoration*. Menlo Park, Calif.: Lane Book Co., 1963.

B195 *Lighting Your Home*. [1st ed.]. Menlo Park, Calif.: Lane Book Co., 1963.

B196 *Men Cooking, by 474 Outstanding Men Cooks*. Menlo Park, Calif.: Lane Book Co., 1963. (A Sunset Book).

B197 *Mexico*. 3d ed. Menlo Park, Calif.: Lane Book Co., 1963. (A Sunset discovery book).

B198 *Official Guide to Pacific Northwest and Century 21 Exposition*. Menlo Park, Calif.: Lane Book Co., 1963.

B199 *Pacific Northwest and British Columbia*. [2d ed.]. Menlo Park, Calif.: Lane Book Co, 1963.

B200 *The Sunset Cook Book of Breads*. Menlo Park, Calif.: Lane Book Co, 1963.

B201 *Sunset Cook Book of Desserts*. Menlo Park, Calif.: Lane Book Co, 1963.

B202 *Western Campsite Directory*. Menlo Park, Calif.: Lane Pub. Co., 1963.

B203 *Northern California Boating Atlas*. Clarence Elmer Erickson. 1st ed. Menlo Park, Calif.: Lane Book Co., 1963. (Sunset book).

B204 *Stagecoach Days*. Vickie Hunter and Elizabeth Hamma. Menlo Park, Calif.: Lane Book Co., 1963.

B205 *The Dinner Party Cook Book*. Dorothy Krell. Menlo Park, Calif.: Lane Book Co, 1963.

B206 *Modern Bathrooms*. Joseph F. Schram. Menlo Park, Calif.: Lane Book Co, 1963.

B207 *Adventures in Food*. 1st ed. Menlo Park, Calif.: Lane Book Co, 1964.

B208 *The California Missions: a Pictorial History*. Menlo Park, Calif.: Lane Book Co, 1964.

B209 *Carports and Garages*. Menlo Park, Calif.: Lanc Book Co, 1964.

B210 *Garden & Patio Building Book: Five Complete Sunset Books in One Volume to Cover Your Basic Outdoor Building Needs*. [1st ed.]. Menlo Park, Calif.: Lane Book Co., 1964.

B211 *Golf Course Directory for California*. Menlo Park, Calif.: Lane Book Co, 1964.

B212 *How to Build Patio Roofs*. 2d ed. Menlo Park, Calif.: Lane Books Co., 1964.

B213 *Lawns and Ground Covers*. 3d ed. Menlo Park, Calif.: Lane Book Co., 1964.

B214 *Northern California*. [2d ed.]. Menlo Park, Calif.: Lane Book Co, 1964.

B215 *Southern California*. Rev. Menlo Park, Calif.: Lane Book Co, 1964.

B216 *The Sunset Cook Book; Food With a Gourmet Touch, by the Sunset Editorial Staff*. Menlo Park, Calif.: Lane Book Co, 1964.

B217 *My Life With Animals*. Carey Baldwin. Menlo Park, Calif.: Lane Book Co, 1964.

B218 *How to Fish the Pacific Coast; a Manual for Salt Water Fisherman*. Raymond Cannon. 2d ed. Menlo Park, Calif.: Lane Book Co, 1964.

B219 *Trains, Tracks & Trails; How the Railroads Reached the West*. Norris Ewing. Menlo Park, Calif.: Lane Book Co., 1964.

B220 *Sailers, Whalers & Steamers: Ships That Opened the West*. Edith Thacher Hurd, Lyle Galloway, and John Haskell Kemble. 1st ed. Menlo Park, Calif.: Lane Book Co., 1964.

B221 *Earthquake Country*. Robert Iacopi. Menlo Park, Calif.: Lane Book Co., 1964.

B222 *Peter McIntyre's New Zealand*. Peter McIntyre. Menlo Park, Calif.: Lane Magazine & Book Co., 1964.

B223 *Australia*. Frederic M. Rea. Menlo Park, Calif.: Lane Book Co., 1964. (A Sunset Travel Book).

B224 *Japan*. Frederic M. Rea. Menlo Park, Calif.: Lane Book Co, 1964.

B225 *New Zealand*. Frederic M. Rea. Menlo Park, Calif.: Lane Book Co., 1964. (A Sunset Travel Book).

B226 *How to Make Pottery & Ceramic Sculpture*. Herbert H. Sanders. Menlo Park, Calif.: Lane Books, 1964.

B227 *How to Plan, Establish, and Maintain Rock Gardens*. George Walden Schenk. Menlo Park, Calif.: Lane Book Co., 1964.

B228 *National Parks in California*. Dorr Graves Yeager. 2d ed. Menlo Park, Calif.: Lane Books, 1964.

B229 *Casserole Book*. Menlo Park, Calif.: Lane, 1965.

B230 *Garden Pools, Fountains & Waterfalls*. Menlo Park, Calif.: Lane Books, 1965. (A Sunset book).

B231 *Gifts You Can Make*. Menlo Park, Calif.: Lane Books, 1965.

B232 *Ground Beef Cook Book*. Menlo Park, CA: Lane Books, 1965.

B233 *National Parks of the West*. Menlo Park, Calif.: Lane Magazine & Book Co, 1965.

B234 *Planning and Landscaping Hillside Homes*. Menlo Park, Calif.: Lane Books, 1965.

B235 *The Sunset Appetizer Book*. Menlo Park, Calif.: Lane Books, 1965.

B236 *Sunset Ideas for Garden Color*. 2d rev. Menlo Park, Calif.: Lane Books, 1965.

B237 *Western Campsite Directory*. Menlo Park, Calif.: Lane Pub. Co., 1965.

B238 *Hawaii*. Nancy Bannick. [3d ed.]. Menlo Park, Calif.: Lane Books, 1965. (A Sunset travel book).

B239 *The Monterey Peninsula*. William Wyatt Davenport. Menlo Park, Calif.: Lane Books, 1965.

B240 *Decorative Stitchery*. Marian May. [1st ed.]. Menlo Park, Calif.: Lane Books, 1965.

B241 *Bonsai: Culture and Care of Miniature Trees*. Jack McDowell. [1st ed.]. Menlo Park, Calif.: Lane Books, 1965.

B242 *Fresh-Water Fishing Illustrated; How to Catch a Fish in the West*. Erwin G Morrison. Menlo Park, Calif.: Lane Books, 1965. (A Sunset book).

B243 *Flower Arranging by Tat; Step-by-Step Instruction Showing How to Create and Use Flower Arrangements*. Tat Shinno. Menlo Park, Calif.: Lane books, 1965.

B244 *Hong Kong*. Mary Benton Smith and Frederic M. Rea. Menlo Park, Calif.: Lane Books, 1965. (A Sunset Travel Book).

B245 *Alaska*. [2d rev. ed.]. Menlo Park, Calif.: Lane Books, 1966.

B246 *Beachcombers' Guide to the Pacific Coast*. Menlo Park, Calif.: Lane Books, 1966.

Books

B247 *Breakfasts & Brunches*. Menlo Park, Calif.: Lane Books, 1966.

B248 *Garden Plans*. [1st ed.]. Menlo Park, Calif.: Lane Books, 1966.

B249 *How to Build Walks, Walls, Patio Floors*. [2d ed.]. Menlo Park, Calif.: Lane Books, 1966.

B250 *Ideas for Storage: Bookshelves, Cupboards, Cabinets*. [2d ed.]. Menlo Park, Calif.: Lane Books, 1966.

B251 *Landscaping for Modern Living*. Menlo Park, Calif.: Lane Pub. Co., 1966.

B252 *Quick & Easy Dinners*. Menlo Park, Calif.: Lane Books, 1966.

B253 *Sculpture With Simple Materials*. [1st ed.]. Menlo Park, Calif.: Lane Books, 1966.

B254 *Sunset Cook Book of Breads*. Menlo Park, Calif.: Lane Books, 1966.

B255 *Sunset Cook Book of Chicken & Turkey, Other Poultry, Game Birds*. Menlo Park, Calif.: Lane Books, 1966.

B256 *Sunset Salad Book*. [3d ed.]. Menlo Park, Calif.: Lane Books, 1966.

B257 *Swimming Pools*. Rev. Menlo Park, Calif.: Lane Books, 1966.

B258 *Western Campsite Directory*. Menlo Park, Calif.: Lane Books, 1966.

B259 *The Sea of Cortez*. Raymond Cannon. Menlo Park, Calif.: Lane Magazine and Book Co, 1966.

B260 *Art Treasures in the West*. William Wyatt Davenport. Menlo Park, Calif.: Lane Magazine & Book Co, 1966.

B261 *California State Parks*. John Robinson and Alfred Calais. [2d ed.]. Menlo Park, Calif.: Lane Books, 1966.

B262 *Islands of the South Pacific*. Mary Benton Smith. Menlo Park, Calif.: Lane Books, 1966. (A sunset travel book).

B263 *The 76 Bonanza; the Fabulous Life and Times of the Union Oil Company of California*. Earl M. Welty and Frank J. Taylor. Menlo Park, Calif.: Lane Magazine & Book Co, 1966.

B264 *Sunset Cook Book of Favorite Recipes*. Emily Chase. Menlo Park, Calif.: Lane Books, 131966.

B265 *Barbecue Cook Book*. [4th ed.]. Menlo Park, Calif.: Lane Books, 1967.

B266 *Cabins and Vacation Houses*. [2d ed.]. Menlo Park, Calif.: Lane Books, 1967.

B267 *Cook Book of Soups & Stews*. Menlo Park, Calif.: Lane Books, 1967.

B268 *Cooking Bold & Fearless*. 2d ed. Menlo Park, Calif.: Lane Books, 1967.

B269 *Desert Gardening*. 1st ed. Menlo Park, Calif.: Lane Books, 1967.

B270 *The Dinner Party Cook Book*. [2d ed.]. Menlo Park, Calif.: Lane Books, 1967.

B271 *Favorite Recipes for Soups & Stews*. 1st ed. Menlo Park, Calif.: Lane Pub. Co., 1967.

B272 *Gardening in Containers*. 2d ed. Menlo Park, Calif.: Lane Books, 1967.

B273 *Ideas for Planning Your New Home*. 2d ed. Menlo Park, Calif.: Lane Books, 1967.

B274 *Mexico*. [4th ed.]. Menlo Park, Calif.: Lane Books, 1967.

B275 *Planning & Remodeling Your Kitchen*. [3d ed.]. Menlo Park, Calif.: Lane Books, 1967.

B276 *Seafood Cook Book*. Menlo Park, Calif.: Lane Books, 1967.

B277 *Side Trips & Discoveries in Europe*. 1st ed. Menlo Park, Calif.: Lane Books, 1967. (A Sunset travel book).

B278 *Sunset Salad Book*. 3d ed. Menlo Park, Calif.: Lane Books, 1967.

B279 *Sunset Travel Guide to Arizona*. [3d ed.]. Menlo Park, Calif.: Lane Books, 1967.

B280 *Sunset Western Garden Book*. New ed., 3d ed. Menlo Park, Calif.: Lane Magazine & Book Co., 1967.

B281 *How to Fish the Pacific Coast: a Manual for Salt Water Fishermen*. Raymond Cannon. 3d ed. Menlo Park, Calif.: Lane Books, 1967.

B282 *Cook Book for Entertaining*. Menlo Park, Calif.: Lane Pub. Co., 1968.

B283 *Crafts for Children*. [1st ed.]. Menlo Park, Calif.: Lane Pub. Co., 1968.

B284 *Gold Rush Country: Guide to California's Mother Lode & Northern Mines*. 3d ed. Menlo Park, Calif.: Lane Books, 1968.

B285 *How to Grow and Use Camellias*. [3d ed.]. Menlo Park, Calif.: Lane Books, 1968.

B286 *How to Grow Bulbs*. [2d ed.]. Menlo Park, Calif.: Lane Books, 1968.

B287 *How to Grow House Plants*. [1st ed.]. Menlo Park, Calif.: Lane Books, 1968.

B288 *Landscaping for Western Living*. 2d ed, [Rev. ed.]. Menlo Park, Calif.: Lane Books, 1968.

B289 *Mexico*. New ed. Menlo Park, Calif.: Lane Books, 1968. (A Sunset Travel Book).

B290 *Sunset Cook Book of Desserts*. [2d ed.]. Menlo Park, Calif.: Lane Books, 1968.

B291 *Sunset Discovery Trips in the Rockies*. [1st ed.]. Menlo Park, Calif.: Lane Books, 1968.

B292 *Sunset Ideas for Recreation Rooms*. [1st ed.]. Menlo Park, Calif.: Lane Books, 1968.

B293 *Sunset Landscaping Book*. [Rev., i.e. 2d ed.]. Menlo Park, Calif.: Lane Books, 1968.

B294 *Sunset Travel Guide to Oregon*. Menlo Park, Calif.: Lane Books, 1968.

B295 *Sunset Travel Guide to Washington*. Menlo Park, Calif.: Lane Books, 1968.

B296 *Woodworking Projects*. [1st ed.]. Menlo Park, Calif.: Lane Pub. Co., 1968.

B297 *Los Angeles: Portrait of an Extraordinary City*. Paul C. Johnson. 1st ed. Menlo Park, Calif.: Lane Magazine and Book Co., 1968. (A Sunset pictorial).

B298 *Sunset Ideas for Japanese Gardens*. Jack McDowell. [1st ed.]. Menlo Park, Calif.: Lane Books, 1968.

B299 *Australia*. Frederic M. Rea. [2d ed.]. Menlo Park, Calif.: Lane Books, 1968. (A Sunset travel book).

B300 *New Zealand*. Frederic M. Rea. [2d ed.]. Menlo Park, Calif.: Lane Books, 1968. (A Sunset Travel Book).

B301 *Southeast Asia*. Mary Benton. Smith. [1st ed.]. Menlo Park, Calif.: Lane Books, 1968. (A Sunset Travel Book).

B302 *Taiwan; China's "Island Beautiful."*. Mary Benton Smith and Frederic M. Rea. Menlo Park, Calif.: Lane Books, 1968. (A Sunset Travel Book).

B303 *California Wine Country*. Bob Thompson. Menlo Park, Calif.: Lane Books, 1968.

B304 *California National Parks*. [3d ed.]. Menlo Park, Calif.: Lane Books, 1969.

B305 *Cook Book of Favorite Recipes*. [2d ed.]. Menlo Park, Calif.: Lane Books, 1969.

B306 *Garden & Patio Building Book*. Menlo Park, Calif.: Lane Books, 1969.

B307 *Ideas for Remodeling Your Home*. Menlo Park, Calif.: Lane Pub. Co., 1969.

B308 *Mexican Cookbook*. [1st ed.]. Menlo Park, Calif.: Lane Books, 1969.

B309 *Planning & Remodeling Bathrooms*. [New ed.]. Menlo Park, Calif.: Lane Books, 1969.

B310 *Sunset Cook Book of Favorite Recipes*. 2d ed. Menlo Park, Calif.: Lane Books, 1969.

B311 *Sunset Menu Cook Book*. Menlo Park, Calif.: Lane Magazine & Book Co, 1969.

B312 *Sunset Travel Guide to Idaho*. [1st ed.]. Menlo Park, Calif.: Lane Books, 1969.

B313 *Western Campsite Directory*. Menlo Park, Calif.: Lane Books, 1969.

B314 *Hawaii*. Nancy Bannick. [4th rev. ed.]. Menlo Park, Calif.: Lane Books, 1969. (A Sunset travel book).

B315 *Rhododendrons and Azaleas*. Philip Edinger. [1st ed.]. Menlo Park, Calif.: Lane Books, 1969.

B316 *Outdoor Lighting*. Bob Horne. [1st ed.]. Menlo Park, Calif.: Lane Books, 1969.

B317 *From Sails to Rails : Sailing Ships, Stagecoaches and Trains That Opened Up California*. Edith Thacher Hurd. Menlo Park, Calif.: Lane Magazine & Book Co., 1969. (A Sunset Book).

Books

B318 *Earthquake Country*. Robert Iacopi. [Rev. ed.]. Menlo Park, Calif.: Lane Books, 1969.

B319 *Redwood Country and the Big Trees of the Sierra*. Robert Iacopi. [1st ed.]. Menlo Park, Calif.: Lane Books, 1969. (A Sunset book).

B320 *Furniture Finishing and Refinishing*. James B. Johnstone. [1st ed.]. Menlo Park, Calif.: Lane Books, 1969.

B321 *Beautiful California*. Dorothy Krell. [2d ed.]. Menlo Park, Calif.: Lane Magazine & Book Co, 1969.

B322 *San Francisco*. Jack McDowell. Menlo Park, Calif.: Lane Books, 1969.

B323 *Hong Kong*. Mary Benton Smith and Frederic M. Rea. [Rev. ed.]. Menlo Park, Calif.: Lane Books, 1969.

B324 *Children's Rooms and Play Yards*. [2d ed.]. Menlo Park, Calif.: Lane Books, 1970.

B325 *National Parks of the West*. [2d ed.]. Menlo Park, Calif.: Lane Magazine & Book Co, 1970.

B326 *Southwest Indian Country: Arizona, New Mexico, Southern Utah, and Colorado*. [1st ed.]. Menlo Park, Calif.: Lane Books, 1970.

B327 *Sunset Oriental Cook Book*. [1st ed.]. Menlo Park, Calif.: Lane Books, 1970.

B328 *Sunset Travel Guide to Northern California*. [3d ed.]. Menlo Park, Calif.: Lane Books, 1970.

B329 *Swimming Pools*. [4th ed.]. Menlo Park, Calif.: Lane Books, 1970.

B331 *Sunset Travel Guide to Southern California*. Dixie Taylor Barlow. [3d ed.]. Menlo Park, Calif.: Lane Books, 1970.

B332 *Sunset Travel Guide to Western Canada*. Mimi Bell. [1st ed.]. Menlo Park, Calif.: Lane Books, 1970.

B333 *Furniture Upholstery and Repair*. James B. Johnstone. [1st ed.]. Menlo Park, Calif.: Lane Books, 1970. (A Sunset Book).

B334 *How to Grow Orchids*. Jack Kramer. [1st ed.]. Menlo Park, Calif.: Lane Books, 1970.

B335 *Succulents and Cactus*. Jack Kramer. [1st ed.]. Menlo Park, Calif.: Lane Books, 1970.

B336 *The Beautiful Northwest*. Dorothy Krell. Menlo Park, Calif.: Lane Magazine & Book Co, 1970.

B337 *Peter McIntyre's West*. Peter McIntyre. Menlo Park, Calif.: Lane Magazine & Book Co, 1970.

B338 *Soul Power Cook Book*. Calif. Students Ravenswood High School (Palo Alto). Menlo Park, Calif.: Lane Magazine & Book Co, 1970.

B339 *Sunset Camping Handbook*. John Robinson. [3d ed.]. Menlo Park, Calif.: Lane Books, 1970.

B340 *Papier Mache*. William J. Shelley and Barbara Linse. [1st ed.]. Menlo Park, Calif.: Lane Books, 1970.

B341 *California Wine Country*. Bob Thompson. Menlo Park, Calif.: Lane Books, 1970.

1971–1980

B342 *Basic Home Repairs Illustrated*. [1st ed.]. Menlo Park, Calif.: Lane Books, 1971.

B343 *Building Barbecues*. [2d ed.]. Menlo Park, Calif.: Lane Books, 1971.

B344 *Cook Book for Entertaining*. Abridged 2d ed. Menlo Park, Calif.: Lane Magazine & Book Co., 1971.

B345 *Furniture You Can Make*. [2d ed.]. Menlo Park, Calif.: Lane Books, 1971.

B346 *Guide to Organic Gardening*. [1st ed.]. Menlo Park, Calif.: Lane Pub. Co., 1971.

B347 *How to Build Fences & Gates*. [3d ed.]. Menlo Park, Calif.: Lane Books, 1971.

B348 *Ideas for Building Barbecues*. [2d ed.]. Menlo Park, Calif.: Lane Pub. Co., 1971.

B349 *Macrame*. Menlo Park, Calif.: Lane Books, 1971.

B350 *Nevada*. [1st ed.]. Menlo Park, Calif.: Lane Books, 1971.

B351 *Patio Book*. [3d ed.]. Menlo Park, Calif.: Lane Books, 1971.

B352 *Sunset Barbecue Building Book*. [2d ed.]. Menlo Park, Calif.: Lane Pub. Co., 1971.

B353 *Sunset Travel Guide to Utah*. [1st ed.]. Menlo Park, Calif.: Lane Books, 1971.

B354 *Baja California*. Ken Bates and Caroline Bates. [1st ed.]. Menlo Park, Calif.: Lane Books, 1971.

B355 *Ghost Towns of the West*. William Carter. Menlo Park, Calif.: Lane Magazine & Book Co, 1971.

B356 *Earthquake Country*. Robert Iacopi. [3d ed.]. Menlo Park, Calif.: Lane Books, 1971.

B357 *Woodcarving: Techniques & Projects*. James B. Johnstone. [2d ed.]. Menlo Park, Calif.: Lane Books, 1971.

B358 *How to Grow African Violets*. Jack Kramer. 4th. Menlo Park, Calif.: Lane Books, 1971.

B359 *New Zealand*. Frederic M. Rea. [2d ed.]. Menlo Park, Calif.: Lane Books, 1971. (A Sunset Travel Book).

B360 *Chafing Dish & Fondue Cook Book*. Jan Thiesen. [1st ed.]. Menlo Park, Calif.: Lane Books, 1971.

B361 *Sunset Back Roads of California: Sketches and Trip Notes*. Earl Thollander. Menlo Park, Calif.: Lane Magazine & Book Co., 1971. (A Sunset pictorial).

B362 *Australia*. Menlo Park, Calif.: Lane Pub. Co., 1972. (A Sunset Travel Book).

B363 *Basic Carpentry Illustrated*. [1st ed.]. Menlo Park, Calif.: Lane Books, 1972.

B364 *Discovery Trips in Europe*. [2d ed.]. Menlo Park, Calif.: Lane Books, 1972.

B365 *Furniture Upholstery and Repair*. Menlo Park, Calif.: Lane Books, 1972.

B366 *Ideas for Japanese Gardens*. Menlo Park, Calif.: Lane Books, 1972.

B367 *Ideas for Landscaping*. 3d ed. Menlo Park, Calif.: Lane Books, 1972.

B368 *Italian Cook Book*. [1st ed.]. Menlo Park, Calif.: Lane Pub. Co., 1972.

B369 *Pruning Handbook*. [New ed.]. Menlo Park, Calif.: Lane Books, 1972.

B370 *Sunset Barbecue Cook Book*. [Abridged 4th ed.]. Menlo Park, Calif.: Lane Books, 1972.

B371 *Sunset Christmas Ideas and Answers*. 2d ed. Menlo Park, Calif.: Lane Pub. Co., 1972.

B372 *Sunset Salad Book*. 3d ed. Menlo Park, Calif.: Lane Books, 1972.

B373 *Things to Make for Children: Toys, Togs, Party Fun*. [1st ed.]. Menlo Park, Calif.: Lane Books, 1972.

B374 *Western Campsite Directory*. 11th ed. Menlo Park, Calif.: Lane Magazine & Book Co., 1972.

B375 *Gold Rush Country*. Barbara Braasch. 4th ed.]. Menlo Park, Calif.: Lane Books, 1972.

B376 *Islands of the South Pacific*. Frances Coleberd. 2d ed.]. Menlo Park, Calif.: Lane Books, 1972.

B377 *Cooking With Wine*. Judith A. Gaulke. 1st ed.]. Menlo Park, Calif.: Lane Books, 1972.

B378 *Dinner Party Cook Book*. Judith A. Gaulke. 3d ed.]. Menlo Park, Calif.: Lane Books, 1972.

B379 *The Beautiful Southwest*. Paul C. Johnson. 1st ed.]. Menlo Park, Calif.: Lane Magazine & Book Co., 1972.

B380 *Beautiful Hawaii. [Edited by Dorothy Krell. Design: John Flack. Cartography: Basil C. Wood]*. Dorothy Krell. Menlo Park, Calif.: Lane Magazine & Book Co., 1972.

B381 *Needlepoint*. Susan Sedlacek Lampton. 1st ed.]. Menlo Park, Calif.: Lane Books, 1972.

B382 *How to Grow Herbs*. Richard Osborne. 1st ed., second printing May 1972. Menlo Park, Calif.: Lane Books, 1972.

Books

B383 *California State Parks.* John Robinson. 3d ed.]. Menlo Park, Calif: Lane Books, 1972.

B384 *Basic Gardening Illustrated.* Menlo Park, Calif.: Lane Book Co., 1973. (A Sunset book).

B385 *Color in Your Garden.* [3d ed.]. Menlo Park, Calif.: Lane Books, 1973.

B386 *How to Build Decks.* [2d ed.]. Menlo Park, Calif.: Lane Books, 1973.

B387 *How to Build Patio Roofs.* [3d ed.]. Menlo Park, Calif.: Lane Books, 1973.

B388 *How to Build Walks, Walls & Patio Floors.* [3d rev. ed.]. Menlo Park, Calif.: Lane Books, 1973.

B389 *How to Grow Bulbs.* [3d ed.]. Menlo Park, Calif.: Lane Books, 1973.

B390 *How to Plan and Build Fireplaces.* [3d ed.]. Menlo Park, Calif.: Lane Books, 1973.

B391 *Ideas for Cooking Vegetables.* 1st ed.]. Menlo Park, Calif.: Lane Pub. Co., 1973.

B392 *Quilting & Patchwork.* [1st ed.]. Menlo Park, Calif.: Lane Books, 1973.

B393 *Recipes for Ground Beef and Other Ground Meats.* [2d rev. ed.]. Menlo Park, Calif.: Lane Books, 1973.

B394 *Sunset Ideas for Improving Your Home.* Menlo Park, Calif.: Sunset Magazine, Special Services Dept, 1973.

B395 *Sunset Ideas for Remodeling Your Home.* 2. Menlo Park, Calif.: Lane Books, 1973.

B396 *Sunset Travel Guide to Arizona.* 4th. Menlo Park, Calif.: Lane Books, 1973.

B397 *Sunset Western Garden Book.* 3d ed., rev. Menlo Park, Calif.: Lane Magazine & Book Co., 1973.

B398 *Things to Make for Children.* [Rev. ed.]. Menlo Park, Calif.: Lane Books, 1973.

B399 *Terrariums & Miniature Gardens.* Kathryn Arthurs. 1st ed. Menlo Park, Calif.: Lane Books, 1973.

B400 *Sunset Travel Guide to Washington.* Robert G. Bander. 3d rev. Menlo Park, Calif.: Lane Books, 1973.

B401 *Hawaii.* Nancy Bannick. 7th print., rev. Menlo Park, Calif.: Lane Books, 1973. (A Sunset travel book).

B402 *Australia.* Lawrence A. Clancy, Frances Coleberd, Valerie McGlenighan, and Frederic M. Rea. [3d rev. ed.]. Menlo Park, Calif.: Lane Books, 1973. (A Sunset Travel Book).

B403 *Japan.* Frances Coleberd. 2d ed. Menlo Park, Calif.: Lane Books, 1973.

B404 *How to Grow Roses.* Philip Edinger. 3d ed.]. Menlo Park, Calif.: Lane Books, 1973.

B405 *Ceramics: Techniques & Projects.* Jane Horn. 1st ed.]. Menlo Park, Calif.: Lane Books, 1973.

B406 *Mexico.* Jack McDowell. [1st ed.]. Menlo Park, Calif.: Lane Magazine & Book Co, 1973.

B407 *Things to Make With Leather: Techniques & Projects.* Richard Osborne. Menlo Park, Calif.: Lane Books, 1973.

B408 *California Wine.* Bob Thompson. [1st ed.]. Menlo Park, Calif.: Lane Magazine, 1973.

B409 *California Wine Country.* Bob Thompson. Rev. Menlo Park, Calif.: Lane Books, 1973.

B410 *Attracting Birds to Your Garden.* Menlo Park, Calif.: Lane Books, 1974.

B411 *Cooking With Spices & Herbs.* 1st ed.]. Menlo Park, Calif.: Lane Books, 1974.

B412 *Garden Pools, Fountains & Waterfalls.* 2d ed. Menlo Park, Calif.: Lane Books, 1974.

B413 *How to Build Patio Roofs.* Menlo Park, Calif.: Lane Pub. Co., 1974.

B414 *How to Grow Annuals.* [2d ed.]. Menlo Park, Calif.: Lane Books, 1974.

B415 *How to Grow House Plants.* Menlo Park, Calif.: Lane Pub. Co., 1974. (A Sunset book).

B416 *Ideas for Hanging Gardens.* Menlo Park, Calif.: Lane Pub. Co., 1974.

B417 *Ideas for Leisure Rooms.* 2d ed. Menlo Park, Calif.: Lane Pub. Co., 1974.

B418 *Low Maintenance Gardening.* Menlo Park, Calif.: Lane Books, 1974.

B419 *Mexico.* [5th rev. ed.]. Menlo Park, Calif.: Lane Books, 1974.

B420 *Quick & Easy Dinners.* [2d ed.]. Menlo Park, Calif.: Lane Pub. Co., 1974.

B421 *Scandinavian Cook Book.* Menlo Park, Calif.: Lane Pub. Co., 1974.

B422 *Sunset Christmas Ideas and Answers.* 4th ed. Menlo Park, Calif.: Sunset, 1974.

B423 *Planning & Remodeling Kitchens.* Kathryn Arthurs. 4th ed. Menlo Park, Calif.: Lane Pub. Co., 1974. (A Sunset Book).

B424 *Sunset Travel Guide to Southern California.* Barbara Braasch. 4th rev. Menlo Park, Calif.: Lane Pub. Co., 1974.

B425 *Weaving; Techniques & Projects.* Alyson Smith Gonsalves. 1st ed.]. Menlo Park, Calif.: Lane Books, 1974.

B426 *Rivers of the West.* Elizabeth R. Hogan. 1st ed. Menlo Park, Calif.: Lane Pub. Co., 1974.

B427 *Alaska.* Dorothy Krell. 1st ed., 1974. Menlo Park, Calif.: Lane Pub. Co., 1974.

B428 *Stitchery: Embroidery, Applique, Crewel.* Lynne R. Morrall. 1st ed. Menlo Park, Calif.: Lane Pub. Co., 1974.

B429 *Mexico.* Robyn E Shotwell. [1st ed.]. Menlo Park, Calif.: Lane Magazine & Book Co., 1974. (A Sunset Travel Book).

B430 *How to Make Bookshelves & Cabinets.* Donald W. Vandervort. 1st ed. Menlo Park, Calif.: Lane Pub. Co., 1974.

B431 *Basic Plumbing Illustrated.* Menlo Park, Calif.: Lane Pub. Co., 1975.

B432 *Cabins & Vacation Houses.* 3d ed. Menlo Park, Calif.: Lane Pub. Co., 1975.

B433 *Crochet: Techniques & Projects.* 1st ed. Menlo Park, Calif.: Lane Pub. Co., 1975.

B434 *Favorite Recipes for Soups & Stews.* Menlo Park, Calif.: Lane Books, 1975.

B435 *Ideas for Storage.* 3d ed. Menlo Park, Calif.: Lane Pub. Co., 1975.

B436 *Jewelry You Can Make.* 1st ed. Menlo Park, Calif.: Lane Pub. Co., 1975.

B437 *Macrame.* 2d ed. Menlo Park, Calif.: Lane Pub. Co. Co., 1975.

B438 *Sunset Barbecue Cook Book.* [Abridged 4th ed.]. Menlo Park, Calif.: Lane Books, 1975.

B439 *Travel Guide to Northern California.* 4th. Menlo Park, Calif.: Lane Pub. Co., 1975.

B440 *Vegetable Gardening.* 2d ed. Menlo Park, Calif.: Lane Pub. Co., 1975.

B441 *Woodworking Projects.* 2d ed. Menlo Park, Calif.: Lane Pub. Co., 1975.

B442 *Sunset Travel Guide to the Orient: Japan, South Korea, Taiwan, Hong Kong, Macau, China.* Lawrence A. Clancy and Cornelia Fogle. Menlo Park, Calif.: Lane Pub. Co., 1975.

B443 *Sunset Travel Guide to Southeast Asia.* Cornelia Fogle, Lawrence A Clancy, and Frederic M. Rea. [2d rev. ed.]. Menlo Park, Calif.: Lane Pub. Co., 1975.

B444 *Home Canning.* Judith A. Gaulke. Menlo Park, Calif.: Lane Pub. Co., 1975.

B445 *Ceramics: Techniques & Projects.* Jane Horn. "New edition." [i.e. 4th print.]. Menlo Park, Calif.: Lane Books, 1975. (A Sunset Book).

B446 *Basic Gardening Illustrated.* Will Kirkman. 2d ed., 1st printing. Menlo Park, Calif.: Lane Pub. Co., 1975.

B447 *Hawaii: a Guide to All the Islands.* Dorothy Krell. Menlo Park, Calif.: Lane Pub. Co., 1975.

B448 *Discovering the California Coast.* Jack McDowell. 1st ed. Menlo Park, Calif.: Lane Pub. Co., 1975.

B449 *Garden Trees.* Richard Osborne and Philip Edinger. 1st ed. Menlo Park, Calif.: Lane Pub. Co., 1975.

Books

B450 *California Wine Country*. Bob Thompson. Menlo Park, Calif.: Lane Books, 1975.

B451 *Planning & Remodeling Bathrooms*. Maureen Williams Zimmerman. 3d ed. Menlo Park, Calif.: Lane Pub. Co., 1975.

B452 *Bonsai: Culture and Care of Miniature Trees*. 2d ed., New. Menlo Park, Calif.: Lane Pub. Co., 1976.

B453 *Easy-to-Make Tables & Chairs*. 1st ed. Menlo Park, Calif.: Lane Pub. Co., 1976.

B454 *French Cook Book*. Menlo Park, Calif.: Lane Pub. Co., 1976.

B455 *Greenhouse Gardening*. 1st ed. Menlo Park, Calif.: Lane Pub. Co., 1976.

B456 *Hors D'Oeuvres: Appetizers, Spreads & Dips*. Menlo Park, Calif.: Lane Pub. Co., 1976.

B457 *How to Grow House Plants*. 3d ed. Menlo Park, Calif.: Lane Pub. Co., 1976.

B458 *Planning & Remodeling Kitchens*. 5th rev. ed. Menlo Park, Calif. : Lane Pub. Co., 1976. (A Sunset book).

B459 *Sunset Christmas Ideas and Answers*. 5th ed. Menlo Park, Calif.: Lane Pub. Co., 1976.

B460 *Sunset Joy of Gardening*. Menlo Park, Calif.: Sunset Magazine, Special Services Dept, 1976.

B461 *Western Campsite Directory*. Menlo Park, Calif.: Lane Pub. Co., 1976.

B462 *Western Garden Book*. Menlo Park, Calif.: Lane Pub. Co., 1976.

B463 *Sunset Home Remodeling Guide to Paneling, Painting & Wallpapering*. Robert G. Bander. 1st ed. Menlo Park, Calif.: Lane Pub. Co., 1976.

B464 *Australia*. Lawrence A. Clancy, Frances Coleberd, and Valerie McGlenighan. 3d ed., updated. Menlo Park, Calif.: Lane Books, 1976. (A Sunset Travel Book).

B465 *Sunset Low-Cost Cookery: Great Meals at Real Savings*. Jerry Anne DiVecchio and Holly Lyman. Menlo Park, Calif.: Lane Pub. Co., 1976.

B466 *Sunset Travel Guide to Oregon*. Cornelia Fogle. 3d ed. Menlo Park, Calif.: Lane Pub. Co., 1976.

B467 *Travel Guide to Oregon*. Cornelia Fogle. 3d ed. Menlo Park, Calif.: Lane Pub. Co., 1976.

B468 *Knitting: Techniques and Projects*. Robyn Shotwell Metcalfe. 1st ed. Menlo Park, Calif.: Lane Pub. Co., 1976.

B469 *Plant Containers You Can Make*. Robyn Shotwell Metcalfe. 1st ed. Menlo Park, Calif.: Lane Pub. Co., 1976.

B470 *Microwave Cook Book*. Cynthia Scheer. Menlo Park, Calif.: Lane Pub. Co., 1976.

B471 *Children's Crafts*. Susan Warton, Dennis Ziemienski, and Darrow M. Watt. 2d ed. Menlo Park, Calif.: Lane Pub. Co., 1976.

B472 *Cook Book of Breads*. 3d ed. Menlo Park, Calif.: Lane Pub. Co., 1977.

B473 *Easy-to-Make Furniture*. Menlo Park, Calif.: Lane Pub. Co., 1977.

B474 *Ideas for Hanging Gardens*. 1st ed., 6th printing. Menlo Park, Calif.: Lane Pub. Co., 1977.

B475 *Needlepoint: Techniques and Projects*. 2d ed. Menlo Park, Calif.: Lane Pub. Co., 1977.

B476 *Oriental Cook Book*. Menlo Park, Calif.: Lane Pub. Co., 1977.

B477 *Patio Book*. 3d ed. Menlo Park, Calif.: Lane Pub. Co., 1977.

B478 *Sunset Mexican Cook Book*. 2d ed. Menlo Park, Calif.: Lane Pub. Co., 1977.

B479 *Sunset Salad Book*. Menlo Park, Calif.: Lane Pub. Co., 1977.

B480 *Sunset Travel Guide to Mexico*. Barbara Braasch. 6th. Menlo Park, Calif.: Lane Pub. Co., 1977.

B481 *Gardening in Containers*. Linda Brandt. 3d ed./ research and text, Linda Brandt. Menlo Park, Calif.: Lane Pub. Co., 1977.

B482 *Australia*. Lawrence A. Clancy, Frances Coleberd, and Valerie McGlenighan. 3d ed., 4th print., updated. Menlo Park, Calif.: Lane Books, 1977. (A Sunset Travel Book).

B483 *Clothing Decoration*. Alyson Smith Gonsalves. 1st ed. Menlo Park, Calif.: Lane Pub. Co., 1977.

B484 *Beautiful California*. Elizabeth R. Hogan. 3d ed. Menlo Park, Calif.: Lane Pub. Co., 1977.

B485 *How to Grow African Violets*. Jack Kramer. 6th ed. Menlo Park, Calif.: Lane Pub. Co., 1977.

B486 *How to Grow Orchids*. Jack Kramer. Menlo Park, Calif.: Lane Pub. Co., 1977.

B487 *Alaska*. Dorothy Krell. [1st ed.]. Menlo Park, Calif.: Lane Magazine & Book Co., 1977. (A Sunset pictorial).

B488 *Beautiful Hawaii*. Dorothy Krell. 2d ed. Menlo Park, Calif.: Lane Pub. Co., 1977.

B489 *The Beautiful Northwest*. Dorothy Krell. 2d ed. Menlo Park, Calif.: Lane Pub. Co., 1977.

B490 *Hawaii: a Guide to All the Islands*. Dorothy Krell. Menlo Park, Calif.: Lane Pub. Co., 1977.

B491 *Sunset Seafood Cook Book*. Holly Lyman. 1st ed. Menlo Park, Calif.: Lane Pub. Co., 1977.

B492 *San Francisco*. Jack McDowell and Dorothy Krell. 2d rev. ed. Menlo Park, Calif.: Lane Pub. Co., 1977.

B493 *Furniture Finishing & Refinishing*. Christopher Payne. 2d ed. Menlo Park, Calif.: Lane Pub. Co., 1977.

B494 *Basic Home Wiring Illustrated*. Linda J. Selden. Menlo Park, Calif.: Lane Pub. Co., 1977.

B495 *Back Roads of California: Sketches and Trip Notes*. Earl Thollander. 2d ed. Menlo Park, Calif.: Lane Pub. Co., 1977.

B496 *California Wine*. Bob Thompson. [2d ed.]. Menlo Park, Calif.: Lane Pub. Co., 1977.

B497 *Soft Toys & Dolls*. Susan Warton. Menlo Park, Calif.: Lane Pub. Co., 1977.

B498 *Do-It-Yourself Insulation & Weatherstripping*. 1st ed. Menlo Park, Calif.: Lane Pub. Co., 1978.

B499 *Remodeling With Tile*. 1st ed. Menlo Park, Calif.: Lane Pub. Co., 1978.

B500 *Sunset Cook Book of Desserts*. 2d ed. Menlo Park, Calif.: Lane Pub. Co., 1978.

B501 *Sunset Travel Guide to Southeast Asia*. 2d ed., 3d ed. print. (updated). Menlo Park, Calif.: Lane Pub. Co., 1978.

B502 *Western Travel Adventures*. Premiere edition 1978. Menlo Park, Calif.: Lane, 1978.

B503 *Sunset Homeowner's Guide to Solar Heating*. Holly Lyman Antolini. Menlo Park, Calif.: Lane Pub. Co., 1978.

B504 *Small-Space Gardens*. Kathryn Arthurs. 1st ed. Menlo Park, Calif.: Lane Pub. Co., 1978.

B505 *Sunset Ideas for Landscaping & Garden Remodeling*. Robert G. Bander. 4th. Menlo Park, Calif.: Lane Pub. Co., 1978.

B506 *Gold Rush Country*. Barbara Braasch. 4th. Menlo Park, Calif.: Lane Books, 1978.

B507 *Travel Guide to Alaska*. Barbara Braasch. 3d ed. Menlo Park, Calif.: Lane Pub. Co., 1978.

B508 *Cactus and Succulents: [House Plants & Landscaping Ideas in Color]*. Linda Brandt. 2d ed. Menlo Park, Calif.: Lane Pub. Co., 1978.

B509 *Ghost Towns of the West*. William Carter and Jack McDowell. Rev. Menlo Park, Calif.: Lane Pub. Co., 1978.

B510 *How to Grow Roses*. Philip Edinger. 3d ed. Menlo Park, Calif.: Lane Pub. Co., 1978. (A Sunset book).

Books

B511 *Sunset Travel Guide to New Zealand.* Cornelia Fogle. 3d ed. Menlo Park, Calif.: Lane Pub. Co., 1978.

B512 *Sunset Wok Cook Book.* Judith A. Gaulke. 1st ed. Menlo Park, Calif.: Lane Pub. Co., 1978.

B513 *Sunset Travel Guide to Arizona.* Rene Klein. 6th ed. Menlo Park, Calif.: Lane Pub. Co., 1978.

B514 *Beautiful Northwest.* Dorothy Krell. Menlo Park, Calif.: Lane Pub. Co., 1978.

B515 *Hawaii: a Guide to All the Islands.* Dorothy Krell. Menlo Park, Calif.: Lane Pub. Co., 1978.

B516 *Sunset Ideas for Remodeling Your Home.* Dorothy Krell and Karen A. Paulsen. 3d ed. Menlo Park, Calif.: Lane Pub. Co., 1978.

B517 *Discovering the California Coast.* Jack McDowell. 2d ed. Menlo Park, Calif.: Lane Pub. Co., 1978.

B518 *Sunset Add-a-Room Book: Successful Ideas for More Living Space.* Jack McDowell and Buff Bradley. 1st ed. Menlo Park, Calif.: Lane Pub. Co., 1978.

B519 *Sunset Food Processor Cook Book.* Janeth Johnson Nix. Menlo Park, Calif.,: Lane Pub. Co., 1978.

B520 *Sunset Cooking for Two… or Just for You.* Cynthia Scheer. Menlo Park, Calif.: Lane Pub. Co., 1978.

B521 *Sunset Travel Guide to Washington.* Bob Thompson. Menlo Park, Calif.: Lane Pub. Co., 1978. (Sunset travel & recreation.

B522 *Chinese Cook Book.* 1st ed. Menlo Park, Calif.: Lane Pub. Co., 1979.

B523 *Favorite Recipes for Salads.* 4th. Menlo Park, Calif.: Lane Pub. Co., 1979.

B524 *Homeowner's Guide to Wood Stoves.* Menlo Park, Calif.: Lane, 1979.

B525 *New Western Garden Book.* 4th. Menlo Park, Calif.: Lane Pub. Co., 1979.

B526 *Picture Framing & Wall Display.* 1st ed. Menlo Park, Calif.: Lane Pub. Co., 1979.

B527 *Sunset Ideas for Hot Tubs, Spas & Home Saunas.* 1st ed. Menlo Park, Calif.: Lane Pub. Co., 1979.

B528 *Sunset Western Travel Adventures.* 2d ed. Menlo Park, Calif.: Sunset Magazine, Special Services Department, 1979.

B529 *Sunset Western Travel Adventures, V.2.* 2d ed. Menlo Park, Calif.: Lane Pub. Co., 1979.

B530 *Lawns & Ground Covers.* Kathryn Arthurs. 4th. Menlo Park, Calif.: Lane Pub. Co., 1979.

B531 *Slipcovers & Bedspreads.* Christine Barnes, Maureen Williams Zimmerman, and Diane Petrica Tapscott. 1st ed. Menlo Park, Calif.: Lane Pub. Co., 1979.

B532 *Sunset Travel Guide to Southern California.* Barbara Braasch and William C. Alpin. 5th. ed. Menlo Park, Calif.: Lane Pub. Co., 1979.

B533 *Sunset Barbecue Cook Book.* Linda Brandt. 5th. ed. Menlo Park, Calif.: Lane Pub. Co., 1979.

B534 *Islands of the South Pacific.* Joan Erickson. 3d ed.]. Menlo Park, Calif.: Lane Pub. Co., 1979.

B535 *Sunset Ideas for Patios & Decks.* Barbara Gordon Gibson. 4th. Menlo Park, Calif.: Lane Pub. Co., 1979.

B536 *The California Missions: a Pictorial History.* Dorothy Krell. Soft cover. Menlo Park, Calif.: Lane Pub. Co., 1979.

B537 *Curtains, Draperies & Shades.* Diane Petrica Tapscott. Menlo Park, Calif.: Lane Pub. Co., 1979. (A Sunset book).

B538 *Guide to California's Wine Country.* Bob Thompson. 2d ed. Menlo Park, Calif.: Lane Pub. Co., 1979.

B539 *Planning & Remodeling Family Rooms, Dens & Studios.* Anne K. Turley. 1st ed. Menlo Park, Calif.: Lane Pub. Co., 1979.

B540 *Easy-to-Make Outdoor Furniture.* Donald W. Vandervort. 1st ed. Menlo Park, Calif.: Lane Pub. Co., 1979.

B541 *Basic Home Repairs Illustrated.* [rev. ed.]. Menlo Park, Calif.: Lane Pub. Co., 1980.

B542 *Breakfast & Brunch.* 3d ed. Menlo Park, Calif.: Lane Pub. Co., 1980.

B543 *How to Build Decks.* 3d ed. Menlo Park, Calif.: Lane Pub. Co., 1980.

B544 *How to Plan and Build Fireplaces.* 4th. Menlo Park, Calif.: Lane Pub. Co., 1980.

B545 *How to Plan & Build Decks.* 3d ed. Menlo Park, Calif.: Lane Pub. Co., 1980.

B546 *Ideas for Children's Rooms & Play Yards.* 3d ed. Menlo Park, Calif.: Lane Pub. Co., 1980.

B547 *Pasta Cook Book.* Menlo Park, Calif.: Lane Pub. Co., 1980.

B548 *Sunset Home Improvement Study, September 1980.* Menlo Park, Calif.: Lane Pub. Co., 1980.

B549 *Sunset Ideas & Recipes for Breakfast & Brunch.* 3d ed. Menlo Park, Calif.: Lane Pub. Co., 1980.

B550 *Western Travel Adventures.* 3d ed. Menlo Park, Calif.: Lane Pub. Co., 1980.

B551 *Sunset Homeowner's Guide to Solar Heating and Cooling.* Holly Lyman Antolini. 1st ed. Menlo Park, Calif.: Lane Pub. Co., 1980.

B552 *How to Make Pillows.* Christine Barnes. 1st ed. Menlo Park, Calif.: Lane Pub. Co., 1980.

B553 *Sunset Travel Guide to Northern California.* Barbara Braasch and Julie Anne Gold. 5th. ed. Menlo Park, Calif.: Lane Pub. Co., 1980.

B554 *Sunset Casserole Cook Book.* Linda Brandt. 3d ed. Menlo Park, Calif.: Lane Pub. Co., 1980.

B555 *How to Grow Roses.* Philip Edinger. 4th. Menlo Park, Calif.: Lane Pub. Co., 1980.

B556 *Travel Guide to Australia.* Joan Erickson. 4th. Menlo Park, Calif.: Lane Pub. Co., 1980.

B557 *Discovery Trips in Europe.* Cornelia Fogle. 3d ed. Menlo Park, Calif.: Lane Pub. Co., 1980.

B558 *Planning & Remodeling Bathrooms.* Barbara Gordon Gibson and Maureen Williams Zimmerman. 4th ed. Menlo Park, Calif.: Lane Pub. Co. Co., 1980.

B559 *Convection Oven Cook Book.* Elizabeth R. Hogan and Cynthia Scheer. 1st ed. Menlo Park, Calif.: Lane, 1980.

B560 *National Parks of the West.* Dorothy Krell. [3d ed.]. Menlo Park, Calif.: Lane Pub. Co., 1980.

B561 *Decorating With Indoor Plants.* Denise Van Lear. Menlo Park, Calif.: Lane Pub. Co., 1980.

B562 *Furniture Upholstery.* Denise Van Lear. 2d ed. Menlo Park, Calif.: Lane Pub. Co., 1980.

B563 *Remodeling & Decorating Bedrooms.* Maureen Williams Zimmerman. 1st ed. Menlo Park, Calif.: Lane Pub. Co., 1980.

1981–1990

B564 *Canning, Freezing & Drying.* 2d ed. ed. Menlo Park, Calif.: Lane Pub. Co., 1981.

B565 *Country French Cooking.* 2d ed. Menlo Park, Calif.: Lane, 1981.

B567 *How to Plan and Build Fences & Gates.* 4th ed. Menlo Park, Calif.: Lane Pub. Co., 1981.

B568 *Ideas for Swimming Pools.* 5th. ed. Menlo Park, Calif.: Lane Pub. Co., 1981.

B569 *Kitchen Storage: Ideas & Projects.* 1st ed. Menlo Park, Calif.: Lane Pub. Co., 1981.

B570 *Menus & Recipes for Vegetarian Cooking.* 1st ed. Menlo Park, Calif.: Lane, 1981.

B571 *Microwave Cook Book.* 2d ed. Menlo Park, Calif.: Lane Pub. Co., 1981.

Books

B572 *Sunset Seafood Cook Book*. 4th ed. Menlo Park, Calif.: Lane Pub. Co., 1981. (Sunset cook books).

B573 *Travel Guide to Oregon*. 4th ed. Menlo Park, Calif.: Lane Pub. Co., 1981.

B574 *Quilting - Patchwork, Applique*. Christine Barnes, Sally Shimizu, and Steve W. Marley. 2d ed. Menlo Park, Calif.: Lane Pub. Co., 1981. (Sunset hobby & craft books).

B575 *Sunset Italian Cook Book*. Jerry Anne DiVecchio. 2d ed. Menlo Park, Calif.: Lane Pub. Co., 1981.

B576 *Sunset Gardening With Shade*. Suzanne Normand Eyre. Menlo Park, Calif.: Sunset Pub. Corp., 1981.

B577 *Basic Masonry Illustrated*. Scott Fitzgerrell. 1st ed. Menlo Park, Calif.: Lane Pub. Co., 1981.

B578 *Wall Systems and Shelving*. Scott Fitzgerrell and Scott Atkinson. 1st ed. Menlo Park, Calif.: Lane Pub. Co., 1981.

B579 *Do-It-Yourself Roofing & Siding*. Lee Foster, Donald W. Vandervort, and Elton Welke. 1st ed. Menlo Park, Calif.: Lane Pub. Co. Co., 1981. (Sunset building, remodeling & home design books).

B580 *Garden Color: Annuals & Perennials*. John K. McClements and Philip Edinger. 1st ed. Menlo Park, Calif.: Lane Pub. Co., 1981.

B581 *Do-It-Yourself Energy Saving Projects*. Michael Scofield and Bill Tanler. 1st ed. Menlo Park, Calif.: Lane Pub. Co., 1981.

B582 *Decorating With Plants*. Denise Van Lear. 1st ed. Menlo Park, Calif.: Lane Pub. Co., 1981.

B583 *Introduction to Basic Gardening*. Maureen Williams Zimmerman. 3d ed. Menlo Park, Calif.: Lane Pub. Co., 1981.

B584 *Azaleas, Rhododendrons, Camellias*. 1st ed. Menlo Park, Calif.: Lane Pub. Co., 1982.

B585 *Easy Basics for Good Cooking*. 1st ed. Menlo Park, Calif.: Lane Pub. Co., 1982.

B586 *Garage, Attic & Basement Storage*. 1st ed. Menlo Park, Calif.: Lane, 1982.

B587 *How to Grow Vegetables & Berries*. 1st ed. Menlo Park, Calif.: Lane Pub. Co., 1982.

B588 *Ideas for Bedroom & Bath Storage*. Menlo Park, Calif.: Lane Pub. Co., 1982.

B589 *Picnics and Tailgate Parties*. 1st ed. Menlo Park, Calif.: Lane Pub. Co., 1982.

B590 *Solar Remodeling*. 1st ed. Menlo Park, Calif.: Lane Pub. Co., 1982.

B591 *Sunset Cook Book of Favorite Recipes I*. Menlo Park, Calif.: Lane Pub. Co., 1982.

B592 *Sunset Cook Book of Favorite Recipes II*. 1st ed. ed. Menlo Park, Calif.: Lane Pub. Co., 1982.

B593 *Windows & Skylights*. 1st ed. Menlo Park, Calif.: Lane Pub. Co., 1982.

B594 *How to Grow Roses*. Philip Edinger. 4th ed. updated June 1982, Menlo Park, Calif.: Lane Pub. Co 1982.

B595 *Southeast Asia*. Joan Erickson. 3d ed. Menlo Park, Calif.: Lane Pub. Co., 1982.

B596 *Wall Coverings: Wallpaper, Fabric, Paint, Paneling*. Alice Rich Hallowell. 1st ed. Menlo Park, Calif.: Lane Pub. Co., 1982.

B597 *Sunset Easy Basics for Good Cooking*. Janeth Johnson Nix and Elaine R. Woodard. 1st ed. Menlo Park, Calif.: Lane Pub. Co., 1982.

B598 *Home Lighting*. Sarah S. Norton and Michael Scofield. 1st ed. Menlo Park, Calif.: Lane Pub. Co., 1982.

B599 *Do-It-Yourself: Flooring*. Bill Tanler. 1st ed. Menlo Park, Calif.: Lane Pub. Co., 1982.

B600 *Guide to California's Wine Country*. Bob Thompson. 3d ed. Menlo Park, Calif.: Lane Pub. Co., 1982.

B601 *Bathrooms, Planning & Remodeling*. 5th. ed. Menlo Park, Calif.: Lane Pub. Co., 1983.

B602 *Children's Clothes & Toys*. Menlo Park, Calif.: Lane Pub. Co., 1983.

B603 *Garden & Patio Building Book*. 2d ed. Menlo Park, Calif.: Lane, 1983.

B604 *Gardener's Answer Book*. 1st ed. Menlo Park, Calif.: Lane, 1983.

B605 *House Plants*. 4th ed. Menlo Park, Calif.: Lane Publications, 1983.

B606 *Kitchens: Planning & Remodeling*. 6th. Menlo Park, Calif.: Lane Pub. Co., 1983.

B607 *Quick Meals...With Fresh Foods*. 1st ed. ed. Menlo Park, Calif.: Lane, 1983.

B608 *Sunset Vegetable Cook Book*. 2d ed. Menlo Park, Calif.: Lane Pub. Co., 1983.

B609 *Vegetarian Favorites*. 1st ed. Menlo Park, Calif.: Lane, 1983.

B610 *Sunset Basic Plumbing, Illustrated*. Karen A. L. Boswell, Michael Scofield, and Scott Atkinson. 2d ed. Menlo Park, Calif.: Lane Pub. Co., 1983.

B611 *Mexico Travel Guide*. Barbara Braasch. 7th. Menlo Park, Calif.: Lane Pub. Co., 1983.

B612 *Orient Travel Guide*. Barbara Braasch. 2d ed. Menlo Park, Calif.: Lane Pub. Co., 1983.

B613 *Pruning Handbook*. Philip Edinger. 3d ed. Menlo Park, Calif.: Lane Pub. Co., 1983.

B614 *Hawaii: a Guide to All the Islands*. Dorothy Krell. 5th. ed. Menlo Park, Calif.: Lane Pub. Co., 1983.

B615 *Sunset International Vegetarian Cook Book*. Maureen Williams Zimmerman. Menlo Park, Calif.: Lane Pub. Co., 1983.

B616 *Basic Carpentry Illustrated*. 2d ed. Menlo Park, Calif.: Lane Pub. Co., 1984.

B617 *Breads: Step by Step Techniques*. 4th ed. Menlo Park, Calif.: Lane Pub. Co., 1984.

B618 *Easy Basics for International Cooking*. 1st ed. Menlo Park, Calif.: Lane Pub. Co., 1984.

B619 *Entertaining for All Seasons*. 1st ed. Menlo Park, Calif.: Lane Pub. Co., 1984.

B620 *Hawaii: a Guide to All the Islands*. Rev. Menlo Park, Calif.: Lane Pub. Co., 1984.

B621 *How to Grow Fruits, Nuts & Berries*. 1st ed. Menlo Park, Calif.: Lane Pub. Co., 1984.

B622 *Landscaping Illustrated*. 1st ed. Menlo Park, Calif.: Lane, 1984.

B623 *New Zealand Travel Guide*. 4th ed. Menlo Park, Calif.: Lane Pub. Co., 1984.

B624 *Oriental Cook Book*. Menlo Park, Calif.: Lane Pub. Co., 1984.

B625 *Sunset Complete Home Storage*. 1st ed. Menlo Park, Calif.: Lane Pub. Co., 1984.

B626 *Sunset Woodworking Projects II*. 1st ed. Menlo Park, Calif.: Lane Pub. Co., 1984.

B627 *Walks, Walls & Patio Floors*. 3d ed. Menlo Park, Calif.: Lane Pub. Co., 1984.

B628 *Sunset Southern California Travel Guide*. Barbara Braasch and William C. Alpin. 5th ed., 4th prtg. updated. Menlo Park, Calif.: Lane Pub. Co., 1984.

B629 *Sunset Appetizers: Hors D'Oeuvres to Light Meals*. Cynthia Scheer. 1st ed. Menlo Park, Calif.: Lane Pub. Co., 1984.

B630 *Container Gardening*. A. Cort Sinnes. 4th ed. Menlo Park, Calif.: Lane Pub. Co., 1984.

B631 *Bulbs for All Seasons*. Menlo Park, Calif.: Lane Pub. Co., 1985.

B632 *Children's Furniture*. 1st ed. Menlo Park, Calif.: Lane Pub. Co., 1985.

B633 *Cooking for Two*. 2d ed. Menlo Park, Calif.: Lane Pub. Co., 1985.

Books

B634 *Dolls & Soft Toys.* 1st ed. Menlo Park, Calif.: Lane Pub. Co., 1985.

B635 *Food Processor Cook Book.* 2d ed. Menlo Park, Calif.: Lane Pub. Co., 1985.

B636 *Home Repair Handbook.* 1st ed. Menlo Park, Calif.: Lane Pub. Co., 1985.

B637 *How to Grow Bulbs.* 4th ed. Menlo Park, Calif.: Lane Pub. Co., 1985.

B638 *Pies & Pastries: Step-by-Step Techniques.* Menlo Park, Calif.: Lane Pub. Co., 1985.

B639 *Sunset Cookies: Step-by-Step Techniques.* 1st ed. Menlo Park, Calif.: Lane Pub. Co., 1985.

B640 *Sunset Landscaping for Privacy.* 1st ed. Menlo Park, Calif.: Lane, 1985.

B641 *Home Repair Handbook.* Cynthia Overbeck Bix and others. 1st ed. Menlo Park, Calif.: Lane Pub. Co., 1985.

B642 *Arizona Travel Guide.* Barbara Braasch. 6th. Menlo Park, Calif.: Lane Pub. Co., 1985.

B643 *Homemade Soups.* Claire Coleman. 1st ed. Menlo Park, Calif.: Lane Pub. Co., 1985.

B644 *Southeast Asia Travel Guide.* Joan Erickson. 3d ed., 2d printing (updated). Menlo Park, Calif.: Lane Pub. Co., 1985.

B645 *Barbecue Building Book.* [2d ed.]. Menlo Park, Calif.: Lane Pub. Co., 1986.

B646 *Basic Woodworking Illustrated.* Menlo Park, Calif.: Lane Pub. Co., 1986.

B647 *Bookshelves & Cabinets.* Menlo Park, Calif.: Lane Pub. Co., 1986.

B648 *Cheese: How to Choose, Serve & Enjoy.* 1st ed. Menlo Park, Calif.: Lane Pub. Co., 1986.

B649 *Flooring.* Menlo Park, Calif.: Lane, 1986.

B650 *Good Cook's Handbook.* 1st ed. Menlo Park, Calif.: Lane Pub. Co., 1986.

B651 *Hawaii: a Guide to All the Islands.* 6th ed. ; updated 1986. Menlo Park, Calif.: Lane Pub. Co., 1986.

B652 *Home Offices & Work Spaces.* Menlo Park, Calif.: Lane Pub. Co., 1986.

B653 *Light Cuisine.* Menlo Park, Calif.: Lane Pub. Co., 1986.

B654 *Remodeling Ideas for More Living Space.* Menlo Park, Calif.: Lane Pub. Co., 1986.

B655 *Sunset Barbecue Cook Book.* 6th. Menlo Park, Calif.: Lane Pub. Co., 1986.

B656 *Sunset California Travel Guide.* 1st ed. Menlo Park, Calif.: Lane Pub. Co., 1986.

B657 *Sunset South Pacific Travel Guide.* Menlo Park, Calif.: Lane Pub. Co., 1986.

B659 *Things You Can Make for Children.* 1st ed. Menlo Park, Calif.: Lane Pub. Co., 1986.

B660 *Western Garden Book.* 4th ed., updated. Menlo Park, Calif.: Lane Pub. Co., 1986.

B661 *Cactus and Succulents.* Linda Brandt. Menlo Park, Calif.: Lane Pub. Co., 1986. (A Sunset book).

B662 *Sunset California Freeway Exit Guide.* Bill Cima and Saundra Cima. Menlo Park, Calif.: Lane Pub. Co., 1986.

B663 *Decks.* Barbara Gordon Gibson. 3d ed. Menlo Park, Calif.: Lane Pub. Co., 1986.

B664 *Patios & Decks.* Barbara Gordon Gibson. 4th ed. Menlo Park, Calif.: Lane Pub. Co., 1986.

B665 *Sunset Fresh Ways With Chicken.* Elaine Johnson. 1st ed. Menlo Park, Calif.: Lane Pub. Co., 1986.

B666 *Spas, Hot Tubs & Home Saunas.* Susan Warton and Paul Spring. 2d ed. Menlo Park, Calif.: Lane Pub. Co., 1986.

B667 *Beautiful California : Sunset Pictorial.* Menlo Park, Calif.: Lane Pub. Co., 1987.

B668 *The Best of Sunset: Recipes From the Magazine of Western Living.* 1st ed. Menlo Park, Calif.: Lane, 1987.

B669 *Christmas Treasury.* 1st ed. Menlo Park, Calif.: Lane Pub. Co., 1987.

B670 *Fresh Ways With Salads.* 5th. ed. Menlo Park, Calif.: Lane Pub. Co., 1987.

B671 *Home Remodeling Illustrated.* 1st ed. Menlo Park, Calif.: Lane Pub. Co., 1987.

B672 *Maui Travel Guide.* 1st ed. Menlo Park, Calif.: Lane Pub. Co., 1987.

B673 *Oregon Travel Guide.* 5th. ed. Menlo Park, Calif.: Lane Pub. Co., 1987.

B674 *Quick Cuisine.* Menlo Park, Calif.: Lane Pub. Co., 1987.

B675 *Sunset Bookshelves & Cabinets.* 2d ed. Menlo Park, Calif.: Lane Pub. Co., 1987.

B676 *Sunset Fresh Produce.* 1st ed. Menlo Park, Calif.: Lane, 1987.

B677 *Sunset Light Desserts.* 1st ed. Menlo Park, Calif.: Lane, 1987.

B678 *Sunset Pocket Road Atlas : United States Canada Mexico.* Menlo Park, Calif.: Lane Pub. Co., 1987. (A Sunset Book).

B679 *Sunset Road Atlas: United States, Canada, Mexico.* Menlo Park, Calif.: Lane :in conjunction with the H.M. Gousha Co., San Jose, 1987.

B680 *Sunset Tile Remodeling Handbook.* 2d ed. Menlo Park, Calif.: Lane Pub. Co., 1987.

B681 *Vegetable Gardening.* 3d ed. Menlo Park, Calif.: Lane Pub. Co., 1987.

B682 *Highway Services Directory.* Bill Cima and Saundra Cima. 1st ed. Menlo Park, Calif.: Lane Pub. Co., 1987. (Highway services directory series).

B683 *Australia Travel Guide.* Joan Erickson. 5th. ed. Menlo Park, Calif.: Lane Pub. Co., 1987.

B684 *New Zealand Travel Guide.* Cornelia Fogle. 4th ed., 4th printing (updated). Menlo Park, Calif.: Lane Pub. Co., 1987. (Sunset Books).

B685 *Southwest Cook Book.* Joan Griffiths and Mary Jane Swanson. Menlo Park, Calif.: Lane Pub. Co., 1987.

B686 *Road Atlas : United States, Canada, Mexico.* H.M. Gousha Company. 1987 ed. Menlo Park, Calif.: Lane Pub. Co., 1987.

B687 *Las Vegas, the Entertainment Capital.* Donn Knepp. Menlo Park, Calif.: Lane Pub. Co., 1987.

B688 *Taxsaver : Automobile.* Jay Knepp. 1st ed. Menlo Park, Calif.: Lane Pub. Co., 1987. (Taxsaver).

B689 *Taxsaver : Home Office.* Jay Knepp. 1st ed. Menlo Park, Calif.: Lane Pub. Co., 1987.

B690 *Taxsaver : Homeowners.* Jay Knepp. 1st ed. Menlo Park, Calif.: Lane Pub. Co., 1987. (Taxsaver).

B691 *Taxsaver : Itemized Deductions.* Jay Knepp. 1st ed. Menlo Park, Calif.: Lane Pub. Co., 1987. (Taxsaver).

B692 *Taxsaver : Outside Sales.* Jay Knepp. 1st ed. Menlo Park, Calif.: Lane Pub. Co., 1987.

B693 *Taxsaver : Real Estate.* Jay Knepp. 1st ed. Menlo Park, Calif.: Lane Pub. Co., 1987.

B694 *National Parks of the West.* Dorothy Krell. Menlo Park, Calif.: Lane Pub. Co., 1987.

B695 *Basic Home Wiring Illustrated.* Linda J. Selden. 2d ed. Menlo Park, Calif.: Lane Pub. Co., 1987.

B696 *Sunset Basic Home Wiring Illustrated.* Linda J. Selden. 2d ed. Menlo Park, Calif.: Lane, 1987.

B697 *Wine Country California.* Rod Smith. [4th ed.]. Menlo Park, Calif.: Lane Pub. Co., 1987.

B698 *Sunset Washington Travel Guide.* Bob Thompson and Maureen Williams Zimmerman. 5th. ed. Menlo Park, Calif.: Lane Pub. Co., 1987.

B699 *Entertaining for All Seasons.* Kenneth R. Burke and Jerry Anne DiVecchio. Menlo Park, Calif.: Lane Pub. Co., 1987.

B700 *Alaska Travel Guide.* 4th ed. Menlo Park, Calif.: Lane Pub. Co., 1988.

B701 *Children's Rooms & Play Yards.* 4th ed. Menlo Park, Calif.: Lane Pub. Co., 1988.

Books

B702 *The Complete Wok Cook Book*. 1st ed. Menlo Park, Calif.: Lane Pub. Co., 1988.

B703 *Decorating With House Plants*. 2d ed. Menlo Park, Calif.: Lane Pub. Co., 1988.

B704 *Family Rooms & Activity Areas*. 2d ed. Menlo Park, Calif.: Lane Pub. Co., 1988.

B705 *The Get-Away Gourmet*. Menlo Park, Calif.: Lane Pub. Co., 1988.

B706 *Gifts From Your Kitchen*. 1st ed. Menlo Park, Calif.: Lane Pub. Co., 1988.

B707 *Hawaii: a Guide to All the Islands*. 6th ed., 4th printing, updated June 1988. Menlo Park, Calif.: Lane Pub. Co., 1988.

B708 *Holiday Cook Book*. 1st ed. Menlo Park, Calif.: Lane Pub. Co., 1988.

B709 *Home Lighting Handbook*. 2d ed. Menlo Park, Calif.: Lane Pub. Co., 1988.

B710 *Potluck Cook Book*. 1st ed. Menlo Park, Calif.: Lane Pub. Co., 1988.

B711 *Stir-Fry Cook Book*. 1st ed. Menlo Park, Calif.: Lane Pub. Co., 1988.

B712 *Sunset Bedroom & Bath Storage*. 2d ed. Menlo Park, Calif.: Lane Pub. Co., 1988.

B713 *Sunset Kitchens & Bathrooms; Planning & Remodeling*. Menlo Park, Calif.: Lane Pub. Co., 1988.

B714 *Sunset Mexico Travel Guide: [From Baja to the Yucatan]*. 8th. Menlo Park, Calif.: Lane, 1988.

B715 *Sunset Orient Travel Guide*. 3d ed. Menlo Park, Calif.: Lane Pub. Co., 1988.

B716 *Sunset Recipe Annual: Every Sunset Magazine Recipe and Food Article From 1987*. 1988. Menlo Park, Calif.: Lane Pub. Co., 1988.

B717 *Western Garden Book*. 5th. ed. Menlo Park, Calif.: Lane Pub. Co., 1988.

B718 *The Frequent Traveler's City Atlas*. Creative Sales Corp and American Map Corporation. Menlo Park, Calif.: Lane Pub. Co., 1988.

B719 *The Frequent Traveler's State & City Atlas*. Creative Sales Corp and American Map Corporation. Menlo Park, Calif.: Lane Pub. Co., 1988.

B720 *Easy-Care Gardening*. Philip Edinger. 1st ed. Menlo Park, Calif.: Lane Pub. Co., 1988.

B721 *Back Roads of California: Sketches and Trip Notes*. Earl Thollander. 3d ed. Menlo Park, Calif.: Lane Pub. Co., 1988.

B722 *Making Your Home Child-Safe*. Donald W. Vandervort. 1st ed. Menlo Park, Calif.: Lane Pub. Co., 1988.

B723 *Patio Roofs & Gazebos*. Donald W. Vandervort and Fran Feldman. 1st ed. Menlo Park, Calif.: Lane Pub. Co., 1988.

B724 *6 Ingredients or Less*. 1st ed. Menlo Park, Calif.: Lane Pub. Co., 1989.

B725 *Children's Play Yards*. Menlo Park, Calif.: Lane Pub. Co., 1989.

B726 *Complete Home Storage*. 2d ed. Menlo Park, Calif.: Lane Pub. Co., 1989.

B727 *Fireplaces & Wood Stoves*. 1st ed. Menlo Park, Calif.: Lane Pub. Co., 1989.

B728 *Fish & Shellfish*. 1st ed. Menlo Park, Calif.: Lane Pub. Co., 1989.

B729 *Kitchen Storage*. 2d ed. Menlo Park, Calif.: Lane Pub. Co., 1989.

B730 *Less Than 7 Ingredients Cook Book*. 1st ed. Menlo Park, Calif.: Sunset Pub. Co., 1989.

B731 *New England Travel Guide*. 1st ed. Menlo Park, Calif.: Lane Pub. Co., 1989.

B732 *Roses*. 5th. ed. Menlo Park, Calif.: Lane Pub. Co., 1989.

B733 *Sunset Fences & Gates*. 4th ed., 7th printing Sept. 1989. Menlo Park, Calif.: Lane Pub. Co., 1989.

B734 *Sunset Recipe Annual: Every Sunset Magazine Recipe and Food Article From 1988*. 1989. Menlo Park, Calif.: Lane Pub. Co., 1989.

B735 *Sunset Road Atlas: United States, Canada, Mexico*. 1989. Menlo Park, Calif.: Lane Pub. Co., 1989.

B736 *Sunset Western Garden Calendar*. Menlo Park, Calif.: Lane Pub. Co., 1989.

B737 *Wok Cook Book*. 2d ed. Menlo Park, Calif.: Lane Pub. Co., 1989.

B738 *Garden Pools, Fountains & Waterfalls*. Scott Atkinson. 3d ed. Menlo Park, Calif.: Lane Pub. Co., 1989.

B739 *Waterwise Gardening*. Kathryn Stechert Black. 1st ed. Menlo Park, Calif.: Lane Pub. Co., 1989.

B740 *Make-Ahead Cook Book*. Sue Brownlee. Menlo Park, Calif.: Lane Pub. Co., 1989.

B741 *Sunset Mexican Cook Book*. Tori Ritchie Bunting. 3d ed. Menlo Park, Calif.: Lane Pub. Co., 1989.

B742 *Southeast Asia Travel Guide*. Joan Erickson. 3d ed., 3d printing (updated). Menlo Park, Calif.: Lane Pub. Co., 1989.

B743 *Sunset Lawns & Ground Covers*. Fran Feldman. 5th. ed. Menlo Park, Calif.: Lane Pub. Co., 1989.

B744 *Discovery Trips in Europe*. Cornelia Fogle. 4th ed. Menlo Park, Calif.: Lane Pub. Co., 1989.

B745 *The Ultimate Grill Book*. Joan Griffiths, Mary Jane Swanson, and Deborah Thomas Kramer. 1st ed. Menlo Park, Calif.: Lane Pub. Co., 1989.

B746 *Seafood Cook Book*. Cynthia Scheer. 5th. ed. Menlo Park, Calif.: Lane Pub. Co., 1989.

B747 *Decks*. 4th ed. Menlo Park, Calif.: Lane Pub. Co., 1990.

B748 *An Illustrated Guide to Attracting Birds*. 1st ed. Menlo Park, Calif.: Sunset Pub., 1990.

B749 *Sunset Appetizers*. 2d ed. Menlo Park, Calif.: Lane Pub. Co., 1990.

B750 *Sunset Fresh Ways With Pasta*. 1st ed. Menlo Park, Calif.: Lane Pub. Co., 1990.

B751 *Sunset Recipe Annual: Every Sunset Magazine Recipe and Food Article From 1989*. 1990. Menlo Park, Calif.: Lane Pub. Co., 1990.

B752 *The Complete Patio Book*. Scott Atkinson. 1st ed. Menlo Park, Calif.: Lane Pub. Co., 1990.

B753 *Light & Healthy Cook Book*. Tori Ritchie Bunting. 1st ed. Menlo Park, Calif.: Sunset Pub. Corp., 1990.

B754 *Road Atlas : United States, Canada, Mexico*. Creative Sales Corporation. 1990 ed. Menlo Park, Calif.: Lane Pub. Co., 1990.

B755 *Microwave Main Dishes*. Joan Griffiths and Mary Jane Swanson. Menlo Park, Calif.: Sunset Pub. Corp., 1990.

B756 *Sunset Low Cholesterol Cook Book*. Patricia Kearney. 1st ed. Menlo Park, Calif.: Lane Pub. Co., 1990.

1991–1998

B757 *The Best of Sunset : Over 500 All-Time Favorite Recipes From the Magazine of Western Living*. 1st ed. Menlo Park, Calif.: Sunset Pub. Co., 1991.

B758 *California Travel Guide*. 2d ed. Menlo Park, Calif.: Sunset Pub. Corp., 1991.

B759 *Ideas for Great Kitchens*. Menlo Park, Calif.: Sunset Pub. Corp., 1991.

B760 *An Illustrated Guide to Organic Gardening*. 2d ed. Menlo Park, Calif.: Sunset Pub. Corp., 1991.

B761 *Light Ways With Beef, Lamb & Pork*. Menlo Park, Calif.: Sunset Pub. Corp., 1991.

B762 *Poultry Cook Book*. Menlo Park, Calif.: Sunset Pub. Co., 1991.

B763 *Sunset Cooking for Two*. 3d ed. Menlo Park, Calif.: Sunset Pub. Corp., 1991.

B764 *Sunset Drought Survival Guide for Home and Garden*. Menlo Park, Calif.: Sunset Pub. Corp., 1991.

B765 *Sunset Quick & Easy Cook Book*. 1st ed. Menlo Park, Calif.: Sunset Pub. Corp., 1991.

Books

B766 *Sunset Recipe Annual: Every Sunset Magazine Recipe and Food Article From 1990.* Menlo Park, Calif.: Sunset, 1991.

B767 *Decorating With Paint & Wall Coverings.* Scott Atkinson. Menlo Park, Calif.: Sunset Pub., 1991.

B768 *Ideas for Great Bathrooms.* Scott Atkinson. Menlo Park, Calif.: Sunset Pub. Corp., 1991.

B769 *Home Repair Handbook.* Cynthia Overbeck Bix and Karen A. L. Boswell. Menlo Park, Calif.: Sunset Pub. Co., 1991.

B770 *Northern California Travel Guide.* Barbara Braasch. Menlo Park, Calif.: Sunset Pub. Corp., 1991.

B771 *Sunset California Travel Guide.* Barbara Braasch and Phyllis Elving. 2d ed. Menlo Park, Calif.: Sunset, 1991.

B772 *Ground Covers.* Philip Edinger. 1st ed. Menlo Park, Calif.: Sunset Pub. Corp., 1991.

B773 *Sunset Deck Plans.* Philip Edinger and Walheim Lance. 1st ed. Menlo Park, Calif.: Sunset, 1991.

B774 *The Ultimate Grill Book.* Joan Griffiths, Mary Jane Swanson, and Deborah Thomas Kramer. 2d ed. Menlo Park, Calif.: Lane Pub. Co., 1991.

B775 *Best Home Plans.* Menlo Park, Calif.: Sunset Pub., 1992.

B776 *Best Home Plans: Affordable Living.* Menlo Park, Calif.: Sunset Pub., 1992.

B777 *Best Home Plans: Country Living.* Menlo Park, Calif.: Sunset Pub., 1992.

B778 *Best Home Plans: One-Story Living.* Menlo Park, Calif.: Sunset Pub., 1992.

B779 *Best Home Plans: Traditional Homes.* Menlo Park, Calif.: Sunset Pub., 1992.

B780 *Best Home Plans: Vacation Homes.* Menlo Park, Calif.: Sunset Pub., 1992.

B781 *Decks.* 4th ed. Menlo Park, Calif.: Sunset Pub. Corp., 1992.

B782 *Sunset Best of the Holidays.* Menlo Park, Calif.: Sunset Pub. Corp., 1992.

B783 *Sunset Furniture Finishing.* 3d ed. Menlo Park, Calif.: Sunset Pub. Corp., 1992.

B784 *Sunset Recipe Annual: Every Sunset Magazine Recipe and Food Article From 1991.* Menlo Park, Calif.: Sunset, 1992.

B785 *Walks, Walls & Patio Floors.* Scott Atkinson. [4th ed.]. Menlo Park, Calif.: Sunset Pub. Corp., 1992.

B786 *Landscaping for Small Spaces.* Cynthia Overbeck Bix. 1st ed. Menlo Park, Calif.: Sunset Pub. Corp., 1992.

B787 *Best Kids Cook Book.* Sue Brownlee, R. W. Alley, and Tom Wyatt, Menlo Park, Calif.: Sunset Pub. Corp., 1992.

B788 *Fresh Ways With Italian Cooking.* Tori Richie Bunting and Cornelia Fogle. Menlo Park, Calif.: Sunset Pub. Corp., 1992.

B789 *Perennials.* Philip Edinger. Menlo Park, Calif.: Sunset Pub. Corp., 1992.

B790 *Ideas for Great Wall Systems.* Lynne Gilberg. 1st ed. Menlo Park, Calif.: Sunset Pub. Corp., 1992.

B791 *Ideas for Great Window Treatments.* Lynne Gilberg. Menlo Park, Calif.: Sunset Pub. Corp., 1992.

B792 *Basic Plumbing Illustrated.* Lynne Gilberg and Donald W. Vandervort. 3d ed. Menlo Park, Calif.: Sunset Pub. Corp., 1992.

B793 *Beautiful California.* Elizabeth R. Hogan. 4th ed. Menlo Park, Calif.: Sunset Pub. Corp., 1992.

B794 *Crockery Cook Book.* Cynthia Scheer. Menlo Park, Calif.: Sunset, 1992.

B795 *Low-Fat Cook Book.* Cynthia Scheer. 1st ed. Menlo Park, Calif.: Sunset Pub. Corp., 1992.

B796 *Annuals.* Lance Walheim. Menlo Park, Calif.: Sunset Pub. Corp., 1992.

B797 *Best Kids Garden Book.* Lance Walheim, Patricia Parrott West, Sally Wittman, Sandra Forrest and Viki Marugg. 1st ed. Menlo Park, Calif.: Sunset Pub. Corp., 1992.

B798 *All-Time Favorite Recipes.* 1st ed. Menlo Park, Calif.: Sunset Pub. Corp., 1993.

B799 *Best Home Plans: Indoor/Outdoor Living.* Menlo Park, Calif.: Sunset Pub. Corp., 1993.

B800 *Creative Decorative Painting.* Menlo Park, Calif.: Sunset Pub. Corp., 1993.

B801 *Garden Pests & Diseases.* Menlo Park, Calif.: Sunset Pub., 1993.

B802 *Hawaii: a Guide to All the Islands.* Menlo Park, Calif.: Sunset Pub. Corp., 1993.

B803 *Home Canning.* 3d ed. Menlo Park, Calif.: Sunset Pub. Corp., 1993.

B804 *More Low-Fat Recipes.* Menlo Park, Calif.: Sunset Pub. Co., 1993.

B805 *Sunset Annuals & Perennials.* Menlo Park, Calif.: Sunset Pub. Corp., 1993.

B806 *Sunset Recipe Annual : Every Sunset Magazine Recipe and Food Article From 1992.* 1993 ed. Menlo Park, Calif.: Sunset Pub. Co., 1993.

B807 *Ideas for Great Windows & Doors.* Scott Atkinson. 1st ed. Menlo Park, Calif.: Sunset Pub. Corp., 1993.

B808 *Curtains, Draperies & Shades.* Christine Barnes. 2d ed. Menlo Park, Calif.: Sunset Pub. Corp., 1993.

B809 *Best Kids Love-the-Earth Activity Book.* Cynthia Overbeck Bix, Sydney L. Donahoe, Patricia Parrott West, Sandra Forrest, and Scott Atkinson. 1st ed. Menlo Park, Calif.: Sunset Pub. Corp., 1993.

B810 *Beautiful Things to Make for Baby: Knitting, Sewing, Crochet, Embroidery.* Sheryl Braden. Menlo Park, Calif.: Sunset Pub. Corp., 1993.

B811 *Best Kids Cookie Book.* Sue Brownlee, Paige Billin-Frye and Tom Wyatt. 1st ed. Menlo Park, Calif.: Sunset Pub. Corp., 1993.

B812 *Herbs: an Illustrated Guide.* Philip Edinger. 2d ed. Menlo Park, Calif.: Sunset Pub. Corp., 1993.

B813 *Trees & Shrubs.* Philip Edinger. Menlo Park, Calif.: Sunset Pub. Corp., 1993.

B814 *Lawns.* Fran Feldman. 1st ed. Menlo Park, Calif.: Sunset Pub. Corp., 1993.

B815 *Best Home Plans. Energy-Efficient Homes.* Elizabeth L. Hogan. Menlo Park, Calif.: Sunset Pub., 1993.

B816 *Creative Dried Flowers.* Elizabeth L. Hogan. Menlo Park, Calif.: Sunset Pub. Corp., 1993.

B817 *The California Missions: a Pictorial History.* Dorothy Krell. Soft cover. Menlo Park, Calif.: Sunset Pub. Corp., 1993.

B818 *Ideas for Great Kids' Rooms.* Susan Lang. Menlo Park, Calif.: Sunset Pub., 1993.

B819 *Creative Fun Crafts for Kids.* Jennie Mackenzie. Menlo Park, Calif.: Sunset Pub. Corp., 1993.

B820 *Complete Vegetarian Cook Book.* Cynthia Scheer. Menlo Park, Calif.: Sunset Pub. Co., 1993.

B821 *Bathrooms: Planning & Remodeling.* 6th. Menlo Park, Calif.: Lane Pub. Co., 1994.

B822 *The Best of Sunset Low-Fat Cook Book.* Menlo Park, Calif.: Sunset Pub. Corp., 1994.

B823 *Breads.* 5th. ed. Menlo Park, Calif.: Lane Pub. Co., 1994.

B824 *Chicken : Sunset Creative Cooking Library.* Menlo Park, Calif.: Sunset Pub. Corp., 1994.

B825 *Cookies.* Menlo Park, Calif.: Sunset Pub Corp., 1994. (Sunset creative cooking library).

B826 *Ideas for Great Bedrooms.* 1st ed. Menlo Park, Calif.: Sunset Pub. Corp., 1994.

B827 *Ideas for Great Patios & Decks.* 1st ed. Menlo Park, Calif.: Sunset Pub. Co., 1994.

B828 *Kebabs on the Grill.* 1st ed. Menlo Park, Calif.: Sunset, 1994.

Books

B829 *Kitchens & Bathrooms: Planning & Remodeling.* 2d ed. Menlo Park, Calif.: Sunset Pub. Corp., 1994.

B830 *Kitchens: Planning & Remodeling.* 7th. Menlo Park, Calif.: Lane Pub. Co., 1994.

B831 *Low-Fat Pasta.* 1st ed. Menlo Park, Calif.: Sunset Pub. Co., 1994.

B832 *Pasta : Sunset Creative Cooking Library.* Menlo Park, Calif.: Sunset Pub. Corp., 1994.

B833 *Roofing & Siding.* 2d ed. Menlo Park, Calif.: Sunset Pub. Corp., 1994.

B834 *Sloping Lots.* 1st ed. Menlo Park, Calif.: Sunset Pub. Co., 1994. (Sunset Best home plans).

B835 *Stir-Fry.* Menlo Park, Calif.: Sunset Pub. Corp., 1994. (Sunset creative cooking library).

B836 *Sunset Recipe Annual: Every Sunset Magazine Recipe and Food Article From 1993.* 1994 ed., 1st ed. Menlo Park, Calif.: Sunset Pub. Corp., 1994.

B837 *Trader Joe's Favorite Sunset Recipes.* 1st ed. Menlo Park, Calif.: Sunset Pub. Co., 1994.

B838 *Two-Story Living.* 1st ed. Menlo Park, Calif.: Sunset Pub. Co., 1994. (Sunset Best home plans).

B839 *Western Garden Annual.* 1st ed. Menlo Park, Calif.: Sunset Pub. Corp., 1994.

B840 *Garlic.* Orla Broderick. Menlo Park, Calif.: Sunset Pub. Corp., 1994. (The Gourmet kitchen).

B841 *Sun-Dried Tomatoes : Sunset Creative Cooking Library.* Orla Broderick. Menlo Park, Calif: Sunset Pub. Corp., 1994.

B842 *All-Time Favorite Recipes.* Lisa Chaney, Annabel Post, and Tori Ritchie. 1st ed. Menlo Park, Calif.: Sunset Pub. Co., 1994.

B843 *Mushrooms : Sunset Creative Cooking Library.* Jacqueline Clark. Menlo Park, Calif.: Sunset Pub. Corp., 1994.

B844 *Bonsai.* Philip Edinger. 3d ed. Menlo Park, Calif.: Sunset Pub. Corp., 1994.

B845 *Low-Fat Mexican Cook Book.* Karyn I. Lipman. Menlo Park, Calif.: Sunset Pub. Corp., 1994.

B846 *Starbucks Passion for Coffee.* Starbucks Coffee Company. Menlo Park, Calif.: Sunset Pub., 1994.

B847 *Olive & Other Oils.* Gina Steer. Menlo Park, Calif.: Sunset Pub. Corp., 1994. (The gourmet kitchen).

B848 *Vinegars.* Gina Steer. 1st ed. Menlo Park, Calif.: Sunset Pub. Co., 1994. (The Gourmet kitchen).

B849 *Chillies & Other Peppers : Sunset Creative Cooking Library.* Johanna Younger and James Fisher. Menlo Park, Calif.: Sunset Pub. Corp., 1994.

B850 *Basic Carpentry.* 3d ed. Menlo Park, Calif.: Sunset Pub. Co., 1995.

B851 *Basic Home Repairs.* 2d ed. Menlo Park, Calif.: Sunset Pub. Corp., 1995.

B852 *Basic Masonry.* Menlo Park, Calif.: Sunset Pub. Corp., 1995.

B853 *Basic Plumbing.* 4th ed. Menlo Park, Calif.: Sunset Pub. Corp., 1995.

B854 *Basic Woodworking.* 2d ed. Menlo Park, Calif.: Sunset Pub. Corp., 1995.

B855 *Best Home Plans : Affordable Living.* 2d ed. Menlo Park, Calif.: Sunset Pub. Co., 1995. (Best home plans)

B856 *Best Home Plans Encyclopedia.* Menlo Park, Calif.: Sunset Pub. Corp., 1995.

B857 *Best Home Plans : Getaway Homes.* Menlo Park, Calif.: Sunset Pub. Co., 1995. (Sunset Best home plans).

B858 *Best Home Plans : Luxury Homes.* Menlo Park, Calif.: Sunset Pub. Co., 1995.

B859 *Best Home Plans : Western Living.* Menlo Park, Calif.: Sunset Pub. Co., 1995.

B860 *Creating Storage.* 1st ed. Menlo Park, Calif.: Sunset Pub. Corp., 1995.

B861 *Fish & Seafood on the Grill.* 1st ed. Menlo Park, Calif.: Sunset, 1995.

B862 *Gardening With Color.* Menlo Park, Calif.: Sunset Pub. Corp., 1995.

B863 *Ideas for Great Home Offices.* Menlo Park, Calif.: Sunset Pub. Corp., 1995.

B864 *Low-Fat Stir Fry Cookbook.* 1st ed. Menlo Park, Calif.: Sunset Pub. Corp, 1995.

B865 *Low-Fat Vegetarian Cookbook.* 1st ed. Menlo Park, Calif.: Sunset Pub. Corp., 1995.

B866 *Sauces & Salsas for the Grill.* 1st ed. Menlo Park, Calif.: Sunset Pub. Corp., 1995.

B867 *Sunset Recipe Annual : Every Sunset Magazine Recipe and Food Article From 1994.* 1995 ed. Menlo Park, Calif.: Sunset Pub. Co., 1995.

B868 *Sunset Western Garden Book.* [40th anniversary ed., completely rev. and updated]. Menlo Park, Calif.: Sunset Pub. Corp., 1995.

B869 *Vegetables on the Grill.* 1st ed. Menlo Park, Calif.: Sunset Books, 1995.

B870 *Working With Tile.* 1st ed. Menlo Park, Calif.: Sunset Pub. Corp., 1995.

B871 *Trattoria: the Best of Casual Italian Cooking.* Mary Beth Clark and Peter Johnson. Menlo Park, Calif.: Sunset Books, 1995. (Casual cuisines of the world).

B872 *Bistro: the Best of Casual French Cooking.* Gerald Hirigoyen. Menlo Park, Calif.: Sunset Pub., 1995. (Casual cuisines of the world).

B873 *Beads.* Jo Moody. 1st ed. Menlo Park, Calif.: Sunset Pub. Corp., 1995. (Keepsake crafts).

B874 *Buttons.* Jo Moody. 1st ed. Menlo Park, Calif.: Sunset Pub. Corp., 1995. (Keepsake crafts).

B875 *Ribbons.* Hilary More. 1st ed. Menlo Park, Calif.: Sunset Pub. Corp., 1995. (Keepsake crafts).

B876 *Wreaths.* Gloria Nicol. 1st ed. Menlo Park, Calif.: Sunset Pub. Corp., 1995. (Keepsake crafts).

B877 *Kitchen Cabinet.* Cynthia Scheer. Menlo Park, Calif.: Sunset Pub. Corp., 1995.

B878 *Christmas Tree Decorations.* Deborah Schneebeli-Morrel. 1st ed. Menlo Park, Calif.: Sunset Pub. Corp., 1995. (Keepsake crafts).

B879 *Pleasures of Summer.* Mary Townsend, John Phillip Carroll, and Starbucks Coffee Company. 1st ed. Menlo Park, Calif.: Sunset Books, 1995.

B880 *Candles.* Pamela Westland. 1st ed. Menlo Park, Calif.: Sunset Pub. Corp., 1995. (Keepsake crafts).

B881 *Diner: the Best of Casual American Cooking.* Diane Rossen Worthington and Allan Rosenberg. Menlo Park, Calif.: Sunset Pub., 1995. (Casual cuisines of the world).

B882 *Best Home Plans.* 2d ed. Menlo Park, Calif.: Sunset Pub. Co., 1996. (Sunset Best home plans).

B883 *Best Home Plans. Homes for Entertaining.* 1st ed. Menlo Park, Calif.: Sunset Pub. Corp., 1996.

B884 *Best Home Plans. One-Story Living.* 2d ed. Menlo Park, Calif.: Sunset Pub. Corp., 1996.

B885 *Best Home Plans : Starter & Retirement Homes.* Menlo Park, Calif.: Sunset Pub. Co., 1996.

B886 *Citrus.* 1st ed. Menlo Park, Calif.: Sunset Pub. Corp., 1996.

B887 *Complete Book of Low-Fat Cooking.* 1st ed. Menlo Park, Calif.: Sunset Pub. Co., 1996.

B888 *Complete Deck Book.* 1st ed. Menlo Park, Calif.: Sunset Pub. Corp., 1996.

B889 *Creating Beautiful Floors.* 1st ed. Menlo Park, Calif.: Sunset Pub. Corp., 1996.

B890 *Decks.* 1st ed. Menlo Park, Calif.: Sunset Pub. Corp., 1996.

B891 *Diabetic Cookbook.* Menlo Park, Calif.: Sunset Pub., 1996.

B892 *Fences & Gates.* 1st ed. Menlo Park, Calif.: Sunset Pub., 1996.

B893 *Ideas for Great Home Decorating.* 1st ed. Menlo Park, Calif.: Sunset Pub. Corp., 1996.

B894 *Low-Fat Italian Cookbook.* Menlo Park, Calif.: Sunset Books, 1996.

Books

B895 *Quick Light and Healthy*. 1st ed. Menlo Park, Calif.: Sunset Pub. Co., 1996.

B896 *Sheds & Garages*. 1st ed. Menlo Park, Calif.: Sunset Pub Corp., 1996.

B897 *Sunset Quick, Light and Healthy*. 1st ed. Menlo Park, Calif.: Sunset Pub. Corp., 1996.

B898 *Sunset Recipe Annual : Every Recipe From the Past Year's Issues*. 1997 ed. Menlo Park, Calif.: Sunset Pub. Co., 1996.

B899 *Sunset Recipe Annual : Every Sunset Magazine Recipe and Food Article From 1995*. 1996 ed. Menlo Park, Calif.: Sunset Pub. Co., 1996.

B900 *Western Garden Annual*. 1996 ed. Menlo Park, Calif.: Sunset Pub. Co., 1996.

B901 *Chicken and Other Poultry*. Jerry Anne Di Vecchio, Betty Hughes, and Weber (Firm). 1st ed. Menlo Park, Calif.: Sunset Pub. Corp., 1996. (Grill by the book).

B902 *Steaks, Chops, and Burgers*. Jerry Anne Di Vecchio, Betty Hughes, and Weber (Firm). 1st ed. Menlo Park, Calif.: Sunset Pub. Corp., 1996. (Grill by the book).

B903 *Great American Grilling*. Jerry Anne DiVecchio and Betty A. Hughes. Menlo Park, Calif.: Sunset Pub. Co., 1996.

B904 *Fish and Shellfish*. Jerry Anne DiVecchio, Betty Hughes, and Weber (Firm). 1st ed. Menlo Park, Calif.: Sunset Pub. Corp., 1996. (Grill by the book).

B905 *Weekday Meals*. Jerry Anne DiVecchio, Betty Hughes, and Weber (Firm). 1st ed. Menlo Park, Calif.: Sunset Pub. Corp., 1996. (Grill by the book).

B906 *Sunset Gardening With Shade*. Suzanne Normand Eyre. Menlo Park, Calif.: Sunset Pub. Corp., 1996.

B907 *Cantina: the Best of Casual Mexican Cooking*. Susan Feniger and Mary Sue Milliken. Menlo Park, Calif.: Sunset, 1996. (Casual cuisines of the world).

B908 *Taverna: the Best of Casual Mediterranean Cooking*. Joyce Esersky Goldstein. Menlo Park, Calif.: Sunset Pub. Corp., 1996. (Casual cuisines of the world).

B909 *Far East Cafe: the Best of Casual Asian Cooking*. Joyce Jue. Menlo Park, Calif.: Sunset Pub. Corp., 1996. (Casual cuisines of the world).

B910 *Windows & Skylights*. Heather Mills and Alfred Lemaitre. 1st ed. Menlo Park, Calif.: Sunset Pub., 1996.

B911 *Affordable Home Plans : 200 Best Buys*. Menlo Park, Calif.: Sunset Books, 1997.

B912 *Best Home Plans : 200+ Smart Buys*. Menlo Park, Calif.: Sunset Books, 1997.

B913 *Best Home Plans : 500 Best-Selling Home Plans*. Menlo Park, Calif.: Sunset Pub. Co., 1997.

B914 *Best Home Plans : 500 Best Vacation Home Plans*. Menlo Park, Calif.: Sunset Pub. Co., 1997.

B915 *Best Home Plans : Country Home Plans*. Menlo Park, Calif.: Sunset Pub. Co., 1997.

B916 *Best Home Plans : Luxury Homes*. Menlo Park, Calif.: Sunset Pub. Co., 1997.

B917 *Best Home Plans : Traditional Home Plans*. Menlo Park, Calif.: Sunset Pub. Co., 1997.

B918 *Complete Home Storage*. 1st ed. Menlo Park, Calif.: Sunset Books, 1997.

B919 *Home Plans Encyclopedia : Over 400 Popular Plans, Featuring Top-Rated Ktichens and Bathrooms*. Menlo Park, Calif.: Sunset Books, 1997.

B920 *National Garden Book*. Menlo Park, Calif.: Sunset Books, 1997.

B921 *One-Story Home Plans*. Menlo Park, Calif.: Sunset Pub. Co., 1997.

B922 *Sunset Recipe Annual*. 1998 ed. Menlo Park, Calif.: Sunset Books, 1997.

B923 *Vacation Home Plans : Our Best 200 Plans for Vacation Retreats*. Menlo Park, Calif.: Sunset Books, 1997.

B924 *Water Gardens*. Menlo Park, Calif. : Sunset Books, 1997.

B925 *Western Garden Annual*. 1997 ed. Menlo Park, Calif.: Sunset Pub. Co., 1997.

B926 *Sunset Western Landscaping Book*. Kathleen Norris Brenzel. 1st ed. Menlo Park, Calif.: Sunset Books, 1997.

B927 *New Easy Basics Cookbook*. Jerry Anne DiVecchio. 1st ed. Menlo Park, Calif.: Sunset Books Inc., 1997.

B928 *Pizzeria: the Best of Casual Pizza Oven Cooking*. Evan Kleiman. Menlo Park, Calif.: Sunset Books, 1997. (Casual cuisines of the world).

B929 *Country Inn: the Best of Casual Country Cooking*. George Mahaffey. Menlo Park, Calif.: Sunset Books, 1997. (Casual cuisines of the world).

B930 *30 Minutes or Less Cookbook*. Linda J. Selden and Rebecca LeBrun. 1st ed. Menlo Park, Calif.: Sunset Books, 1997.

B931 *Simply Slipcovers*. Linda J. Selden and Carol Spier. Menlo Park, Calif.: Sunset Books , 1997.

B932 *Children's Play Areas*. Jon Arno and Jim Lutes Rob St. Remy Multimedia/McRae. 1st ed. Menlo Park, Calif.: Sunset Books, 1998.

B933 *Swimming Pools & Spas*. Pierre Home-Douglas, Jim McRae, and St. Remy Multimedia. 1st ed. Menlo Park, Calif.: Sunset Books, 1998.

B934 *Ideas for Great Tile*. Linda J. Selden and Scott Atkinson. 2st ed. Menlo Park, Calif.: Sunset Books, 1998.

B935 *Simply Pillows*. Linda J. Selden and Carol Spier. 1st ed. Menlo Park, Calif.: Sunset Books, 1998.

B936 *Bookshelves & Cabinets*. Don Vandevort, St. Remy Multimedia, Jim McRae, and Pierre Arno Jon Home-Douglas. 1st ed. Menlo Park, Calif.: Sunset Books, 1998.

B937 *Entryways*. Don Vandevort, St. Remy Multimedia, Jim McRae, and Rob Lutes. 1st ed. Menlo Park, Calif.: Sunset Pub. Co., 1998.

Right: However whimsical the treatment, there is a serious message to this September 1932 cover: This magazine, as well as gardening, is to be shared between husband and wife. (Artist: Heath Anderson)

SUNSET

September 1932.　　10 Cents

featuring...
Autumn Gardening

Index of Subjects and Authors

Index of Subjects and Authors

Index of Subjects and Authors

Index of Subjects and Authors

Index of Subjects and Authors

Index of Subjects and Authors

Index of Subjects and Authors

Index of Subjects and Authors

Index of Subjects and Authors

Index of Subjects and Authors

Index of Subjects and Authors

Index of Subjects and Authors

Index of Subjects and Authors

Index of Subjects and Authors

Index of Subjects and Authors

Index of Subjects and Authors

Index of Subjects and Authors

Index of Subjects and Authors

Index of Subjects and Authors

Index of Subjects and Authors

Index of Subjects and Authors

Index of Subjects and Authors

Index of Subjects and Authors

Index of Subjects and Authors

Index of Subjects and Authors

Index of Subjects and Authors

Index of Subjects and Authors

Index of Subjects and Authors

Index of Subjects and Authors

Index of Subjects and Authors

Index

Resources

For assistance in locating
out-of-print booksellers

*Antiquarian Booksellers' Association
of America
20 West 44th Street, Fourth Floor
New York, NY 10035
(telephone) 212-944-8291
(fax) 212-944-8293
http://www.abaa
booknet.com/booknet.html*

Sunset articles may be obtained
from the following
document retrieval service
(as well as others)

*Information Express
3221 Porter Drive
Palo Alto, CA 94304
(telephone) 650-494-8787
(electronic mail) service@express.com
http://www.express.com*

Sunset magazine on the
World Wide Web

http://www.sunsetmagazine.com

Subscriptions to Sunset magazine

800-777-0117

World Wide Web version of the
Sunset centennial bibliography
(this book)

*http://www.sunset-magazine.
stanford.edu*

Colophon

Design

*Chuck Byrne
Chuck Byrne/Design*

Typefaces

*Stone Cycles and Stone Print
Stone Typefoundry*

Scanning and
separations of original
Sunset covers

Hunza Graphics

Scanning and
preparation of original
Sunset editorial images

Chuck Byrne/Design

Printing

Shoreline Printing